Frommer's®

POSTCARDS

FROM

NEW YORK CITY

No matter how many times you've seen it, the Manhattan skyline is simply astounding. See chapter 7 for details on all the architectural landmarks. © Greg Pease/Tony Stone Images.

MoMA boasts masterworks by Picasso and just about every other major artist of the 20th century. See chapter 7. © Catherine Karnow Photography.

Discover the art and architecture of medieval Europe at The Cloisters. See chapter 7. © Rudi von Briel Photography.

The Met is the nation's premier art museum. See chapter 7. © Bob Krist Photography.

Downtown in the Village and SoHo, you can still find lots of mom-and-pop shops and unique stores, though many shoppers head straight for the big names like Bloomingdale's. See chapter 8. Both images © Catherine Karnow Photography.

View of the twin towers of the World Trade Center as seen from beneath the Brooklyn Bridge. See chapter 7. © Rudi Von Briel Photography.

Central Park is New York's most famous place to play. See chapter 7. © Kelly/Mooney Photography.

Tavern on the Green is known for its spectacular setting and décor. See chapter 6 for a complete review. © Catherine Karnow Photography.

Delis are one of the quintessential New York dining experiences. See chapter 6. © Catherine Karnow Photography.

There's no place more festive than New York during the holidays. Shoppers flock to the stores, and thousands of visitors attend Radio City's annual Christmas Spectacular. See chapter 9. © Color Day/The Image Bank.

New York has become a great place for a family vacation. Your kids will love the newly revitalized Times Square and the dinosaurs at the Museum of Natural History. See chapter 7. Both photos © Rudi Von Briel Photography.

Walking across the Brooklyn Bridge is one of our all-time favorite New York experiences. See chapter 7. © Kelly/Mooney Photography.

Mulberry Street, lined with restaurants and cafes, is the heart of Little Italy. See chapters 4 and 6. © Rudi Von Briel Photography.

The Chrysler Building is perhaps the city's most romantic architectural achievement. See chapter 7. © Andrea Pistolesi Photography.

New York cabbies hail from all over the world. See chapter 4 for helpful tips. © Catherine Karnow Photography.

Wall Street is the hub of the financial world. See chapter 7 for details on how to tour the Stock Exchange. © Rudi Von Briel Photography.

St. Patrick's is the largest Catholic cathedral in the United States. See chapter 7. © Robert Landau Photography.

The Flatiron Building, a triangular masterpiece, was one of the city's first skyscrapers. See chapter 7. © Rudi Von Briel Photography.

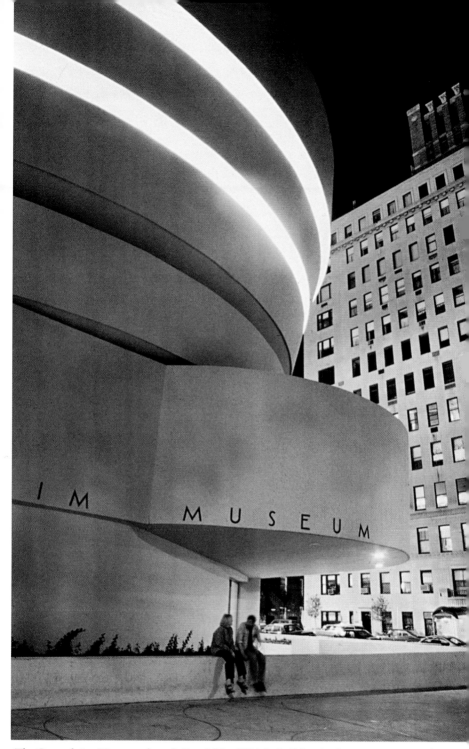

*The Guggenheim Museum, the only Frank Lloyd Wright building in the city, is more noted for its controversial design than for the collection of modern art it houses. See chapter 7.
© John Carucci Photography.*

No other monument so embodies the nation's ideals of political freedom and economic prosperity as the Statue of Liberty. See chapter 7. © Jon Ortner/Tony Stone Images.

Frommer's® 2000

New York City

by Cheryl Farr Leas

with research assistance from Nathaniel R. Leas
and Elena M. Dixon
Online Directory by Michael Shapiro

MACMILLAN • USA

ABOUT THE AUTHOR

Cheryl Farr Leas was a senior editor at Macmillan Travel before embarking on a freelance writing career. She also authors *Frommer's New York City from $80 a Day* and *The Complete Idiot's Travel Guide to Hawaii,* contributes to *Frommer's USA* and *The Complete Idiot's Honeymoon Guide,* and is hard at work on *The Complete Idiot's Travel Guide to California.* When she's not traveling, she's at home in Park Slope, Brooklyn, with her groovy husband, Rob, and their happy dog, Monty. Feel free to write her directly at rncleas@yahoo.com.

MACMILLAN TRAVEL

Macmillan General Reference USA, Inc.
1633 Broadway
New York, NY 10019

Find us online at **www.frommers.com**.

Copyright © 1999 by Macmillan General Reference USA, Inc.
Maps copyright © by Macmillan General Reference USA, Inc.

MACMILLAN is a registered trademark of Macmillan, Inc.
FROMMER'S is a registered trademark of Arthur Frommer. Used under license.

ISBN 0-02-863035-1
ISSN 1090-7335

Editor: Lisa Renaud
Production Editor: Michael Thomas
Walking Tour by Reid Bramblett
Design by Michele Laseau
Staff Cartographers: John Decamillis, Roberta Stockwell
Photo Editor: Richard Fox
Page Creation: Ellen Considine and Sean Monkhouse

SPECIAL SALES

Bulk purchases (10+ copies) of Frommer's and selected Macmillan travel guides are available to corporations, organizations, mail-order catalogs, institutions, and charities at special discounts, and can be customized to suit individual needs. For more information write to Special Sales, Macmillan General Reference, 1633 Broadway, New York, NY 10019.

Manufactured in the United States of America

5 4 3 2 1

Contents

List of Maps

AN INVITATION TO THE READER

In researching this book, we discovered many wonderful places—hotels, restaurants, shops, and more. We're sure you'll find others. Please tell us about them so we can share the information with your fellow travelers in upcoming editions. If you were disappointed with a recommendation, we'd love to know that, too. Please write to:

Frommer's New York City 2000
Macmillan Travel
1633 Broadway
New York, NY 10019

AN ADDITIONAL NOTE

Please be advised that travel information is subject to change at any time—and this is especially true of prices. We therefore suggest that you write or call ahead for confirmation when making your travel plans. The authors, editors, and publisher cannot be held responsible for the experiences of readers while traveling. Your safety is important to us, however, so we encourage you to stay alert and be aware of your surroundings. Keep a close eye on cameras, purses, and wallets, all favorite targets of thieves and pickpockets.

WHAT THE SYMBOLS MEAN

✪ Frommer's Favorites

Our favorite places and experiences—outstanding for quality, value, or both.

The following abbreviations are used for credit cards:

AE	American Express	EURO	Eurocard
CB	Carte Blanche	JCB	Japan Credit Bank
DC	Diners Club	MC	MasterCard
DISC	Discover	V	Visa
ER	EnRoute		

FIND FROMMER'S ONLINE

Arthur Frommer's Budget Travel (www.frommers.com) offers more than 6,000 pages of up-to-the-minute travel information—including the latest bargains and candid, personal articles updated daily by Arthur Frommer himself. No other Web site offers such comprehensive and timely coverage of the world of travel.

The Best of the Big Apple

Welcome to New York City—the only city on the planet brazen enough to call itself "The Capital of the World." New York has never been subtle, self-effacing, or coy. This is the Muhammad Ali of cities: We Are the Greatest!

It's precisely this kind of urban machismo that makes people either love New York or hate it—or both. Either you'll be enthralled by the tempo, glamour, and sheer excitement of it all, or you'll be stunned by the noise, the intimate mingling of inhuman poverty and unimaginable wealth, the smog, and the callousness that's an everyday occurrence on these city streets. If your emotional metronome swings back and forth from one moment to the next, take heart: We New Yorkers have a never-ending love-hate relationship with this awful, wonderful town. We talk endlessly about escaping for the weekend, commiserate about subways that arrive late, and bemoan the noise, the rents, the crowds, the cab drivers who don't seem to know Lincoln Center from the Lower East Side. Yet still we stay.

The questions beg to be asked: Why do we stay? And what is it about New York City that makes you, dear reader, want to join us?

Any attempt to define New York today recalls the Zen wisdom that you can't step in the same stream twice. The city is so mutable, so constantly changing, that it's almost impossible to get a fix on. Restaurants and nightclubs become trendy overnight, then die under the weight of their own popularity. (Yogi Berra, of course, had the perfect phrase for that very phenomenon: "Nobody goes there anymore; it's too crowded.") Fashions, almost by definition, change in the time it takes to try on a pair of vinyl pants. Broadway shows, exercise fads, even neighborhoods are all subject to the same Big Apple fickleness. But within this ebb and flow lies the answer: No other place keeps any of us on our toes quite like New York City. Nowhere else is the challenge so tough, the pace so relentless, the stimuli so everchanging and insistent—and the payoff so rewarding. Simply put, New York never gets boring. Anything can happen here.

The city has a special magnetism—a charisma, if you will—that pulls in the intelligent, the creative, the determined, the overbearing, and the overblown from all over the world. Just about any language and any dialect is spoken here, from Mandarin to Brooklynese; no other dot on the map is quite so ethnically, culturally, and socially diverse. This is the nerve center of world finance and trade. The international hub of advertising, publishing, entertainment, and fashion.

The creative core for the arts. The top showcase for pure celebrity. And, now as never before, a huge magnet for travelers from all over the country and around the globe, in search of a brief glimpse of it all.

You've probably heard the good news: The city is in top form, its finest in more than fifty years. The economy is up, and crime is down. Everywhere you look, things are being refurbished and the city is steadily improving. It has even become, believe it or not, *family friendly*—just look at the new peep show– and porn-free Times Square. New Yorkers love to complain about "Hizzoner," Mayor Rudy Giuliani, because he likes to take the lion's share of credit—more than he deserves, methinks. But few alive today have ever seen the city so radiant, so manageable, and he's had the good fortune to usher in the renaissance. New Yorkers love to wax nostalgic about the good-old, bad-old days, but the fact is that we're reveling in our own good fortune. Now is a great time to be in New York.

Visitors, pumped with curiosity about this "new" New York, are arriving by the millions, swarming the city's streets, sights, hotels, museums, restaurants, nightclubs, and theaters. And the city, aglow in its newfound optimism, is welcoming them, and you, with open arms. So come—and be prepared to be overwhelmed, exasperated, delighted, and utterly charmed. That, after all, is what the Big Apple is all about.

1 Frommer's Favorite New York City Experiences

- **Sailing to the Statue of Liberty.** If you have time to do only one thing on your visit to New York, this is what it should be. No monument so embodies the nation's, and the world's, notion of political freedom and economic potential more than Lady Liberty. As silly as this may sound, the view never loses its power—and neither do the skyline views of Manhattan, which are breathtaking from this perspective. The ferry that takes you out to **Liberty Island** also stops at the historic federal immigration station on **Ellis Island,** gateway to America for nearly half of the nation's forefathers. The museum's exhibits illustrate, with moving simplicity, what coming to the promised land was all about. If you want the view but prefer to skip the tourist crowds, consider catching the free Staten Island ferry, a city icon unto itself, instead. See chapter 7.

- **Visiting the Museums.** The **Metropolitan Museum of Art,** the **American Museum of Natural History,** the **Museum of Modern Art,** the **Whitney Museum of American Art,** the **Guggenheim**—museum hopping just doesn't get any better than this. The number of masterworks housed in this city is mind-boggling. But don't just stick to the biggies; New York boasts a wealth of smaller, lower-profile museums that speak to specific interests—from folk art to photography to financial history—and house some phenomenal treasures. For a complete rundown, see chapter 7.

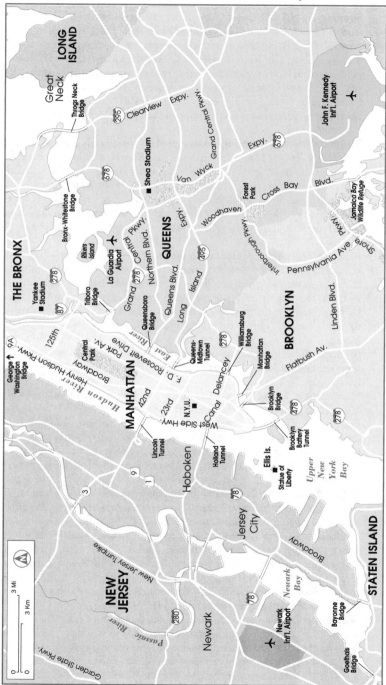

- **Strolling the Neighborhoods.** One of the greatest things about New York is the distinct character of each of its neighborhoods. Rather than trying to quick-scan them all, I highly recommend picking one and really getting to know it. Wend your way through the historic streets of **Greenwich Village,** saunter the cast-iron canyons of **SoHo,** or explore the lovely, trendy **Flatiron District.** All you really need is a map and a sense of adventure. If you prefer a little structure, consider taking one of the many excellent walking tours that are available—there's no better way to get to know a neighborhood than with an expert at the helm. See chapters 4 and 7.
- **Walking the Brooklyn Bridge.** A marvel of civic engineering when it first connected Brooklyn to Manhattan in 1883, the **Brooklyn Bridge** is still able to inspire awe even in jaded New Yorkers. I never tire of admiring its Gothic-inspired stone pylons and intricate steel-cable webs. Get an up-close look, and some marvelous views of Manhattan, by taking the easy stroll from end to end. Start at the Brooklyn end for best effect, and consider preceding your walk with a stroll through historic Brooklyn Heights for a leafy, lovely afternoon. See chapter 7.
- **Being on Top of the World.** Go to the top. Straight to the top—higher than you've ever been before. New York is made to be seen from above, in the full light of day or in the full glitter of night—it's your choice. Better yet, get both perspectives. Head up to the Top of the World observation deck at the **World Trade Center** where, if you're lucky, you'll be able to go out on the rooftop promenade, the world's highest open-air observation deck. If you'd rather avoid the tourist crowds, book a table at Windows on the World or enjoy a cocktail at the Greatest Bar on Earth, which boast the same incredible views. And don't forget about the **Empire State Building**—not quite as high up, but doubly romantic. See chapters 6, 7, and 9.
- **Star Gazing at Grand Central Terminal.** Always a beaux arts gem, this majestic 1913 railroad station has gotten a remarkable facelift that has made it a must-see. Every surface glitters with renewed optimism—but none more than the masterful ceiling, once again brilliant with 24-karat gold zodiac constellations against a gorgeous blue-green sky. Walk in, throw your head back, and watch the stars gleam. For a longer view, consider dining at Michael Jordan's—The Steak House, the mezzanine-level restaurant that opens onto the stellar view. See chapters 6 and 7.
- **Ogling the City's Art Deco Marvels.** Nothing embodies the city's historic sense of optimism more than its streamline masterpieces. And nowhere is the art deco style more passionately realized than at **Rockefeller Center,** the business-and-entertainment center at the heart of midtown. The most romantic of the city's skyscrapers, the chrome-topped **Chrysler Building,** is another art deco gem; look for the gargoyles, looking suspiciously like streamline-Gothic hood ornaments, jutting out from the upper floors. And when you visit the marvelous **Empire State Building,** don't miss the streamline mural in the lobby in your rush to get to the top. See chapter 7.
- **Wandering Central Park.** This beautiful accident of civic planning makes the otherwise uninterrupted urban jungle tolerable for workaday New Yorkers. Without this great green park, I couldn't imagine life in the city. Be sure to seek out Strawberry Fields, the living memorial to John Lennon, which exhorts us all to IMAGINE. Book a table at Park View at the Boathouse for the most magical alfresco dining in the city. See chapters 6 and 7.
- **Watching Your Favorite Talk Show Being Taped.** If you have the forethought (to send away months in advance) or the patience (to wait in the standby line),

you can watch Dave, Conan, Rosie, Jon Stewart, the ladies of *The View,* or even Regis and Kathie Lee work their TV magic. If sketch comedy or sitcoms are more your speed, think *Spin City, Cosby,* or—the holy grail of TV audience wannabes—*Saturday Night Live.* To start planning, see chapter 7.

- **Dining Out.** New York is the world capital of great eating. This city boasts some of the finest fine dining in the entire world. Consider splurging on a meal at Chanterelle, Le Cirque, Gramercy Tavern, Nobu, or one of the city's other top-flight restaurants, a surprising number of which are capable of creating lifelong culinary memories. But the true beauty of New York's restaurant scene is that you don't have to spend a fortune to eat well. You'll find cheap but dazzling Chinese in Chinatown, pastrami to die for at any number of Jewish delis, pasta that even your Italian grandmother could love . . . the list goes on and on. See chapter 6.
- **Shopping 'til You Drop.** There's no more glorious shoppers' paradise in the country—maybe even the world—than New York City. You want it? New York's got it. Check out chapter 8 to find it.
- **Watching the Curtain Rise on a Play.** There's nothing like the immediacy and excitement of a stage production in action. Movie and TV stars know it, which is why more and more are strutting their stuff on the New York stages. Make it a priority to catch a live theater production while you're in town. If musicals are your thing, stick to the Great White Way; if you prefer cutting-edge drama, try Off Broadway. See chapter 9 for tips on getting tickets.
- **Catching a Ball Game.** There's no better place to experience the trademark "Noo Yawk" attitude than in the grandstand. New York fans have a love/hate relationship with their sports teams—they're saints when they win, bums when they lose. There's never a dull moment: Everybody has an opinion, and it's all part of the show. Check out the Yankees at **Yankee Stadium,** the Mets at **Shea,** and, if you can score tickets, the Knicks or the Rangers at **Madison Square Garden.** See chapter 7.
- **Bar Hopping & Nightclubbing.** It doesn't matter whether you're the Stoli martini or the draft beer type, whether cabaret or stand-up comedy or electronica is your thing: New York has the after-dark hangout for you. They don't call this "The City That Never Sleeps" for nothing. See chapter 9 for all the options.
- **Celebrating the Holidays in the City.** As millions of my neighbors head out of town to the shores and the mountains, I love to stay behind. On July 4, a peaceful hush comes over the city—until the fireworks explode overhead, lighting up the night sky with patriotic flair. Nobody does Labor Day like the "ladies" of Wigstock. On Halloween, more than the usual ghouls walk among us in Greenwich Village. The huge hot-air balloons of the Macy's Thanksgiving Day Parade bring out the kid in all of us. No place is more festive than Rockefeller Center at Christmastime. And on Chinese New Year, a bright dragon promises great fortune ahead. For details on these events and others, see the "Calendar of Events" in chapter 2.

2 Best Hotel Bets

This city boasts some of the best hotels in the world—and, believe it or not, some great affordable choices, too. For the details on these and other New York City hotels, see chapter 5.

- **Best New Year's Eve Lookouts:** Even if the century hasn't already turned by the time you read this, you're not going to have much luck booking a room for the ring-in-the-millennium party if you don't have one by now. But watching the

New Year's ball drop is an event worthy of celebration any year. Hotels boasting great views of the action include the **Crowne Plaza Manhattan,** 1605 Broadway (☎ **800/243-NYNY**); the **Millennium Broadway,** 145 W. 44th St. (☎ **800/ 622-5569**); and **New York Marriott Marquis,** 1535 Broadway (☎ **800/ 843-4898**). But none of these monoliths can beat the intimate **Casablanca Hotel,** 147 W. 43rd St. (☎ **888/922-7225**), for vantage. This charming Moroccan-themed hotel has a wonderful rooftop deck (for guests only, natch) that couldn't be better situated for the midnight excitement—it's practically a private show.

- **Best Landmark Hotel:** Hands down, the newly and exquisitely restored **Algonquin,** 59 W. 44th St. (☎ **800/555-3000**), is the winner. The birthplace of *The New Yorker* and home to Dorothy Parker's legendary Round Table in the '20s, this venerable beauty has managed to recreate the glamour of the past without pricing itself out of the reach of regular folks. Even if you don't stay here, stop into the wonderful oak-paneled and velvet-seated lobby—one of the most comfortable and welcoming in the city—for afternoon tea or a post-theater cocktail.
- **Best for Classic New York Elegance:** There's lots of competition in this category, but the low-key **Sherry-Netherland,** 751 Fifth Ave. (☎ **800/247-4377**), steals the show. This gargoyled neo-Romanesque residence hotel is the epitome of understated service and elegance. The rooms and suites provide a chance to experience the glamour of uptown apartment living, and the location—at the southeast of Central Park, presiding grandly over Fifth Avenue at its most fabulous—couldn't be more spectacular. Quintessentially New York in every way.
- **Best Trendy Hotels:** The **Soho Grand,** 310 W. Broadway (☎ **800/ 637-7200**), with its cool Downtown location and even cooler retro-modern design, competes for star power with Ian Schrager's endlessly hip **Royalton,** 44 W. 44th St. (☎ **800/635-9013**), which is primed to transcend yet another decade with its trendiness still intact.
- **Best Service if Money Is No Object:** For the ultimate pampering, you'd be hard pressed to do better than the **Carlyle,** 35 E. 76th St. (☎ **800/227-5737**), where the staff-to-guest ratio is a phenomenal two-to-one; you won't want for anything here. But these days, the Carlyle is getting a run for its money from **Trump International Hotel & Tower,** 1 Central Park West (☎ **888/44-TRUMP**). Your very own Trump Attaché will fulfill your every whim, keeping meticulous notes all the while for your next stay, when you won't even have to *ask.* Of course, such personal attention in Manhattan doesn't come cheap—but you'll be in supreme comfort as you max out that platinum card!
- **Best Service for the Budget-Minded:** The professional staff at the **Broadway Inn,** 264 W. 46th St. (☎ **800/826-6300**), just may be the most helpful in the city. They're so committed to making their guests feel welcome and at home in New York that they give you a hotline number upon check-in so you can call when you're out and about if you need directions, advice on where to eat, or any other assistance. When you come home from your long day of sightseeing, they'll be happy to order in delivery from any of the nearby restaurants for you. And you thought New York wasn't friendly!
- **Best for Business Travelers:** The **Millenium Hilton,** 55 Church St. (☎ **800/ 835-2220**), is the best hotel in the Financial District, with an ideal location (just across the street from the World Trade Center), first-rate amenities, and stellar views. In midtown, **The Peninsula–New York,** 700 Fifth Ave. (☎ **800/ 262-9467**), is the ultimate address for power brokers; each room has a terrific L-shaped executive workstation with desk-level inputs, direct-line fax, and

dual-line speakerphones, plus other high-tech amenities for ladder-climbing execs. If your expense account isn't that big, book in at the **Doubletree Guest Suites,** 1568 Broadway (☎ 800/222-TREE), where you can get a two-room suite with all the comforts of home *and* office for the same money you'd pay for a standard hotel room; there are even some conference suites available if you want to hold an ensuite meeting.

- **Best for Families:** The **Doubletree Guest Suites,** 1568 Broadway (☎ 800/222-TREE), isn't just for business travelers—it's great for families, too. There's an entire floor of childproof suites, complete with living room for spreading out and kitchenette for preparing light meals. And your young ones will love the Kids Club (for ages 3 to 12), which boasts a playroom, an arts-and-crafts center, and computer and video games. For more kid-friendly suggestions, see "Family-Friendly Hotels" in chapter 5.
- **Best for a Romantic Getaway:** Even harried New Yorkers have been known to stow away for a love-in weekend at the **Inn at Irving Place,** 56 Irving Place (☎ 800/685-1447). Like a page stolen from a Gilded Age novel, the inn is historically evocative. Luxury is the rule, from an antique Victorian drawing room to graciously appointed guest rooms. Its Gramercy Park address and no-children-under-12 policy make for a peaceful, very adult setting.
- **Best Moderately Priced Hotel:** The **Hotel Metro,** 45 W. 35th St. (☎ 800/356-3870), is a midtown gem that gives you a surprisingly good deal, including a marble bath. I also love the **Wyndham,** 42 W. 58th St. (☎ 800/257-1111), a family-owned charmer with simply enormous rooms on a great block and only steps away from Fifth Avenue shopping and Central Park. And on the Upper West Side is the **Lucerne,** 201 W. 79th St. (☎ 800/492-8122), a sophisticated hotel that's big on comforts and service but not on price.
- **Best Budget Hotel:** If you don't mind sharing a bath, the charming **Larchmont Hotel,** in the heart of Greenwich Village at 27 W. 11th St. (☎ 212/989-9333), is the best budget deal in town. If you want your very own facilities, you can't lose with the **Cosmopolitan Hotel–Tribeca,** 95 W. Broadway (☎ 888/895-9400), with small but comfy IKEAish rooms and petite but immaculate private bathrooms.
- **Best Alternative Accommodations:** If you're a youth-minded traveler looking for an artsy environment, the wild **Gershwin Hotel,** 7 E. 27th St. (☎ 212/545-8000), is the place for you. Billy Name is the house photog—what more do I need to say? If you're a grown-up looking for something special, book into **Country Inn the City,** on W. 77th Street (☎ 212/580-4183), one of the most impeccably done guest houses I've ever seen—and superbly located in prime Upper West Side territory.
- **Best Health Club:** **Le Parker Méridien,** 118 W. 57th St. (☎ 800/543-4300), is home to Club La Racquette, a comprehensive fitness center with a rooftop pool and racquetball, squash, and handball courts. But it's hard to beat **The Peninsula–New York,** 700 Fifth Ave. (☎ 800/759-3000), which boasts a trilevel 35,000-square-foot fitness center with a gorgeous pool and complete spa services. If these luxury hotels are out of your price range, consider the **Crowne Plaza Manhattan,** 1605 Broadway (☎ 800/243-NYNY), a somewhat more affordable hotel that boasts it own branch of the New York Sports Club, complete with Olympic-size pool and steam rooms.
- **Best Amenity for A-Types:** The **Lowell,** 28 E. 63rd St. (☎ 800/221-4444), boasts a suite with a private gym that, not surprisingly, Madonna has called home from time to time.

- **Best Weekend Packages:** For a great Theater District deal, see what's on offer from the **Millennium Broadway,** 145 W. 44th St. (☎ **800/622-5569**); be sure to check www.millenniumbroadway.com for Web page–only deals. At the unaffilliated downtown **Millenium Hilton,** 55 Church St. (☎ **800/835-2220**), vacationers can make phenomenal deals on luxury rooms abandoned for the weekend by Wall Street business travelers.

- **Best Suite Deals:** You'd be hard-pressed to find a better deal than the **Hotel Beacon,** 2130 Broadway (☎ **800/572-4969**). Located on the Upper West Side, one of the city's most desirable residential neighborhoods, the Beacon has spacious suites that boast all the comforts, including microwaves in the kitchenettes and well-furnished living rooms with pull-out sofas. Most New York families don't live in two-bedroom apartments as big as the ones you'll find here—and they even have a second bath. With suites running just $205 to $450, this place fills up fast, so book early. If you'd rather be in Midtown, try **The Kimberly,** 145 E. 50th St. (☎ **800/683-0400**), where the prices of these cozy suites can climb high in the busiest seasons, but the off-season deals are remarkable.

- **Best for Disabled Travelers:** Disabled travelers no longer have to spend a fortune to stay in a hotel that can accommodate them. The affordable **Gorham,** 136 W. 55th St. (☎ **800/735-0710**), features rooms equipped for the wheelchair bound, smoke detectors for the hearing impaired, braille and audible floor indicators in elevators, and braille electronic key cards. And at press time, the **Milburn,** 242 W. 76th St. (☎ **800/833-9622**), was adding five new lobby-level wheelchair-accessible rooms to their selection of comfortable, budget-minded accommodations.

- **Best for Your Pooch:** If you really want to pamper your pup, head to the Hartz Mountain–owned **Soho Grand Hotel,** 310 W. Broadway (☎ **800/965-3000**), where there's a pet-friendly room-service menu available 24 hours a day, and the guest services desk will be happy to arrange anything from grooming and nail care to dog walking and custom clothing. Et tu, Bowser!

- **Best In-Room Tchotchke:** They get some stiff competition from W New York (where you get a windowbox of fresh green lawn to tend), but the **Soho Grand,** 310 West Broadway (☎ **800/637-7200**), comes out the clear winner in this category. Each guestroom features a pretty goldfish in a bowl to keep you company for the duration of your stay. You also get a take-out carrier for Goldie, so your temporary pet can help you paint the town red.

3 Best Dining Bets

One of the great joys of being in New York is that there's fabulous food at nearly every turn. You can flex your gold card on some of the most memorable fine dining in the world, or go ethnic—Chinese, Jewish, Italian, and much, much more—to indulge in the best cheap eats you'll find anywhere. For the details on these and other terrific New York City restaurants, see chapter 6.

- **Best Spot for a Break-the-Bank Celebration:** For understated elegance, perfect service, and sublime New French cuisine, there's **Chanterelle,** 2 Harrison St. (☎ **212/966-6960**), which can cause even the most jaded gourmands to swoon. For pure New York excitement, the choice is **Le Cirque 2000,** 455 Madison Ave. (☎ **212/303-7788**), whose legendary panache simply can't be beat.

- **Best for Romance:** Downtown, reserve at **One If By Land, Two If By Sea,** 14 Barrow St. (☎ **212/228-0822**), where candles and lush piano music take you back in time and put you in the mood. In Midtown, try **March,** 405 E. 58th St. (☎ **212/754-6272**), for a sublime meal in a cozy town house.

On New York

It's a city where everyone mutinies but no one deserts.

—Harry Hershfield

The end [of the world] wouldn't come as a surprise here. Many people already bank on it.

—Saul Bellow

- **Best View:** Without a doubt, the winner is **Windows on the World,** high atop 1 World Trade Center (☎ **212/524-7011**). No matter how many years I live in this city, the spectacular view never fails to take my breath away. And thanks to new chef Michael Lomanaco, the cuisine is garnering similar raves.
- **Best Spot for a Business Lunch:** The landmark **"21" Club,** 21 W. 52nd St. (☎ **212/582-7200**), is the classic choice of New York's old-school power set. If you prefer more casual, more convenient, and want to impress with your New York acumen, head to the **Oyster Bar,** in Grand Central Terminal (☎ **212/490-6650**), another New York classic that's a perfect spot to seal the deal.
- **Best Spot for a Ladies-Who-Lunch Lunch:** There's no meal I enjoy more than a society lunch. What's more decadent than lingering over three courses and a couple of glasses of wine for a few hours in the middle of the day, when regular folks are hard at work? **Café Boulud,** 20 E. 76th St. (☎ **212/772-2600**), is the ideal place to rub elbows with the Upper East Side society dames who've made this a way of life.
- **Best Spot for Brunch:** For Uptown elegant, try **Café des Artistes,** 1 W. 67th St. (☎ **212/877-3500**). For Uptown casual, head to **Sarabeth's Kitchen,** 423 Amsterdam Ave. (☎ **212/496-6280**). For Downtown elegant, head to **Windows on the World,** 1 World Trade Center (☎ **212/524-7000**), where the top-of-the-tower views just can't be beat. For Downtown casual, **Le Gigot,** 18 Cornelia St. (☎ **212/627-3737**) is the Village's best-kept secret—until now, that is.
- **Best Pre-Theater Choice:** There's **Chez Josephine,** 414 W. 42nd St. (☎ **212/594-1925**), a wonderful choice for its sexy appeal and abundance of nostalgia *à la française.* If you're heading to Lincoln Center, you can't do better than sublime **Jean Georges,** in the Trump International Hotel & Tower, 1 Central Park West (☎ **212/299-3900**), where the faultless waitstaff will make sure you're wowed well before curtaintime.
- **Best Early-Bird Dinner Deal:** If you don't mind dining early and you have the willpower to stick to the prix-fixe menu, the two-course $20 dinner at **Alison on Dominick Street,** at 38 Dominick St. in SoHo (☎ **212/727-1188**), is a smokin' deal. Since seatings are between 5 and 6:30pm, you can even take advantage of Alison on Dominick as a pre-theater choice, as long as you allow yourself time to hop a cab uptown.
- **Best Dessert:** There are a lot of stellar pastry chefs in town, but you'd be hard-pressed to do better than the remarkable confections at **Payard Pâtisserie & Bistro,** 1032 Lexington Ave. (☎ **212/717-5252**), which is well located for a pastry break during a day of Upper East Side museum-hopping or shopping.
- **Best Contemporary American Cuisine: Gramercy Tavern,** 42 E. 20th St. (☎ **212/477-0777**), does everything just right. The beautiful dining room is the perfect blend of urban sophisitication and heartland rusticity, the service is warm and friendly, and its New American menu is pleasing from start to finish. Excellent through and through.

- **Best Chinese Cuisine:** With all the culinary wonders that Chinatown has to offer, this is a tough choice. But whenever I think about the steamy soup dumplings at **Joe's Shanghai,** 9 Pell St. (☎ 212/233-8888), I can't help but swoon.
- **Best French Cuisine:** Downtown, magical **Chanterelle,** 2 Harrison St. (☎ 212/966-6960), is the obvious choice, serving ethereal French with welcome comtemporary twists. Uptown, there's **Daniel,** 60 E. 65th St. (☎ 212/288-0033), where superstar chef Daniel Boulud's French country fare is sublime. For more affordable French, your best bet is **Le Gigot,** a true slice of St-Germain at 18 Cornelia St. (☎ 212/627-3737).
- **Best Italian Cuisine: San Domenico**, 240 Central Park South (☎ 212/265-5959), gets high marks for owner Tony May's consistently excellent Northern Italian fare. For the best-bang-for-your-buck Italian, head to **Bar Pitti,** 268 Sixth Ave. (☎ 212/982-3300), a wonderfully authentic Tuscan-style trattoria.
- **Best Japanese Cuisine:** In a category all its own is the inventive **Nobu,** 105 Hudson St. (☎ 212/219-0500), where unusual textures, daring combinations, and surprising flavors add up to a first-rate dining adventure that you won't soon forget. For sushi as high art, head to super-fashionable **BondSt,** 6 Bond St. (☎ 212/777-2500), where you'll find faultlessly fresh, beautifully prepared raw fish, some of it flown in from Japan daily.
- **Best Home-Style Cooking:** No other restaurant warms my heart more than the aptly named **Home,** 20 Cornelia St. (☎ 212/243-9579), where the cumin-crusted pork chop sits in a bed of homemade barbecue sauce that's better than Dad used to make, and the silky-smooth chocolate pudding even Mom would admit is better than hers.
- **Best Jewish Deli:** Kosher **Second Avenue Deli,** 156 Second Ave. (☎ 212/677-0606), is New York's deli among those who know their kreplach, matzo, and pastrami. No cutesy sandwiches named for celebrities here—just top-notch Jewish classics.
- **Best Burger and Beer:** Ask a hundred New Yorkers, and you'll get a hundred opinions. But for my money, there's no better choice than **Old Town Bar & Restaurant,** 45 E. 18th St. (☎ 212/529-6732). Whether you go low-fat turkey or bacon-chili-cheddar, the burgers at this venerable 19th-century pub are perfect every time. The fries are addictively crisp, the Buffalo wings are slathered in spicy sauce, and there's a whole selection of great beers on tap.
- **Best Pizza:** Pizza doesn't get any better than the coal oven–baked, fresh mozzarella-topped pies at **Patsy Grimaldi's Pizzeria,** 19 Old Fulton St., Brooklyn Heights (☎ 718/858-4300). If you're unwilling to travel across the river for real Noo Yawk pizza, head to **Lombardi's,** 32 Spring St. (☎ 212/941-7994), which has been baking up its own coal-oven pies since 1905.
- **Best Seafood:** The black bass ceviche alone—not to mention everything else that comes out of its blue-ribbon kitchen—keeps **Le Bernardin,** 155 W. 51st St. (☎ 212/489-1515), at the top of the world's great fish restaurants. If your budget isn't quite big enough to handle such a splurge, head to **Pisces,** 95 Ave. A (☎ 212/260-6660).
- **Best for Celebrity Spotting:** It's the luck of the draw, really. But for the best odds, head to **Le Cirque 2000,** in the New York Palace Hotel, 455 Madison Ave. (☎ 212/303-7788), where the crowd is full of big-name movie stars, politicos, and socialites; I personally spotted Whoopi just moments after walking through the front door. And forget Moomba: Your other best bet is **Mr. Chow,** 324 E. 57th St. (☎ 212/751-9030), a favorite among Uptown celebs like Mark

Wahlberg, Madonna, and the latest names in hip hop—and where you'll be treated like a star, too.

- **Best Late-Night Hangout:** Half authentic French bistro, half all-American diner, **Florent,** 69 Gansevoort St. (☎ **212/989-5779**), is the hipster crowd's favorite after-hours hangout. Thanks to its good food, great people-watching, and wonderful sense of humor, it's mine, too.

- **Best Alfresco Dining: Park View at the Boathouse,** on the lake in Central Park, near 72nd Street and Park Drive North (☎ **212/517-2233**), is without rival. It's both quintessentially New York and wonderfully removed from the urban hustle and bustle. If you're visiting in summer, don't miss this one-of-a-kind dining experience.

- **Best Wine List:** A whole fleet of young sommeliers have landed on the city's restaurant scene, bringing fresh ideas and a wonderful enthusiasm to wine lists all around town, from the respected cellar at **Windows on the World,** 1 World Trade Center (☎ **212/524-7011**), to upstarts like **Babbo,** 110 Waverly Place (☎ **212/777-0303**), where Italian grapes are the stars of a very exciting show. But it's hard to beat **Le Cirque 2000,** in the New York Palace hotel, 455 Madison Ave. (☎ **212/303-7788**), where the keen sommeliers staff will be happy to help you choose among their superb—and surprisingly well-priced—collection of French, Italian, and American vintages.

- **Best Wine Deals:** Tuesday isn't just Tuesday anymore—at least not at the **Bridge Cafe,** 279 Water St. (☎ **212/227-3344**), where it's Wine Discovery Tuesday. Every bottle on the restaurant's already–well priced all-American wine list is 30% off. **Cité,** 120 W. 51st St. (☎ **212/956-7100**), offers a nightly deal from 8pm to midnight that's almost too good to be true: For $59.50, you get a three-course meal—your choice of appetizer, main course, and dessert—and you can enjoy unlimited quantities of the four wines on offer *at no extra charge.* And you're not getting the cheap stuff: Choices on recent offer included a '90 Mondavi cabernet, a '97 Acacia chardonnay, a '94 Chalone Vinyard pinot noir reserve, and Taittinger brut for celebrating. These deals should still be on while you're in town, but call ahead to be sure.

- **Best Newcomer:** With **Babbo,** 110 Waverly Place (☎ **212/777-0303**), TV Food Network chef Mario Batali has created the ideal setting for his exciting Northern Italian cooking. The setting is beautiful, the service warm and gracious, and the food excellent. Nobody does pasta better—I can't wait to go back.

- **Best Service:** With an almost-unheard-of 27 (out of a possible 30) rating for service from Zagat's, **Chanterelle,** 2 Harrison St. (☎ **212/966-6960**), simply can't be beat. The service somehow manages to be impeccable without being too formal or stuffy. Other restaurants try, but this is how it's supposed to be. A magical experience, and worth every penny.

2

Planning Your Trip to New York City

In the pages that follow, you'll find everything you need to know to handle the practical details of planning your trip in advance: airlines and area airports, a calendar of events, resources for those of you with special needs, and much more.

Note that there's no need to rent a car for your visit to New York. Driving is a nightmare and parking is ridiculously expensive (or near-to-impossible in some neighborhoods). It's much easier to get around using public transportation and taxis. If you're going to visit Aunt Erma on Long Island or you have some other need to travel beyond the five boroughs, call one of the major car-rental companies, such as **Hertz** (☎ **800/654-3131;** www.hertz.com), **National** (☎ **800/ 227-7368;** www.nationalcar.com), or **Avis** (☎ **800/230-4898;** www. avis.com), all of which have airport and Manhattan locations.

1 Visitor Information

For information before you leave home, your best source (besides this book, of course) is the **New York Convention & Visitors Bureau** (NYCVB), 810 Seventh Ave., New York, NY 10019. You can call the bureau's 24-hour hotline at ☎ **800/NYC-VISIT** or 212/397-8222 to order a **Big Apple Visitors Kit,** detailing hotels, restaurants, theaters, attractions, events, and more. It costs $5.95 to receive the packet (payable by credit card), which will arrive at most U.S. addresses within a week or two. If you don't want to pay the six bucks, they'll send you the guide that's the heart of the kit for free, but expect it to take 4 to 6 weeks to reach you. The bureau also has a terrific website at **www.nycvisit.com**. To speak to a travel counselor who can answer specific questions, call ☎ **212/ 484-1222** Monday through Friday from 9am to 5pm EST (multilingual counselors are available).

For visitor center and information desk locations once you arrive, see "Visitor Information" in chapter 4.

FOR BRITISH VISITORS In late 1998, an **NYCVB Visitor Infor-mation Center** opened in London at 33–34 Carnaby St (☎ **0171/ 437-8300**). The new center offers a wealth of information and free one-on-one travel-planning assistance to New York–bound travelers. It's open Monday through Friday from 10am to 4pm.

SITE SEEING: THE BIG APPLE ON THE WEB

The NYCVB's **www.nycvisit.com** is a terrific online resource offering tons of information on the city, from trip-planning basics to tips on where to take the kids.

But there's much more to be learned from the web than the official line. Sure, there's a lot of junk out there in cyberspace—but the net boasts some terrific sites on the city, the best of which can supply up-to-the minute news, current events calendars, information for those of you with special interests, or just another point of view. Here are our favorite general information sites (we'll also recommend lots of subject-specific sites in the chapters that follow):

- **www.newyork.sidewalk.com**   The Microsoft-backed **Sidewalk** is an excellent source for up-to-the-minute information on what's happening in the city. It's particularly good for the latest nightlife information—you'll find reviews of current theater, music, and other performing arts events, and most club listings even feature day-to-day schedules. I also like Sidewalk for the latest restaurant dish and sample sales, but competitor Citysearch's (see below) shopping listings are more comprehensive. Be patient, because Sidewalk can be a bit slow to download at times, and it may take wading through a few pages to get where you want.

- **www.newyork.citysearch.com**   Done in cooperation with the *Daily News* and *Time Out* magazine—hands down the best weekly magazine source for what's going on in the city—**Citysearch** is much more well organized than Sidewalk, with the home page directly linking you wherever you want to go, and much quicker to load. They're also all over current happenings, with direct links to recommended events. The listings are as comprehensive as Sidewalk's, sometimes more so, but new stuff almost always hits Sidewalk first. I suggest checking them both out—that's what I do!

- **www.nytoday.com**   The *New York Times* created this site as a gift to those of us who wanted access to the *Times'* cultural coverage without having to wade through the main site (**www.nytimes.com**), which requires you to register and pay archiving fees on past articles. Set up in an easy-access daily calendar format, the site is an expanded version of the paper's cultural coverage. You'll find even more events listings and critics' reviews in this electronic version, including museum schedules and sports events, plus the *Times'* definitive restaurant reviews.

- **www.papermag.com**   The online version of the glossy alterna-monthly *Paper* serves as good prep for those of you who want to experience the hipper side of the city. There's opinionated coverage on clubs and bars (including extensive gay scene coverage)—virtually all downtown, of course.

- **www.panix.com/clay/nyc**   Commonly referred to as New York City Reference, this handy site is a virtual hyperlink index of New York–related sites. Begun in 1995, it's regularly updated, and at press time there were about 2,000 links covering every subject area from "The Best Public Toilets in New York City" (**www.angelfire.com/ny/NYCtoilets,** if you want to bypass the middleman) to "Webcams: Live Pictures of New York City."

- **www.TheInsider.com/nyc**   This straightforward site presents an archive of features ranging from New York survival tips to the city's best coffee bars. I find both Sidewalk and Citysearch to be more authoritative, but the photo links offer an exciting visual preview of your Gotham visit.

2 Money

You never have to carry too much cash in New York, and while the city's pretty safe these days, it's best not to overstuff your wallet (although always make sure you have at least $20 in taxi fare on hand). Credit cards and travelers checks are accepted almost everywhere—plastic is even accepted in the subway system now—and ATMs are almost always on hand in case you need the green stuff.

ATMS

Almost all New York City ATMs are linked to a national network that most likely includes your bank at home. **Cirrus** (☎ 800/424-7787; www.mastercard.com/atm) and **Plus** (☎ 800/843-7587; www.visa.com/atms) are the two most popular networks; check the back of your ATM card to see which network your bank belongs to. The city's biggest ATM networks belong to Citibank, Chase, and Fleet banks, which belong to both networks.

In the most popular Manhattan neighborhoods, there's a bank with ATM machines on every other corner or so. The only places you may have some difficulty in are more far-flung neighborhoods, like the far East Village or far uptown in Harlem. If you don't easily spot an ATM, use the 800 numbers to locate one in your destination.

New York's Consumer Affairs chief has tried to ward off additional ATM charges for consumers, but it seems to be a losing battle. At press time, the last holdout from additional charges was **Republic National Bank,** which has ATM locations throughout the city, including 1185 Sixth Ave., between 46th and 47th streets; 661 Eighth Ave., at 42nd Street; and on the southeast concourse of the World Trade Center. You'll find a Republic National Bank locator online at **www.rnb.com**.

Otherwise expect to pay $1 or $1.50 each time you withdraw money from an ATM, in addition to what your home bank charges. Try to stay away from commercial machines, like those in hotel lobbies and corner delis, which often charge $2 or more per transaction.

TRAVELER'S CHECKS

Traveler's checks are something of an anachronism from the days before the ATM made cash accessible at any time. These days, they seem less necessary because 24-hour ATMs allow you to withdraw small amounts of cash as needed—and thus avoid the risk of carrying a fortune around. But New York is an expensive city, capable of sucking money right out of your pocket. And if you're withdrawing money every day, you might be better off with traveler's checks—provided that you don't mind showing identification every time you want to cash one.

You can get traveler's checks at almost any bank. **American Express** offers checks in denominations of $10, $20, $50, $100, $500, and $1,000. You'll pay a service charge ranging from 1 to 4%. You can also get American Express traveler's checks over the phone by calling ☎ 800/221-7282; by using this number, Amex gold and platinum cardholders are exempt from the 1% fee. AAA members can obtain checks without a fee at most AAA offices.

Safety Tip

Avoid poorly lit or out-of-the-way ATMs, especially at night. Use an indoor machine, or one at a well-trafficked, well-lit location. Put your money away discreetly; don't flash it around or count it in a way that could attract the attention of thieves.

Visa offers traveler's checks at Citibank branches nationwide, as well as several other banks. The service charge ranges between 1½ and 2%; checks come in denominations of $20, $50, $100, $500, and $1,000. **MasterCard** also offers traveler's checks. Call ☎ **800/223-9920** for a location near you.

If you opt to carry traveler's checks, be sure to keep a record of their serial numbers (separately from the checks, of course), so you're ensured a refund in case they're lost or stolen.

CREDIT CARDS

Credit cards are invaluable when traveling. They're a safe way to carry money and provide a convenient record of all your expenses. **American Express, Master Card,** and **Visa** are accepted virtually everywhere in New York. **Discover** is also popular, and **Carte Blanche** and **Diner's Club** are making a comeback, especially in hotel circles. Since New York has such a heavy influx of international visitors, cards like **enRoute** and **JCB** are also widely accepted, particularly at hotels.

Still, it can be smart to keep some cash on hand for small expenses, like cab rides, or for that rare occasion when a restaurant or small shop doesn't take plastic, which can happen if you're dining at a neighborhood joint or buying from a small vendor.

THEFT   Almost every credit card company has an emergency 800 number that you can call if your wallet or purse is stolen. They may be able to wire you a cash advance off your credit card immediately, and in many places, they can deliver an emergency credit card in a day or two. The issuing bank's 800 number is usually on the back of the credit card—though that doesn't help you much if the card was stolen. The toll-free credit card information directory will provide the number if you dial ☎ **800/ 555-1212.** Citicorp **Visa's** U.S. emergency number is ☎ **800/336-8472. American Express** cardholders and traveler's check holders should call ☎ **800/221-7282** for all money emergencies. **MasterCard** holders should call ☎ **800/307-7309.**

Odds are that if your wallet is gone, the police won't be able to recover it for you. However, after you realize that it's gone and you cancel your credit cards, it's still worth informing the authorities. Your credit card company or insurer may require a police report number.

3 When to Go

Summer or winter, rain or shine, there's always great stuff going on in New York City, so there's no real "best" time to go.

If you're planning a visit with specific interests in mind, certain times of year may be better than others. Culture hounds might come in fall, winter, and early spring, when the theater and performing-arts seasons predictably reach their heights. During summer, many of the top cultural institutions, especially Lincoln Center, offer free (or nearly free) and alfresco entertainment. Those who want to see the biggest hits on Broadway usually have the best luck getting tickets in the theaters' slower months of January and February.

Gourmands might find it easier to get the best tables during July and August, when New Yorkers escape the city's muggy air for weekends in places like the Hamptons. If you prefer to walk every city block to take in the sights, spring and fall prove best for the mildest and most pleasant weather.

New York is a non-stop holiday party from early December through the start of the new year. Celebrations of the season abound in festive holiday windows and events like the lighting of the Rockefeller Center tree and the Radio City Christmas Spectacular—not to mention those terrific seasonal sales that take over the city, making New York a holiday shopping bonanza. However, keep in mind that hotel prices go sky high (more on that below), and the crowds are almost intolerable.

If you'd rather have more of the city to yourself—better chances at restaurant reservations and Broadway show tickets, as well as easier access to museums and other attractions—choose another time of year to visit.

MONEY MATTERS   If money is your biggest concern, you might want to visit in winter, between the first of the year and early April. Sure, the weather can suck, but hotels are suffering from the post-holiday blues, and rooms often go for a relative song. In the winter of '99, you could even get a room at the Waldorf-Astoria for as little as $189 on select nights, and the truly comfortable Comfort Inn Midtown had rooms for as low as $79.

Spring and fall are the busiest, and most expensive, seasons after holiday time. Don't expect hotels to be handing you deals, but you may be able to negotiate a decent rate.

New York's spit-shined image means that the city is drawing more families these days, and they usually visit in the summer. Still, the prospect of heat and humidity keeps some people away, making June, July, and the first half of August a generally cheaper time to visit than later in the year, and good hotel deals are often available.

At Christmas, all bets are off—expect to pay top dollar for everything. But Thanksgiving can be a great time to come, believe it or not: Business travelers have gone home for the holiday, and the holiday shoppers haven't yet arrived. It's a little-known secret that most hotels away from the Thanksgiving Day Parade route have empty rooms sitting, and they're usually willing to make great deals to fill them.

WEATHER   The worst weather in New York is during that long week or 10 days that arrives each summer between mid-July and mid-August, when temperatures go up to around 100°F with 90% humidity. You feel sticky all day, the streets smell horrible, everyone's cranky, and the concrete canyons become furnaces. It can be no fun walking around in this weather. Don't get put off by this—summer has its compensations, such as wonderful free open-air concerts and other events, as I've already mentioned—but bear it in mind. And you may luck out—the last few summers have been downright lovely. But if you are at all temperature sensitive, your odds of getting comfortable weather are better in June or September.

Another period when you might not like to stroll around the city is during January or February, when temperatures are commonly in the 20s (-6°C) and those concrete canyons turn into wind tunnels. The city looks gorgeous just after a snowfall, but the streets soon become an ugly, slushy mess. Again, you never know—temperatures have regularly been in the mild 40s during the past few winters. If you hit the weather jackpot, you could have a bargain bonanza (see "Money Matters" directly above).

Fall and spring are the best times in New York. From April to June and September to November, temperatures are mild and pleasant, and the light is beautiful. With the leaves changing in Central Park and just the hint of crispness in the air, October is a fabulous time to be here—but expect to pay for the privilege (see "Money Matters" above).

If you want to know how to pack just before you go, check the Weather Channel's online 5-day forecast at **www.weather.com**.

New York's Average Temperature & Rainfall

	Jan	Feb	Mar	Apr	May	June	July	Aug	Sept	Oct	Nov	Dec
Daily Temp. (°F)	38	40	48	61	71	80	85	84	77	67	54	42
Daily Temp. (°C)	3	4	9	16	22	27	29	29	25	19	12	6
Days of Rain	11	10	11	11	11	10	11	10	8	8	9	10

New York City Calendar of Events

As with any schedule of events, the following information is always subject to change. Always confirm information before you make plans around an event. Call the venue or the city's visitors bureau at ☎ **212/484-1222** (Mon–Fri 9am–5pm EST), or go to **www.nycvisit.com/cgi/calendar.html** for the latest details on these or other events taking place within the span of your trip.

January

- **New York National Boat Show.** Slip on your docksiders and head to the **Jacob K. Javits Convention Center** for the 90th edition, which promises a leviathan fleet of boats and marine products from the world's leading manufacturers. Call ☎ **212/922-1212.** January 8–16.
- **Winter Antiques Show at the Seventh Regiment Armory.** This is New York's most important, prestigious, and expensive antiques show. If you can come by an invitation to the benefactors' opening night, you'll see high-society ladies swoop down like hungry raptors to pick up the cream of the crop before us regular folks get through the doors. Call ☎ **718/292-7392.** January 14–25 (preview January 13).
- **Antiques at the Other Armory.** Younger, trendier dealers with more affordable collectibles show at the **26th Street Armory** (at Lexington Avenue) during the first weekend of the Winter Antiques Show. A free shuttle runs between the two locations. Call ☎ **212/255-0020.** January 14–16.

February

- **Chinese New Year.** Every year Chinatown rings in its own New Year (based on a lunar calendar) with two weeks of celebrations, including parades with dragon and lion dancers, vivid costumes of all kinds, and fireworks (though the city has been cracking down on using fireworks in recent years). The year 2000 (4698 in the Chinese designation) is the Year of the Dragon, and the Chinese New Year falls on February 5. Call the NYCVB hotline at ☎ **212/484-1222** or the Chinese Center at 212/373-1800.
- **Valentine's Day Marriage Marathon at the World Trade Center.** Once again, 110 people will be married at the top of the city's tallest skyscraper during the annual Valentine's Day Marriage Marathon. Applicants for "marrying slots" will be accepted from January 1, 2000; a maximum of 55 couples will be selected by February 1. To be considered, contestants are usually required to write a one-page typewritten essay entitled "Why We Want to Get Married at the Highest Place in New York"; call ☎ **212/580-9548.** A similar event is held on the observation deck at the **Empire State Building;** call ☎ **212/736-3100** or visit **www.esbnyc.org**.
- ✪ **Westminster Kennel Club Dog Show.** The ultimate purebred pooch fest. Some 30,000 dog fanciers from the world over congregate at **Madison Square Garden** for the "World Series of Dogdom." All 2,500 dogs are American Kennel Club Champions of Record, competing for the Best in Show trophy. Call ☎ **800/455-3647** for information. Tickets become available after January 1 through **Ticketmaster** (☎ **212/307-7171** or 212/307-1212; www.ticketmaster.com). February 14–15.
- **International Cat Show.** More than 800 fabulous felines, from rare and exotic purebreds to household pets, also compete for Best of Show honors at **Madison Square Garden.** Lectures by vets, special competitions (including cat photo contests), and the largest "feline shopping mall" anywhere are all part of the fun. Call

☎ **212/465-6741.** Tickets usually become available after February 1 through **Ticketmaster** (☎ **212/307-7171** or 212/307-1212; www.ticketmaster.com). Late February or early March.

March

✪ **Manhattan Antiques and Collectibles Triple Pier Expo.** The city's largest and most comprehensive antiques show takes place over two consecutive weekends, as more than 600 dealers exhibit their treasures, ranging from ephemera to jewelry to home furnishings, on three piers along the Hudson River between 48th and 51st streets. **Pier 88** features 20th-century collectibles from the '20s to the '70s; **Pier 90** has all manner of Americana, including country rustic, folk art, and Arts and Crafts; and **Pier 92** houses 18th- and 19th-century formal European antiques. Call ☎ **212/255-0020** or point your web browser to **www.antiqnet. com/Stella** for this year's dates. Usually mid-March, and again in mid-November.

• **St. Patrick's Day Parade.** More than 150,000 marchers join in the world's largest civilian parade, as Fifth Avenue from 44th to 86th streets rings with the sounds of bands and bagpipes, and an inordinate amount of beer is consumed (much of it green). The parade usually starts at 11am, but go extra-early if you want a good spot. Wear green and insist you're Irish if anyone asks—you are, at least for today. Call ☎ **212/484-1222.** March 17.

• **Ringling Bros. and Barnum & Bailey Circus.** The circus comes to town in grand style as elephants and bears and other performing animals parade down the city streets from the railroad at Twelfth Avenue and 34th Street to Madison Square Garden early on the morning before the first performance (usually well before daybreak). Call ☎ **212/465-6741** for this year's dates, or **Ticketmaster** (☎ **212/307-7171** or 212/307-1212; www.ticketmaster.com) for tickets. Usually late March to early April.

✪ **New Directors/New Films.** The kleig lights are turned on up-and-coming directors at this film series co-sponsored by the Museum of Modern Art (MoMA) and the Film Society of Lincoln Center, and screened at **MoMA.** Notable debuts in recent years have included *Smoke Signals, Buffalo '66,* and π. Call ☎ **212/ 875-5610** or point your web browser to **www.filmlinc.com** for this year's calendar.

April

✪ **The Easter Parade.** This isn't a traditional parade, per se: There are no marching bands, no baton twirlers, no protesters. Once upon a time, New York's gentry came out to show off their tasteful but discreet toppings. Today, if you were planning to slip on a tasteful little number—say something delicately woven in straw with a simple flower or two that matches your gloves—you will *not* be the grandest lady in this springtime hike along Fifth Avenue from 48th to 57th streets. It's more about flamboyant exhibitionism, with hats and costumes that get more outrageous every year—and anybody can join right in for free. The parade generally runs Easter Sunday from about 10:30am to 3pm. Call ☎ **212/ 484-1222.** April 23.

• **Greater New York International Auto Show.** Hot wheels from all over the world whirl into the **Jacob K. Javits Convention Center** for the largest auto show in the United States. Many concept cars show up that will never roll off the assembly line, but are fun to dream about nonetheless. Call ☎ **800/282-3336** or 212/216-2000. One week in early or mid-April.

May

✪ **Bike New York: The Great Five Boro Bike Tour.** The largest mass-participation cycling event in the United States attracts about 30,000 cyclists from all over the world. After a 42-mile ride through the five boroughs, finalists are greeted with a traditional New York-style celebration of food and music. Starting line is at Battery Park in Manhattan; the finish line is at Fort Wadsworth Naval Station on Staten Island. If you plan on entering, expect a stop-and-start ride. (Ever been caught in bike gridlock? Another New York first.) Call ☎ 212/932-0778 or visit **www.bikenewyork.org** to register. May 7.

- **Ninth Avenue International Food Festival.** Cancel dinner reservations and spend the day sampling sizzling Italian sausages, homemade pierogi, spicy curries, and an assortment of other ethnic dishes. Street musicians, bands, and vendors add to the festive atmosphere at one of the city's best street fairs, stretching along Ninth Avenue from 37th to 57th streets. Call ☎ 212/581-7217. One weekend in mid-May.

✪ **Fleet Week.** About 10,000 Navy and Coast Guard personnel are "at liberty" in New York for the annual Fleet Week at the end of May. Usually from 1 to 4pm daily, you can visit the ships and aircraft carriersas they dock in at the piers on the west side of Manhattan, and watch some dramatic exhibitions by the U.S. Marines. The whole celebration is hosted by the *Intrepid* Sea-Air-Space Museum, and kids love it. But even if you don't take in any of the events, you'll know it's Fleet Week, since those 10,000 sailors invade midtown in their starched white uniforms. It's simply wonderful—just like *On the Town* come to life. Call ☎ 212/245-2533, or visit **www.uss-intrepid.com**. Late May.

- **Washington Square Outdoor Art Exhibition.** This Greenwich Village tradition, in its 69th year, features the works of 250 artists displayed on 20 blocks in and around **Washington Square Park.** Call ☎ 212/982-6255. May 27–29 and June 3–5, and again in September.

June

- **The Belmont Stakes.** The third jewel in the Triple Crown is held at the **Belmont Park Race Track** in Elmont, Long Island. If a triple crown winner is to be named, it will happen here. For information, call ☎ 516/667-5055 or 718/641-4700. Early June.

✪ **Lesbian and Gay Pride Week and March.** A week of cheerful happenings, from simple parties to major political fund-raisers, precedes a zany parade commemorating the Stonewall Riot of June 27, 1969, which for many marks the beginning of the gay liberation movement. Fifth Avenue goes wild as the gay/lesbian community celebrates with bands, marching groups, floats, and plenty of panache. The parade starts on upper Fifth around 52nd Street and continues into the Village, where a street festival and a waterfront dance party with fireworks cap the day. Call ☎ 212/807-7433. Mid- to late June.

✪ **SummerStage.** A summer-long festival of free or low-cost outdoor concerts in **Central Park,** featuring world music, pop, folk, and jazz artists ranging from Ziggy Marley to Yoko Ono to Morrissey. Call ☎ 212/360-2777. June through August.

- **Metropolitan Opera in the Parks.** Free evening performances are given in the city parks. Past performers have included the likes of Luciano Pavarotti and Kathleen Battle. Call ☎ 212/362-6000 or visit **www.metopera.org**. June through July.

✪ **Shakespeare in the Park.** The Delacorte Theater in **Central Park** is the setting for first-rate free performances under the stars, often with stars on the stage. Recent visiting performers have included Patrick Stewart (*The Tempest*) and Andre Braugher (*Henry V*). Be prepared to line up hours in advance for tickets; you're allowed to collect two. For more details, see "Park It! Shakespeare, Music & Other Free Fun" in chapter 9. Call ☎ 212/539-8750 or 212/539-8500, or point your web browser to **www.publictheater.org**. June through August.

✪ **Restaurant Week.** Dine for only $20 at some of New York's finest restaurants. Participating places vary each year, so watch for the full-page ads in the *New York Times* or call ahead to the visitors bureau, since they usually have a list of who's participating by mid- or late May. *Reserve instantly.* One week in late June; some restaurants extend their offers through summer to Labor Day.

• **JVC Jazz Festival.** The biggest names in jazz play sites like **Avery Fisher Hall, Carnegie Hall,** the **Beacon Theater,** and **Town Hall;** free concerts at **Bryant Park** may also be in this year's mix. Call ☎ **212/501-1390,** or point your web browser to **www.jvc-america.com/jazz.** Late June to early July.

July

✪ **Independence Day Harbor Festival and Fourth of July Fireworks Spectacular.** Start the day amid the patriotic crowds at the Great July Fourth Festival in Lower Manhattan, watch the tall ships sail up the Hudson River in the afternoon, and then catch Macy's great fireworks extravaganza (one of the country's most fantastic) over the East River (the best vantage point is from the FDR Drive, which closes to traffic several hours before sunset). Call ☎ **212/484-1222,** or Macy's Special Events at 212/494-2922. July 4.

✪ **Lincoln Center Festival 2000.** This festival celebrates the best of the performing arts from all over the world—theater, ballet, contemporary dance, opera, even puppet and media-based art. Recent editions have featured performances by Ornette Coleman, the Royal Opera, the Royal Ballet, and the New York Philharmonic. Schedules are usually available in mid-March, and tickets go on sale in late May or early June. Call ☎ **212/546-2656,** or visit **www. lincolncenter.org**. July.

✪ **Midsummer Night's Swing.** Dancing duos head to the **Lincoln Center Fountain Plaza** for romantic evenings of big band swing, salsa, and tango under the stars to the sounds of top-flight bands. Dance lessons are offered with the purchase of a ticket. Call ☎ **212/875-5766,** or visit **www.lincolncenter.org**. July and August.

• **Mostly Mozart.** World-renowned ensembles and soloists (Alicia de Larrocha and André Watts have performed in the past) are featured at this month-long series at **Avery Fisher Hall.** Schedules are usually available in mid-April. Call ☎ **212/875-5103** or 212/546-2656, or visit **www.lincolncenter.org**. July and August.

August

• **Lincoln Center Out-of-Doors.** This series of free music and dance performances is held outdoors at **Lincoln Center.** Schedules are available in July. Call ☎ **212/875-5108,** or visit **www.lincolncenter.org**. August to September.

• **New York Fringe Festival.** Held in a variety of tiny Lower East Side venues for a mainly hipster crowd, this arts festival presents alternative as well as traditional theater, musicals, dance, comedy, and all manner of performance art, including new media. Literally hundreds of events are held at all hours over about ten days in late August. The quality can vary wildly (lots of performers use Fringe as a workshop to develop their acts and shows) and some performances really push the envelope, but you'd be surprised at how many shows are actually *good.* Call ☎ **888/FRINGENYC** or 212/307-0229, or point your Web browser to **www. fringenyc.org**. Mid- to late August.

✪ **U.S. Open Tennis Championships.** The final Grand Slam event of the tennis season is held at the slick new facilities at **Flushing Meadows Park** in Queens. Tickets go on sale in May. The event sells out far in advance, since many of the tickets are held by corporate sponsors who hand them out to customers. (It's worth it to check the list of sponsors to determine if anyone you know has a connection for getting tickets.) You can usually scalp tickets outside the complex (an illegal practice, of course), which is right next to **Shea Stadium.** The last few matches of the tournament are most expensive, but you'll see a lot more tennis early on, when your ticket allows you to wander the outside courts and view several different matches. Call ☎ **718/760-6200** or Telecharge at ☎ **800/ 524-8440** for tickets as far in advance as possible; visit **www.usopen.org** for additional information. Two weeks surrounding Labor Day.

- **Harlem Week.** The world's largest black and Hispanic cultural festival actually spans about two weeks, including the Black Film Festival and the Taste of Harlem Food Festival. Expect a whole slate of music, from gospel to hip hop, and lots of other festivities. Call ☎ 212/862-7200 or 212/484-1222 for this year's schedule of events and locations. Mid-August.

September

- **West Indian–American Day Parade.** This annual Brooklyn event is New York's largest street celebration. Come for the extravagant costumes, pulsating rhythms (soca, calypso, reggae), bright colors, folklore, food (jerk chicken, oxtail soup, Caribbean soul food), and 2 million hip-shaking revelers. The parade runs down Eastern Parkway in Brooklyn. Call ☎ **212/484-1222** or 718/774-8807. Labor Day (September 6 in 1999, September 4 in 2000).

- ○ **Wigstock.** Come see the Lady Bunny, Hedda Lettuce, Lypsinka, and even RuPaul—plus hundreds of other fabulous drag queens—strut their stuff. The crowd is usually wilder than the stage acts. A true East Village event, Wigstock outgrew its original location, Tompkins Square Park, and has been held on the pier at 11th Street on the Hudson River in recent years, but another move could be in the offing. For a preview, see Goldwyn's *Wigstock: The Movie.* For information, point your web browser to **www.wigstock.nu** or call ☎ **800/494-TIXS** or the Lesbian and Gay Community Services Center at ☎ 212/620-7310. Labor Day weekend.

- **Washington Square Outdoor Art Exhibition.** The May event returns for Labor Day, when the works of 250 artists are displayed in and around **Washington Square Park.** Call ☎ **212/982-6255.** September 2–4 and 9–10.

- **Broadway on Broadway.** This free afternoon show features the songs and casts from virtually every Broadway production performing on a stage erected in the middle of **Times Square.** Call ☎ **212/768-1560.** Early or mid-September.

- **Feast of San Gennaro.** An atmospheric Little Italy street fair honoring the patron saint of Naples, with great food, traditional music, carnival rides, games, and vendors set up along Mulberry Street north of Canal Street. Expect big crowds. And who knows? You may even spot a Godfather or two. Usually mid-September.

- ○ **New York Film Festival.** Legendary hits *Pulp Fiction* and *Mean Streets* both had their U.S. premieres at the Film Society of Lincoln Center's two-week festival, a major stop on the film fest circuit. Schedules in recent years have included advance looks at *The Sweet Hereafter, Gods and Monsters,* and *Rushmore.* Screenings are held in various **Lincoln Center** venues throughout the days of the festival; advance tickets are a good bet always, and a necessity for certain events (especially evening and weekend screenings). Call ☎ **212/875-5610,** or point your web browser to **www.filmlinc.com.** Two weeks from late September to early October (Sept 24–Oct 10 in 1999, Sept 22–Oct 9 in 2000).

- ○ **BAM Next Wave Festival.** One of the city's most important cultural events takes place at the **Brooklyn Academy of Music.** The months-long festival showcases experimental new dance, theater, and music works by both renowned and lesser-known international artists. Recent celebrated performances have included Astor Piazzolla's *Maria de Buenos Aires* (featuring Piazzolla disciple Gidon Kremer), the 25th anniversary of the Kronos Quartet, and choreographer Bill T. Jones's *We Set Out Early . . . Visibility Was Poor* (set to the music of Stravinsky, John Cage, and Peteris Vask). Call ☎ **718/636-4100** or visit **www.bam.org**. September through December.

October

- **Ice-Skating.** Show off your skating style in the limelight at the diminutive **Rockefeller Center** rink (☎ **212/332-7654**), open from mid-October to mid-March (you'll skate under the magnificent Christmas tree for the month of December), or at the larger **Wollman Rink** in Central Park, at 59th Street and Sixth Avenue (☎ **212/396-1010**), which usually closes in early April.

- ✪ **Feast of St. Francis.** Animals from goldfish to elephants are blessed as thousands of Homo sapiens look on at the **Cathedral of St. John the Divine.** A magical experience; pets, of course, are welcome. A festive fair follows the blessing and music events. Buy tickets in advance, because they can be hard to come by. Call ☎ **212/316-7540** or visit **www.stjohndivine.org**. Early October.

- **International Fine Arts and Antiques Dealers Show.** Considered by many as the opening of the fall arts season, this show attracts dealers and collectors from all over the world to the **Seventh Regiment Armory.** Call ☎ **212/642-8572** or 212/877-0202. Mid-October.

- ✪ **Greenwich Village Halloween Parade.** This is Halloween at its most outrageous. You may have heard Lou Reed singing about it on his classic album *New York*—he wasn't exaggerating. Drag queens and assorted other flamboyant types parade through the village in wildly creative costumes. The parade route has changed over the years, but most recently it has started after sunset at Spring Street and marched up Sixth Avenue to 23rd Street or Union Square. Check the papers for the exact route so you can watch—or participate, if you have the threads and the imagination. October 31.

November

- ✪ **New York City Marathon.** Some 25,000 hopefuls from around the world participate in the largest U.S. marathon, and at least a million fans will cheer them on as they follow a route that touches on all five New York boroughs and finishes at Central Park. Call ☎ **212/860-4455,** or point your web browser to **www.nyrrc.org**. November 7 in 1999; call for the 2000 date (most likely to be November 4 or 11).

- **Ice Skating at the South Street Seaport.** The rink is petite, but the waterfront setting is grand. Call ☎ **212/SEA-PORT** or 212/809-6080. November through March.

- **Radio City Music Hall Christmas Spectacular.** A rather gaudy extravaganza, but lots of fun nonetheless. Starring the Radio City Rockettes and a cast that includes live animals (just try to picture the camels sauntering in the Sixth Avenue entrance!). For information, call ☎ **212/247-4777** or visit **www.radiocity.com;** buy tickets at the box office or via Ticketmaster's **Radio City Hotline** (☎ **212/307-1000**). Mid-November to early January.

- ✪ **Manhattan Antiques and Collectibles Triple Pier Expo.** The city's largest antiques show takes place over two consecutive weekends, usually just before Thanksgiving; for details, see March, above. Call ☎ **212/255-0020** or visit **www.antiqnet.com/Stella** for this year's dates.

✪ **Macy's Thanksgiving Day Parade.** The procession from Central Park West and 77th Street and down Broadway to Herald Square at 34th Street continues to be a national tradition. Huge hot-air balloons in the forms of Rocky and Bullwinkle, Snoopy, Underdog, the Pink Panther, Bart Simpson, and other cartoon favorites are the best part of the fun. The night before, you can usually see the big blow-up on Central Park West at 79th Street; call in advance to see if it will be open to the public again this year. Call ☎ 212/494-5432 or 212/494-2922. November 25 in 1999, November 23 in 2000.

✪ **Big Apple Circus.** New York City's homegrown, not-for-profit circus is a favorite with children and the young at heart. A tent is pitched in **Damrosch Park** at **Lincoln Center.** Call ☎ 212/268-2500. November to January.

• *The Nutcracker.* Tchaikovsky's holiday favorite is performed by the New York City Ballet at **Lincoln Center.** Tickets are usually available starting in early October. Call ☎ 212/870-5570, or point your web browser to **www.nycballet. org.** Late November through early January.

December

✪ **Lighting of the Rockefeller Center Christmas Tree.** The annual lighting ceremony is accompanied by an ice-skating show, singing, entertainment, and a huge crowd. The tree stays lit around the clock until after the new year. Call ☎ 212/632-3975. Early December.

✪ **Holiday Trimmings.** Stroll down festive Fifth Avenue, and you'll see doormen dressed as wooden soldiers at **FAO Schwarz,** a 27-foot sparkling snowflake floating over the intersection outside **Tiffany's,** the **Cartier** building ribboned and bowed in red, wreaths warming the necks of the **New York Public Library's** lions, and fanciful figurines in the windows of **Saks Fifth Avenue** and **Lord & Taylor.** Throughout December.

• **Christmas Traditions.** In addition to the **Radio City Music Hall Christmas Spectacular** and the New York City Ballet's staging of *The Nutcracker* (see November, above), traditional holiday events include *A Christmas Carol* at the Theater at **Madison Square Garden** (☎ 212/465-6741 or www.thegarden. com, ☎ 212/307-7171 or www.ticketmaster.com for tickets), usually featuring a big name or two to draw in the crowds (Roger Daltrey in 1998). At **Avery Fisher Hall** is the National Chorale's sing-along performance of Handel's *Messiah* (☎ 212/875-5030; www.lincolncenter.org). Don't worry if the only words you know are "Alleluia, Alleluia!"—a lyrics sheet is given to ticket holders.

• **Lighting of the Hanukkah Menorah.** Everything is done on a grand scale in New York, so it's no surprise that the world's largest menorah (32 feet high) is at Manhattan's **Grand Army Plaza,** Fifth Avenue and 59th Street. Hanukkah celebrations begin December 4 in 1999 and December 22 in 2000 with the lighting of the first of the giant electric candles.

✪ **New Year's Eve.** The biggest party of them all happens in **Times Square,** where hundreds of thousands of raucous revelers count down in unison the year's final seconds until the new lighted ball drops at midnight at 1 Times Square. I personally don't understand it, since it's always a crowded, cold, boozy madhouse, but hey! Call ☎ 212/354-0003 or 212/484-1222. December 31.

There's also **First Night,** a liquor-free gala celebration held at venues all around town. Just purchase a button for admission to any of these; they're available throughout December at various locations around the city. Events include swing dancing in the magnificent concourse of **Grand Central Terminal,** taking in the view at the **Empire State Building** observation deck, world music concerts, children's events, and more. Call the **First Night Hotline** at ☎ 212/922-9393.

Other unique events include **fireworks** followed by a **5-mile midnight run** sponsored by the New York Road Runners Club (☎ 212/860-4455; www.nyrrc.org) in **Central Park**. The **Cathedral of St. John the Divine** (☎ 212/316-7540; www.stjohndivine.org) is known for its New Year's Eve concert.

4 Health & Insurance

It can be hard to find a doctor you can trust when you're in an unfamiliar place. Try to take proper precautions the week before you depart to avoid falling ill while you're away from home. Amid the last-minute frenzy that often precede a vacation break, make an extra effort to eat and sleep well—especially if you feel an illness coming on. It's a drag to be sick on vacation, and a head cold can make a plane flight intolerable.

WHAT TO DO IF YOU GET SICK AWAY FROM HOME

If you worry about getting sick away from home, you may want to consider **medical travel insurance** (see "Travel Insurance" section, below). In most cases, however, your existing health plan will provide all the coverage you need. Be sure to carry your identification card in your wallet.

If you suffer from a chronic illness, consult your doctor before your departure. For conditions like epilepsy, diabetes, or heart problems, wear a **Medic Alert Identification Tag** (☎ 800/825-3785; www.medicalert.org), which will immediately alert doctors to your condition and give them access to your records through Medic Alert's 24-hour hotline. Membership is $35, plus a $15 annual fee.

Pack prescription medications in your carry-on luggage. Carry written prescriptions in generic, not brand-name form, and dispense all prescription medications from their original labeled vials. If you wear contact lenses, pack an extra pair in case you lose one.

FINDING A DOCTOR   If you do get sick, ask the concierge at your hotel to recommend a local doctor, even his or her own. This will probably yield a better recommendation than any 800 number would. There are also several walk-in medical centers, like the **New York Healthcare Immediate Care**, 55 E. 34th St., between Park and Madison avenues (☎ 212/252-6001), for non-emergency illnesses. The clinic, affiliated with Beth Israel Medical Center, is open Monday to Thursday 8am to 8pm, Friday 8am to 7pm, Saturday 9am to 3pm, and Sunday 9am to 2pm. A 24-hour referral service for doctors who make house calls can be reached by calling ☎ 212/737-2333.

If you have dental problems, a nationwide referral service known as **1-800-DENTIST** (☎ 800/336-8478) will provide the name of a nearby dentist or clinic. **Preventive Dental Associates** at (☎ 212/683-2530) accepts same-day appointments and has a 24-hour answering service.

If you can't find a doctor who can help you right away, try the emergency room at the local hospital. Many emergency rooms have walk-in-clinics for emergency cases that are not life threatening. You may not get immediate attention, but you won't pay the high price of an emergency room visit (usually a minimum of $300 just for signing your name, plus the price of whatever treatment you receive). For a list of local hospitals, see "Fast Facts: New York City," in chapter 4.

TRAVEL INSURANCE

There are three kinds of travel insurance: trip-cancellation, medical, and lost-luggage coverage. **Trip-cancellation insurance** is a good idea if you have paid a large portion

Travel Tip

If you're buying a package vacation or tour, don't buy your trip-cancellation insurance from your tour operator—talk about putting all of your eggs in one basket! Buy it from an outside vendor instead.

of your vacation expenses up front (say, by purchasing a package deal). The other two types of insurance, however, don't make sense for most travelers. Rule number one: check your existing policies before you buy any additional coverage.

Your existing health insurance should cover you if you get sick while on vacation (though if you belong to an HMO, you should check to see whether you are fully covered when away from home). For independent travel health-insurance providers, see below.

Your homeowner's or renter's insurance should cover stolen luggage. The airlines are responsible for losses up to $1,250 on domestic flights if they lose your luggage; if you plan to carry anything more valuable than that, keep it in your carry-on bag.

The differences between **travel assistance** and insurance are often blurred, but in general, the former offers on-the-spot assistance and 24-hour hotlines (mostly oriented toward medical problems), while the latter reimburses you for travel problems (medical, travel, or otherwise) after you have filed the paperwork. The coverage you should consider will depend on how much protection is already contained in your existing health insurance or other policies. Some credit- and charge-card companies may insure you against travel accidents if you buy plane, train, or bus tickets with their cards. Before purchasing additional insurance, read your policies and agreements over carefully. Call your insurers or credit/charge-card companies if you have any questions.

Some credit cards (American Express and certain gold and platinum Visa and MasterCards, for example) offer automatic **flight insurance** for death or dismemberment in case of an airplane crash.

If you do require additional insurance, try one of the companies listed below. But don't pay for more than you need. If you need only trip-cancellation insurance, don't purchase coverage for lost or stolen property, which should be covered by your homeowner's or renter's policy. Trip-cancellation insurance costs approximately 6 to 8% of the total value of your vacation.

Among the reputable issuers of travel insurance are:

Access America, 6600 W. Broad St., Richmond, VA 23230 (☎ **800/284-8300;** www.accessamerica.com); **Travel Guard International,** 1145 Clark St., Stevens Point, WI 54481 (☎ **800/826-1300;** www.travel-guard.com); **Travel Insured International,** Inc., P.O. Box 280568, East Hartford, CT 06128 (☎ **800/243-3174**); **Travelex Insurance Services,** P.O. Box 9408, Garden City, NY 11530-9408 (☎ **800/228-9792**).

5 Tips for Travelers with Special Needs
FOR FAMILIES

You don't have to leave the kids home, Mom and Dad. New York is a playground for the younger set, too.

For the last few years, as a result of the startling decrease in crime and the sudden increase in family-oriented entertainment (exemplified by the "new" Times Square), the city's sidewalks are full of pint-sized visitors who love its eye-popping delights. There are hundreds of ways to keep the kids entertained, from kid-oriented museums and theater to theme park-style shopping and restaurants.

For the best places to stay and eat, see "Family-Friendly Hotels" in chapter 5 and "Family-Friendly Restaurants" in chapter 6. For details on sightseeing, check out the section called "Especially for Kids" in chapter 7.

Those of you who want a guide devoted exclusively to travel with children might buy a copy of *Frommer's New York City with Kids.*

Good bets for the most timely information include: the "Weekend" section of Friday's *The New York Times,* which has a whole section dedicated to the week's best kid-friendly activities; weekly *New York* magazine, which has a full calendar of children's events in its "Cue" section; and *Time Out New York,* which also has a great weekly kid's section with a bit of an alternative bent.

Good web sources for up-to-date information and advice include **New York Family** (☎ 914/381-7474) which features an online calendar and other family-friendly Big Apple advice at **www.family.go.com/Local/nyfm;** and **Big Apple Parent** (☎ 212/533-2277) offering similar information and links at **www.family.go.com/Local/bapp.** Both *New York Family* and the *Big Apple Parents' Paper* are usually available for free at children's stores and other locations in Manhattan. Call to find out how to order advance copies.

FINDING A BABYSITTER   The first place to look for babysitting is in your hotel (better yet, ask about babysitting when you reserve). Many hotels have babysitting services or will provide you with lists of reliable sitters. If this doesn't pan out, there's the **Baby Sitters' Guild** (☎ 212/682-0227) or the **Frances Stewart Agency** (☎ 212/439-9222). The sitters are licensed, insured, and bonded, and can even take your child on outings.

FOR TRAVELERS WITH DISABILITIES

A disability shouldn't stop anyone from traveling. The Americans with Disabilities Act and state and local laws require an increasing number of buildings and other public spaces to accommodate people with disabilities, making New York more accessible to disabled travelers than ever before. The city's bus system is wheelchair-friendly, and most of the major sightseeing attractions are easily accessible. Even so, always call first to be sure that the places you want to go to are fully accessible.

Most hotels are ADA compliant, with suitable rooms for wheelchair-bound travelers as well as those with other disabilities. But before you book, **ask lots of questions** based on your needs. Many city hotels are housed in older buildings that have had to be modified to meet requirements; still, elevators and bathrooms can both be on the small side, and other impediments may exist. If you have mobility issues, you'll probably do best to book into one of the city's newer hotels, which tend to be more spacious and accommodating.

Some Broadway theaters and other performance venues provide total wheelchair accessibility; others provide partial accessibility. Many also offer lower-priced tickets for disabled theatergoers and their companions, though you'll need to check individual policies and reserve in advance.

GENERAL TRAVEL INFORMATION   The **Moss Rehab Hospital** (☎ 215/456-9600) has been providing friendly and helpful phone advice and referrals to disabled travelers for years through its **Travel Information Service** (☎ 215/456-9603). You can hook up with a number of travel agents who specialize in planning trips for disabled travelers, as well as a wealth of other travel-related information, by logging onto their website at **www.mossresourcenet.org**.

If you're looking for a travel agent that offers tours or can plan trips for travelers with disabilities, another great Internet source is **www.access-able.com**. You'll also find relay and voice numbers for hotels, airlines, and car-rental companies on this user-friendly site, as well as links to accessible accommodations, attractions, transportation, tours, local medical resources and equipment repairers, and much more.

You can join **The Society for the Advancement of Travel for the Handicapped** (SATH), 347 Fifth Ave. Suite 610, New York, NY 10016 (☎ **212/447-7284;** fax 212-725-8253; www.sath.org), for $45 annually ($30 for seniors and students), to gain access to their vast network of connections in the travel industry. They provide information sheets on destinations and referrals to tour operators that specialize in traveling with disabilities. Their quarterly magazine, *Open World for Disability and Mature Travel*, is full of good information and resources.

CITY-SPECIFIC INFORMATION Hospital Audiences, Inc., has an information hotline (☎ **888/424-4685,** Mon–Fri 9am–5pm), that proves details about accessibility at cultural institutions, hotels, restaurants, and transportation as well as cultural events adapted for people with disabilities. Trained staff members answer specific questions based on your particular physical needs and the dates of your trip. This nonprofit organization also publishes *Access for All,* a guidebook on accessibility at many of the city's cultural institutions, available by sending a $5 check to **Hospital Audiences, Inc.,** 220 W. 42nd St., 13th floor, New York, NY 10036 (☎ **212/575-7676;** TTY 212/575-7673; www.hospitalaudiences.org). They also have a range of other services, including "Describe!", which allows visually impaired theatergoers to enjoy theater events, and an omnibus program that transports the disabled to cultural events.

Another terrific source for disabled travelers coming to New York City is **Big Apple Greeter** (☎ **212/669-8159;** TTY: 212/669-8273; www.bigapplegreeter.org). Their Greeter Access Project is geared to travelers with disabilities interested in getting to know the Big Apple. All of their employees are extremely well-versed on accessability issues. They can provide a resource list of agencies that serve the city's disabled community, and sometimes have special discounts available to theater and music performances. Big Apple Greeter even offers one-to-one tours that pair volunteers with disabled visitors; they can even introduce you to the public transportation system if you like. Reserve at least one week ahead.

Other helpful organizations are: the **American Foundation for the Blind,** 11 Penn Plaza, Suite 300, New York, NY 10001 (☎ **800/232-5463** or 212/502-7600); **The Lighthouse, Inc.,** 111 E. 59th St., New York, NY 10022 (☎ **800/829-0500** or 212/821-9200; www.lighthouse.org), which arranges activities for people with impaired vision and sells Braille subway maps; and the **New York Society for the Deaf,** 817 Broadway, 7th floor, New York, NY 10003 (☎ **212/777-3900**).

GETTING AROUND Gray Line Air Shuttle (☎ **800/451-0455** or 212/ 315-3006) operates minibuses with lifts from JFK, La Guardia, and Newark airports to midtown hotels by reservation; be sure to arrange pick-up three or four days in advance.

A liscensed ambulette company, **Upward Mobility Limousine Service** (☎ **718/ 645-7774;** www.brainlink.com/~phil) is a wheelchair-accessible car service that can provide door-to-door airport shuttle service as well as taxi service anywhere in the metropolitan area. Arrange airport pick-ups with as much advance notice as possible.

Taxis are required to carry people who have folding wheelchairs and Seeing-Eye or hearing-ear dogs. However, don't be surprised if they don't run each other down trying to get to you; even though you shouldn't have to, you may have to wait a bit for a friendly (or fare-desperate) driver to come along.

Public buses are an inexpensive and easy way to get around New York. All buses' back doors are supposed to be equipped with wheelchair lifts (though the city has had complaints that not all are in working order). Buses also "kneel," lowering their front steps for people who have difficulty boarding. Passengers with disabilities pay half-price fares (75¢). Call the **Accessable Line** at ☎ 718/596-8585 (daily 6am–9pm) for bus and subway transit info, or point your web browser to **www.mta.nyc.ny.us/nyct**.

The **subway** isn't yet fully wheelchair accessible, but a free brochure about subway accessibility, *Accessible Transfer Points,* is available by contacting MTA Customer Assistance, 370 J St., Room 702, Brooklyn, NY 11201 (☎ **718/330-3322**; TTY: 718/596-8273). A list of accessible subway stations is also on the MTA Web site.

You're better off not trying to rent your own car to get around the city. But if you consider it the best mode of transportation for you, **Wheelchair Getaways** (☎ **800/ 379-3750** or 516/939-0372; www.wheelchair-getaways.com) rents specialized vans with wheelchair lifts and other features for travelers with disabilities throughout the New York metropolitan area.

FOR SENIOR TRAVELERS

One of the benefits of age is that travel often costs less. New York subway and bus fares are half price (75¢) for people 65 and older. Many museums and sights (and some theaters and performance halls) offer discounted entrance and tickets to seniors, so don't be shy about asking. Always bring an ID card, especially if you've kept your youthful glow.

Also mention the fact that you're a senior when you first make your travel reservations. Both **Amtrak** (☎ **800/USA-RAIL;** www.amtrak.com) and **Greyhound** (☎ **800/752-4841;** www.greyhound.com) offer discounts to persons over 62, and most of the major domestic airlines offer discount programs for senior travelers. Many hotels also offer senior discounts; **Choice Hotels** (which include Comfort Inns, some of my favorite affordable midtown hotels; see chapter 5), for example, gives 30% off their published rates to anyone over 50, provided you book your room through their nationwide toll-free reservations number (that is, not directly with the hotels or through a travel agent). For a complete list of Choice Hotels, visit **www.hotelchoice. com**.

Members of the **American Association of Retired Persons (AARP)**, 601 E St. NW, Washington, DC 20049 (☎ **800/424-3410** or 202/434-2277; www.aarp.org), get discounts not only on hotels but on airfares and car rentals, too. The AARP offers members a wide range of special benefits, including *Modern Maturity* magazine and a monthly newsletter. If you're not already a member, do yourself a favor and join.

Mature Outlook, P.O. Box 9390, Des Moines, IA 50306 (☎ **800/336-6330;** www.sears.ca/e/travel/outlook.htm), began as a travel organization for people over 50, though it now caters to people of all ages. Members receive discounts on hotels and receive a bimonthly magazine. Annual membership is $19.95, which entitles members to discounts and, often, free coupons for discounted merchandise from Sears.

Golden Companions, P.O. Box 5249, Reno, NV 89513 (☎ **702/324-2227**), helps travelers 45 years-plus find compatible companions through a personal voice-mail service. Contact them for more information.

The Mature Traveler, a monthly 12-page newsletter on senior travel is a valuable resource. It's available by subscription ($30 a year) from GEM Publishing Group, Box 50400, Reno, NV 89513-0400. GEM also publishes *The Book of Deals,* a collection of more than 1,000 senior discounts on airlines, lodging, tours, and attractions around the country; it's available for $9.95 by calling ☎ **800/460-6676.** Another helpful publication is *101 Tips for the Mature Traveler,* available from Grand Circle Travel, 347 Congress St., Suite 3A, Boston, MA 02210 (☎ **800/597-3644** or 617/350-7500; fax 617/346-6700; www.gct.com).

Some thugs and unscrupulous tricksters try to take advantage of seniors. Be as skeptical as a New Yorker whenever you're approached, especially by someone who has a long story that promises to give you something for nothing. For safety tips, see "Playing It Safe" in chapter 4. Your experience and common sense equips you with more savvy than most hucksters will ever have.

FOR GAY & LESBIAN TRAVELERS

Gay and lesbian culture is as much a part of New York's basic identity as yellow cabs, high-rises, and Broadway theater. Indeed, in a city with one of the world's largest, loudest, and most powerful gay and lesbian populations, homosexuality is hardly seen as an "alternative" these days—it's squarely in the urban mainstream. So city hotels tend to be neutral on the issue, and gay couples shouldn't have a problem. You'll want to see "The Lesbian & Gay Scene" in chapter 9 for nightlife suggestions.

If you want help planning your trip to New York, **The International Gay & Lesbian Travel Association** (IGLTA; ☎ **800/448-8550** or 954/776-2626; fax 954/776-3303; www.iglta.org), can link you up with the appropriate gay-friendly service organization or tour specialist. With around 1,200 members, it offers quarterly newsletters, marketing mailings, and a membership directory that's updated quarterly. Members are kept informed of gay and gay-friendly hoteliers, tour operators, and airline and cruise-line representatives.

Out and About, 8 W. 19th St., no. 401, New York, NY 10011 (☎ **800/929-2268** or 212/645-6922; www.outandabout.com), has been hailed for its "straight" reporting about gay travel. It offers a monthly newsletter ($49 a year) packed with good information on the global gay and lesbian scene. Out and About's guidebooks are available at most major bookstores and through **A Different Light Bookstore,** 151 W. 19th St. (☎ **800/343-4002** or 212/989-4850; www.adlbooks.com), while its website features links to gay and lesbian tour operators and other gay-themed travel links. *Our World,* 1104 North Nova Rd., Suite 251, Daytona Beach, FL 32117 (☎ **904/441-5367;** www.pimps.com/ourworld) is a slicker monthly promoting and highlighting travel bargains and opportunities. Annual subscription rates are $35 in the United States, $45 outside the U.S.

All over Manhattan, but especially in neighborhoods like the **West Village** (particularly Christopher Street, famous the world over as the main drag of New York gay-male life) and **Chelsea** (especially Eighth Avenue from 16th to 23rd streets and West 17th to 19th streets from Fifth to Eighth avenues), shops, services, and restaurants have a lesbian and gay flavor. A Different Light (above) and the **Oscar Wilde Bookshop,** 15 Christopher St. (☎ **212/255-8097;** www.oscarwildebooks.com), are the city's best two gay and lesbian bookstores; both are good sources for information on the city's gay community.

Stonewall Remembered

Many gay visitors will want to visit the Stonewall Bar, 53 Christopher St., at Seventh Avenue (☎ **212/463-0950**), in nearly the same location as where the famed Stonewall Inn once stood. (Neighbors have recently been threatening to have the bar closed for disturbing their peace. The bar has put in soundproofing in response, so it might survive the onslaught.)

On the night of June 27, 1969, customers at the original Stonewall, tired of constant police harassment, decided to fight back. That milestone marks the beginnings of the contemporary gay liberation movement. The usually celebratory, always engaging Lesbian and Gay Pride March is held in late June to commemorate the Stonewall "Riots"—see the calendar of events earlier in this chapter.

The **Lesbian and Gay Community Services Center** is at 1 Little W. 12th Street, between Ninth Avenue and Hudson Street, one block south of West 13th Street (☎ 212/620-7310; www.gaycenter.org), and is open daily 9am to 10:30pm. (This is its temporary home for about two years while its headquarters at 208 W. 13th St. is being renovated.) The center is the meeting place for more than 400 lesbian, gay, and bisexual organizations. The center also runs 26 programs of its own. You can call to request the Community Calendar of Events that lists happenings like lectures, dances, concerts, readings, and films.

Another good source for lesbian and gay events during your visit is *Homo Xtra (HX)*, a weekly magazine you can pick up in appropriate bars, clubs, and stores throughout town. Lesbians now have their own version, *HX for Her*. Both mags have information online at **www.hx.com.** In addition, the weekly *Time Out New York* boasts a terrific gay and lesbian section. For other online information sources, see "Site Seeing" under "Visitor Information" earlier in this chapter.

In addition, there are lesbian and gay musical events, such as performances by the **Gay Men's Chorus** (☎ 212/924-7770; www.nycgmc.org); health programs sponsored by **Gay Men's Health Crisis** (GMHC), 119 W. 24th St. (☎ 212/807-6664; AIDS hotline 212/807-6655; www.gmhc.org); the **Gay and Lesbian Switchboard of New York** (☎ 212/989-0999; www.glnh.org), offering peer counseling and information on upcoming events; and many other organizations. If you're a traveler with HIV, this city just might be the best place to visit. Its support and medical services are unrivaled.

FOR SINGLE TRAVELERS

Many people prefer traveling alone—save for the relatively steep cost of booking a single room. **Travel Companion** (☎ 516/454-0880) is one of the nation's oldest roommate finders for single travelers. Register with them and find a trustworthy travel mate who will split the cost of the room with you and be around as little, or as often, as you like during the day.

FOR STUDENTS

Many museums, sights, and theaters offer reduced admission to students, so don't forget to bring your valid student ID and valid proof of age.

Your best resource is the **Council on International Educational Exchange,** or CIEE. They can set you up with an International Student ID card, and their travel branch, **Council Travel** (☎ 800/226-8624; www.counciltravel.com), the world's biggest student travel agency, can get you discounts on plane tickets and the like. City locations include 254 Greene St., between Waverly and 8th Street in the Village (☎ 212/254-2525).

Contact **Hostelling International–American Youth Hostels,** 733 15th St. NW, Suite 840, Washington, DC 20005 (☎ 800/444-6111 or 202/783-6161; www.hiayh.org) for reservations to youth hostels in New York City.

For more complete reviews of city hostels and other budget accommodations than you'll find in this book, see *Frommer's New York City from $75 a Day.*

6 Getting There

BY PLANE

Three major airports serve New York City: **John F. Kennedy International Airport** (☎ 718/244-4444) in Queens, about 15 miles (or one hour's driving time) from midtown Manhattan; **LaGuardia Airport** (☎ 718/533-3400), also in Queens, about

8 miles (or 30 minutes) from midtown; and **Newark International Airport** (☎ **201/ 961-6000**) in nearby New Jersey, about 16 miles (or 45 minutes) from midtown. Online information on all three airports is available at **www.panynj.gov**.

Almost every major domestic carrier serves at least one of these airports; most serve two or all three. Among them are **America West** (☎ **800/235-9292;** www. americawest.com), **American** (☎ **800/433-7300;** www.americanair.com), **Continental** (☎ **800/525-0280** or 800/523-3273; www.flycontinental.com), **Delta** (☎ **800/221-1212;** www.delta-air.com), **Northwest** (☎ **800/225-2525;** www.nwa. com), **TWA** (☎ **800/221-2000;** www.twa.com), **US Airways** (☎ **800/ 428-4322;** www.usairways.com), and **United** (☎ **800/241-6522;** www.ual.com).

In recent years there has been rapid growth in the number of start-up, no-frills airlines serving New York. These smaller, sometimes struggling airlines may offer lower fares—but don't expect the same kind of service you get from the majors. You might check out **AirTran** (☎ **800/AIRTRAN;** www.airtran.com), **Frontier** (☎ **800/ 432-1359;** www.frontierair.com), **Spirit Airlines** (☎ **800/772-7117;** www.spiritair. com), **Midway** (☎ **800/446-4392;** www.midwayair.com), **Midwest Express** (☎ **800/452-2022;** www.midwestexpress.com), **Tower Air** (☎ **800/34-TOWER** or 718/553-8500; www.towerair.com), **ATA** (☎ **800/I-FLY-ATA;** www.ata.com), **SunJet International** (☎ **800/4-SUNJET;** www.sunjet.com), and **Sun Country** (☎ **800/752-1218;** www.suncountry.com). In addition, a new airline, **New Air,** is scheuduled to begin serving New York at great discounts in fall 1999, but no other details were available at press time. And the nation's leading discount airline, **Southwest** (☎ **800/435-9792;** www.iflyswa.com), announced flights to MacArthur Airport on Long Island, 40 miles east of Manhattan, but there are no current plans to fly into the city's airports.

Most major international carriers also serve New York; see chapter 3 for details.

Keep in mind that it's more convenient to fly into Newark than Kennedy if your destination is Manhattan, and consider that fares to Newark are often cheaper than the other airports. Newark can also be the most convenient if your hotel is in Midtown West or downtown near the World Trade Center.

FLYING FOR LESS: TIPS FOR GETTING THE BEST AIRFARES

Passengers within the same airplane cabin rarely pay the same fare for their seats. Business travelers who need to purchase tickets at the last minute, change their itinerary at a moment's notice, or get home before the weekend pay the premium rate, known as the full farc. Passengers who can book their ticket in advance and commit to a fixed itinerary will pay a fraction of the full fare. On most flights, even the shortest hops, the full fare is close to $1,000 or more, but you'll most likely pay a lot less if you buy a 7-day or 14-day advance purchase ticket. Here are a few other easy ways to save.

- Periodically, airlines lower prices on their most popular routes, which often include New York. Check your newspaper for advertised discounts or call the airlines directly and ask if any **promotional rates or special fares** are available. You'll almost never see a sale during the peak summer vacation months of July and August, or during the Thanksgiving or Christmas seasons; in periods of low-volume travel, however, you should pay no more than $400 for a cross-country flight.

   Note, however, that the lowest-priced fares are often nonrefundable, require advance purchase of one to three weeks and a certain length of stay, and carry penalties for changing dates of travel. So, when you're quoted a fare, make sure you know exactly what the restrictions are before you commit.

Money-Saving Tip

If your schedule is flexible, you can almost always secure a cheaper fare by staying over a Saturday night or by flying during midweek. Many airlines won't volunteer this information, so be sure to ask.

- **Consolidators,** also known as bucket shops, are a good place to find low fares, often below even the airlines' discounted rates. There's nothing shady about the reliable ones—basically, they're just big travel agents that get discounts for buying in bulk and pass some of the savings on to you. Before you pay, however, ask for a confirmation number from the consolidator and then call the airline itself to confirm your seat. Be prepared to book your ticket with a different consolidator—there are many to choose from—if the airline can't confirm your reservation. Also be aware that consolidator tickets are usually non-refundable or come with stiff cancellation penalties.

  Small ads for consolidators usually run in the Sunday travel section of major newspapers at the bottom of the page. But I recommend going with one of these reliable companies: I've gotten great deals on a number of occasions from **Cheap Tickets** (☎ **800/377-1000** or 212/570-1179; www.cheaptickets.com). **Council Travel** (☎ **800/226-8624;** www.counciltravel.com) and **STA Travel** (☎ **800/ 781-4040;** www.sta.travel.com) cater especially to young travelers, but their bargain-basement prices are available to people of all ages. **Travel Bargains** (☎ **800/AIR-FARE;** www.1800airfare.com) was formerly owned by TWA but now offers the deepest discounts on many other airlines, with a four-day advance purchase. Other reliable consolidators include **1-800-FLY-4-LESS; Cheap Seats** (☎ **800/451-7200;** www.cheapseatstravel.com); **1-800-FLY-CHEAP** (**www. 1800flycheap.com**); and "rebators" such as **Travel Avenue** (☎ **800/333-3335** or 312/876-1116) and the **Smart Traveller** (☎ **800/448-3338** or 305/448-3338), which rebate part of their commissions to you.

- Search the **Internet** for cheap fares—though it's still best to compare your findings with the research of a dedicated travel agent, if you're lucky enough to have one, especially when you're booking more than just a flight. A few of the better-respected virtual travel agents are **Travelocity** (**www.travelocity.com**) and **Microsoft Expedia** (**www.expedia.com**). Each has its own little quirks—Travelocity and Expedia both require you to register with them—but they all provide variations of the same service. Just enter the dates you want to fly and the cities you want to visit, and the computer roots out the lowest fares. Expedia's site will e-mail you the best airfare deal once a week if you so choose. Travelocity uses the SABRE computer reservations system that most travel agents use, and has a "Last Minute Deals" database that advertises really cheap fares for those who can get away at a moment's notice. Another good bet is **Arthur Frommer's Budget Travel** (**www.frommers. com**), which offers detailed information on 200 destinations around the world, plus ways to save on flights, hotels, car reservations, and cruises. Book an entire vacation online, or direct your travel questions to Arthur himself. The newsletter is updated daily to keep you abreast of the latest-breaking ways to save.

- Great last-minute deals are also available through **E-savers,** which are free e-mail services provided directly by the airlines. Each week, the airline sends you a list of discounted flights, usually leaving the upcoming Friday or Saturday and returning the following Monday or Tuesday. You can sign up at each airline's Web site (see "By Plane" above for Web addresses).

Better yet, save yourself the headache and register with **Smarter Living** (**www.smarterliving.com**). Every week you'll get a customized e-mail summarizing the discount fares available from your departure city. Smarter Living tracks more than 15 different airlines, so it's a worthwhile time-saver. The site also features concise lists of links to hotel, car rental, and other hot travel deals.

TRANSPORTATION TO & FROM THE NEW YORK AREA AIRPORTS

Since there's no need to rent a car for a visit to New York, you're going to have to figure out how you want to get from the airport to your hotel and back.

For complete transportation information for all three airports (JFK, La Guardia, and Newark), call **Air-Ride** (☎ **800/247-7433**); it gives recorded details on bus and shuttle companies and private car services registered with the New York and New Jersey Port Authority.

On the arrivals level at each airport, the Port Authority also has Ground Transportation Information counters where you can get information and book on all manner of transport. Most transportation companies also have courtesy phones near the baggage-claim area.

Generally, travel time between the airports and midtown Manhattan by taxi or car is one hour for JFK, 45 minutes for La Guardia, and 50 minutes for Newark. Always allow extra time, though, especially during rush hour, peak holiday travel times, and if you're taking a bus.

SUBWAYS & PUBLIC BUSES   For the most part, your best bet is to stay away from the MTA when traveling to and from the airport. You might save a few dollars, but subways and buses that currently serve the airports involve multiple transfers and staircases up and down which you must drag your luggage. On some subways you'd be traveling through undesirable neighborhoods. Spare yourself the drama.

The only exception to this rule that I feel comfortable with is the subway service to and from JFK—but you should only consider it if money is extremely tight *and* you're already well-versed in the ways of New York. It's a huge hassle, and you should expect it to take 90 minutes or more, but you can take the **A train,** which connects to one of two free **shuttle buses** that serve all the JFK terminals. Upon exiting the terminal, pick up the shuttle bus (marked **LONG TERM PARKING LOT**) out front; it takes you to the **Howard Beach station,** where you pick up the A train to the west side of Manhattan. Service is every 10 to 15 minutes during rush hour and every 20 minutes at midday, and the subway fare is $1.50. If you're traveling to JFK from Manhattan, be sure to take the A train that says **FAR ROCKAWAY** or **ROCKAWAY PARK**—*not* LEFFERTS BOULEVARD. Get off at the Howard Beach/JFK Airport station and connect to the shuttle bus, A or B, that goes to your terminal (they're clearly marked, and there's usually a guide to point you to the right one). The subway can actually be more reliable than taking a car or taxi at the height of rush hour, but *a few words of warning:* This isn't the right option for you if you're bringing more than a single piece of luggage, since there's a good amount of walking and some stairs involved in the trip, and you'll have nowhere to put it on the subway train. And *do not* use this method if you're traveling to or from the airport after dark, or too early in the morning—it's just not safe. For additional subway information, see "Getting Around" in chapter 4.

TAXIS   Taxis are a quick and convenient way to travel to and from the airports. They're available at designated taxi stands outside the terminals, with uniformed dispatchers on hand during peak hours (follow the **GROUND TRANSPORTATION** or **TAXI** signs). There may be a long line, but it generally moves pretty quickly. Fares, whether fixed or metered, do not include bridge and tunnel tolls ($3.50 to $4) or a tip

Money-Saving Package Deals

Before you start your search for the lowest airfare, you may want to consider booking your flight as part of a travel package.

Package tours are not the same as escorted tours. They are simply a way to buy airfare and accommodations (and sometimes extras like sightseeing tours and hard-to-get theater tickets) at the same time. For visiting New York, a package can be a smart way to go. In many cases, a package that includes airfare, hotel, and transportation to and from the airport will cost you less than your hotel bill alone would have had you booked it yourself. That's because packages are sold in bulk to tour operators, who then resell them to the public at a cost that drastically undercuts standard rates.

Packages, however, vary widely. Some offer a better class of hotels than others. Some offer the same hotels for lower prices. With some packagers, your choice of accommodations and travel days may be limited. Which package is right for you depends entirely on what you want.

Here are a few tips to help you tell one package from another, and figure out which one is right for you:

- **Read this guide.** Do a little homework; read up on New York. Compare the rack rates that we've published to the discounted rates being offered by the packagers to see what kinds of deals they're offering—if you're actually being offered a substantial savings, or if they've just gussied up the rack rates to make their offer *sound* like a deal. If you're being offered a stay in a hotel I haven't recommended, do more research to learn about it, especially if it isn't a reliable franchise like Holiday Inn or Hyatt. It's not a deal if you end up at a dump.

- **Read the fine print.** Make sure you know *exactly* what's included in the price you're being quoted, and what's not. Are hotel taxes and airport transfers included, or will you have to pay extra? Conversely, don't pay for a rental car you don't need—and you won't need one in New York. Before you commit to a package, make sure you know how much flexibility you have, say, if your kid gets sick or your boss suddenly asks you to adjust your vacation schedule. Some packagers require iron-clad commitments, while others are will go with the flow, charging only minimal fees for changes or cancellations.

- **Use your best judgment.** Stay away from fly-by-nights and shady packagers. If a deal appears to be too good to be true, it probably is. Go with a reputable firm with a proven track record. This is where your travel agent can come in handy; he or she should be knowledgeable about different packagers, the deals they offer, and the general rate of satisfaction among their customers.

for the cabbie (15% to 20% is customary). They do include all passengers in the cab and luggage—never pay more than the metered or flat rate, except for tolls and a tip (from 8pm to 6am a 50¢ surcharge also applies on New York yellow cabs). Taxis have a limit of four passengers, so if there are more in your group, you'll have to take more than one cab. For more on taxis, see "Getting Around" in chapter 4.

- **From JFK:** At press time, the flat rate of $30 to and from Manhattan (plus any tolls and tip) was still in effect. The meter will not be turned on and the surcharge will not be added. If the flat rate has been overturned by the time you arrive (the cabbies really hate it), expect the fare to be metered and run $30 to $40.

So how do you find a package deal?

The best place to start your search is the travel section of your local Sunday newspaper. Also check the ads in the back of national travel magazines like *Travel & Leisure, National Geographic Traveler,* and *Condé Nast Traveler.*

One of the biggest packagers in the Northeast, **Liberty Travel** (☎ 888/ 271-1584; www.libertytravel.com) boasts a full-page ad in many Sunday papers. You won't get much in the way of service, but you will get a good deal. They offer great-value 2- to 7-night New York packages that usually include such freebies as a Circle Line cruise and discounts at Planet Hollywood, plus lots of good hotels to choose from.

The major airlines offering good-value packages to New York include **Continental Airlines Vacations** (☎ 800/634-5555; www.coolvacations.com), which featured a limited selection of hotels at press time (but among the choices was the Hotel Metro, one of my mid-priced favorites). **Delta Vacations** (☎ 800/ 872-7786; www.deltavacations.com), boasts a very good selection of hotels, including the Hotel Metro, the Doubletree Guest Suites (a great family choice), and the luxurious Waldorf Astoria. **United Vacations** (☎ 800/328-6877; www. unitedvacations.com) and **US Airways Vacations** (☎ 800/455-0123; www. usairwaysvacations.com) each offer a pleasing range of hotels, plus Broadway tickets as part of their list of add-on options. **American Airlines Vacations** (☎ 800/321-2121; aav3.aavacations.com) has an extensive but mixed selection of hotels, so be careful where you book (skip the Ameritania and the Park Central altogether). **Northwest WorldVacations** (☎ 800/800-1504; www. nwa.com/vacpkg) is another option, but their prices weren't that attractive last time I checked. You may want to choose the airline that has frequent service to your hometown or the one on which you accumulate frequent flyer miles (you may even be able to pay with your trip using miles).

For one-stop shopping on the Web, go to **www.vacationpackager.com,** a search engine that will link you to many different package-tour operators offering New York City vacations, often with a company profile summarizing the company's basic booking and cancellation terms.

In New York, many **hotels** also offer package deals, especially for weekend stays. Some of the best deals in town are those that include theater tickets, sometimes for otherwise sold-out shows like *The Lion King.* (Most aren't air/land combos, however; you'll have to book your airfare separately.) I've included tips on hotels that regularly offer them in chapter 5, but always ask about available packages when you call any hotel.

- **From La Guardia.** $20 to $25, metered.
- **From Newark.** The dispatcher for New Jersey taxis gives you a slip of paper with a flat rate ranging from $30 to $45 (toll and tip extra), depending on where you're going in Manhattan, so you'll have to be precise about your destination. New York yellow cabs aren't permitted to pick up passengers at Newark. The yellow-cab fare from Manhattan to Newark is the meter amount plus $10 and tolls (about $40 to $50, perhaps a few dollars more with tip). New Jersey taxis aren't permitted to take passengers from Manhattan to Newark.

An Airport Warning

Never accept a car ride from the hustlers who hang out in the terminal halls. They're illegal, don't have proper insurance, and aren't safe. You can tell who they are because they'll approach you with a suspicious conspiratorial air and ask if you need a ride. Not from them, you don't. Sanctioned city cabs and car services wait outside the terminals.

PRIVATE CAR & LIMOUSINE SERVICES Private car and limousine companies provide convenient 24-hour door-to-door airport transfers. The advantage they offer over taking a taxi is that you can arrange your pick-up in advance and avoid the hassles of the taxi line. Call at least 24 hours in advance (even earlier on holidays), and a driver will meet you near baggage claim or at your hotel for a return trip. You'll probably be asked to leave a credit card number to guarantee your ride; you'll likely be offered the choice of indoor or curbside pickup. Vehicles range from sedans to vans to limousines and tend to be relatively clean and comfortable. Prices vary slightly by company and the size of car reserved, but expect to pay around the same as you would for a taxi if you request a basic sedan and have only one stop; toll and tip policies are the same. (Note that car services are not subject to the flat-rate rule that taxis have for rides to and from JFK.) Ask when booking what the fare will be and if you can use your credit card to pay for the ride so there are no surprises at drop-off time. There may be waiting charges tacked on if the driver has to wait an excessive amount of time for your plane to land when picking you up, but the car companies will usually check on your flight beforehand to get an accurate landing time.

I've had the best luck with **Carmel** (☎ **800/922-7635** or 212/666-6666); **Legends** (☎ **800/LEGENDS** or 718/788-1234); **Executive Town Car & Limousines** (☎ **800/716-2799** or 516/538-8551), which also serves New Jersey and Connecticut; and **Allstate** (☎ **800/453-4099** or 212/741-7440). All have good cars, responsive dispatchers, and polite drivers.

PRIVATE BUSES & SHUTTLES Buses and shuttle services provide a comfortable and less expensive (but usually more time-consuming) option for airport transfers than do taxis and car services.

Gray Line Air Shuttle and **Super Shuttle** serve all three airports; **New York Airport Service** serves JFK and La Guardia; **Olympia Trails** serves Newark. These services are my favorite option for getting to and from Newark during peak travel times because the drivers usually take lesser-known surface streets that make the ride much quicker than if you go with a taxi or car, which will virtually always stick to the traffic-clogged main route.

Gray Line Air Shuttle (☎ **800/451-0455** or 212/315-3006; www.graylinenewyork.com) vans depart JFK, La Guardia, and Newark every 20 minutes between 7am and 11:30pm. They will drop you off at **most hotels between 23rd and 63rd streets in Manhattan**, or **Port Authority** (34th Street and Seventh Avenue) or **Grand Central** (42nd Street and Park Avenue) terminals if you need to catch a subway to another part of town or a train to the 'burbs. No reservation is required; just go to the ground-transportation desk or use the courtesy phone in the baggage-claim area and ask for Gray Line. Service from most major mid-Manhattan hotels to all three airports operates 5am to 7pm; you must call a day in advance to arrange a hotel pickup. The one-way fare to and from JFK is $19, to and from La Guardia is $16, and to and from Newark is $19, but you can save a few bucks by pre-paying your round-trip at the airport ($28 for JFK and Newark, $26 for LaGuardia).

The familiar blue vans of **Super Shuttle** (☎ 800/258-3826 or 718/482-9703; www.supershuttle.com/nyc.htm) serve all three area airports, providing door-to-door service to Manhattan and points on Long Island every 15 to 30 minutes around the clock. As with Gray Line, you don't need to reserve your airport-to-Manhattan ride; just go to the ground-transportation desk or use the courtesy phone in the baggage-claim area and ask for Super Shuttle. Hotel pickups for your return trip require 24 to 48 hours' advance booking. One-way fares are $15 to and from JFK, $14 to and from LaGuardia, and $17 to and from Newark.

New York Airport Service (☎ 718/706-9658) buses travel from JFK and La Guardia to the **Port Authority Bus Terminal** (42nd Street and Eighth Avenue), **Penn Station** (34th Street and Seventh Avenue), **Grand Central Terminal** (Park Avenue between 41st and 42nd streets), or your **midtown hotel,** plus the **Jamaica LIRR Station in Queens,** where you can pick up a train for Long Island. Follow the GROUND TRANSPORTATION signs to the curbside pickup or look for the uniformed agent. Buses depart the airport every 20 to 70 minutes (depending on your departure point and destination) between 6:30am and midnight. Buses to JFK and La Guardia depart the Port Authority and Grand Central Terminal on the Park Avenue side every 15 to 30 minutes, depending on the time of day and the day of the week. To request direct shuttle service from your hotel, call the above number at least 24 hours in advance. One-way fare for JFK is $13, and $10 to and from La Guardia; children under 12 ride free with a parent.

Olympia Trails (☎ 888/662-7700 or 212/964-6233; www.olympiabus.com) provides service every 5 to 15 minutes (less frequently during off hours) from Newark Airport to four Manhattan locations: the **World Trade Center** (on West Street, next to the Marriott World Trade Center Hotel), **Penn Station** (the pickup point is the northwest corner of 34th Street and Eighth Avenue and the drop-off point the southwest corner), the **Port Authority Bus Terminal** (on 42nd Street between Eighth and Ninth avenues), and **Grand Central Terminal** (41st Street between Park and Lexington). Passengers to and from the Grand Central Terminal location can connect to Olympia's midtown shuttle vans, which service most hotels between 30th and 65th streets. From the above departure points in Manhattan, service runs every 15 to 30 minutes depending on your pickup point; call for exact schedule. The one-way fare is $10, or $15 if you connect to the hotel shuttle.

BY TRAIN

Amtrak (☎ 800/USA-RAIL; www.amtrak.com) runs frequent service to New York City's Penn Station (Seventh Avenue between 31st and 33rd streets), where you can easily pick up a taxi, subway, or bus to your hotel. To get the best rates, book early (as much as six months in advance) and travel on weekends.

BY BUS

Buses arrive at the **Port Authority Terminal** (Eighth Avenue between 40th and 42nd streets), where you can easily transfer to your hotel by taxi, subway, or bus. I don't suggest taking the bus, because the ride is long and uncomfortable, and fares are usually no cheaper than the much quicker and more comfortable train. But if for some reason bus is your preferred mode of transportation, call **Greyhound Bus Lines** (☎ 800/231-2222 or check your local phone book).

BY CAR

From the **New Jersey Turnpike** (I-95) and points west, there are three Hudson River crossings into the city's west side: the **Holland Tunnel** (lower Manhattan), the **Lincoln Tunnel** (midtown), and the **George Washington Bridge** (upper Manhattan).

Airport Transportation Tips

If you're traveling to a borough other than Manhattan, call **ETS Air Service** (☎ 888/467-4996 or 718/221-5341) for shared door-to-door service. For Long Island service, see **Super Shuttle,** above. For service to Westchester County or Connecticut, contact **Connecticut Limousine** (☎ 800/472-5466 or 203/878-6867).

If you're traveling to points in New Jersey from Newark Airport, call **Olympic Limousine** (☎ 800/822-9797 or 908/938-4300) for Ocean and Monmouth counties; the **Princeton Airporter** (☎ 800/385-4000 or 609/587-6600) to Middlesex and Mercer counties; or **State Shuttle** (☎ 800/427-3207 or 973/729-0030) for other Jersey destinations.

From **upstate New York,** take the **New York State Thruway** (I-87), which crosses the Hudson on the Tappan Zee Bridge and becomes the **Major Deegan Expressway** (I-87) through the Bronx. For the east side, continue to the Triborough Bridge and then down the FDR Drive. For the west side, take the Cross Bronx Expressway (I-95) to the Henry Hudson Parkway or the Taconic State Parkway to the Saw Mill River Parkway to the Henry Hudson Parkway south.

From **New England,** the **New England Thruway** (I-95) connects with the **Bruckner Expressway** (I-278), which leads to the Triborough Bridge and the FDR on the east side. For the west side, take the Bruckner to the Cross Bronx Expressway (I-95) to the Henry Hudson Parkway south.

Note that you'll have to pay (hefty) tolls along some of these roads and at most crossings.

Once you arrive in Manhattan, park your car in a garage (expect to pay at least $20 to $35 per day) and leave it there. Don't use your car for traveling within the city. Public transportation, taxis, and walking will easily get you where you want to go without the headaches of parking, gridlock, and dodging crazy cabbies.

For Foreign Visitors $\boldsymbol{3}$

You've seen it all already—the high-rises, the bustling crowds, the glittering nightlife and shopping. New York's global media profile might make it appear familiar, but movies and TV, music videos, and news images all distort as much as they reflect. The gap between image and reality can make certain situations puzzling for the foreign—or even domestic—visitor. This chapter will help prepare you for the more common problems that you may encounter.

1 Preparing for Your Trip

ENTRY REQUIREMENTS

Immigration laws are a hot political issue in the United States these days, and the following requirements may have changed somewhat by the time you plan your trip. Check at any U.S. embassy or consulate for current information and requirements, or plug into the U.S. State Department's website at **http://travel.state.gov**. Go to **http://travel. state.gov/visa_services.html** for the latest entry requirements, while **http://travel.state.gov/links.html** will provide you with contact information for U.S. embassies and consulates worldwide.

VISAS The U.S. State Department has a **Visa Waiver Pilot Program** allowing citizens of certain countries to enter the United States without a visa for stays of up to 90 days.

At press time, this visa waiver program applied to citizens of these countries: Andorra, Argentina, Australia, Austria, Belgium, Brunei, Denmark, Finland, France, Germany, Iceland, Ireland, Italy, Japan, Liechtenstein, Luxembourg, Monaco, the Netherlands, New Zealand, Norway, San Marino, Slovenia, Spain, Sweden, Switzerland, and the United Kingdom.

Citizens of these countries need only a valid passport and a round-trip air or cruise ticket in their possession upon arrival. If they first enter the United States, they may also visit Mexico, Canada, Bermuda, and/or the Caribbean islands and return to the United States without a visa. Further information is available from any U.S. embassy or consulate.

Canadian citizens may enter the United States without visas; they need only proof of residence.

Citizens of all other countries must have: (1) a valid passport that expires at least six months later than the scheduled end of their visit to the United States; and (2) a tourist visa, which may be obtained without charge from any U.S. consulate.

Obtaining a Visa   To obtain a visa, you must submit a completed application form (either in person or by mail) with a 1½-inch-square photo, and must demonstrate binding ties to a residence abroad. Usually you can obtain a visa at once or within 24 hours, but it may take longer during the summer rush from June through August. If you cannot go in person, contact the nearest U.S. embassy or consulate for directions on applying by mail. Your travel agent or airline office may also be able to provide you with visa applications and instructions. The U.S. consulate or embassy that issues your visa will determine if you will be issued a multiple- or single-entry visa and any restrictions regarding the length of your stay.

British subjects can obtain up-to-date passport and visa information by calling the **U.S. Embassy Visa Information Line** (☎ **0891/200-290**) or the **London Passport Office** (☎ **0990/210-410**) for recorded information.

IMMIGRATION QUESTIONS   Telephone operators will answer your inquiries regarding U.S. immigration policies or laws at the **Immigration and Naturalization Service's Customer Information Center** (☎ **800/375-5283**). Representatives are available Monday through Friday from 9am to 3pm. The INS also runs a 24-hour automated information service, for commonly asked questions, at ☎ **800/755-0777.** You'll find them online at **www.ins.usdoj.gov.**

MEDICAL REQUIREMENTS   Unless you're arriving from an area known to be suffering from an epidemic (particularly cholera or yellow fever), inoculations or vaccinations are not required for entry into the United States. If you have a disease that requires treatment with narcotics or syringe-administered medications, carry a valid signed prescription from your physician to allay any suspicions that you may be smuggling narcotics (a serious offense that carries severe penalties in the U.S.).

For HIV-positive visitors, requirements for entering the United States are somewhat vague and change frequently. According to the latest publication of *HIV and Immigrants: A Manual for AIDS Service Providers,* "although INS doesn't require a medical exam for every one trying to come into the United States, INS officials may keep out people who they suspect are HIV positive. INS may stop people because they look sick or because they are carrying AIDS/HIV medicine."

If an HIV-positive noncitizen applying for a non-immigrant visa knows that HIV is a communicable disease of public health significance but checks "no" on the question about communicable diseases, INS may deny the visa because it thinks the applicant committed fraud. If a non-immigrant visa applicant checks "yes," or if INS suspects the person is HIV positive, it will deny the visa unless the applicant asks for a special waiver for visitors. This waiver is for people visiting the United States for a short time, to attend a conference, for instance, to visit close relatives, or to receive medical treatment.

For up-to-the-minute information concerning HIV-positive travelers, contact the Center for Disease Control's **National Center for HIV** (☎ **404/332-4559;** www.hivatis.org) or the **Gay Men's Health Crisis** (☎ **212/367-1000;** www.gmhc.org).

DRIVER'S LICENSES   Foreign driver's licenses are mostly recognized in the U.S., although you may want to get an international driver's license if your home license is not written in English.

PASSPORT INFORMATION

Safeguard your passport in an inconspicuous, inaccessible place like a money belt. If you lose this, visit the nearest consulate of your native country as soon as possible for a replacement (a list of major consulates can be found in "Fast Facts" at the end of this chapter). Passport applications are downloadable from the Internet sites listed below.

FOR RESIDENTS OF CANADA   You can pick up a passport application at one of 28 regional passport offices or most travel agencies. A passport is valid for five years and costs $60. Children under 16 may be included on a parent's passport but they will need their own passport to travel if unaccompanied by the parent. Applications, which must be accompanied by two identical passport-sized photographs and proof of Canadian citizenship, are available at travel agencies throughout Canada or from the central **Passport Office, Department of Foreign Affairs and International Trade,** Ottawa, Ont. K1A 0G3 (☎ **800/567-6868;** www.dfait-maeci.gc.ca/passport). Processing takes five to ten days if you apply in person, or about three weeks by mail.

FOR RESIDENTS OF THE UNITED KINGDOM   As a member of the European Union, you need only an identity card, not a passport, to travel to other EU countries. However, if you already possess a passport, it's always useful to carry it. To pick up an application for a regular 10-year passport (the Visitor's Passport has been abolished), visit your nearest passport office, major post office, or travel agency. You can also contact the London Passport Office at ☎ **0171/271-3000** or search its Web site at **www.open.gov.uk/ukpass/ukpass.htm**. Passports are £21 for adults and £11 for children under 16.

FOR RESIDENTS OF IRELAND   You can apply for a 10-year passport, costing IR£45, at the Passport Office, Setanta Centre, Molesworth Street, Dublin 2 (☎ **01/671-1633;** www.irlgov.ie/iveagh/foreignaffairs/services). Those under age 18 and over 65 must apply for a 3-year passport that costs IR£10. You can also apply at 1A South Mall, Cork (☎ **021/272-525**) or over the counter at most main post offices.

FOR RESIDENTS OF AUSTRALIA   Apply at your local post office or passport office or search the government Web site at **www.dfat.gov.au/passports**. Passports for adults are A$126 and A$63 for those under 18.

FOR RESIDENTS OF NEW ZEALAND   You can pick up a passport application at any travel agency or Link Centre. For more info, contact the Passport Office, P.O. Box 805, Wellington (☎ **0800/225-050**). Passports for adults are NZ$80 and NZ$40 for those under 16.

CUSTOMS

WHAT YOU CAN BRING IN   Every visitor over 21 years of age may bring in, free of duty, the following: (1) one liter of wine or hard liquor; (2) 200 cigarettes, 100 cigars (but not from Cuba), or three pounds of smoking tobacco; and (3) $100 worth of gifts. These exemptions are offered to travelers who spend at least 72 hours in the United States and who have not claimed them within the preceding six months. It is altogether forbidden to bring into the country foodstuffs (particularly fruit, cooked meats, and canned goods) and plants (vegetables, seeds, tropical plants, and the like). Foreign tourists may bring in or take out up to $10,000 in U.S. or foreign currency with no formalities; larger sums must be declared to U.S. Customs upon entering or leaving, which includes filing form CM 4790. For more specific information regarding U.S. Customs, contact your nearest U.S. embassy or consulate, or the **U.S. Customs** office at ☎ **202/927-1770** or www.customs.ustreas.gov.

WHAT YOU CAN BRING HOME   U.K. citizens returning from a non-EC country have a customs allowance of: 200 cigarettes; 50 cigars; 250g of smoking tobacco; 2 liters of still table wine; 1 liter of spirits or strong liqueurs (over 22% volume); 2 liters of fortified wine, sparkling wine or other liqueurs; 60cc (ml) perfume; 250cc (ml) of toilet water; and £145 worth of all other goods, including gifts and souvenirs. People under 17 cannot have the tobacco or alcohol allowance. For more information, contact HM Customs & Excise, Passenger Enquiry Point, 2nd

Floor Wayfarer House, Great South West Road, Feltham, Middlesex, TW14 8NP (☎ **0181/910-3744;** from outside the U.K. 44/181-910-3744), or consult their Web site at **www.open.gov.uk**.

For a clear summary of **Canadian** rules, write for the booklet *I Declare*, issued by **Revenue Canada,** 2265 St. Laurent Blvd., Ottawa K1G 4KE (☎ **613/993-0534**). Canada allows its citizens a $500 exemption, and you're allowed to bring back duty-free 200 cigarettes, 2.2 pounds of tobacco, 40 imperial ounces of liquor, and 50 cigars. In addition, you're allowed to mail gifts to Canada from abroad at the rate of Can$60 a day, provided they're unsolicited and don't contain alcohol or tobacco (write on the package: "Unsolicited gift, under $60 value"). All valuables should be declared on the Y-38 form before departure from Canada, including the serial numbers of valuables you already own, such as expensive foreign cameras. *Note:* The $500 exemption can only be used once a year and only after an absence of seven days.

The duty-free allowance in **Australia** is A$400 or, for those under 18, A$200. Personal property mailed back from England should be marked "Australian goods returned" to avoid payment of duty. Upon returning to Australia, citizens can bring in 250 cigarettes or 250 grams of loose tobacco, and 1,125ml of alcohol. If you're returning with valuable goods you already own, such as foreign-made cameras, you should file form B263. A helpful brochure, available from Australian consulates or Customs offices, is *Know Before You Go*. For more information, contact **Australian Customs Services,** GPO Box 8, Sydney NSW 2001 (☎ **02/9213-2000**).

The duty-free allowance for **New Zealand** is NZ$700. Citizens over 17 can bring in 200 cigarettes, or 50 cigars, or 250 grams of tobacco (or a mixture of all three if their combined weight doesn't exceed 250 grams), plus 4.5 liters of wine and beer, or 1.125 liters of liquor. New Zealand currency does not carry import or export restrictions. Fill out a certificate of export, listing the valuables you are taking out of the country; that way, you can bring them back without paying duty. Most questions are answered in a free pamphlet available at New Zealand consulates and Customs offices: *New Zealand Customs Guide for Travellers, Notice no. 4*. For more information, contact New Zealand Customs, 50 Anzac Ave., P.O. Box 29, Auckland (☎ **09/359-6655**).

INSURANCE

Although it's not required of travelers, health insurance is highly recommended. Unlike many European countries, the United States does not usually offer free or low-cost medical care to its citizens or visitors. Doctors and hospitals are expensive, and in most cases will require advance payment or proof of coverage before they render their services. Travel insurance policies can cover everything from the loss or theft of your baggage and trip cancellation to the guarantee of bail in case you're arrested. Good policies will also cover the costs of an accident, repatriation, or death. See "Health & Insurance" in chapter 2 for more information. Packages such as **Europ Assistance** in Europe are sold by automobile clubs and travel agencies at attractive rates. **Worldwide Assistance Services, Inc.** (☎ **800/821-2828**) is the agent for Europe Assistance in the United States.

Though lack of health insurance may prevent you from being admitted to a hospital in nonemergencies, don't worry about being left on a street corner to die: The American way is to fix you now and bill the living daylights out of you later.

FOR BRITISH TRAVELERS   Most big travel agents offer their own insurance, and will probably try to sell you their package when you book a holiday. Think before you sign. **Britain's Consumers' Association** recommends that you insist on seeing the policy and reading the fine print before buying travel insurance. **The Association of British Insurers** (☎ **0171/600-3333**) gives advice by phone and publishes the free

Holiday Insurance, a guide to policy provisions and prices. You might also shop around for better deals: Try **Columbus Travel Insurance Ltd.** (☎ **0171/375-0011**) or, for students, **Campus Travel** (☎ **0171/730-2101**).

FOR CANADIAN TRAVELERS   Canadians should check with their provincial health plan offices or call **HealthCanada** (☎ **613/957-2991**) to find out the extent of their coverage and what documentation and receipts they must take home in case they are treated in the United States.

MONEY

CURRENCY   The U.S. monetary system is painfully simple: The most common bills (all ugly, all green) are the $1 (colloquially, a "buck"), $5, $10, and $20 denominations. There are also $2 bills (seldom encountered), $50 bills, and $100 bills (the last two are usually not welcome as payment for small purchases). Note that a newly redesigned $100 and $50 bill were introduced in 1996, and a redesigned $20 bill in 1998. Expect to see redesigned $10 and $5 notes in the year 2000. Despite rumors to the contrary, the old-style bills are still legal tender.

There are six denominations of coins: 1¢ (1 cent, or a penny); 5¢ (5 cents, or a nickel); 10¢ (10 cents, or a dime); 25¢ (25 cents, or a quarter); 50¢ (50 cents, or a half dollar); and, prized by collectors, the rare $1 piece (the older, large silver dollar and the newer, small Susan B. Anthony coin). A new gold $1 piece will be introduced by the year 2000.

The "foreign-exchange bureaus" so common in Europe are rare even at airports in the United States, and nonexistent outside major cities. You'll find them in New York's prime tourist areas like Times Square, but expect to get extorted on the exchange rate. **American Express** (☎ **800/AXP-TRIP;** www.americanexpress.com) has many offices throughout the city, including at the New York Hilton, 1335 Sixth Ave., at 53rd Street (☎ 212/664-7798); the New York Marriott Marquis, 1535 Broadway, in the 8th floor lobby (☎ 212/575-6580); on the mezzanine level at Macy's Herald Square, 34th Street and Broadway (☎ 212/695-8075); and 65 Broadway, between Exchange Place and Rector Street (☎ 212/493-6500). **Thomas Cook Currency Services** (☎ **212/753-0132;** www.thomascook.com) has locations at JFK Airport; 1590 Broadway, at 48th Street (☎ 212/265-6049); 317 Madison Ave., at 42nd Street (☎ 212/883-0040); and 511 Madison Ave., at 53rd St. (☎ 212/753-2398).

It's best not to change foreign money (or traveler's checks denominated in a currency other than U.S. dollars) at a small-town bank, or even a branch in New York or any other American city. In fact, it's best to just leave any currency other than U.S. dollars at home—it may prove a greater nuisance to you than it's worth.

TRAVELER'S CHECKS   Though traveler's checks are widely accepted, make sure that they're denominated in U.S. dollars, as foreign-currency checks are often difficult to exchange. The three traveler's checks that are most widely recognized—and least likely to be denied—are **Visa, American Express,** and **Thomas Cook.** Be sure to record the numbers of the checks, and keep that information separately in case they get lost or stolen. Most businesses are pretty good about taking traveler's checks, but you're better off cashing them in at a bank (in small amounts, of course) and paying in cash. Remember: You'll need identification, such as a driver's license or passport, to change a traveler's check.

CREDIT CARDS & ATMS   Credit cards are the most widely used form of payment in the United States: **Visa** (BarclayCard in Britain), **MasterCard** (EuroCard in Europe, Access in Britain, Chargex in Canada), **American Express, Diners Club, Discover,** and **Carte Blanche;** you'll also find that New York vendors may also accept international

---

Travel Tip

Be sure to keep a copy of all your travel papers separate from your wallet or purse, and leave a copy with someone at home should you need it faxed in an emergency.

---

cards like **enRoute, EuroCard,** and **JCB,** but not as universally as AmEx, MasterCard, or Visa. There are, however, a handful of stores and restaurants that do not take credit cards, so be sure to ask in advance. Most businesses display a sticker near their entrance to let you know which cards they accept. And be aware that often businesses require a minimum purchase price, usually around $10 or $15, to use a credit card.

It is strongly recommended that you bring at least one major credit card. Hotels, car-rental companies, and airlines usually require a credit-card imprint as a deposit against expenses, and in an emergency a credit card can be priceless.

You'll find automated teller machines (ATMs) on just about every block in Manhattan. Some ATMs will allow you to draw U.S. currency against your bank and credit cards. Check with your bank before leaving home, and remember that you will need your personal identification number (PIN) to do so. Most accept Visa, MasterCard, and American Express, as well as ATM cards from other U.S. banks. Expect to be charged up to $3 per transaction, however, if you're not using your own bank's ATM.

SAFETY

Tourist areas in Manhattan are generally safe, and the city has experienced a dramatic drop in its crime rate in recent years. Still, crime is a national problem, and U.S. urban areas tend to be less safe than those in Europe or Japan. You should always stay alert, use common sense, and trust your instincts. If you feel you're in an unsafe area or situation, you probably are and should leave as quickly as possible.

GENERAL SAFETY SUGGESTIONS   Leave your valuables at home if you can live without them. Don't display expensive cameras, flashy jewelry, or electronic equipment as you walk around the city. If you are using a map, consult it as discreetly as possible, with one eye on what's going on around you at all times. Hold your pocketbook across your shoulder and in front of you at all times, and place your billfold in an inside pocket. In theaters, restaurants, subways, and other public places, keep a hand on your possessions at all times. Put your purse at your feet rather than slinging it over the back of a chair, where it can be lifted without you knowing it.

Remember also that hotels are open to the public, and in a large hotel, security may not be able to screen everyone entering. Always lock your room door—don't assume that once inside your hotel you are automatically safe and no longer need to keep an eye on your valuables or be aware of your surroundings.

Avoid deserted areas, especially at night, and don't go into public parks at night unless there's a concert or similar occasion that will attract a crowd.

For more about personal security in Manhattan, see "Playing It Safe" in chapter 4.

DRIVING   An inviolable rule of thumb for New York: Don't even think of driving within the city (especially not in neighborhoods you don't know, including parts of Harlem, the Bronx, and Brooklyn). Like many cities, New York has its own arcane rules of the road, confusing one-way streets, incomprehensible street-parking signs, and outrageously expensive parking garages. Public transport—whether buses, subways, or taxis—will get you anywhere you want to go quickly and easily, and that's where you'll be most comfortable.

If you do drive to New York in a rental car, return it as soon as you arrive and rent another when you're ready to leave the city. If you dare to arrive in your own car, park it in one of those garages that have monthly charges about equal to a mortgage payment, and then don't take your vehicle out again until you leave the city. Always keep your car doors locked. Never leave any packages or valuables in sight, because thieves will break car windows. If someone attempts to rob you or steal your car, don't resist. Report the incident to the police department immediately.

2 Getting to the United States

In addition to the domestic airlines listed in chapter 2, many international carriers serve John F. Kennedy International and Newark airports. **British Airways** (☎ 0345/222-111 in the U.K.; www.british-airways.com) has daily service from London as well as direct flights from Manchester and Glasgow. **Virgin Atlantic** (☎ 01293/747-747 in the U.K.; www.fly.virgin.com) flies from London's Heathrow to New York.

Canadian readers might book flights on **Air Canada** (☎ 800/776-3000; www.aircanada.ca), which offers direct service from Toronto, Montréal, Ottawa, and other cities, or on **Canadian Airlines** (☎ 800/426-7000; www.cdair.ca).

Continental (☎ 01293/776-464 in the U.K.; www.flycontinental.com) flies to Newark from London, Manchester, Madrid, Paris, and Frankfurt. **Aer Lingus** flies from Dublin and Shannon to New York (☎ 01/844-4747 in Dublin or 061/415-556 in Shannon; www.aerlingus.ie). **TWA** (☎ 800/892-4141 in the U.K.; www.twa.com) has nonstop service to New York from Barcelona, Madrid, Milan, Paris, and Rome. **United** (☎ 0181/990-9900 in the U.K.; www.ual.com) serves those cities and London, Amsterdam, Brussels, and Zurich. **American** (☎ 0181/572-5555 in the U.K.; www.americanair.com) flies nonstop from London, Manchester, Paris, Brussels, and Zurich. **Delta** (☎ 0800/414-764 in the U.K.; www.delta-air.com) flies to New York from most major European cities.

Qantas (☎ 13-12-11 in Australia; www.qantas.com.au) and **Air New Zealand** (☎ 13-2476 in New Zealand; www.airnewzealand.co.nz) fly to the West Coast and will book you straight through to New York City on a partner airline.

AIRLINE DISCOUNTS   The idea of traveling abroad on a budget is something of an oxymoron, especially when pricey New York is your destination, but you can reduce the price of a plane ticket by several hundred dollars if you take the time to shop around. For example, overseas visitors can take advantage of the APEX (Advance Purchase Excursion) reductions offered by all major U.S. and European carriers. For more money-saving airline advice, see "Getting There" in chapter 2. For the best rates, compare fares and be flexible with the dates and times of travel.

Operated by the ETN (European Travel Network), **Discount Tickets** (**www.discount-tickets.com**) is a great online source for regular and discounted airfares to New York and other destinations around the world. You can also use this site to compare rates and book accommodations, car rentals, and tours. Click on "Special Offers" for the latest package deals.

IMMIGRATION & CUSTOMS CLEARANCE   Visitors arriving by air, no matter what the port of entry, should cultivate patience and resignation before setting foot on

Money-Saving Tip

If you're on a tight budget and you're coming from Europe, you might want to consider traveling to New York between January and March. That's when airlines like British Airways and Virgin Atlantic pull out all the stops to fill their post-holiday flights, and fares plummet. Hotels are also suffering the after-Christmas blues, and rooms often go for a relative song.

U.S. soil. Getting through immigration control may take as long as two hours on some days, especially on summer weekends, so be sure to have this guidebook or something else to read. Add the time it takes to clear Customs, and you'll see that you should make a two- to three-hour allowance for delays when you plan your connections between international and domestic flights.

In contrast, for the traveler arriving by car or rail from Canada, the border-crossing formalities have been streamlined to the vanishing point. People traveling by air from Canada, Bermuda, and some places in the Caribbean can sometimes clear Customs and Immigration at the point of departure, which is much quicker.

3 Getting Around the United States

If you'll be traveling beyond New York, you'll have to think about how you'd like to get around.

BY PLANE   The United States is a massive country, so the fastest way to cover large distances is by airplane. Some large airlines (for example, Northwest and Delta) offer travelers on their transatlantic or transpacific flights special discount tickets under the name **Visit USA,** allowing mostly one-way travel from one U.S. destination to another at very low prices. These discount tickets are not on sale in the United States and must be purchased abroad in conjunction with your international ticket. This system is the best and easiest way to see the United States at low cost. You should obtain information well in advance from your travel agent or the office of the airline concerned, since the conditions attached to these discount tickets can be changed without advance notice.

BY TRAIN   If you're making a short hop to another East Coast city, such as Boston, Philadelphia, or Washington, D.C., rail is the best way to go. **Amtrak** (☎ **800/ USA-RAIL;** www.amtrak.com) trains leave from New York's Pennsylvania Station, at Seventh Avenue and 34th Street. Although bus travel is available for short hops, it can also be slow and uncomfortable, and no less expensive than the far more luxurious trains.

If you're visiting more than one city, you may want to consider purchasing a **USA Railpass,** available to international visitors only and good for 15 or 30 days of unlimited travel on Amtrak. The pass is available through many foreign travel agents. Prices in 1999 for a 15-day pass are $285 off-peak, and $425 peak; a 30-day pass costs $375 off-peak, and $535 peak. (With a foreign passport, you can also buy passes at some Amtrak offices in the U.S., including New York.) Reservations are generally required and should be made for each part of your trip as early as possible.

BY CAR   After airplanes, the most cost-effective, convenient, and comfortable way to travel around the United States is by car. The interstate highway system connects cities and towns all over the country; in addition to these high-speed, limited-access roadways, there's an extensive network of federal, state, and local highways and roads. Some of the national car-rental companies include **Avis** (☎ 800/331-1212), **Budget** (☎ 800/527-0700), **Dollar** (☎ 800/800-4000), **Hertz** (☎ 800/654-3131), and **National** (☎ 800/227-7368).

To rent a car in the United States you need a valid driver's license, a passport, and a major credit card. The minimum age is usually 25, but some companies will rent to younger people and add a surcharge. It's a good idea to buy maximum insurance coverage unless you're positive your own auto or credit-card insurance is sufficient. All major car-rental agencies have branches in Manhattan; check the Yellow Pages directory under "Automobile Renting" for locations. Rates vary, so it pays to call around. Stick to the major companies (Avis, Budget, Dollar, Enterprise, Hertz, National) because what you might save with smaller companies might not be worth the headache if you have mechanical troubles on the road.

In New York it's sometimes much less expensive to rent a car from a nearby smaller town or from an airport rather than from the city center. You might consider taking the train to a destination outside the city and then renting and returning your car there. Compare the rates—and figure in the transportation costs and inconveniences—before you decide on this option.

If you're planning to buy or borrow a car, automobile-association membership is recommended; see "Fast Facts," below, for details.

Fast Facts: For the Foreign Traveler

Also see "Fast Facts" in chapter 4 for more New York City–specific information.

Automobile Organizations   Auto clubs will supply maps, suggested routes, guidebooks, accident and bail-bond insurance, and emergency road service. The **American Automobile Association (AAA)** is the major auto club in the United States. If you belong to an auto club in your home country, inquire about AAA reciprocity before you leave. You may be able to join AAA even if you're not a member of a reciprocal club; to inquire, call ☎ **800/222-4357.** AAA is actually an organization of regional auto clubs, so look under "AAA Automobile Club" in the White Pages of the telephone directory. AAA has a nationwide emergency road service telephone number (☎ **800/AAA-HELP**).

Business Hours   See "Fast Facts: New York City" in chapter 4.

Currency & Currency Exchange   See "Money" under "Preparing for Your Trip," earlier in this chapter. For the latest market conversion rates, point your Internet browser to **www.cnn.com/travel/currency**.

Drinking Laws   The legal age for purchase and consumption of alcoholic beverages is 21; proof of age is required and often requested at bars, nightclubs, and restaurants, so it's always a good idea to bring ID when you go out. Liquor stores, the only retail outlets for wine as well as hard liquor in New York, are closed on Sundays, holidays, and election days while the polls are open. Beer can be purchased in grocery stores and delis all day Monday to Saturday and Sunday after noon.

Do not carry open containers of alcohol in your car or any public area that isn't zoned for alcohol consumption. The police can, and probably will, fine you on the spot. And nothing will ruin your trip faster than getting a citation for DUI ("driving under the influence"), so don't even think about driving while intoxicated.

Electricity   Like Canada, the United States uses 110 to 120 volts AC (60 cycles), compared to 220 to 240 volts AC (50 cycles) in most of Europe, Australia, and New Zealand. If your small appliances use 220 to 240 volts, you'll need a 110-volt transformer and a plug adapter with two flat parallel pins to operate them here. Downward converters that change 220-240 volts to 110-120 volts are difficult to find in the United States, so bring one with you.

Embassies/Consulates   All embassies are in Washington, D.C. Some countries have consulates general in major U.S. cities, and most have a mission to the United Nations in New York City. If your country isn't listed below, call for directory information in Washington, D.C. (☎ **202/555-1212**) or point your Web browser to **www.embassy.org/embassies** for the number of your national embassy.

Australia: Embassy, 1601 Massachusetts Ave. NW, Washington, D.C. 20036
(☎ 202/797-3000; www.austemb.org). Consulate General, 630 Fifth Ave., New
York, NY 10111 (☎ 212-351-6500). **Canada:** Embassy, 501 Pennsylvania Ave.
NW, Washington, D.C. 20001 (☎ 202/682-1740; www.cdnemb-washdc.org).
Consulate General, 1251 Ave. of the Americas, New York, NY 10020 (☎ 212/
596-1600). **Ireland:** Embassy, 2234 Massachusetts Ave. NW, Washington, D.C.
20008 (☎ 202/462-3939; www.irelandemb.org). Consulate General, 345 Park
Ave., New York, NY 10154-0037 (☎ 212/319-2555). **Japan:** Embassy, 2520
Massachusetts Ave. NW, Washington, DC 20008 (☎ 202/238-6700; www.
embjapan.org). **New Zealand:** Embassy, 37 Observatory Circle NW, Washington, D.C. 20008 (☎ 202/328-4800; www.emb.com/nzemb). Consulate
General, 780 Third Ave., New York, NY, 10017 (☎ 212/832-4938). **United
Kingdom:** Embassy, 3100 Massachusetts Ave. NW, Washington, D.C. 20008
(☎ 202/462-1340). Consulate General, 845 Third Ave., New York, NY 10022
(☎ 212/745-0202).

Emergencies   Call ☎ **911** to report a fire, call the police, or get an ambulance
anywhere in the United States. This is a toll-free call (no coins are required at
public telephones).

If you have a medical emergency that doesn't require an ambulance, you can
walk into a hospital's 24-hour emergency room (usually a separate entrance). For
a list of hospitals, see "Fast Facts: New York City" in chapter 4. Because emergency rooms are often crowded and waits are long, one of the walk-in medical
centers listed under "Finding a Doctor" under "Health & Insurance" in chapter
2 might be a better option. Otherwise, call ☎ **212/737-2333,** a referral service
available 8am to midnight, for doctors who make house calls. Don't be surprised
if the first question you are asked is, "Do you have medical insurance?"

Gasoline (Petrol)   Petrol is known as gasoline (or simply "gas") in the United
States, and petrol stations are known as both gas stations and service stations.
Gasoline costs about half as much here as it does in Europe (about $1.05 per
gallon at press time), and taxes are already included in the printed price. One
U.S. gallon equals 3.8 liters or .85 Imperial gallons.

Holidays   Banks, government offices, post offices, and many stores, restaurants,
and museums are closed on the following legal national holidays: January 1 (New
Year's Day), the third Monday in January (Martin Luther King, Jr. Day), the
third Monday in February (Presidents' Day, Washington's Birthday), the last
Monday in May (Memorial Day), July 4 (Independence Day), the first Monday
in September (Labor Day), the second Monday in October (Columbus Day),
November 11 (Veterans' Day/Armistice Day), the fourth Thursday in November
(Thanksgiving Day), and December 25 (Christmas). Also, the Tuesday following
the first Monday in November is Election Day and is a federal government holiday in presidential-election years (held every four years, and next in 2000).

Legal Aid   The foreign tourist will probably never become involved with the
American legal system. If you are stopped for a minor infraction (for example, of
the highway code, such as speeding), never attempt to pay the fine directly to a
police officer; this could be construed as attempted bribery, a much more serious
crime. If it's a traffic infraction, do not get out of the car; stay seated and with
your hands on the steering wheel until the officer approaches you. Pay fines by
mail, or directly into the hands of the clerk of the court. If accused of a more
serious offense, say and do nothing before consulting a lawyer. Here the burden
is on the state to prove a person's guilt beyond a reasonable doubt, and everyone

has the right to remain silent, whether he or she is suspected of a crime or actually arrested. Once arrested, a person can make one telephone call to a party of his or her choice. Call your embassy or consulate.

Mail   If you aren't sure what your address will be in the United States, mail can be sent to you, in your name, c/o General Delivery at the main post office in New York City, at Eighth Avenue between 31st and 33rd streets, which is open 24 hours. To receive general-delivery mail in New York City, call ☎ **212/330-3099.** The addressee must pick mail up in person and must produce proof of identity (driver's license, passport, etc.). Most post offices will hold your mail for up to one month.

Generally found at intersections, mailboxes are blue with a white eagle logo and carry the inscription U.S. MAIL. If your mail is addressed to a U.S. destination, don't forget to add the five-digit postal code (or ZIP code), after the two-letter abbreviation of the state to which the mail is addressed.

At press time, domestic postage rates were 20¢ for a postcard and 33¢ for a letter. For international mail, a first-class letter of up to one-half ounce costs 60¢ (46¢ to Canada and 40¢ to Mexico); a first-class postcard costs 50¢ (40¢ to Canada and 35¢ Mexico); and a preprinted postal aerogramme costs 50¢. Point your web browser to **www.usps.gov** for complete U.S. postal information, or call ☎ **800/275-8777** for information on the nearest post office. Most branches are open Monday to Friday from 8am to 5 or 6pm, and Saturday from 9am to 3pm.

Newspapers/Magazines   In addition to the *New York Times* and other city papers, many newsstands in New York City carry a selection of international newspapers and magazines. For nearly all major newspapers and magazines from around the world, head to **Universal News & Magazines,** 977 Eighth Ave., at 57th Street (☎ **212/459-0932**), or **Hotalings News Agency,** 142 W. 42nd St., between Broadway and Sixth Avenue (☎ **212/840-1868**).

Taxes   In the United States there is no value-added tax (VAT) or other indirect tax at the national level. Every state, county, and city has the right to levy its own local tax on all purchases, including hotel and restaurant checks, airline tickets, and so on. Sales tax is usually not included in the price tags on merchandise but is added at the cash register. These taxes aren't refundable. In New York City, the **sales tax** is 8.25%, but there has been talk of reducing or eliminating it at some point on clothing purchases under $500. The **hotel tax** is 13.25% plus $2 per room per night (including sales tax). The **parking garage tax,** added to already high basic fees, is 18.25%.

Telephone, Telegraph, & Fax   The telephone system in the United States is run by private corporations, so rates, especially for long-distance service and operator-assisted calls, can vary widely. Generally, hotel surcharges on long-distance and local calls are astronomical, so you're usually better off using a **public pay telephone,** which you'll find clearly marked in most public buildings and private establishments as well as on the street. Convenience grocery stores and gas stations always have them. Many convenience groceries and packaging services sell **prepaid calling cards** in denominations up to $50; these can be the least expensive way to call home. Many public phones at airports now accept American Express, MasterCard, and Visa credit cards. **Local calls** made from public pay phones usually cost 25¢ for the first five minutes, but sometimes it's 35¢. Pay phones do not accept pennies, and few will take anything larger than a quarter.

In New York, I advise caution when using pay phones. In fact, I use only pay phones bearing the distinctive green-and-blue **Bell Atlantic** logo, or the sleek new multimedia phone booths from **AT&T,** another reliable company. Many other phones belong to unscrupulous companies that provide bad service and charge unconscionably high rates. Pay phones located directly against the outside wall of a store or other commercial space might belong to fly-by-night phone companies; the store owner usually receives a commission for allowing the phone to be proximate to his or her property but will disavow any responsibility for returning your money if the phone doesn't work properly.

Most long-distance and international calls can be dialed directly from any phone. **For calls within the United States and to Canada,** dial 1 followed by the area code and the seven-digit number. **For other international calls,** dial 011 followed by the country code, city code, and the telephone number of the person you are calling. Some country and city codes are as follows: **Australia** 61, Melbourne 3, Sydney 2; **Ireland** 353, Dublin 1; **New Zealand** 64, Auckland 9, Wellington 4; **United Kingdom** 44, Belfast 232, Birmingham 21, Glasgow 41, London 71 or 81. If you're calling the **United States** from another country, the country code is 01.

For **reversed-charge, collect, operator-assisted, and person-to-person calls,** dial 0 (the number zero, not the letter O) followed by the area code and number you want; an operator will then come on the line, and you should specify that you are calling collect, or person-to-person, or both. If your operator-assisted call is international, ask for the overseas operator.

For **local directory assistance** ("information"), dial 411; for long-distance information, dial 1, then the appropriate area code and 555-1212.

Telegraph services are provided primarily by Western Union. You can bring your telegram into the nearest Western Union office (there are hundreds across the country) or dictate it over the phone (☎ **800/325-6000**). You can also telegraph money or have it telegraphed to you very quickly over the Western Union system, but this service can cost as much as 15 to 20% of the amount sent.

Most hotels have **fax machines** available for guest use (be sure to ask about the charge to use it), and many hotel rooms are even wired for guests' fax machines. A less expensive way to send and receive faxes may be at stores such as **Mail Boxes Etc.,** a national chain of packing service shops (look in the Yellow Pages directory under "Packing Services").

There are two kinds of telephone directories in the United States. The so-called **White Pages** list private households and business subscribers in alphabetical order. The inside front cover lists emergency numbers for police, fire, ambulance, the Coast Guard, poison-control center, crime-victims hotline, and so on. The first few pages will tell you how to make long-distance and international calls, complete with country codes and area codes. Government numbers are usually printed on blue paper within the White Pages. Printed on yellow paper, the so-called **Yellow Pages** list all local services, businesses, industries, and houses of worship according to activity with an index at the front or back.

Travel Tip

Calls to area codes **800, 888,** and **877** are toll-free. However, calls to numbers in area codes **700** and **900** (chat lines, bulletin boards, "dating" services, and so on) can be very expensive—usually a charge of 95¢ to $3 or more per minute, and they sometimes have minimum charges that can run as high as $15 or more.

(Drugstores/pharmacies and restaurants are also listed by geographic location.) The Yellow Pages also include city plans or detailed area maps, postal ZIP codes, and public transportation routes. Useful online yellow pages for finding phone numbers and addresses in New York and other U.S. cities include **www.yp. ameritech.net.**

Time   The continental United States is divided into **four time zones:** eastern standard time (EST), the time zone New York is in, which is five hours behind Greenwich Mean Time (GMT); central standard time (CST); mountain standard time (MST); and Pacific standard time (PST). Alaska and Hawaii have their own zones. For example, noon in New York City (EST) is 11am in Chicago (CST), 10am in Denver (MST), 9am in Los Angeles (PST), 8am in Anchorage (AST), and 7am in Honolulu (HST).

Daylight saving time is in effect from 1am on the first Sunday in April through 1am the last Sunday in October, except in Arizona, Hawaii, part of Indiana, and Puerto Rico. Daylight saving time moves the clock one hour ahead of standard time. When daylight saving time is in effect, New York is only four hours behind Greenwich Mean Time.

For the correct local time in New York, dial ☎ **212/976-1616.**

Tipping   Tips are a very important part of certain workers' salaries, so it's necessary to leave appropriate gratuities. Unlike in most of Europe, tips aren't automatically added to restaurant and hotel bills. **In restaurants,** a tip to the waitperson of 15 to 20% of the total check is customary (in New York City, just double the 8.25% tax to figure the appropriate tip).

Other tipping guidelines: 15 to 20% of the fare to taxi drivers, 10 to 15% of the tab to bartenders, $1 to $2 per bag to bellhops, $1 per day to hotel maids, $1 per item to checkroom attendants, $1 to valet parking attendants, and 15 to 20% to hairdressers. Tipping theater ushers, gas station attendants, and cafeteria and fast-food restaurant employees isn't expected.

Toilets   In general, you won't find public toilets or "rest rooms" on the streets in New York, but they can be found in hotel lobbies, bars, restaurants, museums, department stores, or railway and bus stations. See "Rest Rooms" under "Fast Facts: New York City" in chapter 4.

Traveler's Assistance   See "Fast Facts: New York City" in chapter 4.

4 Getting to Know New York City

This chapter gives you an insider's take on Manhattan's most distinctive neighborhoods and streets, tells you how to get around town, and serves as a handy reference to everything from personal safety to libraries and liquor.

1 Orientation

VISITOR INFORMATION
INFORMATION OFFICES

Here are convenient addresses where you can collect details about the city:

- ✪ **The Times Square Visitors Center,** 1560 Broadway, between 46th and 47th streets (where Broadway meets Seventh Avenue), across from the TKTS booth (☎ 212/768-1560; www.timessquarebid.org), is the city's top info stop. Run by the Times Square Business Improvement District and occupying the renovated 1925 Embassy Theatre, this pleasant and attractive center features a helpful information desk offering loads of citywide information. There's also a tour desk selling tickets for Gray Line bus tours and Circle Line boat tours; a Metropolitan Transportation Authority (MTA) desk staffed to sell MetroCard fare cards, provide public transit maps, and answer all of your questions on the transit system; a Broadway Ticket Center providing show information and selling full-price show tickets (although we suggest you get your tickets across the street from the discount TKTS booth or directly at the box office); ATMs and currency exchange machines; computer terminals with free Internet access courtesy of Yahoo; an international newsstand; and more. It's open daily from 8am to 8pm.

- At press time, the New York Convention and Visitors Bureau had just opened the **NYCVB Visitor Information Center** at 810 Seventh Ave., between 52nd and 53rd streets. In addition to loads of information on citywide attractions and a multilingual information counselor on hand to answer questions, the center also has interactive terminals that provide free touch-screen access to visitor information via Citysearch and sell advance tickets to major attractions (which can save you from standing in long ticket lines once you arrive). There's also an ATM, a gift shop, and a bank of phones that connect you directly with American Express card member services. The center is open Monday through Friday from 8:30am to 5:30pm, and Saturday and Sunday from 9am to 5pm. For over-the-phone assistance, call ☎ 212/484-1222 weekdays from 9am to 5pm EST.

- **Grand Central Partnership,** at Grand Central Terminal, East 42nd Street at the corner of Vanderbilt Avenue (☎ 212/818-1777). There's an information window inside the newly restored Grand Central Terminal and a cart out front, open Monday to Friday from 8:30am to 6:30pm and Saturday and Sunday from 9am to 6pm.
- **34th Street Partnership,** in Penn Station, Seventh Avenue between 31st and 33rd streets (☎ 212/868-0521). This window is open Monday to Friday 8:30am to 5:30pm and Saturday and Sunday 9am to 6pm. The group also maintains carts at the Empire State Building (year-round), Fifth Avenue and 34th Street; outside Madison Square Garden, Seventh Avenue at 32nd Street (except when it's colder than 30°F outside); and in Greeley Square, 32nd Street where Broadway and Sixth Avenue cross (summer only). The carts are open daily from 9:15am to 4:45pm.
- **Manhattan Mall,** Sixth Avenue and 32nd Street (☎ 212/465-0500). Travelers' tips are available on the first floor of this vertical series of shops Monday to Saturday from 10am to 8pm and Sunday from 11am to 6pm.
- **Lower East Side Business Improvement District,** 261 Broome St., between Orchard and Allen streets (☎ 888/VALUES-4-U or 212/226-9010). The Lower East Side's Visitor Center is open Sunday through Friday from 10am to 4pm; stop in for an Orchard Street Bargain District shopping guide (which they can also send you in advance), plus other neighborhood information. They also have public rest rooms.

PUBLICATIONS

For comprehensive listings of films, concerts, performances, sporting events, museum and gallery exhibits, street fairs, and special events, there are many local publications to choose from. The following are your best bets:

- The *New York Times* (www.nytimes.com) features terrific arts and entertainment coverage, particularly in the two-part Friday "Weekend" section and the Sunday "Arts & Leisure" section. Both days boast full guides to the latest happenings in Broadway and off-Broadway theater, classical music, dance, pop and jazz, film, and the art world. Friday is particularly good for cabaret, family fun, and general-interest recreational and sightseeing events.
- *Time Out New York* (www.timeoutny.citysearch.com) is my favorite weekly magazine. Dedicated to weekly goings-on, it's attractive, well organized, and easy to use. *TONY* features excellent coverage in all categories, from live music, theater, and clubs (gay and straight) to museum shows, dance events, book and poetry readings, and kids' stuff. The regular "Check Out" section, unequaled in any other listings magazine, will fill you in on upcoming sample and closeout sales, crafts and antiques shows, and other shopping-related scoop. A new issue hits newsstands every Thursday.
- The free weekly *Village Voice* (www.villagevoice.com), the city's legendary alterna-paper, is available late Tuesday downtown and early Wednesday in the rest of the city. From classical music to clubs, the arts and entertainment coverage couldn't be more extensive, and just about every live music venue advertises its shows here. But I find the paper a bit unwieldy to navigate, and the exposé tone of its features can be tiresome.

Other useful weekly rags with city information and events listings include the glossy *New York* magazine (**www.newyorkmag.com**), whose "Cue" section is a selective guide to city arts and entertainment; *The New Yorker,* which features an artsy "Goings On About Town" section at the front of the magazine; and the alternative *New York Press* newspaper, available free in caddies around Manhattan. Monthly *Paper* (**www.papermag.com**) is a glossy alterna-mag that's serves as good prep for those of you who want to experience the hipper side of the city.

CITY LAYOUT

Open the sheet map that comes free with this book and you'll see the city is comprised of five boroughs: **Manhattan,** where most of the visitor action is; the **Bronx,** the only borough connected to the mainland United States; **Queens,** where Kennedy and La Guardia airports are located and which borders the Atlantic Ocean and occupies part of Long Island; **Brooklyn,** south of Queens, which is also on Long Island and is famed for its attitude, accent, and Atlantic-front Coney Island; and **Staten Island,** the least populous borough, bordering Upper New York Bay on one side and the Atlantic Ocean on the other.

But it is Manhattan, the long finger-shaped island pointing southwest off the mainland—surrounded by the Harlem River to the north, the Hudson River to the west, the East River (really an estuary) to the east, and the fabulous expanse of Upper New York Bay to the south—that most visitors think of when they envision New York. Despite the fact that it's the city's smallest borough (13½ miles long, 2¼ miles wide, 22 square miles), Manhattan contains the city's most famous attractions, buildings, and cultural institutions. For that reason, all of the accommodations and most of the restaurants suggested in this book are in Manhattan.

In most of Manhattan, finding your way around is a snap because of the logical, well-executed grid system by which the streets are numbered. If you can discern uptown and downtown, and East Side and West Side, you can find your way around pretty easily. In real terms, **Uptown** means north of where you happen to be and **Downtown** means south, although sometimes these labels have vague psychographical meanings (generally speaking, "Uptown" chic vs. "Downtown" bohemianism).

Avenues run north and south (uptown and downtown). Most are numbered. **Fifth Avenue** divides the East Side from the West Side of town, and serves as the eastern border of Central Park north of 59th Street. **First Avenue** is all the way east and **Twelfth Avenue** is all the way west. The three most important unnumbered avenues on the East Side you should know are between Third and Fifth Avenues: **Madison** (east of Fifth), **Park** (east of Madison), and **Lexington** (east of Park, just west of Third). Important unnumbered avenues on the West Side are **Avenue of the Americas,** which all New Yorkers call Sixth Avenue; **Central Park West,** which is what Eighth Avenue north of 59th Street is called as it borders Central Park on the west (hence the name); **Columbus Avenue,** which is what Ninth Avenue is called north of 59th Street; and **Amsterdam Avenue,** or Tenth Avenue north of 59th.

Broadway is the exception to the rule—the only major avenue that doesn't run uptown–downtown. It cuts a diagonal path across the island, from the northwest tip down to the southeast corner. As it crosses most major avenues, it creates **squares** (Times Square, Herald Square, Madison Square, and Union Square, for example).

Streets run east–west (crosstown) and are numbered consecutively as they proceed uptown from Houston Street. So to go uptown, simply walk north of, or to a higher-numbered street, than where you are. Downtown is south of (or a lower-numbered street than) your current location. If you can see a major landmark like the Empire State Building or the World Trade Center, it's easy to determine uptown from downtown if you know what street you are on and remember that the former is on 34th Street and the latter is almost on the southern tip of the island.

As I've already mentioned, Fifth Avenue is the dividing line between the **East Side** and **West Side** of town (except below Washington Square, where Broadway serves that function). On the East Side of Fifth Avenue, streets are numbered with the distinction East, on the West Side of that avenue they are numbered West. East 51st Street, for example, begins at Fifth Avenue and runs to the East River, and West 51st Street begins at Fifth Avenue and runs to the Hudson River.

If you're looking for a particular address, remember that even-numbered street addresses are on the south side of streets and odd-numbered addresses are on the north. Street addresses increase by about 50 per block starting at Fifth Avenue. For example, nos. 1 to 50 East are just about between Fifth and Madison avenues, while nos. 1 to 50 West are just about between Fifth and Sixth avenues. Traffic generally runs east on even-numbered streets and west on odd-numbered streets, with a few exceptions, like the major east–west thoroughfares—**14th, 23rd, 34th, 42nd, 57th, 72nd, 79th, 86th,** and so on—which have two-way traffic. Therefore 28 W. 23rd St., is a short walk west of Fifth Avenue; 325 E. 35th Street would be a few blocks east of that road.

Avenue addresses are irregular. For example, 994 Second Avenue is at East 51st Street but so is 320 Park Avenue. Thus, it's important to know a building's cross street to find it easily.

Unfortunately, these rules don't apply to neighborhoods in Lower Manhattan, south of 14th Street—like Wall Street, Chinatown, SoHo, TriBeCa, the Village—since they sprang up before engineers devised this brilliant grid scheme. A good map is essential when exploring these areas.

STREET MAPS   You'll find a useful pull-out street-by-street map of Manhattan at the back of this book. There's also a decent one available for free as part of the **Big Apple Visitors Kit** if you write ahead for information (see "Visitor Information" in chapter 2); you can also pick it up for free at most of the visitor centers listed above.

Even with all these freebies at hand, I suggest investing in a map with more features if you really want to zip around the city like a pro. **Hagstrom** maps are terrific because they feature block-by-block street numbering—so instead of trying to guess what the cross street for 125 Prince Street is, you can see right on your map that it's Greene Street. Another great bet is H.M. Gousha's **Fastmap,** which folds in only three places and is laminated. Easy to handle on the run and pack away into a purse or pocket, it can also be read discreetly, which is a major deterrent to crime. Van Dam's **New York Unfolds,** a pop-up map that unfolds and refolds like an origami flower, serves the

---

Orientation Tips

I've indicated the cross streets for all destinations in this book, but be sure to ask for the cross street (or avenue) if you're ever calling for an address.

When you give a taxi driver an address, **always specify the cross streets.** New Yorkers, even most cab drivers, probably wouldn't know where to find 994 Second Ave., but they do know where to find 51st and Second. If you're heading to the restaurant Le Bernadin, for example, tell them that it's on 51st Street between Sixth and Seventh avenues. The exact number (in this case, no. 155) is given only as a further precision.

If you have only the numbered address on an avenue and need to figure out the cross street, put new batteries in your calculator and refer to the address locator at the front of the Yellow Pages.

same function. Spiral- or staple-bound notebook-size maps are another good idea, but many of these cover all five boroughs, which is probably more information than you need. These and other visitor-friendly maps are available at just about any good bookstore, including the Barnes & Noble and Borders Books & Music branches around town; see "Shopping A to Z" in chapter 8 for locations.

Manhattan's Neighborhoods in Brief

Since they grew up over the course of hundreds of years, all of Manhattan neighborhoods have multiple, splintered personalities and fluid boundaries. Still, it's relatively easy to agree upon what they stand for in general terms—so if you stop a New Yorker on the street and ask them to point you to, say, the Upper West Side or the Flatiron District, they'll know where you want to go. From south to north, here is how I've defined Manhattan's neighborhoods for use throughout this book. It's a good idea to refer to the foldout map in the back of this book as you review this section in order to get your bearings.

DOWNTOWN

Lower Manhattan: South Street Seaport & the Financial District   For hundreds of years, this was New York. Originally established by the Dutch in 1625 (hence the city's original name, Nieuw Amsterdam), the first settlements sprung up here, on the southern tip of Manhattan island, and everything uptown was farm country and wilderness. While all that's changed, this is still the best place to search for the past. George Washington was first inaugurated president here. Fraunces Tavern, on Pearl Street, was the site of countless great moments in city history. The now-touristy South Street Seaport area is surrounded by reminders of when shipping was the raison d'etre of the city. The Brooklyn Bridge stands proudly as the symbol of a new world of engineering marvels that came to the city in the 19th century. Wall Street—now a state of mind much grander than the actual narrow street—dominates the global mindset with the New York Stock Exchange and the towering World Trade Center (also known as the Twin Towers). Battery Park City is where downtown residents are found, while Battery Park itself is your point of departure for the Statue of Liberty, Ellis Island, and Staten Island. (The Wall Street and Financial District walking tour in chapter 7 offers can guide you through Lower Manhattan's past.)

Lower Manhattan constitutes everything south of Chambers Street. Battery Park is on the very south tip, while South Street Seaport lies a bit north on the east coast (just south of the Brooklyn Bridge). The rest of the area is considered the Financial District, which is anchored by the World Financial Center, the World Trade Center, and Battery Park City to the west and Wall Street running crosstown to the south. City Hall is at the northern border of the district, abutting Chambers Street (look for City Hall Park on the map). Most of the streets of this neighborhood are narrow concrete canyons, with Broadway serving as the main uptown–downtown artery.

Just about all of the major subway lines congregate here before they either end or head to Brooklyn (the Sixth Avenue B, D, F, Q line being the chief exception—it crosses into Brooklyn from the Lower East Side, over the Manhattan Bridge).

During the week this neighborhood is the heart of capitalism and city politics, and the sidewalks are crowded with the business-suit set. But despite the fact that some office buildings have been redeveloped into high-end apartments, the neighborhood still feels rather desolate after work and on the weekends. This may sound like the most romantic time to explore the area, but it's actually more fun to be here at the height of the hustle and bustle, between 8am and 6pm on weekdays. Still, you might consider staying down here, especially if you're visiting on the weekend or during the

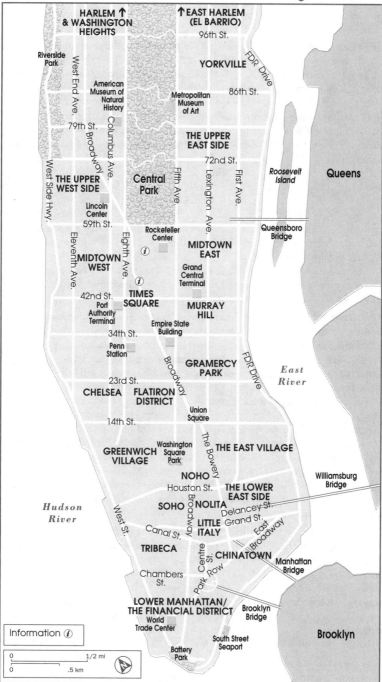

HARLEM ↑
& WASHINGTON
HEIGHTS

↑EAST HARLEM
(EL BARRIO)
96th St.

Riverside
Park

West End Ave.

YORKVILLE

FDR Drive

American
Museum of
Natural
History

Metropolitan
Museum
of Art

86th St.

79th St.

Columbus Ave.

Broadway

THE UPPER
EAST SIDE

72nd St.

West Side Hwy.

THE UPPER
WEST SIDE

Central
Park

Fifth Ave.

Lexington Ave.

First Ave.

Roosevelt
Island

Queens

Lincoln
Center

59th St.

Eleventh Ave.

Eighth Ave.

Rockefeller
Center

ⓘ

MIDTOWN
EAST

Queensboro
Bridge

MIDTOWN
WEST

ⓘ

Grand
Central
Terminal

42nd St.
Port
Authority
Terminal

TIMES
SQUARE

MURRAY
HILL

34th St.

Empire State
Building

Penn
Station

Broadway

GRAMERCY
PARK

FDR Drive

East
River

23rd St.

CHELSEA

FLATIRON
DISTRICT

14th St.

Union
Square

GREENWICH
VILLAGE

Washington
Square
Park

The Bowery

THE EAST VILLAGE

NOHO

Williamsburg
Bridge

Houston St.

THE LOWER
EAST SIDE

Hudson
River

West St.

SOHO

Broadway

NOLITA

Delancey St.

LITTLE
ITALY

Grand St.

Canal St.

East Broadway

TRIBECA

Park Centre St.

CHINATOWN

Manhattan
Bridge

Chambers
St.

Park Row

LOWER MANHATTAN/
THE FINANCIAL DISTRICT

Brooklyn
Bridge

World
Trade Center

South Street
Seaport

Brooklyn

Battery
Park

Information ⓘ

0   1/2 mi
0   .5 km

holidays, when your dollars can go a lot further in the luxury hotels that business travelers have abandoned for home.

TriBeCa   Bordered by the Hudson River to the west, the area north of Chambers Street, west of Broadway, and south of Canal Street is the *Tri*angle *Be*low *Ca*nal Street, or TriBeCa. Since the 1980s, as SoHo became saturated with chic, the spillover has been quietly transforming TriBeCa into one of the city's hippest residential neighborhoods, where celebrities and families quietly coexist in cast-iron warehouses converted into spacious, expensive loft apartments. Artists' lofts and galleries as well as hip antiques and design shops pepper the area, as do as some of the city's best restaurants. Robert DeNiro gave the neighborhood a tremendous boost when he established the Tribeca Film Center, and Miramax headquarters gave the area further capitalist-chic cachet. Still, historic streets like White (especially the Federal-style building at no. 2) and Harrison (the complete stretch west from Greenwich Street) evoke a bygone, more human-scaled New York, as do a few hold-out businesses and old-world pubs. I love this neighborhood, because it seems to have brought together the old city and the new without bastardizing either. And because retail spaces are usually a few doors apart rather than right on top of one another, it also manages to be more peaceful than similarly popular neighborhoods.

The main uptown–downtown drag is West Broadway (two blocks to the west of Broadway), and the main subway line is the 1/9, which stops at Franklin in the heart of the 'hood. Take your map; the streets are a maze.

Chinatown   New York City's most famous ethnic enclave is bursting past its traditional boundaries and encroaching on Little Italy, much to the chagrin of civic fathers there. The former marshlands northeast of City Hall and below Canal Street, from Broadway to the Bowery, are where Chinese immigrants arriving from San Francisco were forced in the 1870s. This booming neighborhood is now a conglomeration of Asian populations. As such, it offers tasty cheap eats in cuisines from Szechuan to Hunan, Cantonese to Fujian, Vietnamese to Thai. Exotic shops offer strange foods, herbs, and souvenirs. Bargains on clothing and leather are plenty. The area is also home to sweatshops, however, and doesn't have quite the quaint character you'd find in San Francisco. Still, it's a blast to walk down Canal Street, peering into the myriad electronics and luggage stores and watching crabs cut loose from their handlers at the exotic fish markets.

The Grand Street (B, D, Q) and Canal Street (J, M, Z, N, R, 6) street stations will get you to the heart of the action. The streets are crowded during the day and empty out after around 9pm; they remain quite safe, but the neighborhood is more enjoyable during the bustle.

Little Italy   Nearby is Little Italy, just as ethnic if not quite so vibrant, and compelling for its own culinary treats. Traditionally the area east of Broadway between Houston and Canal streets, the community is shrinking today, due to the encroachment of thriving Chinatown. It's now limited mainly to Mulberry Street, where you'll find most restaurants, and just a few offshoots. With rents going up in the increasingly trendy Lower East Side, a few chic spots are moving in, further intruding upon the old-world landscape. To reach Little Italy, your best bet is to walk up Mulberry Street from the Grand Street Station, or east from the Spring Street station on the no. 6 line. September is a great time to visit, when Mulberry Street comes alive during the Feast of San Gennaro.

The Lower East Side   In 1894, the four square miles that made up the Lower East Side were the most densely populated on earth. Of all the successive waves of immigrants and refugees who passed through here from the mid-19th century to the 1920s, it was the Eastern European Jews who left the most lasting impression on the neighborhood, which runs between Houston and Canal streets, and east of the Bowery.

Impressions

Can we actually "know" the universe? It's hard enough finding your way around Chinatown.

—Woody Allen

Drugs and crime ultimately supplanted the Jewish communities that first popped up here, dragging the Lower East Side into the gutter until recently. While the Lower East Side has been gentrifying over the last few years—lots of hip bars and clubs have sprung up, prompting complaints from old-time residents who seem to have preferred the desolation and crime of the old days—the area can still be very dicey in spots, and should generally be avoided late at night. There are some remnants of what was once the largest Jewish population in America along Orchard Street, where you'll find great bargain hunting in its many fabric and clothing stores. There's a good visitor center run by the neighborhood business improvement district, where you can get your bearings and pick up a shopping guide, just around the corner from Orchard Street at 261 Broome St. Keep in mind that as an Orthodox Jewish community, many places (including the visitor center) close early on Friday afternoon and all day on Saturday (the Jewish Sabbath). The trendy set can be found mostly along Ludlow Street, north of Delancey, with the biggest concentration of action being just south of Houston.

This area is not well served by the subway system (one cause for its years of decline), so your best bet is to take the F train to Second Avenue and walk east on Houston; when you see Katz's Deli, you'll know you've arrived.

SoHo & NoLiTa   No relation to the London neighborhood of the same name, **SoHo** got its moniker as an abbreviation of "South of Houston Street" (pronounced HOUSE-ton). This super-fashionable neighborhood extends down to Canal Street, between Sixth Avenue to the west and Lafayette Street (one block east of Broadway) to the east.

The neighborhood is easily accessible by subway: Take the B, D, F, or Q train to the Broadway–Lafayette stop; the N, R to the Prince Street Station; or the C, E to Spring Street.

An industrial zone during the 19th century, SoHo retains the impressive cast-iron architecture of the era, and in many places, cobblestone peeks out from beneath the street's asphalt. In the early 1960s, cutting-edge artists began occupying the drab and deteriorating buildings, soon turning it into the trendiest neighborhood in the city. SoHo is now a prime example of urban gentrification and a major New York attraction thanks to its impeccably restored buildings, influential arts scene, fashionable restaurants, and stylish boutiques. On weekends, the cobbled streets and narrow sidewalks are crowded with gallery goers and shoppers, with the prime action being between Broadway and Sullivan Street north of Grand Street.

Some critics claim that SoHo is becoming a victim of its own popularity—witness the recent departure of several imaginative galleries and independent boutiques to TriBeCa and Chelsea as well as the influx of suburban mall-style stores like J. Crew, Victoria's Secret, and Smith & Hawken. However, the neighborhood is still one of the best shopping neighborhoods in the city, and few are more fun to browse. High-end street peddlers set up along the boutique-lined sidewalks, hawking silver jewelry, coffee-table books, and their own art. At night, the neighborhood is transformed into a terrific, albeit pricey, dining and bar-hopping neighborhood. You can even stay here now, thanks to the introduction of two super-trendy hotels, the Mercer and the Soho Grand.

In recent years SoHo has been crawling its way east, taking over Mott and Mulberry streets—and white-hot Elizabeth Street in particular—north of Kenmare Street, an area now known as **NoLiTa** for its *No*rth of *Li*ttle *Ita*ly location. NoLiTa is becoming increasingly well known for its hot shopping prospects, which include a number of pricey antiques and home design stores. Taking the 6 to Spring Street will get you closest by subway, but it's just a short walk east from SoHo proper.

The East Village & NoHo   The **East Village,** which extends between 14th Street and Houston Street, from Broadway east to First Avenue and beyond to Avenues A, B, C, and D, is where the city's real Bohemia has gone. Once, flower children tripped along St. Mark's Place and listened to music at the Fillmore East; now the East Village is a fascinating mix of affordable ethnic and trendy restaurants, upstart clothing designers and kitschy boutiques, punk-rock clubs (yep, still) and folk cafes, all of which give the neighborhood a youthful vibe. A half-dozen off-Broadway theaters also call this place home.

The gentrification that has swept the city has made a huge impact on the East Village, but there's still a seedy element that some of you won't find appealing. Now yuppies and other ladder-climbing types make their homes alongside old-world Russian immigrants who have lived in the neighborhood forever, as well as the cross-dressers and squatters who settled here in between. The neighborhood still embraces great ethnic diversity, with strong elements of its Ukrainian and Irish heritage, while more recent immigrants have taken over Sixth Street between First and Second avenues, turning it into a haven of cheap eats known as Little India.

The East Village isn't very accessible by subway; unless you're traveling along 14th Street (the L Line will drop you off at Third and First avenues), your best bet is to take the N, R to 8th Street or the 6 to Astor Place and walk east. Always stay alert in the East Village. The landscape changes from one block to the next, especially the farther east you go. Venture only with care into Alphabet City (avenues A, B, C, and D)—drug dealers still peddle openly here, and these streets can be dangerous.

The southwestern section, around Broadway and Lafayette between Bleecker and 4th streets, is called **NoHo** (for *No*rth of *Ho*uston), and has a completely different character. As you might have guessed from its name, this area is developing much more like its neighbor to the south, SoHo. Here you'll find a growing crop of trendy lounges, stylish restaurants, cutting-edge designers, and upscale antiques shops. NoHo is wonderful fun to browse; the Bleecker Street stop on the no. 6 line will land you right in the heart of it, and the Broadway–Lafayette stop on B, D, F, Q lines will drop you right at its edge.

Greenwich Village   Tree-lined streets crisscross and wind, following ancient streams and cow paths. Each block reveals yet another row of Greek Revival town houses, a well-preserved Federal-style house, or a peaceful courtyard or square. This is "the Village," from Broadway west to the Hudson River, bordered by Houston Street to the south and 14th Street to the north. It defies Manhattan's orderly grid system with streets that predate it, virtually every one choc-a-block with activity, and unless you live here it may be impossible to master the lay of the land—so be sure to have a map on hand as you explore.

The Seventh Avenue line (1, 2, 3, 9) is the area's main subway artery, while the West 4th Street stop (where the A, C, E lines meet the B, D, F, Q lines), serves as its central hub.

Nineteenth-century artists like Mark Twain, Edgar Allan Poe, Henry James, and Winslow Homer first gave the Village its reputation for embracing the unconventional. Groundbreaking artists like Edward Hopper and Jackson Pollack were drawn in, as were writers like Eugene O'Neill, e.e. cummings, and Dylan Thomas. Radical thinkers from John Reed to Upton Sinclair basked in the neighborhood's liberal ethos, and beatniks Allen Ginsberg, Jack Kerouac, and William Burroughs dug the free-swinging atmosphere.

Gentrification and escalating land values have conspired to push out the artistic element, but culture and counterculture still rub shoulders in cafes, internationally renowned jazz clubs, neighborhood bars, off-Broadway theaters, and an endless variety of tiny shops and restaurants.

The Village is probably the most chameleon-like of Manhattan's neighborhoods; indeed, it changes faces depending on what block you're on. Some of the highest-priced real estate in the city runs along lower Fifth Avenue, which dead-ends at Washington Square Park. Serpentine Bleecker Street stretches through most of the neighborhood, and is emblematic of the area's historical bent. The tolerant, anything-goes attitude in the Village has fostered a large gay community, which is still largely in evidence around Christopher Street and Sheridan Square. The streets west of Seventh Avenue, an area known as the West Village, boast a more relaxed vibe and some of the city's most charming and historic brownstones. Three colleges—New York University, Parsons School of Design, and the New School for Social Research—keep the area thinking young—hence the popularity of Eighth Street, lined with shops selling cheap, hip clothes to bridge-and-tunnel kids and the college crowd.

Streets are often crowded with weekend warriors and teenagers looking for a taste of what used to be, especially on Bleecker, West 4th, 8th, and surrounding streets. Keep an eye on your wallet when navigating the weekend throngs. And Washington Square Park was cleaned up a couple of years back, but there's never any telling when the drug dealers will be back; stay away after dark.

MIDTOWN

Chelsea   This neighborhood is coming on strong of late as a hip address, especially for the gay community. A low-rise composite of town houses, tenements, lofts, and factories, Chelsea comprises roughly the area west of Sixth Avenue from 14th to 30th streets. (Sixth Avenue itself below 23rd Street is actually considered part of the Flatiron District; see below.) Its main arteries are Seventh and Eighth avenues, and it's primarily served by the C, E and 1, 9 subway lines.

The Chelsea Piers sports complex to the far west and a host of shops (both unique boutiques and big names like Williams-Sonoma), well-priced bistros, and thriving bars along the main drags have contributed to the area's rebirth. Even the Hotel Chelsea—

Touring Tip

If you're looking to tour a specific neighborhood with an expert guide, call **Big Apple Greeter** (☎ **212/669-8159;** www.bigapplegreeter.org), preferably at least one week ahead of your arrival. It's a non-profit organization of specially trained New Yorkers who volunteer to take visitors around town for a free two- to four-hour tour of a particular neighborhood. And they say New York isn't friendly! The office is open Monday to Friday from 10am to 5:30pm.

the neighborhood's most famous architectural and literary landmark, where Thomas Wolfe and Arthur Miller wrote, Bob Dylan composed "Sad-Eyed Lady of the Low Land," Viva and Edie Sedgwick of Andy Warhol fame lived, and Sid Vicious killed girlfriend Nancy Spungeon—has undergone a renovation. You'll find a number of very popular flea markets set up in parking lots along Sixth Avenue, between 24th and 27th streets, on the weekends.

One of the most influential trends in Chelsea has been the establishment of a "gallery row" on far West 22nd Street and its vicinity; this is where you'll find the cutting edge of today's New York art scene. The power of art can also be found at the Joyce Theater, New York's principal modern-dance venue.

The Flatiron District, Union Square & Gramercy Park   These adjoining and at places overlapping neighborhoods are some of the city's most appealing. Dotted with four small historic parks (Union Square, Gramercy, Madison Square, and Stuyvesant), their streets have been rediscovered by New Yorkers and visitors alike thanks to great shopping and dining opportunities. The commercial spaces are often large loftlike expanses with witty designs and graceful columns.

The **Flatiron District** lies south of 23rd Street to 14th Street, between Broadway and Sixth Avenue, and centers around the historic Flatiron Building on 23rd (so named for its triangular shape) and Park Avenue South, which has become a sophisticated new Restaurant Row. Below 23rd Street along Sixth Avenue (once known as the Ladies' Mile shopping district), mass-market discounters like Filene's Basement, Bed Bath & Beyond, Old Navy, and others have moved in. The shopping gets classier on Fifth Avenue, where you'll find a mix of national names (including Emporio Armani, Kenneth Cole, Banana Republic, and the super-trendy Restoration Hardware) and hip boutiques. Lined with Oriental carpet dealers and high-end fixture stores, Broadway is becoming the city's home-furnishings alley; its crowning jewel is the justifiably famous ABC Carpet & Home, with eight floors of gorgeous textiles, homewares, and gifts on one side of Broadway, and an equally dazzling display of floor coverings on the other.

Union Square is the hub of the entire area; the N, R, 4, 5, 6, and L trains stop here, making it easy to reach from most other city neighborhoods. Long in the shadows of the more bustling (Times and Herald) and high-toned (Washington) city squares, Union Square has experienced a major renaissance in the last decade. Local businesses joined forces with the city to rid the park of drug dealers, and now it's a delightful place to spend an afternoon. Union Square is perhaps best known as the setting for New York's premier greenmarket every Monday, Wednesday, Friday, and Saturday. Musical acts often play the small pavilion at the north end of the park, and in-line skaters take over the market space in the after-work hours. A number of hip restaurants rim the square, as do superstores like Toys 'Я' Us, the city's best Barnes & Noble superstore, and a brand-new Virgin Megastore. The shopping gets dubious along 14th Street, which also becomes rather unsightly as you move away from the square.

From about 16th to 23rd streets, east from Park Avenue South to about Second Avenue, is the leafy, largely residential district known as **Gramercy Park.** The pity of the Gramercy Park district is that so few can enjoy the park of the same name: Built by Samuel Ruggles in the 1830s to attract buyers to his other property in the area, it is the only private park in the city and is locked to all but those who live on its perimeter (the rule is that your windows have to look over the park for you to have a key). Located at the southern endpoint of Lexington Avenue (at 21st Street), it is one of the most peaceful spots in the city. If you know someone who has a magic key, go there. Or better yet, book a room at the Gramercy Park Hotel, whose guests have park privileges.

At the northern edge of the area, fronting the Flatiron Building on 23rd Street and Fifth Avenue, is another of Manhattan's lovely little parks, **Madison Square.** Across from its northeastern corner once stood Stanford White's original Madison Square Garden (in whose roof garden White was murdered in 1906 by possibly deranged, but definitely jealous, millionaire Harry K. Thaw). It's now majetically presided over by the massive New York Life Insurance building, the masterful New York State Supreme Court, and the Metropolitan Life Insurance Company, whose tower in 1909 was the tallest building in the world at 700 feet.

Times Square & Midtown West   Midtown West, the vast area from 34th to 59th streets west of Fifth Avenue to the Hudson River, encompasses several famous names: Madison Square Garden, the Garment District, Rockefeller Center, the Theater District, and Times Square. This is New York's tourism central, where you'll find the bright lights and bustle that draws people from all over the world. As such, this is also the city's biggest hotel neighborhood, with choices running the gamut from budget to deluxe.

The 1, 2, 3, 9 subway line serves the massive neon station at the heart of Times Square, at 42nd Street between Broadway and Seventh Avenue, while the B, D, F, Q line runs up Sixth Avenue to Rockefeller Center. The N, R line cuts diagonally across the neighborhood, following the path of Broadway before heading up Seventh Avenue at 42nd Street. The A, C, E line serves the west side, running along Eighth Avenue.

If you know New York but haven't been here in a few years, you'll be quite surprised by the "new" **Times Square.** Longtime New Yorkers like to kvetch nostalgic about the glory days of the old peep-show-and-porn-shop Times Square that this cleaned-up, Disney-fied one supplanted, but the truth is that it's a hugely successful regentrification. Grand old theaters have come back to life as Broadway and children's playhouses, and scores of new family-friendly restaurants and shops have opened (including the terrific Virgin Megastore on Broadway as well as Disney and Warner Bros. studio stores). Plenty of businesses have moved in—MTV studios overlook Times Square at 1515 Broadway, and, taking a key note from the far more successful *Today* show, *Good Morning America* is in the process of launching its own street-facing studio at Broadway and 44th Street, which should be up and running by the time you arrive. The neon lights have never been brighter, and middle America has never been more welcome.

Most of the great Broadway theaters light up the streets just off Times Square, in the West 40s just east and west of Broadway. At the heart of the Theater District, where Broadway meets Seventh Avenue, is the TKTS booth, where crowds line up daily to buy discount tickets for tonight's shows.

Unlike neighboring Times Square, gorgeous **Rockefeller Center** needs no renovation. Situated between 46th and 50th streets from Sixth Avenue east to Fifth, this art deco complex contains some of the city's great architectural gems that house hundreds of offices, a number of NBC studios (including *Saturday Night Live, Late Night with Conan O'Brien,* and the famous glass-walled *Today* show studio at 48th Street), and some pleasing upscale boutiques (attention, shoppers: Saks Fifth Avenue is just on the other side of Fifth). Holiday time is a great time to be here, as ice skaters take over the central plaza and the huge Christmas tree twinkles against the night sky.

Along Seventh Avenue south of 42nd Street is the **Garment District,** of little interest to tourists except for its sample sales, where some great new fashions are sold off cheap to serious bargain hunters willing to scour the racks. Other than that, it's a pretty grim commercial area. Between Seventh and Eighth avenues and 31st and 33rd streets, Penn Station sits beneath Madison Square Garden, where the Rangers and the Knicks play. Taking up all of 34th Street between Sixth and Seventh Avenues is Macy's, the world's largest department store; exit Macy's at the southeast corner and you'll find more famous-label shopping around **Herald Square.**

Farther north, despite the presence of grand dame Carnegie Hall, West 57th Street has become a theme restaurant bonanza, with Planet Hollywood (for now, anyway, until it moves to the in-the-works Planet Hollywood Hotel in Times Square), the Harley-Davidson Cafe, the Motown Cafe, Brooklyn Diner USA, and the venerable Hard Rock in residence. There are a good number of hotels in all price categories in this area, and their convenience to Central Park (which starts at 59th Street) is an extra plus.

If you're looking for something a little more culture-rich than an over-priced burger and a logo T-shirt, Midtown West is also home to the Museum of Modern Art, Radio City Music Hall, and the *Intrepid* Sea-Air-Space Museum.

Midtown East & Murray Hill   **Midtown East,** the area including Fifth Avenue and everything east from 34th to 59th streets, is the more upscale side of the midtown map. This side of town is short of subway trains, served primarily by the Lexington Avenue 4, 5, 6 line.

Midtown East is where you'll find the city's finest collection of grand hotels, mostly along Lexington Avenue and near the park at the top of Fifth. The stretch of Fifth Avenue from Saks at 49th Street extending to FAO Schwarz at 59th is home to the city's most high-profile haute shopping, including Tiffany & Co., Cartier, and Bergdorf Goodman, but more mid-priced names like Banana Republic, Ann Taylor, and Liz Claiborne have moved their superstores in of late. The stretch of 57th Street between Fifth and Lexington avenues is also known for high-fashion boutiques (Chanel, Hermès) and high-ticket galleries, but change is underway since Warner Brothers (at the intersection with Fifth), Levi's, and Niketown squeezed in. You'll find plenty of spillover along Madison Avenue, a great strip for shoe shopping in particular.

Magnificent architectural highlights include the recently repolished Chrysler Building, with its stylized gargoyles glaring down on passersby; the beaux arts tour de force that is the newly renovated Grand Central Terminal; magnificent St. Patrick's Cathedral; and the glorious Empire State Building, offering oh-so-romantic views from its observation deck.

Far east, swank Sutton and Beekman places are enclaves of beautiful town houses, luxury living, and tiny pocket parks that look out over the East River. Along this river is the United Nations, which isn't officially in New York City, or even the United States, but is on a parcel of international land belonging to member nations.

Claiming the territory east from Madison Avenue, **Murray Hill** begins somewhere north of 23rd Street (the line between it and Gramercy Park is fuzzy), and is most clearly recognizable north of 34th Street to 42nd Street. This residential quarter, lined with lovely brownstones, is largely a quiet residential neighborhood, most notable for its handful of good budget and mid-priced hotels.

UPTOWN

The Upper West Side   North of 59th Street and encompassing everything west of Central Park, the Upper West Side contains Lincoln Center, arguably the world's premier performing-arts venue; the American Museum of Natural History, whose renovated Dinosaur Halls garner justifiably rave reviews; and a number of mid-priced hotels whose larger-than-midtown rooms and nice residential location make them particularly good bets for families. Unlike the more stratified Upper East Side, the Upper West Side is home to an egalitarian mix of middle-class yuppiedom, laid-back wealth (lots of celebs and monied media types call the grand apartments along Central Park West home), and ethnic families who were here before the gentrification.

The neighborhood runs all the way up to Harlem, around 125th Street, and encompasses Morningside Heights, where you'll find Columbia University and the perennial construction project known as the Cathedral of St. John the Divine. But prime Upper West Side—and the part you're most likely to explore—is the area running from Columbus Circle at 59th Street into the 80s, between the park and Broadway. North of 59th Street is where Eighth Avenue becomes Central Park West, the eastern border of the neighborhood (and the western border of Central Park); Ninth Avenue becomes Columbus Avenue, lined with attractive boutiques and cafes; and Tenth Avenue becomes Amsterdam Avenue, less appealing than Columbus to the east and less trafficked than bustling Broadway to the west, whose highlights are the gourmet mega-marts Zabar's and Fairway. You'll find Lincoln Center at the lower end of the neighborhood, in the mid-60s, where Broadway cross-cuts Amsterdam.

Two major subway lines service the area: the 1, 2, 3, 9 line runs up Broadway, while the B and C trains run up glamorous Central Park West, stopping right at the historic Dakota apartment building (where John Lennon was shot and Yoko still lives, albeit without an all-grown-up Sean) at 72nd Street, and at the Museum of Natural History at 81st Street.

The Upper East Side   North of 59th Street and east of Central Park is some of the most expensive residential real estate in the city—and probably the world. This is New York at its most gentrified: Walk along Fifth and Park avenues, especially between 60th and 80th streets, and you're sure to encounter some of the wizened WASPs and Chanel-suited socialites that make up the most rarefied of the city's population. Madison Avenue to 79th Street is the monied crowd's main shopping strip, recently vaunting ahead of Hong Kong's Causeway Bay to become to most expensive retail real estate *in the world*—so bring your platinum card. You can also use it to stay at one of the neighborhood's remarkably luxurious hotels, such as the Carlyle or the Mark, or to dine at four-star wonders like Le Cirque 2000 and Daniel.

The main attraction of this neighborhood is Museum Mile, the stretch of Fifth Avenue fronting Central Park that's home to no fewer than ten terrific cultural institutions, including Frank Lloyd Wright's Guggenheim, and anchored by the mind-boggling Metropolitan Museum of Art. But the elegant rows of landmark townhouses are worth a look alone: East 70th Street, from Madison east to Lexington, is one of the world's most charming residential streets. If you want to see where real people live, move east to Third Avenue and beyond; that's where affordable restaurants and active street life start popping up.

A second subway line is in the works, but it's still no more than an architect's blueprint. For now, the Upper East Side is served solely by the Lexington Avenue line (4, 5, 6 trains), so wear your walking shoes (or bring taxi fare) if you're heading up here to explore.

Harlem   Harlem is really two areas. Harlem proper stretches from river to river, beginning at 125th Street on the West Side and 96th Street on the East Side. Spanish Harlem (El Barrio), an enclave east of Fifth Avenue, runs between East 100th and East 125th streets.

Parts of Harlem are benefiting from the same kinds of revitalization that has swept so much of the city, with national-brand retailers moving in and visitors arriving to tour historic sites related to the Golden Age of African-American culture. In the '20s and '30s, great bands like the Count Basie and Duke Ellington orchestras played at the Cotton Club and Sugar Cane Club, and literary giants like Langston Hughes and James Baldwin soaked up the scene. Some houses date back to a time when the area was something of a country retreat, and represent some of the best brownstone mansions in the city. On Sugar Hill (from 143rd Street to 155th Street, between St. Nicholas and Edgecombe avenues) and Striver's Row (West 139th Street between Adam Clayton Powell Jr. and Frederick Douglass boulevards) are a significant number of fine town houses. For cultural visits, there's the Morris-Jumel Mansion, the Schomburg Center, the Studio Museum, and the Apollo Theater.

By all means, come see Harlem—it's one of the city's most vital and historic neighborhoods. But your best bet is to take a guided tour (see chapter 7). Sights tend to be far apart, and neighborhoods change quickly. Don't wander thoughtlessly through Harlem, especially at night.

Washington Heights & Inwood Located at the northern tip of Manhattan, Washington Heights (the area from 155th Street to Dyckman Street, with adjacent Inwood running to the tip) is home to a large segment of Manhattan's Latino community. Fort Tryon Park and the Cloisters are the two big reasons to come up this way. The Cloisters houses the Metropolitan Museum of Art's stunning medieval collection; in a building perched atop a hill, with excellent views across the Hudson to the Palisades. Committed off-the-beaten-path sightseers might also want to visit the Dyckman Farmhouse, a historic jewel built in 1783 and the only remaining Dutch Colonial structure in Manhattan.

2 Getting Around

Frankly, Manhattan's transportation systems are a marvel. It's simply miraculous that so many people can gather on this little island and move around it. For the most part, you can get where you're going pretty quickly and easily using some combination of subways, buses, and cabs; this section will tell you how to do just that.

But between traffic gridlock and subway delays, sometimes you just can't get there from here—unless you walk. Walking can be the fastest way to navigate the island. During rush hours, you'll easily beat car traffic while on foot, as taxis and buses stop and groan at gridlocked corners (don't even *try* going crosstown in a cab or bus in Midtown at midday). You'll also just see a whole lot more by walking than you will if you ride beneath the street in the subway or fly by in a cab. So pack your most comfortable shoes and hit the pavement—it's the best, cheapest, and most appealing way to experience the city.

BY SUBWAY

The much-maligned subway system is actually the best way to travel around New York, especially during rush hours. Some 3½ million people a day seem to agree with me, as it's their primary mode of transportation. The subway is quick, inexpensive, relatively safe, and pretty efficient, as well as being a genuine New York experience that you really shouldn't miss.

The subway runs 24 hours a day, seven days a week. The rush-hour crushes are roughly from 8am to 9:30am and from 5pm to 6:30pm on weekdays; the rest of the time the trains are relatively uncrowded.

PAYING YOUR WAY

The subway fare is $1.50 (half-price for seniors and those with disabilities), and children under 44 inches tall ride free (up to three per adult). **Tokens** still exist (although there is some talk of phasing them out altogether), but most people pay fares these

On the Sidewalks

What's the primary means New Yorkers use for getting around town? The subway? Buses? Taxis? Nope. Walking. They stride across wide, crowded pavements without any regard for the light, weaving through crowds at high speeds, dodging taxis and buses whose drivers are forced to interrupt the normal flow of traffic to avoid flattening them. **Never take your walking cues from the locals.** Wait for walk signals, and always use crosswalks—don't cross in the middle of the block. Do otherwise, and you could quickly end up with a jaywalking ticket—or as a flattened statistic.

Always pay attention to the traffic flow. Walk as if you're driving, staying to the right. Pay attention to what's happening in the street, even if you have the right of way. At intersections, keep an eye out for drivers who don't yield, turn without looking, or think a yellow traffic light means "Hurry up!" as you cross. Unfortunately, most bicyclists seem to think that the traffic laws don't apply to them; they'll often blithely fly through red lights and dash the wrong way on one-way streets, so be on your guard.

For more important safety tips, see "Playing it Safe" later in this chapter.

days with the **MetroCard,** a magnetically encoded card that debits the fare when swiped through the turnstile, or the farebox on any city bus. Once you're in the system, you can transfer freely to any subway line that you can reach without exiting your station. MetroCards—not tokens—also allow you **free transfers** between the bus and subway within a two-hour period.

The MetroCard can be purchased in a few different configurations:

Pay-Per-Ride MetroCards, which can be used for up to four people by swiping up to four times (bring the whole family). You can put any amount from $3 (two rides) to $80 on your card. Every time you put $15 on your Pay-Per-Ride MetroCard, it's automatically credited 10%—that's one free ride for every $15. You can buy Pay-Per-Ride MetroCards in any denomination at any subway stations; an increasing number of stations now have automated MetroCard vending machines, which allow you to buy MetroCards using your major credit card. MetroCards are also available from shops and newsstands around town in $15 and $30 values. You can refill your card at any time until the expiration date on the card, usually about a year from the date of purchase, at any subway station.

Unlimited-Use MetroCards, which can't be used for more than one person at a time or more frequently than 18-minute intervals, are available in four values: the **daily Fun Pass,** which allows you a day's worth of unlimited subway and bus rides for $4; the **7-Day MetroCard,** for $17; and the **30-Day MetroCard,** for $63. Seven-and 30-day Unlimited-Use MetroCards can be purchased at any subway station or a MetroCard merchant. Fun Passes, however, cannot be purchased at token booths— you can only buy them from a MetroCard merchant such as Rite Aid drugstores; at the MTA information desk at the Times Square Visitor Center, 1560 Broadway, between 46th and 47th streets; or at a station that has a MetroCard vending machine, including 59th Street/Columbus Circle and 68th Street/Lexington Avenue. Unlimited-Use MetroCards go into effect not at the time you buy them, but the first time you use them—so if you buy a card on Monday and don't begin to use it until Wednesday, Wednesday is when the clock starts ticking on your MetroCard. A Fun Pass is good from the first time you use it until 3am the next day, while 7- and 30-day MetroCards run out at midnight on the last day. These MetroCards cannot be refilled; you throw it out once it's been used up and buy a new one.

Tips for using your MetroCard: The MetroCard-swiping mechanisms at turnstiles have been the source of much grousing among subway riders ever since the MetroCard was introduced. If you swipe too fast or too slow, the turnstile will ask you to swipe again. If this happens, *do not move to a different turnstile,* or you may end up paying twice. If you've tried a bunch of times and really can't make your MetroCard work, tell the token booth clerk; chances are good, though, that you'll get the movement down after a couple of uses.

If you're not sure how much money you have left on your MetroCard, or what day it expires, use the station's MetroCard Reader, usually located near the station entrance or the token booth (on buses, the fare box will also provide you with this information).

To locate the nearest MetroCard merchant, or for any other MetroCard questions, call ☎ **800/METROCARD,** or 212/METROCARD, or point your Web browser to **www.mta.nyc.ny.us/metrocard**.

USING THE SYSTEM

As you can see from the full-color subway map on the inside front cover of this book, the subway system basically mimics the lay of the land above ground, with most lines in Manhattan running north and south, like the avenues, and a few lines east and west, like the streets.

To go up and down the east side of Manhattan (and to the Bronx and Brooklyn), take the 4, 5, or 6 train.

To travel up and down the west side (and also to the Bronx and Brooklyn), take the 1, 2, 3, or 9 line; the A, C, E, or F line; or the B or D line.

The N and R lines first cut diagonally across town from east to west and then snake under Seventh Avenue before shooting out to Queens.

The crosstown S line, the Shuttle, runs back and forth, back and forth, between Times Square and Grand Central Terminal. Farther downtown, across 14th Street, the L line works its own crosstown magic.

Lines have assigned colors on subway maps and trains—red for the 1, 2, 3, 9 line; green for 4, 5, 6 trains; and so on—but nobody ever refers to them by color. Always refer to them by number or letter when asking questions. Within Manhattan, the distinction between different numbered trains that share the same line is usually that some are express and others local. Express trains often skip about three stops for each one that they make; express stops are indicated on subway maps with a white (rather than solid) circle. Regular stops usually come about nine blocks apart.

Directions are almost always indicated using "Uptown" (northbound) and "Downtown" (southbound), so be sure to know what direction you want to head in. The outsides of some subway entrances are marked UPTOWN ONLY or DOWNTOWN ONLY; read carefully, as it's easy to head in the wrong direction. Once you're on the platform, check the signs overhead to make sure that the train you're waiting for will be traveling in the right direction. If you do make a mistake, it's a good idea to wait for an express station, like 14th Street or 42nd Street, so you can get off and change for the other direction without paying again.

The days of graffiti-covered cars are gone, but the stations—and an increasing number of trains—are not nearly as clean as they could be. Trains are air-conditioned (move to the next car if yours isn't), though during the dog days of summer, the platforms can be sweltering. In theory, all subway cars have PA systems to allow you to hear the conductor's announcements, but they don't always work well. It's a good idea to move to a car with a working PA system in case any sudden service changes are announced that you'll want to know about.

For **subway safety tips,** see "Playing It Safe" later in this chapter.

For More Bus & Subway Information

For additional transit information, call the **MTA/New York City Transit's Travel Information Center** at ☎ **718/330-1234.** Extensive automated information is available at this number 24 hours a day, and travel agents are on hand to answer your questions and provide directions daily from 6am to 9pm. For online information, point your Web browser to **www.mta.nyc.ny.us**.

To request system maps or the *Token Trips Travel Guide* brochure, which gives subway and bus travel directions to more than 120 popular sites, call the **Customer Assistance Line** at ☎ **718/330-3322** (Mon–Fri 9am–5pm). For transit info for disabled riders, call the **Accessible Line** at ☎ **718/596-8585** (daily 6am–9pm).

You can get bus and subway maps and additional transit information at most tourist information centers (see "Visitor Information" earlier in this chapter); there's a particularly helpful MTA transit information desk at the Times Square Visitor Center, 1560 Broadway, between 46th and 47th streets. Maps are sometimes available in subway stations (ask at the token booth), but rarely on buses.

BY BUS

Less expensive than taxis and more pleasant than subways (they provide a mobile sightseeing window on Manhattan), buses are a good transportation option. Their very big drawback: They can get stuck in traffic, sometimes making it quicker to walk. They also stop every couple of blocks, rather than the eight or nine blocks that local subway traverse between stops. So for long distances, the subway is your best bet; but for short distances or traveling crosstown, try the bus.

PAYING YOUR WAY

Like the subway fare, the **bus fare** is $1.50, half-price for seniors and riders with disabilities, free for children under 44 inches (up to three per adult). The fare is payable with a **MetroCard, token** (for now, anyway), or **exact change.** Bus drivers don't make change, and fare boxes don't accept dollar bills or pennies. You can't purchase Metro-Cards or tokens on the bus, so you'll have to have them before you board; for details, see "Paying Your Way" under "By Subway" above.

If you pay with a MetroCard, you can freely transfer to another bus or to the subway for up to two hours. If you use a token, you must request a **free transfer** slip that allows you to change to an intersecting bus route only (legal transfer points are listed on the transfer paper) within one hour of issue. Transfer slips cannot be used to enter the subway.

USING THE SYSTEM

You can't flag a city bus down—you have to meet it at a bus stop. **Bus stops** are located every two or three blocks on the right-side corner of the street (facing the direction of traffic flow). They're marked by a curb painted yellow and a blue-and-white sign with a bus emblem and the route number or numbers. Guide-A-Ride boxes at most stops display a route map and a hysterically optimistic schedule.

Almost every major avenue has its own **bus route.** They run either north or south: downtown on Fifth, uptown on Madison, downtown on Lexington, uptown on Third, and so on. There are **crosstown buses** at strategic locations all around town: 8th Street (eastbound); 9th (westbound); 14th, 23rd, 34th, and 42nd (east- and westbound); 49th (eastbound); 50th (westbound); 57th (east- and westbound); 65th (eastbound across the West Side, through the park, and then north on Madison, continuing east on 68th to York Avenue); 67th (westbound on the East Side to Fifth Avenue and then south on Fifth, continuing west on 66th Street through the park and across the West Side to West End Avenue); and 79th, 86th, 96th, 116th, and 125th (east- and westbound). Some bus routes, however, are erratic: The M104, for example, starts at the East River, then turns at Eighth Avenue and goes up Broadway. The buses of the Fifth Avenue line go up Madison or Sixth and follow various routes around the city. Most routes operate 24 hours a day, but service is infrequent at night. Some say that New York buses have a herding instinct: They come only in groups. During rush hour, main routes have "limited" buses, identifiable by the red card in the front window; they stop only at major cross streets.

To make sure the bus you're boarding goes where you're going, check the maps on the bus signs, get your hands on a route map (see "For More Bus & Subway Information," above), or **just ask.** The drivers are helpful, as long as you don't hold up the line too long.

While traveling, look out the window, not only to take in the sights but also to keep track of cross streets so you know when to get off. Signal for a stop by pressing the tape strip above and beside the windows and along the metal straps, about two blocks before you want to stop. Exit through the pneumatic back doors (not the front door) by pushing on the yellow tape strip; the doors open automatically—pushing on the handles is useless unless you're as buffed as Hercules. Most city buses are equipped with wheelchair lifts, making buses the preferable mode of public transportation for wheelchair-bound travelers; for more on this topic, see "Tips for Travelers with Special Needs" in chapter 2. Buses also "kneel," lowering down to the curb to make boarding easier.

BY TAXI

If you don't want to deal with the hustle and bustle of public transportation, finding an address that might be a few blocks from the subway station, or sharing your ride with 3½ million other people, then take a taxi. The biggest advantages are, of course, that cabs can be hailed on any street (providing you find an empty one—often simple, yet at other times nearly impossible) and will take you right to your destination. I find they're best used at night when there's little traffic to keep them from speeding you to your destination and when the subway may seem a little daunting. In midtown at midday, you can usually walk to where you're going more quickly.

Official New York City taxis, licensed by the Taxi and Limousine Commission, are yellow, with the rates printed on the door and a light with a medallion number on the roof. You can hail a taxi on any street. *Never* accept a ride from any other car except an official city yellow cab (private livery cars are not allowed to pick up fares on the street).

The base fare on entering the cab is $2 (a surcharge of 50¢ is added from 8pm to 6am). The cost is 30¢ for every ⅕ mile or 20¢ per minute in stopped or very slow-moving traffic (or for waiting time). There's no extra charge for each passenger or for

---

Taxi-Hailing Tips

- When you're waiting on the street for an available taxi, look at the medallion light on the top of the coming cabs. If the light is out, the taxi is in use. When the center part (the number) is lit, the taxi is available—this is when you raise your hand to flag the cab. If all the lights are on, the driver is off duty.
- A taxi can't take more than four people, so expect to split up if your group is larger.

luggage. However, you must pay bridge or tunnel tolls (sometimes the driver will front the toll and add it to your bill at the end; most times, however, you pay the driver before the toll). A 15 to 20% tip is customary.

Forget about hopping into the back seat and having some double-chinned, cigar-chomping, all-knowing driver slowly turn and ask nonchalantly, "Where to, Mac?" Nowadays taxi drivers speak only an approximation of English and drive in engagingly exotic ways. Always wear your seat belt—taxis are required to provide them.

The TLC has posted a **Taxi Rider's Bill of Rights** sticker in every cab. Drivers are required by law to take you anywhere in the five boroughs, to Nassau or Westchester counties, or to Newark Airport. They are supposed to know how to get you to any address in Manhattan, and all major points in the outer boroughs. They are also required to provide air conditioning and turn off the radio on demand, and they cannot smoke while you're in the cab. They are also required to be polite.

You are allowed to dictate the route that is taken. It's a good idea to look at a map before you get in a taxi. Taxi drivers have been known to jack up the fare on visitors who don't know better by taking a circuitous route between point A and point B. Know enough about where you're going to know that something's wrong if you hop in a cab at Sixth Avenue and 57th Street to go to the Empire State Building (Fifth Avenue and 34th Street), say, and you suddenly find yourself on Ninth Avenue.

On the other hand, listen to drivers who propose an alternate route. These guys spend eight or ten hours a day on these streets, and they know them well—where the worst midday traffic is, where Con Ed has dug up an intersection that should be avoided. A knowledgeable driver will know how to get you to your destination quickly and efficiently.

Another important tip: **Always make sure the meter is turned on at the start of the ride.** You'll see the red LED read-out register the initial $2 and start calculating the fare as you go. I've witnessed a good number of unscrupulous drivers buzzing unsuspecting visitors around the city with the meter off, and then overcharging them at drop-off time.

Always ask for the receipt—it comes in handy if you need to make a complaint or have left something in a cab. In fact, it's a good idea to make a mental note of the driver's four-digit medallion number (usually posted on the divider between the front and back seats) just in case you need it later. You probably won't, but it's a good idea to play it safe.

For driver complaints and lost property, call the 24-hour Consumer Hotline at ☎ **212/NYC-TAXI.** For details on getting to and from the local airports by taxi, see "By Plane" under "Getting There" in chapter 2. For further taxi information—including a complete run-down of your rights as a taxi rider—point your web browser to **www.ci.nyc.ny.us/taxi**.

BY CAR

Forget driving yourself around the city. It's not worth the headache. Traffic is horrendous; you don't know the rules of the road (written or unwritten) or the arcane alternate-side-of-the-street parking regulations (in fact, precious few New Yorkers do). You don't want to find out the monstrous price of parking violations or the Kafka-esque tragedy of liberating a vehicle from the tow pound. Not to mention the security risks.

Impressions ───

Traffic signals in New York are just rough guidelines.

—David Letterman

───

If you do arrive in New York City by car, park it in a garage (expect to pay in the neighborhood of $20 to $30 per day) and leave it there for the duration of your stay. If you drive a rental car in, return it as soon as you arrive and rent another on the day you leave. Just about all of the major car-rental companies, including **Hertz** (☎ 800/654-3131), **National** (☎ 800/227-7368), and **Avis** (☎ 800/230-4898), have airport and Manhattan locations.

FROM THE CITY TO THE SUBURBS

The **PATH** (☎ 800/234-7284; www.panynj.gov/path) system connects urban communities in New Jersey, including Hoboken and Newark, to Manhattan by subway-style trains. Stops in Manhattan are at the World Trade Center, Christopher and 9th streets, and along Sixth Avenue at 14th, 23rd, and 33rd streets. The fare is $1.

New Jersey Transit (☎ 973/762-5100; www.njtransit.state.nj.us) operates commuter trains from Penn Station, and buses from the Port Authority at Eighth Avenue and 42nd Street, to points throughout New Jersey.

The **Long Island Rail Road** (☎ 718/217-5477; www.mta.nyc.ny.us/lirr) runs from Penn Station, at Seventh Avenue between 31st and 33rd streets, to Queens (ocean beaches, Shea Stadium, Belmont Park) and points beyond on Long Island, to even better beaches and summer hot spots like Fire Island and the Hamptons.

Metro North (☎ 800/638-7646 or 212/532-4900; www.mta.nyc.ny.us/mnr) departs from Grand Central Terminal, 42nd Street and Lexington Avenue, for areas north of the city, including Westchester County, the lovely Hudson Valley, and Connecticut.

If you'd like to investigate the areas beyond the city, check out *Frommer's Wonderful Weekends from New York City.*

3 Playing It Safe

Sure, there's crime in New York City, but millions of people spend their lives here without being robbed and assaulted. In fact, New York is safer than any other big American city, and is listed by the FBI as somewhere around 150th in the nation for total crimes. While that's quite encouraging for all of us, it's important to take precautions. Visitors especially should remain vigilant, as swindlers and criminals are expert at spotting newcomers who appear disoriented or vulnerable.

Men should carry their wallets in their front pockets and women should keep constant hold of their purse straps. Cross camera and purse straps over one shoulder, across your front, and under the other arm. Never hang a purse on the back of a chair or on a hook in a bathroom stall; keep it in your lap or between your feet with one foot through a strap and up against the purse itself. Avoid carrying large amounts of cash. You might carry your money in several pockets so that if one is picked, the others might escape. Skip the flashy jewelry and keep valuables out of sight when you're on the street.

Panhandlers are seldom dangerous but should be ignored (more aggressive pleas should firmly be answered, "Not today"). I hate to be cynical, but experience teaches that if a stranger walks up to you on the street with a long sob story ("I live in the

The Top Safety Tips

Trust your instincts, because they're usually right. You'll rarely be hassled, but it's always best to walk with a sense of purpose and self-confidence, and don't stop in the middle of the sidewalk to pull out and peruse your map. Anywhere in the city, if you find yourself on a deserted street that feels unsafe, it probably is; leave as quickly as possible. If you do find yourself accosted by someone with or without a weapon, remember to keep your anger in check and that the most reasonable response (maddening though it may be) is not to resist.

---

suburbs and was just attacked and don't have the money to get home") it should be ignored—it's a scam. If someone approaches you with any kind of elaborate tale, it's most definitely a confidence game. Walk away and don't feel bad. Be wary of an individual who "accidentally" falls in front of you or causes some other commotion, because he or she may be working with someone else who will take your wallet when you try to help. And remember: You *will* lose if you place a bet on a sidewalk card game or shell game.

Certain areas should be avoided late at night. I don't recommend going to the Lower East Side or the East Village unless you know where you're going; head straight for your destination and don't wander onto side streets. It's probably best to keep your wits about you in Alphabet City, in the far East Village. The areas above 96th Street aren't the best, either. Times Square isn't as bad as it once was; it's been cleaned up quite a bit, and there'll be crowds around until 11pm or midnight, when theatergoers leave the area. Still, stick to the main streets, such as Broadway. The areas west and south of Times Square are not worth going to and should be avoided. Take a cab or bus when visiting the Jacob Javits Center on 34th Street and the Hudson River. Don't go wandering the parks after dark, unless you're going to a performance; if that's the case, stick with the crowd.

If you plan on visiting the outer boroughs, go only during the daylight hours. If the subway doesn't go directly to your destination (such as the Bronx Zoo or the Brooklyn Museum of Art), your best bet is to take a taxi, and don't wander the side streets. Many areas in the outer boroughs are perfectly safe, but neighborhoods change quickly, and it's easy to get lost.

All this said, don't panic. Remember that New York has experienced a dramatic drop in crime and is generally safe these days, especially in the neighborhoods visitors are prone to frequent. There's a good police presence on the street, so don't be afraid to stop an officer, or even a friendly looking New Yorker (trust me—you can tell), if you need help getting your bearings.

SUBWAY SAFETY TIPS   In general, the subways are safe, especially in Manhattan. There are panhandlers and questionable characters like anywhere else in the city, but subway crime has gone down to 1960s levels. Still, stay alert and trust your instincts. Always keep a hand on your personal belongings.

When using the subway, don't wait for trains near the edge of the platform or on extreme ends of a station. During non-rush hours, wait for the train in view of the token booth clerk or under the the yellow DURING OFF HOURS TRAINS STOP HERE signs, and ride in the train operator's or conductor's car (usually in the center cars of the train; you'll see his or her head stick out when the doors open). Choose crowded cars over empty ones—there's safety in numbers.

Avoid subways late at night, and splurge on a cab after about 10 or 11pm—it's money well spent to avoid a long wait on a deserted platform. Or take the bus.

Fast Facts: New York City

Ambulance & Emergencies Dial ☎ **911.**

American Express Travel service offices are at many Manhattan locations, including the New York Hilton, 1335 Sixth Ave., at 53rd Street (☎ 212/664-7798); the New York Marriott Marquis, 1535 Broadway, in the 8th floor lobby (☎ 212/575-6580); on the mezzanine level at Macy's Herald Square, 34th Street and Broadway (☎ 212/695-8075); and 65 Broadway, between Exchange Place and Rector Street (☎ 212/493-6500). Contact American Express at ☎ **800/AXP-TRIP** or point your web browser to **www.americanexpress.com** for other city locations or general information.

Area Codes From late 1998, there'll be three area codes in the city: two in Manhattan, **212** and **646,** and two in the outer boroughs, **718** and (new in fall 1999) **347.** At press time, dialing procedures for local calls hadn't been determined. Before making a call, check for instructions in a phone book or on a phone booth or dial 0 and ask the operator. It may always be necessary to dial 11 digits (1, the area code, and the number), even when making a call within the same 212 or 646 or 718 area codes.

Business Hours In general, **retail stores** are open Monday to Saturday from 10am to 6pm or 7pm, Thursday from 10am to 8:30 or 9pm, and Sunday from noon to 5pm (see chapter 8). **Banks** tend to be open Monday to Friday from 9am to 3pm and sometimes Saturday mornings.

Dentists See "Health & Insurance" in chapter 2.

Doctors For medical emergencies requiring immediate attention, head to the nearest emergency room (see "Hospitals" below). For less urgent health problems, see "Health & Insurance" in chapter 2 for walk-in medical centers and doctor's offices that will accept appointments.

Embassies/Consulates See "Fast Facts: For the Foreign Traveler" in chapter 3.

Emergencies Dial ☎ **911** for fire, police, and ambulance. The **Poison Control Center** is at ☎ **212/764-7667** or 212/340-4494.

Fire Dial ☎ **911.**

Hospitals **Downtown:** New York Downtown Hospital, 170 William St., at Beekman Street (☎ **212/312-5000**); St. Vincent's Hospital, Seventh Avenue and 11th Street (☎ **212/604-7000**); and Beth Israel Medical Center, First Avenue and 16th Street (☎ **212/420-2000**). **Midtown:** Bellevue Hospital Center, 462 First Avenue and 27th Street (☎ **212/562-4141;** New York University Medical Center, 560 First Avenue and 33rd Street (☎ **212/263-7300**); and Roosevelt Hospital Center, Tenth Avenue and 59th Street (☎ **212/523-4000**). **Upper West Side:** St. Luke's Hospital Center, Amsterdam Avenue and 114th Street (☎ **212/523-4000**). **Upper East Side:** New York Hospital's Emergency Pavilion, York Avenue and 70th Street (☎ **212/746-5050**), and Lenox Hill Hospital, 77th Street between Park and Lexington avenues (☎ **212/434-2000**). Don't forget your insurance card.

Hot Lines The 24-hour **Crime Victims Hot Line** is ☎ **212/577-7777.** You can reach **Alcoholics Anonymous** at ☎ **212/870-3400** (general office) or 212/647-1680 (intergroup, for alcoholics who need immediate counseling from a sober recovering alcoholic). Other useful numbers include: **Sex Crimes Report Line** ☎ 212/267-7273; **Suicide Prevention Help Line** ☎ 212/532-2400;

Samaritans' Suicide Prevention Line ☎ 212/673-3000; local **police precincts** ☎ 212/374-5000; **Department of Consumer Affairs** ☎ 212/487-4444 or 718/286-2994; **Taxi complaints** ☎ 212/NYC-TAXI.

Internet Centers   The **Times Square Visitors Center,** 1560 Broadway, between 46th and 47th streets (☎ **212/768-1560**), has computer terminals with free Internet access courtesy of Yahoo; you can even send an electronic postcard with a photo of yourself home to Mom. The **Internet Cafe,** 82 E. 3rd St., between First and Second avenues in the East Village (☎ **212/614-0747;** www.bigmagic.com), offers direct Internet access at $10 per hour; students get a 10% discount with ID. **Cybercafe,** 273 Lafayette St., at Prince Street in SoHo (☎ **212/334-5140;** www.cyber-cafe.com), is more expensive at $12.80 an hour, but their T1 connectivity gives you much speedier access, and they offer a full range of other cyber services.

Libraries   The main research branch of the **New York Public Library** is on Fifth Avenue at 42nd Street (☎ **212/340-0849**). This beaux arts beauty houses more than 38 million volumes, and the beautiful reading rooms have been restored to their former glory. More efficient and modern, if less charming, is the mid-Manhattan branch at 40th Street and Fifth Avenue, across the street from the main library. There are other branches in almost every neighborhood; you can find a list online at **www.nypl.org**.

Liquor Laws   The minimum legal age to purchase and consume alcoholic beverages in New York is 21. Liquor and wine are sold only in licensed stores, which are closed on Sundays, holidays, and election days while the polls are open. Beer can be purchased in grocery stores and delis 24 hours a day, except Sundays before noon.

Newspapers/Magazines   There are three major daily newspapers: the *New York Times,* the *Daily News,* and the *New York Post.* For details on where to find arts and entertainment listings, see "Publications" under "Orientation" earlier in this chapter.

In addition to the dailies, many newsstands in New York City carry a selection of newspapers and magazines. If you want to find your hometown paper, try **Universal News & Magazines,** 977 Eighth Ave., at 57th Street (☎ **212/ 459-0932**), or **Hotalings News Agency,** 142 W. 42nd St., between Broadway and Sixth Avenue (☎ **212/840-1868**). Both have huge selections of international and domestic newspapers and magazines.

Pharmacies   There are two 24-hour pharmacies, both branches of **Duane Reade:** one at Broadway and 57th Street (☎ **212/541-9708**) and the other at Third Avenue and 74th Street (☎ **212/744-2668**).

Police   Dial ☎ **911** in an emergency; otherwise, call ☎ **212/374-5000** for the number of the nearest precinct.

Post Office   The main New York City post office is on 421 Eighth Ave., between 31st and 33rd streets and is open 24 hours a day (☎ **212/967-8585**). There's a second branch with extended hours (Mon–Fri 7am–midnight, Sat 7am–4pm) just north of the World Trade Center at 90 Church Street, between Barclay and Vesey streets (☎ **212/330-5313**). There are branches and drop boxes throughout the city. Call ☎ **800/275-8777** to locate the nearest post office. Most branches are open Monday to Friday from 8am to 5 or 6pm, and Saturday from 9am to 3pm. For information on receiving general delivery mail in the city, see "Mail" under "Fast Facts: For the Foreign Traveler" in chapter 3.

Rest Rooms   Public rest rooms are as hard to come by as an empty taxi in a downpour. The visitors centers in midtown (1560 Broadway, between 46th and 47th streets; and 810 Seventh Ave., between 52nd and 53rd streets) have facilities. Grand Central Terminal, at 42nd Street between Park and Lexington avenues, has cleaned up its rest rooms. But only out of desperation should you take your chances with the facilities at places like Penn Station and the Port Authority bus terminal, where cleanliness is not highly regarded. Your best bet is to head to hotel lobbies (especially the big midtown ones) and department stores like Macy's and Bloomingdale's. Restaurants often post intimidating signs like REST ROOMS FOR CUSTOMERS ONLY, but if you look clean-cut and ask nicely (or beeline it to the john), you shouldn't have a problem; better yet, just pay for a Coke to avoid a problem. On the Lower East Side, stop into the Lower East Side BID visitor center, 261 Broome St., between Orchard and Allen streets (open Sunday to Friday 10am to 4pm). There's a program to install pay toilets in the parks, but I wouldn't count on it.

Smoking   Smoking is prohibited on all public transportation, in the lobbies of hotels and office buildings, in taxis, and in most shops. Smoking also may be restricted or not permitted in restaurants; for more on this, see chapter 6.

Taxes   Sales tax is 8.25% on meals, most goods, and some services, though there has been political chatter about reducing or eliminating it, especially on clothing under $500. **Hotel tax** is 13.25% plus $2 per room per night (including sales tax). **Parking garage tax** is 18.25%.

Transit Information   For information on getting to and from the airport, see "Getting There" in chapter 2 or call **Air-Ride** at ☎ **800/247-7433.** For information on subways and buses, see "Getting Around" earlier in this chapter.

Traveler's Assistance   Travelers Aid is an organization that helps distressed travelers with all kinds of problems, including accidents, sickness, and lost or stolen luggage. The Manhattan office is on the second floor of 1451 Broadway, at 41st Street (☎ **212/944-0013**), although it was in danger of becoming the victim of budget cuts at press time. There is also an office (scheduled to remain open) in the international arrivals building at JFK Airport (☎ **718/656-4870**).

Telephone Information   Dial ☎ **411,** or the area code of the area you wish to reach plus 555-1212.

Time   For the correct time, dial ☎ **212/976-1616.**

Weather   For the current temperature and next day's forecast, look in the upper-right corner of the *New York Times* or call ☎ **212/976-1212.** If you want to know how to pack before you arrive, point your Web browser to **www.cnn.com/weather** or **www.weather.com** for the four- or five-day forecast.

Accommodations 5

As you're probably well aware, New York is more popular than it's been in decades. On one hand, that's terrific: It's a reflection of how well the city's doing, and how well it's projecting that positive image to the rest of the world. This popularity makes the city feel vital and self-assured; you can practically feel the excitement and energy as you walk down the street.

Now the downside: With increased demand comes higher prices—Economics 101, pure and simple. Occupancy rates are higher than they've been since the pre-war years, and rates have responded accordingly. Average room rates are now hovering around $195, higher than ever before in the city's history. With rates at these levels—remember, just for an *average* hotel room—accommodations are likely to be the biggest financial commitment of your trip. Choose carefully.

That doesn't mean that there aren't a few bargains out there—so even if money is tight, don't give up yet. In the pages that follow, I'll tell you about some truly wonderful places to stay that won't break your bank account. But when deciding what you're willing to afford vs. what you're willing to put up with, keep in mind that this is the land of $200-a-night Holiday Inns and HoJos—so if you only want to spend 100 bucks a night, you're going to have to put up with some inconveniences. For instance, you may have to stay in a residential district rather than your first-choice neighborhood. Or you may have to give up New York's rarest asset: space. New York gives everybody a whole new perspective on "small," and that's particularly true for budget travelers. Don't be surprised if your room isn't much bigger than the bed that's in it. For the best bargains in town, you'll have to get used to the idea of sharing a bath. If you're willing to do so (Europeans seem to have a much easier time with this than Americans do), you can get a lot of bang for your buck.

Even those who can afford a bit of luxury—or even just a few mid-priced conveniences—still want to get the most for their money. I'll show you how to do that, too.

Manhattan is a small island, but the **neighborhood** you'd like to stay in should figure in your considerations. Of course, your location may be dictated by budget; it's generally more expensive to stay on the Upper East Side than in Murray Hill. But also consider your interests: Are you here to see as many Broadway shows as you can squeeze in? Then the Theater District (included in the area I call Times Square and Midtown West) is the place to stay. If you want to shop 'til you drop, Midtown East—ideally, between Fifth and Madison avenues—might be the neighborhood for you. If you fancy yourself an off-the-beaten-path traveler, and you prefer funky boutique shopping and club hopping, consider SoHo or Greenwich Village. If you have the kids in tow, look to the larger-than-average rooms on the residential Upper West Side. For more help in choosing a location, take a close look at "Manhattan's Neighborhoods in Brief" in chapter 4 before you delve into the hotel listings.

For an easy-to-scan introduction to the best of what the city has to offer, take a moment to check out **"Best Hotel Bets"** in chapter 1, if you haven't already.

ON THE LISTINGS IN THIS CHAPTER   The rates quoted in the listings below are the **rack rates**—the maximum rates that a hotel charges for rooms. It's the rate you'd get if you walked in off the street and asked for a room without bargaining. I've used these rack rates to divide the hotels into four price categories, ranging from "Very Expensive" to "Inexpensive," for easy reference.

But rack rates are only guidelines. Hardly anybody pays these prices, and there are many ways around them; see "Tips for Saving on Your Hotel Room," below.

Many **features** come standard in most hotel rooms these days. If you stay in a hotel listed under the "Very Expensive" or "Expensive" categories below, you can assume that your room will have an alarm clock, hair dryer, an in-room safe, an iron and ironing board, and voice mail and dataport on the telephone unless I've otherwise noted. But in hotels listed under "Moderate" and "Inexpensive," these features aren't a given, so I've explicitly noted what's included.

PET POLICIES   I've indicated in the listings below those hotels that admitted that they would accept pets. However, understand that this policy may have limitations, such as weight and breed restrictions; may require a deposit and/or a signed waiver against damages; and may be revoked at any time. Always inquire when booking if you're bringing Bowser or Fluffy along—*never* just show up with him or her in tow.

TIPS FOR SAVING ON YOUR HOTEL ROOM

In the listings below, I tried to give you an idea of the kind of deals that may be available at particular hotels: Which ones have the best discounted packages, which ones offer AAA and other discounts, which ones allow kids to stay with Mom and Dad for free, and so on. But there's no way of knowing what the offers will be when you're booking, so also consider these general tips:

- **Choose your season carefully.** The biggest factor that will affect how much you pay for your hotel room is the season in which you travel. The rate you'll pay for a room can vary dramatically—by hundreds of dollars in some cases—depending on what time of year you visit. The general rules of thumb: Winter from January to mid-April is best for bargains, with summer from June to mid-August being second-best. Spring and fall are the busiest and most expensive seasons after Christmas, but negotiating a decent rate is do-able, especially in spring. All bets are off at Christmas—expect to pay top dollar for everything—but Thanksgiving can be great for bargain hunters. For more on this subject, see "Money Matters" under "When to Go" in chapter 2.
- **Visit over a weekend.** If your trip includes a weekend, you might be able to save big bucks. Business hotels tend to empty out, and rooms that go for $300 or more Monday through Thursday can drop dramatically once the mid-level execs have headed home. At the Millenium Hilton, for instance, a $300–$350 room goes for as little as $120. These deals are especially prevalent in the Financial District hotels, but they're often available even in tourist-friendly Midtown. Look in the Travel section of the Sunday *New York Times* for some of the best weekend deals. They're also often advertised on the hotel's Web site. Or just ask when you call.

- **Don't be afraid to bargain.** Always ask for a lower price than the first one quoted. Most rack rates include commissions of 10 to 25% or more for travel agents, which many hotels will cut if you make your own reservations and haggle a bit. Always ask politely whether a less expensive room is available than the first one mentioned, or whether any special rates apply to you. You may qualify for corporate, student, military, senior citizen, or other discounts. Be sure to mention membership in AAA, AARP, frequent-flyer programs, or trade unions, which may entitle you to special deals as well. The big chains, such as Sheraton, tend to be good about trying to save you money, but reservation agents often won't volunteer the information—you have to pull it out of them.
- **Dial direct.** When booking a room in a chain hotel, call the hotel's local line, as well as the toll-free number, and see where you get the best deal. The clerk who runs the place is more likely to know about booking patterns and will often grant deep discounts in order to fill up.
- **Call a travel agent.** Certain hotels give travel agents discounts in exchange for steering business their way, so if you're shy about bargaining, an agent may be better equipped to negotiate discounts for you.
- **Shop online.** Hotels often offer "Internet only" deals that can save you 10 to 20% over what you'd pay if you booked over the telephone. Also, hotels often advertise all of their available deals on their Web sites, so you don't have to rely on a reservation agent to fill you in. In addition, some of the discount reservations agencies (see below) have sights that allow you to book online.
- **Consider a suite.** If you are traveling with your family, a suite can be a terrific way to go. They're always cheaper than two hotel rooms. The living room almost always features a sofa bed, and there's often a kitchenette where you can save money by preparing coffee and light meals for yourself. If you're traveling with a large family or another couple, you may be able to snag a two-bedroom suite (sometimes even with a second bathroom!) for less money than two rooms would cost, without having to compromise on comfort. Remember that some places charge for extra guests beyond two, some don't.
- **Investigate reservation services.** These outfits usually work as consolidators, buying up or reserving rooms in bulk, and then dealing them out to customers at a profit. They do garner special deals that range from 10 to 50% off, but remember, these discounts apply to rack rates, inflated prices that people rarely end up paying. You're probably better off dealing directly with a hotel, but if you don't like bargaining, this is certainly a viable option. Most of them offer online reservation services as well. A few of the more reputable providers are: **Accommodations Express** (☎ **800/950-4685;** www.accommodationsxpress. com); **Hotel Reservations Network** (☎ **800/96HOTEL;** www.180096HOTEL.com); and **Microsoft Expedia** (**www.expedia.com**), which features an online "Travel Agent" that will also direct you to affordable lodgings. Another good bet is **Hotel ConXions** (☎ **800/522-9991** or 212/840-8686; www.hotelconxions.com), a consolidator that handles hotels in only a few select destinations, including New York. Not only can they check pricing and availability on a number of hotels with just one phone call, they can also save you up to 40% off rack rates. Also, because Hotel ConXions has guaranteed room blocks in select properties, they can often get you into a hotel that's otherwise sold out.

  Important tip: Never just rely on a reservations service. Do a little homework; compare the rack rates that we've published to the discounted rates being offered by the service to see what kind of deal they're offering—that way you'll know if you're actually being offered a substantial savings, or if they've just gussied up the rack rates to make their offer sound like a deal. If you're being offered a stay in a hotel I haven't recommended, do more research to learn about it, especially if it isn't a reliable chain name like Holiday Inn or Hyatt. It's not a deal if you end up at a dump.

- **Buy a money-saving package deal.** A travel package that gets you your plane tickets and your hotel stay for one price may just be the best bargain of all. In some cases, you'll get airfare, accommodations, transportation to and from the airport, plus extras—maybe an afternoon sightseeing tour, or restaurant and shopping discount coupons—for less than the hotel alone would have cost had you booked it yourself. For the lowdown on where and how to get the best package, see "Money-Saving Package Deals" in chapter 2.

1 South Street Seaport & the Financial District

See the "Downtown Accommodations" map (p. 81) to locate hotels in this section.

EXPENSIVE

In addition to the choices below, you might also consider the **Marriott Financial Center,** 85 West St. (☎ 800/242-8685 or 212/385-4900), and the **Marriott World Trade Center,** 3 World Trade Center (☎ **800/228-9290** or 212/938-9100), both excellent branches of the reliable chain catering primarily to business travelers. Particularly recommendable is the Marriott World Trade Center, which boasts an excellent location, connected to the Twin Towers, and a great health club with a pool, jogging track, racquetball court, and saunas; the Financial Center location also features a health club with pool and sauna, plus Roy's New York, the first east coast restaurant by venerable Hawaiian chef Roy Yamaguchi. Be sure to inquire when you call, or check **www.marriott.com,** for deeply discounted weekend rates and other promotions.

✪ **The Millenium Hilton.** 55 Church St. (btw. Fulton and Dey sts.), New York, NY 10017. ☎ **800/835-2220** or 212/693-2001. Fax 212/571-2316. www.hilton.com. 561 units. A/C MINIBAR TV TEL. $300–$350 double, $400 junior suite, $700–$1,550 suite. Rates drop to $120–$199 double on weekends, depending on season; continental breakfast usually included in weekend rates. Corporate, senior, and other promotions may also be available. Extra person $30. Children under 18 stay free in parents' room. AE, CB, DC, DISC, JCB, MC, V. Valet or self-parking $35. Subway: 1, 9, N, R to Cortlandt St.; C, E to World Trade Center.

This Mobil four-star, AAA four-diamond hotel is the top choice in the Financial District for bulls and bears, but it's great for vacationers, too—especially on weekends, when it becomes one of the best values in town. Facing the World Trade Center but reaching only halfway up, the 58-story tinted-glass monolith opened in 1992. In 1994 Hilton took over, renaming it—obviously without running a spell check—and remaking it into the neighborhood's best hotel. This area goes from bustling to near-desolate on weekends, but multiple subway lines are nearby, ready to whisk you uptown in no time.

The rooms are light and bright on every floor, but the Lower Manhattan and bay views become more and more glorious as you go up. The accommodations are extremely comfortable, with excellent platform beds fitted with cushioned quilts, firm mattresses, and down pillows. Other appealing in-room features include well-designed built-ins that maximize work and storage space; big bathrooms with lots of counter space; two-line phones; fax/printer/copiers; and cushy bathrobes. I saw some wear in the wood furnishings in some rooms, but everything else was in beautiful shape.

Dining/Diversions: Two American restaurants—one upscale, one casual—serve just-fine-but-nothing-special fare; there's also a comfortable bar.

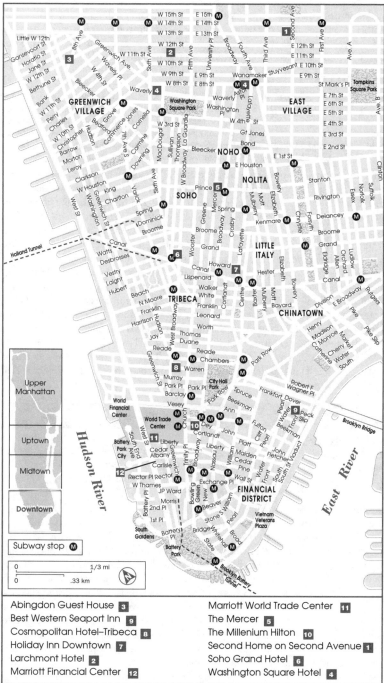

Abingdon Guest House **3**
Best Western Seaport Inn **9**
Cosmopolitan Hotel–Tribeca **8**
Holiday Inn Downtown **7**
Larchmont Hotel **2**
Marriott Financial Center **12**

Marriott World Trade Center **11**
The Mercer **5**
The Millenium Hilton **10**
Second Home on Second Avenue **1**
Soho Grand Hotel **6**
Washington Square Hotel **4**

Amenities: Business center with conference room, well-equipped fitness center with a great pool and a dry sauna, concierge, 24-hour room service, twice-daily maid service, express checkout, complimentary car service to midtown, gift shop and newsstand. Secretarial services available; lots of meeting space.

MODERATE

Best Western Seaport Inn. 33 Peck Slip (2 blocks north of Fulton St., btw. Front and Water sts.), New York, NY 10038. ☎ **800/HOTEL-NY** or 212/766-6600. Fax 212/ 766-6615. www.bestwestern.com. 72 units. A/C TV TEL. $169–$209 double. Rates include continental breakfast. Corporate rates from $149; family, senior, and weekend discounts may also be available. Extra person $10. Children under 15 stay free in parents' room using existing bedding. AE, CB, DC, DISC, MC, V. Parking $20 nearby. Subway: 2, 3 to Fulton St.

Catering primarily to business travelers, this well-kept chain hotel is a good bet for vacationers, too. It's located in cobblestoned South Street Seaport, within walking distance of the ferries to the Statue of Liberty, Ellis Island, and Staten Island. Though they're housed in an 1852 building with a beautifully restored exterior, the guest rooms are more in keeping with what you'd expect from a Best Western, but they're quite comfortably outfitted. Each is equipped with a work desk, phone with dataport, refrigerator, VCR, hair dryer, clock radio, and safe; some have small dining tables, sleeper sofas, steam baths, whirlpools, and/or terraces with fine views of the seaport. On the downside, some closets consist only of racks on the walls and the towels are motel-thin, but there are luggage-sized benches in each room and the bathrooms are spacious. Go with a corner room if you'd like extra space—they boast two queen beds and lots of windows, some with wonderful water views. Light sleepers should ask for an inside room, since the Fulton Fish Market is right next door, and it's in full swing daily from 11pm to 8am.

Video rentals and valet service are available. There's no room service, but nearby restaurants are happy to deliver, and just around the corner is the landmark Bridge Cafe (see chapter 6).

2 TriBeCa

INEXPENSIVE

✪ Cosmopolitan Hotel–Tribeca. 95 W. Broadway (at Warren St., 1 block south of Chambers St.), New York, NY, 10007. ☎ **888/895-9400** or 212/566-1900. Fax 212/566-6909. www.cosmohotel.com. 104 units. A/C TV TEL. $99–$139 double. AE, CB, DC, JCB, MC, V. Parking $20 (with validation) 1 block away. Subway 1, 2, 3, 9, A, C, E to Chambers St.

Hiding behind a plain-vanilla Tribeca awning is the best hotel deal in Manhattan for budget travelers who don't want to sacrifice the luxury of a private bathroom to save. Every room comes with its own small but spotless bath, telephone with dataport, air conditioning, satellite TV, alarm, and ceiling fan, all for as little as 99 bucks a night. Everything is strictly budget, but nice: The modern IKEAish furniture includes an armoire (a few rooms have a dresser and hanging rack instead) and a work desk; for a few extra bucks, you can also have a loveseat, too. Beds are comfy, and sheets and towels are better quality than in many more expensive hotels. Rooms are small but make the most of the limited space, and the whole place is pristine. The two-level mini-lofts have lots of character, but expect to duck on the second level: Downstairs is the bath, TV, closet, desk, and club chair, while upstairs is a low-ceilinged bedroom with a second TV and phone. The neighborhood is safe, hip, and subway-convenient; the Financial District is just a walk away. There's no room service, but a range of great restaurants, from budget to deluxe, will deliver. All services are kept at a bare minimum to keep costs down, so you must be a low-maintenance guest to be happy here. If you are, this place is a smokin' deal.

3 Chinatown

See the "Downtown Accommodations" map (p. 81) to locate this hotel.

MODERATE

Holiday Inn Downtown. 138 Lafayette St. (at Howard St., 1 block north of Canal St.), New York, NY 10013. ☎ **800/HOLIDAY** or 212/966-8898. Fax 212/966-3933. www.newyork. citysearch.com or www.holiday-inn.com (for online reservations). 227 units. A/C TV TEL. $169–$219 double, $229–$249 junior suite. Children 19 and under stay free in parents' room. AAA, AARP, and other discounts may be available. AE, CB, DC, DISC, JCB, MC, V. Valet parking $25. Subway: 6 to Canal St.

This Holiday Inn is everything you'd expect from this good-value chain: clean, well-outfitted, reliable, and very comfortable. The guest rooms are chain-standard but have everything you need, including a desk with easy-access dataport, two phones with voice mail, an in-room safe, iron and ironing board, and lots of counter space in the bathroom. Most junior suites have in-room fax machines as well. You'll find Asian touches throughout, a nod to the hotel's location: At the northern edge of Chinatown, just steps away from SoHo, it's safe and well-situated for those who prefer downtown's shopping, dining, and club scenes. On site is a well-respected Cantonese restaurant, Pacifica, and a cocktail bar. Other amenities include a fax machine for guests' use, concierge, limited room service, and privileges at a nearby Crunch health club for a fee. You really can't go wrong here.

4 SoHo

See the "Downtown Accommodations" map (p. 81) for hotels in this section.

VERY EXPENSIVE

The Mercer. 99 Prince St. (at Mercer St.), New York, NY 10012. ☎ **888/918-6060** or 212/966-6060. Fax 212/965-3838. www.themercer.com. 75 units. A/C MINIBAR TV TEL. $350–$400 double, $430–$450 studio, from $875 suite. AE, DC, MC, V. Parking $26 nearby. Subway: N, R to Prince St.

André Balazs, a longtime Manhattan nightcrawler and owner of L.A.'s chic Chateau Marmont, opened the Mercer in April 1997, and the beautiful people have been keeping the place booked ever since. The lobby feels like a postmodern library lounge, with design books lining the shelves and a hip staff scurrying about in Isaac Mizrahi finery. Word is that the hotel is more service-oriented than competitors like the Royalton, but I found its ultra-cool, almost frosty air a little offputting. Even the entrance, guarded by heavy curtains, feels almost uninviting.

The high-ceilinged guest rooms, by French designer Christian Liaigre, are more welcoming, with simple, clean-lined furnishings in beautiful African wenge wood (the material of the moment in design circles). The linens are gorgeous textured cottons. There's comfortable seating and a large work table in every room that easily can double as a dining table. The austerely beautiful tile-and-marble bathrooms have a steel cart for storage, oversized shower stalls (request a tub when booking if you want one), and Face Stockholm toiletries. Nice extras include ceiling fans, VCRs and video games, stereos with CD players, minibars stocked with goodies from Dean & Deluca, and free local phone calls.

Dining/Diversions: Mercer Kitchen is the downtown domain of superstar chef Jean-Georges Vongerichten, of JoJo, Vong, and Jean Georges (see chapter 6). The experimental French/Asian fusion cuisine is good, but not quite good enough for what they're charging. Still, it's about as hip as a scene gets these days. On the lobby level is Mercer Cafe, serving breakfast, lunch, and cocktails.

Amenities: Concierge, 24-hour room service from Mercer Kitchen, valet service, free access to nearby David Barton Gym, meeting rooms.

✪ Soho Grand Hotel. 310 W. Broadway (btw. Grand and Canal sts.), New York, NY 10013. ☎ **212/965-3000.** Fax 212/965-3200. www.sohogrand.com. 373 units. A/C MINIBAR TV TEL. $334–$414 double; penthouse suite prices available upon request. AE, CB, DC, DISC, EURO, JCB, MC, V. Valet parking $30. Subway: A, C, E, 1, 9, N, R to Canal St. Pets welcomed.

New in 1996, this stop-off for the image-conscious was the first hotel to open in SoHo in more than a century. Built from the ground up, the hotel was designed as a modern ode to the neighborhood's cast-iron past; the result is a Industrial Age–meets–21st century environment that will probably have a longer shelf life than wholly modern rivals like the Mercer and W New York. Here, they got the mix right: the self-conscious modern design that overwhelms at the Mercer is toned down and warmed up with a '90s affinity for natural textures and materials, but without the contrivance that reigns at W.

The guest rooms boast retro-reproduction furnishings with an Asian slant, including desks that resemble artists' drafting tables and end tables that look like sculptors' stands. The natural colors are warm and soothing, William Morris fabrics abound, and there's beautiful lighting throughout (including Edison bulbs in the public spaces). The beds are fitted with Frette linens, cushioned naugahyde head-boards, and gorgeous coverlets. Decked out in ceramic subway tile, the bathrooms are beautiful but simple. In-room conveniences include full-length mirrors, VCRs and stereos with CD players, double-paned windows that open, two-line phones with free local calls, and your very own fish in a bowl—courtesy of owners Hartz Mountain, of course.

Dining/Diversions: Awarded two stars by the *New York Times,* Canal House serves sophisticated New England–style tavern fare; word is that the macaroni and cheese (made with three-year-aged cheddar) is excellent. Voted one of the city's hottest bar scenes by Zagat's, the Grand Bar is a clubby retro-hip bar that's so popular the action often spills out into the lobby's living room–like "salon." On street level is Caviarteria, a wonderful caviar-and-champagne bar.

Amenities: Fitness center, concierge, 24-hour room service (including a menu for your pooch or kitty), valet service, newspaper delivery, express checkout, conference room. Butler's pantry with complimentary coffee, tea, and hot chocolate on every floor. On street level is Privé, a chic salon.

5 The East Village

See the "Downtown Accommodations" map (p. 81) to locate this hotel.

INEXPENSIVE

Second Home on Second Avenue. 221 Second Ave. (btw. E. 13th and 14th sts.), New York, NY 10003. ☎ and fax **212/677-3161.** www.citysearch.com/nyc/secondhome. 7 units (2 with private bathroom). A/C TV TEL. $65–$110 double with shared bathroom, $130 double with private bathroom, $155 suite. Extra person $25. 3-night minimum stay required. AE, ER, MC, V. Parking about $20 nearby. Subway: L to 3rd Ave.; N, R, 4, 5, 6 to Union Square.

Here's a nice guest house for young, independent-minded travelers who'd prefer the restaurant- and club-heavy East Village over more tourist-heavy neighborhoods. The rooms are large and decently, if eclectically, furnished, with some surprisingly nice touches here and there. Each is outfitted with two full beds, good closet space, and a large TV with VCR and a CD player in every room (otherwise unheard of in this price category). If there's more than two of you, the suite, which has a separate living room with a nice leather sofa that pulls out into a queen bed and a big private bath-room, is a good bet. Bathrooms are older but clean. One of the features that makes this a recommendable choice is the fully outfitted common kitchen, with full stove and fridge, toaster oven, coffee maker, and dishwasher, plus free coffee and tea on hand at all times.

A few words of caution, though: Don't expect lots in the way of service; you're really on your own here. Rooms are on the third and fourth floors, so this isn't the place for visitors with mobility issues. And the guest house is popular with European travelers, who like to smoke, so stay elsewhere if the odor bothers you.

6 Greenwich Village

See the "Downtown Accommodations" map (p. 81) for hotels in this section.

MODERATE

✪ **Abingdon Guest House.** 13 Eighth Ave. (btw. W. 12th and Jane sts.), New York, NY 10014. ☎ **212/243-5384.** Fax 212/807-7473. www.abingdonguesthouse.com. 9 units (7 with private bathroom). A/C TV TEL. High season (May–June and Sept–Dec) $110–$135 double with shared bathroom, $155–$195 double with private bathroom; low season (Jan–Apr and July–Aug) $95–$120 double with shared bathroom, $135–$175 with private bathroom. $10–$15 less for single travelers. Extra person $25. 4-night minimum on weekends, 2-night minimum on weekdays; longer minimum stays may be required for holidays. AE, DC, DISC, MC, V. Parking $20 nearby. Subway: A, C, E to 14th St.; 1, 2, 3, 9 to 14th St.

Steve Austin, who has a hotel management degree, and his partner, Zachary Stass, educated in interior design, now run this lovely guest house (and its downstairs coffee bar, Brewbar) in a wonderful West Village neighborhood. Both men have an eye for style and take the guest-house business seriously, and their commitment shows—the Abingdon is beautifully outfitted and professionally run. All the rooms are done in bold colors and outfitted with well-chosen art and furnishings; each can be previewed on their Web site, so your best bet is to choose the one that best fits your personal style and budget. I suggest opting for one with a new bathroom (they're large and well done). But no matter which one you choose, you'll get a superior-quality mattress and linens (better than at most hotels that cost more), hair dryer, soft polyfleece bathrobes, alarm, a small TV, and telephone with your own answering machine (a splitter can be provided for your laptop); five rooms also have ceiling fans. The best (and most expensive) is the Ambassador Room, which has a witty British Raj theme and comes with a kitchenette (with microwave), VCR, and sleeper sofa for a third person.

The neighborhood is terrific, especially for those who want to be close to good restaurants and boutiques, but it's a bit off the beaten path if you're planning on lots of midtown sightseeing. And the Abingdon is best for independent-minded travelers since there's no regular staff on site; if you want cozy but expect to need a lot of guidance, consider the Broadway Inn (p.100) instead. No smoking.

INEXPENSIVE

✪ **Larchmont Hotel.** 27 W. 11th St. (btw. Fifth and Sixth aves.), New York, NY 10011. ☎ **212/989-9333.** Fax 212/989-9496. www.citysearch.com/nyc/larchmonthotel. 55 units (none with private bathroom). A/C TV TEL. $60–$70 single; $85–$99 double. Rates include continental breakfast. Children under 13 stay free in parents' room. AE, CB, DC, DISC, MC, V. Parking $20 nearby. Subway: 4, 5, 6, N, R, L to Union Square; A, C, E, B, D, F, Q to West 4th St. (use 8th St. exit); F to 14th St.

Excellently located on a beautiful tree-lined block in a quiet residential part of the Village, this European-style hotel is simply a gem. If you're willing to put up with the inconvenience of shared bathrooms, you can't do better for the money. The entire place has a wonderful air of warmth and sophistication; the butter-yellow lobby even *smells* good. Each bright guest room is tastefully done in rattan and outfitted with a writing desk, a wash basin, a mini-library of books, an alarm clock, and a few extras that you normally have to pay a lot more for, such as cotton bathrobes and ceiling fans. Every floor has two shared bathrooms and a small, simple kitchen. The management is constantly renovating, so everything feels clean and fresh. Free continental breakfast, including fresh-baked goods every morning, is the crowning touch that makes the Larchmont an unbeatable deal. And with some of the city's best shopping, dining, and sightseeing, plus your choice of subway lines, just a walk away, you couldn't be better situated. As you might expect, the hotel is always full, so book *well* in advance (the management suggests six to seven weeks' lead time).

Washington Square Hotel. 103 Waverly Place (btw. Fifth and Sixth aves.), New York, NY 10011. ☎ **800/222-0418** or 212/777-9515. Fax 212/979-8373. www.wshotel.com. 180 units. A/C TV TEL. $116 single, $136–$146 double, $167 quad. Rates include continental breakfast. AE, MC, JCB, V. Parking $22. Subway: A, B, C, D, E, F, Q to West 4th St.

The best thing about this hotel is its great location, right in the heart of Greenwich Village overlooking Washington Square Park. The pretty facade and marble-and-brass lobby come as quite a surprise—not exactly what you expect from a budget hotel.

Recent rate hikes have made the tiny, plain rooms not quite the deal they used to be, but they're still a decent value. Each comes with a private bathroom, a deposit-activated phone with voicemail and dataport, and a small closet with a pint-sized safe; irons and hair dryers are available from the front desk. Beds are firm but the pillows are flat, and a little more elbow grease could go into the detailing of some of the petite baths. Still, for the money, you could do worse. It's worth paying a few extra dollars for a south-facing room on a high floor, since others can be a bit dark. There's a basic gym and a very good restaurant, CIII, that even draws locals with its well-priced bistro fare, friendly staff, two-for-one happy hours (Mon–Fri 5–7pm), and Sunday jazz brunch that Zagat's calls "marvelous." However, the hotel staff can be terse and we've received complaints about their unresponsiveness to guest requests, so be on your guard and let me know if you have any problems.

7 The Flatiron District & Gramercy Park

See the "Midtown Accommodations" map (pp. 88-89) for hotels in this section.

EXPENSIVE

The Inn at Irving Place. 56 Irving Place (btw. 17th and 18th sts.), New York, NY 10003. ☎ **800/685-1447** or 212/533-4600. Fax 212/533-4611. www.innatirving.com. 12 units. A/C MINIBAR TV TEL. $295–$375 double, $425–$450 suite. Rates include continental breakfast. AE, CB, DC, JCB, MC, V. Parking $20. Subway: 4, 5, 6, N, R to Union Square. Children under 12 not accepted.

In adjoining 1834 Greek Revival townhouses, carefully restored by owner Naomi Blumenthal, this jewel is arguably New York's most intimate, romantic, and historically evocative hotel. It's a favorite with honeymooners, world travelers, and New York couples on amorous weekend retreats snuggling in four-posters between lush Frette linens. The decor is lavishly Victorian—each unique room has a fireplace (nonworking) and antiques, period paintings, Oriental rugs, and fresh flowers. All rooms have VCRs, CD players, and dual-line phones with dataport. One drawback is that some rooms have limited storage space, so ask if you're an overpacker like me. The cozy parlor is the perfect place to loll through Edith Wharton's *Age of Innocence*. (The writer was born nearby on 23rd Street, and there's a room here named for Countess Olenska, one of the novel's characters.) The inn is on a charming little street just south of Gramercy Park.

Dining/Diversions: Lady Mendel's Tea Salon serves a supremely elegant five-course afternoon tea that high tea lovers shouldn't miss; in the evening, the salon becomes a sophisticated fireplace-lit lounge, serving cocktails, select liqueurs, appetizers, and desserts as well as Lady Mendel's exotic teas and coffees. Verbena (☎ **212/260-5454**), run separately from the hotel, serves wonderful contemporary American cuisine. Fine cigars, cocktails, and appetizers are available at the chic Cibar (see chapter 9).

Amenities: Concierge, room service for continental breakfast and in the evening from Verbena, free *New York Times*. In-room massage and light shopping service available. Laptops and fax machines available on request. Nearby health club privileges for a fee.

MODERATE

Gramercy Park Hotel. 2 Lexington Ave. (btw. 21st and 22nd sts.), New York, NY 10010. ☎ **800/221-4083** or 212/475-4320. Fax 212/505-0535. 360 units. A/C TV TEL. $165–$170 single, $180 double, from $210 suite. Extra person $10. Children under 12 stay free in parents' room. AE, CB, DC, DISC, EURO, JCB, MC, V. Parking: $20 nearby. Subway: 6 to 23rd St.

Opened in 1924, this Old World hotel has one of the best settings in the city. It's in one of New York's loveliest neighborhoods, ideally located on the edge of the private park—restricted to just a few area residents and to hotel guests, who can also get a key—that gives Gramercy Park the air of a quiet London square. Unfortunately, the hotel has been plagued by claims of neglect in recent years, but management seems to be responding well, and the old place is looking pretty good these days. You'll still have to overlook the finer details—expect a smoky lobby, chipped paint here and there, Brady Bunch–era shag carpeting in some halls, mix-and-match baths that have been updated haphazardly, and ancient TVs. But rooms are big by city standards, decently furnished, and comfortable, and the hotel has a surprisingly appealing old New York vibe. Standard doubles have a king bed or two doubles, and some suites have pullout sofas that make them large enough to sleep six; all have big closets, unstocked minifridges, and hair dryers and fluffy towels in the roomy bathrooms. Best of all is the old-style pricing scheme: Request a park-facing room, which costs no more but features a great view and a small kitchenette. There's a continental restaurant and a lounge with nightly entertainment off the bustling knotty pine-paneled lobby, plus a beauty salon and newsstand. Valet service and limited room service are available.

INEXPENSIVE

✪ **Gershwin Hotel.** 7 E. 27th St. (btw. Fifth and Madison aves.), New York, NY 10016. ☎ **212/545-8000.** Fax 212/684-5546. www.gershwinhotel.com. 94 doubles, 31 4-person dorms. TV TEL (in doubles only). $109–$139 double, $119–$149 triple, $129–$159 quad, depending on season; $22 per person in dorm. Check Web site for seasonal deals. AE, MC, V. Parking $20 nearby. Subway: N, R, 6 to 28th St.

If you see glowing horns protruding from a lipstick-red facade, you're in the right place. An upscale version of the Carlton Arms (see "Midtown East & Murray Hill," later in this chapter), this budget-conscious, youth-oriented hotel caters to up-and-coming artistic types with its bold modern art collection and wild style. The lobby is a colorful, post-modern cartoon of kitschy furniture and pop art by Lichtenstein, Warhol, de Koonig, and lesser names. The standard rooms are clean and saved from the budget doldrums by bright colors, Picasso-style wall murals, Starck-ish takes on motel furnishings, and more modern art. All have private bathrooms; none of the bathrooms are bad, but try to nab yourself one of the cute, colorful new ones. The cheapest accommodations are four- and eight-bedded dorms: just basic rooms with IKEA bunk beds sharing a bath, but better than a hostel, especially if you're traveling with a group and can claim one as your own.

One of the best things about the Gershwin is its great, Factory-esque vibe, sort of like an artsy frat or sorority house. The hotel is more service-oriented than you usually see at this price level, and there's always something going on, whether it's live

Midtown Accommodations

The Algonquin **43**
The Avalon **55**
The Barbizon **1**
Best Western Manhattan **52**
Broadway Inn **34**
Carlton Arms **58**
Casablanca Hotel **40**
Chelsea Savoy Hotel **61**
Clarion Hotel Fifth Avenue **46**
Comfort Inn Manhattan **50**
Comfort Inn Midtown **39**
Crowne Plaza
  at the United Nations **48**
Crowne Plaza Manhattan **33**
Doubletree Guest Suites **38**
Essex House **6**
Fitzpatrick Grand Central **47**
Four Seasons Hotel New York **11**
Gershwin Hotel **59**
The Gorham **27**
Gramercy Park Hotel **62**
Helmsley Middletowne Hotel **13**
Holiday Inn Broadway **53**
Hotel Chelsea **60**
Hotel Edison **36**
Hotel Elysée **21**
Hotel Metro **51**
Hotel 17 **64**
Hotel 31 **57**
Hotel Wolcott **54**
The Inn at Irving Place **63**
The Kimberly **16**
Le Parker Meridien **7**
Loews New York **17**
The Lowell **2**

continues on
opposite page

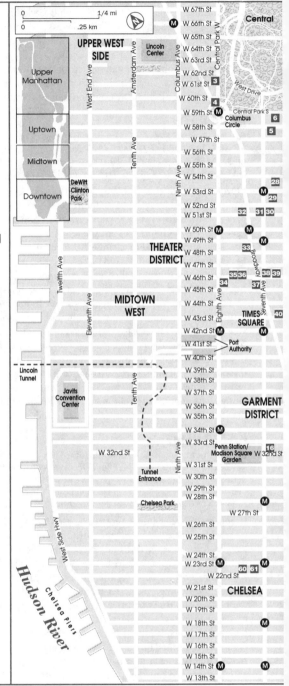

NA-0146

88

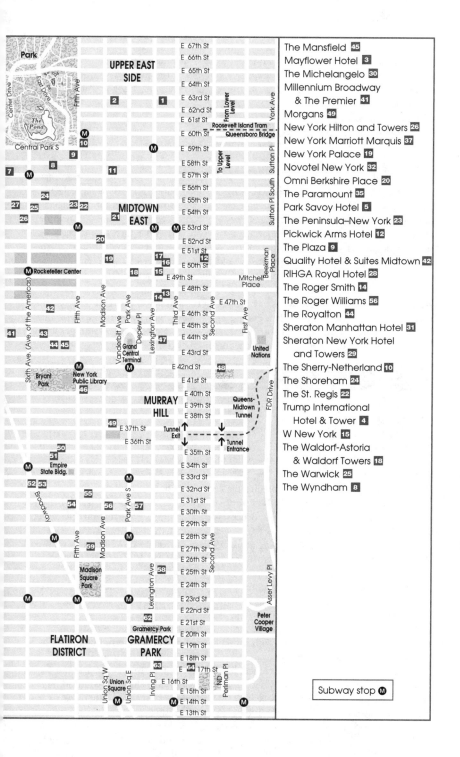

The Mansfield **45**
Mayflower Hotel **3**
The Michelangelo **30**
Millennium Broadway
    & The Premier **41**
Morgans **49**
New York Hilton and Towers **26**
New York Marriott Marquis **37**
New York Palace **19**
Novotel New York **32**
Omni Berkshire Place **20**
The Paramount **35**
Park Savoy Hotel **5**
The Peninsula–New York **23**
Pickwick Arms Hotel **12**
The Plaza **9**
Quality Hotel & Suites Midtown **42**
RIHGA Royal Hotel **28**
The Roger Smith **14**
The Roger Williams **56**
The Royalton **44**
Sheraton Manhattan Hotel **31**
Sheraton New York Hotel
    and Towers **29**
The Sherry-Netherland **10**
The Shoreham **24**
The St. Regis **22**
Trump International
    Hotel & Tower **4**
W New York **15**
The Waldorf-Astoria
    & Waldorf Towers **18**
The Warwick **25**
The Wyndham **8**

Subway stop **M**

comedy or jazz in the beer and wine bar, a film screening or barbecue on the rooftop garden, or an opening at the hotel's own art gallery. At press time, a new vendor had just taken over the funky Gallery Cafe, and room service was in the works. Air conditioning was also in the planning stage, but make sure before you book an August stay.

Hotel 17. 225 E. 17th St. (btw. Second and Third aves.), New York, NY 10003. ☎ **212/ 475-2845.** Fax 212/677-8178. www.citysearch.com/nyc/hotel17. 130 units (none with private bathroom). AC TV TEL. $98–$130 double, $200 3-person suite. All prices include tax. No credit cards. Parking $25. Subway: 4, 5, 6 to 14th St.; L to Third Ave.

In the last couple of years, Hotel 17 has managed to garner a reputation as the hippest budget hotel in Manhattan, no doubt thanks (at least in part) to the fact that Madonna, David Bowie, and Maxwell have all been photographed in the eclectic, eccentric rooms. But it's not all hype. Hotel 17 has a lot to recommend it: The neighborhood is great, the block peaceful, and the individually decorated rooms surprisingly attractive. Look beyond the stylish veneer, though, and you'll find rooms that are small, dark, and basic—definitely not for travelers looking for creature comforts. Each has its own sink; the shared bathrooms are older but kept very clean. Recent renovation has softened the edge, adding A/C, TVs, hair dryers, and alarm clocks to all rooms. The lobby has a funky streamline moderne feel to it, but the security glass separating you from the front-desk staff detracts from the ambience. There's a roof garden and self-service laundry. All in all, a good deal for the money, especially if you're the sort who requires some individuality in your lodgings. Expect lots of younger and international travelers, who don't mind the inconveniences.

8 Chelsea

See the "Midtown Accommodations" map (pp. 88-89) for hotels in this section.

MODERATE

Hotel Chelsea. 222 W. 23rd St. (btw. Seventh and Eighth aves.), New York, NY 10011. ☎ **212/243-3700.** Fax 212/675-5531. www.hotelchelsea.com. 400 units, 100 available to travelers (most with private bathroom). A/C (in most rooms) TV TEL. $150–$285 double or junior suite, from $300 suite. AE, JCB, MC, V. Valet parking $18. Subway: 1, 9, C, E to 23rd St.

If you're looking for dependable, predictable comforts, book a room next door at the Chelsea Savoy. But if it's Warhol's New York you're here to discover—or Sarah Bernhardt's or Eugene O'Neill's or Lenny Bruce's—the Hotel Chelsea is the only place to stay. Thomas Wolfe wrote *You Can't Go Home Again* at the Chelsea; Arthur Miller penned *After the Fall* in its welcoming arms; William Burroughs moved in to work on *Naked Lunch;* and in a defining moment of punk history, Sid Vicious killed screechy girlfriend Nancy Spungeon here. No other hotel boasts so much genuine atmosphere—you may even have an encounter with a ghost or two. Currently, most of the 400 rooms are inhabited by long-term residents of the creative bent, so the bohemian spirit and sense of community are as strong as ever.

A designated landmark, the 1884 redbrick Victorian boasts graceful cast-iron balconies and a bustling lobby filled with museum-quality works by prominent current and former residents. A recent renovation has taken the seediness out of the allure— these days, the hotel is looking very nice. It's still very quirky, mind you, and not for everybody: Most of the individually decorated rooms and suites have air-conditioning, and they tell me that all rooms have TVs and telephones now, but otherwise it's a crapshoot. The accommodations tend to be sparsely furnished, but they're almost universally large and virtually soundproof (you can see how this would be a plus for unbridled creation). I loved no. 520, a pretty purple-painted junior suite with two double beds, a ceiling fan, sofa, and a pantry kitchenette. Everything is clean, but don't expect new. The hotel is service-oriented, but in an appropriately fluid way: There's no room or valet service, but the bellmen will be happy to deliver takeout to your room or run your dirty clothes to the cleaners.

INEXPENSIVE

✪ **Chelsea Savoy Hotel.** 204 W. 23rd St. (at Seventh Ave.), New York, NY 10011. ☎ **212/929-9353.** Fax 212/741-6309. www.citysearch.com/nyc/chelseasavoy. 90 units. A/C TV TEL. $99–$115 single, $125–$155 double, $155–$185 quad. Rates include continental breakfast. Children under 13 stay free in parents' room. AE, MC, V. Parking $16 nearby. Subway: 1, 9 to 23rd St.

This two-year-old hotel is our top choice in Chelsea, a neighborhood abloom with art galleries, restaurants, and weekend flea markets but formerly devoid of nice, affordable hotels. The six-story Savoy was built from the ground up, so it isn't subject to the eccentricities of the mostly older hotels in this price range: The hallways are attractive and wide, the elevators are swift and silent, and the generic but cheery rooms are good-sized and have big closets and roomy, immaculate bathrooms with tons of counter space. Creature comforts abound: The rooms boast mattresses, furniture, textiles, and linens of high quality, plus the kinds of amenities you usually have to pay more for, like hair dryers, minifridges, alarm clocks, irons and ironing boards, in-room safes, and toiletries (VCRs were scheduled to be added at press time). Most rooms are street-facing and sunny; corner rooms tend to be brightest and noisiest. Ask for a darker, back-facing room if you crave total silence. There's a plain but pleasant sitting room off the lobby where you can relax and enjoy your morning coffee over a selection of newspapers and magazines. The staff is young and helpful, and the increasingly hip neighborhood makes a good base for exploring both midtown and downtown.

9 Times Square & Midtown West

See the "Midtown Accommodations" map (pp. 88–89) for hotels in this section.

VERY EXPENSIVE

In addition to the choices below, you might also consider the super-deluxe, all-suite **RIHGA Royal Hotel,** at 151 W. 54th St. (☎ **800/937-5454** or 212/307-5000; www.ny.rihga.com), a darling of international entertainment industry execs—and priced accordingly.

Essex House. 160 Central Park South (btw. Sixth and Seventh aves.), New York, NY 10019. ☎ **800/645-5687** or 212/247-0300. Fax 212/315-1839. www.essexhouse.com. 597 units. A/C MINIBAR TV TEL. $330–$475 double, $425–$3,000 suite. Two children under 18 stay free in parents' room. AE, CB, DC, DISC, JCB, MC, V. Valet parking $37. Subway: 1, 9, A, B, C, D to Columbus Circle. Pets accepted.

A few years back, Japan's Nikko Hotels completed a $75-million renovation that properly restored the lobby, an art deco masterpiece, and enlarged the rooms, equipping them with TVs with VCRs, dual-line phones, and fax machines. Now under new management, the hotel as fabulous and sophisticated as ever. The rooms are done in an elegant faux-Chippendale and chintz style, and come with all the amenities you expect from a hotel of this caliber. With double sinks, separate tubs and showers, and soft robes, the marble-and-chrome bathrooms are fit for an emperor. The rooms overlooking Central Park are more expensive, of course, but the views are spectacular. Service is particularly attentive.

Dining/Diversions: Return visitors should note that lavish Les Célébrités closed in early 1999, after the departure of longtime chef Christian Delouvrier left the kitchen foundering and reviewers less than thrilled. Journeys is a clubby, wood-paneled cocktail bar.

Amenities: Fitness center, concierge, 24-hour room service, valet service, twice-daily maid service, newspaper delivery, express checkout, business center, conference rooms. Secretarial services and baby-sitting available. Complimentary weekday car service to Wall Street.

Le Parker Meridien. 118 W. 57th St. (btw. Sixth and Seventh aves.), New York, NY 10019. ☎ **800/543-4300** or 212/245-5000. Fax 212/307-1776. www.parkermeridien.com. 700 units. A/C (summer only) MINIBAR TV TEL. $350–$380 double, from $450 suite. Children (under 12 on weekdays, under 18 on weekends) stay free in parents' room. AE, CB, DC, DISC, ER, EURO, JCB, MC, V. Valet and self-parking $32. Subway: N, R, B, Q to 57th St. Pets under 15 pounds accepted.

Originally owned by Air France and now run by the London-based Forte Hotel Group, the first French hotel in New York maintains its distinctly Gallic ambiance—but with none of the haughty attitude. A three-story atrium lobby leads to elegant neo-classic guest rooms. Done in a sophisticated palette of beige and black, they feature all the latest amenities, including VCRs, CD players, phones with call waiting, fax machines, and marble bathrooms. Some suites have full kitchens (complete with china, cookware, and microwave) and two-line phones. Rooms are very comfortable, but it's the extensive—and top-notch—facilities that make the hotel a keeper.

Dining/Diversions: Nowhere is the morning meal treated with such reverence, and decadence, than at Norma's, a soaring, ultramodern ode to breakfast food where beautifully presented versions of the classic favorites as well as creative reinterpretations are served daily until 3pm; it's well worth a visit even if you're not staying here. Seppi's is the uptown version of Prince Street's Raoul's, a classic New York French bistro. Jack's is an ultramodern lobby bar that's reborn as an espresso bar in the morning.

Amenities: Concierge, 24-hour room service, valet service, twice-daily maid service, newspaper delivery, complimentary weekday car service to Wall Street, express checkout, business center, conference rooms, gift shop. Baby-sitting and secretarial services available. The excellent Club La Raquette is 15,000 square feet of workout space with state-of-the-art equipment, classes, jogging track, squash and racquetball courts, a fabulous rooftop pool with sundeck, saunas, and spa services.

The Michelangelo. 152 W. 51st St. (btw. Sixth and Seventh aves.), New York, NY 10019. ☎ **800/237-0990** or 212/765-1900. Fax 212/541-6604. www.summithotels.com. 178 units. A/C MINIBAR TV TEL. $360–$395 double, $475 junior suite, $635–$950 1-bedroom suite, $1,300 2-bedroom suite. Rates include Italian-style continental breakfast. Check Web site or inquire about weekend rates (which can go as low as $240) and other promotions. AE, CB, DC, DISC, JCB, MC, V. Valet parking $28. Subway: 1, 9 to 50th St.; B, D, E to 53rd St. Pets accepted with prior approval.

The American flagship of the Florence-based Starhotels group, the Michelangelo gets full credit for truth in advertising: It really is intimate, elegant, and very Italian, just as they say it is. With Italian marble, and oil paintings, and Vivaldi playing in the background, the welcoming lobby instantly transports you to a palazzo in Italy. The theme continues with imported mineral water and Baci chocolates at turndown. The guest rooms are decorated in styles ranging from art deco to French country, but all are oversized and boast king beds and VCRs (CD players are available). The bathrooms are done in Italian marble and have imported toiletries, Frette terry robes, and luxury tubs that just may be the largest in the city. Techies will be happy to find that every room comes equipped with a fax/printer/copier they can plug their laptops into, plus a state-of-the-art phone system; if that's not enough, the staff will deliver a "smart desk" with computer and laser printer to your room. All employees are trained in basic Italian, so feel free to practice your *buon giorno* on them.

Dining/Diversions: Limoncello features elegant but expense account–priced classic Italian cuisine. The Grotto features lighter fare, cocktails, a selection of fine cigars, and live jazz piano on Thursdays.

Amenities: Concierge, 24-hour room service, small fitness center (plus access to nearby health club), valet service, twice-daily maid service, newspaper delivery, free coffee and refreshments in lobby, free weekday car service to Wall Street, express checkout. Baby-sitting and a full range of business services available.

✪ **Millennium Broadway & The Premier.** 145 W. 44th St. (btw. Sixth Ave. and Broadway), New York, NY 10036. ☎ **800/622-5569** or 212/768-0847. Fax 212/768-0847. www.millenniumbroadway.com. 752 units. A/C MINIBAR TV TEL. $295–$345 double at Millennium, $395–$450 double at the Premier; from $650 suite. Children under 13 stay free in parents' room. Inquire about special deals and weekend packages, and check for Internet-only rates. AE, DC, CB, JCB, MC, V. Valet parking $35. Subway: 1, 2, 3, 9, N, R to Times Square; B, D, F, Q to 42nd St.

The Millennium Broadway (which, unlike the unaffiliated Millenium downtown, knows how to spell) is one of the top business hotels in the city, but its prime Times Square location and well-priced packages make it a good bet for leisure travelers, too. The spacious rooms have a lovely art deco style, with black-and-white photos, rich red mahogany, and black lacquer details. The textiles are of excellent quality, the bathrooms have lots of marble counter space, and nice extras include a writing desk, comfy streamline club chairs, and two-line phones with all the gadgets. Club rooms, on floors 46 to 52, feature larger-than-normal desks, fax machines, coffeemakers, turndown service, and free continental breakfast and evening cocktails at the top-floor Club Lounge.

Adjoining the Millenium is the brand-new **Premier,** housing 125 high-tech luxury rooms done in a more contemporary style, with blond ash, green glass, and natural fibers. The Omaha mattresses—the same ones used in the far more expensive Four Seasons—done up in Frette linens just may be the most glorious beds in town. The rooms also feature larger-than-average workspace with all the necessary gadgets, a love seat with its own cable-knit throw for curling up, coffeemaker, fax machine, CD player, and oversized bathrooms with soaking tubs and separate showers. The Premier also boasts its own lounge with continental breakfast, cocktails, and large flat-screen TV.

Dining: With very good New American cuisine and a friendly staff, the highly regarded restaurant Charlotte is a classy choice for pre- and post-theater dining as well as Sunday brunch.

Amenities: Fitness center with sauna, concierge, 24-hour room service, valet service, twice-daily maid service, newspaper delivery, express checkout, business center. Five-floor Manhattan Conference Center, with 33 dedicated meeting rooms and 11,000 square feet of exhibition space. Secretarial services, limo service, baby-sitting, and in-room massage available.

✪ **The Royalton.** 44 W. 44th St. (btw. Fifth and Sixth aves.), New York, NY 10036. ☎ **800/635-9013** or 292/869-4400. Fax 212/869-8965. 205 units. A/C MINIBAR TV TEL. $350–$550 double, from $500 suite. Ask about promotional rates (sometimes as low as $260) and weekend deals. AE, DC, EURO, MC, V. Valet parking $35. Subway: B, D, F, Q to 42nd St.

This was the second entry into the hotel market for Ian Schrager and the late Steve Rubell, who first tested the waters with Morgans (see "Midtown East & Murray Hill," later in this chapter) after the glory days of their 1970s disco heaven Studio 54 were a distant memory. More than a decade later, thanks to the pioneering design of French superstar Phillippe Starck, the Royalton is still an ultra-modern show stopper: lighting fixtures that look like rhinoceros horns, attractive service people dressed in de rigueur black, furniture—even carpet—with attitude. Even more importantly, Starck and

Schrager have reinvented the idea of hotel: This is hotel as public space, as gathering space, as *scene*. Never have you seen a lobby quite like this, buzzing with beautiful people and energy. This ain't exactly your average Hilton, baby.

Thankfully, comfort was never sacrificed for style. Beautifully designed with a loose cruise-ship theme in rich mahogany, cool slate, and white cotton duck, even the smallest guest room is spacious enough to have a cushioned banquette for reclining, a good-sized work desk, and a roomy bathroom with a five-foot round tub or an oversized shower stall (request one or the other when you book if it matters to you). All have a VCR, CD player, groovy Kiehl's toiletries, and two two-line speaker phones with direct-dial numbers and conference calling; some even have working fireplaces.

Dining/Diversions: 44 serves reliably good New American cuisine to publishing bigwigs and other power types; service can be lax if you're not one of the in-crowd. The perennially popular lobby features comfy seating nooks, an extensive martini list, a light menu of excellent finger foods, and the Round Bar, a 20-seat circular enclave done in high *Jetsons* style.

Amenities: Concierge, 24-hour room service, valet service, turndown service, *USA Today* delivery, video library, fitness room. Business/secretarial services, personal trainers, and massage available.

EXPENSIVE

In addition to the choices below, you might also consider the **Sheraton New York Hotel and Towers,** 811 Seventh Ave., at 53rd Street (☎ 800/325-3535 or 212/581-1000; www.sheraton.com), a monster of a business and convention hotel, with well-outfitted, relatively spacious rooms; and the **Sheraton Manhattan Hotel,** across the street at 790 Seventh Ave. (☎ 800/325-3535 or 212/581-3300; www.sheraton.com), much smaller than its sibling hotel and largely catering to business travelers with oversized desks and in-room HP OfficeJet printer/fax/copiers.

There's also the **Holiday Inn Broadway,** 49 W. 32nd St., at Broadway (☎ 888/NYHOLIDAY or 212/736-3800; www.holiday-inn.com), a fine branch of this reliable chain but more expensive than you might think—only stay here if you can get a deeply discounted rate (or if you're traveling with a pet). Ditto with the **New York Hilton and Towers** at Rockefeller Center, 1335 Sixth Ave. (☎ 800/HILTONS or 212/586-7000; www.hilton.com), a 2,100-room monstrosity whose cubbyhole-sized rooms overflow with business travelers and conventioneers.

○ **The Algonquin.** 59 W. 44th St. (btw. Fifth and Sixth aves.), New York, NY 10036. ☎ 800/555-3000 or 212/840-6800. Fax 212/944-1419. www.camberleyhotels.com. 165 units. A/C TV TEL. $189–$329 double, $329–$529 suite. Rates include continental breakfast. Extra person $25. AE, CB, DC, DISC, EURO, JCB, MC, V. Parking $25 across the street. Subway: B, D, F, Q to 42nd St.

This 1902 hotel is one of the Theater District's best-known landmarks: This is where the *New Yorker* was born, where Lerner and Loewe wrote *My Fair Lady,* and—most famously—where some of the biggest names in 1920s literati, among them Dorothy Parker, met to trade boozy quips at the celebrated Algonquin Round Table. I'm happy to report that the past isn't just a memory here anymore—a complete 1998 restoration returned this venerable hotel to its full Arts-and-Crafts splendor. True to its tradition, the Algonquin is a very social hotel: The splendid oak-paneled lobby is the comfiest and most welcoming in the city, made to linger over afternoon tea or a post-theater cocktail. While posher than ever, the small rooms are comfortable but cramped—fine for tourists out on the town all day, but not suitable for business travelers who may need to spread out and get some work done. Extras include stocked candy jars (a nice touch). The freshened bathrooms boast short but deep soaking tubs, hair dryers, and bathrobes. Twins are the roomiest doubles. For the ultimate New York vibe, opt for one of the literary-themed suites.

Dining/Diversions: Cocktails, tea, coffee, and an all-day menu are served in the lobby and adjacent Rose Room. The Oak Room is one of the city's top cabaret rooms, featuring such big names as Andrea Marcovicci. The Monday-night Spoken Word program continues, with speakers as diverse as Spalding Gray, Stanley Tucci, and Paul Theroux. Pub fare is available in the Blue Bar, home to a rotating collection of Hirschfeld drawings.

Amenities: Well-outfitted fitness and business centers, concierge, room service (daily 7am–11pm), twice-daily maid service, valet service; baby-sitting available.

○ **Casablanca Hotel.** 147 W. 43rd St. (just east of Broadway), New York, NY 10036. ☎ **888/922-7225** or 212/869-1212. Fax 212/391-7585. www.casablancahotel.com. 48 units. A/C MINIBAR TV TEL. $245–$265 double, $375 suite. Rates include continental breakfast and afternoon snacks. Two children under 13 stay free in parents' room. Check Web site for Internet deals. AE, DC, JCB, MC, V. Parking $18 next door. Subway: 1, 2, 3, 9, N, R to 42nd St./Times Square.

This stylish Moroccan-themed boutique hotel is a real winner. With vibrant mosaic tiles, warm woods and rattan, potted palms, and North African–themed art gracing both the public spaces and guest rooms, the vibe is just right—the only thing missing is Bogart and Bergman. The rooms aren't big, but they're nicely outfitted with comfortable platform beds, ceiling fans, VCR, two-line phone, full-length mirror, and double-paned windows for peace and quiet. The minibar is stocked, believe it or not, with reasonably priced water, sodas, and snacks. The bathrooms are beautifully done with gorgeous Andalusian tile, and even the smallest is spacious enough for an oversized shower stall (request a tub when booking if you want one). Suites have pullout sofas that convert to single beds, but they're really too small to accommodate families. Everything is high-quality, and beautiful touches like Murano glass sconces and framed Moroccan carpets in the halls add an extra flair. The small staff is very attentive, and the ambitious manager is constantly at work improving the property. Book well ahead, as an increasing number of happy repeat guests and corporate clients fill this place up fast.

Dining/Diversions: The comfortable second-floor lounge serves continental breakfast, complimentary refreshments throughout the day, and wine and cheese in the evening. There's also a serve-yourself cappuccino machine and an extra-large TV; high-speed data lines are installed, and computers with Internet access should be available by the time you arrive. A tiled second-floor courtyard is ideal for summer lounging, and the rooftop deck is a perfect vantage for watching the New Year's ball drop.

Amenities: Free access to nearby New York Sports Club, with pool and sauna; valet service, video library, small high-tech conference room. Secretarial services available.

The Time. 224 W. 49th St. (btw. Broadway and Eighth Ave.), New York, NY 10019. ☎ **877/ TIME-NYC** or 212/246-5252. www.thetimenyc.com. Fax 212/320-2926. 192 units. A/C MINIBAR TV TEL. $250–$400 double, from $375 suite. AE, DC, DISC, MC, V. Parking $20. Subway: 1, 9, C, E to 50th St.; N, R to 49th St.

This brand-new hotel will be fully up and running by the time you read this. The design buffs among you are likely to have heard the buzz on this first hotel designed by Adam Tihany, the man behind such incredible spaces as Le Cirque 2000, Jean-Georges, and Wolfgang Puck's Spago restaurants.

Despite the high-design pedigree and boutique-chic air that pervades the place, the guest rooms are surprisingly practical. They're done in a minimalist style in one of three primary color schemes: your choice of red, yellow, or blue, accented with black and gray. Everything is top quality but understated—think clean lines, low furnishings, and soft backlighting (including the cleverest bedside lighting I've seen). Nicely designed touches like a coffeemaker caddy and built-in valet make the rooms extra-efficient (some have double closets instead of drawer space, though, so ask if it matters to you). Amenities include a printer/copier/fax machine on the big worktable, Web TV, and Bose radios. Things get a bit silly with color-matched scents (yours to invoke only if you wish) and fruits, but the gimmicks don't intrude. Some of the bathrooms are on the smaller side, but all have double-wide showers (suites have whirlpool tubs) and clever cubbyholes that provide additional storage space.

Dining/Diversions: The first New York restaurant from celebrity chef Jean-Louis Palladin, master of nouveau French cooking and mentor to such big-name chefs as such Eric Ripert of Le Bernadin, Palladin is highly anticipated to be a major player on the restaurant scene. Time^2, the lobby-level lounge, is set to be another hotspot in the Royalton vein, with a tapas bar providing an individual twist.

Amenities: Concierge, 18-hour room service, valet service, turndown service, express checkout, gift shop, international newsstand, conference room, and fitness room. VCR and videos, mobile phones, and personal shopper service available.

Crowne Plaza Manhattan. 1605 Broadway (btw. 48th and 49th sts.), New York, NY 10019. ☎ **800/243-NYNY** or 212/977-4000. Fax 212/333-7393. www.crowneplaza.com. 770 units. A/C MINIBAR TV TEL. $229–$489 double, $479–$1,000 1-bedroom suite, $700–$1,350 2-bedroom suite. Ask about weekend rates, senior rates, and other discounts; check Web site for special deals. Two children under 19 free in parents' room using existing bedding. AE, CB, DC, DISC, EURO, JCB, MC, V. Valet parking $35. Subway: 1, 9 to 50th St.; N, R to 49th St.

When Holiday Inn went upscale in 1994 with its new Crowne Plaza line, this became its international flagship. In the heart of Times Square and near most Broadway theaters, the 46-story glass tower is as good as a mass-market chain hotel gets—and you couldn't be better located for Midtown's top attractions. The comfortable guest rooms boast contemporary furnishings and marble bathrooms, plus extras like coffeemakers and all the features you've come to expect, like in-room safes. The top four floors are devoted to Crowne Plaza Club rooms, which also feature free continental breakfast, evening hors d'oeuvres, and other extras. Noted designer Adam Tihany is at work here through '99, so expect new zest in the public spaces. Rack rates are high, but discounted rates are often available, especially for weekend travelers.

Dining/Diversions: There are three satisfactory, if unmemorable, restaurants, including the well-situated Samplings Bar, which serves contemporary pre- and post-theater meals overlooking the lights of Broadway. The Lobby Bar is a comfortable lounge that invites you to sink into a club chair, order up a martini, and stay awhile.

Amenities: Excellent fitness center with 50-foot pool and sauna, concierge, 24-hour room service, valet service, newspaper delivery, express checkout, business center, conference rooms, tour desk. Secretarial services available.

♦ Doubletree Guest Suites. 1568 Broadway (47th St. at Seventh Ave.), New York, NY 10036. ☎ **800/222-TREE** or 212/719-1600. Fax 212/921-5212. www.doubletreehotels.com. 460 units. A/C MINIBAR TV TEL. $239–$350 two-room suite, from $400 family or conference suite. Extra person $20. Children under 12 free in parents' suite. Senior discounts and corporate rates available. Inquire about weekend package deals, which at press time included tickets to *The Lion King*. AE, DC, DISC, JCB, MC, V. Valet parking $30. Subway: N, R to 49th St.

For less than the cost of a normal room in many nearby Times Square hotels, you can get a suite at the Doubletree with a separate bedroom and living room with a pull-out sofa bed, a dining/work table, a refrigerator, a wet bar, a microwave, a coffeemaker, two TVs, and three phones with voice mail. For businesspeople, conference suites feature work stations with convenient dataports and outlets to plug in your laptop, and they're large enough for small meetings. What's more, this is a family-friendly hotel with a floor of childproof suites and special amenities for kids, such as the Kids Club, designed by Philadelphia's Please Touch Museum for children 3 to 12, featuring a playroom, an arts-and-crafts center, and computer and video games. Cribs and strollers are available, and there's a kids' room-service menu.

Dining/Diversions: There's a restaurant serving hotel-standard continental and American cuisine, plus a pleasant Broadway-themed piano bar.

Amenities: Fitness center, Kids Club with children's programs, concierge, 24-hour room service, valet service, newspaper delivery, express checkout, coin-op laundry room, guest services desk, business center with secretarial services available, newsstand and gift shop, meeting and banquet rooms.

✪ The Gorham. 136 W. 55th St. (btw. Sixth and Seventh aves.), New York, NY 10019. ☎ **800/735-0710** or 212/245-1800. Fax 212/582-8332. www.gorhamhotel.com. 115 units. A/C TV TEL. $215–$400 single or double, $235–$475 suite. Children under 16 stay free in parents' room. Check Web site for seasonal deals and packages. AE, CB, DC, EURO, JCB, MC, V. Parking $20. Subway: B, D, E to 53rd St.; B, N, R, Q to 57th St.

A major 1993 renovation reestablished the Gorham as an affordable contemporary choice in Midtown West, and a 1998 face-lift refreshed the bright new look. It's an especially good deal, considering that all of the large, pleasingly contemporary rooms have fully equipped kitchenettes with microwaves; 27-inch TVs with Nintendo; a spacious work desk; three multi-line phones with call waiting (four in suites); two queen-size or one king bed; and marble bathrooms with makeup mirrors and digital temperature controls. The suites feature a separate sitting room with a pull-out sofa bed and velour robes (two have Jacuzzi tubs). The location, not far from Times Square and the theme restaurants there and on 57th Street, make the Gorham a favorite with kids (don't even get them started on the Nintendo).

At press time, the hotel was offering theater packages that included in-demand tickets to *The Lion King;* check the hotel's Web site or inquire whether this or other packages are available when you call.

Dining: Breakfast is served in a private breakfast room ($8.50 continental, $11.50 all-you-can-eat buffet).

Amenities: Fitness center, concierge, room service (daily 7am–10pm), valet service, express checkout, conference rooms. Secretarial services, baby-sitting, in-room massage, and access to nearby health club available.

New York Marriott Marquis. 1535 Broadway (btw. 45th and 46th sts.), New York, NY 10036. ☎ **800/843-4898** or 212/398-1900. Fax 212/704-8930. www.marriott.com. 1,919 units. A/C MINIBAR TV TEL. $210–$395 double, $250–$435 Concierge-level double, from $450 suite. Ask about AAA, AARP, and corporate discounts when booking. AE, CB, DC, DISC, JCB, MC, V. Parking $30. Subway: 1, 2, 3, 9, N, R to Times Square; N, R to 49th St. Pets accepted.

The construction of the 50-story Marriott Marquis was a milestone for Times Square in 1985. Advocates hailed it as a sign of the neighborhood's resurgence, but the Helen Hayes and Morosco theaters were destroyed to make room for it, leading theater lovers to argue that it portended the end of Broadway. Both the hotel and the Great White Way have thrived in ways no one could've predicted. Though many New Yorkers continue to love to hate the pedestrian-unfriendly John Portman–designed hotel, it's a top choice of travelers. Its centerpieces are Portman's signature atrium, rising 37 floors to be the world's tallest, and the glass-enclosed elevators that zip up the atrium's center at knee-buckling speed. The surprisingly large guest rooms have two-line phones and coffeemakers. Concierge Level amenities include free continental breakfast and evening hors d'oeuvres. In 1997, the hotel completed a $20-million redecoration, which, among many improvements, added work desks and ergonomic chairs to every room.

Dining/Diversions: If it's a clear night, head up to the three-story revolving rooftop restaurant, aptly named the View, for cocktails and skyline views, but dine elsewhere. There are several restaurants and lounges in the atrium and many better ones just steps from the hotel (see chapter 6 for recommendations).

Amenities: Health club with whirlpool and sauna, concierge, 24-hour room service, valet service, express checkout, business center, gift shop and newsstand, salon, American Express travel desk.

Novotel New York. 226 W. 52nd St. (at Broadway), New York, NY 10019. ☎ **800/ NOVOTEL** or 212/315-0100. Fax 212/765-5369. www.accor.com. 480 units. A/C MINIBAR TV TEL. $189–$319 single or double, $600–$705 suite. Two children under 16 stay free in parents' room. Inquire about Broadway theater and other packages. AE, CB, DC, JCB, MC, V. Parking $16 nearby. Subway: 1, 9 to 50th St.; N, R to 49th St. Pets accepted.

The Novotel New York was built over an existing four-story building, so don't be surprised by the small street-level entrance. Once you've taken the elevator up to the seventh-floor Sky Lobby looking down Broadway to Times Square, you'll find a perfectly nice French-modern hotel with some spectacular views. The decor isn't anything special, but the guest rooms are soundproof and come equipped with a king or two double beds, plus a sofa and desk, as well as two phones, a large movie selection, and spacious bathrooms. The Novotel is particularly kid-friendly: Two children under 16 can sleep free in their parents' room, and both receive complimentary breakfast in the hotel's restaurant; in the lobby, the Children's Corner has a Lego table, and Café Nicole has a kids' menu.

Dining/Diversions: Café Nicole offers affordable European-style bistro fare and seventh-floor terrace dining. There's live entertainment nightly in the piano bar.

Amenities: Concierge, room service (daily 6:30am–midnight), valet service, newspaper delivery, express checkout, small fitness center, car-rental and tour desks. Business travelers can make use of a computer and fax machine in the lobby's Business Corner, as well as laptop and cell phone rental.

The Paramount. 235 W. 46th St. (just east of Eighth Ave.), New York, NY 10036. ☎ **800/ 225-7474** or 212/764-5500. Fax 212/354-5237. 618 units. A/C MINIBAR TV TEL. $145 single, $235–$300 double, from $550 suite. Children under 12 stay free in parents' room. Ask about promotional rates (sometimes as low as $160 double) and weekend deals. AE, DC, MC, V. Parking $18 nearby. Subway: 1, 2, 3, 9 to Times Square; A, C, E to 42nd St./Port Authority.

Here's your chance to enjoy the superslick stylings of hotels like Morgans and the Royalton at a more wallet-friendly rate. The Paramount bears all the Ian Schrager hallmarks, from the over-the-top Philippe Starck design to the don't-hate-me-because-I'm-beautiful staff. The tiny rooms are unmistakably Starck: all whites and grays, with compact stainless-steel bathroom, silk-screen headboards (*The Lacemaker*, by Vermeer, is one of four classic works that might hover larger than life over your dreams), cartoonish cafe table and side chairs, and swiveling armoires hiding the small TV and VCR. Other features include a bedside two-line phone (no in-room safes, though). It's a tight fit—you'll need an extra room or a suite if there's more than two of you—but worth the sacrifice if you want to live in high Schrager style. The art deco-meets-industrial lobby isn't the buzzy scene that the Royalton's lobby is, but it's still a good perch for people-watching.

Dining/Diversions: Owned by celebrity husband Rande Gerber (Mr. Cindy Crawford), the Whiskey bar is eternally trendy and inexcusably haughty; instead, head up to the little-known Mezzanine bar (on the balcony level overlooking the lobby) for quieter, pretension-free cocktails. Dean & DeLuca runs a charming cafeteria-style cafe at street level, featuring gourmet sandwiches, salads, and sweets. For full-scale dining, there's the just-fine Mezzanine restaurant and Coco Pazzo Teatro, a colorful and pleasing Tuscan-style trattoria that's great for pre- and post-theater dining (you may even spot a Broadway name or two later in the evening).

Amenities: Fitness center, extensive video library, concierge, 24-hour room service, express checkout, international news and magazine shop, children's playroom, business center, conference rooms. Secretarial services, baby-sitting, in-room massage available.

The Warwick. 65 W. 54th St. (at Sixth Ave.), New York, NY 10019. ☎ **800/223-4099,** 800/203-3232 or 212/247-2700. Fax 212/957-8915. www.warwickhotels.com. 422 units. A/C MINIBAR TV TEL. $265–$320 double, $450–$600 1-bedroom suite, $550–$1,200 2-bedroom suite. Children under 17 stay free in parents' room. Ask about corporate rates and other discounts. AE, DC, DISC, JCB, MC, V. Parking $28. Subway: B, Q to 57th St.; B, D to 53rd St.

The 36-story art deco Warwick was built in 1926 by publishing tycoon William Randolph Hearst as an apartment building for his Hollywood friends, including his mistress, Marion Davies, who had a specially designed floor. After some years of decline, the Warwick is back and better than ever as the flagship property of Warwick International Hotels, with service to match the high standards the chain is known for. All rooms have been completely redone as part of a $20 million renovation, with technological improvements (two-line phones, dataports, and so on) bringing them up to the current standard, and new mahogany furniture, attractive floral textiles, and marble bathrooms adding a bit of deluxe pizazz. Because the building was originally residential, the rooms are oversized and have spacious closets and large bathrooms. Some suites even have wraparound terraces (ask for the wonderful no. 2706, which was Cary Grant's residence for 12 years).

Dining/Diversions: Ciao Europa is a charming and attractive restaurant serving up very good Northern Italian cuisine at fair prices; the $24.95 pre-theater dinner is a great deal. Randolph's bar, a great after-work/cocktails place, has a light menu of salads and sandwiches.

Amenities: Fitness center, concierge, 24-hour room service, valet service, newspaper delivery, twice-daily maid service, express checkout, business center, conference rooms. Secretarial services, in-room massage available.

MODERATE

In addition to the choices below, also consider the **Best Western Manhattan,** 17 W. 32nd St. (☎ **800/551-2303** or 212/736-1600; www.applecorehotels.com). This is another Apple Core Management hotel (along with the Comfort Inn Midtown and the Quality Hotel & Suites) with modest but well-kept rooms ranging from $109 to $249. If you can get a room on the lower end of that scale, it's a good deal, especially when free continental breakfast and small business and fitness centers sweeten the pie.

✪ **Belvedere Hotel.** 319 W. 48th St. (btw. Eighth and Ninth aves.), New York, NY 10036. ☎ **888/HOTEL58** or 212/245-7000. Fax 212/265-7778. www.newyorkhotel.com/belvedere. 350 units. A/C TV TEL. $125–$240 double, depending on season (rates start at $150 in summer, $170 in fall and at holiday time). AAA discounts available; check Web site for special Internet deals. AE, DC, DISC, MC, V. Parking $17 on next block. Subway: C, E to 50th St.

Here's another excellent hotel from the Empire Hotel Group, the people behind the Upper West Side's Lucerne and Newton. Done with a sharp retro-modern deco flair, the public spaces are much more impressive than you'd expect to find in this price range. They lead to sizable, comfortable, attractive rooms with smallish but very nice bathrooms with hair dryers as well as pantry kitchenettes with fridges, sinks, and microwaves (BYO utensils). Beds are nice and firm, textiles are of high quality, and you'll find voice mail and dataports on the telephones. The decor is pleasing in all rooms, but ask for a renovated one, where you'll get good-quality cherry-wood furnishings, plus an alarm clock and work desk (in all but a few). Also ask for a high floor (8 and above) for great views; usually they'll cost no more (ask when booking).

Extras that make the Belvedere one of the city's top values include dry cleaning and laundry service, a self-serve Laundromat, electronic luggage lockers, fax and Internet-access machines, a brand-new stylish breakfast room and light-bites cafe for guests, and the terrific Churrascaria Plataforma Brazilian restaurant (see chapter 6). At press time, two change rooms for guests with late flights and a cocktail lounge were in the works. The Theater District neighborhood is loaded with great restaurants along Ninth Avenue and nearby Restaurant Row.

✪ **Broadway Inn.** 264 W. 46th St. (at Eighth Ave.), New York, NY 10036. ☎ **800/ 826-6300** or 212/997-9200. Fax 212/768-2807. www.broadwayinn.com. 40 units. A/C TV TEL. $85–$95 single, $115–$170 double, $195 suite. Extra person $10. Rates include continental breakfast. AE, DC, DISC, MC, V. Parking $16 at lot 3 blocks away. Subway: 1, 2, 3, 7, 9, S to 42nd St./Times Square; A, C, E to 42nd St.; N, R to 49th St.

More like a San Francsico B&B than a Theater District hotel, this lovely, welcoming inn is a real charmer. The second-floor lobby sets the homey, easygoing tone with stocked bookcases, cushy seating, and cafe tables where breakfast is served. The rooms are basic but comfy, outfitted in an appealing neo-deco style with firm beds and good-quality linens and textiles. The whole place is impeccably kept—neatniks won't have a quibble. Two rooms have king beds and Jacuzzi tubs, but the standard doubles are just fine for two if you're looking to save some dough. If there's more than two of you, or you're looking to stay awhile, the suites—with pullout sofa, microwave, minifridge, and lots of closet space—are a great deal. The location can be noisy, but double-paned windows keep the rooms surprisingly peaceful; still, ask for a back-facing one if you're extra-sensitive.

The inn's biggest asset is its terrific staff, who go above and beyond to make guests happy and at home in New York. And this corner of the Theater District is now porn-free and gentrifying nicely; it makes a great home base, especially for theatergoers. The inn has inspired a loyal following, so reserve early. However, there's no elevator in the four-story building, so overpackers and travelers with limited mobility should book elsewhere.

Comfort Inn Manhattan. 42 W. 35th St. (Fifth and Sixth aves.), New York, NY 10001. ☎ **800/228-5150** or 212/947-0200. Fax 212/594-3047. www.comfortinnmanhattan.com. 131 units. A/C TV TEL. Jan–July $129–$189 double; Aug–Dec $189–$349 double. Rates include continental breakfast. Ask about senior, AAA, corporate, and promotional discounts; check www.comfortinn.com for online booking discounts. Parking $16–$18 in nearby garage. Subway: B, D, F, Q, N, R to 34th St.

This centrally located hotel is a good choice, especially for those who prefer to go with a national chain with a familiar profile and a proven reputation. It's on a fine block just a stone's throw from some of Midtown's biggest attractions, including the Empire State Building and Macy's. Don't expect lots of personality: This is a standard, basically characterless chain hotel, but the rooms are clean, well maintained, and remarkably large by Manhattan standards. Nice extras include big closets, hair dryers, in-room safes, on-command movies, and voice mail. About 20 rooms have microwaves and minifridges, and about 30 king-bedded rooms come with sleeper sofas. The lobby is attractive enough to invite lounging, and the front desk staff is friendly and helpful. Rack rates are high, especially in the busy season, but it's usually possible to get a room for less than $200 even around holiday time. The substantial continental breakfast spread that's included in the rates is a big plus; there's also room service (7am–8pm) from the cute cafe adjacent to the hotel.

☉ Comfort Inn Midtown. 129 W. 46th St. (btw. Sixth Ave. and Broadway), New York, NY 10036. ☎ **800/567-7720** or 212/221-2600. Fax 212/790-2760. www.applecorehotels. com. 80 units. A/C TV TEL. $109–$249 double, depending on season. Children under 14 stay free in parents' room. Rates include continental breakfast. Ask about senior, AAA, corporate, and promotional discounts; check www.comfortinn.com for online booking discounts. AE, DC, DISC, MC, V. Parking: $20 nearby. Subway: 1, 2, 3, 9 to 42nd St./Times Square; N,R to 49th St.; B, D, F, Q to 47–50th sts./Rockefeller Center.

A major 1998 renovation brightened the former Hotel Remington's public spaces and small guest rooms, which now boast nice floral patterns, neo-Shaker furnishings, and nice marble and tile bathrooms (a few have showers only, so be sure to request a tub if it matters). Everything's fresh, comfortable, and new. Nice in-room extras include hair dryers, coffeemakers (oddly situated in the bathroom, but great for a morning cup o' joe nonetheless), blackout drapes, pay movies, and voice mail. Other plusses include a small fitness center (Stairmaster, treadmill, bike) and a business center; a coffee shop was in the works at press time. This one's considerably cheerier than the Comfort Inn Manhattan (see above), but stay there if you need your space. The location is excellent, steps from Times Square, Rockefeller Center, and the Theater District. We're not thrilled with Apple Core Hotels' (the management company that handles this Comfort Inn franchise) wide-ranging price schedule, but we found that it was relatively easy to get a well-priced room ($150 or less) even around holiday time, and rates drop as low as $79 in the off-season.

☉ Hotel Metro. 45 W. 35th St. (btw. Fifth and Sixth aves.), New York, NY 10001. ☎ **800/356-3870** or 212/947-2500. Fax 212/279-1310. 175 units. A/C TV TEL. $165–$250 double, $200–$325 suite. Extra person $25. Rates include continental breakfast. Off-season discounts may be available; check with airlines and other package operators for package deals. AE, DC, MC, V. Parking $20 nearby. Subway: B, D, F, Q, N, R to 34th St.

The Metro is the best choice in midtown for those who don't want to sacrifice either style or comfort for affordability. This lovely art deco-ish jewel has larger rooms than you'd expect for the price. They're outfitted with smart retro furnishings, playful textiles, and extras like voice mail and dataport on the phone, as well as hair dryers and huge mirrors in the small but well-appointed bathrooms. The neo-deco design gives the whole place an air of New York glamour that I've not otherwise seen in this price range. A great collection of black-and-white photos, from Man Ray classics in the halls to Garbo and Dietrich portraits in the lobby, adds to the vibe. Only about half the baths have tubs, but the others have shower stalls big enough for two. One of the really nice things about this hotel is its welcoming public spaces: The comfy lounge area off the lobby, where buffet breakfast is laid out and the coffeepot's on all day, is a popular hangout, and the well-furnished rooftop terrace (a great place to order up room service) boasts one of the most breathtaking views of the Empire State Building I've ever seen. Valet service, room service from the stylish Metro Grill (see chapter 6), and a sizable fitness room add to the great value.

Quality Hotel & Suites Midtown. 59 W. 46th St. (btw. Fifth and Sixth aves.), New York, NY 10036. ☎ **800/567-7720** or 212/719-2300. Fax 212/921-8929. www.applecorehotels. com. 193 units. A/C TV TEL. $109–$249 double, $149–$299 suite, depending on the season. Rates include continental breakfast. Children under 19 stay free in parents' room. Ask about senior, AAA, corporate, and promotional discounts. AE, DC, DISC, MC, V. Parking $20 nearby. Subway: B, D, F, Q to 47th–50th sts./Rockefeller Center.

Here's a fine choice for those looking for your basic clean, well-outfitted hotel room for not too much money. Nice extras include coffeemakers with free coffee; decent closets with iron and ironing board, and safe; smallish but fine bathrooms with hair dryers; and phones with voice mail, dataport, and free local calls (an excellent plus).

The suites have king beds, pullout sleeper sofas in the living room, and two TVs, making them great for families. The 1902 landmark building, with a beaux arts facade and an attractive lobby, has been recently renovated to include a nice exercise room with cardio machines, two meeting rooms, and a business center with credit card–activiated Internet access and fax and copy machines, as well as an ATM. The location, in the Diamond District between Rockefeller Center and Times Square, is great for both business and pleasure. We're not thrilled with the management's wide-ranging price schedule, but we found that it was relatively easy to negotiate a good rate ($139 or less) even around holiday time, and rates drop as low as $79 in the off-season (you might even be able to get a suite for 99 bucks if your timing is right).

INEXPENSIVE

Even if you're set on a bargain-basement rate, don't forget to consider many of the properties listed under "Moderate" directly above. Even though their rack rates are too high to list them as inexpensive, these Times Square–area hotels—particularly the ones with recognizable names, such as Comfort Inn—are particularly sensitive to the market in both directions. Because they hate to see rooms sit empty, they'll often negotiate astounding rates, particularly at the last minute and in the off-season. Often, you can get far more for your money if you're willing to make a few extra phone calls.

✪ **Hotel Edison.** 228 W. 47th St. (btw. Broadway and Eighth Ave.), New York, NY 10036. ☎ **800/637-7070** or 212/840-5000. Fax 212/596-6850. www.edisonhotelnyc.com. 869 units. A/C TV TEL. $125 single, $140 double, $155–$170 triple or quad, $160–$200 suite. Extra person $15. AE, CB, DC, DISC, MC, V. Valet parking $22. Subway: N, R to 49th St.; 1, 9 to 50th St.

There's no doubt about it—the Edison is one of the Theater District's best hotel bargains, if not the best. No other area hotel is so consistently value-priced. About 90% of the rooms were refurbished in 1998 (the rest should be done by the time you arrive), and they're much nicer than what you'd get for just about the same money at the nearby Ramada Inn Milford Plaza (which ain't exactly the "Lullabuy of Broadway!" these days). Don't expect much more than the basics, but you will find a firm bed (flat pillows, though), motel decor that's more attractive than most I've seen in this category, a phone with dataport, and a clean, perfectly adequate tile bathroom. Most double rooms feature two twins or a full bed, but there are some queens; request one at booking and show up early in the day for your best chance at one. Triple/quad rooms are larger, with two doubles.

Off the attractive deco-style lobby is Cafe Edison, a hoot of an old-style Polish deli that's a favorite among ladder-climbing theater types and downmarket ladies who lunch; Sofia's, an Italian restaurant; a tavern with live entertainment most nights; and a gift shop. Services are kept at a bare minimum to keep rates down, but there is a beauty salon and a guest services desk where you can arrange tours, theater tickets, and transportation. The hotel fills up with tour groups from the world over, but since it has nearly 1,000 rooms, you can carve out some space if you call early enough.

Hotel Wolcott. 4 W. 31st St. (at Fifth Ave.), New York, NY 10001. ☎ **212/268-2900.** Fax 212/563-0096. www.wolcott.com. 250 units. A/C TV TEL. $120 double, $140 triple, $170 suite. Discounted AAA, AARP, and promotional rates may be available. AE, JCB, MC, V. Parking $16 next door. Subway: B, D, F, Q, N, R to 34th St.

The Wolcott was one of the grande dames of Manhattan hotels at the start of the 20th century. Somewhat less than that now, it has been reinvented as a good-value option for bargain-hunting travelers. Only the lobby hints at the hotel's former grandeur; these days, the rooms are motel-standard, but they're well-kept and quite serviceable. Plusses include spacious bathrooms and voice mail, plus mini-fridges in most rooms.

On the downside, some of the mattresses aren't as firm as I might like, and the closets tend to be on the small side. And some of the triples are poorly configured—the front door to one I saw hit up right against a bed—but they're plenty big enough for three, and come with two TVs to avoid before-bedtime conflicts (as do the suites). All in all, you get your money's worth here. One of the hotel's most recommendable features is its basement coin-op laundry, a rarity for Manhattan. There's also a tour desk and a snack shop where you can get your morning coffee; an Internet center was in the works at press time.

Park Savoy Hotel. 158 W. 58th St. (btw. Sixth and Seventh aves.), New York, NY 10019. ☎ **212/245-5755.** Fax 212/765-0668. www.neon.net/parksavoy. 70 units. A/C (May–Oct) TV TEL. $70 single, $85–$155 double. All rates include tax. AE, MC, V. Parking $20 nearby. Subway: A, B, C, D, 1, 9 to 59th St./Columbus Circle; N, R to 57th St.

The Park Savoy isn't quite as nice as its sister hotel, the Chelsea Savoy (see above), but the lower prices reflect the quality difference, making it a good deal nonetheless. The hotel has been recently renovated so that all rooms have nice new black-and-white–tiled private bathrooms, which are petite (with showers only) but attractive and clean. If your budget is tight, two of you can make do in the smallest rooms; the biggest ones can accommodate three or four in two double beds. Rooms are basic—don't expect frills like hair dryers and alarm clocks—and a few I saw were in need of a fresh coat of paint, but they do the job. All have voice mail, most have walk-in closets, and a few have mini-fridges. Services are kept to a minimum to keep rates low, but there's a good Pasta Lovers restaurant in the building that gives guests 10% off and will deliver to your room. Best of all is the attractive and convenient location—a block from Central Park and a stone's throw from Carnegie Hall, Lincoln Center, and the Columbus Circle subway lines, which give you easy access to the rest of the city.

✪ **The Wyndham.** 42 W. 58th St. (btw. Fifth and Sixth aves.), New York, NY 10019. ☎ **800/257-1111** or 212/753-3500. Fax 212/754-5638. 140 units. AC TV TEL. $125–$140 single, $140–$155 double, $180–$225 1-bedroom suite, $320–$365 2-bedroom suite. AE, DC, MC, V. Parking $35 next door. Subway: N, R to Fifth Ave.; B, Q to 57th St.

This family-owned charmer is one of midtown's best hotel deals—and it's perfectly located to boot, on a great block steps away from Fifth Avenue shopping and Central Park. The Wyndham is stuck in the '70s on all fronts—don't expect so much as an alarm clock or hair dryer in your room, much less a dataport—but its guest rooms are enormous by city standards, comfortable, and loaded with character. The entire hotel features a wild collection of wallpaper, from candy stripes to crushed velvets, so some rooms definitely cross the ticky-tacky line. But others are downright lovely, with such details as rich oriental carpets and well-worn libraries, and the eclectic art collection that lines the walls boasts some real gems. Most important, you get a lot for your money: The rooms are universally large, and all feature huge walk-in closets (the biggest I've ever seen). The surprisingly affordable suites also have full-fledged living rooms, dressing areas, and cold kitchenettes (fridge only). If you're put in a room that's not to your taste, just ask politely to see another one; the staff is usually happy to accommodate. Valet service is available, as is limited room service (the restaurant should be in full swing by the time you arrive).

10 Midtown East & Murray Hill

See the "Midtown Accommodations" map (pp. 88-89) for hotels in this section.

VERY EXPENSIVE

Four Seasons Hotel New York. 57 E. 57th St. (btw. Park and Madison aves.), New York, NY 10022. ☎ **800/332-3442** in the U.S., 800/268-6282 in Canada, or 212/758-5700.

Fax 212/758-5711. www.fourseasons.com. 370 units. A/C MINIBAR TV TEL. $565–$750 double, $1,050–$5,000 1-bedroom suite, $2,300–$2,800 2-bedroom suite; room with terrace $50 extra. One child under 19 stays free in parents' room. Check Web site for current package deals. AE, CB, DC, DISC, ER, JCB, MC, V. Valet parking $40. Subway: 4, 5, 6, N, R to 60th St.

Hollywood meets Manhattan in the grand but frosty lobby of this ultra-luxury, ultra-modern hotel. Aging rock stars spice the brew, as can anyone with a generous expense account or a wad of cash to drop. Designed by I. M. Pei in 1993, the limestone-clad tower rises 52 stories, providing hundreds of rooms with a view. You'll immediately know this place is special, even in super-luxe New York, where anything goes. The soaring lobby has marble floors and a high back-lit onyx ceiling. The white-on-white guest rooms are among New York's largest (averaging 600 square feet) and have entrance foyers, sitting areas, desks with leather chairs, and sycamore-paneled dressing areas. The Florentine marble bathrooms have separate tubs and showers. Other special touches include goose-down pillows, Frette linens, oversized bath towels, and cushy robes. You'd expect less? For this much money, you deserve *more*.

Dining/Diversions: Fifty-Seven, Fifty-Seven is a fine contemporary New American grill and popular power-breakfast and lunch spot. The snazzy Bar offers an extensive martini menu to wash down light meals. The Lobby Lounge features lunch, afternoon tea, cocktails, and hors d'oeuvres.

Amenities: Luxurious fitness center with Jacuzzi and sauna, concierge, 24-hour room service, valet service, twice-daily maid service, free newspaper delivery, express checkout, free coffee in lobby 5:30–7am, business center, conference rooms. Baby-sitting, secretarial services, and in-room massage available.

Hotel Elysée. 60 E. 54th St. (btw. Madison and Park aves.), New York, NY 10022. ☎ **800/ 535-9733** or 212/753-1066. Fax 212/980-9278. http://members.aol.com/elysee99. 99 units. A/C TV TEL. $295–$315 double, $350–$900 suite. Rates include continental breakfast. AE, DC, JCB, MC, V. Valet parking $24. Subway: E, F to 53rd St./Park Ave.

A favorite with the power elite and a discerning European clientele, the Elysée sets the standard for the growing trend of service-oriented boutique hotels. The striking deco-ish lobby leads to stylish, comfortable rooms. Small but ample, they're outfitted with antiques, unstocked mini-fridges with free bottled water and iced tea, and VCRs; some also have sundecks. (There are no in-room safes, though, so you'll have to lock your valuables up at the front desk.) The Italian marble bathrooms come with Caswell-Massey toiletries. The Piano Suite boasts a Steinway that once belonged to Vladimir Horowitz. Complimentary breakfast, afternoon tea, and cocktail-hour wine and cheese are served in the attractive second-floor sitting room and library. A good choice for those who can afford fancy but want something more intimate than your average luxury hotel.

Dining/Diversions: The legendary Monkey Bar serves very good New American cuisine in a swank Old Hollywood setting; it's also a late-night gathering spot for the see-and-be-seen crowd.

Amenities: Concierge; room service during breakfast, lunch (weekdays only), and dinner hours; valet service; twice-daily maid service; video library; small conference room; free access to nearby health club. Baby-sitting, in-room massage available.

✪ Morgans. 237 Madison Ave. (btw. 37th and 38th sts.), New York, NY 10016. ☎ **800/ 334-3408** or 212/686-0300. Fax 212/779-8352. 113 units. A/C MINIBAR TV TEL. $310–$375 double, from $425 suite. Rates include continental breakfast and afternoon tea. AE, DC, DISC, MC, V. Valet parking $33. Subway: 6 to 33rd St.; 4, 5, 6, 7, S to Grand Central.

Ian Schrager's first boutique hotel (also see the Paramount and the Royalton) opened in 1984 as a low-profile "anti-hotel" without a sign or a staff experienced in hotel management. There's still little to give away its Murray Hill location except for the limos occasionally dropping off some high-profile type, but today the staff is experienced and competent. The hotel's original designer, Andrée Putman, also renovated the stylish interior in 1995; it eschews the over-the-top elements of the Starck-designed Paramount and Royalton for a more low-key, grown-up sensibility. The rooms are done with gorgeous tactile fabrics in a soothing palette of taupe, ivory, and black. They're not huge, but furnishings designed low to the ground and beautiful custom maple-eye built-ins—including storage and cushioned window seats for both lounging and out-of-sight luggage storage—make them feel more spacious. Other pleasing extras include a VCR, CD player, spacious work desk, and a state-of-the-art phone system. The small bathrooms are a Putman signature, with black-and-white checkered tile and stainless-steel sinks; most have double-wide stall showers, so request a tub when booking if you require one.

Dining/Diversions: The Philippe Starck–designed Asia de Cuba serves surprisingly good fusion cuisine to a trendsetting crowd, becoming a white-hot velvet-rope bar scene later in the evening. In the cellar is Morgans Bar, a Rande Gerber (of the Whiskey bars) late-night hotspot for musicians, artists, and models, this time done up as a postmodern salon. The lovely breakfast room is for guests only.

Amenities: Concierge, 24-hour room service, valet service, newspaper delivery on request, free access to nearby New York Sports Club. Fax machines, cell phones, and laptops available for use.

New York Palace. 455 Madison Ave. (btw. 50th and 51st sts.), New York, NY 10022. ☎ **800/NY-PALACE** or 212/888-7000. Fax 212/303-6000. www.newyorkpalace.com. 891 units. A/C MINIBAR TV TEL. $425–$550 double, from $900 suite. Two children under 19 stay free in parents' room. Check Web site or inquire about special weekend packages, when rates can go as low as $245 in main hotel, $365 in Towers. AE, CB, DC, DISC, ER, EURO, JCB, MC, V. Valet parking $47. Subway: 6 to 51st St.

The Sultan of Brunei bought this convenient Midtown palace from the Queen of Mean, Leona Helmsley, restoring the public rooms with an opulence befitting nouveau royalty and putting complaints of mediocre rooms to rest. A member of the Leading Hotels of the World organization, the Palace is comprised of the landmark McKim, Mead & White–designed Villard Houses (1882) and a 55-story modern tower. Outfitted with every luxury, all of the rooms are the height of elegance and modern convenience. Which building you choose is all a matter of taste: The main Hotel is rich with old-world style, while the Towers, which functions as its own hotel-within-a-hotel, has a sophisticated contemporary-deco style and the added bonus of around-the-clock butler service. The Executive Hotel, housed on the high floors of the Villard Houses, offers extra amenities like a dedicated concierge and continental breakfast and hors d'oeuvres in the lounge. The views are incredible from the Towers, but they're great from the Hotel too, thanks to the Villard Houses' U-shaped design.

Dining/Diversions: As the new home of the revered Le Cirque, the hotel stars center stage in gourmets' dreams (see chapter 6). Istana, a Mediterranean cafe and restaurant, should not be overlooked: It transcends its hotel-restaurant class with wonderful food, fine ports, a welcoming staff, and even its own olive bar, with more than 30 varieties of the fabulous fruit.

Amenities: There's a new 7,000-square-foot fitness center with all the latest equipment as well as personal trainers, steam rooms, and spa treatments. Concierge, 24-hour room service, valet service (including 1-hour pressing service), newspaper delivery, complimentary weekday shuttle to Wall Street, excellent business center with secretarial and translation services, full high-tech meeting center.

✪ **The Peninsula–New York.** 700 Fifth Ave. (at 55th St.), New York, NY 10019. ☎ **800/ 262-9467** or 212/956-2888. Fax 212/903-3949. www.peninsula.com. 241 units. A/C MINIBAR TV TEL. $560–$680 double, from $850 suite. Extra person $20; 1 child under 12 stays free in parents' room. AE, CB, DC, DISC, EURO, JCB, MC, V. Valet parking $38. Subway: E, F to 53rd St./Fifth Ave. Small pets accepted.

After $45 million and ten months of downtime, the Peninsula reopened in November 1998 as a state-of-the-art stunner. Inside, all that's left of the beaux arts past is the marvelous wedding-cake ceiling in the lobby. Work your way past the redecorated public floors and everything's brand new; the guest-room floors were totally gutted and laid out afresh, allowing for high-tech wiring, better room configurations, and what may be the most fabulous bathrooms in the city.

Rooted in an elegant gold-cream-black palette, the decor is a rich mix of art nouveau, vibrant Asian elements (including gorgeous silk bedcovers), and contemporary art. Every room boasts lots of storage and counter space, and fabulous linens (including the cushiest bathrobes I've seen). But the real news is the technology, which includes a room-wide speaker system and mood lighting; an executive workstation with desk-level inputs, direct-line fax, and dual-line speakerphones; a bedside panel for everything, from climate controls to the DO NOT DISTURB sign; even a doorside weather display. But wait, there's more: In the huge marble bathrooms, a tub-level panel allows you to control the speaker system, answer the phone, and, if you're in any room above the lowest (superior) level, control the bathroom TV. Simply fabulous— but why go this far and put VCRs and CD players in the suites only?

Dining/Diversions: Redone with a fresh contemporary feel, Adrienne now serves an admirable eclectic menu with Asian touches, plus lighter meals in the adjoining bistro. With comfortable seating and a wonderful library-like vibe, the Gotham Lounge offers an excellent afternoon tea, cocktails, and snacks. The Pen-Top Bar and Terrace (see chapter 9) offers rooftop cocktails and some of midtown's most dramatic views.

Amenities: Three-level rooftop health club and spa (one of New York's best), with heated pool, exercise classes, Jacuzzi, sauna, and sundeck. Concierge, 24-hour room service, valet service, newspaper delivery, twice-daily maid service, express checkout, business center, conference rooms, tour desk, salon. Secretarial services, baby-sitting, in-room massage available.

The Plaza. 768 Fifth Ave. (btw. 58th and 59th sts.), New York, NY 10019. ☎ **800/ 759-3000** or 212/759-3000. Fax 212/759-3167. www.fairmont.com/newyork. 872 units. A/C MINIBAR TV TEL. $335–$580 double, from $450 suite. Inquire about weekend packages and other special promotions. AE, DC, DISC, JCB, MC, V. Valet parking $40. Subway: N, R to Fifth Ave.

Designed by Henry J. Hardenbergh (who also gave us the landmark Dakota Apartments on the Upper West Side), this 1907 French Renaissance palace rightfully deserves its National Historic Landmark status. Having glamorously appeared in dozens of movies from *North by Northwest* to *Home Alone 2*, the Plaza is an internationally recognized symbol of New York—there is no more impressive address. The blinding gold leaf and gaudy chandeliers of the Donald Trump days have been toned down, but you'd still be hard-pressed to find a grander hotel. The guest rooms have been spruced up, but beware: They can be small, especially those that don't face the park, and they feel even smaller at these prices. But the amenities are always first class: crystal chandeliers, beautiful Frette linens, and two-line phones; some rooms also feature 14-foot ceilings, carved marble fireplaces, and gorgeous mahogany doors. If money is no object, consider one of the specialty suites, some of which replicate stately English country homes.

Dining/Diversions: The gardenlike Palm Court is a favorite for tea or a spectacular Sunday brunch. The clubby Oak Room and the classic Edwardian Room both serve well prepared but wildly expensive formal American fare. The Oak Bar is popular for drinks, and the Oyster Bar (not to be confused with the better one at Grand Central) is a casual fish house/pub.

Amenities: Clef d'Or concierge, 24-hour room service, valet service, packing service, ticket desk, barber shop, salon, newsstand, boutiques, meeting and banquet rooms. Business center with secretarial and messenger service available. Exercise room, plus use of nearby health club; a spa was in the works at press time.

✪ The Sherry-Netherland. 751 Fifth Ave. (at 59th St.). ☎ **800/247-4377** or 212/355-2800. Fax 212/319-4306. www.sherrynetherland.com. 77 units. A/C TV TEL. $295–$450 double, $550–$825 1-bedroom suite, from $830 2-bedroom suite. Rates include continental breakfast at Cipriani's. AE, DC, DISC, ER, JCB, MC, V. Valet parking $40. Subway: N, R to Fifth Ave.

For a taste of genteel New York apartment living, come to the Sherry-Netherland. Housed in a wonderful 1927 neo-Romanesque building overlooking Fifth Avenue and Central Park, the Sherry is one of a kind: both a first-class hotel and a quietly elegant residential building where the guest rooms are privately owned co-ops. As a result, they vary greatly in style, but each is grandly proportioned with high ceilings, big bathrooms, and walk-in closets. These are the largest rooms I've seen in the city, and every one features high-quality furnishings and art, VCR, fax machine, Godiva chocolates upon arrival, and fridge with free soft drinks (voice mail was not yet in place at this writing, so check before you book if that matters). About half are suites with kitchenettes that have a cooktop or microwave, often both. The hotel is expensive, but at least you get a lot for your dollar here.

The most wonderful thing about the Sherry is its homeyness—even the standard doubles have a residential feel. You'll pay more for a lighter, park- or street-facing room; the views are stunning, but the lower floors can be noisy for light-sleepers. Interior-facing rooms are appreciably darker and quieter but no less fabulous, and a lot cheaper. One of my favorite suites is no. 814, an interior one-bedroom done in a playful art deco-contemporary style, with a gorgeous marble bathroom, a terrific kitchen with bar, and a wealth of luxurious space. If you'd prefer a more traditionally styled room, let the excellent staff know. The hotel is old-world formal—there are even attendants in gold-trimmed jackets manning the elevators around the clock—but not the least bit stuffy. A true New York classic.

Dining/Diversions: Packed with Armani-suited moguls, million-dollar models, and East Side denizens, bustling Cipriani's is the ultimate power spot. The wildly expensive food is excellent (especially the papardelle with in-season mushrooms), as is the tuxedoed service. Well worth the splurge.

Amenities: Concierge, room service (7am–midnight), valet service, newspaper delivery of any paper you choose, twice-daily maid service, fitness room, meeting room, barber shop, beauty salon, newsstand. Free access to library stocked with the *New York Times* best-sellers and a complete catalogue of Oscar-winning films.

The St. Regis. 2 E. 55th St. (at Fifth Ave.), New York, NY 10022. ☎ **800/759-7550** or 212/753-4500. Fax 212/787-3447. www.starwoodlodging.com. 314 units. A/C MINIBAR TV TEL. $520–$640 double, from $895 suite. AE, CB, DC, DISC, ER, EURO, JCB, MC, V. Valet parking $38. Subway: E, F to Fifth Ave.

In 1991, a $200-million restoration revived the old-world elegance of this classic beaux arts hotel—and the cost was passed on to guests, resulting in some of New York's highest room rates. You do, however, get what you pay for: grand public spaces and guest rooms filled with Louis XV–style furnishings, chandeliers, and original works of art, as well as luxurious marble bathrooms with double sinks and separate tubs and shower stalls. Your clothing (two items per person) is pressed as soon as you arrive, tea or coffee arrives daily immediately following your wake-up call, a fresh fruit plate and sweets are another daily occurrence, and there's always a butler on hand to attend to your needs. If that's not enough, free local phone calls are included. Suite guests also benefit from CD players, VCRs, cell phones, fax machines, and bouquets of roses delivered daily. This is classic luxury at its grandiose best.

Dining/Diversions: Ruth Reichl of the *New York Times* just awarded Lespinasse the top prize of four stars again in late 1998, but the Asian-accented French cuisine and Louis XIV ambience fail to wow me; still, hotel dining hardly gets better. The King Cole Room (see chapter 9), where the Bloody Mary was invented, is a great setting for cocktails—and its Maxfield Parrish mural is an art deco gem. The Astor Court serves a very sophisticated afternoon tea.

Amenities: Fitness center with sauna, Clef d'Or concierge, 24-hour room service, valet service, twice-daily maid service, newspaper delivery, business center, conference rooms, salon, boutiques. Baby-sitting, limousine service, in-room massage available.

EXPENSIVE

In addition to the choices below, you might also want to consider the **Omni Berkshire Place,** 21 E. 52nd St. (☎ **800/THE-OMNI** or 212/753-5800; www.omnihotels. com), which sometimes offers excellent weekend promotions; and the brand-new **Fitzpatrick Grand Central,** 141 E. 44th St. (☎ **800/367-7701** or 212/351-6800; www.fitzpatrickhotels.com), a pleasing Irish-themed hotel from the Dublin-based Fitzpatrick chain.

The Avalon. 16 E. 32nd St. (btw. Fifth and Madison aves.), New York, NY 10016. ☎ **888/ HI-AVALON** or 212/299-7000. Fax 212/299-7001. www.theavalonny.com. 100 units. A/C MINIBAR TV TEL. $195–$350 double, $250–$390 junior suite, $300–$600 deluxe or executive suite. Rates include continental breakfast. Check Web site for special offers. AE, DC, MC, V. Valet parking $23. Subway: 6 to 33rd St.

New York's newest boutique hotel is a mostly suite-filled, amenity-laden ode to luxury—I challenge you to find another hotel in the city that offers 5-foot body pillows in every room (Craig Stoltz of the *Washington Post* claimed that one of these gave him his best night's sleep *ever*). The George Patero–designed interiors are attractively done in muted colors in a sophisticated but comfy Americana style. The basic doubles (there are only 20) are on the small side, but even they come with desks with easy-access dataport and outlets, double-paned windows to block out noise, 27-inch TVs (VCRs on request), two-line speaker phones with conferencing (credit card and toll-free calls are free!), Egyptian cotton and Irish linens, lighted makeup mirrors in the marble bathroom, fluffy Frette bathrobes, coffeemakers with free fixin's, and more—even umbrellas. All suites have pullout sofas and two TVs; expect even more in the most expensive ones, such as whirlpool tubs, cordless phones, and Bose radios. The stylish staff is professional, if a little aloof; still, you can expect to have all your desires met.

Dining/Diversions: The Coach House is the domain of star chef Larry Forgione (of An American Place), so come prepared to have your taste buds tantalized. An expanded continental breakfast is served in the library (7–11am), and tea is available in the afternoons.

Amenities: Clef d'Or concierge, room service (7am–midnight), valet service, newspaper delivery, high-tech conference room, secretarial services; airport "meet and greet" services available. A fitness center was in the plans at press time, but guests have complimentary access to a nearby Bally's Sports club.

Crowne Plaza at the United Nations. 304 E. 42nd St. (just east of Second Aves.), New York, NY 10017. ☎ **800/879-8836** or 212/986-8800. Fax 212/986-1758. www. crowneplaza-un.com or www.crowneplaza.com. 314 units. A/C MINIBAR TV TEL. $229–$379 double, $259–$600 suite. Ask about weekend packages and other discounts, and check online for Internet-only deals. AE, CB, DC, DISC, JCB, MC, V. Valet parking $30 weekdays, $26 weekends. Subway: 4, 5, 6, 7, S to Grand Central.

Here's a very nice chain hotel that boasts all the expected comforts, plus a surprising bit of personality. Housed in a lovely neo-Tudor building, the guest rooms are newly renovated and very well done, with excellent-quality linens and textiles (the towels could be plusher, but the sheets are fabulous) and such extras as 2 two-line phones with dataports and voice mail, good workspace, bedside control panels for everything from air to lights, double-paned windows to shut out street noise, coffeemakers, irons and ironing boards, trouser presses, safes, and Italian marble bathrooms with hair dryers and makeup mirrors. Executive rooms and suites also feature whirlpool tubs, bidets, and a pullout sofa or loveseat. A surprisingly attractive collection of French prints and historic New York City photos gives the entire hotel a nice sense of style. Some may find the far-east location a bit out of the way (Grand Central is a five-minute walk away), but visitors interested in a quiet, attractive neighborhood will find it fits the bill.

Dining/Diversions: Cecil's Bistro features an expansive breakfast buffet staffed by an omelet maker, plus continental fare at lunch and dinner. The smoke-free Regency Lounge is open for cocktails; there's also a bar that allows smoking adjacent to Cecil's.

Amenities: Fitness center with treadmills, lifecycles, Stairmaster, free weights, saunas, and massage. Clef d'Or concierge, 24-hour room service, valet service, newspaper delivery, secretarial services, express checkout, business center. The Crowne Plaza Club lounge for executive and suite guests has a big-screen TV, Internet access, fax, complimentary continental breakfast, and cocktails.

✪ **The Kimberly.** 145 E. 50th St. (btw. Lexington and Third aves.), New York, NY 10022. ☎ **800/683-0400** or 212/755-0400. Fax 212/486-6915. www.citysearch.com/nyc/kimberly. 184 units. A/C TV TEL. $229–$339 double, $279–$799 1-bedroom suite, $429–$689 2-bedroom suite. Extra person $25. Children under 17 stay free in parents' room. Check for online specials or ask about weekend and other special rates. AE, DC, DISC, JCB, MC, V. Valet parking $25. Subway: 6 to 51st St.

Surprisingly good rates on suites mean that you could be standing on your private balcony overlooking Manhattan for a lot less than you'd pay for a cell-like room in many other Midtown hotels. Suites with dining areas, living rooms, fully equipped kitchens, marble baths with deep tubs, and private balconies make up most of the Kimberly, but its regular rooms are handsome and comfortable too, with double beds and minifridges. Additional in-room amenities include two TVs, two-line phones, a fax machine, and plush bathrobes. The entire hotel is done in an attractive and cozy traditional style. Rates can climb in the high seasons, but I was quoted a remarkably good rate of $315 for a one-bedroom accommodating two adults and one child in May, one of the city's busier months. I can't promise that the deals will be that attractive when you call, but in winter '99, one-bedrooms were going for as little as $209—an amazing deal.

Dining/Diversions: American bistro fare is served at the Tam-Tam Bar, while Tatou is a sexy supper club for dinner and dancing that has hosted entertainers ranging from Tony Bennett to Joan Rivers; hotel guests get 25% off menu prices (check to make sure this policy is still in effect when you book). On weekends, three-hour sunset cruises circle Manhattan on the 75-foot New York Health & Racquet Club yacht.

Amenities: Clef d'Or concierge, 24-hour room service, valet service, newspaper delivery, meeting room. Free access to the fabulous New York Health & Racquet Club includes a pool, tennis, squash, and racquetball courts, indoor golf, and any machine you could want. Massages, facials, manicures, and other spa treatments are available at discounted and package rates, with free transportation to the spa included.

The Roger Smith. 501 Lexington Ave. (btw. 47th and 48th), New York, NY 10017. ☎ **800/445-0277** or 212/755-1400. Fax 212/758-4061. www.rogersmith.com. 130 units. A/C TV TEL. $240–$260 double, $295–$400 1-bedroom suite. Rates include continental breakfast. Corporate and weekend rates may be available; check Web site for seasonal Internet specials. AE, CB, DC, DISC, JCB, MC, V. Valet parking $24. Subway: 6 to 51st St.

Here's a great place to stay for those who want the creature comforts of an upscale midtown hotel but like the idea of a few artsy twists. Owner James Knowles has a passion for contemporary art, and his hotel is infused with a real independent spirit. Knowles's own bronzes will greet you at the entrance; he even created the main door pulls in his Connecticut foundry. With a regular clientele oddly made up of Swedish businessmen, Spanish honeymooners, tennis pros, and low-key rockers (Victoria Williams, Barenaked Ladies, Rufus Wainwright) who like the easygoing vibe, the hotel has a quirky appeal that's a welcome relief from the standard East Side stuffiness, but it's straightforward in its comforts. The rooms, larger than most in the neighborhood, are individually decorated, largely in a classic Americana style. All feature firm beds with good pillows, minifridge, coffeemaker, and writing desk (VCRs should be in all rooms by the time you arrive). Suites have well-stocked pantries with microwave. Most bathrooms are older but nicely kept; you'll pay about $20 more to stay on the VIP floors, which have brand-new granite baths with a whirlpool tub. Not perfect—a few minor details could use attention—but an appealing choice nonetheless.

Dining/Diversions: A restaurant/bar serves moderately priced American cuisine with a German flair. The hotel hosts an ongoing series of events, including an annual Iberian Festival in February, regular brown-bag lecture lunches, artist suppers, and rotating fine art shows at the Roger Smith Gallery.

Amenities: Valet service, free local calls, iMac in lobby for e-mail and Internet access, newspapers at breakfast, free video library, 24-hour delivery from local restaurants (with dishes and utensils provided by housekeeping), conference rooms, rooftop deck, access to nearby health club with pool. In-room massage and salon services (facials, nail care) available.

The Waldorf-Astoria and Waldorf Towers. 301 Park Ave. (btw. 49th and 50th sts.), New York, NY 10022. ☎ **800/WALDORF,** 800/774-1500, or 212/355-3000. Fax 212/872-7272 (Astoria) or 212/872-4799 (Towers). www.hilton.com. 1,280 units (119 in the Towers). A/C MINIBAR TV TEL. Waldorf-Astoria: $229–$415 double, $300–$475 suite. Waldorf Towers: $309–$525 double, from $389–$1,445 suite. Ask about corporate, senior, seasonal, and weekend discounts; check online for special packages, with rates sometimes as low as $189 at the Astoria. AE, CB, DC, DISC, EURO, JCB, MC, V. Valet parking $37. Subway: 6 to 51st St.

Other than the Plaza, there's hardly a more elegant address in town, and the legend lives on in much better shape thanks to the $200 million Hilton Hotels spent to renovate this legendary art deco masterpiece. Each room in the main hotel is uniquely decorated, but all feature marble bathrooms and the luxury amenities befitting a hotel of this level. And Hilton deserves extra points for keeping rates comparatively affordable for a property of this stature.

The exquisite, and more exclusive, Waldorf Towers occupies floors 27 to 42 and has a separate entrance. These rooms and suites feature authentic and reproduction English and French antiques, and many have dining rooms, full kitchens, and maid's quarters. The Towers is renowned for its excellent butler service and respect for privacy. The Presidential Suite is aptly named, having cosseted many world leaders. It's quite a dramatic scene when the President is in residence, with paparazzi armed guards out front, stopped traffic in the street, and helicopters buzzing overhead.

Dining/Diversions: There are a number of restaurants to choose from, the most notable being Peacock Alley, the revitalized formal dining room, which deserves the praise it has received thanks to the creative French cooking of Laurent Gras; and Inagiku, serving excellent Japanese food. Sir Harry's Bar is quiet and clubby, but I prefer the Cocktail Terrace, where you can enjoy afternoon tea or evening drinks while a pianist tinkles the ivories on Cole Porter's very own Steinway Grand.

Amenities: Fitness center, concierge, 24-hour room service, valet service, weekday newspaper delivery (executive rooms only), express checkout, business center. Tower services include butler service and two concierges.

W New York. 541 Lexington Ave. (btw. 49th and 50th sts.), New York, NY 10022. ☎ **877/ W-HOTELS** or 212/755-1200. Fax 212/319-8344. www.whotels.com. 717 units. A/C TV MINIBAR TEL. $279–$425 double, from $525 suite. Senior, corporate, or other discounts may be available, as well as weekend rates; inquire or check online booking. AE, CB, DC, DISC, MC, V. Valet parking $34. Subway: 6 to 51st St.

Kudos to Starwood Hotels chief Barry Sternlicht, who has proven that Ian Schrager is not the final word in urban boutique hotels. As conceived by David Rockwell (the man behind such dramatic spaces as Nobu and the newly renovated Grand Central), the brand-new W is meant to be an oasis in the urban jungle, a nature-inspired sanctuary from the stresses of city life—a high-falutin' concept, sure, but one that largely works. The hotel is modern in a thoroughly late '90s way, done in a natural palate with exotic touches and an easygoing shabby-chic style. At its heart is a living room–style lobby, designed to draw in hip New Yorkers as well as guests to its social scene. All warmth and light, it's a great place to lounge over a cocktail or a game of chess.

You'll need the lobby to spread out, because the guest rooms are *small*. They have a beautiful nature-inspired style and feature a heavenly featherbed atop a firm mattress. Other plusses include a 27" TV with VCR and Internet service, CD player, two-line speaker phone, a safe big enough for a laptop, and a signature box of green wheat grass that implores you, in perfect Smith & Hawken style, to WATER ME. The bathrooms boast plush towels but little counter space. The signature rooms are in demand thanks to their unique setup, with a bed floating in the middle of the room and a witty desk that's bigger on style than work space, but go for a standard instead, which gets you a club chair and a bit more space for about the same money.

Dining/Diversions: Heartbeat offers fresh, seasonal cuisine with a healthy bent that the *New York Times'* Ruth Reichl lauded as "a pleasure." There's also Cool Juice, a health bar that purportedly counts Sarah, Duchess of York, among its fans; the lobby Oasis bar; and Whiskey Blue, a new hotspot from nightlife impresario Rande Gerber that's much warmer and more inviting than his Whiskey bar at the Paramount.

Amenities: Excellent 10,000-square-foot spa and health club with tons of equipment, classes, and treatments. Concierge, 24-hour room service, valet service, newspaper delivery, newsstand, high-tech conference facilities, and ballroom. A business center and video and CD library were in the works at press time.

MODERATE

You might also want to consider **Loews New York,** 569 Lexington Ave., at 51st Street (☎ **800/836-6471** or 212/752-7000; www.loewshotels.com/newyork), a perfectly nice chain hotel with business and fitness centers. Rack rates start at $189, but you can often do better—especially if you ask for corporate, AAA, or senior discounts—and cribs and rollaways for the kids are free.

Clarion Hotel Fifth Avenue. 3 E. 40th St. (at Fifth Ave.), New York, NY 10016. ☎ **800/ 252-7466** or 212/447-1500. Fax 212/213-0972. www.hotelchoice.com. 189 units. A/C TV TEL. $159–$375 double. Extra person $15. Children under 18 stay free in parents' room. Ask about senior, AAA, corporate, and promotional deals; check Web site for online booking discounts. AE, CB, DC, DISC, EURO, JCB, MC, V. Parking $19 2 blocks away. Subway: B, D, F, Q to 42nd St.

The location, price, and quality of the accommodations make this former Quality Hotel the best value on Midtown's East Side. Across Fifth Avenue from the New York Public Library, near Grand Central, Rockefeller Center, and Times Square, the hotel is close to Times Square but a notch down on the hustle-and-bustle level. It isn't the most stylish place in town, but it's clean and comfortable, and a full renovation (in progress at press time) will only make things better. Rooms come with either one or two double beds or a queen, a work area, coffeemaker, clock radio, iron and ironing board, and a phone with dataport and free local calls (a great value-added touch). For the best view, ask for a high-floor room ending with the number 5. Wonderful extras that you don't usually find in hotels in this price category include complimentary morning coffee and weekday newspaper, concierge service, limited room service, valet service, business services, and express checkout. You'll have access to a nearby health club for $15.

Helmsley Middletowne Hotel. 148 E. 48th St. (btw. Third and Lexington aves.), New York, NY 10017. ☎ **800/221-4982** or 212/755-3000. Fax 212/832-0261. www.helmsleyhotels. com. 194 units. A/C TV TEL. $170–$270 double, $275–$560 suite. Two children under 12 stay free in parents' room. Ask about special weekend packages. AE, CB, DC, JCB, MC, V. Valet parking $30. Subway: 6 to 51st St.

A converted apartment building that still feels like one, the Middletowne doesn't have room service, a restaurant, or a health club. What it does have are large, relatively affordable rooms and suites (studios and one- and two-bedrooms). Every room has a refrigerator, three two-line phones with dataport, makeup mirrors and hair dryers in the bathroom, and two large closets. The larger suites have fully equipped walk-in kitchenettes, making this an attractive choice for families who want to save on the high cost of eating out (ask for a room with a pull-out sofa bed if you want one). Business travelers can request an in-room fax machine. The Midtown East location is nice and convenient, making this a pretty good deal on all fronts.

INEXPENSIVE

Carlton Arms. 160 E. 25th St. (btw. Lexington and Third aves.), New York, NY 10010. ☎ **212/679-0680** (reservations) or 212/684-8337 (guests). 54 units (20 with private bathrooms). $57–$90 single–triple with shared bathroom, $68–$101 single–triple with private bathroom. Discounts for students and foreign visitors. 10% discount on seven-night stays paid upon arrival. MC, V. Parking $16 nearby. Subway: 6 to 23rd St.

The motto at the Carlton Arms is THIS AIN'T NO HOLIDAY INN—and boy, ain't that the truth. The true spirit of bohemianism and artistic freedom reigns in this backpacker's delight of a hotel, where every room is a work of art executed by an edgy artist given full license to go hog wild. Some spaces are sublime, such as Robin Banks's Cartoon Room (#5B), Thias Charbonet's Underwater Room (#1A), the ocean-blue lobby (complete with fishes in the TV), and the stunning first-floor mosaic bathroom. Others are simply bizarre. Whether you end up with a mermaid mural or a wall of teddy bears, you'll see why this is the most extraordinary hotel in the city.

But if you're looking for creature comforts and modern conveniences, this is *not* the place for you. The cramped rooms are basic—*very* basic. The beds are lumpy, there's no air-conditioning, and everything's old and on the crusty side. Each room has a sink, but you'll most likely end up sharing a hallway bathroom with your fellow budget travelers: mainly students, foreign travelers, and fellow existentialists looking for an experience beyond the ordinary. The place is kept clean, but there's no maid service during your stay. On the upside, the staff is super-friendly, and they'll be happy to take phone messages for you in the office (there's a pay phone in the lobby for outgoing calls). Reserve

ⓗ Family-Friendly Hotels

Once upon a time, traveling children were regarded by New York hotels as little more than an inconvenience. Then New York was reborn as a family-friendly city, and many New York hotels now make it attractive for parents to take along the younger set.

Doubletree Guest Suites *(p. 96)*   Your young ones will have their very own Kids Club (for ages 3 to 12), with a playroom, an arts-and-crafts center, and computer and video games. For after playtime, there's an entire floor of child-proof suites, complete with kitchenettes and living rooms, for just about the same price you'd pay for a standard room in another hotel.

The Gorham *(p. 97)*   This well-located Midtown choice is another good deal for families, since the large rooms are big enough for two queen beds, and the well-priced suites feature pull-out sofas in the living rooms to accommodate the kids. A fully equipped kitchenette with microwave will make the 'rents happy, and Nintendo on the TV will keep Junior occupied for hours.

Gramercy Park Hotel *(p. 87)*   There are no special amenities that make this moderately priced, old-world hotel particularly kid-friendly, but you'll see a lot of youngsters cruising the wood-paneled lobby nonetheless. That's because parents end up with a lot of space for their money here: Standard doubles are big enough for two double beds, still with play space to spare, and some suites have pullout sofas that make them large enough to sleep six.

Novotel New York *(p. 98)*   This Midtown West branch of the French chain is particularly kid-friendly: Two children under 16 can sleep free in their parents' room, and both receive complimentary breakfast in the hotel's restaurant. In the lobby, the Children's Corner has a Lego table, and the cafe boasts a kids' menu.

Hotel Beacon *(p. 116)*   Ideally located in one of the city's most kid-friendly neighborhoods, the Beacon is one of the best deals in town for families. Fitted with two double beds, virtually all of the spacious standard rooms are big enough for wallet-watching families. For a bit more money, the one- and two-bedroom suites are great bargains that give families room to spread out. Every room features a fully stocked kitchenette that makes breakfast and snacktime a cinch, and there's a laundromat on site to make mom and dad's life easier.

The Milburn *(p. 119)*   This budget-minded neighbor to the Beacon also offers rooms with kitchenettes in the same great neighborhood, but for less. The Milburn may not be quite as nice as the Beacon, but it offers equal value for your dollar, and the one-bedroom suites with a pullout queen sofa are a great bargain for families.

one to two months in advance, because despite the inconveniences, this place is almost always full.

Hotel 31. 120 E. 31st St. (btw. Park and Lexington aves.), New York, NY 10016. ☎ **212/685-3060.** Fax 212/532-1232. www.citysearch.com/nyc/hotel17. 90 units (about half with private bathroom). A/C TV TEL. $85–$130 double. Rates include tax. No credit cards. Parking about $20 on next block. Subway: 6 to 33rd St.

This sibling to trendy Hotel 17 (see "The Flatiron District & Gramercy Park," above) is situated in a quiet, mostly residential neighborhood that's not quite as lovely as the 17th Street location, but just fine nonetheless. The former SRO (the hotel still houses a number of permanent single-room-occupancy tenants) has been reinvented in much the same way as Hotel 17, with quirkily attractive but very basic rooms. They're dark and downright miniscule, but come with air-conditioning, alarm clocks, hair dryers, and voice mail. About half have private bathrooms; if you choose to save a few dollars and share, you'll have access to nice, newish bathrooms. Not all of the no-bath rooms have their own sinks, so be sure to request one when booking. The management renovates as tenants leave, so also ask for a recently renovated room, as I spotted a few beginning signs of wear in the older ones. Since the hotel is most popular with—and most suited to—younger travelers and Europeans, there's lots of smoking going on, and ashtrays in the public spaces don't exactly discourage it; as a result, the narrow hallways tend to smell like cigarettes. Avid non-smokers may want to book elsewhere.

Pickwick Arms Hotel. 230 E. 51st St. (btw. Second and Third aves.), New York, NY 10022. ☎ **800/PICKWIK** in the U.S., 800/874-0074 in Canada, or 212/355-0300. Fax 212/755-5029. 320 units (200 with private bathroom). A/C TV TEL. $70–$99 single, $125–$160 double. AE, CB, DC, MC, V. Parking $28 nearby. Subway: 6 to 51st St.

What keeps the Pickwick booked up well in advance is its prices—for a Midtown hotel on the East Side, this is like entering an economic time warp. The location, in one of the city's most prestigious neighborhoods, couldn't be better. The older, sometimes astoundingly small rooms are spare (think monk's cell), but they're well kept, and the entire place is safe and well-run. This former SRO has a few doubles and twins with private bathrooms (the larger deluxe twins can accommodate a rollaway for a third person), but the majority of rooms are singles with private, semi-private, or shared hall bathrooms. Two friends traveling together can take advantage of the semi-private situation: Two singles—each with their own sink, TV, desk, small closet, and telephone—that share a bathroom can be had for the same price as a twin room. All of the bathrooms are worn-looking and have showers only, but they're clean. A renovation is spiffing up the halls and some rooms a bit. Still, don't expect anything more than the basics—but if you want a great location and you're on a tight budget, this is a good choice. On site is a rooftop patio with skyline views; Scarabee, a good but pricey French-Mediterranean restaurant; and a wine bar that also serves breakfast.

11 The Upper West Side

See the "Uptown Accommodations" map (pp. 116-117) for hotels in this section.

VERY EXPENSIVE

✪ **Trump International Hotel & Tower.** 1 Central Park West (at 60th St.), New York, NY 10023. ☎ **888/44-TRUMP** or 212/299-1000. Fax 212/299-1150. www.citysearch/nyc/trumphotel. 167 units. A/C MINIBAR TV TEL. $475–$525 double, $750–$950 1-bedroom suite, $1,500 2-bedroom suite. Children stay free in parents' room. AE, CB, DC, JCB, MC, V. Valet parking $42. Subway: 1, 9, A, B, C, D to Columbus Circle.

Forget all your preconceptions about The Donald—this is a surprisingly cultivated venture from the ultimate 1980s Bad Boy.

New in 1997, Trump International is housed on 14 lower floors of a freestanding 52-story mirrored monolith at the southwest corner of Central Park, with unobstructed views on all sides. The rooms are on the small side, but high ceilings and smart design make them feel uncluttered. They're beautifully done in an understated contemporary style, with clean-lined furniture, beautiful fabrics, and soothing earth tones. Floor-to-ceiling windows maximize the spectacular views, which are especially breathtaking on the park-facing side. In addition to the standard luxury amenities, each room is equipped with a fax machine, VCR, CD stereo, Jacuzzi tub in the marble bathroom, excellent bathrobes, umbrellas, and a telescope for taking in the views. Suites also have a European-style kitchen stocked with china and crystal.

But what really sets this hotel apart is its signature services. Each guest is assigned a Trump Attaché who basically functions as your own personal concierge, providing comprehensive business and personal services and, following your stay, recording your preferences to have on hand for your next visit. For the ultimate in romance and convenience, you can arrange in advance to have a chef from Jean Georges cook and prepare a mulitcourse meal right in your suite's own kitchen.

Dining: Awarded the coveted four stars by the *New York Times,* Jean Georges serves excellent contemporary French cuisine by one of the city's most celebrated chefs (see chapter 6). Unfortunately, word is that not enough reservations are put aside for guests, so be sure to book a table well ahead.

Amenities: Amazing 6,000-foot health and fitness spa with pool, steam rooms, saunas, personal trainers, and a full slate of spa treatments. Personal attaché service, 24-hour room service, valet service (with complimentary overnight pressing), free local phone calls, newspaper delivery, business center. Cell phones, computers, and printers upon request.

MODERATE

✪ **Country Inn the City.** W. 77th St. (btw. Broadway and West End Ave.), New York, NY 10024. (Exact address omitted by request of owner.) ☎ **212/580-4183.** Fax 212/874-3981. www.countryinnthecity.com. 4 units. A/C TV TEL. $160–$185 double. No sales tax added for stays of 7 nights or more. No credit cards. 3-night minimum. Maximum 2 guests per apartment. No credit cards. Parking $25 nearby. Subway: 1, 9 to 79th St. No children under 12.

This charming townhouse is rich with original details, impeccable Americana-style decor, and more homey comforts than you'll find anywhere else for the price. Each guestroom is actually a full studio apartment, with a cozy sofa, dining area, and a gorgeous, supremely comfortable queen bed in the large, high-ceilinged bedroom, as well as a big, fully outfitted galley kitchenette and a spacious, pretty bathroom. The whole place is bright and elegant, and the appointments, from the Oriental carpets covering the hardwood floors to the (nonworking) fireplaces that grace every room, couldn't be finer. Wonderful portraits in oil, tasteful collectibles, and brandy and fresh fruit on hand make these rooms really feel like home—maybe even much nicer than home. My favorite is no. 4, done in soft yellow with a high poster bed and whitewashed floorboards, but which one you'll like best all depends on your tastes. Front-facing no. 5 has another four-poster with a soft-as-can-be denim bedcover, plus a great new kitchen and bath. No. 2 is a bit darker and features the most beautiful tile fireplace I've ever seen. No. 6 is the smallest, with a pretty sleigh bed in the corner, a smaller kitchenette, and a shower only in the bathroom, but its fabulous private terrace more than makes up the difference. Everything is immaculate, thanks to a resident housekeeper who provides maid service every other day. A quiet, peaceful air pervades the house, and the neighborhood couldn't be nicer. An excellent choice in every respect. No smoking is allowed.

Excelsior Hotel. 45 W. 81st St. (off Central Park West), New York, NY 10024. ☎ **800/ 368-4575** or 212/362-9200. Fax 212/721-2994. 169 rms. A/C TV TEL. $179–$209 double, $229–$309 1-bedroom suite, $409–$528 2-bedroom suite. AE, DISC, MC, V. Parking $27 2 blocks away. Subway: B, C to 81st St./Museum of Natural History.

Located across the street from the Museum of Natural History on an excellent block, this former budget hotel has been upgraded to suit its chic location, and now makes a good choice for mid-price travelers looking for a nice residential setting. The freshly redone guest rooms are bright and boast commodious closets (with irons and ironing boards), voice mail and dataports on the two-line phones, alarms, hair dryers, and full-length dressing mirrors (a nice touch). The pretty new bathrooms are most impressive—not big, but they make the most of their limited space. Expect to pay more for the sunny museum-facing rooms. Renovations are ongoing at press time: By the time

Uptown Accommodations

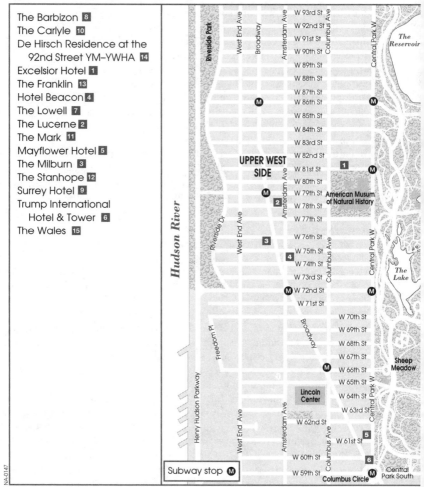

The Barbizon **8**
The Carlyle **10**
De Hirsch Residence at the
    92nd Street YM–YWHA **14**
Excelsior Hotel **1**
The Franklin **13**
Hotel Beacon **4**
The Lowell **7**
The Lucerne **2**
The Mark **11**
Mayflower Hotel **5**
The Milburn **3**
The Stanhope **12**
Surrey Hotel **9**
Trump International
    Hotel & Tower **6**
The Wales **15**

Subway stop Ⓜ

you arrive, you should find an expanded lobby and a breakfast room, plus fitness and business centers. Concierge and valet service are already available. Around the corner from Columbus Avenue's boutiques and less than a block from Central Park, the location is prime Upper West Side—don't be surprised if you spot a celebrity or two cruising the 'hood. I like the Beacon and the Lucerne better—both have better services, are more convenient to the subway, and have features that make them much better values (see below). Still, the Excelsior is a good, comfortable choice.

✪ **Hotel Beacon.** 2130 Broadway (at 75th St.), New York, NY 10023. ☎ **800/572-4969** or 212/787-1100. Fax 212/724-0839. www.beaconhotel.com. 210 units. A/C TV TEL. $145–$165 single, $170–$185 double, $205–$450 suite. Extra person $15. Children under 17 stay free in parents' room. AE, DC, DISC, MC, V. Parking $25 nearby. Subway: 1, 2, 3, 9 to 72nd St.

Ideally located in one of the city's most desirable neighborhoods, only a few blocks from Lincoln Center, Central Park, and the Museum of Natural History, the Beacon is one the best deals in town, especially for families. Every generously sized room features a fully stocked kitchenette (with cooktop, coffeemaker, minifridge, and microwave),

roomy closet, alarm, voice mail on the phone, and new marble bathroom with hair dryer. Rooms won't win any personality awards, but they're freshly done in muted florals, and linens are plush. Virtually all standard rooms feature two double beds, and they're spacious enough to sleep a family on a budget. The big one- and two-bedroom suites are some of the best bargains in the city; each has two closets and a pull-out sofa in the well-furnished living room. The two-bedrooms have a second bathroom, making them well-outfitted enough to house a small army. Another fab family-friendly extra is the self-service laundromat. There's no room service, but with gourmet markets like Zabar's and Fairway nearby, cooking is an attractive alternative, and there are plenty of restaurants nearby. Concierge and valet service are available, plus access to a terrific nearby health club for a daily fee. All in all, a great place to stay—and a great value to boot.

✪ **The Lucerne.** 201 W. 79th St. (at Amsterdam Ave.), New York, NY 10024. ☎ **800/ 492-8122** or 212/875-1000. Fax 212/579-2408. www.newyorkhotel.com/lucerne. 250 units. AC TV TEL. $150–$230 double, $190–$240 junior (queen) suite, $220–$450 1-bedroom suite. AAA discounts offered; check Web site for special Internet deals. AE, DC, DISC, MC, V. Parking $16 nearby. Subway: 1, 9 to 79th St.

Want top-notch comforts and service without paying top-dollar prices? Then book into this Mobil four-star, AAA three-diamond hotel, one of the best values in the city. As soon as the morning-suited doorman greets you at the entrance to the 1903 land-mark building, you'll know you're getting more for your money than you expected. The bright marble lobby leads to comfortable guest rooms done in a tasteful Ameri-cana style. The standard rooms are big enough for a king, queen, or two doubles (great for those traveling with kids). All rooms have Nintendo, coffeemakers, alarms, two-line phones with voice mail and dataport (although not always near the work desk), irons and ironing boards, and attractive bathrooms with hair dryers, spacious traver-tine counters, and good toiletries. Everything is fresh and immaculate. The suites also boast very nice kitchenttes with microwave and minifridge, terry robes, and sitting rooms with sofas and extra TVs and Nintendo sets. The queen suites are a great deal for couples willing to spend a few extra dollars, while the larger suites with two queens or a king and pullout sofa give families the room they need (although Mom and Dad might get more space for their money at the Beacon).

The Lucerne prides itself on its excellent service record, so expect your needs to be promptly attended to. Amenities include a better-than-average fitness center with cardio machines and free weights, room service (7am–midnight), valet service, secre-tarial services (a business center was in the works at press time), and meeting space with a terrific rooftop sundeck. On site is Wilson's, a Upper West Side hotspot fea-turing good Continental fare and even better live jazz three or four nights a week.

Mayflower Hotel. 15 Central Park West (at 61st St.), New York, NY 10023. ☎ **800/ 223-4164** or 212/265-0060. Fax 212/265-0227. www.mayflowerhotel.com. 365 units. A/C TV TEL. $180–$220 single, $195–$235 double, $230–$310 suite, $500–$1,000 penthouse ter-race or 2-bedroom suite. AE, CB, DC, DISC, ER, JCB, MC, V. Parking $28 nearby. Subway: 1, 9, A, B, C, D to Columbus Circle. Small pets accepted.

Set on the edge of Central Park near Lincoln Center, the Mayflower has a spectacular location—in prime Upper West Side territory, but just a stone's throw from the hustle and bustle of Midtown. The rooms are spacious (with two doubles, two queens, or a king) and all feature walk-in closets, a service pantry with a fridge, and voice mail. Bathrooms are fine, although some could use regrouting; all boast hair dryers, and makeup mirrors were in the works at press time. You'll pay more for park views, but they're fabulous. On site you'll find the good Conservatory restaurant and a well-outfitted fitness center, plus ATM, fax, and currency exchange machines in the lobby. Free newspapers are also available in the lobby, and coffee and cookies are set out on weekends. Valet service and limited room service (7am to midnight) are available. All in all, not a great deal—the Beacon is a better value, as are the suites at the Lucerne—but a perfectly fine place to stay. We've received some complaints in the past about inconsistent service, however, so please let us know if you have a problem.

INEXPENSIVE
✪ **Hotel Newton.** 2528 Broadway (btw. 94th and 95th sts.), New York, NY 10025. ☎ **888/ HOTEL58** or 212/678-6500. Fax 212/678-6758. www.newyorkhotel.com/newton. 120 units (10 with shared bathroom). A/C TV TEL. $85 single or double with shared bathroom, $99–$135 single or double with private bathroom, $150 suite. Extra person $15. Children under 17 stay free. AAA discounts available; check Web site for special Internet deals. AE, DC, DISC, MC, V. Parking $14 nearby. Subway: 1, 2, 3, 9 to 96th St.

Finally—an inexpensive hotel that's actually *nice.* Unlike many of its peers, the Newton doesn't scream "budget!" at every turn, or require you to have the carefree atti-tude of a college student to put up with it. As you enter the pretty lobby, you're greeted by a uniformed staff that's attentive and professional. The rooms are generally large, with good, firm beds, a work desk, and a sizable new bathroom, plus roomy closets in

most (a few of the cheapest have wall racks only). Some are big enough to accommodate families with two doubles or two queen beds. The suites feature two queen beds
in the bedroom, a sofa in the sitting room, plus niceties like a microwave, minifridge,
iron and board, and hair dryer, making them well worth the few extra dollars. The
bigger rooms and suites have been upgraded with cherry-wood furnishings, but even
the older laminated furniture is much nicer than I usually see in this price range. The
AAA-approved hotel is impeccably kept, and there was lots of sprucing up going on—
new drapes here, fresh paint there—during my last visit. The nice neighborhood
boasts lots of affordable restaurants, and a cute diner in the same block provides room
service from 6am to 1am. The 96th Street express subway stop is just a block away,
providing convenient access to the rest of the city. A great bet all the way around.

✪ **The Milburn.** 242 W. 76th St. (btw. Broadway and West End Ave.), New York, NY 10023.
☎ **800/833-9622** or 212/362-1006. Fax 212/721-5476. www.milburnhotel.com. 111
units. A/C TV TEL. $119–$145 studio double, $149–$175 1-bedroom suite, depending on
season. Extra person $10. Children under 12 stay free in parents' room. AE, CB, DC, MC, V.
Parking $16–$20. Subway: 1, 2, 3, 9 to 72nd St.

On a quiet side street a block from the Beacon, the Milburn also offers rooms with
kitchenettes in the same great neighborhood for less. The Milburn may not be quite
as nice as the Beacon, but it offers equal value for your dollar, and arguably better in
the less busy seasons, when a double studio goes for just $119. Every room is rife with
amenities: dining area, safe, iron and ironing board, hair dryer, two-line phone with
dataport, alarm, nice newish bath, and kitchenette with minifridge, microwave, coffeemaker (with free coffee!), hot plate on request, and all the necessary equipment. The
one-bedroom suites also boast a pullout queen sofa and a work desk. Don't expect
much from the decor, and the laminated furniture is clearly a cheaper grade than what
you'll get at the Beacon, but everything is attractive and in good shape. In fact, the
whole place is spotless. But what makes the Milburn a real find is that it's more
service-oriented than most hotels in this price range. The friendly staff will do everything from providing free copy, fax, and e-mail services to picking up your laundry at
the dry cleaners next door. Additional facilities include a self-serve laundromat, VCR
rentals, wheelchair-accessible rooms, discount dining programs at local restaurants,
and use of the nearby Equinox health club for a special $15 fee (usually $35). At press
time, a small workout room was in the works.

12 The Upper East Side

See the "Uptown Accommodations" map (pp. 116-117) for hotels in this section.

VERY EXPENSIVE

✪ **The Carlyle.** 35 E. 76th St. (at Madison Ave.), New York, NY 10021. ☎ **800/227-5737**
or 212/744-1600. Fax 212/717-4682. 180 units. A/C MINIBAR TV TEL. $375–$650 double,
$600–$2,500 suite. AE, DC, MC, V. Valet parking $39. Subway: 6 to 77th St. Pets accepted.

If you've ever wondered how the rich and famous live, check into the Carlyle. Countless movie stars and international heads of states (including JFK, who was supposedly
once visited by Marilyn here) have lain their heads on the fluffy pillows. Why they
choose the Carlyle is clear—its hallmark attention to detail. With a staff-to-guest ratio
of about two-to-one, service is simply the best. The English manor–style decor is luxurious but not excessive, creating the comfortably elegant ambiance of an Upper East
Side apartment. The guest rooms range from singles to seven-room suites, some with
terraces and pantries. All have marble bathrooms with whirlpool tubs and all the
amenities you'd expect from a hotel of this caliber—even CD players and fax machines
in every room.

Dining/Diversions: Outfitted with the requisite Chinese screens and English hunting prints, the Carlyle Restaurant features formal French dining in the evening as well as lavish breakfast and lunch buffets. Less stuffy but still dressy is Cafe Carlyle, the supper club where living legend Bobby Short and other big names entertain, which makes for an expensive but memorable night on the town (see chapter 9). Both rooms serve up a legendary Sunday brunch, à la carte in the restaurant and buffet-style in the cafe. Charming Bemelmans Bar (named after children's book illustrator Ludwig Bemelmans, who created the Madeline books and painted the mural here) is a wonderful spot for cocktails, and the Gallery serves afternoon tea.

Amenities: High-tech fitness center with sauna and massage room, concierge, 24-hour room service, valet service, twice-daily maid service, banquet rooms. Business and secretarial services—as well as just about anything else you might need—are available.

✪ **The Lowell.** 28 E. 63rd St. (btw. Park and Madison aves.), New York, NY 10021. ☎ **800/221-4444** or 212/838-1400. Fax 212/605-6808. www.preferredhotels.com. 65 units. A/C MINIBAR TV TEL. $345 single, $445 double, $545–$915 1-bedroom suite, from $1,015 2-bedroom suite. Extra person $35. Inquire about weekend rates and romance packages. AE, DC, ER, JCB, MC, V. Valet parking $45. Subway: B, Q to Lexington Ave. Small pets (less than 15 lbs.) accepted.

Housed in a historic landmark building on a lovely tree-lined street, this quietly elegant boutique hotel is a real gem. From the moment you enter the refined deco-French Empire lobby with its signed Edgar Brandt console, you know you're in a posh place. The Lowell has a distinct air of exclusivity about it, but without being snobbish. About two-thirds of the rooms are suites. In addition to fine old-world antiques, expect all the luxuries, from VCRs, multiline phones, and fax machines to Scandinavian down comforters, king-size feather pillows, and Frette terry robes. The marble-and-brass baths have makeup mirrors and Gilchrist & Soames toiletries. Each suite has a fully equipped kitchenette but is otherwise unique, with such features as wood-burning fireplaces, full dining rooms, a garden terrace, or even a private gym (this is the one Madonna chose, natch), so be sure to inquire about the available options.

Dining/Diversions: Called one of the ten best steakhouses in America by *Wine Spectator,* the highly regarded Post House serves giant steaks and lobsters in a classic American setting. Festooned in English chintz, the Pembroke Room serves breakfast, weekend brunch, and a supremely elegant afternoon tea that's perfect for purists (seasonal, so call ahead).

Amenities: Concierge, 24-hour room service, fitness center, valet service, free daily newspaper delivery, twice-daily maid service, express checkout, conference rooms. In-room massage, baby-sitting, video rentals, secretarial services available.

✪ **The Mark.** 25 E. 77th St. (btw. Fifth and Madison aves.), New York, NY 10021. ☎ **800/THE-MARK** in the U.S., 800/223-6800 in Canada, or 212/744-4300. Fax 212/744-2749. www.themarkhotel.com. 180 units. A/C MINIBAR TV TEL. $455–$530 double, from $650 suite. Extra person $30. Children under 16 stay free in parents' room. Corporate rates available; ask about weekend packages, which can go as low as $299. AE, CB, DC, DISC, JCB, MC, V. Valet parking $35. Subway: 6 to 77th St.

After a $35-million renovation, the Mark positioned itself as the Carlyle's chief rival. Located in the heart of a tony neighborhood that makes an ideal base for museum goers and boutique shoppers, it's superbly elegant and somewhat more contemporary in feeling than the Carlyle. Behind the 1929 building's art deco facade is a neoclassical decor and a wonderful air of tranquility. The lobby's custom-designed Biedermeier furniture and marble floors prepare you for the lovely guest rooms, which are larger than most and feature king-size beds with Frette triple sheeting, overstuffed chairs, upholstered sofas, and museum-quality art. Fresh flowers, two-line phones, fax machines,

In case you want to see the world.

At American Express, we're here to make your journey a smooth one. So we have over 1,700 travel service locations in over 130 countries ready to help. What else would you expect from the world's largest travel agency?

do more **AMERICAN EXPRESS** Travel

Call 1 800 AXP-3429 or visit
www.americanexpress.com/travel

In case you want to be welcomed there.

We're here to see that you're always welcomed at establishments everywhere. That's why millions of people carry the American Express® Card – for peace of mind, confidence, and security, around the world or just around the corner.

do more AMERICAN EXPRESS

Cards

To apply, call 1 800 THE-CARD
or visit www.americanexpress.com

In case you're running low.

We're here to help with more than 190,000 Express Cash locations around the world. In order to enroll, just call American Express at 1 800 CASH-NOW before you start your vacation.

do more   AMERICAN EXPRESS

Express Cash

And in case you'd rather be safe than sorry.

We're here with American Express® Travelers Cheques. They're the safe way to carry money on your vacation, because if they're ever lost or stolen you can get a refund, practically anywhere or anytime. To find the nearest place to buy Travelers Cheques, call 1 800 495-1153. Another way we help you do more.

do more AMERICAN EXPRESS

Travelers Cheques

VCRs, terry robes, and even umbrellas are standard, and many rooms even have fully outfitted kitchenettes. The bathrooms have oversized tubs, heated towel racks, and luxury toiletries. The GM has been named one of the top ten in the world, so it comes as no surprise that the service is beyond reproach.

Dining/Diversions: One of the best hotel restaurants in the city, Mark's serves chef David Paulstich's consistently—and deservedly—high-rated New American–fusion cuisine in an elegant wood-paneled setting. The three-course pre-theater dinner is an excellent value and the Sunday brunch is one of New York's all-time best, while afternoon tea is a new institution among Upper East Side ladies. Mark's Bar serves hors d'oeuvres and cocktails.

Amenities: Award-winning concierge, 24-hour room service, fitness center with sauna, valet service, free newspaper delivery, twice-daily maid service, conference and banquet rooms, complimentary weekday car service to Wall Street, and Friday and Saturday evening car service to Theater District. Secretarial services, baby-sitting, and in-room massage available.

The Stanhope. 995 Fifth Ave. (at 81st St.), New York, NY 10028. ☎ **800/828-1123** or 212/288-5800. Fax 212/517-0088. www.citysearch/nyc/thestanhope or www.thestanhope. com. 185 units. A/C MINIBAR TV TEL. $395 deluxe double, $475 junior suite, $525–$1,450 luxury suite. AE, CB, DC, DISC, ER, EURO, JCB, MC, V. Valet parking $38. Subway: 6 to 77th St.

If you can afford it, here's the ideal hotel for museum lovers: The Stanhope is in prime museum territory, right on Fifth Avenue across from the Metropolitan Museum of Art and Central Park. The Stanhope's new owners have reconfigured the guest rooms, but the essential style remains unchanged. Still, it has a nouveau-hip vibe, thanks to the trendy Blue Bongo Bar, plus recent visits from hot celebs like Winona Ryder and Lenny Kravitz. The Versailles-inspired lobby shows off Louis XIV antiques, gold-leaf moldings, and museum-quality Gobelin tapestries. The guest rooms are furnished in a luxe French Empire style with chinoiserie accents. Besides the standard high-tech amenities (VCR, 2 two-line phones, and so on), other fabulous touches include Egyptian cotton sheets and thick terry robes. The suites on the park are gorgeous. Service is impeccable.

Dining/Diversions: With a kitchen headed by celebrity chef Matthew Kenney, Cafe M serves up terrific Mediterranean cuisine in a slick, modern dining room. The Terrace has upper Fifth Avenue's only sidewalk cafe, offering incomparable people-watching. The Gerard Room is a clubby cigar lounge, while the retro-luxe, ultra-hip Blue Bongo Bar is a tribute to New York's jazz age, complete with vintage jukebox spinning Charlie Parker, Miles Davis, and friends.

Amenities: State-of-the-art fitness center with sauna, concierge, 24-hour room service, twice-daily maid service, valet service, newspaper delivery, express checkout, conference rooms, and lending library. Baby-sitting, business and secretarial services, weekday car service to Midtown and Wall Street, evening car service to Broadway theaters, and in-room massage available.

Surrey Hotel. 20 E. 76th St. (at Madison Ave.), New York, NY 10021. ☎ **800/ME-SUITE** or 212/320-8027. Fax 212/465-3697. www.mesuite.com. 130 units. A/C TV TEL. From $328 studio suite, from $383 1-bedroom suite, from $699 2-bedroom suite. Extra person $20. Children under 13 stay free in parents' room. Check Web site for special offers. AE, DC, DISC, JCB, MC, V. Valet parking $35. Subway: 6 to 77th St.

Thanks in large part to the presence of world-renowned chef Daniel Boulud, the Surrey has gone from best-kept secret to sought-after hotel. But the Surrey can hold its own even though the four-star restaurant Daniel has moved to other digs (the more relaxed Café Boulud has taken its place; see below). This all-suite lodging is ideally located in a pristine (if prim) Upper East Side neighborhood, near Central Park, Madison Avenue boutiques, and Museum Mile. Done in an 18th-century English parlor style, the lobby sets the tone for the well-appointed guest rooms. Rates are high, but at least you get a lot for your money: Each suite comes with a fully equipped kitchen with microwave (the staff will even stock up for you upon request), two-line speaker phones, a dining area and/or sitting area (the one- and two-bedrooms have both), and a large bathroom with terry robes.

Dining: The domain of one of the country's best chefs, Daniel Boulud, Café Boulud serves pricey traditional French and seasonal cuisine that's worth every penny—and then some, in fact (see chapter 6).

Amenities: Concierge, room service from Café Boulud (daily 7–10pm), fitness center, self-service laundromat, valet service, newspaper delivery, grocery shopping service, conference rooms. Secretarial services available.

EXPENSIVE

The Barbizon. 140 E. 63rd St. (at Lexington Ave.), New York, NY 10021. ☎ **800/ 223-1020** or 212/838-5700. Fax 212/888-4271. 300 units. A/C MINIBAR TV TEL. $230–$350 double, $400–$1,200 suite. Children under 12 stay free in parents' room using existing bedding. AE, DC, DISC, MC, V. Valet parking $29. Subway: B, Q to 63rd St.

This neo-Gothic building has been famous since the 1920s, when it began as a women-only hostelry where Grace Kelly, Candace Bergen, and Sylvia Plath (who wrote about it in *The Bell Jar*) all stayed over the years. Then it served as a nothing-special hotel, perfect for putting up visiting parents who wanted to stay safely and conveniently in Midtown near Bloomingdale's and Central Park. But after a $40-million renovation in 1997, the Barbizon has been transformed. Tower Suites have been added, the art deco elegance of the lobby has returned, and the rooms are decorated with custom iron headboards and contemporary furniture and artwork. In-room amenities include two-line speakerphones and CD players (the hotel maintains a musical lending library).

Dining/Diversions: There's a breakfast room (continental $14.50 per person, full $17.50), a lobby bar and lounge, and a health-food cafe in the fitness club.

Amenities: Complimentary access to on-site Equinox Fitness Club, with a pool and spa, concierge, 24-hour room service, valet service, newspaper delivery. Business/ secretarial services available.

INEXPENSIVE

De Hirsch Residence at the 92nd Street YM–YWHA. 1395 Lexington Ave. (at 92nd St.), New York, NY 10128. ☎ **888/699-6884,** or 212/415-5650. Fax 212/415-5578. www.92ndsty.org. 372 units (none with private bathroom). A/C. $69 single, $90 double; long-term stays (2 months or more) $795/month single, $1,100–$1,300/month double. Must be at least 18, and no older than 30 for long-term stays. AE, MC, V. Parking $20 nearby. Subway: 4, 5, 6 to 86th St.; 6 to 96th St.

Travelers on a tight budget should contact the 92nd Street Y well in advance. The de Hirsch Residence offers basic but comfortable rooms, each with either one or two single beds, a dresser, and bookshelves. Each floor has a large communal bathroom, a fully equipped kitchen/dining room with microwave, and laundry facilities. The building is rather institutional looking but it's well kept and secure, the staff is friendly, and the location is terrific. This high-rent Upper East Side neighborhood is just blocks from Central Park and Museum Mile, and there's plenty of cheap eats and places to pick up meal fixings within a few blocks. Daily maid service and use of the Y's state-of-the-art fitness facility (pool, weights, racquetball, aerobics) are included in the daily rates, making this a stellar deal. This is a great bet for lone travelers in particular, since the 92nd Street Y is a community center in a true sense of the word, offering a real sense of kinship and a mind-boggling slate of top-rated cultural happenings (see chapter 9).

Dining 6

Attention, foodies: Welcome to Mecca. Without a doubt, New York is the best restaurant town in the country, and one of the top in the world. Other cities might have particular specialties—Paris has better bistros, of course, Hong Kong better Chinese, Los Angeles better Mexican, Austin better barbecue—but no culinary capital spans the globe so successfully as the Big Apple.

That's due in part to New York's vibrant immigrant mix. Let a newcomer arrive and see that his or her native foods aren't being served and *zap!*—there's a new restaurant, cafe, or grocery to fill the void. Yet we New Yorkers can be fickle: One moment a restaurant is hot; the next it's passé. So restaurants close with a frequency we wish applied to the arrival of subway trains. Always call ahead.

But there's one thing we all have to face sooner or later: Eating in New York just ain't cheap. The primary cause? The high cost of real estate, which is reflected in what you're charged. Wherever you're from, particularly if you're from the reasonably priced American heartland, New York's restaurants will seem *expensive.* Yet good value abounds, especially if you're willing to eat ethnic, and venture beyond tourist zones into the neighborhoods where budget-challenged New Yorkers eat, like Chinatown and the Upper West Side. (The East Village is particularly good for getting a lot of bang for your buck.) But even if you have no intention of venturing beyond Times Square, don't worry: I've included inexpensive restaurants in every neighborhood, including some of the city's best-kept secrets, so you'll know where to get good value for your money no matter where you are in Manhattan.

WHAT'S HAPPENING

Thanks to a booming economy and an optimistic outlook, New York is home to more good restaurants than ever before. Whole new districts have sprouted up; the Flatiron District has become a "Restaurant Row" unto itself, sparkling with wonderful splurge-worthy restaurants. The East Village has become ground zero for affordable quality dining, with excellent restaurants at every turn. For the best of what the city has to offer, take a moment to check out "Best Dining Bets" in chapter 1, if you haven't already.

New York is always a hotbed of experimentation, and the current scene is no exception: The cuisines of the moment are South American, Indian, and Belgian—but fads come and go so quickly, who knows what will be in by the time you arrive? Always-popular Japanese is bigger than ever before, with long lines snaking out of even mediocre sushi joints.

Less successful has been Indian fusion, a new hybrid cuisine that blends Eastern spices with Western cooking techniques. It's a cuisine that's not yet fully formed, and the restaurants I've tried have been lacking. If the idea tickles your tastebuds anyway, word is that your best bet is the $48 prix-fixe at Danny Meyer's **Tabla**, 11 Madison Ave., at 25th Street (☎ **212/889-0667**). Meyer, the man behind Union Square Cafe and Gramercy Tavern, is a restaurant genius, so you shouldn't be disappointed.

There are three major trends that transcend culinary lines, all products of a thriving dining scene. The first is what I like to call The Big Squeeze: The increasing tendency of restaurants to be unable to say "no" to diners dying to get in and spend wads of cash. As a result, more and more tables are being squeezed into smaller and smaller spaces. Elbow room is a thing of the past, even in some of the city's finer restaurants, where you'd think your money would buy you better. In the listings below, I've tried to consistently mention those restaurants where the tables are on the small side and the seating is tight. As you can see from my reviews, I don't consider this a reason to stay away; some of my favorite restaurants suffer from this problem. However, keep it in mind when you're making your choice. If you want romance and quiet conversation, or simply lots of leg room, choose carefully.

The second is the increasing popularity of the understated entrance. Somehow, restaurants are flourishing *without signs*—or with cryptic signs, or tiny signs you can hardly see. All of this may be well and good for a hot spot's exclusivity factor, but it can make them a bear to find. Again, I've tried to point out in the listings below when you have to be on the lookout for this phenomenon, but your best bet is to always bring the restaurant's exact street address with you when you head out to your reservation.

The last big trend that's worth noting is the increasing tendency for waiters to come on like aggressive salespeople. If you're offered a special, feel free to ask how much it is, even in the fanciest restaurant—there's nothing gauche about it. Many waiters will try to push extra starters and sides, but don't feel pressured—if you wanted fries, you would've asked for fries in the first place. The biggest bugaboo in this category has been bottled water: Many servers will ask "sparkling or still?" as if perfectly good New York City tap water was not an option. It is. Don't get roped in if *l'eau Giuliani* is all you want; otherwise you can end up with an additional $10 or $15 charge (yep, that's right) for something you didn't really want in the first place.

On a nostalgic note, I'm saddened to report the demise of the Rainbow Room. The city's ultimate celebratory spot, this legendary restaurant will be sorely missed.

WHAT'S MISSING?

There's no way that I can review each and every New York City restaurant for you in the pages that follow. You'd never want to carry around such a heavy tome! So I've made some hard choices about what to include, giving you the best in every neighborhood and price range across a spectrum of cuisines.

But anybody who attempts to do such a thing is bound to ruffle some feathers, especially when it comes to what's left out. There are some big-name restaurants I haven't included in this chapter—not because they're bad, but because I simply can't recommend them as highly as other restaurants offering similar experiences for the money. **The Four Seasons,** 99 E. 52nd St. (☎ **212/754-9494**), may be a New York institution, but for this much money (you're pretty much committed to $200 for dinner for two), you should get *a lot* more attention than we received on our last visit. I don't have any specific complaints about *New York Times* four-star award winner **Lespinasse,** in the St. Regis hotel, 2 E. 55th St. (☎ **212/339-6719**), but I've dined there on a couple of occasions now, and it has failed to wow me. Ditto for **Bouley Bakery,** 120 W. Broadway in Tribeca (☎ **212/964-2525**), where the innovative French cuisine isn't the equal of the original, oft-lamented Bouley; here's hoping for a return to the sublime for chef David Bouley's in-the-works projects. If you want über-fancy, I suggest Le Bernardin (p. 160), Chanterelle (p. 134), Daniel (p. 183), or the River Cafe (p. 188) instead.

Tribeca Grill, 375 Greenwich St. (☎ **212/941-3900**), has traditionally been the place for celebrity spotting, whether it's co-owner Robert DeNiro, Miramax chiefs Bob and Harvey Weinstein, or a whole host of other stars. But complaints have been mounting as a result of inconsistent quality and an almost intolerable noise level when the place is crowded. Ditto for **Moomba,** 133 Seventh Ave. So. (☎ **212/ 989-1414**), where you could end up next to anyone from Marilyn Manson to Leo himself—and expect to be duly neglected as a result. The desserts are fabulous, but for 26 bucks my chicken shouldn't have been dry. And why does a restaurant that takes reservations need a velvet rope and a bouncer at 8:30pm on a weeknight? Go if you must, but I suggest skipping the pretensions and heading elsewhere. For top-notch celeb-spotting and a first-rate dining experience, Le Cirque 2000 (p. 170), Mr. Chow (p. 172), Daniel (p. 183), and Gramercy Tavern (p. 153) are all much better bets. I personally scored sightings of Cindy Crawford and Whoopi Goldberg at Gramercy and Le Cirque, respectively. Uptown celebs like Sean Penn and the latest names in hip hop tend to hang out at Mr. Chow, and simply *everybody's* going to Daniel.

Superstar chef Jean-Georges Vongerichten went downtown casual this year with **Mercer Kitchen,** in the Mercer Hotel, 99 Prince St. (☎ **212/966-5454**). If the menu and wine list were five or seven bucks cheaper across the board, I'd say go and experiment with his French/Asian fusion cuisine. But for $20 to $35 an entree, you can do far better uptown at his Vong (p. 173) or Jo Jo (p. 184), and they're both easier to get into. Or stick with stellar neighbor Quilty's (p. 139). Or hell, just spend a little more and blow the wad at sublime Jean Georges (p. 176), where you simply can't go wrong. Daniel Boulud of Daniel has had much greater success scaling down at Cafe Boulud (p. 184).

But my biggest disappointment this year was an old favorite, **Union Square Cafe,** 21 E. 16th St. (☎ **212/243-4020**), which has been New York's most popular restaurant for years now thanks to excellent bistro-style food and utter lack of pretension. Unfortunately, USC seems to be taking that popularity for granted these days—or maybe they're just trying too hard to please. On my last visit, there were so many diners shoehorned into the restaurant that patrons were eating full $25-a-course dinners *at the bar*—which meant that expectant diners had to line up uncomfortably against a wall, expensive cocktail in hand, to wait for their tables. The whole place, which used to have a nice easygoing vibe, felt overcrowded and cramped, and service suffered for it. Book yourself into sister restaurant Gramercy Tavern instead (p. 153), which is still in top form.

RESERVATIONS

Reservations are always a good idea in New York, and a virtual necessity if your party is bigger than two. Do yourself a favor and call ahead as a rule of thumb so you won't be disappointed. If you're booking dinner on a weekend night, it's a good idea to call a few days in advance if you can.

For bookings at the city's most popular restaurants, call far ahead—a month is a good idea. Most eateries start taking reservations exactly 30 days in advance, so if you want to eat at a hot restaurant at a popular hour—Saturday at 8pm, say, at Jean Georges—be sure to mark your calendar and start dialing at 9am. If you're booking a holiday dinner, call earlier.

But if you didn't call well ahead and your heart's set on dinner at Le Cirque or Gramercy Tavern, don't despair. Often, early or late hours—between 6 and 7pm, or after 10pm—are available, especially on weeknights. And try calling the day before or first thing in the morning, when you may be able to take advantage of a last-minute cancellation. Or go for lunch, which is usually much easier to book without lots of advance notice. And if you're staying at a hotel with a concierge, don't be afraid to use them—they can often get you into hot spots that you couldn't get into on your own.

But What If They Don't *Take* Reservations?   Lots of city restaurants, especially at the affordable end of the price continuum, don't take reservations at all. One of the ways they're able to keep prices down is by packing people in as quickly as possible. This means that the best cheap and mid-priced restaurants often have a wait. Again, your best bet is to go early. Often, you can get in more quickly on a weeknight. Or just go knowing that you're going to have to wait if you head to a popular spot like Boca Chica, and hunker down with a margarita at the bar, taking in the festivities around you.

THE LOWDOWN ON SMOKING

Following the national trend, New York City enacted strict no-smoking laws a few years back that made most of the city's dining rooms blessedly smoke-free. However, that doesn't mean that smokers are completely prohibited from lighting up. Here's the deal: Restaurants with more than 35 seats cannot allow smoking in their dining rooms. They can, however, allow smoking in their bar or lounge areas, and most do. Restaurants with fewer than 35 seats—and there are more of those in the city than you'd think—can allow or prohibit smoking as they see fit. This ruling has turned some of the city's restaurants into particularly smoker-friendly establishments, which might be a turn-off for non-smokers.

Whether you're a smoker or non-smoker, your best bet is to call ahead and ask about the smoking policy if it matters to you. If you're hell-bent on enjoying an after-dinner cigarette indoors, make sure that the restaurant has a bar or lounge that allows smoking. Some restaurants, such as Clementine and Bar Pitti, even offer dinner tables in their lounges where you can puff away all during the meal if you so choose. And smoking is usually allowed in alfresco dining areas, but never assume—always ask. If you're a non-smoker who doesn't want to be bothered by second-hand smoke, make sure your seat is well away from the bar; at Moomba, for instance, some of the tables in the first-floor dining room are perilously close to the puffing.

TIPPING

Tipping is easy in New York. The way to do it: Double the 8¼% sales tax and voilà!, happy waitperson. In fancier venues, another 5% is appropriate for the captain. If the wine steward helps, hand him or her 10% of the bottle's price.

In the restaurant reviews below, I've made notes about what you can expect in terms of service. However, keep in mind that it all depends on the luck of the draw, and your waitperson's personality. In some of the most popular restaurants, service can become neglectful on occasion for those of us who aren't perceived as VIPs, especially if Puff Daddy or some other big-name bigwigs are in the house. Remember: No matter where you eat, if you get good service, reward your waitperson accordingly. But if you genuinely feel like you were short-shrifted, feel free to let the tip reflect it.

Leave a dollar per item, no matter how small, for the checkroom attendant.

1 Restaurants by Cuisine

AMERICAN

America (p. 157)
Bendix Diner (p. 160)
Big Nick's (p. 181)
Brooklyn Diner USA (p. 168)
Cafeteria (p.159)
EJ's Luncheonette (p. 186)
Empire Diner (p. 160)
Fanelli's Cafe (p. 140)
Hamburger Harry's (p. 166)
Hard Rock Cafe (p. 168)
Harley-Davidson Cafe (p. 169)
Hi-Life Restaurant & Lounge
  (p.186)
Jekyll & Hyde Club (p. 169)
Joe Allen (p. 162)
Kitchenette (p. 135)
Mars 2112 (p. 169)
McDonald's (p. 133)
The Odeon (p. 136)
Old Town Bar & Restaurant (p. 157)
Official All-Star Cafe (p. 169)
Planet Hollywood (p. 169)
Popover Cafe (p. 182)
Prime Burger (p. 175)
Serendipity 3 (p. 187)
SoHo Kitchen & Bar (p. 141)
"21" Club (p. 161)
Wall Street Kitchen & Bar (p. 132)
Wild Blue (p. 132)

ASIAN FUSION

Mercer Kitchen (p. 125)
Union Pacific (p. 152)
Vong (p. 173)

BELGIAN

Cafe de Bruxelles (p. 149)

BRITISH

The British Open (p. 174)
North Star Pub (p. 133)

CHINESE

Hunan Park (p. 182)
Joe's Shanghai (p. 137)
Mr. Chow (p. 172)
New York Noodletown (p. 137)

CONTEMPORARY AMERICAN

Alley's End (p. 159)
Aureole (p. 183)
Bridge Cafe (p. 132)
Clementine (p. 148)
Gramercy Tavern (p. 153)
Home (p. 150)
March (p. 171)
Metro Grill (p. 165)
Moomba (p. 125)
Park View at the
  Boathouse (p. 184)
Quilty's (p. 139)
The River Café (p. 188)
Sarabeth's Kitchen (p. 181)
Savoy (p. 139)
Time Cafe (p. 150)
Tribeca Grill (p. 125)
Union Square Cafe (p. 125)
Water's Edge (p. 189)
Windows on the World (p. 129)

CONTINENTAL

Café des Artistes (p. 176)
Cité (p. 162)
The Four Seasons (p. 125)
One If By Land, Two If By Sea
  (p. 147)

Petrossian (p. 164)
Tavern on the Green (p. 177)

ETHIOPIAN

Meskerem (p. 169)

FRENCH

Alison on Dominick Street (p. 138)
Balthazar (p. 138)
Cafe Boulud (p. 184)
Cafe Luxembourg (p. 180)
Chanterelle (p. 134)
Chez Josephine (p. 162)
Danal (p. 143)
Daniel (p. 183)
Florent (p. 151)
Jean Georges (p. 176)
Jo Jo (p. 184)
La Bonne Soupe (p. 168)
Le Bernardin (p. 160)
Le Cirque 2000 (p. 171)
Le Gigot (p. 149)
Lespinasse (p. 125)
Montrachet (p. 134)
Payard Pâtisserie & Bistro (p. 186)
Steak Frites (p. 156)
Tartine (p. 152)

GOURMET SANDWICHES/DELI

Ess-A-Bagel (p. 174)
Island Burgers & Shakes (p. 167)
Mangia (p. 133)

GREEK

Estiatorio Milos (p. 163)
Molyvos (p. 164)

HISPANIC

Old San Juan (p. 167)

INDIAN/INDIAN FUSION

Bombay Dining (p. 145)
Cafe Spice (p. 151)
Gandhi (p. 145)
Haveli (p. 145)
Mitali East (p. 145)
Passage to India (p. 145)
Salaam Bombay (p. 136)
Tabla (p. 124)

ITALIAN

Babbo (p. 148)

Barbetta (p. 161)
Bar Pitti (p. 150)
Caffe Bondí Ristorante (p. 156)
Caffe Grazie (p. 185)
Carmine's (p. 165)
Coco Pazzo Teatro (p. 163)
Cucina di Pesce (p. 146)
Il Cortile (p. 136)
Orso (p. 162)
San Domenico (p. 161)

JAPANESE

Blue Ribbon Sushi (p. 140)
BondSt (p. 142)
Haru (p. 180)
Iso (p. 143)
Next Door Nobu (p. 134)
Nobu (p. 134)
Shabu Tatsu (p. 147)

JEWISH

Carnegie Delicatessen &
    Restaurant (p. 146)
Kaplan's (p. 146)
Katz's Delicatessen (p. 146)
Second Avenue Deli (p. 146)
Stage Deli (p. 146)

KOREAN

Bop (p. 142)
Hangawi (p. 170)
Won Jo (p. 170)
Woo Chon (p. 170)

MALAYSIAN

Franklin Station Cafe (p. 135)

MEDITERRANEAN

Julian's (p. 167)
Layla (p. 135)
Medusa (p. 156)
Picholine (p. 177)

MEXICAN/TEX-MEX

Burritoville (p. 132)
Taco & Tortilla King (p. 176)
Zarela (p. 174)

PAN-ASIAN

Kelley & Ping (p. 140)
Republic (p. 158)

PIZZA
John's Pizzeria (p. 167)
Lombardi's (p. 141)
Patsy Grimaldi's Pizzeria (p. 189)
Pintaile's Pizza (p. 187)
Sofia's Fabulous Pizza (p. 187)
Totonno's Pizzeria Napolitano (p. 187)
Two Boots to Go (p. 151)

RUSSIAN/CAVIAR
Petrossian (p. 164)

SCANDINAVIAN
The Cafe at Aquavit (p. 164)

SEAFOOD
Blue Water Grill (p. 156)
Estiatorio Milos (p. 163)
Le Bernardin (p. 160)
Oyster Bar (p. 173)
Pisces (p. 143)

SOUP
Soup Kitchen International (p. 170)

SOUL FOOD
Sylvia's (p. 188)

SOUTH AMERICAN
Boca Chica (p. 145)
Bolivar (p. 185)
Churrascaria Plataforma (p. 165)
Rice 'n' Beans (p. 167)

SOUTHERN/BARBECUE
Virgil's Real BBQ (p. 166)

SOUTHWESTERN
Citrus (p. 180)
Mesa Grill (p. 153)

SPANISH
La Paella (p. 143)

STEAKS
Michael Jordan's–The Steak House (p. 172)
Peter Luger Steakhouse (p. 188)

SWISS
Roetelle A.G. (p. 144)

THAI
Chanpen (p. 170)
Pongsri Thai Restaurant (p. 170)
Siam Inn Too (p. 170)
Thailand Restaurant (p. 138)

UKRANIAN
Veselka (p. 147)

VEGETARIAN/HEALTH-CONSCIOUS
Angelica Kitchen (p. 144)
Josie's Restaurant & Juice Bar (p. 182)
Spring Street Natural Restaurant (p. 141)
Zen Palate (p. 158)

VIETNAMESE
Nha Trang (p. 137)

2 South Street Seaport & the Financial District

See the "Downtown Dining" map (p. 130–131) for restaurants in this section.

VERY EXPENSIVE

☺ **Windows on the World.** 1 World Trade Center, 107th Floor (enter on West St., between Liberty and Vesey sts.). ☎ **212/524-7000.** Reservations recommended well in advance. Jacket required. Main courses $25–$35; sunset prix-fixe (before 6pm) $35; prix-fixe brunch $32.50. AE, CB, DC, DISC, MC, V. Mon–Thurs 5–10:30pm, Fri–Sat 5–11:30pm, Sun 5–10pm; brunch Sun 11am–3pm. Limited seating is available for non-members Mon–Fri noon–2pm; a surcharge may apply. Subway: C, E to World Trade Center; 1, 9, N, R to Cortlandt St. Valet parking off West St. $18. CONTEMPORARY AMERICAN.

The interior is more hotel dining than high design, but that's just fine: Who needs to look at the inside when all New York's out the window? This restaurant boasts the most spectacular views in the city, as well as a New American menu that's more than admirable now that Michael Lomonaco, the former executive chef of the "21" Club,

Downtown Dining

Alison on Dominick Street
Angelica Kitchen
Babbo
Balthazar
Bar Pitti
Bendix Diner
Blue Ribbon Sushi
Boca Chica
Bombay Dining
BondSt
Bridge Cafe
Burritoville
Cafe de Bruxelles
Chanterelle
Clementine
Cucina di Pesce
Danal
Drovers Tap Room
EJ's Luncheonette
Fanelli's Cafe
Florent
Franklin Station Cafe
Frutti de Mare
Gandhi
Haveli
Home
Il Cortile
Iso
Joe's Shanghai
John's Pizzeria
Katz's Delicatessen
Kelley & Ping
Kitchenette
La Paella

continues on
opposite page

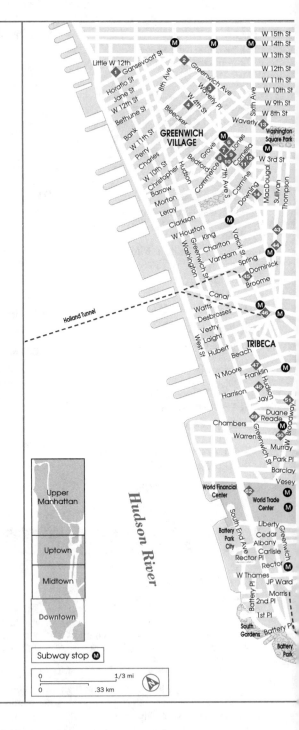

NA-0148

130

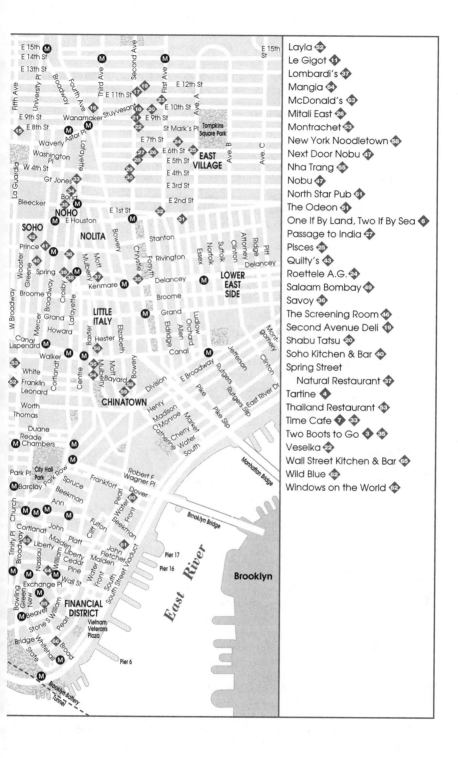

Layla 52
Le Gigot 11
Lombardi's 37
Mangia 64
McDonald's 63
Mitali East 26
Montrachet 53
New York Noodletown 58
Next Door Nobu 47
Nha Trang 55
Nobu 47
North Star Pub 61
The Odeon 51
One If By Land, Two If By Sea 6
Passage to India 27
Pisces 25
Quilty's 43
Roettele A.G. 24
Salaam Bombay 49
Savoy 36
The Screening Room 46
Second Avenue Deli 19
Shabu Tatsu 20
Soho Kitchen & Bar 40
Spring Street
   Natural Restaurant 37
Tartine 4
Thailand Restaurant 53
Time Cafe 7 33
Two Boots to Go 3 35
Veselka 22
Wall Street Kitchen & Bar 65
Wild Blue 62
Windows on the World 62

is at the helm. Windows is also home to one of the city's most respected wine cellars. The sommelier will be happy to point you in the right direction, whether you're a serious oenophile looking for a one-of-a-kind find or a casual wine lover who wants a good-value bottle to carry you from the stout-braised black Angus short ribs to the poached Maine lobster pot pie (both Lomonaco signatures).

New to the 107th floor is **Wild Blue** (☎ 212/524-7107), a more intimate, less formal, and slightly less expensive (main courses $18 to $28) alternative to big sister Windows. The straightforward American-chophouse menu boasts few surprises, but the room is warm and inviting and the views are, of course, magnificent.

MODERATE

Bridge Cafe. 279 Water St. (at Dover St., just north of South Street Seaport). ☎ 212/227-3344. www.bridgecafe.com. Reservations recommended. Main courses $12–$22; prix-fixe Sun brunch (until 4pm) $14.95; prix-fixe Sun dinner $19.95. AE, CB, DC, MC, V. Sun–Mon 11:45am–10pm, Tues–Fri 11:45am–midnight, Sat 5pm–midnight. Subway: 4, 5, 6 to Brooklyn Bridge/City Hall. Free parking after 6pm at the Edison parking lot, 1 block south. CONTEMPORARY AMERICAN.

It just ain't easy to find a decent and affordable place to eat in Lower Manhattan. Luckily, there's the Bridge Cafe. Housed in the oldest woodframe building in the city (built in 1794), this romantic little restaurant is a great place to dine after a long day of Seaport area sightseeing. It's on a block that (thankfully) hasn't been gentrified, a few blocks north of the Seaport but definitely worth the couple of minutes' walk (take a cab if you're not good with maps). The room is a brick-walled charmer, and the service attentive and friendly. The menu changes quarterly, but expect seasonal variations on chicken (the fall version was marinated with chanterelles), roast duck, a few well-prepared fishes, and some additional choices, such as brisket of beef or smoked chops. There's always a vegetarian choice, plus a wallet-friendly pasta or two. The all-American wine list boasts lots of good values, especially on **Wine Discovery Tuesdays,** when every bottle is 30% off.

INEXPENSIVE

If you want to rub elbows with Wall Street's after-work crowd, head to the **Wall Street Kitchen & Bar,** which, like its sister restaurant **Soho Kitchen & Bar** (p. 141), serves up reasonably priced bar food along with 50 beers on tap and "flight" menus of wines and microbrews for tasting. Housed in a spectacular former bank building in the heart of the financial district at 70 Broad St. (☎ 212/797-7070), it's worth a stop for a beer and a burger.

Burritoville. 36 Water St. (at Broad St.). ☎ 212/747-1100. Main courses $4.25–$9.95. AE, DISC, MC, V. Daily 11am–midnight. Subway: 2, 3 to Wall St.; 1, 9 to South Ferry. TEX-MEX.

For a quick, healthy, and inexpensive lunch in the Seaport area, Burritoville fits the bill. These storefront taco shops serve up forward-thinking Mexican fare, all prepared with the freshest and healthiest ingredients. Everything is prepared fresh daily using no lard, preservatives, or canned goods—even the tortillas are pressed every day. Options range from well-stuffed taco and burrito standards to only-at-Burritoville creations like a spicy white chicken chili with cumin and a number of choice veggie wraps. Just about every menu item features nutty brown rice and ten-spiced, beer-stewed black beans. As you might expect, there are lots of choices for vegetarians as well as anyone looking for a quick bite on the go.

There are a whole handful of Burritovilles throughout the city, including 141 Second Ave., between St. Mark's and 9th Street, in the East Village (☎ 212/260-3300); 298 Bleecker St., at Seventh Avenue, in Greenwich Village (☎ 212/633-9249);

You Want Fries With That?

Wall Street's famous **McDonald's,** 160 Broadway, between Maiden Lane and Liberty Street (☎ 212/385-2063), elevates the Happy Meal to a whole new level. Ever been to another McDonald's where a doorman in tails greets you, a hostess finds you a table and sets it with place mats, and a tux-clad pianist twinkles the ivories at a candelabra-topped baby grand? But lest you fear that Ronald has abandoned his winning formula, don't worry: Everything else, from the quarter pounders to the ice-milk shakes, is comfortingly familiar.

264 W. 23rd St., between Seventh and Eighth avenues, in Chelsea (☎ 212/ 367-9844); and 166 W. 72nd St., at Amsterdam Avenue, on the Upper West Side (☎ 212/580-7700). Call ☎ 212/964-1119 or consult the White Pages for additional locations.

Mangia. 40 Wall St. (btw. Nassau and William sts.). ☎ 212/425-4040 or 212/363-9536. Main courses $5.95–$9.95. AE, DC, MC, V. Mon–Fri 7am–8pm. Subway: 4, 5 to Wall St.; J, M, Z to Broad St. GOURMET DELI.

This big, bustling gourmet cafeteria is an ideal place to take a break during your day of Financial District sightseeing. Between the giant salad and soup bars, the sandwich and hot entree counters, and an expansive cappuccino-and-pastry counter at the front of the cavernous room, even the most finicky eater will have a hard time deciding what to eat. Everything is freshly prepared and beautifully presented. The soups and stews are particularly good (there are always a number of daily choices), and a cup goes well with a fresh-baked pizzette (a mini-pizza). Pay-by-the-pound salad bars don't get any better than this, hot meal choices (such as grilled mahi-mahi or cumin-marinated lamb kabob) are cooked to order, and sandwiches are freshly made as you watch. This place is packed with Wall Streeters between noon and 2pm, but things move quickly and there's enough seating that usually no one has to wait. Come in for a late breakfast or an afternoon snack, and you'll virtually have the place to yourself.

In addition to the Wall Street location, Mangia also has two cafeteria-style cafes in Midtown that offer similar, if not such expansive, menus: at 50 W. 57th St., between Fifth and Sixth avenues (☎ 212/582-5882); and at 16 E. 48th St., just east of Fifth Avenue (☎ 212/754-7600).

North Star Pub. At South Street Seaport, 93 South St. (at Fulton St.). ☎ 212/509-6757. Main courses $7.50–$12.95. AE, CB, DC, MC, V. Daily 11:30am–10:30pm. Subway: 2, 3, 4, 5 to Fulton St. BRITISH.

This friendly place right at the entrance to the Seaport is a refreshing bit of authenticity in the mallified, almost theme park–like historic district. It's the spitting image of a British pub, down to the chalkboard menus boasting daily specials like kidney pie and the Guinness, Harp, and Fullers ESB on tap. We love the ale-battered fish 'n' chips, good-quality fish deep-fried just right (not too greasy); the excellent golden-browned shepherd's pie (just like grandma used to make); the bangers 'n' mash, made with grilled Cumberland sausage; and the traditional Ploughman's, including very good pâté, a sizable hunk of cheddar or stilton, fresh bread, and all the accompaniments (even Branston pickle!). All in all, a fun, relaxing place to hang out and eat and drink heartily (and cheaply). In keeping with the theme, there's also an expansive menu of single-malt scotches and Irish whiskeys.

3 TriBeCa

See the "Downtown Dining" map (pp. 130–131) for restaurants in this section.

VERY EXPENSIVE

✪ **Chanterelle.** 2 Harrison St. (btw. Hudson and Greenwich sts.). ☎ **212/966-6960.** Reservations recommended well in advance. Prix-fixe lunch $35, à la carte lunch $18.50–$24; prix-fixe dinner $75, tasting menu $89. AE, CB, DC, DISC, MC, V. Mon 5:30–11pm, Tues–Sat noon–2:30pm and 5:30–11pm. Subway: 1, 9 to Franklin St. CONTEMPORARY FRENCH.

Here's a true special-occasion restaurant. One of only five places to hold four stars from the *New York Times*, Chanterelle leaves you saying not only "The food was superb" or "The wine was sublime," but also "Thank you for a marvelous time." Overseen by husband-and-wife co-owners David and Karen Waltuch, the first-rate waitstaff—the best in the city—makes sure of it. There's no stuffiness here at all; everyone is encouraged to feel at home and relaxed. Your server will know the handwritten menu in depth and be glad to describe preparations in detail and suggest complementary combinations. The artful cuisine is based on traditional French technique, but Pacific and pan-European notes sneak into the culinary melodies, and lots of dishes are lighter than you'd expect. The seasonal menu changes every few weeks, but one signature dish appears on almost every menu: a marvelous grilled seafood sausage. Cheese lovers should opt for a cheese course—the presentation and selection can't be beat. The dining room is simple but beautiful, with a pressed-tin ceiling, widely spaced large tables, comfortable chairs, and gorgeous flowers. Master sommelier Roger Dagorn has assembled a superlative wine list, but we wish there were more affordable options. Still, you don't come to Chanterelle on the cheap—you come to celebrate. Very expensive, but magnificent.

EXPENSIVE

✪ **Montrachet.** 239 W. Broadway (btw. White and Walker sts.). ☎ **212/219-2777.** Reservations highly recommended. Main courses $26–$32; 3-course prix-fixe dinners $35 and $42; 6-course tasting menu $75. AE, MC, V. Mon–Thurs and Sat 5:30–10:30pm; Fri noon–2:30pm and 5:30–10:30pm. Subway: 1, 9 to Franklin St. FRENCH BISTRO.

Opened in 1985, this TriBeCa pioneer is the baby of restauranteur Drew Nieporent, who's gone on to launch such other city favorites as Tribeca Grill, Layla, and Nobu. Montrachet earned raves from the moment it opened, and won its three stars from the *New York Times* anew at the end of 1998 when Frenchman Rémi Lauvand, late of Le Cirque, took over the kitchen. Now considered one of Manhattan's "new classics," Montrachet never fails to wow. The food is more French than ever thanks to Lauvand, whose menu is in turn heartily traditional, classically fancy, and playfully creative, depending on what you choose. The fois gras terrine is a consummate example of his country-style cooking; consider the warm oysters in creamy champagne sauce if you want a supremely elegant dish. For simpler tastes, even the roasted chicken is everything it should be. A *Wine Spectator* award of excellence winner, the wine list is very good, and the sommelier will be happy to point out the best values to you. The room is attractive and casual and the service friendly, making Montrachet perfect for those who consider uptown stuffiness a turn-off. For bargain hunters, the prix-fixe dinners are one of the city's best dining values.

✪ **Nobu/Next Door Nobu.** 105 Hudson St. (at Franklin St.). ☎ **212/219-0500** for Nobu; ☎ **212/334-4445** for Next Door Nobu. Reservations required far in advance at Nobu; reservations taken only for parties of 6 or more at Next Door Nobu. Most dishes $8–$32; sushi $3–$10 per piece. AE, DC, MC, V. Mon–Fri 11:45am–2:15pm, daily 5:45–10:15pm at Nobu; Mon–Thurs 5:45pm–midnight, Fri–Sat 5:45pm–1am. Subway: 1, 9 to Franklin St. NEW JAPANESE.

Dining Zone: TriBeCa

TriBeCa abounds with great restaurants in every price range. At attractive **Salaam Bombay,** 317 Greenwich St., between Duane and Reade streets (☎ 212/ 226-9400), the pan-Indian food is a cut above the standard fare, and the weekday $10.95 all-you-can-eat lunch buffet is a steal. **Kitchenette,** 80 W. Broadway, at Warren St. (☎ 212/267-6740), is a contender on the comfort-food circuit thanks to Hungry Man–sized breakfasts and more just-like-home cooking. For warm and cozy, stop in at **Franklin Station Cafe,** 222 W. Broadway, at Franklin Street (☎ 212/274-8525), for affordable Malaysian noodle bowls and French-inspired sandwiches, prepared by a health-minded kitchen with all-natural ingredients.

Chef Nobu Matsuhisa took New York by storm in 1994 with his innovative, pan-cultural preparations, and Nobu has been flying high ever since. Deeply rooted in Japanese tradition but heavily influenced by Latin American and Western techniques, his cooking bursts with creative spirit. Unusual textures, impulsive combinations, and surprising flavors add up to a first-rate dining adventure that you won't soon forget. Virtually every creation hits its target, whether you opt for the new-style sashimi; seared whitefish in olive oil seasoned with garlic, ginger, and sesame; light-as-air rock shrimp tempura; or sublime broiled black cod in sweet miso, the best dish in the house. If Kobe beef is available, try this delicacy tataki style (with soy, scallions, and daikon). The knowledgeable staff will be happy to guide you. However, since most dinners are structured as a series of tasting plates, be aware that the bill can soar—wallet-watchers should keep a close eye on the tally. The excitement is heightened by the witty modern decor (check out the chopstick-legged chairs at the sushi bar). The only disappointment is the traditional sushi, which doesn't live up to the more creative dishes; head elsewhere for a full sushi meal.

But you can't get a reservation at Nobu? Take heart, for now there's **Next Door Nobu,** the slightly more casual, slightly less expensive (in theory, anyway) version that has a firm no-reservations policy. This is great news in this exclusionary town: Just show up, wait your turn, and you get a table. Since waits can be as long as 90 minutes, the secret is to go early: We walked in at 6:30pm on a weeknight and the place was half-empty. This isn't cut-rate Nobu—you get the full treatment here, too. The modern room is highly stylized but comfortable, all the house specialties are available, and the service is equal to the main restaurant. Noodle dishes add a moderately priced dimension to the menu, but it takes a lot of willpower to keep the tab low. There's also a raw bar, the star of which is sea urchin served in the shell, a perfect juxtaposition of textures for bold palates.

MODERATE

Layla. 211 W. Broadway (at Franklin St.). ☎ **212/431-0700.** Reservations recommended. Mezzes $6–$13, main courses $20–$27, $42 prix-fixe Layla's feast; $2 entertainment charge for belly-dancing show. AE, DC, MC, V. Mon–Thurs 5:30–11pm, Fri noon–2:30pm and 5:30–11:30pm, Sat 5:30–11:30pm, Sun 5:30–9:30pm. Subway: 1, 9 to Franklin St. MEDITER-RANEAN/MIDDLE EASTERN.

Here's yet another wonderful TriBeCa restaurant from Drew Nieporent's Robert DeNiro–backed Myriad Group, the brains behind such big names as Nobu, Montrachet, and Tribeca Grill. Unlike the others, though, which generally eschew themes, this one is like a page out of the *Arabian Nights*—there's even a belly dancer to entertain. A stylized take on a sultan's den, the fanciful dining room is the perfect setting for Layla's modern-meets-Middle East cuisine. Dinner can be expensive, but I list Layla in the "moderate" category because I wouldn't dream of coming here and ordering a traditional (and too pricey) appetizer-and-entree meal. The fun, high-energy setting and expansive, affordable mezze menu are made for family-style sharing. In fact, this is such a popular option that there's a $20 per person food minimum in the dining room, which you can circumvent if you wish by eating at the bar. The beautifully presented cuisine has a strong Greek influence, so expect well-prepared hummus, taramasalata, and baba gannoush. But the mezzes quickly get more creative, with such excellent specialties as coriander-crusted scallops over chickpeas and grilled flatbread topped with spicy lamb. If you wander over to the entree list, consider the Moroccan couscous with braised lamb and the vegetable pastilla, an ideal dish for sharing.

The Odeon. 145 W. Broadway (at Thomas St.). ☎ **212/233-0507.** Reservations recommended for parties of 4 or more. Main courses $9–$25. AE, DC, MC, V. Mon–Wed noon–2am, Thurs–Fri noon–3am, Sat 11:30am–3am, Sun 11:30am–2am. Subway: 1, 2, 3, 9 to Chambers St. (walk 3 blocks north). AMERICAN/FRENCH.

The Odeon is always the first place that comes to mind when I crave a late-night meal, but this attractive hotspot is satisfying at any time of day. The striking deco-ish room is perennially trendy but universally welcoming—no velvet ropes here. Sure, De Niro might be a couple of tables away, but it's the food that's the real draw. The restaurant crosses budget and culture lines: It's easy to eat cheap here if you stick to the burgers, vegetarian chili, and sandwiches, or you can spend a little more and go for excellent steak frites, roasted free-range chicken, braised lamb shank, and other top-notch brasserie-style dinners. The prices are lower than they have to be for food like this, and the wine list is equally reasonable. With rich wood paneling, Formica-topped tables, and leather banquettes, the Odeon even manages to be swanky and comfortable at the same time. As proof of its egalitarianism, there's even a kid's menu—and the chocolate pudding is scrumptious.

4 Chinatown & Little Italy

See the "Downtown Dining" map (pp. 130–131) for restaurants in this section.

MODERATE

Il Cortile. 125 Mulberry St. (btw. Canal and Hester sts.). ☎ **212/226-6060.** Reservations recommended. Pastas $8.50–$22, meats and fish $16.50–$32. AE, DC, DISC, MC, V. Sun–Thurs noon–midnight, Fri–Sat noon–1am. Subway: 6, N, R to Canal St. NORTHERN ITALIAN.

The best restaurant in Little Italy stands out on Mulberry Street thanks to its warm, sophisticated demeanor amid the bright lights and bold decor of its lesser neighbors. The interior has a dramatic skylit atrium; I prefer the cozier front room. There's a certain Old World elegance to the menu: Like a *billet doux* from the chef, it's folded and sealed with gold foil. The second sign that you're out of the Little Italy ordinary arrives with the warm basket of focaccia, crusty small loaves, golden-brown crostini, and crunchy breadsticks. The Northern Italian fare is well prepared and pleasing: The greens fresh and crisp, the sauces appropriately seasoned, the pastas perfectly al dente. This is traditional cuisine, but not without a few welcome twists: The filet mignon carpaccio is rolled with onions and parsley, thick cut, and seared; shiitakes give an unexpected flair to the rigatoni. On my last visit, the best dish at our table was the polenta with mushrooms in a savory white wine sauce, a bargain at $10.50. The waitstaff, made up of career neighborhood waiters, is attentive and reserved in an appealing Old World style. The extensive wine cellar, hidden at the front of the restaurant behind a beautiful wooden door that looks as if it may have been liberated from a grand European castle, contains a good number of well-priced selections.

INEXPENSIVE

✪ **Joe's Shanghai.** 9 Pell St. (btw. Bowery and Mott sts.). ☎ **212/233-8888.** Reservations recommended for 10 or more. Main courses $4.25–$12.95. No credit cards. Sun–Thurs 11am–10pm, Fri–Sat 11am–10:30pm. Subway: N, R, 6 to Canal St; B, D, Q to Grand St. SHANGHAI CHINESE.

Tucked away on a little elbow of a side street just off the Bowery is this Chinatown institution, which serves up authentic cuisine to enthusiastic crowds nightly. The stars of the huge menu are the signature soup dumplings, quivering steamed pockets filled with hot broth and your choice of pork or crab, accompanied by a side of seasoned soy. Listed on the menu as "steamed buns" (item numbers 1 and 2), these culinary marvels never disappoint. Neither does the rest of the authentic Shanghai-inspired menu, which boasts such main courses as whole yellowfish bathed in spicy sauce; excellent "mock duck," a saucy bean-curd dish similar to Japanese yuba that's a hit with vegetarians and carnivores alike; and lots of well-prepared staples. The room is set mostly with round tables of ten or so, and you'll be asked if you're willing to share. I encourage you to do so; it's a great way to watch and learn from your neighbors (many of whom are Chinese), who are usually more than happy to tell you what they're eating. If you want a private table, expect a wait.

Joe's Shanghai now a second Manhattan location, in midtown at 24 W. 56th St., just west of Fifth Avenue (☎ **212/333-3868**).

✪ **New York Noodletown.** 28½ Bowery (at Bayard St.). ☎ **212/349-0923.** Reservations accepted. Main courses $3.95–$10.95. No credit cards. Daily 9am–4am. Subway: N, R, 6 to Canal St. SEAFOOD/CHINESE.

This just may be the best Chinese food in New York City. Among its fans are Ruth Reichl, restaurant critic for the *New York Times,* who constantly puts it at the top of the heap. But don't expect fancy—this is two-star food served in no-star ambiance. So what if the room is reminiscent of a school cafeteria? The food is fabulous. The mushroom soup is a lunch in itself, thick with earthy chunks of shiitakes, vegetables, and thin noodles. Another appetizer that can serve as a meal is the hacked roast duck in noodle soup. The kitchen excels at seafood preparations, so be sure to try at least one: Looking like a snow-dusted plate of meaty fish, the salt-baked squid is sublime. The quick-woked Chinese broccoli or the crisp sautéed baby bok choy make great accompaniments. Other special dishes are various sandy pot casseroles, hearty, flavorful affairs slow-simmered in clay vessels. Unlike most of its neighbors, New York Noodletown keeps very long hours, which makes it the best late-night bet in the neighborhood, too.

Nha Trang. 87 Baxter St. (btw. Canal and Bayard sts.). ☎ **212/233-5948.** Reservations recommended for large parties. Main courses $4–$12.50. No credit cards. Daily 10:30am–9:30pm. Subway: N, R, 6 to Canal St. VIETNAMESE.

The decor may be standard-issue, no-atmosphere Chinatown (glass-topped tables, linoleum floors, mirrored walls), but this friendly, bustling place serves up the best Vietnamese in Chinatown. A plate of six crispy, finger-sized spring rolls is a nice way to start; the slightly spicy pork-and-shrimp filling is nicely offset by the wrapping of lettuce, cucumber, and mint. The pho noodle soup comes in a quart-sized bowl brimming with bright vegetables and various meats and seafood. But my favorite dish is the simple barbecued pork chops—sliced paper-thin, soaked in a soy/sugar-cane marinade, and grilled to utter perfection. Everything is well prepared, though, and your waiter will be glad to help you design a meal to suit your tastes. If there's a line, stick around; it won't take long to get a table.

Thailand Restaurant. 106 Bayard St. (at Baxter St.). ☎ **212/349-3132.** Reservations recommended. Main courses $4.95–$12.95. AE. Daily 11:30am–11pm. Subway: N, R, 6 to Canal St. THAI.

Thai has also been added to the expanding menu in Chinatown, and this kitchen turns out first-rate dishes—aromatic, searing, full of zest and colors. When you say spicy you'd better mean it, because your tongue will sizzle like a midtown sidewalk in August. The sliced charcoal steak with onions, hot pepper, lemon juice, and mint is a fabulously fiery, flavorful appetizer. The tasty green curry with coconut milk, eggplant, bamboo shoots, and green chiles comes with your choice of chicken, beef, pork, lamb, or shrimp. Sautéed rice noodles are a good choice to offset the tangier dishes. The whole fish, especially sea bass, are delicately crispy outside, moist and flaky inside. The coconut milk dessert, with slices of ice cubes, is the perfect finish.

5 SoHo

See the "Downtown Dining" map (pp. 130–131) for restaurants in this section.

EXPENSIVE

❍ **Alison on Dominick Street.** 38 Dominick St. (btw. Hudson and Varick sts.; from Varick St., turn west at the Manhattan Mini-Storage facility). ☎ **212/727-1188.** Reservations highly recommended. Main courses $27–$34; pre-theater (5–6:30pm) 2-course prix-fixe dinner $20 ($30 with dessert). AE, DC, MC, V. Tues–Fri 5:30–10:30pm, Sun–Mon 5:30–9:30pm. Subway: 1, 9 to Canal St.; C, E to Spring St. CONTEMPORARY FRENCH.

It's bound to happen: You're on Varick looking for little Dominick Street, and you think, "This can't be the right place." This is far west SoHo but it looks like warehouse-filled TriBeCa on a *really* quiet night, except for the cars with Jersey plates trying to shoehorn their way into the Holland Tunnel. It's not a bad neighborhood by any means—just not the kind of place where you'd expect to find a sophisticated restaurant. But that's only the first of the surprises, the best of which is the pre-theater dinner, one of the best dining values in town. Sit down between 5:15 and 6pm and you can enjoy two stellar courses for just twenty bucks. There are three starters and three entrees to choose from, usually a market-fresh fish, a terrific roast chicken, and an excellent braised lamb with aromatic vegetables, white beans, and basil. If you can't make it for the prix-fixe, come anyway for a worthwhile splurge. The full menu of light, modern French fare is irresistible; we particularly love the mustard-crusted beef short ribs and the roast quail stuffed with wild mushrooms, pancetta, and savoy cabbage. The room is the epitome of gorgeous simplicity, from the midnight blue-velvet drapes to the long mahogany bar. Perfect for an off-the-beaten-track romantic rendezvous.

Balthazar. 80 Spring St. (at Crosby St., 1 block east of Broadway). ☎ **212/965-1414.** Reservations recommended well in advance. Main courses $16–$26; raw bar platters $56 and $98. AE, MC, V. Breakfast daily 7:30am–11:30am; Mon–Fri noon–5pm and 6pm–12am; oyster bar Sun–Thurs noon–2am, Fri–Sat noon–3am; brunch Sat–Sun 11:30am–5pm. Subway: C, E to Spring St. FRENCH BISTRO.

Balthazar has been one of the hottest scenes in town since its doors opened a few years back, and it shows every sign of remaining high on the hip list. We fully understand why. With all the trappings of an authentic Parisian brasserie, the space is simply gorgeous. The classic French bistro fare, ranging from steak frites and grilled calf's liver to a wonderful brook trout with honey mustard glaze, is surprisingly affordable; and the expansive raw bar offerings are beautifully displayed and make a worthy splurge. But we have some serious complaints: The lofty room is so tightly packed and the tables so uncomfortably close that private conversation is a pipe dream. And this is the loudest restaurant we've ever been in—my husband and I found ourselves yelling at each other across the tiny table, which made the whole dining experience less than relaxing. Still, if you're willing to put up with the discomforts, this is about as exciting as a downtown scene gets. The long mirrored bar is a hopping spot unto itself that attracts beautiful people galore, and the boulangerie sells fresh-baked breads, desserts, and sandwiches to go.

✪ **Quilty's.** 177 Prince St. (btw. Sullivan and Thompson sts.). ☎ **212/254-1260.** Reservations highly recommended. Main courses $10–$18.50 at lunch, $19.50–$29 at dinner; weekend brunch $8–$18.50. AE, DC, DISC, MC, V. Mon 6–11pm, Tues–Sat noon–3pm and 6–11pm, Sun 11am–3pm and 6–10pm. Subway: C, E to Spring St.; N, R to Prince St. CONTEMPORARY AMERICAN.

No matter how many restaurants I visit in this city, Quilty's remains one of my absolute favorites. Chef Katy Sparks and her crew just get it all right. The subtle, softly lit room is intimate and relaxing, with decently sized and spaced tables, comfortable seating, and an elegantly casual SoHo-goes-pastoral vibe that makes the restaurant feel special without being formal or stuffy. The greeting is warm, and the service professional yet personable. The feisty New American menu changes with the seasons, but you can expect bold, complex flavors that wow without overwhelming. There's always a lot going on in the dishes, but they're always harmonious. Last time I dined here (from the autumn menu), the fresh cepes baked in parchment and paired with harmony croutons and ricotta salata was a delicate symphony. And a reisling coriander jus was the ideal twist to the perfect comfort food: roasted organic chicken with buttermilk-battered onion rings. For dessert, the caramelized golden pineapple with vanilla bean–anise sauce was an ideal reinvention of the tropical fruit. The wine list is on the high side, but tends toward special vintages and rare labels; lively descriptions make it fun to choose, but the knowledgeable waitstaff is happy to suggest pairings if you prefer. Any way you look at it, Quilty's is a winner.

Savoy. 70 Prince St. (at Crosby St.). ☎ **212/219-8570.** Reservations highly recommended. Main courses $10–$14 at lunch, $19–$24 at dinner; prix-fixe dinner $52. AE, DISC, MC, V. Mon–Sat noon–3pm; Mon–Thurs 6–10:30pm, Fri–Sat 6–11pm, Sun 6–10pm. Subway: N, R to Prince St.; B, D, F, Q to Broadway–Lafayette St.; 6 to Spring St. CONTEMPORARY AMERICAN.

On a charming brick-paved street, behind a facade with a warm patina-like glow, hides this SoHo treasure. An innovative à la carte menu is served downstairs where, despite the cozy dining room's small size, it's easy to have an intimate conversation since the noise level is controlled by an ingeniously screened sound-absorbing ceiling. The brilliance of chef/owner Peter Hoffmann's creative, Mediterranean-accented contemporary cuisine is its subtlety—he wins diners over with gentle flavors and pleasing combinations. The menu changes constantly, but a signature dish is the excellent salt-crusted baked duck. Last time I dined here, cured pork loin with tomatillo sauce, sweet-and-sour cabbage, and butternut squash was also a winner, as was perfectly fileted brook trout on a bed of cornmeal sauce with braised mushrooms and kale. Upstairs there's a cozy bar and a second dining room, seating no more than 15 or so, where the four-course prix-fixe dinner is served; almost entirely prepared in the room's brick fireplace, it makes for a memorable evening. The desserts are delectable, and the eclectic wine list offers enough choices under $45 to keep things reasonable. Service is a bit formal for the setting—almost French—but appropriately attentive.

MODERATE

Blue Ribbon Sushi. 119 Sullivan St. (btw. Prince and Spring sts.). ☎ **212/343-0404.** Reservations not accepted. À la carte sushi and rolls $2.75–$15.50 (specials may be higher); sushi combos and main courses $11.50–$25. AE, DISC, MC, V. Daily 4pm–2am. Subway: C, E to Spring St.; N, R to Prince St. SUSHI.

This lovely, almost zen-like closet of a restaurant is a terrific choice for sushi lovers, especially those with adventurous palates. This is hipper-than-thou SoHo and Blue Ribbon is hot, hot, hot, so don't expect a bargain. But you will get your money's worth here: The fish is as fresh as can be, the top-notch chefs know how to handle it, and the selection is marvelous. Almost evenly split between the Pacific and the Atlantic, the dazzling menu offers up the obvious (ruby-red tuna, meaty yellowtail, creamy sea urchin in the shell) and the out there (blue crab roll, Maine lobster, Japanese mountain yam, even jellyfish). There's a changing array of inventive, Nobu-ish appetizers— we had an incredible, almost foie gras-like monkfish liver last time I was there—and an equally impressive sake list. The staff is a bit harried, but they're very knowledgeable and do a remarkable job keeping up with demand. The biggest downside, of course, is that reservations aren't taken, so come early, come late, or expect a wait. Also, while the booths are very comfortable for two or four, seating can be tight for larger parties.

INEXPENSIVE

Fanelli's Cafe. 94 Prince St. (at Mercer St.). ☎ **212/226-9412.** Reservations not accepted. Main courses $5–$12. AE, MC, V. Mon–Wed 10am–2am, Thurs–Sat 10am–4am, Sun noon–2am. Subway: N, R to Prince St. AMERICAN.

Once upon a time, SoHo consisted of a few daring galleries, a gaggle of artists living illegally in loft space that no one wanted, a few Italian bakeries, and Fanelli's. Matters couldn't be more different now: The galleries have given way to Banana Republic, the bakeries have moved over for Balthazar, and absolutely everyone wants those lofts. Thankfully, however, Fanelli's remains the same. This place is a classic New York pub. The long bar is propped up by regulars, and its corner door and pressed-tin ceiling have locked in the 1847 atmosphere (this is the second-oldest continuously operating establishment in the city, after the Bridge Cafe). A lot of smoking gets done in front, so if fumes annoy you, ask to be seated in the back. There's not much point in getting fancy with your order: The burgers are great, the pastas fresh and offered with a selection of sauces straight from Little Italy, the beer tapped into pint glasses. The daring will give the dandy mussels a shot. Wine? House red. No kidding. If you're coming for dinner, especially on a weekend, your best bet is to arrive before 7pm, when the noise level really starts to escalate.

Kelley & Ping. 127 Greene St. (btw. Houston and Prince sts.). ☎ **212/228-1212.** Reservations not accepted. Main courses $3.95–$7.50 at lunch, $7.95–$16.95 at dinner. AE, MC, V. Daily 11:30am–11pm. Subway: N, R to Prince St. PAN-ASIAN.

At the northern edge of SoHo lies this convivial noodle restaurant, which is almost unbelievably low-priced for the neighborhood and hipness quotient. The dark wood-and-glass decor, which evokes a sort of Shanghai-market look, is an ideal setting for the pan-Asian cuisine, which criss-crosses the continent from Korea to Malaysia to Japan, with a little fusion thrown in for good measure. The menu is heavy on spicy soups, dumplings, and noodle dishes. We particularly like the shrimp-and-peanut pad thai, a traditionalist's delight; the excellent wonton and roast duck soup; and the flavorful curries. In keeping with the menu and the ambiance, there's an exhaustive tea selection. Expect lots of downtown gallery and aspiring model types, who practically consider this their second home (or first, for as much as they probably cook). Unfortunately, this place can be a little too popular—don't be surprised if you have to wait for a table at dinnertime. Things move a little faster at lunch, when you belly up to the kitchen counter, cafeteria-style, to place your order.

Lombardi's. 32 Spring St. (Mott and Mulberry sts.). ☎ **212/941-7994.** Reservations accepted for parties of 6 or more. Small pies (6 slices) $10.50–$16, large pies $12.50–$20. No credit cards. Mon–Thurs 11:30am–11pm, Fri–Sat 11:30am–midnight, Sun 11:30am–10pm. Subway: 6 to Spring St.; N, R to Prince St. PIZZA.

Lombardi's is a living gem in the annals of the city's culinary history. First opened in 1905, "America's first licensed pizzeria" still cooks some of New York's best pizza in its original coal brick oven. The wonderful, crispy-thin crust (a generations-old family recipe that Gennaro Lombardi hand-carried from Naples at the turn of the century) is topped with fresh mozzarella, basil, and tomatoes, Pecorino romano cheese, and virgin olive oil. From there, the choice is yours. Topping options are suitably old-world (pancetta, calamata olives, Italian sausage, and the like), but Lombardi's specialty is the fresh clam pie, with hand-shucked clams, oregano, garlic, romano, and pepper (no sauce). The main dining room is narrow but pleasant, with the usual checkered tablecloths and exposed brick walls. A big draw is the garden out back. (Walk past the kitchen and up a flight of stairs to reach this lovely second-floor deck, where tables sport Cinzano umbrellas and a flowering tree shoots up through the concrete.) Another plus: In a city where rudeness is a badge of honor, Lombardi's wait staff is extremely affable.

Soho Kitchen & Bar. 103 Greene St. (btw. Spring and Prince sts.). ☎ **212/925-1866.** Reservations accepted for parties of 6 or more. Main courses $7.75–$18.50. AE, MC, V. Mon–Thurs 11:30am–midnight, Fri–Sat 11:30am–2am, Sun 12:30–11pm. Subway: N, R to Prince St.; C, E to Spring St. AMERICAN.

Even though the food is nothing special, the fun, easygoing atmosphere makes Soho Kitchen a regular stop on my agenda. This large, lofty space attracts an animated after-work and late-night crowd to its central bar, which dispenses more 21 beers on tap, a whole slew of microbrews by the bottle, and more than 100 wines by the glass, either individually or in "flights" for comparative tastings. The menu offers predictable but affordable bar fare: buffalo wings, oversize salads, good burgers, and a variety of sandwiches and thin-crust pizzas. You won't spend more than 12 bucks or so on your main meal unless you graduate to entrees like the New York sirloin, which makes this a great bet for wallet-watchers.

If you're in lower Manhattan and you're looking for similar fare, head to the **Wall Street Kitchen & Bar,** housed in a spectacular former bank building in the heart of the Financial District at 70 Broad St. (☎ **212/797-7070**).

Spring Street Natural Restaurant. 62 Spring St. (at Lafayette St.) ☎ **212/966-0290.** www.citysearch.com/nyc/springstnatural. Reservations not necessary. Main courses $7–$16. AE, DC, MC, V. Sun–Thurs 11:30am–midnight, Fri–Sat 11:30am–1am. Subway: 6 to Spring St. HEALTH-CONSCIOUS.

This 25-year-old spot is as comfortable and easygoing as your old college hangout—and just about as affordable, too. The expansive brick-walled room is filled with leafy greenery and anchored by an old oak bar. This is the kind of place where you can set yourself down at a table and camp for a while, poring over a good book while you nosh on a farm-fresh entree-sized salad or a terrific tempeh burger; the staff will happily refill your coffee mug as you relax. But while the cuisine is all-natural and prepared with good health in mind, it's not strictly vegetarian: There's also fresh-off-the-boat seafood and free-range chicken and turkey. The menu isn't restricted to soups, sandwiches, and salads, as it is in many other health-minded restaurants. You can come for a full meal, dining on such entrees as broiled New England bluefish with shiitake mushrooms, roasted chicken with pommery mustard glaze, or any number of pastas and stir frys. Everything is well-prepared and satisfying. The kitchen can also satisfy sugar, dairy, and other dietary restrictions. Brunch is served on weekends until 4pm, and there's pleasant outdoor seating along Lafayette Street in good weather.

6 The East Village & NoHo

See the "Downtown Dining" map (pp. 130–131) for restaurants in this section.

EXPENSIVE

✪ **BondSt.** 6 Bond St. (1 block north of Bleecker St., btw. Broadway and Lafayette St.). ☎ **212/777-2500.** Reservations highly recommended. À la carte sushi and rolls $6–$18; main courses and sushi combos $14–$26; omikase from $60. AE, MC, V. Mon–Sat 6pm–midnight; lounge Mon–Sat 5pm–2am. Subway: 6 to Bleecker St.; B, D, F, Q to Broadway–Lafayette St. SUSHI.

Go to Nobu for the most creative hot Japanese food in the city—but come to BondSt if you want to experience sushi as high art. This super-designed, über-trendy NoHo hotspot does offer some creative cooked dishes, including a beautiful charred Chilean sea bass in Saikyo miso, but BondSt is really all about raw fish. Chef Hiroshi Nakahara has managed to add creative twists to the sushi tradition without skewering it. A number of fishes are flown in from Japan daily, so expect to see choices that don't usually surface on this continent. Purists will love the super-fresh yellowtail, the terrific selection of blue fin and big eye tunas, and the perfectly presented eels, both anago (sea eel) and unagi (freshwater). For the best deal on roes and urchins, go with the Caviar 006 plate, which allows you to sample all of the choices, including herring and mullet roes and osetra caviar sushi (superflously topped with gold leaf, but sublime nevertheless), as well as the obvious choices, for a fraction of what it would cost to order them all individually. For the most intriguing selection, start with a few of the creative appetizers, which include fugu sashimi (yep, blowfish) in ponzu sauce— a splurge at $30, but worth a try for adventurous eaters. The sake selection is excellent. Service is fashionably aloof, but the stick-thin waitstaff knows the menu well. Reservations usually require a week's notice, but you might be able to grab a spot at the sushi bar if you stop in (earlier is always better).

MODERATE

In addition to the choices below, also consider the NoHo branch of **Time Cafe** (p. 150), 380 Lafayette St., at Great Jones Street (☎ **212/533-7000**), which has a wonderful Moroccan-themed lounge called Fez Under Time Cafe (see chapter 9 for details).

✪ **Bop.** 325 Bowery (at 2nd St.). ☎ **212/254-7887.** Reservations accepted for parties of 4 or more. Main courses $12.95–$18.95. AE, MC, V. Mon–Sat 6pm–midnight, Sun 6–11pm; bar open daily from 5pm. Subway: 6 to Bleecker St.; F to 2nd Ave. KOREAN.

Bop may be on the fringes of Chinatown, but don't expect your average brightly lit ethnic restaurant serving up the staples. The brainchild of hip restaurateur Brad Kelley, also of Kelley & Ping in SoHo (p. 140), among other hot spots, Bop is a gorgeous space designed with the beautiful people in mind and dimly lit for ultimate effect. But that's where the pretensions end: The friendly, attentive staff serves wonderful modern Korean cuisine with pan-Asian twists. The signature dish is *bi bim bop*, rice served either sizzling in a hot stone bowl or warm in a wooden bowl with wild mountain vegetables, kimchee, and raw tuna or shredded beef. We prefer the sizzling variety, which actually cooks as you mix the ingredients with chili paste (you define the temperature by how much you add). For an even more interactive meal, dine at one of the tabletop barbecues, where you can have such specialties as short ribs brushed with sake and soy or squid marinated in chili sauce cooked right in front of you. Cocktail lovers shouldn't pass on the soju, a yummy, lightly sweet Korean vodka made from sweet potatoes that's beautifully served in a martini glass with cucumber slices.

Danal. 90 E. 10th St. (btw. Third and Fourth aves.). ☎ **212/982-6930.** Reservations accepted for dinner. Main courses $15–$23. AE, MC, V. Tues–Fri 6–10pm, Sat–Sun 10am–3pm and 6–10pm. Subway: 6 to Astor Place. FRENCH COUNTRY.

This delightful restaurant resembles a Vermont farmhouse kitchen transplanted to New York. Weekend brunch is a favorite: aromatic coffee in bistro press pots, smoked salmon with dill pancakes, scrambled eggs with chicken-apple sausage, and grilled chicken salad with pears and bleu cheese. Dinner is hearty and satisfying, too. The menu changes daily, but might include a spinach, grilled onion, and goat cheese tart among the starters, and main dishes like rabbit ragout with dijon and bacon sauce, grilled monkfish with roasted mushrooms and shallot vinaigrette, and seared tuna salad with french lentils for lighter tastes. I can't shake the feeling that the dishes are a little higher priced than they should be, but everything is well prepared and the shabby-chic room just oozes charm. A great date place. Try not to miss the crème brûlée tart, Kahlúa cheesecake, blueberry bread pudding, and chocolate-raspberry tart.

Iso. 175 Second Ave. (at 11th St.). ☎ **212/777-0361.** Reservations not accepted. À la carte sushi $2.50–$6; sushi rolls $4.50–$12.50; sushi combos and main courses $13.50–$21. AE, MC, V. Mon–Sat 5:30pm–midnight. Subway: 6 to Astor Place. SUSHI.

Iso is the top choice in town for fresh and beautifully presented sushi at affordable prices. The sushi and sashimi combos make a good-value starting point; supplement with your favorites or a few of the daily special fishes, which may include blue fin toro (tuna belly) or Japanese aji (horse mackerel). The menu also features light, greaseless tempura and entrees like chicken teriyaki and beef negamaki for the sushiphobes in your party. The attractive Keith Haring–themed room is tightly packed but still manages to be relatively comfortable, and service is better than at other sushi joints in this price range. Unless you arrive before 6pm, expect a line—but the high-quality fish and wallet-friendly pricing make Iso worth the wait.

La Paella. 214 E. 9th St. (at Second Ave.). ☎ **212/598-4321.** Reservations accepted for 6 or more. Tapas $4.50–$9; paella for 2 $22–$36. MC, V. Sun–Thurs 5–11pm, Fri–Sat 5–11:30pm. Subway: 6 to Astor Place. SPANISH.

La Paella's tapas are the best in town, and the paella can hardly be outdone. This is fun eating, the kind of place where patrons return again and again to wash down fish croquettes, chorizos, and green olives with bottles of chilled Negro Modela, a dark Mexican brew that goes perfectly with the flavorful menu of (primarily) grilled delights, or the terrific sangria, served in generous pitchers by the frisky waitstaff, many of whom seem as though they just blew in from Madrid. Tapas here are more generously apportioned than at many other places; the grilled calamari is a perfectly sized appetizer without being overwhelming. The tapas and paellas are well priced, but it's easy to run up a tab in the festive setting, which tends to attract large parties after 8pm. There are two dining rooms: Upstairs is baroque-lite, with walls glazed to a gentle, earthen tone; a funkier, moodier, and more masculine vibe rules downstairs.

✪ **Pisces.** 95 Ave. A (at 6th St.). ☎ **212/260-6660.** Reservations recommended. Main courses $8.95–$19.95; 2-course prix-fixe dinner (Mon–Thurs 5:30–7pm, Fri–Sun 5:30–6:30pm) $14.95. AE, CB, DC, MC, V. Mon–Thurs 5:30–11:30pm, Fri 5:30pm–1am, Sat 11:30am–3:30pm and 5:30pm–1am, Sun 11:30am–3:30pm and 5:30–11:30pm. Subway: 6 to Astor Place. SEAFOOD.

This excellent fish house serves up the best moderately priced seafood in the city. All fish is top-quality and fresh daily, and all smoked items are prepared in the restaurant's own smoker. But it's the creative kitchen, which shows surprising skill with vegetables as well as fish, that makes Pisces a real winner. The mesquite-smoked whole trout in sherry oyster sauce is sublime, better than trout I've had for twice the price; start with the phyllo-fried shrimp or the tuna ceviche with curried potato chips and roasted pepper coulis, and the world is yours. Other winning dishes include flaky pan-fried skate in a burgundy reduction with garlicky mashed potatoes and roasted pearl onions. There are daily specials in addition to the menu; last time we dined here, I feasted on an excellent grilled mako shark with chard in a cockle stew. The wine list is appealing and very well priced, the decor suitably nautical without being kitschy, and the service friendly and attentive. For wallet-watchers, the early-bird prix-fixe makes an already terrific value even better. The Alphabet City locale gives Pisces serious hip, but it's laid-back enough that even Grandma will be comfortable here. Tables spill out onto the sidewalk on warm evenings, giving you a ringside seat for the funky East Village show.

Roettele A.G. 126 E. 7th St. (btw. First Ave. and Ave. A). ☎ **212/674-4140.** Reservations recommended, especially on weekends. Main courses $7–$16; fondue for two $30–$34. AE, DC, DISC, MC, V. Tues–Sat 12pm–3pm and 5:30–11:30pm, Sun 5:30–10pm. Subway: L to First Ave.; 6 to Astor Place. SWISS.

This Swiss chalet hideaway is New York's only authentic Swiss restaurant, and it's a winner. The cheese fondue, a hearty dinner for two or a generous appetizer for four, is perfectly smooth and beautifully presented with crusty bread and fresh vegetables. Build your meal around it by supplementing with other Alpine and house specialties, such as air-dried beef, classic raclette and wienerschnitzl, duck liver mousse, and terrific sautéed wild mushrooms over fresh herbs and polenta—plus spaetzle on the side, of course. They stock Swiss and German wines and beers, plus a few French bottles; try the medium-bodied Spatenlager to help wash down all that melted cheese. In keeping with the theme, a wide selection of tempting French and German pastries are available. The only thing that keeps me from awarding a star to this East Village fave is the harried service, which is friendly but seems stymied by the kitchen. It's not a big problem—just come armed with a little patience.

INEXPENSIVE

Also consider the East Village branch of **Bendix Diner** (p. 160), 167 First Ave., between 10th and 11th streets (☎ 212/260-4220) for hipster takes on homestyle favorites. There's also **Burritoville** (p. 132), at 141 Second Ave., between St. Mark's and 9th Street (☎ 212/260-3300), which is great for a quick bite.

☉ Angelica Kitchen. 300 E. 12th St. (just east of Second Ave.). ☎ **212/228-2909.** Reservations accepted for six or more Mon–Thurs. Main courses $5.95–$14.25; lunch deal (Mon–Fri 11:30am–5pm) $6.75. No credit cards. Daily 11:30am–10:30pm. Subway: L, N, R, 4, 5, 6, to 14th St./Union Sq. ORGANIC VEGETARIAN.

If you like to eat healthy, take note: This cheerful restaurant is serious about vegan cuisine. The kitchen prepares everything fresh daily; they guarantee that at least 95% of all ingredients are organically grown, with sustainable agriculture and responsible business practices additionally required before food can cross the kitchen's threshold. But good-for-you (and good-for-the-environment) doesn't have to mean boring—this is flavorful, beautifully prepared cuisine served in a lovely country kitchen–style setting. Salads spill over with sprouts and all kinds of crisp veggies and are crowned with homemade dressings. The Dragon Bowls, a specialty, are heaping portions of rice, beans, tofu, and steamed vegetables. The daily seasonal specials feature the best of what's fresh and in season in such dishes as fiery three-bean chili, slow-simmered with sundried tomatoes and a blend of chile peppers; baked tempeh nestled in a sourdough baguette and dressed in mushroom gravy; and lemon-herb baked tofu layered with roasted vegetables and fresh pesto on mixed-grain bread. Breads and desserts are fresh baked and similarly wholesome (and made without eggs, of course).

Boca Chica. 13 First Ave. (at 1st St.). ☎ **212/473-0108.** Reservations accepted for parties of 6 or more Mon–Thurs only. Main dishes $7.50–$19.75 (most under $13). AE, MC, V. Sun–Thurs 6–11pm, Fri–Sat 6pm–midnight. Subway: F to Second Ave. SOUTH AMERICAN.

This lively, colorful joint is always packed with a gleefully mixed crowd working its way through a round of margaritas or a few pitchers of beer. The cuisine is a down-market version of the pan-Latino favorites that have captivated palates farther uptown, most notably at Bolivar on the Upper East Side. The food at Boca Chica is a little closer to its hearty South American roots: well-prepared pork, beef, fish, and vegetarian dishes, most pleasingly heavy on the sauce and spice, accompanied by plantains, rice, and beans. There's also a bevy of interesting appetizers, including black bean soup well-seasoned with lime juice and terrific coconut-fried shrimp. While this approach to cooking now tends to be well out of reach of the under-$25 crowd, Boca Chica keeps things at an affordable level, much to the delight of those of us without bottomless wallets. *Be forewarned:* Getting in on weekends is about as hard as sneaking into Havana.

Dining Zone: Little India

The stretch of East Sixth Street between First and Second avenues in the East Village is known as "Little India," thanks to the dozen or more Indian restaurants that line the block (subway: F to Second Avenue). Dining here isn't exactly high style, but Little India's restaurants do offer decent Indian food at discount prices, sometimes accompanied by live sitar music. It's loads of fun to grab a bottle of wine or a six pack from one of the corner stores on Second Avenue (many of Little India's restaurants don't serve alcohol, but even those who do will often let you bring in your own) and cruise the strip, deciding which one most appeals to you. In warm weather, each usually stations a hawker out front to convince you what makes theirs *so* much better than the competition, which gives the street a lively bazaar feel.

Some people speculate that there's one big kitchen in the alley behind East 6th, but a few of Little India's restaurants deserve special attention. **Bombay Dining,** at 320 E. 6th St. (☎ 212/260-8229), is a standout, serving excellent *samosa* (crisp vegetable-and-meat patties), *pakora* (banana fritters), and *papadum* (crispy bean wafers with coarse peppercorns). Also satisfying are **Gandhi,** 344 E. 6th St. (☎ 212/614-9718), for a touch of low-light romance; **Mitali East,** 336 E. 6th St. (☎ 212/533-2508), the king of curry; and **Passage to India,** 308 E. 6th St. (☎ 212/ 529-5770), for North Indian tandoori. The Phyllis Diller of Little India, Christmas light–bedecked **Rose of India,** 308 E. 6th St. (☎ 212/533-5011), used to be a kitschy favorite, but the food has been disappointing the last few times out.

Around the corner—and a giant step up in quality—from Little India is ✪ **Haveli,** 100 Second Ave. (☎ 212/982-0533), where the authentically prepared dishes, setting, and service are far superior to what you'll find on East 6th Street. Prices are a little steeper—solidly in the $10 to $16 range—but the Haveli experience is worth the extra dough.

The New York Deli News

There's simply nothing more Noo Yawk than hunkering down over a mammoth pastrami sandwich or a lox-and-bagel plate at an authentic Jewish deli, where anything you order comes with a bowl of lip-smacking sour dills and a side of attitude. All of the following are the real deal—you gotta problem wid'dat?

Opened in 1937, the **Stage Deli,** 834 Seventh Ave., between 53rd and 54th streets (☎ **212/245-7850**), may be New York's oldest continuously run deli. The Stage is noisy and crowded and packed with tourists, but it's still as authentic as they come. Connoisseurs line up to sample the 36 famous specialty sandwiches named after many of the stars whose photos adorn the walls. The celebrity sandwiches, ostensibly created by the personalities themselves, are jaw-distending mountains of top-quality fixings: The Tom Hanks is roast beef, chopped liver, onion, and chicken fat, while the Dolly Parton is—drumroll, please—twin rolls of corned beef and pastrami.

For the quintessential New York experience, head to the **Carnegie Deli,** 854 Seventh Ave., at 55th Street (☎ **212/757-2245**), where it's worth subjecting yourself to surly service, tourist-targeted pricing, and elbow-to-elbow seating for the best pastrami and corned beef in town. Even big eaters may be challenged by mammoth sandwiches with names like "fifty ways to love your liver" (chopped liver, hard-boiled egg, lettuce, tomato, and onion). Main courses range from goulash to roasted chicken, and the heavenly blintzes come stuffed with cheese or fruit. Cheesecake can't get more divine, so save room!

The ✪ **Second Avenue Deli,** 156 Second Ave., at 10th Street (☎ **212/ 677-0606**), is the best kosher choice in town (for all you goyem out there, that means no milk, butter, or cheese is served). There's no bowing to tourism here— this is the real deal. The service is brusque, the decor is nondescript, and the sandwiches don't have cute names, but the dishes served here are true New York classics: gefilte fish, matzoh ball soup, chicken livers, potato knishes, nova lox and eggs. And for $11 to $13—several bucks cheaper than Midtown's Carnegie, it's worth noting—you get a monster triple decker sandwich (try wrapping your gums around the corned beef, tongue, and salami) with a side of fries. The crunchy dills are to die for. Keep an ear tuned to the Catskills-quality banter among crusty wait staff. It don't get more Noo Yawk than this.

Other outstanding choices are **Kaplan's** at the Delmonico, 59 E. 59th St., between Madison and Park avenues (☎ **212/755-5959**), for East Side class and good sandwiches; and **Katz's Delicatessen,** 205 E. Houston St., at hipster-hot Ludlow Street on the Lower East Side (☎ **212/254-2246**), for their beloved all-beef hot dogs.

Cucina di Pesce. 87 E. 4th St. (at Second Ave.). ☎ **212/260-6800.** Reservations accepted. Main dishes $6.95–$10.95 (specials may be slightly higher); 3-course early-bird dinner (offered daily 3:30–6:30pm) $9.95. No credit cards. Daily 4pm–midnight. Subway: F to Second Ave. ITALIAN.

This crowded East Village Italian is legendary for its good value—and it's surprisingly charming, too, if a little on the loud side. The focus is on Old World basics like hearty beef lasagna, marinara-topped pasta, shrimp scampi, and veal marsala. Every once in a while somebody in the kitchen goes too far with a shellfish-and-mollusk combo, but by and large the offerings really satisfy. The wide selection of basic pastas (fettuccine primavera, linguine with clam sauce—you get the picture) are always fresh and properly sauced, the veal nicely tender, and the fried calamari well seasoned and perfectly crisped. The great meal/low price combo means that the place can be a mob scene, but free mussels marinara at the bar makes the sometimes-long wait easier to take. The only disappointment is the wine list, which leaves a lot to be desired; your best bet is to stick with the house red, or opt for beer instead.

If the wait is just too excruciatingly long, head across the street to **Frutti de Mare,** 84 E. 4th St. (☎ **212/979-2034**), which offers up basically the same schtick, minus the mussels at the bar.

☺ Shabu Tatsu. 216 E. 10th St. (First and Second aves.). ☎ **212/477-2972.** Reservations accepted for parties of 4 or more. Full shabu-shabu dinners for two $28–$34. AE, DC, MC, V. Sun–Thurs 5–11:45pm, Fri–Sat 3pm–2am. Subway: L to First Ave., 6 to Astor Place. JAPANESE SHABU-SHABU.

This casual place features shabu-shabu, a dish you prepare yourself in the hotpot of boiling water built into the center of your table. The interactive fun begins when the waiter brings a plate piled high with raw beef (turkey is also available) and vegetables and gives an introductory lesson on how to make "shabu." It's lots of fun poking into the pot with your chopsticks, watching your piece of meat or veggies cook to your satisfaction, then dipping them in one of two sauces, one peanuty and the other of vinegar and soy sauce. After you're done, noodles are piled in and the broth is turned into a yummy after-dinner soup. The food is fresh, high-quality, and appealing even to those who otherwise don't care for Japanese food. The pure entertainment value makes this a great place to take kids or a group, and completely impractical for single diners. Duos can snare a table, but since you can't reserve ahead, don't be surprised if there's a wait; the restaurant is always busy, so it's best to go early or late.

Other locations are on the Upper East Side at 1414 York Ave. and 75th Street (☎ **212/472-3322**), and on the Upper West Side at 483 Columbus Ave., between 83rd and 84th streets (☎ **212/874-5366**).

Veselka. 144 Second Ave. (at 9th St.). ☎ **212/228-9682.** Sandwiches $1.95–$6.50; main courses $5–$12. AE, MC, V. Daily 24 hours. Subway: 6 to Astor Place. UKRAINIAN DINER.

Whenever the craving hits for hearty Eastern European fare at old-world prices, Veselka fits the bill with *pierogi* (small doughy envelopes filled with potatoes, cheese, or sauerkraut), *kasha varnishkes* (cracked buckwheat and noodles with mushroom sauce), stuffed cabbage, grilled polish kielbasa, freshly-made potato pancakes, and classic soups like a sublime scarlet borscht, voted best in the city by the *New York Times* and *New York* magazine. Try the buckwheat pancakes for a perfect breakfast or brunch. Despite the authentic fare, the diner is comfortable and appealing, with an artsy slant. Thanks to Veselka's we-never-close policy, it's a favorite after-hours hangout with club kids and other night owls.

7 Greenwich Village

See the "Downtown Dining" map (pp. 130–131) for restaurants in this section.

VERY EXPENSIVE

☺ One If By Land, Two If By Sea. 17 Barrow St. (btw. W. 4th St. and Seventh Ave. South). ☎ **212/228-0822.** Reservations strongly recommended. Jacket recommended; tie optional. Main courses $29–$39; tasting menu $68. AE, DC, DISC, MC, V. Daily 5:30–11:30pm. Subway: 1, 9 to Christopher St. CONTINENTAL.

Ask just about any New Yorker to point you to the city's most romantic restaurant and you'll end up at this candlelit, rose-filled 18th-century carriage house once owned by Aaron Burr. This beautiful, intimate space has been a haven of lovers (and those who hope to be) for nearly 30 years. The fireplace crackles and a pianist fills the room with melody as you are escorted to your table for two by the tuxedoed maitre'd. Given the emphasis on romance, it's no wonder that food has always come second here. It has never been bad—just committedly retro in the way that makes food snobs turn up their noses ("Beef Wellington? Ugh!"). But now that chef David McInerney has taken over the kitchen, even gourmands are giving One If By Land a second look. It's still pleasingly Continental-classic, but a few modern touches have given the menu new life. Among the best appetizers are the foie gras terrine with wild field greens and warm brioche, and rosy seared tuna with fresh wasabi, baby fennel, and shiitakes. The pan-roasted duck breast is greaseless and perfectly accompanied by cherries and black lentils, and the rack of lamb is lightly smoked and roasted. And, of course, there's the beef Wellington with bordelaise sauce—still a classic, and outstanding. The formal service is attentive without being intrusive. The wine list boasts no bargains, but does have a number of celebratory champagnes.

EXPENSIVE

✪ **Babbo.** 110 Waverly Place (just east of Sixth Ave.). ☎ **212/777-0303.** Reservations highly recommended. Pastas $16–$19, meats and fish $19–$25; tasting menus $49–$59. AE, DC, DISC, MC, V. Tues–Sat 5:30–11:30pm, Sun 4–9:30pm. Subway: A, B, C, D, E, F, Q to W. 4th St. (use 8th St. exit). NORTHERN ITALIAN.

Chef Mario Batali may not be Emeril (yet), but his zesty, adventurous cooking has attracted a lot of attention since he began appearing on the Food Network. And justifiably so—Babbo is my pick for 1998's top new restaurant. Batali also runs Pó on Cornelia Street, but this restaurant is now the best forum for enjoying his mind-bogglingly good cuisine.

As soon as we saw Babbo's inviting butter-yellow facade, we knew we were in for something special. The restaurant is warm and intimate, with well-spaced tables and a relaxed air that makes dining here feel special but comfortable, not formal. The greeting is welcoming and the service smart and friendly. That's a good thing, because you may need help choosing from the risk-taking menu. Batali has reinvented the notion of antipasti with such starters as fresh anchovies beautifully marinated in lobster oil, and legendary Faicco sopressata accented with roasted beets, shaved fennel, and Macintosh vinegar. The chef has no equal when it comes to creative pastas; ask anyone who's dined here and they'll wax poetic about the spicy lamb sausage in delicate clouds called mint love letters, quickly becoming Babbo's signature dish. Heavy with offals and game meats, the *secondi* menu features such wonders as tender fennel-dusted sweetbreads; smoky grilled quail in a gamey but heavenly fig and duck liver vinaigrette; and spicy two-minute calamari, a paragon of culinary simplicity. The knowledgeable sommelier can help you choose from the unusual but excellent wine list, all Italian and well priced.

Clementine. 1 Fifth Ave. (at 8th St.). ☎ **212/253-0003.** Reservations recommended. Main courses $15–$25; late-night menu $7–$13. AE, DC, CB, DISC, MC, V. Daily 5pm–4am; dinner menu served Sun–Thurs 6pm–11:30pm, Fri–Sat 6pm–12:30am. Subway: A, B, C, D, E, F, Q to W. 4th St. (use 8th St. exit). CONTEMPORARY AMERICAN.

Reminiscent of an elegant art deco ocean liner, Clementine sports portholelike sconces, circular mohair booths, and an incongruous gurgling fountain at the heart of the main dining room. A long bar with a brass rail dominates the swanky but comfortable front-room lounge.

Clementine attracts a mix of trendsetters and devoted foodies. I was thrilled with chef John Schenk's daring cooking style; his flavors are bold and complex but not heavy, thanks to lots of reductions and natural juices. Appetizers are impressive, most notably the salad of fried green tomatoes and braised spare ribs served off the bone with white beans and watercress, or Schenk's signature grilled squid stuffed with spicy merguez sausage and couscous in a cumin-flavored tomato broth. Mahi mahi with collard greens, hush puppies, and toasted corn is a pleasing Southern surprise, while barbecued squab and chile-rubbed pork loins are classics in the making. There's a good number of well-priced wines to choose from, as well as a full menu of Clementine cocktails. We experienced good service from the youngish staff, but I've heard rumblings that not all servers are created equal at Clementine. And don't come here for romance—the tables for two are set close to one another, enough to scare a dallying couple away on our last visit.

✪ **Le Gigot.** 18 Cornelia St. (btw. Bleecker and W. 4th sts.). ☎ **212/627-3737.** Reservations highly recommended. Main courses $18–$22. AE. Tues–Sat 11am–2:30pm and 5pm–11pm, Sun 11am–2:30pm and 5–10pm. Subway: A, B, C, D, E, F, Q to W. 4th St. (use W. 3rd St. exit). FRENCH BISTRO.

Conceived as a moderate rather than a special-occasion restaurant, Le Gigot is a bit on the high side, but it's well worth the money. With buttercup walls, white linens, and bentwood cafe chairs, the tiny restaurant is so traditional that it's like a slice of Left Bank Paris transplanted to Greenwich Village. Fittingly, the menu is full of French bistro classics, and they're excellent across the board. There's a nod to the sea with a shellfish-heavy bouillabaise and a couple of fish preparatations, but Le Gigot is really a meat-lover's paradise, with prime cuts and creamy sauces. The steak au poivre is aged sirloin flambéed in cognac; free-range chicken is perfectly roasted, dressed in a heavenly Beaujolais shallot and mushroom sauce, and accompanied by crisply crusted gratin potatoes; escargot swims in rich butter and parsley; and traditional cassoulet and steak frites are first-rate realizations. Desserts are as classic and decadent as you'd expect, and there's a small but well-chosen wine list. Brunch is a neighborhood secret, with excellent omelets and crisp fried potatoes. Be aware, though, that the narrow space isn't suitable for large parties or those who need lots of leg room. Design alert: The bathrooms are the city's most lovely, with a gorgeous French country style and unusually beautiful brass fixtures.

MODERATE

Cafe de Bruxelles. 118 Greenwich Ave. (at Horatio St.). ☎ **212/206-1830.** Reservations recommended. Main courses $10.95–$19.50. AE, DC, MC, V. Tues–Thurs noon–11:30pm, Friday–Sat noon–midnight, Sun–Mon noon–10:30pm. Subway: A, C, E, 1, 2, 3, 9 to 14th St. BELGIAN.

This wonderfully low-key, lace-curtained restaurant is the city's top stop for Belgian-style mussels, frites, and beers. Yummy starters include wild mushrooms in puff pastry, thick-cut country pâté, and escargot in rich roquefort sauce. You might want to follow with the *carbonade flamande,* beef stew made with dark Belgian beer; *boudin blanc* with apples and onions; Belgian seafood casserole; or one of eight varieties of mussels, the best of which is the simple mariniere—nothing more than a large bowl of the mollusks cooked in onion, garlic, and white wine. No matter what you choose, your order is accompanied by a metal tin of sublime crispy fries with the traditional accompaniment, mayonnaise. Winning choices from the excellent selection of Trappist ales and lambics include the Affligem Abbey, smooth, rich, and fruity; and my favorite, the Chimay Rouge, a great choice for dark beer lovers.

⭘ **Home.** 20 Cornelia St. (btw. Bleecker and W. 4th sts.) ☎ **212/243-9579.** Reservations highly recommended. Main courses $14–$18 at dinner. AE. Mon–Fri 9–11am, 11:30am–3pm, and 6–11pm; Sat–Sun 11am–4pm and 6–11pm. Subway: A, B, C, D, E, F, Q to W. 4th St. (use W. 3rd St. exit). CONTEMPORARY AMERICAN HOME COOKING.

We just love Home. This cozy restaurant is the domain of a husband-and-wife team, chef David Page and co-owner Barbara Shinn, who have made homestyle cooking something to celebrate. Page and Shinn keep things fresh, popularly priced, and welcoming; as a result, their narrow, tin-roofed dining room is always packed. The menu changes regularly, but look for such signature dishes as the rich-and-creamy blue cheese fondue; an excellent cumin-crusted pork chop on a bed of homemade barbecue sauce; a filleted-at-your-table brook trout accompanied by an apple fig pancake and smoked bacon shallot dressing; and perfectly moist roasted chicken with a side of spicy onion rings. Chocolate lovers should save room for the silky-smooth pudding. Weekend brunch is another great time to visit, with fluffy pancakes and excellent egg dishes. This is a quintessential Village restaurant, loaded with sophisticated charm, but it is tiny. Seating isn't uncomfortable and you won't feel intruded upon by your neighbors, but the tight room isn't built for large parties or those who want to spread out. The lovely garden is heated year-round, but is most charming in warm weather; book an outside table well ahead.

Page and Shinn also run **Drovers Tap Room,** around the corner at 9 Jones St. (☎ **212/627-1233**). It's their Midwest-comes-to-Manhattan take on the small-town tavern. The all-American comfort food is delicious, reservations tend to be easier to come by, and the comfortable room is more suited to larger parties than Home is.

Time Cafe. 87 Seventh Ave. South (at Barrow St.). ☎ **212/220-9100.** Reservations recommended on weekends. Main courses $4–$13.50 at breakfast and brunch, $7.50–$13.75 at lunch, $7.50–$22 at dinner. AE, MC, V. Sun–Thurs noon–midnight, Fri noon–2am, Sat 10:30am–2am, Sun 10:30am–midnight. Subway: 1, 9 to Christopher St./Sheridan Sq. CONTEMPORARY AMERICAN.

This easygoing, affordable spot can provide a night's entertainment or the perfect sidewalk brunch. Although the NoHo location was the first, I prefer this one, which boasts one of the best outdoor spaces in Gotham. At street level is the cafe, an airy modern space that opens on to the street, with a good-sized bar and excellent people-watching potential. The spacious, umbrella-covered alfresco dining area is one flight up on the roof. The kitchen features a large selection of contemporary fare with a healthy bent, such as a grilled rare tuna sandwich with organic daikon sprouts and sesame wasabi on seven-grain bread; herb-roasted free-range chicken with roasted garlic hominy grits and sautéed spinach; and a host of creative thin-crust pizzas on lavash-style crust. The food isn't the best in town, but it's fine, and I like the healthy preparations and the casual, laid-back vibe.

In addition to this one, there's also the terrific NoHo location at 380 Lafayette St., at Great Jones St. (☎ **212/533-7000**), where I've spotted Michael Stipe more than once.

INEXPENSIVE

In addition to the choices below, there's also a branch of the retro all-American diner known as **EJ's Luncheonette** (p. 186) at 432 Sixth Ave., between 9th and 10th streets (☎ **212/473-5555**); and a nice branch of **Burritoville** (p. 132) at 298 Bleecker St., at Seventh Avenue (☎ **212/633-9249**).

⭘ **Bar Pitti.** 268 Sixth Ave. (btw. Bleecker and Houston sts.). ☎ **212/982-3300.** Reservations only accepted for 4 or more. Main courses $5.50–$12.50 (some specials may be higher). No credit cards. Daily noon–midnight. Subway: A, B, C, D, E, F, Q to W. 4th St. (use 3rd St. exit). TUSCAN ITALIAN.

Pizza! Pizza!

In the mood for a slice or two . . . or three? The Village is the perfect place to be. The original location of **John's Pizzeria** (p. 167), 278 Bleecker St. between Sixth and Seventh avnues (☎ **212/243-1680**), is a New York original and still one of the city's best. The pies are thin-crusted, properly sauced, and fresh, and served up piping hot in an authentic old-world setting. Sorry, no slices.

For something a little more artsy, head to **Two Boots to Go,** 201 W. 11st St. (at Seventh Avenue; ☎ **212/633-9096**), and 74 Bleecker St. (between Broadway and Crosby St.; ☎ **212/777-1033**), where creative variations on the traditional pie are precisely the point. Both are predominately takeout and delivery locations, but there are a few tiny tables for in-house eaters.

This indoor/outdoor Tuscan-style trattoria is a perennially hip sidewalk scene, and one of downtown's best dining bargains. Waiting for a table can be a chore (the wait list never seems very organized), but all is forgiven once you take a seat, thanks to authentic, affordably priced cuisine and some of the friendliest waiters in town. Despite the tightly packed seating, Bar Pitti wins you over with its rustic Italian charm—it's the kind of place where the waiter brings over the list of daily specials to your table on a well-worn blackboard, and if you want more cheese, a block of Parmesan and a grater suddenly appears. Peruse the laminated menu, but don't get your heart set on anything until you see the board, which boasts the best of what the kitchen has to offer; the last time we dined here, they wowed us with a fabulous veal meatball special. Winners off the regular menu, which focuses heavily on pastas and panini, include excellent rare beef carpaccio; grilled country bread with prosciutto, garlic, and olive oil; and spinach and ricotta ravioli in a creamy sage and parmesan sauce. The all-Italian wine list is high-priced compared to the menu, but you'll find a few good value choices.

Cafe Spice. 72 University Place (at 11th St.). ☎ **212/253-6999.** Full dinners $13.50–$18. Mon–Wed 11:30am–3pm and 5pm–10:30pm, Thur–Fri 11:30am–3pm and 5pm–11:30pm, Sat–Sun 1–10:30pm. AE, MC, V. Subway: L, N, R, 4, 5, 6 to Union Square. INDIAN FUSION.

The owners of Dawat have opened an edgy, affordably priced restaurant that many (including yours truly) consider to be even better than their haute Indian uptowner. Two steps up from Little India and more well-developed than fusion hotspots like Surya, Cafe Spice is a terrific bet. The restaurant has a groovy modern style; the room is all geometric shapes and vibrant colors. Each dish is artfully displayed and presented—a telltale sign of the not-quite-there-yet Indian fusion rage that has taken Manhattan this year. But, thankfully, the only thing that's really fusion about this menu is that it criss-crosses the sub-continent itself, from Punjab to Goa and back again, with a substantial side trip to southern India for spicy vegetarian along the way. The dishes are classic and confident. A great way to start is with the *palak papri chaat,* a well-spiced blend of spinach crisps, potatoes, and chickpeas in yogurt in tamarind; or with stuffed samosas, seasoned chicken or potatoes (skip the spiced tuna) in a light pastry shell. The tandooris (chicken, assorted veggies, or catch of the day) are all well prepared and pleasing, as are the other Indian basics: paneers, tikkas, and so on. All dinners come with basmati rice, fluffy naan, lentils, and a seasonal vegetable of the day, making this an all-around great deal.

✪ **Florent.** 69 Gansevoort St. (2 blocks south of 14th St. and 1 block west of Ninth Ave., btw. Greenwich and Washington sts.). ☎ **212/989-5779.** Reservations recommended for dinner. Main courses $7.95–$17.95; 3-course prix-fixe dinner $16.50 before 7:30pm, $18.50 7:30pm–midnight. No credit cards. Mon–Fri 9am–5am, Sat–Sun 24 hours. Subway: A, C, E, L to 14th St. FRENCH BISTRO/DINER.

So you get a craving at 3am for homemade rillettes, boudin noir, or steak frites and can't decide whether you'd like to eat with club kids, partying celebrities, cross-dressed revelers, truckers from Jersey, or the odd stockbroker? Then get thee down to Florent, the nearly 24-hour French bistro dressed up as a 50s-style diner, where you can have it all. Located in the far West Village area known as the Meat Packing District, Florent is a perennial hotspot no matter what the time of day. But it's after the clubs close when the joint really jumps. Tables are tightly packed, almost uncomfortably so in some cases, but it's all part of the late-night festivities. This place has a real sense of humor (check out the menu boards above the bar) and a CD catalog full of the latest indie sounds, all adding to the hipster fun. The food's not half-bad, either: The grilled chicken with herbs and mustard sauce is a winner, moist and flavorful, as is the french onion soup crowned with melted gruyere. There are always diner faves like burgers and chili in addition to Gallic standards like moules frites, and the comfort food specialties such as chicken pot pie make regular appearances. Try not to miss the fries, which are light, crispy, and addictive.

Tartine. 253 W. 11th St. (at W. 4th St.). ☎ **212/229-2611.** Reservations not accepted. Main courses $8–$16. No credit cards. Tues–Fri 9am–10pm, Sat 9am–10:30pm, Sun 9am–10pm. Subway: 1, 2, 3, 9 to 14th St. FRENCH BISTRO.

Authentic French isn't just for rich New Yorkers anymore thanks to the half-dozen or so affordable, authentic spots that have opened in Manhattan in recent years. The best of the bunch, by far, is Tartine. Tucked well west in Greenwich Village, this BYOB stalwart has been cooking up chicken pot pies and croque monsieurs for a friendly crowd for more than a decade. Packed at lunch, then packed again after 7pm until closing, Tartine is as famous for its mignonettes of beef, served with a mountain of delectable golden frites. The made-on-the-premises food (including all bread and baked goods) is so good that crowds are willing to put up with long lines and harried service. The only way to avoid the wait is to arrive early; otherwise, be prepared to hang around for an hour, but the great food at even better prices make patience quite a virtue for bargain hunters. Even more good news: There's no corkage fee.

8 The Flatiron District, Union Square & Gramercy Park

See the "Midtown Dining" map (pp. 154-155) for restaurants in this section.

VERY EXPENSIVE

✪ **Union Pacific.** 111 E. 22nd St. (btw. Park Ave. South and Lexington Ave.). ☎ **212/995-8500.** Reservations highly recommended. Prix-fixe lunch $29–$35, 3-course prix-fixe dinner $65 (plus optional 3 to 5-course appetizer flights $20–$30); tasting menus $72–$135. AE, CB, DC, MC, V. Mon–Sat noon–1:45pm and 5:30–10:15pm. Subway: 6 to 23rd St. PACIFIC RIM/ASIAN FUSION.

A city of innovators, New York drops the ball every once in awhile. It took until 1998 for truly excellent Pacific Rim–fusion cuisine to arrive in the city, but chef Rocco DiSpirito has really gotten it right.

The soaring, bi-level restaurant is serene and beautiful, with elegant Japanese touches and a lovely wall of water at the entrance (keep an eye out for the low-profile sign). Tables are well spaced and suited to private conversation, but you're best off asking to be seated along one of the banquettes. The menu may seem contrived at first (young rabbit with glazed turnips and a cane sugar conundrum?), but the combinations are extraordinary. While Mr. DiSpirito's French influences are strong, it's the flavors of Japan and the Pacific that gives his menu its edge. Still, this is not Nobu. Stellar appetizers include bluefin tuna with yuzu and fresh wasabi, ragout of Maryland blue crab with chanterelles, and caramelized sweetbreads with sorrels and muskmelon. The coldwater fish selections—such as east coast halibut with cracklin' shallot and young ginger, and Chatham cod with mustard greens and bright lovage broth—also keep the menu firmly rooted: This is a New Yorker's Pacific Rim menu. I've not found anything on the menu that isn't excellent, and Ruth Reichl of the *New York Times* has made the same claim, awarding the restaurant three prestigious stars. Wine pairings are available for both appetizers and entrees, with a surprising number of German and Austrian labels among the selections, adding a whole new dimension to the meal. Expensive, but excellent through and through.

EXPENSIVE

✪ **Gramercy Tavern.** 42 E. 20th St. (btw. Broadway and Park Ave. South). ☎ **212/ 477-0777.** Reservations required well in advance. Main courses $18–$21 at lunch; 3-course prix-fixe lunch $33; 3-course prix-fixe dinner $62. AE, DC, DISC, MC, V. Sun–Thurs noon–2pm and 5:30–10pm, Fri and Sat noon–2pm and 5:30–11pm. Subway: 6, R to 23rd St. CONTEMPORARY AMERICAN.

Thanks to warm service, a beautiful dining room that's the perfect blend of urban sophisitication and heartland rusticity, and faultless New American cuisine, Gramercy Tavern is one of the top dining rooms in the city. At the height of its game these days, it's a cut above almost any other contemporary restaurant in the city, including big sister Union Square Cafe. Owner Danny Meyer and chef Tom Colicchio assure that the restaurant exceeds expectations at every turn. You simply can't go wrong here.

The menu, which changes based on what's fresh and in season, is pleasing from start to finish. The foie gras appetizer exquisitely juxtaposes tender liver with a crunchy, acidic rhubarb relish. The seared pepper-crusted tuna is fanned out on a bed of wilted arugula, white beans, and squash with lemon confit. Saddle of rabbit will wow game lovers, and lowly chicken is elevated to new heights when it's poached and braised with salsify, pistachio, and truffles. The excellent cheese tray features top-notch farmstead selections from New York State, France, Spain, Italy, and England. Desserts, like warm lemon tart soufflé with blueberry compote and ginger ice cream, are equally divine. Expensive, but well worth every penny.

If the main dining room is too rich for your blood, or you simply can't get a reservation, consider the less expensive, more casual Tavern Room (see "Moderate," below).

Mesa Grill. 102 Fifth Ave. (btw. 15th and 16th sts.). ☎ **212/807-7400.** Reservations recommended. Main courses $15–$18 at lunch, $18–$29 at dinner. AE, DC, DISC, MC, V. Mon–Fri noon–2:30pm; Sun–Thurs 5:30–10:30pm, Fri–Sat 5:30–11pm; brunch Sat–Sun 11:30am–2:30pm. Subway: L, N, R, 4, 5, 6 to 14th St./Union Sq. SOUTHWESTERN.

A must for those interested in new American cooking, this spicy-hot restaurant has been made into a new classic by chef/owner Bobby Flay, star of the Food Network's *Hot Off the Grill with Bobby Flay*. His menu is almost thrillingly inventive: The tangerine and red chile–glazed tuna is invariably perfectly cooked, with bracing spices. Yucatan-spiced venison is tempered with caramelized cranberry sauce and sweet potato gratin. The grilled black Angus steak comes with Mesa Grill's sparky housemade steak sauce and a double-baked horseradish potato for extra flair. Sweet potato and Scotch bonnet ravioli with cremini mushroom sauce makes a quirkily appealing appetizer, but I can never resist starting with the blue corn pancake with zesty barbecued duck and habañero sauce. The only downside is the cavernous Roy Rogers–meets–Andy Warhol dining room, which is bright and festive, but can be way too noisy for comfortable conversation at times. Try to snag a table on the upstairs balcony if you can.

Midtown Dining

Alley's End
America
Aureole
Bolivar
Barbetta
Bendix Diner
Blue Water Grill
The British Open
Brooklyn Diner USA
Burritoville
The Cafe at Aquavit
Cafe Spice
Cafeteria
Caffe Bondí Ristorante
Carmine's
Carnegie Deli
Chanpen
Chez Josephine
Churrascaria Plataforma
Cité
Coco Pazzo Teatro
Daniel
Destinée
Ellen's Stardust Diner
Empire Diner
Ess-A-Bagel
Estiatorio Milos
Gramercy Tavern
Hamburger Harry's
Hangawi
Hard Rock Cafe
Harley-Davidson Cafe
Island Burgers & Shakes
Jean Georges
Jekyll & Hyde Club
Joe Allen
Joe's Shanghai
John's Pizzeria
Jo Jo
Julian's
Kaplan's
La Bonne Soupe
Le Bernardin
Le Cirque 2000

continues on
opposite page

NA-0146

Mangia 25 63
March 7
Mars 2112 48
Medusa 71
Mesa Grill 76
Meskerem 65
Metro Grill 65
Michael Jordan's–
    The Steak House 35
Molyvos 51
Motown Cafe 21
Mr. Chow 30
Official All Star Cafe 42
Old San Juan 50
Old Town Bar & Restaurant 80
Orso 59
Oyster Bar 35
Petrossian 16
Picholine 3
Pintaile's Pizza 74
Planet Hollywood 21
Pongsri Thai Restaurant 45
Prime Burger 37
Republic 77
Rice 'n' Beans 52
San Domenico 14
Serendipity 3 9
Siam Inn Too 54
Soup Kitchen International 18
Stage Deli 20
Steak Frites 78
Taco & Tortilla King 66
Tavern on the Green 1
The Tavern Room
    at Gramercy Tavern 72
"21" Club 38
Union Pacific 70
Virgil's Real BBQ 41
Vong 31
Won Jo 66
Woo Chon 64
Zarela 32
Zen Palate 57 73

Subway stop Ⓜ

MODERATE

Blue Water Grill. 31 Union Sq. West (at 16th St.). ☎ **212/675-9500.** Reservations recommended. Main courses $14.95–$24.95 (most less than $20). AE, MC, V. Mon–Thurs 11:30am–12:30am, Fri–Sat 11:30am–1am, Sun 5:30pm–midnight; brunch Sun 11am–4pm. Subway: L, N, R, 4, 5, 6 to 14th St./Union Sq. SEAFOOD.

This stylish seafooder serves up good-quality fish to an energetic crowd. There's usually a good selection of raw fish to choose from, whether sushi, oysters, or shrimp cocktail is your thing. Look for both Asian and Mediterranean influences on the extensive main course menu, which makes the most of the catches of the day. The best selections—often Atlantic salmon, wild striped bass, and Pacific mahi, among others—come from the kitchen's wood-burning grill. Lobster is well-priced and cooked to order. There's a good free-range chicken, a filet mignon, and a few pastas for the non-fish eaters in your crowd. If the weather's good, try to snag a table on the lovely narrow terrace overlooking Union Square. There's a live jazz combo in the art deco-influenced downstairs dining room nightly.

Caffe Bondí Ristorante. 7 W. 20th St. (btw. Fifth and Sixth aves.). ☎ **212/691-8136.** Reservations recommended. Pastas $9–$15, meat and fish main courses $16–$25; 4-course prix-fixe dinner $29 Sun–Thurs, 5-course prix-fixe dinner $39 Fri–Sat. AE, DC, JCB, MC, V. Mon–Sat 11am–11pm, Sun 11am–9pm. Subway: N, R, F to 23rd St. SICILIAN.

This charmingly authentic Italian cafe serves Sicilian delicacies with skill and care. The dedication of the Settepani brothers, who own and run the place, shows at every level, from the quality of the food to the friendliness of the staff. You might start with the *conca d'oro*, a lively salad of oranges, fennel, black olives, and red onions in an oil-and-vinegar dressing. The *insalata di fagiolini* is string beans, potatoes, and tomatoes mixed with oregano, olive oil, and vinegar. The fish soup is from an 11th-century Saracen recipe: sole, grouper, mussels, clams, and shrimp in a sauce of capers, saffron, garlic, pine nuts, and laurel leaves. Among the notable entrees are braised rabbit with white wine and sautéed shrimp in wine and béchamel sauce served with carrot-almond purée. The garden is a delight.

Medusa. 239 Park Ave. South (btw. 19th and 20th sts). ☎ **212/477-1500.** Reservations recommended. Pastas $10–$13, seafood and meat main courses $14–$19. Subway: L, N, R, 4, 5, 6 to 14th St./Union Square. MEDITERRANEAN.

If Medusa were just a little more expensive—a few dollars here, a few dollars there—there would be nothing special about it. It would be lost in the sea of overpriced Mediterranean boites that regularly come and go in the city. But what Medusa has going for it is value. In the increasingly high-rent, high-profile Flatiron District, Medusa has managed to keep its prices down to earth while still maintaining all the trappings of a downtown see-and-be-seen hotspot. And what's more, the food is good. The grilled octopus with baby greens, tomatoes, and steamed potatoes is a great way to start, and a bargain at $9. Or go with the attention-grabbing toasted herbed Medusa bread, topped with kefalotyri cheese flambéed in Sambuca—the restaurant's own successful twist on saganaki. All the pastas are fresh and well prepared, as are mostly seafood mains like oven-roasted Chilean sea bass. We've always been pleased with our meals at romantic, stylish Medusa; this is a place that manages to feel grown-up without the requisite high tab. There are a few concessions, such as on-the-cheap cafe chairs, but they're all but unnoticable in the romantically candlelit tomato-red space. Let's hope the people behind Medusa can keep up the good work.

Steak Frites. 9 E. 16th St. (between Fifth Ave. and Broadway/Union Sq. West). ☎ **212/463-7101.** Reservations recommended. Main courses $8.50–$17.50 at lunch, $13.95–$21.95 at dinner. AE, DC, MC, V. Mon–Thurs noon–11:30pm, Fri–Sat noon–12:30am, Sun noon–10pm. Subway: L, N, R, 4, 5, 6 to 14th St./Union Sq. FRENCH BISTRO.

Meat lovers, arm yourselves. The menu offers other choices (pasta, chicken, salads), but order the steak frites for two—certified black Angus perfectly grilled, pink inside, blackened outside. Or go with the mussels, which come in a number of presentations, the best of which is the white wine and fresh herbs or the hearty Belgian beer. The frites are better at Cafe de Bruxelles, but they're good here, too, and you'll get good ol' American ketchup on the side rather than Euro-style mayo. The big room is loud and the service isn't quite as attentive as I might like, but the food is well priced (especially the steak frites, a deal at $21.95) and well prepared. And I love the bustling, slice-of-St-Germain atmosphere, complete with mahogany-and-brass bar and Toulouse Lautrec–style murals on the walls. There's a good selection of wines and Belgian beers to choose from, as you'd expect from a French brasserie.

✪ **The Tavern Room at Gramercy Tavern.** 42 E. 20th St. (between Broadway and Park Ave. South). ☎ **212/477-0777.** Reservations not accepted. Starters $6–$9.50, main courses $12.50–$18. AE, DC, MC, V. Mon–Thurs and Sun noon–11pm, Fri–Sat noon–midnight. Subway: 6, N, R to 23rd St. CONTEMPORARY AMERICAN.

Unquestionably, Gramercy Tavern's main dining room is one of the finest in the city (see above). However, dining there requires reservations weeks in advance, and the prix-fixe prices almost demand a special occasion. Not so in the front Tavern Room, a friendly, informal bistro-style alternative where you can decide to eat at the last minute and still dine on some of the best food in town—without breaking the bank in the process. The compact but immensely appealing menu offers a lighter, more casual take on chef Tom Colicchio's excellent creative American fare. We love the perfectly roasted baby chicken with butternut squash succotash—nobody does chicken better. And where else are you going to get a filet mignon this good for less than $20? There's a good selection of salads, a terrific tomato garlic-bread soup, and a handful of fish dishes and sandwiches for lighter eaters, plus the restaurant's signature selection of cheeses and desserts. The room is very comfortable, with well-spaced tables and a pleasant energy that still allows for conversation; owner Danny Meyer's blanket no-smoking policy prevents any second-hand smoke from interfering with your meal. Service is top-notch, too. All in all, one of the best dining values in town.

INEXPENSIVE

America. 9 E. 18th St. (btw. Fifth Ave. and Broadway). ☎ **212/505-2110.** Reservations recommended. Main courses $6.95–$18.95. AE, DC, DISC, MC, V. Sun–Thurs 11:30am–midnight, Fri–Sat 11:30am–1am. Subway: L, N, R, 4, 5, 6 to 14th St./Union Sq. AMERICAN.

This attractive, kid-friendly restaurant is nearly as large as a continent, with a seemingly mile-high ceiling. The menu is eclectic (soups, omelets, pancakes, pastas, sandwiches, poultry, salads, meats, fish, burgers, and pizza), with prices you're more likely to see in the heartland than in New York. Each dish has a state or city listed next to it as the inspiration source: Texas five-way chili, Long Island duck pot pie, Mississippi fried catfish, New England clam chowder, and so on. (Get it?) The food isn't exactly gourmet, but so what? It does the job, and at the right price. America also offers a family brunch with a balloon maker and a magician on hand Saturdays and Sundays from noon to 4pm as well as a late kitchen Friday and Saturday nights.

✪ **Old Town Bar & Restaurant.** 45 E. 18th St. (btw. Broadway and Park Ave. South). ☎ **212/529-6732.** Reservations unnecessary. Main courses $6–$15. AE, MC, V. Mon–Sat noon–1am (Kitchen closes at 11:30pm), Sun 1–11:30pm (Kitchen closes at 10:30pm). Subway: 4, 5, 6, L, N, R to 14th St./Union Sq. AMERICAN.

If you've watched TV at all over the last couple of decades, this place should look familiar: It was featured nightly in the old *Late Night with David Letterman* intro, stars as Riff's Bar in *Mad About You,* and appeared in too many commercials to count, as

Pizza! Pizza!

Pintaile's Pizza, 124 Fourth Ave., between 12th and 13th streets (☎ 212/ 475-4977), dresses their daintily crisp organic crusts with layers of plum tomatoes, extra virgin olive oil, and other fabulously fresh ingredients. This new Union Square–area location of the Upper East Side favorite even has lots of seating for in-house eating.

---

well as in such movies as *The Devil's Own*, Woody Allen's *Bullets Over Broadway*, and, most recently, Whit Stillman's *The Last Days of Disco*. But this is no stage set—it's a genuine tin-ceilinged 19th-century bar serving up good pub grub, lots of beers on tap, and a real sense of New York history. Sure, there are healthy salads on the menu, but everybody comes for the burgers. Whether you go low-fat turkey or bacon-chili-cheddar, they're perfect every time. You have your choice of sides, but go with the shoestring fries—what else in a traditional place like this? Other good choices include spicy Buffalo wings with bleu cheese, fiery bowls of chili sprinkled with cheddar cheese and dollopped with sour cream, and a Herculean Caesar salad slathered with mayo and topped with anchovies. Food comes up from the basement kitchen courtesy of ancient dumbwaiters behind the bar, where equally crusty bartenders would rather *not* make you a Cosmopolitan, thank you very much. If you want to escape the cigarettes and the predatory singles scene that pulls in on weekends, head upstairs to the bliss-fully smoke-free dining room.

Republic. 37 Union Sq. West (btw. 16th and 17th sts.). ☎ **212/627-7172.** Reservations not accepted. Main courses $6–$9. AE, DC, MC, V. Sun–Wed noon–11pm, Thurs–Sat noon–midnight. Subway: L, N, R, 4, 5, 6 to 14th St./Union Sq. PAN-ASIAN NOODLES.

Proving once and for all that you don't have to sacrifice high style for wallet-friendly prices, this ultra-chic noodle joint serves up affordable fast food in an area where it's getting harder and harder to find a deal. Cushionless, backless benches pulled up to pine-and-steel refectory tables don't encourage lingering, but that's precisely the point: This is the kind of place that knows how to make you feel hip and happy and get you out the door efficiently. The Chinese-, Vietnamese-, and Thai-inspired noodle menu attracts a steady stream of impossibly chic on-the-go customers. For a one-bowl meal, try the spicy coconut chicken (chicken slices in coconut milk, lime juice, lemongrass, and galangal) or spicy beef (rare beef with wheat noodles in spiced with chiles, garlic, and lemongrass). The long curving bar is perfect for solitary diners.

Zen Palate. 34 Union Square East (at 16th St.). ☎ **212/614-9345.** Reservations recommended. Main courses $6–$16. AE, DC, MC, V. Mon–Thurs 11am–11pm, Fri–Sat 11am–midnight, Sun noon–10:30pm. Subway: L, N, R, 4, 5, 6 to 14th St./Union Square. PAN-ASIAN VEGETARIAN.

The hallmark of Asian dining has long been the health factor, particularly with so many vegetarian dishes (MSG notwithstanding). This might not be true of old-school Chinese, with its viscous sauces, but it certainly is of Zen Palate, which has adopted the less-is-more approach to Asian cuisine. Each location shares the same Japanese-influenced postmodern decor, with teak and patina-ed copper governing the aesthetic; the flagship Union Square location is a standout, with a long counter downstairs for on-the-run eaters and a warren of spare but attractive dining rooms upstairs, including some with Japanese-style seating. Tofu is king here, but you're not limited to it. Stars on the wide-ranging menu include taro spring rolls and basil moo-shu rolls for something creative, as well as steamed veggie dumplings and buns for a more traditional Asian choice. Despite the good-for-you approach, main courses like Rose Petals (homemade soy pasta in a sweet rice ginger sauce with garden vegetables) and Curry Supreme (with tofu, potatoes, and carrots) are very flavorful, and some will particularly appeal to spicy food lovers. All in all, a good bet for health-minded diners. Lest it all sound too good for you, you're welcome to BYOB with no corkage fee in the upstairs dining room.

There are two additional locations: in midtown at 663 Ninth Ave., at 46th Street (☎ 212/582-1669), and on the Upper West Side at 2170 Broadway (☎ 212/501-7768).

9 Chelsea

See the "Midtown Dining" map (pp. 154-156) for restaurants in this section.

MODERATE

Alley's End. 311 W. 17th St. (btw. Eighth and Ninth aves.). ☎ **212/627-8899.** Reservations recommended. Main courses $15–$20. DC, MC, V. Mon–Sat 6–11pm, Sun 11am–3pm and 6–11pm. Subway: A, C, E, L to 14th St. CONTEMPORARY AMERICAN.

Alley's End is a top pick of Chelsea residents and other Manhattanites, who consider it one of the city's few affordable restaurants where they feel safely cosseted from the hustle and bustle outside. You'll have a sense of adventure when you walk through the nearly secret entryway, down an alleyway just west of Eighth Avenue; look for the neon knife and fork, the only indication that there's a restaurant here. At the end you'll find a warren of charming brick-walled dining rooms that are perfect for peaceful conversation. The menu changes frequently depending on what's fresh and in season, but past winning dishes have included heirloom beefsteak tomatoes with grilled chicory and roasted garlic aioli; grilled center-cut pork chop with summer succotash, pancetta, and chipotle sauce; and Coach Farm aged goat cheese ravioli in pumpkin seed pesto with roasted wild fennel. The prices have gone a bit higher than I like in the past year (the $15 ravioli should be $13 max), but everything is carefully prepared, and the soothing setting (an increasing rarity in Manhattan) makes the prices more than palatable. A reasonable wine list, with most choices under $30, also helps.

Cafeteria. 119 Seventh Ave. (at 17th St.). ☎ **212/414-1717.** Reservations recommended. Sandwiches $7.50–$12.95, main courses $10.95–$18.95. AE, DISC, MC, V. Daily 24 hours. Subway: 1, 9 to 18th St. AMERICAN.

The greasy spoon goes glam at this round-the-clock Chelsea hotspot. More über-diner than nouvo automat, Cafeteria is all about high style, from the white-leather banquettes to the waifish waitstaff. Luckily, there's follow-through: Both the food and the service are better than they have to be in this veneer-happy town. The menu features modern takes on the blue-plate classics—meatloaf, chicken pot pie, fried chicken and waffles, and killer mac and cheese made with both cheddar and fontina (yum!)—as well as surprisingly successful neo-American fare, including a well-seared, thick cut tuna loin. On the downside, seating is tight—but that just puts you that much closer to the latest It-girls and boys, right? A great choice for those who want a dose of downtown's hippest crowd without paying the high tab that accompanies dinner at Moomba. Just put on your best basic black and you'll fit right in. Cafeteria is at its hippest after 10pm or so, but be sure to call ahead or you may be turned away at the door.

INEXPENSIVE

In addition to the choices below, there's a dazzling new branch of **Grand Sichuan Chinese Restaurant** at 229 Ninth Ave., at 24th Street (☎ 212/620-5200), which has been garnering rave reviews from restaurant reviewers throughout the city. There's also **Burritoville,** 264 W. 23rd St., between Seventh and Eighth avenues (☎ 212/ 367-9844), good for a quick bite.

Bendix Diner. 219 Eighth Ave. (at 21st St.). ☎ **212/366-0560.** Reservations not accepted. Main courses $5–$15. Tues–Sat 8am–3am; Sun–Mon 8am–midnight. AE, MC, V. Open 24 hours. Subway: C, E to 23rd St. AMERICAN DINER/THAI.

For the same reason that it's just plain pointless to try to order healthy at Bob's Big Boy when you're on a road trip, it's nutty to go for the gentler side of the menu at this funky Chelsea stalwart. Ignore the bizarro Thai dishes (head to a real Thai restaurant for pad thai and curries) and indulge instead in the big, patriotic, all-American grub. The burgers are served deluxe with a heap of french fries; the chili con carne (served "New York style," over rice with onions, peppers, and cheese) is heavy with beef and beans; the meat loaf and mashed potatoes is better than Ma used to make. I love the chicken noodle soup, which is the best I've had in the city, thanks to richer-than-usual broth (no boullion cubes here, brother). Breakfast chow is available any time of day, natch, and it's as hearty and wholesome as you'd expect. Portions are humungous, of course. Sunday brunch gets alarmingly crowded, so bring some sections of the *Times* to occupy yourself while you wait.

Bendix has a second, less-worn location in the East Village at 167 First Ave., between 10th and 11th streets (☎ 212/260-4220).

Empire Diner. 210 Tenth Ave. (at 22nd St.). ☎ **212/243-2736.** Reservations not accepted. Main courses $9.95–$16.95. AE, CB, DC, DISC, MC, V. Daily 24 hours. Subway: C, E to 23rd St. AMERICAN DINER.

Used to be that the Empire was the only thing doing this far west in Chelsea, but the emergence of an alternative-to-SoHo gallery scene in the west 20s has raised the neighborhood's profile a notch. Not that it matters in this throwback shrine to the slicked-up all-American diner, which looks suspiciously like an Airstream camper plunked down on the corner. This classic joint boasts a timeless art deco vibe, honest coffee, and supreme mashed potatoes—Manhattan's best. The food is all basic and good: eggs, omelets, burgers, overstuffed sandwiches, and a very nice turkey platter. There's live music courtesy of a pianist every day at lunch and dinner, and at weekend brunch. If you want quiet, go early. If you want an eyeful, wait for the after-hours crowd; the hours between 1 and 3am offer the best people-watching, when Prada and Gucci meld with Phat Farm and Levi's. When the weather's warm, a sidewalk cafe appears, and the limited traffic this far over—mostly aiming for the Lincoln Tunnel—keeps the soot-and-fumes factor down.

10 Times Square & Midtown West

See the "Midtown Dining" map (pp. 154–155) for restaurants in this section.

VERY EXPENSIVE

✪ **Le Bernardin.** 155 W. 51st St. (btw. Sixth and Seventh aves.). ☎ **212/489-1515.** Reservations required 1 month in advance. Jacket required/tie optional. Prix-fixe lunch $32–$42; prix-fixe dinner $70, tasting menu $120. AE, DISC, MC, V. Mon noon–2:30pm and 6pm–10:30pm, Tues–Thurs noon–2:30pm and 5:30–10:30pm, Fri noon–2:30pm and 5:30–11pm, Sat 5:30–11pm. Subway: 1, 9 to 50th St.; N, R to 49th St. FRENCH/SEAFOOD.

If forced to choose, I'd probably peg Le Bernardin as one of my two favorite restaurants in the city (the other being Chanterelle). The seafood here is the best in New York, if not the world. Food doesn't get better than the flash-marinated black bass ceviche, the freshest fish awash in cilantro, mint, jalapeños, and diced tomatoes. Eric Ripert's tuna tartare always exhilarates, its Asian seasoning a welcome exotic touch. Among lightly cooked dishes that shine are herbed crabmeat in saffron ravioli and shellfish-tarragon reduction; roast baby lobster tail on asparagus-and-cèpe risotto; and an extravagant mix of sea scallops, foie gras, and truffles from the Périgord, wrapped and steamed in a cabbage leaf and splashed with truffle vinaigrette ($15 extra). The crusted cod, served on a bed of haricots verts with potatoes and diced tomatoes, is another favorite. The formal service is impeccable, as is the outrageously pricey wine list, and the room is uptown gorgeous. The prix-fixe lunches are a bargain, given the master in the kitchen. The desserts—especially the frozen rum-scented chestnut soufflé or chocolate dome with crème brûlée on a macaroon—end the meal with a flourish.

✪ **San Domenico.** 240 Central Park South (btw. Broadway and Seventh Ave.). ☎ **212/ 265-5959.** Reservations required. Jacket requested at dinner. Main courses $18.95–$32.50; pre-theater prix-fixe $32.50. AE, CB, DC, MC, V. Mon–Fri noon–2:30pm and 5:30–11pm, Sat 5:30–11pm, Sun 5:30–10:30pm. Subway: N, R to 57th St.; 1, 9 to Columbus Circle. CONTEMPORARY ITALIAN.

Thanks to owner Tony May, San Domenico is one of the few restaurants successful in preserving the best traditions of Italian cooking while adding a modern twist. Inspired by the cuisine of Bologna, San Domenico's menu changes seasonally. Splendid appetizers may include grilled Mediterranean baby octopus with cucumbers and cherry tomatoes, chilled fava bean soup with goat cheese and truffle oil, or a rich mix of lobster, shrimp, king crab, and baby vegetables. Favorite pasta choices: ricotta ravioli with marinated tomatoes and black olives, and the extravagant handmade pasta with chives, caviar, and asparagus. For meat lovers, there's a roasted veal loin with braised radicchio, pearl onions, and creamy bacon sauce. Black sea bass filet in tomato-herb broth and grilled Norwegian salmon with caviar and sour cream are among the excellent fish offerings. The room is swanky, the service impeccable, and the wine list reads like a grade-A list of Italian vineyards. Excellent in every way.

"21" Club. 21 W. 52nd St. (btw. Fifth and Sixth aves.). ☎ **212/582-7200.** Reservations required. Jacket and tie required. Main courses $24–$41 (most $29 or more); prix-fixe lunch $29; pre-theater prix-fixe (5:30–6:30pm) $33; tasting menu $78. AE, DC, DISC, JCB, MC, V. Mon–Thurs noon–2:30pm and 5:30–10:15pm, Fri noon–2:30pm and 5:30–11pm, Sat 5:30–11pm. Closed Aug (or Sept). Subway: B, D, F, Q to 47th–50th sts./Rockefeller Center. AMERICAN.

A former speakeasy in the days of Prohibition, this landmark restaurant is ground zero for New York's old-school business and celebrity power set—and it has recently zoomed its way back onto the list of New York's most interesting dining rooms. After years of being more Ed McMahon than Johnny Carson, the place has a reinvigorated air. And that's due to new owners Orient-Express Hotels, who have made subtle changes in the decor and the menu, while keeping "21" classics like chicken hash, steak tartare prepared tableside, fried oysters, Maine lobster salad, and the famed burger—terribly expensive at $24, but worth it. The historic Bar Room is the best of the dining rooms, with its long mahogany bar, red-checkered tablecloths, and antique toys and other trinkets (many gifts of the celebs who consider "21" their second home) dangling playfully from the ceiling. A real New York classic.

EXPENSIVE

Barbetta. 321 W. 46th St. (btw. Eighth and Ninth aves.). ☎ **212/246-9171.** Reservations recommended. Main courses $22–$32. AE, DC, DISC, MC, V. Tues–Sun noon–2pm and 5pm–midnight. Subway: A, C, E to 42nd St. PIEDMONT ITALIAN.

Open since 1906, this landmark Italian specializes in the cuisine of Italy's northern Piedmont region. Housed in two adjoining townhouses, the restaurant is furnished with 18th-century classical antiques (a passion of owner Laura Maioglio, whose father founded the restaurant). An ungainly acoustical-tile ceiling detracts from the main dining room's old-world elegance, but makes it much more pleasant for conversation. This is a real pre-theater spot—the room goes from bustling to empty at around 7:45, after which a more sedate crowd settles in. Summer is the best time to come, since you can dine in the marvelous outdoor garden—with wrought-iron furniture, century-old trees, and trickling fountain, it's the most romantic spot in Midtown. But other seasons have their draw, too: From October to Christmas, it's truffle season, and Barbetta's white truffles (hunted by the family's own Piedmontese truffle hounds) are the ultimate decadence.

There have been complaints in past years that the food hasn't quite lived up to the setting, but upstart chef Marius Pavlak (formerly of Le Madri and Le Cirque) has revitalized the menu, keeping the best of the traditional dishes while adding some new twists. All of the pastas we tried were excellent, especially the handmade agnolotti and the lingue with olives, as was the risotto with wild porcinis. Among the main courses are a number of game dishes, including a wonderful rack of venison with Hudson River Valley apple, and terrific Maine Diver scallops with a Yukon gold crust. Winner of a *Wine Spectator* Award of Excellence, the all-Italian wine list is a phenomenal collection, especially strong in barolos and barbarescos.

Chez Josephine. 414 W. 42nd St. (btw. Ninth and Tenth aves.). ☎ **212/594-1925.** Reservations recommended. Main courses $17.50–$26.50. AE, DC, JCB, MC, V. Mon–Sat 5pm–1am. Subway: A, C, E to 42nd St. FRENCH BISTRO.

Jean-Claude Baker, one of the sons of the legendary Josephine, who scandalized Americans and seduced the French in the 1920s, is a true New York character. He has made the city his own, and New York would be a touch more *pauvre* without him. He's a warm host who indulges guests with just the right mix of discreet savoir faire and down-to-earth friendliness. The atmosphere somehow combines a pleasing tinge of decadence with respectability, making this perfect for pre- or post-theater dinner or cocktails. Nightly jazz piano keeps things festive, and the whole place is bathed in a magical Paris-in-the-twenties atmosphere. For starters, try the terrine of duck, fried oysters, or lobster bisque. A main-course favorite is cassoulet of lobster, shrimp, scallops, seafood sausage, and black beans in a light shellfish broth. On the way out you can buy Jean-Claude's well-received biography of his mother, *Josephine: The Hungry Heart*, which you can ask him to sign.

✪ **Cité.** 120 W. 51st St. (btw. Sixth and Seventh aves.). ☎ **212/956-7100.** Reservations recommended. Main courses $19.75–$29.75. Pre-theater (5–7:30pm) 3-course prix-fixe $42.50; Taste of the Grape 3-course dinner with wine $59.50 (8pm–midnight). AE, CB, DC, DISC, MC, V. Mon–Fri 11:30am–11:30pm, Sat–Sun 5–11:30pm. Subway: N, R to 49th St.; B, D, E to Seventh Ave. CONTINENTAL/STEAKS.

Dining Zone: Restaurant Row

Just a little to the west of most of the theaters in Times Square, on 46th Street between Eighth and Ninth avenues, is a lively block of 24 restaurants, great for pre- and post-theater dining. The best are ✪ **Joe Allen,** 326 W. 46th St. (☎ **212/581-6464**), for great burgers in a pub atmosphere, with chances for celebrity-spotting; and **Orso,** 322 W. 46th St. (☎ **212/489-7212**), for wonderful contemporary Italian served in a sophisticated rustic setting—after the shows, many stars nip in here.

This pleasing art deco steakhouse has the air of a refined Parisian brasserie, making it a sophisticated—and value-wise—choice for a fine Theater District dinner. The standard pre-theater prix-fixe is a good value unto itself, offering a limited but pleasing number of choices, including the filet mignon steak frites, a mammoth cut that arrives perfectly grilled. But the real deal comes after 8pm, with Cité's fabulous "Taste of the Grape" offer: Choose any appetizer, main course, and dessert from the full dinner menu for $59.50, and enjoy unlimited quantities of the night's four featured wines on offer *at no extra charge*. They're not offering up the cheap stuff—Cité's wine guru Daniel Thames takes this program seriously, and has chosen well. Among the wines on recent offer were an '88 Burgess Cellars cabernet sauvignon, a '97 Acacia chardonnay, a Chalone Vinyard pinot noir reserve from '94, and a Nicolas Feuillate brut for celebrating. The full menu features an excellent selection of chops and steaks plus a fine spit-roasted garlic chicken and a stellar swordfish steak au poivre. Consider launching your meal with the creamy sweet corn chowder, and wrapping up with the classic Floating Island. The professional waitstaff is brisk and attentive, and the overall ambiance much friendlier than at clubbier, more masculine steakhouses.

Coco Pazzo Teatro. At the Paramount hotel, 235 W. 46th St. (just east of Eighth Ave.). ☎ **212/827-4222.** Reservations recommended. Pastas $13–$17 at lunch, $14–$20 at dinner; main courses $16–$22 at lunch, $19–$29 at dinner; 5-course tasting menu (available after 8pm) $65. AE, DISC, DC, MC, V. Mon noon–3pm and 5:30–10pm, Tues–Sat noon–3pm and 5:30pm–midnight, Sun 5–10pm. Subway: A, C, E to 42nd St./Port Authority. ITALIAN.

This colorful and pleasing Tuscan Italian is an after-show favorite with the Broadway set (Alan Alda apparently made it his local when he was starring in *Art* across the street), while the *New York Times* staffers (whose offices are right nearby) keep the place hopping at lunch. The well-prepared Tuscan cuisine can get pricey, but the excellent pastas are a great deal. A very good choice is the hand-rolled garganelli tossed with calamari, baby artichokes, and fresh marjoram; I also like the cappellacci filled with butternut squash and served in a well-balanced butter-sage sauce. If you want something heavier, there's a very satisfying osso buco served over saffron rice, and a well-done roasted pork tenderloin with savory bread pudding. Service is friendly and efficient, especially if you're trying to make curtain time.

Estiatorio Milos. 125 W. 55th St. (btw. Sixth and Seventh aves.). ☎ **212/245-7400.** Reservations recommended. Main courses $18–$32; prix-fixe lunch $29.50. AE, DC, MC, V. Mon–Fri noon–3pm and 5:30pm–midnight, Sat 5:30pm–midnight, Sun 5–11pm. Subway: N, R to 57th St. GREEK SEAFOOD.

The sea stars center stage at this dazzling Greek seafooder, which has managed to earn a terrific rating of "25" for food from Zagat's in just its first full year in the survey. You'll select from the day's catch, seductively displayed on ice and sold by the pound. Appetizers like grilled fresh sardines and charred octopus with onions, capers, and peppers transport you to white-washed villages overlooking the Mediterranean. Grilled whole fish, whether Arctic char, red snapper, loup de mer, or Dover sole, make the best main-course choice: It's brushed with olive oil and herbs, perfectly and simply grilled, and then deboned tableside by the wait staff. Watch the bill, though— that by-the-pound pricing can add up quicker than you can say "opa!" To keep expenses down, consider ordering a selection of appetizers—the menu features creatively prepared octopus and baby squid, Greek-inspired salads, and crab cakes that the *New York Times* called "perfect"—and one whole fish to share. The wine list is excellent, and the cheese tray features about 30 farmhouse selections rarely available outside Greece. For dessert, try the tangy homemade yogurt drizzled with honey and dotted with wild blueberries.

Molyvos. 871 Seventh Ave. (btw. 55th and 56th sts.). ☎ **212/582-7500.** Reservations recommended. Main courses $12.50–$20.50 at lunch, $18.50–$24.50 at dinner; prix-fixe lunch $20. AE, DC, DISC, MC, V. Mon–Fri noon–3pm and 5:30pm–11:30pm, Sat 5pm–midnight, Sun 5–11pm. Subway: N, R to 57th St.; B, D, E to Seventh Ave. GREEK.

Here's another terrific Greek restaurant, this one more like a cozy upscale taverna. Ruth Reichl of the *New York Times* was so thrilled with its high quality and authenticity that she awarded Molyvos three stars (out of a possible four), and I concur wholeheartedly. The menu boasts beautifully prepared favorites—including superb taramosalata, tzatziki, and other traditional spreads—plus a few dishes with contemporary twists. The Greek country salad is generously portioned and as fresh as can be, while the baby octopus starter is grilled over fruit wood to tender, charred perfection. Among the main courses, the lemon and garlic-seasoned roasted free-range chicken is right on the mark: juicy, tender, and dressed with oven-dried tomatoes, olives, and rustic potatoes. More traditional tastes can opt for excellent moussaka; rosemary-skewered souvlaki; or the day's catch, wood-grilled whole with lemon, oregano, and olive oil in traditional Greek style. Baklava fans shouldn't miss the restaurant's moist, nutty version, which is big enough to share. The room is spacious and comfortable, with a warm Mediterranean appeal that doesn't go overboard on the Hellenic themes, and service that's attentive without being intrusive. The sommelier will be happy to help you choose from the surprisingly good list of Greek wines, making Molyvos a winner on all counts.

✪ **Petrossian.** 182 W. 58th St. (at Seventh Ave.). ☎ **212/245-2214.** Reservations recommended. Jacket required. Main courses $28–$34; prix-fixe lunch $22 ($39 with caviar); prix-fixe dinner $35 ($10 supplement for 30g Sevruga caviar). AE, DC, DISC, MC, V. Mon–Sat 11:30am–3pm and 5:30–11:30pm, Sun 11:30am–3pm and 5:30–10:30pm. Subway: B, D, E to Seventh Ave.; N, R to 57th St. RUSSIAN/CONTINENTAL.

Petrossian is North America's (and France's) largest importer of Caspian caviar, so they're able to serve high-quality Sevruga, Osetra, and Beluga for no more than you'd pay if you picked it up at the deli counter down at Balducci's. Oh, but this is no deli counter—nowhere in New York is caviar more exquisitely served. Available all evening, the three-course prix-fixe dinner is almost an unbelievable deal, and definitely the way to go: For $45, you can start with more than an ounce of high-quality Sevruga (elegantly served in silver with toast points), and follow with a full entree, the best of which is the plate of Petrossian Teasers, a gourmand's delight of smoked eel, trout, cod, salmon, and sturgeon, accompanied by excellent foie gras and marinated herring. Champagne by the glass ups the tally, but it's the perfect accompaniment. The art deco room may not live up to the promise of the gorgeous beaux arts exterior, but it's impressive nonetheless, and you're bound to be surrounded by big-haired high-society mavens who are a hoot to ogle. Service is aloof but attentive, just as it should be.

MODERATE

If you're willing to stick with the pastas, also consider **Coco Pazzo Teatro** (above), a wonderful Theater District bet.

✪ **The Cafe at Aquavit.** 13 W. 54th St. (btw. Fifth and Sixth aves.). ☎ **212/307-7311.** Reservations recommended. Main courses $13–$18, 3-course prix-fixe $25–$29 (multicourse menus $58–$75 in main dining room; 3-course pre-theater prix-fixe $39). AE, DC, MC, V. Mon–Fri noon–2:30pm and 5:30–10:30pm, Sat 5:30–10:30pm; main dining room also open Sun noon–3pm (except summer). Subway: E, F to Fifth Ave./53rd St. SCANDINAVIAN.

When Aquavit opened its doors, it opened the eyes of New Yorkers to what fine Scandinavian food could be: Its delicate elegance is reminiscent of Japanese refinement. But that doesn't mean that you have to spend a fortune to enjoy it. The main dining room space is soaring and sleek, with birch trees and an indoor waterfall, but I prefer to dine in the more casual upstairs cafe, another sophisticated Scandanavian modern space that also happens to be one of New York's best dining bargains. There's always a good-value fixed price meal available, but my favorite selections are well-prepared Scandanavian standards from the à la carte cafe menu: the smörgåsbord plate, an assortment of delicacies including perfectly smoked herring and zesty hot-mustard glazed salmon (which also comes as a full-size entree); and Swedish meatballs, a perfect realization of this traditional dish, accompanied by mashed potatoes and lingonberries (beats IKEA by a mile!). The Arctic char, served with cabbage salad, turkey bacon, and red wine sauce, is another good choice. To help you get Scandinavian sleek, the bar offers a wide selection of aquavits, distilled liquors not unlike vodka flavored with fruit and spices and served Arctic cold, which have a smooth finish and are best accompanied by a full-bodied European brew like Carlsberg.

Carmine's. 200 W. 44th St. (btw. Broadway and Eighth Ave.). ☎ **212/221-3800.** Reservations recommended before 6pm, after 6pm accepted only for six or more. Family-style main courses $15–$47. AE, DC, MC, V. Tues–Sat 11:30am–midnight, Sun–Mon 11:30am–11pm. Subway: N, R, S, 1, 2, 3, 7, 9 to 42nd St./Times Square. SOUTHERN ITALIAN FAMILY STYLE.

Everything is done B-I-G at this rollicking, family-style Times Square mainstay. The dining room is vast enough to deserve a map, massive platters of pasta hold Brady Bunch–size portions, and large groups wait to join in the rambunctious atmosphere at this sibling of the original Upper West Sider. This is a value-priced restaurant where the bang for your buck increases for every person you add to your party—but so does the wait, so come early or late to avoid the crowds. Caesar salad and a mound of fried calamari are a perfect beginning, followed by heaping portions of pasta topped with red or white clam sauce, mixed seafood, zesty marinara, and meatballs. The meat entrees include veal parmigiana, broiled porterhouse steak, chicken marsala, and shrimp scampi. The tiramisù is pie-size, thick and creamy, bathed in Kahlúa and marsala. Order half of what you think you'll need.

The original Carmine's at 2450 Broadway (☎ **212/362-2200**) is the same—but even B-I-G-G-E-R.

☼ Churrascaria Plataforma. 316 W. 49th St. (btw. Eighth and Ninth aves.). ☎ **212/245-0505.** Reservations recommended. All-you-can-eat prix-fixe $27 at lunch, $31 at dinner. AE, DC, MC, V. Daily noon–midnight. Subway: C, E to 50th St. BRAZILIAN.

It's a carnival for carnivores at this upscale all-you-can-eat Brazilian rotisserie. A large selection of salad-bar teasers like octopus stew, paella, and carpaccio may tempt you to fill up too quickly, but hold out for the never-ending parade of meat. Roving servers deliver beef (too many cuts to mention), ham, chicken (the chicken hearts are great, trust me), lamb, and sausage—more than 15 delectable varieties—and traditional sides like fried yucca, plantains, and rice right to your table until you cannot eat another bite. The food is excellent, and the service friendly and generous. A fun, festive family affair. The ideal accompaniment is a pitcher of Brazil's signature cocktail, called a *caipirinha:* a margarita-like blend of limes, sugar, crushed ice, and raw sugarcane liquor; those in the know call Plataforma's the best in town.

Metro Grill. In the Hotel Metro, 45 W. 35th St. (btw. Fifth and Sixth aves.). ☎ **212/279-3535.** Reservations recommended. Mon–Fri noon–10pm, Sat–Sun 5–10pm. Main courses $6–$13 at breakfast, $12–$24 at lunch and dinner (most $18 or less). AE, DC, MC, V. Subway: B, D, F, Q, N, R to 34th St. CONTEMPORARY AMERICAN/MEDITERRANEAN.

This stylish restaurant is a Midtown sleeper, serving excellent, moderately priced contemporary cuisine in a beautifully designed series of colorful, comfortable dining rooms. Fashionable but casual, Metro Grill fills a similar niche with its uncomplicated,

Mediterranean-accented fare. The menu changes with the seasons, but expect to find a selection of pizzettes, on grilled semolina flatbread, well-prepared pastas, and a full selection of not-too-fussy entrees. Anyone who knows chef Karen Fohrhaltz Miele's former restaurant, Amsterdam's, knows not to miss the rotisserie chicken, which is always crispy on the outside, juicy on the inside. On my last visit, I thoroughly enjoyed the acorn cornucopia, an acorn squash filled with autumn veggies and porcini mushroom couscous, drizzled with porcini cream. The Atlantic salmon—broiled on the outside, sashimi on the inside—with wasabi dumplings was another winner, as was the Metro burger, a blend of ground beef and lamb accompanied by sweet onions and rosemary fries. If there are two of you, try to snag one of the tables in the middle room, which boast wonderfully cushy corner chairs.

Virgil's Real BBQ. 152 W. 44th St. (btw. Sixth and Seventh aves.). ☎ **212/921-9494.** Reservations recommended. Main courses $5.95–$24.95 (barbecue platters $12.95–$19.95). AE, DC, MC, V. Mon 11:30am–11pm, Tues–Sat 11:30am–midnight, Sun 11:30am–11pm. Subway: 1, 2, 3, 7, 9, N, R to 42nd St./Times Sq. SOUTHERN/BARBECUE.

Virgil's may look like a comfy theme-park version of a down-home barbecue joint, but this place takes its barbecue seriously. The meat is house-smoked with a blend of hickory, oak, and fruitwood chips, and most every regional school is represented, from Carolina pulled pork to Texas beef brisket to Memphis ribs. You may not consider this contest-winning chow if you're from barbecue country, but we less-savvy Yankees are thrilled to have Virgil's in the 'hood. I love to start with the barbecued shrimp, accompanied by yummy mustard slaw, and a plate of buttermilk onion rings with bleu cheese for dipping. The ribs are lip-smackin' good, but the chicken is moist and tender—go for a combo if you just can't choose. Burgers, sandwiches, and other entrees (chicken-fried steak, anyone?) are also available if you can't face up to all that meat 'n' sauce. And cast that cornbread aside for a full order of buttermilk biscuits, which come with maple butter so good it's like dessert. So hunker down, pig out, and don't worry about making a mess; when you're through eating, you get a hot towel for washing up. The bar offers a huge selection of on-tap and bottled brews.

INEXPENSIVE

In addition to listings below, there's also a cafeteria-style branch of **Mangia** at 50 W. 57th St., between Fifth and Sixth avenues (☎ 212/582-5882). See the review in section 2, "South Street Seaport & the Financial District" for details.

Hamburger Harry's. 145 W. 45th St. (btw. Sixth and Seventh aves.). ☎ **212/840-0566.** Reservations recommended for large groups. Burgers and burritos $7.25–$9.95, other main courses $10.95–$15.95. AE, CB, DC, DISC, MC, V. Mon–Thurs 11:30am–11pm, Fri–Sat 11:30am–11:30pm, Sun noon–8pm. Subway: N, R, S, 1, 2, 3, 7, 9 to 42nd St./Times Sq. AMERICAN/BURGERS.

Hamburger Harry's is the perfect stop for everyday refueling at the right price. The casual restaurant has distinguished itself by turning out delicious 7-ounce mesquite-grilled burgers that "may well be the best hamburger in New York City," according to the *New York Times.* I don't know if I can fully agree with that assessment, but they're definitely the best in Times Square. Served with curlique fries, homemade potato salad, or Harry's coleslaw, burger platters are a belly-busting bargain. They come in a range of varieties, from plain and simple to the Ha Ha Burger, topped with Texas chili, cheddar cheese, onion, guacamole, and *pico de gallo.* There are turkey and veggie versions for waist-watchers, too, as well as chicken breast sandwiches, fajitas, southwest-style burritos, Cajun catfish, and New York steak. A great place to take the kids—you can even finish off with an old-fashioned hot fudge sundae.

۞ Island Burgers & Shakes. 766 Ninth Ave. (btw. 51st and 52nd sts.). ☎ **212/ 307-7934.** Reservations not accepted. Main courses $5.50–$8.75. No credit cards. Sat– Thurs 12pm–10:30pm, Fri 12pm–11:15pm. Subway: C, E to 50th St. GOURMET BURGERS/ SANDWICHES.

This excellent aisle-sized diner glows with the wild colors of a California surf shop. A small selection of sandwiches and salads are on hand, but as the name implies, folks come here for the Goliath-sized burgers—either beef hamburgers or, the specialty of the house, churascos (flattened grilled chicken breasts). Innovation strikes with the more than 40 topping combinations: Choose anything from the horseradish, sour cream, and black pepper burger to the Hobie's (with black pepper sauce, bleu cheese, onion, and bacon). Choose your own bread from a wide selection, ranging from soft sourdough to crusty ciabatta. Though Island Burgers serves fries now, you're meant to eat these fellows with their tasty dirty potato chips. Terrifically thick shakes and cookies are also available for those with a sweet tooth.

۞ John's Pizzeria. 260 W. 44th St. (btw. Broadway and Eighth Ave.). ☎ **212/391-7560.** Reservations accepted for 10 or more. Pizzas $9–$12.50 (plus toppings), pastas $6–8. AE, MC, V. Mon–Thurs 11:30am–11:30am, Fri–Sat 11:30am–1am, Sun noon–12:30am. Subway: A, C, E to 42nd St.–Port Authority; 1, 2, 3, 9, N, R, S, 7 to 42nd St.–Times Square. PIZZA.

Thin-crusted, properly sauced, and fresh, the pizza at John's has long been one of New York's best—some even consider these *the* best pies New York has to offer. Housed in the century-old Gospel Tabernacle Church, the split-level dining room is vast and pretty, featuring a gorgeous stained-glass ceiling and chefs working at classic brick ovens right in the room. More importantly, it's big enough to hold pre-theater crowds, so there's never too long of a wait despite the place's popularity. Unlike most pizzerias, at John's you order a whole made-to-order pie rather than by the slice, so come with friends or family. There's also a good selection of traditional pastas to choose from, such as baked ziti, and well-stuffed calzones.

This Theater District location is my favorite, but the original Bleecker Street location, at 278 Bleecker St., between Sixth and Seventh avenues (☎ 212/243-1680), is loaded with old-world atmosphere. The locations near Lincoln Center, 48 W. 65th St. (☎ 212/721-7001), and on the Upper East Side, 408 E. 64th St. (☎ 212/ 935-2895), are also worth checking out.

Dining Zone: Ninth Avenue

Ninth Avenue from 46th to 56th streets has become a well-priced gourmet paradise with dozens of restaurants that are perfect for pre- and post-theater dining.

Rice 'n' Beans, at 744 Ninth Ave., between 50th and 51st streets (☎ 212/ 265-4444), serves up exactly what the name implies: kick-ass, stick-to-your-ribs Brazilian fare. Among the specialties are *feijoada,* a hearty, brackish-looking stew of black beans, pork ribs, and linguiça sausage; and a lovely roast chicken seasoned with tomato and cilantro. Best of all, the bargain-basement prices will have you doing the samba.

Even uninitiated palates will appreciate the Asian-nouvelle vegetarian cuisine at stylish **Zen Palate** (p. 158), at 663 Ninth Ave., at 46th Street (☎ 212/582-1669). **Julian's,** 802 Ninth Ave., between 53rd and 54th streets (☎ 212/262-4800), serves up consistently good mid-priced Mediterranean fare in an attractive setting that includes a lovely alfresco area. And Puerto Rican and Argentinian cuisine doesn't get much better or cheaper than at **Old San Juan,** 765 Ninth Ave., at 52nd Street (☎ 212/262-7013).

Theme Restaurant Thrills!

There's no doubt about it—New York's theme restaurant trend is on the wane. Sure, the Hard Rock, Planet Hollywood, and the All-Star Cafe are still going strong, but you won't see the legendary lines of the '80s forming outside these days. Stand-up–themed **Comedy Nation** and the **Motown Cafe** both shut their doors for good in early 1999. And thankfully, we're *thisclose* to losing the weakest of the bunch, the trouble-plagued **Fashion Cafe,** 51 Rockefeller Plaza, at 51st Street (☎ 212/765-3131), which we all know was never a good idea in the first place; it was officially "closed for renovations" at press time. (Call ahead to see if the promised reopening has actually happened.) This biz will prove to be Darwinist yet.

In addition to those listed below, there are some good ideas in the works. The best is **ESPN Zone,** which should be open at 42nd Street and Broadway by the time you read this. With 42,000 square feet of space slated to house a grill with set replicas from ESPN's hit shows (including *Sportscenter* and *Baseball Tonight*), a lounge with 13 massive TV screens and reclining leather chairs with speakers in the headrests, and a floor of sports-related arcade games, this upscale sports bar and restaurant should prove to be a sports fan's dream come true. (All-Star Cafe? What All-Star Cafe?)

David Copperfield's **Copperfield Magic Underground** should magically appear at Broadway and 49th Street by the time you read this, the **World Wrestling Federation** is in the works for Times Square (Stone Cold Steve cheeseburger, anyone?), and the **Rainforest Cafe** is planning to put down roots in the neighborhood. But until then:

✪ **Brooklyn Diner USA,** 212 W. 57th St., Broadway and Seventh Avenue (☎ 212/581-8900), looks like an old-fashioned diner on the outside, but inside you'll find linen tablecloths and mahogany accents instead of coffee-stained Formica tabletops. The food includes better-than-you'd-expect crab-cakes, tenderloin steak, and Valrhona chocolate fudge sundae. To justify the name, there's a 15-bite Brooklyn hot dog and an Avenue U roast beef sandwich.

Always the perennial favorite, New York's ✪ **Hard Rock Cafe,** 221 W. 57th St., between Broadway and Seventh Avenue (☎ 212/459-9320), is actually one of the originals of the chain, and a terrific realization of the concept. The memorabilia collection is terrific, with lots of great Lennon collectibles. The menu boasts all the Hard Rock standards, including a surprisingly good burger and fajitas, and the comfortable bar mixes up great cocktails.

La Bonne Soupe. 48 W. 55th St. (btw. Fifth and Sixth aves.). ☎ **212/586-7650.** Reservations recommended. Main courses $8.95–$18.25; "les bonnes soupes" prix-fixe $12.95; lunch and dinner prix-fixe $19.95. AE, DC, MC, V. Mon–Sat 11:30am–midnight, Sun 11:30am–11pm. Subway: E, F to Fifth Ave.; B, Q to 57th St. FRENCH BISTRO.

This little slice of Paris has been around forever; I remember discovering the magic of fondue here on a high school French Club field trip that took place more years ago than I care to think about. But for gourmet at good prices, it's still hard to best this authentic bistro, where you'll even see French natives seated elbow-to-elbow in the newly renovated dining room. "Les bonnes soupes" are satisfying noontime meals of salad, bread, a big bowl of soup (mushroom and barley with lamb is a favorite), dessert (chocolate mousse, crème caramel, or ice cream), and wine or coffee—a great bargain

Harley-Davidson Cafe, 1370 Sixth Ave., at 56th Street (☎ **212/245-6000**), brings out the Hell's Angel in all of us. The just-fine munchies do the trick, and memorabilia documents 90 years of Hog history.

Something new to scare you with, my dear? You'll enter the **Jekyll & Hyde Club,** 1409 Sixth Ave., between 57th and 58th streets (☎ **212/541-9505**), through a small dark room with a sinking ceiling, where a corpse warns you of the oddities to come. There are five floors—grand salon, library, laboratory, mausoleum, observatory—of bizarre artifacts, wall hangings that come to life, and other interactive bone chillers. Kids love it. There's a second, more publike location at 91 Seventh Ave. South, between Barrow and Grove streets, in Greenwich Village (☎ **212/989-7701**).

The subterranean red planet-themed restaurant called ✪ **Mars 2112,** 1633 Broadway, at 51st Street (☎ **212/582-2112**), is a hoot, from the simulated red-rock rooms to the Martian-costumed waitstaff to the silly "Man Eats on Mars!" newspaper-style menu. The eclectic food is better than you might expect, but skip the Star Tours–style simulated spacecraft ride at the entrance if you don't want to lose your appetite before you get to your table. The kids won't mind, though—they'll love it, along with the extensive video arcade.

Superstar athletes Andre Agassi, Wayne Gretzky, Ken Griffey Jr., Joe Montana, Shaquille O'Neal, Monica Seles, and Tiger Woods are the names behind the successful **Official All Star Cafe.** 1540 Broadway, at 45th Street (☎ **212/840-8326**). At center court is a full-size scoreboard, on the sidelines are booths shaped like baseball mitts, and video monitors guarantee that the great plays in sports history live forever. The food is straight from the ballpark—hot dogs and hamburgers, St. Louis ribs, Philly cheese steak sandwiches, and the like.

Ellen's Stardust Diner, 1650 Broadway, at 51st Street (☎ **212/956-5151**), is the quintessential '50s-spoof diner, complete with singing waiters, outrageous lampshades, and Bobby Darin on the jukebox. The classic diner food is just fine—and how can you pass on a chocolate malt in a joint like this?

Bruce Willis, Sly Stallone, and Ah-nuld are the moneymongers behind **Planet Hollywood,** 140 W. 57th St., between Sixth and Seventh avenues (☎ **212/333-7827**). Frankly, the movie memorabilia doesn't hold the same excitement as the genuine rock 'n' roll goods over at the Hard Rock (didn't I see the R2D2 and C3PO robots at three *other* PHs?), but it's still plenty of fun for Hollywood buffs nonetheless. Watch for a 2000 move to the new Planet Hollywood hotel in Times Square.

at just $12.95. The menu also features entree-sized salads (including a good niçoise), high-quality steak burgers, and traditional bistro fare like omelets, quiche Lorraine, croque monsieur, and fancier fare like steak frites and filet mignon au poivre. Rounding out the menu are those very French fondues: emmethal cheese, beef, and yummy, creamy chocolate to finish off the meal in perfect style. Bon appetit!

Meskerem. 468 W. 47th St. (btw. Ninth and Tenth aves.). ☎ **212/664-0520.** Reservations recommended. Main courses $7–$11. DISC, MC, V. Daily 11:30am–midnight. Subway: C, E to 50th St. ETHIOPIAN.

Here's an exotic and affordable Theater District choice. Ignore the plain-Jane surroundings, get over the lack of silverware (you eat this African cuisine with your hands), and you'll enjoy a great dining experience here. Ethiopian stews of beef, lamb,

Dining Zone: Koreatown

West 32nd Street between Fifth and Sixth avenues is lit in neon like a block in Seoul, with reliable eateries serving exquisite moderately priced food. ○ **Won Jo,** 23 W. 32nd St. (☎ **212/695-5815**) is favored by many Koreans for its barbecue (sirloin, pork, chicken, or mushroom, accompanied by vegetables, kimchee, and noodles), which you cook yourself (each table has a small grill). Other top selections are **Hangawi,** 12 E. 32 St. (☎ **212/213-0077**), for a pricier but sublimely serene escape on the other side of Fifth; try the tempting pumpkin porridge and Korean vermicelli at this no-meat, no-fish, no-dairy, Asian winner. Farther uptown at 8–10 W. 36th St. is **Woo Chon** (☎ **212/695-0676**), open 24 hours a day and a good bet for first-timers.

chicken, and vegetables are served on communal platters and sopped up with spongy *injera* bread, made from fermented *tef,* an Ethiopian grain. The flavorful dishes range from the mild *doro alecha* (chicken seasoned with onions, garlic, and ginger in a butter sauce) to the spicy ribs dishes, simmered in a spicy berber sauce. The house specialty, *kitfo,* is Ethiopian-style steak tartare—less-adventurous eaters can ask for the beef rare instead of raw. For a little bit of everything, order a combination plate; two combos will easily feed three diners.

Siam Inn Too. 854 Eighth Ave. (btw. 51st and 52nd sts.). ☎ **212/757-4006.** Reservations accepted. Main courses $7.95–$15.95. AE, DC, MC, V. Mon–Fri noon–11:30pm, Sat 4–11:30pm, Sun 5–11pm. Subway: C, E to 50th St. THAI.

Situated on an unremarkable stretch of Eighth Avenue, the Siam Inn is an attractive outpost of very good Thai food. All of your Thai favorites are here, well prepared and served by a brightly attired waitstaff. Tom kah gai soup (with chicken, mushrooms, and coconut milk), chicken satay with yummy peanut sauce, and light, flaky curry puffs all make good starters. Among noteworthy entrees are the masaman and red curries (the former rich and peanuty, the latter quite spicy), spicy sautéed squid with fresh basil and chiles, and perfect pad thai. And unlike many of the drab restaurants in this neighborhood, there's a semblance of decor—black deco tables and chairs, cushy rugs underfoot, and soft lighting.

Siam Inn is my favorite, but this neighborhood abounds with good Thai food. **Pongsri Thai Restaurant,** 244 W. 48th St. between Broadway and Eighth Avenue (☎ **212/582-3392**), courteously serves lovingly cooked Thai specialties; the *tom yum goong* soup (loads of shrimp and straw mushrooms in a broth seasoned with lemongrass, lime juice, coriander, and exotic herbs) may be the best in town. Diners on a tight budget should head to **Chanpen,** 761 Ninth Ave., at 51st Street (☎ **212/586-6808**), which serves bold Thai food at Chinatown prices; the lunch specials, in particular, are remarkable values.

Soup Kitchen International. 259A W. 55th St. (at Eighth Ave.). ☎ **212/757-7730.** Soup $6–$16. Oct–June, Mon–Fri noon–6pm. Closed summer. Subway: C, E to 50th St. SOUP.

It's not hard to find Al Yeganeh, the famously dour soup vendor parodied on *Seinfeld*—just head for 55th Street, and walk to the end of the very long line. Many wait for the novelty, and even hope to be yelled at. (The real-life Kramer once posted a billboard next to the store with "behavior tips," but Yeganeh painted over the sign in red shortly after it appeared.) Here's the deal: It's ridiculously expensive for takeout soup, but it's really that good. Yeganeh labors fiercely, coddling the Hungarian goulash, mushroom barley, and mulligatawny, all subtly spiced and sublime. The seafood bisque gets deserved kudos; I once found an entire lobster claw in mine. The 12 or so soups offered change daily, but don't call because he'll hang up on you. "Whatever soup you want, I have!" he snaps. So come after 2pm to minimize waiting; yes, have your money ready; and no, don't ask to take his picture, since he finds that insulting.

11 Midtown East & Murray Hill

See the "Midtown Dining" map (pp. 154–155) for restaurants in this section.

VERY EXPENSIVE

✪ **Le Cirque 2000.** In the New York Palace hotel, 455 Madison Ave. (at 50th St.). ☎ **212/303-7788.** www.newyork.sidewalk.com/LeCirque. Reservations essential well in advance. Jacket and tie required. Main courses $28–$36; five-course prix-fixe dinner $90. AE, CB, DC, MC, V. Mon–Sat 11:45am–2:45pm and 5:45–11pm, Sun 5:30–10:30pm. Subway: 6 to 51st; E, F to Fifth Ave. FRENCH.

Fine dining goes the way of the big top at Le Cirque 2000, and it's a hit. Iconic restaurateur Sirio Maccioni made a bold move when he relocated his legendary Le Cirque to the New York Palace a few years back, but it turned out to be a master stroke. Designer Adam Tihany festooned the gilded-age mansion's almost rococo interiors with jewel-toned circus colors, bright lights, touches of neon, and furniture with such outrageous lines that it looks like Tex Avery drew it for a Bugs Bunny cartoon. And guess what? It works. The fanciful setting is perfect for a magical night on the town. But that's where the reinvention ends—executive chef Sottha Khunn's haute French menu is classic Le Cirque. The food is excellently prepared if not innovative: lobster roasted with young artichokes and wild mushrooms; paupiette of black sea bass in crispy potatoes with braised leeks; black Angus tenderloin in red wine sauce; and rack of lamb roasted with savory. The starters are almost as pricey as the entrees, but we were won over by the flawlessly sautéed fois gras, and seared sea scallops with wild mushrooms and mesclun in a delicate parmesan basket. The crème brûlée is a perfect realization of the classic dessert, but go with one of the chocolate choices for a suitably decadent finish. The wine list is remarkably well priced, relatively speaking; it seems that Maccioni has thus far avoided the current overcharging trend. There's spectacular courtyard dining in season.

✪ **March.** 405 E. 58th St. (btw. First Ave. and Sutton Place). ☎ **212/754-6272.** Reservations required. Jacket and tie requested. 4-course menus $68, $93 with wines; 7-course tasting menu $90, $125 with wines. AE, DC, DISC, JCB, MC, V. Daily 6–10:30pm. Subway: 4, 5, 6 to 59th St.; N, R to Lexington Ave. CONTEMPORARY AMERICAN.

Here's romantic Manhattan dining as it was meant to be. From start to finish, co-owner/host Joseph Scalice and partner/chef Wayne Nish do things right. The restaurant is in a beautifully restored town house whose intimate rooms create a perfect setting for Nish's marvelously orchestrated meals. The sophisticated crowd may be nattily dressed, but this isn't a see-and-be-seen kind of place—it's all about the experience, and, for lovers, each other.

March skips the usual appetizers-entrees setup for a new approach: a four-course prix-fixe meal that lets you partner smaller portions from vegetarian, seafood, poultry, and meat selections as you wish. Or you can follow four- or seven-course tasting options, in which you follow one of the prescribed menus created by Nish, paired with wines chosen by Wine Director Scalice for best effect. This multi-course approach is terrific because it allows you to fully experience Nish's elegant, excellent cuisine, and adds a beyond-the-ordinary flair that's often missing in special-occasion dining. The menu changes regularly, but expect a host of inventive New American dishes with delicate pan-Asian, even global, touches: Lobster carpaccio is beautifully married with three roes (osetra, mentaiko, and uni); a confit of duck fois gras gets a savory sub-continental twist from Indian spices, crisped black figs, and persimmon chutney; farm-raised veal is dressed with linden honey and aromatic bitters; hot smoked salmon goes transcontinental with German sauerkraut, Irish bacon, and juniper berries. The choices are extensive, so feel free to put yourself in the hands of the first-rate waitstaff. A wonderful, special experience.

EXPENSIVE

✪ **Mr. Chow.** 324 E. 57th St. (btw. First and Second aves.). ☎ **212/751-9030.** Reservations recommended. Main courses $24–$32.50. AE, DC, MC, V. Daily 6–11:45pm. Subway: 4, 5, 6 to 59th St. HAUTE CHINESE.

If you really want to do some great people-watching, skip Moomba and head to Mr. Chow. This wonderful restaurant is a favorite among the celebrity set: Rap star/DJ Ed Lover and his crew were in residence the night we were there, and Madonna, gal pal Sandra Bernhard, and Sean Penn reportedly make regular appearances. But even if you don't spot a famous name, the high-fashion crowd will keep you gloriously entertained—I promise. Michael Chow has been a restaurateur par excellance for three decades now, and his personal style makes this deco dining room extra appealing: This is the kind of place where everyone is treated like a king. I like this egalitarian approach (tsk, tsk, Moomba!), which says your money is just as good as Puff Daddy's.

The food may not be the best haute Chinese in town, but it's close—and the quality of the dining experience makes Mr. Chow well worth the money. You can have a menu if you insist, but the practice is to let your doting, tuxedoed waiter order for you; just tell him what you like and dislike, and he'll build a suitably harmonious meal. The well prepared cuisine is more uptown than Chinatown, so this isn't much of a risk. We loved the lightly spicy green prawns, marinated in basil and other herbs; the generously portioned lobster in ginger sauce; and the tandoori-red chicken satay dressed with a sweet butter-peanut sauce that's a pleasing twist on tradition. It's usually pretty easy to get a table if you call ahead—just show up with your sense of humor and you'll have a great time.

Michael Jordan's–The Steak House. In Grand Central Terminal (mezzanine level), 23 Vanderbilt Ave. ☎ **212/655-2300.** Reservations recommended. Main courses $16.95– $30.95; porterhouse for 2 $58.95. AE, DC, MC, V. Mon–Fri 11:30am–2:30pm and 5–11pm, Sat noon–2:30pm and 5–11pm, Sun 1–2:30pm and 5–10pm. Subway: 4, 5, 6, 7, S to 42nd St./Grand Central. STEAKS.

The name may belong to one sports' greatest heroes, but don't expect an overpriced burger factory with waiters in Bulls jerseys and basketball-shaped plates. Michael Jordan's new restaurant, an elegant steakhouse and richly appointed cigar lounge, is wholly a place for grown-ups. No matter how you feel about his Airness or the game, this gorgeous art deco space makes a great place to dine thanks to its magnificent location, on the open mezzanine level overlooking the main concourse of newly restored Grand Central Terminal. With a perfect view of the legendary sky ceiling, this is more than just the city's best-looking steakhouse—it's an incredible only-in-New York dining experience.

And the food? Pure steakhouse fare: New York steaks, thick-cut filet mignons, tender ribeyes, and well-marbled sirloins, all prime aged cuts. The star of the show is the porterhouse for two, a whopping 44 ounces of top-quality cow, served suitably charred and salty on the outside. Other choices include buffalo sirloin for two, a pleasing lean cut as long as it's ordered on the rare side, and excellent braised short ribs. We didn't have a problem, but word is that on occasion a steak isn't cooked to order, an issue that should disappear as the kitchen establishes itself. In the meantime, don't be shy about sending yours back for another turn on the grill. Skip the more adventuresome starters and sides, such as the disappointing lobster salad, and stick with steakhouse classics like the perfectly creamed spinach, creamy mac and cheese (Mama J's recipe), light-as-air fried onions, and the terrific crimini mushrooms in truffle oil. The wine list is overseen by a helpful sommelier, and service is similarly attentive.

🌀 **Oyster Bar.** In Grand Central Terminal, lower level (btw. Vanderbilt and Lexington aves.). ☎ **212/490-6650.** Reservations recommended. Main courses $9.45–$34.95. AE, CB, DC, DISC, JCB, MC, V. Mon–Fri 11:30am–9:30pm (last seating). Subway: 4, 5, 6, 7, S to 42nd St./Grand Central. SEAFOOD.

Here's one New York institution housed within another: the city's most famous seafood joint in the world's greatest train station, newly renovated Grand Central Terminal. Fully recovered from a 1997 fire, the restaurant is looking spiffy, too, with a main dining room sitting under an impressive curved and tiled ceiling, a more casual luncheonette-style section for walk-ins, and a wood-panelled saloon-style room for smokers. If you love seafood, don't miss this place. A new menu is prepared every day, since only the freshest fish is served. The oysters are irresistible: Kumomoto, Bluepoint, Malepeque, Belon—the list goes on and on. The list of daily catches, which can range from Arctic char to mako shark to ono (Hawaiian wahoo), is equally impressive. Most dinners go for between $19.95 and $24.95, and it's easy to jack up the tab by ordering live lobster (flown in directly from Maine) or one of the rarer daily specialties. But it's just as easy to keep the tab down by sticking with hearty fare like one of the excellent stews and panroasts (from $9.45 for oyster stew to $19.95 for a combo panroast rich with oysters, clams, shrimp, lobster, and scallops) or by pairing the New England clam chowder (at $4.50, an unbeatable lunch) with a smoked starter to make a great meal.

Sparks Steak House. 210 E. 46th St. (btw. Second and Third aves.). ☎ **212/687-4855.** Reservations required. Jacket requested. Main courses $27.95–$31.75. AE, CB, DC, DISC, MC, V. Mon–Fri noon–3pm and 5–11pm, Sat 5–11:30pm. Subway: 4, 5, 6, 7, S to 42nd St./Grand Central. STEAK HOUSE.

When the primal urge strikes, Sparks is where New York's carnivores head. Lobster and other shellfish are prime players, but this macho steakhouse gives its clientele what it really wants: massive, voluptuous, high-quality steaks. The wine list is one of the city's best. The service is as friendly as in a hardware store, but that just adds to the atmosphere. Expect to leave a wad of cash as thick as a steak. A recent meaty expansion gave diners 14,000 more square feet of space.

Vong. 200 E. 54th St. (at Third Ave.). ☎ **212/486-9592.** www.jean-georges.com. Reservations recommended. Jacket and tie recommended. Main courses $20–$36; prix-fixe lunch $28, pre-theater prix-fixe $38; tasting menu $68. AE, DC, MC, V. Mon–Fri noon–2:30pm, Mon–Thurs 6–11pm, Fri–Sat 5:30–11:30pm, Sun 5:30–10pm. Subway: 6 to 51st St.; E, F to Lexington/Third aves. and 53rd St. ASIAN FUSION.

Star chef Jean-Georges Vongerichten (also of Jo Jo, Jean Georges, and Mercer Kitchen) was one of the first to set New York abuzz with imaginative Asian fusion cuisine in the early '90s, and his Vong is still going strong. His brand is a vibrant marriage of Thai spices with French cooking techniques, served up in a room that's as witty and appealing as the exotic cuisine. A Southeast Asian feel is created by salmon and burnt-orange tones, teak wall treatments and bamboo touches throughout, and a pagoda dominating the dining room. This is a proven restaurant used to serving a polished crowd, and the confidence shows in all aspects of preparation, presentation, and service. You really can't go wrong here, whether you opt for the steamed red snapper with mango chutney, cabbage, and watercress; chicken roasted with lemongrass, simply but beautifully paired with sweet rice in a banana leaf; or crisp squab nesting on an egg noodle pancake with honey-ginger-glazed pearl onions. Don't miss the exotic desserts, such as salad of banana and passion fruit with white-pepper ice cream. The tasting menu presents you with a brilliant cross-section of the menu, while the prix-fixe meals are a smokin' deal.

MODERATE

Zarela. 953 Second Ave. (btw. 50th and 51st sts.). ☎ **212/644-6740.** Reservations recommended. Main courses $12.95–$16.95; tasting menu $39. AE, DC, MC. V. Mon–Thurs noon–3pm and 5–11pm, Fri noon–3pm and 5–11:30pm, Sat 5–11:30pm, Sun 5–10pm. Subway: 6 to 51st St.; E, F to Lexington Ave. MEXICAN.

Owner Zarela Martínez really has her finger on the pulse of New York. Her restaurant crowds with a friendly assortment of connoisseurs who come for the unsurpassed authentic Mexican food featuring specials from Oaxaca and Veracruz, margarita lovers (this place serves Manhattan's best), high-profile publishing and business types, and a well-to-do international set who appreciate that Zarela moves in sophisticated circles, writes her own cookbooks (*Food from My Heart*, *The Food and Life of Oaxaca*), and still greets customers herself.

Dine at Zarela's and you'll understand that Mexican food is so much more than you ever thought. Start with the *salpicón de pescado*, a snapper hash with tomatoes, scallions, jalapeños, and aromatic spices. For a main course, try shrimp braised with poblanos, onions, and queso blanco or roasted half duck with a tomato-red chile sauce with dried apricots, prunes, raisins, and pineapple. The fajitas, grilled marinated skirt steak in flour tortillas, melt in your mouth. Order the rice baked with sour cream, white cheddar cheese, poblanos, and corn to complete the eye-opening entrees. Zarela is one Mexican restaurant that prides itself on great desserts, so check out the day's specials.

INEXPENSIVE

In addition to the listings below, there's also a cafeteria-style branch of **Mangia** at 16 E. 48th St., just east of Fifth Avenue (☎ 212/754-7600). See the review in section 2, "South Street Seaport & the Financial District" for details.

The British Open. 320 E. 59th St. (btw. First and Second aves.). ☎ **212/355-8467.** Main courses $7.50–$19.75 (most under $13). AE, DC, DISC, MC, V. Mon–Sat noon–midnight, Sun noon–10pm. Subway: 4, 5, 6 to 59th St. BRITISH.

Here's the perfect pub for golf lovers, or anybody who pines for a pint and some good English grub. This charmer of an alehouse is more sophisticated than most, with a mahogany bar polished to a high sheen, a pretty dining room in back, and friendly, attentive service. Tartan carpet heightens the theme (ah, the Scots would be proud) and little blue lights create a romantic glow. This isn't a copy of a Brit pub—it's the real thing, transplanted from the other side of the Atlantic wholesale, bartender, malt vinegar, and all. The North Star at South Street Seaport is equally genuine, but it's more after-work local than Sunday dinner, if you know what I mean; this is the kind of place you'll be comfortable bringing Grandma to. The extensive menu serves well-prepared versions of the pub staples, plus steaks, chops, and the like. But go for the standards: light, well-battered fish with crispy chips; excellent cottage pie with veggies and perfectly browned mash; plus steak and kidney pie, bangers and mash, and so on. You'll find Guinness, Bass, Fullers ESB, and other British imports on tap, and golf and other sports on the telly at any hour.

✪ Ess-A-Bagel. 831 Third Ave. (at 51st St.). ☎ **212/980-1010.** Sandwiches $1.35–$8.35. AE, DC, DISC, MC, V. Mon–Fri 6:30am–10pm, Sat–Sun 8am–5pm. Subway: 6 to 51st St.; E, F to Lexington Ave. BAGEL SANDWICHES.

Ess-A-Bagel turns out the city's best bagel, edging out rival H&H, who won't make you a sandwich. Baked daily on-site, the giant hand-rolled delicacies come in 12 flavors—plain, sesame, poppy, onion, garlic, salt, whole wheat, pumpernickel, pumpernickel raisin, cinnamon raisin, oat bran, and everything. They're so plump, chewy, and satisfying it's hard to believe they contain no fat, cholesterol, or preservatives. Head to the back counter for a baker's dozen or line up for a sandwich overstuffed with scrumptious salads and spreads. Fillings can range from a generous schmear of cream cheese to

ⓘ Family-Friendly Restaurants

The increasing kid-friendliness of New York City has resulted in a growing number of restaurants that warmly welcome families. While it's always a smart move to call ahead to make sure the restaurant you're interested in can assist parents with such amenities as kids' menus and high chairs, you can count on the following restaurants to be especially accommodating.

America *(p. 157)*   This kid-friendly Flatiron District restaurant is nearly as large as a continent, with a menu to match—even the fussiest kids will find something they like here. America especially caters to kids at their weekend family brunch, which features a balloon maker and a magician along with the good grub.

Carmine's *(p. 165)*   This rollicking family-style Italian was created with kids in mind. Expect Brady Bunch–size portions of all the favorites, including Caesar salad, veal parmigiana, and pasta topped with zesty marinara and little fist-sized meatballs. The bigger the group, the better the bargain.

EJ's Luncheonette *(p. 186)*   These pleasing retro-'50s diners do what they're supposed to do best: serve up great burgers, fries, and blue plate specials. There's even a kids' menu featuring peanut butter and jelly sandwiches along with down-sized versions of the classics. Order up your kid a milkshake on the side, and they'll be in hog heaven.

John's Pizzeria *(p. 167)*   What kid doesn't love pizza? The Times Square location is particularly well located and kid-friendly, with family-sized tables, chefs cooking up pies in brick ovens right in the cavernous room, and a bustling atmosphere where kids are welcome to be kids.

Serendipity 3 *(p. 187)*   Kids will love this whimsical restaurant and ice cream shop, which serves up a huge menu of American favorites, followed up by colossal ice-cream treats. This irony-free charmer even makes grown-ups feel like kids again.

Virgil's Real BBQ *(p. 166)*   This pleasing Times Square barbecue joint welcomes kids with open arms—and Junior will be more than happy, I'm sure, to be *allowed* to eat with his hands.

In addition to these choices, also consider the city's many theme restaurants. Sci fi–minded kids shouldn't miss **Mars 2112** (p. 169), which boasts its very own theme park ride, and a video arcade that can keep the kids busy for hours (or until you run out of quarters). Little groovy ghoulies will love the thrills and chills of the **Jekyll & Hyde Club** (p. 169), while sports-minded kids can drag their baseball dads and soccer moms to the **Official All-Star Cafe** (p. 169). For details on all these choices, see "Theme Restaurant Thrills!" earlier in this chapter.

---

smoked Nova salmon or chopped herring salad (both have received national acclaim) to sun-dried tomato tofu spread. There are also lots of deli-style meats to choose from, plus a wide range of cheeses and salads (egg, chicken, light tuna, and so on). The cheerful dining room has plenty of bistro-style tables.

There's a second, smaller location at 359 First Ave., at 21st Street (☎ **212/260-2252**).

Prime Burger. 5 E. 51st St. (btw. Fifth and Madison aves.). ☎ **212/759-4729.** Reservations not accepted. Main courses $3.25–$7.95. No credit cards. Mon–Fri 5am–7pm, Sat 6am–5pm. Subway: 6 to 51st St.; E, F to Lexington/Third aves. and 53rd St. AMERICAN/ HAMBURGERS.

Just across the street from St. Patrick's Cathedral, this coffee shop is a heavenly find. The burgers and sandwiches are tasty, the fries crispy and generous. The front seats, which might remind you (if you're old enough) of old wooden grammar-school desks, are great fun—especially when ever-so-serious suited-up New Yorkers quietly take their places at these oddities. A great quickie stop during a day of Fifth Avenue shopping.

Taco & Tortilla King. 285 Third Ave. (btw. 22nd and 23rd sts.). ☎ **212/679-8882** or 212/481-3930. Reservations not accepted. Tacos, burritos and sandwiches $1–$6.79; fajitas $12.99–$13.99. No credit cards. Daily 11am–11:30pm. Subway: 6 to 23rd St. MEXICAN.

This place may be slightly off the tourist track, but if you're jonesing for some good, cheap Mexican, it's well worth the walk. This low-profile sleeper is little more than a lunch counter with a few tables and chairs, but the authentic Mexican food can't be beat. Sit down to a couple of tacos and you'll think you've been temporarily transported to one of those super-cheap gourmet Mexican joints your friends in southern California keep raving about. The kitchen won me over with the basics: chunky fresh-made guacamole infused with lime, and flour tortillas made from scratch and baked on premise. All the Mexican staples, from well-stuffed burritos to sizzling fajitas, are authentically prepared, hearty, and satisfying; a good portion of the offerings can be prepared meatless for vegetarians. An all-around winner for a fast meal at an unbeatable price.

12 The Upper West Side

See the "Uptown Dining" map (pp. 178–179) for restaurants in this section.

VERY EXPENSIVE

✪ **Jean Georges.** In the Trump International Hotel & Tower, 1 Central Park West (at 60th St./Columbus Circle). ☎ **212/299-3900.** Reservations required. Jacket required/tie optional. Main courses $22–$30 in Nougatine; lunch prix-fixe $28 in Nougatine, $45 in main restaurant; dinner prix-fixe $85, tasting menu $115. AE, CB, DC, MC, V. Mon–Fri noon–2:30pm and 5:30–11pm, Sat 5:30–11pm. Subway: A, B, C, D, 1, 9 to 59th St./Columbus Circle. FRENCH.

That smarmy Donald Trump can be a very smart guy. When he announced he had secured the services of Jean-Georges Vongerichten (of Vong and Jo Jo) to oversee the restaurant in his new hotel, everyone knew the rave reviews wouldn't be far behind. And they were right—Jean Georges was immediately awarded four coveted stars by the *New York Times.*

Dining here is a sublime experience. In the elegantly restrained Adam Tihany–designed dining room, the menu is the best of Vongerichten's past successes taken one step further. French and Asian touches mingle with a new passion for off-beat harvests, like lamb's quarters, sorrel, yarrow, quince, and chicory. Spring garlic soup with thyme accompanied by a plate of sautéed frogs' legs with parsley makes a great beginning. The Muscovy duck steak with Asian spices and sweet-and-sour jus is carved tableside, while the lobster tartine with pumpkin seed, pea shoots, and a broth of fenugreek (one of Jean-Georges' signature aromatic plants) receives a final dash of spices seconds before you dig in. If the chestnut soup is on the menu, don't miss it. The food is equally excellent but more affordably priced in the more casual cafe Nougatine; don't expect equally comfy chairs or as much elbow room, however. If you're visiting in the warm weather, try to get a table on the lovely outdoor terrace. The professional service is without fault in the main restaurant, and still attentive if not quite as well paced in the cafe. The wine list is also excellent, with a number of unusual choices in every price range.

EXPENSIVE

Café des Artistes. 1 W. 67th St. (btw. Central Park West and Columbus Ave.). ☎ **212/ 877-3500.** Reservations highly required. Jacket required. Main courses $16.50–$26 at lunch and brunch, $22–$40 (most under $30) at dinner; 3-course prix-fixe dinner $37.50. AE, DC, MC, V. Mon–Fri noon–3pm; Mon–Sat 5:30pm–midnight, Sun 5–11pm; brunch Sat, Sun 10am–2:45pm. Subway: 1, 9 to 66th St./Lincoln Center. CONTINENTAL.

Café des Artistes is an ebullient place where playful neo-Renaissance murals of frolicking nymphs set the tone for decadence and romance. Thanks to its superior service and setting, the beautiful restaurant is both a celebrity hangout and a celebratory favorite of locals and visitors alike. The menu is wide ranging, inspired mostly by France but with an occasional nod to Vienna (sturgeon schnitzel, a house specialty, and Austrian beef goulash ladled over spaetzle), Scandinavia (salmon four ways, excellent dill-marinated gravlax), Italy (lush prosciutto di Parma with melon in season), the Mideast (vegetable buffet platter served with pita), and America (Louisiana bluepoints, Washington state mussels). Everything is well prepared and presented with a flourish. The dessert cart, overflowing with gorgeous pies, cakes, and pastries, is fabulous. Café des Artistes isn't the best restaurant in town; if you're looking for unparalleled haute cuisine, head a few blocks away to Jean-Georges. But for romance and special-occasion appeal, it's hard to beat.

The popular à la carte Sunday brunch is also terrific, with a nice cold buffet and egg dishes. Or for a light meal or coffee and pastries, head across the vestibule to **Parlor at Café des Artistes.** This reasonably priced hideaway (open Monday to Saturday 5:30pm to midnight, Sunday 5 to 11pm) is reminiscent of Vienna with a zinc-and-mahogany bar and marble-topped tables.

✪ **Picholine.** 35 W. 64th St. (btw. Central Park West and Broadway). ☎ **212/724-8585.** Reservations required. Main courses $26.50–$36; prix-fixe lunch $25–$35; dinner tasting menus $65 (4 courses) and $85 (7 courses). AE, DC, MC, V. Mon 5:30–11:45pm, Tues–Sat 11:45am–2pm and 5:30–11:45pm, Sun 5–10pm. Subway: 1, 9 to 66th St./Lincoln Center. MEDITERRANEAN.

This *New York Times* three-star winner just keeps getting better. Chef Terrance Brennan has made Picholine a resounding success—around Lincoln Center, few restaurants are as talked about. It's calm and welcoming, but Brennan's inventive take on French Mediterranean classics is what packs them in. Start with the tasty ceviche of Spanish mackerel, full-flavored gnocchi with sheep's milk ricotta, or wonderful grilled octopus with fennel and potato, doused in lemon-pepper dressing. The loin of lamb is spiced with a Moroccan touch and served with a vegetable couscous and minted yogurt. The halibut comes with eggplant pancakes, tomato confit, balsamic vinegar, and basil oil, and the risotto is topped with wild mushrooms and duck with asparagus, fava beans, and white-truffle oil. Make sure someone at your table orders the outstanding duck risotto, and be sure to filch a taste. Cheese whiz Max McCalman presides over the city's only cheese aging room, in which gourmet *fromages* from small producers mature to perfection. In keeping with everything else about Picholine, service is first-rate.

Tavern on the Green. In Central Park, Central Park West and W. 67th St. ☎ **212/873-3200.** Reservations highly recommended, necessary on holidays (reservations available online). Main courses $20–$40; 3-course pre-theater prix-fixe (Mon–Fri until 6:15pm) $30–$40. AE, CB, DC, DISC, MC, V. Mon–Thurs 11:30am–3:30pm and 5:30–11:30pm, Fri 11:30am–3:30pm and 5–11:30pm, Sat 10am–3:30pm and 5–11:30pm, Sun 10am–3:30pm and 5:30–10:30pm. Subway: 1, 9 to 66th St./Lincoln Center. CONTINENTAL/CONTEMPORARY AMERICAN.

This legendary Central Park restaurant is a true one of a kind. Warner LeRoy's fantasy palace has one of the city's best settings, and it's just lovely. Antiques and Tiffany glass fill the space, crystal chandeliers cast a romantic light, tiny twinkling lights glimmer on nearby trees, and the views over the park are wonderful. A festive spirit enlivens the Crystal Room, where you should ask to be seated, especially at Christmas. (A couple of the other dining rooms are so overdone as to cross the line into the realm of tacky, though.) The garden, with its Japanese lanterns and whimsical topiary shrubs, is a lovely place for a drink in summer.

Since the passing of beloved executive chef Patrick Clark, the kitchen gets kudos for maintaining his legacy, though it's hard to be completely consistent in an operation this

Uptown Dining

Aureole ⬥41
Big Nick's Burger Joint ⬥12
Bolivar ⬥39
Burritoville ⬥16
Café Boulud ⬥28
Café des Artistes ⬥31
Cafe Luxembourg ⬥17
Caffe Grazie ⬥18
Carmine's ⬥5
Citrus ⬥14
Daniel ⬥35
EJ's Luncheonette ⬥9 ⬥25
Haru ⬥10 ⬥22
Hi-Life Bar & Grill ⬥7
Hi-Life Restaurant & Lounge ⬥24
Hunan Park ⬥2 ⬥30
Jean Georges ⬥42
John's Pizzeria ⬥33 ⬥37
Jo Jo ⬥36
Josie's Restaurant & Juice Bar ⬥15
Park View at the Boathouse ⬥29
Payard Patisserie & Bistro ⬥26
Picholine ⬥34
Pintaile's Pizza ⬥4
Popover Cafe ⬥6
Republic ⬥8
Sarabeth's Kitchen ⬥3 ⬥11 ⬥27
Serendipity 3 ⬥38
Shabu Tatsu ⬥23
Sofia Fabulous Pizza ⬥19
Sylvia's ⬥1
Tavern on the Green ⬥32
Totonno's Pizzeria Napolitano ⬥20
Zen Palate ⬥13

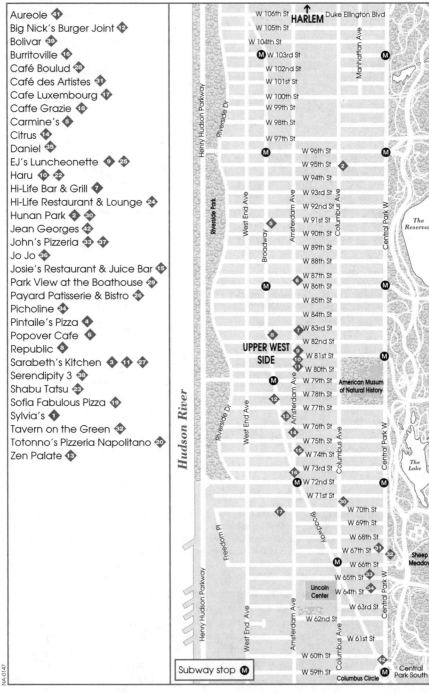

NA-0147

178

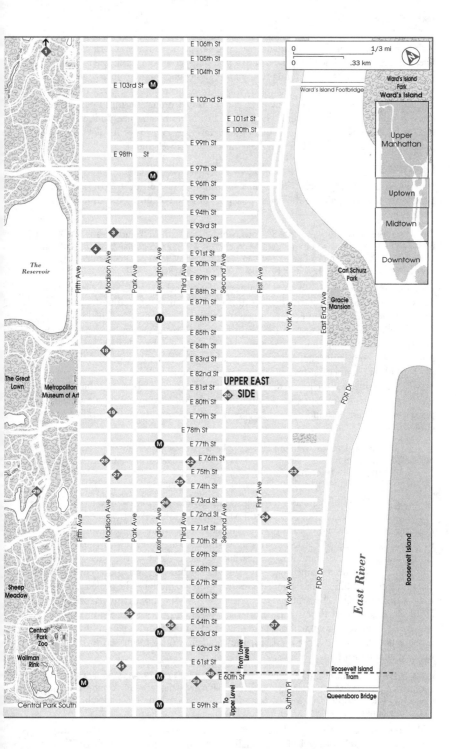

mammoth. The seasonal menus are surprisingly good, particularly if you stick with classic fare. The seared duck foie gras, served with a pear-and-pecan sticky bun and a balsamic-port syrup, is a wonderful beginning to any meal. Other good starters: roasted lobster on lobster polenta, warm house-smoked salmon, and white bean-and-spring vegetable soup. The superb al dente pasta is made by pasta chef Renzo Barcatta. The grilled pork porterhouse is delicious and thick. Salmon is barbecued with Moroccan spices and served with a couscous cake. Despite its big reputation, the Tavern is known for its down-to-earth manner. The crowd can be thick at holiday time, so book well ahead.

MODERATE

For fun, family-style Italian, there's also the original **Carmine's** (p. 165) at 2450 Broadway, between 90th and 91st streets (☎ **212/362-2200**), in addition to the choices below.

Cafe Luxembourg. 200 W. 70th St. (btw. Amsterdam and West End aves.). ☎ **212/ 873-7411.** Reservations recommended. Main courses $17–$27; 3-course prix-fixe lunch or brunch $19.99; 3-course prix-fixe dinner $34. AE, DC, MC, V. Mon–Sat noon–midnight, Sun 11am–midnight. Subway: 1, 2, 3, 9 to 72nd St. FRENCH BISTRO.

Cafe Luxembourg has been a great favorite not far from Lincoln Center ever since it opened. Some might not have predicted this longevity from the feeding frenzy at the time, but it has survived to become a tasteful classic. The clean white-tiled walls, the arch faux art deco touches, and the beautiful people scene at the bar make for an enjoyable evening. The food is basic French brasserie: good steak frites; remarkable grilled lamb chops with ratatouille, potato gratin, and herb-lamb juice; and rabbit pot pie with black trumpet mushrooms, baby onions, carrots, and thyme. The entrees are on the pricey side, but the prix-fixe lunch and dinner are terrific buys and the wine list is well priced, so it's easy to stick to your budget if you're counting on a moderately priced meal. Brunch is another good-value bet. A great pre- or post-Lincoln Center choice.

Citrus. 320 Amsterdam Ave. (at 75th St.). ☎ **212/595-0500.** Reservations recommended, but walk-ins welcome. Main courses $10.75–$17 (specials may be higher). AE, DC, MC, V. Mon 5:30–11pm, Tues–Thurs 5:30pm–midnight, Fri 5:30pm–1am, Sat 5pm–1am; Sun brunch 11:30am–3:30pm, dinner 5pm–1am. Subway: 1, 2, 3, 9 to 72nd St. SOUTHWESTERN.

Boasting a full slate of tequilas and designer margaritas, this place could let the food become an afterthought. But chef Martin Mendoza combines American and Mexican ingredients in surprisingly pleasing ways. The skirt steak with cayenne-flavored onion rings and coffee-infused barbecue sauce is a winner, as is the yellowfin tuna filet on cumin-orange rice and plantains. We also like appetizers such as the blue cornmeal-crusted calamari, the romaine salad with lime caesar dressing and asiago cheese, and any of the creative quesadillas. Some dishes reach too far, though: The pork chops were tough, and the ancho chile-rubbed chicken breast was disappointingly flavorless. But all in all, this is good fusion cuisine at wallet-pleasing prices. And the airy, Southwestern-style space is lively without being cramped—important, since on some nights it seems like the entire Upper West Side is in residence. A tip for dessert lovers: Don't miss the mammoth flan.

Haru. 433 Amsterdam Ave. (btw. 80th and 81st sts.). ☎ **212/579-5655.** Reservations not accepted. À la carte sushi and rolls $3–$8 (special rolls may be higher); sushi combos and main courses $14–$24.50. AE, DC, MC, V. Mon–Thurs 5–11:30pm, Fri 5pm–midnight, Sat–Sun 11:30am–midnight. Subway: 1, 9 to 79th St. SUSHI.

This attractive, sophisticated little restaurant arrived on the Upper West Side, a neighborhood desperately in need of high-quality sushi, like a breath of fresh air. Expect generous, super-fresh cuts of all the classics, plus a good number of vegetable choices (shiitake and cucumber, vegetable tempura) among the hand and cut rolls. I recommend starting with the seaweed salad, which boasts four kinds of seaweed in vinaigrette, king crab shumai, a couple of grilled kushi yaki skewers, and/or a bowl of miso before launching into your raw meal. The good-looking blond-wood room fills up quickly, so don't be surprised if there's a wait; but we've found that it's rather quiet in the pre-theater hour, and Lincoln Center is just a brisk 10- or 15-minute walk away.

If you're on the east side, Haru has a second location at 1329 Third Ave., at 76th Street (☎ **212/579-5655**).

○ **Sarabeth's Kitchen.** 423 Amsterdam Ave. (btw. 80th and 81st sts.). ☎ **212/496-6280.** Reservations accepted for dinner only. Main courses $5–$11 at lunch and brunch, $10–$22 at dinner. AE, CB, DC, DISC, JCB, MC, V. Mon–Thurs 8am–10:30pm, Fri 8am–11pm, Sat 9am–11pm, Sun 9am–9:30pm. Subway: 1, 9 to 79th St. CONTEMPORARY AMERICAN.

Its 200-year-old family recipe for orange-apricot marmalade rooted Sarabeth's Kitchen into New York's consciousness, and now its fresh-baked goods, award-winning preserves, and creative American cooking with a European touch keep a loyal following. This charming country restaurant with a distinct Hamptons feel is best known for its breakfast and weekend brunch, when the menu features such treats as porridge with wheatberries, fresh cream, butter, and brown sugar; pumpkin waffle topped with sour cream, raisins, pumpkin seeds, and honey (a sweet tooth's delight); and a whole host of farm-fresh omelets. But lunch and dinner are just as good and a lot less crowded. Lunch might be a generous Caesar salad with aged Parmesaan, brioche croutons, and a tangy anchovy dressing accompanied by a hearty from-scratch soup, or some beautifully built country-style sandwiches. Dinner is more sophisticated, with such specialties as hazelnut-crusted halibut in an aromatic seven-vegetable broth and oven-roasted lamb crusted in black mushrooms, with grilled leeks and Vidalia onion rings on the side. Leave room for the scrumptious desserts—Sarabeth Levine was just given the James Beard Award for Best Pastry Chef recently, an honor well deserved.

There are also two East Side locations: 1295 Madison Ave. (☎ **212/410-7335**) and inside the Whitney Museum at 945 Madison Ave. (☎ **212/570-3670**).

INEXPENSIVE

In addition to the choices below, there's also a branch of the retro all-American diner known as **EJ's Luncheonette** (p. 186) at 447 Amsterdam Ave., between 81st and 82nd streets (☎ **212/873-3444**). More retro vibes can be had at the **Hi-Life Bar & Grill,** at Amsterdam Avenue and 83rd Street (☎ **212/787-7199**).

Near Lincoln Center, 48 W. 65th St. between Columbus Avenue and Central Park West, there's a nice **John's Pizzeria** (☎ **212/721-7001**), serving up one of the city's best pies (p. 167). You'll also find healthful **Zen Palate** (p. 158) at 2170 Broadway, between 76th and 77th streets (☎ **212/501-7768**); and **Burritoville** at 166 W. 72nd St., at Amsterdam Avenue (☎ **212/580-7700**).

Big Nick's Burger Joint. 2175 Broadway (at 77th St.). ☎ **212/362-9238.** Reservations not necessary. Main courses $3.50–$11. No credit cards. Daily 24 hours. Subway: 1, 9 to 79th St. AMERICAN.

A neighborhood legend since 1962, Big Nick's is one of the best spots in the city for a midnight snack. They offer a full menu 24 hours a day, which includes everything from killer french toast and pancakes to Nick's infamous gourmet beefburgers. The classic char-broiled burgers come in a whole host of varieties, from your all-American cheeseburger to the Mediterranean, stuffed with herbs, spices, and onions and topped with anchovies, feta, and tomato. Or how 'bout a Texasburger, with an egg on top for "egg-stra" energy (Nick's joke, not mine). There's also a good selection of Big Nick-style pizzas, like the Gyromania, topped with well-seasoned gyro meat and onions. As the name suggests, Nick's is a real joint, specializing in homegrown Noo Yawk fare; however, the kitchen gets kudos for developing a dietwatchers menu, with such specialties as pizzas prepared with skim cheese and lean-ground veal and turkey burgers. The atmosphere is suitably lively, with waiters and buspeople scrambling about, cooks calling out orders, and crowded tables full of diners happily chowing down.

Hunan Park. 235 Columbus Ave. (btw. 70th and 71st St.). ☎ **212/724-4411.** Reservations accepted for groups of 5 or more. Main courses $5.25–$10.50 (Peking Duck $24). AE, MC, V. Sun–Thurs noon–11:30pm, Fri–Sat noon–12:30am. Subway: B, C, 1, 2, 3, 9 to 72nd St. HUNAN CHINESE.

This casual place has been earning broad-sweeping kudos for years from everybody from Zagat's to *New York* magazine to Alan Alda for its well-prepared, inexpensive Chinese standards. Everything about it—quality, service, decor—is a cut above the standard. Expect all the familiar favorites, plus satisfying specialties like ginger chicken, spicy four-flavor beef, and crispy sea bass in a rich Hunan sauce. Service is quick and efficient, and the convenient location makes this a cheap and easy post-Central Park or pre-Lincoln Center stop.

If you're farther uptown, there's a second location at 721 Columbus Ave., at 95th Street (☎ **212/222-6511**).

Josie's Restaurant & Juice Bar. 300 Amsterdam Ave. (at 74th St.). ☎ **212/769-1212.** Reservations recommended. Main courses $8–$16. AE, DC, MC, V. Mon 5:30–11pm, Tues–Fri 5:30pm–midnight, Sat 5pm–midnight, Sun 5–11pm. Subway: 1, 2, 3, 9 to 72nd St. HEALTH-CONSCIOUS.

You have to admire the sincerity of an organic restaurant that uses chemical-free milk paint on its walls. Chef/owner Louis Lanza doesn't stop there: His adventurous menu shuns dairy, preservatives, and concentrated fats. Free-range and farm-raised meats and poultry augment vegetarian choices like baked sweet potato with tamari brown rice, broccoli, roasted beets, and tahini sauce; eggless Caesar salad; and a great three-grain vegetable burger with homemade ketchup and caramelized onions. The yellowfin tuna wasabi burger with pickled ginger is another signature. Everything is made with organic grains, beans, and flour as well as organic produce when possible. You don't have to be a health nut to enjoy Josie's; Lanza's eclectic cuisine really satisfies. And nobody's gonna actually make you do without: If wheat grass isn't your thing, a full wine and beer list is served in this pleasing modern space, which boasts enough *Jetsons*-style touches to give the room a playful, relaxed feel.

Popover Cafe. 551 Amsterdam Ave. (btw. 86th and 87th sts.). ☎ **212/595-8555.** Reservations not accepted. Main courses $5.75–$15.50 at breakfast and lunch, $11.95–$17.95 at dinner. AE, MC, V. Mon–Thurs 8am–10pm, Fri 9am–11pm, Sat 9am–11pm, Sun 9am–11pm. Subway: 1, 9 to 86th St. AMERICAN.

The first thing people usually call Popover's is kid-friendly. Not that it isn't—there's the child-size burger, peanut butter and jelly sandwiches, and, of course, cutesy decor chock-a-block with teddy bears—but grownups will like it just as much as kids will. Everybody gets addicted to the namesake item: big, fluffy popovers served with strawberry butter or preserves. Popover's supplements their basic menu with full entrees at dinnertime that are a bit on the pricey side, but their real forte is the kind of comfort food that makes a hearty, and affordable, lunch or brunch: three-egg omelets and scrambles, savory homestyle chili and soups, generous salads and sandwiches with cutesy names like "slim chickens" and "sorry, Charlie" (tuna, natch). A bowl of one of the day's homemade soups (vegetarian three-bean, split pea, and chicken noodle are some of the possible options) accompanied by a popover makes a more-than-satisfying lunch. In fact, eating here feels like you've been welcomed into somebody's big old, hospitable New England home. Well worth a stop.

13 The Upper East Side

See the "Uptown Dining" map (pp. 178–179) for restaurants in this section.

VERY EXPENSIVE

Aureole. 34 E. 61st St. (btw. Madison and Park aves.). ☎ **212/319-1660.** Reservations required 1 month in advance. Jacket and tie required. Prix-fixe dinners $65 and $85; prix-fixe lunches $19.99 (after 2pm) and $32. AE, DC, MC, V. Mon–Fri noon–2:30pm; Mon–Sat 5:30–11pm. Subway: 4, 5, 6 to 59th St.; N, R to Fifth Ave. CONTEMPORARY AMERICAN.

When Aureole opened in 1988, it quickly became one of the first contemporary American restaurants to enjoy the prestige of European-style legends like Lutèce and Le Cirque. Set in a town house where Orson Welles once lived, the romantic 90-seat duplex room is beautiful if cramped, filled with massive flower arrangements and sandstone reliefs; tables are also set in a courtyard garden in warm weather. Winner of a jaw-dropping 28 rating (out of 30) for food from *Zagat*, chef/owner Charlie Palmer excels at striking presentations and bold flavor combinations. The sea scallop sandwich, a signature starter, substitutes crispy potato pancakes for the bread. Tender filet mignon is charcoal grilled and served with red-wine sauce and morels decadently stuffed with foie gras. A potato crust envelops wild striped bass, served with broccoli rabe and black trumpet mushrooms. The sculptural chocolate desserts, stunningly designed by pastry chef Michael Gabriel, are justly famous, and the topflight wine list includes an extensive American selection. A few significant quibbles, though: The service is proficient but a bit too standoffish for my taste, and the space is too tightly packed—you deserve more breathing room for what you'll spend to dine here.

⊙ **Daniel.** 60 E. 65th St. (btw. Madison and Park aves.). ☎ **212/288-0033.** Reservations required 1 month in advance. Jacket and tie required. Prix-fixe lunch $35–$42, 5-course tasting menu $69 at lunch; 3-course prix-fixe dinner $68, 6–8 course tasting menus $90–$120 at dinner. AE, DC, MC, V. Mon–Thurs noon–2:30pm and 5:45–11pm, Fri–Sat noon–2:30pm and 5:45–11:30pm. Subway: 6 to 68th St. FRENCH COUNTRY.

When chef/owner Daniel Boulud first opened Daniel in 1993, Patricia Wells named it one of the *world's* top 10 restaurants. In early '99, Boulud moved Daniel into this much larger space, previously occupied by Le Cirque. A fortune was spent on the renovation, and it shows. If Le Cirque 2000 sounds too over the top for your taste, this is the dining room for you: The room's gorgeous neo-Renaissance features—rich mahogany doors, sensuous arches, elegant Corinthian columns, and soaring terracotta-tiled ceilings—have been beautifully accented with a rich autumn color palette and custom furnishings with subtly playful curves. It's an ideal setting for Boulud's faultless country French cooking.

The menu is heavy with game dishes in elegant but unfussy preparations, plus Daniel signatures like black sea bass in a crisp potato shell, with tender leeks and a light Barolo sauce. Excellent starters include a frisee salad with crisp braised sweetbreads, pistachios, and black truffle, a dish that could convert the most committed offalphile. Don't neglect the specials menu; I was the envy of the table with my warm rabbit confit salad with foie gras. Sublime entrees may include braised Chatham cod with cockles and caviar, or chestnut-crusted venison with sweet potato puree. But you can't really go wrong with anything—the kitchen doesn't take a false turn. The service is a little stuffy for my taste and the sommelier not as interactive as I would like, but the wine list is excellent and features more affordable bottles than I usually see at a restaurant of this ilk. Divided between seasonal fruits and chocolates, the desserts are also uniformly excellent.

EXPENSIVE

✪ **Café Boulud.** At the Surrey Hotel, 20 E. 76th St. (btw. Madison and Fifth aves.). ☎ **212/ 772-2600.** Reservations required. Main courses $24–$32; prix-fixe lunch $28–$35, 4-course prix-fixe dinner $55. Sun–Mon 5:45–11:30pm, Tues–Sat noon–2:30pm and 5:45–11:30pm. Subway: 6 to 77th St. FRENCH/ECLECTIC.

Dying to try the stellar cuisine of Daniel Boulud, New York's best French chef, but can't get in to Daniel? Or the prospect of the bill there makes your wallet tremble with trepidation? Or it just sounds too darn formal for you? Then head to Café Boulud, Boulud's more casual playground for new ideas and culinary cross-pollinations, instead. More casual is a relative term, mind you—this space is still Upper East Side chic. But Daniel's high style has been pleasingly laid back and toned down here. With the food, Boulud has gone eclectic, offering four menus: La Tradition, featuring Boulud's signature French-country classics; Le Potager, a vegetarian menu; La Saison, with seasonal dishes; and Le Voyage, a monthly globe-hopping menu highlighting Tuscany, Thailand, or anything in between. The experimental nature of the wide-ranging menu makes choosing a thrill, and even the most inventive dishes tend to dazzle the palate. But in true Boulud tradition, La Tradition (which always features his divine signature sea bass in potato shell and red wine) and La Saison are where the kitchen really excels. At $28, the two-course prix-fixe lunch is a true bargain; I was thrilled with both my gnocchi starter, delicately seasoned with pumpkin and sage, and the rich, uniquely flavorful braised veal cheeks on soft polenta that followed in perfect juxtaposition. Unfortunately, the service was quite lax on my visit. Based on my previous experiences at the original Daniel, I assume that was an anomaly (here's hoping, anyway). But all in all, a first-rate dining experience at more palatable prices than cuisine this memorable usually costs.

Jo Jo. 160 E. 64th St. (btw. Lexington and Third aves.). ☎ **212/223-5656.** Reservations required. Main courses $19–$35 (most less than $30); 3-course prix-fixe lunch $28; tasting menus $40–$60. AE, DC, MC, V. Mon–Fri noon–2:30pm and 6–11pm, Sat 5:30–11:30pm. Subway: 6 to 68th St.; N, R to Lexington Ave. FRENCH BISTRO.

Chef/owner Jean-Georges Vongerichten garnered his first praise while cooking at the now-defunct Lafayette, where he nearly singlehandedly revolutionized French cooking by replacing butter- and cream-laden sauces with low-fat flavored oils and fresh vegetable juices, and infusing a delicate Asian sensibility. He has drawn crowds to this restaurant continually since 1991, despite opening higher-profile places like Vong, Jean Georges, and Mercer Kitchen since then. This breezy yet elegant East Side townhouse eschews modernism for a warmer, more traditional style that's supremely welcoming: Downstairs, the banquettes are red, the walls a warm yellow; upstairs, parlor-floor windows illuminate the room softly. The compact but inviting menu may offer such lighter-than-usual takes on such French staples like goat cheese (in a potato terrine with baby lettuce and arugula juice), fois gras (with quince and warm lentil salad), squab (served rare with warm potato salad in pommery mustard vinaigrette), and duck (roasted with figs, port wine, and glazed turnips). Prices are high, but the cuisine—and even the wine—is a value considering the excellence of the cooking, service, and setting, and a far better deal than Vongerichten's disappointing Mercer Kitchen. The tasting menus (including a vegetarian menu at dinner) are bargains.

✪ **Park View at the Boathouse.** On the lake in Central Park, near 72nd St. and Park Dr. North (nearest park entrance is 72nd St. and Fifth Ave.). ☎ **212/517-2233.** Reservations highly recommended. Main courses $20–$32; weekend brunch $14–$23. AE, DISC, MC, V. Fall/Winter: Tues–Fri 6–10pm, Sat 11am–3pm and 6–10pm, Sun 11am–3pm. Spring/Summer: Mon–Fri 11:30am–10pm, Sat 11am–11pm, Sun 11am–9pm. Subway: 6 to 77th St. CONTEMPORARY AMERICAN.

Park View is a one-of-a-kind experience—there's no better alfresco dining in the city. What makes it so special? Beautifully set on the edge of the lake and surrounded by great green Central Park, it's quintessentially New York yet magically distant from the urban bustle. And now with acclaimed chef John Villa at the helm, the creative New American cuisine is almost as stellar as the surroundings. Villa particularly excels at dishes with an Asian flair; Indian-spiced salmon tartare with pappadam and plantain crisps made an appealing pan-cultural starter, and coriander spiced tuna loin on a crisp taro cake with mango salsa and cilantro vinaigrette was an ideal marriage of sweet and spice. Not everything works though—red snapper poached in milk?—so ask your waiter to help you steer past the menu's few pitfalls.

The restaurant opened year-round for the first time over the winter 1998–99 season, featuring a game menu served in a glass-walled, fireplace-lit dining room. Summer is the time to come, though; book ahead, since everybody wants to dine here, especially for weekend brunch. Twilight is enchanting, giving Park View the air of a tiny oasis lorded over by the distant twinkling skyline; try to arrive just before sunset if you can, even if it means coming early for a drink at the equally well-situated bar. You've no doubt heard about the dangers of wandering in Central Park after dark, but after 7pm a shuttle runs from Fifth Avenue and 72nd Street (inquire about the current schedule when you reserve).

MODERATE

If you're in the mood for sushi, consider the eastside branch of **Haru** (p. 180), at 1329 Third Ave., at 76th Street (☎ 212/579-5655). If it's an excellent contemporary meal or a sweet treat you're after, head to **Sarabeth's Kitchen** (p. 181), which has two eastside locations: 1295 Madison Ave., at E. 92nd St. (☎ 212/410-7335), and at the Whitney Museum, 945 Madison Ave. (☎ 212/570-3670).

Bolivar. 206 E. 60th St. (near Third Ave.). ☎ **212/838-0440.** Reservations recommended. Main courses $12–$25. AE, DC, DISC, MC, V. Daily noon–3pm and 5:30–11pm. Subway: 4, 5, 6 to 59th St.; N, R to Lexington Ave. SOUTH AMERICAN.

The former Arizona 206 has been transformed into this hotspot for New York's cuisine of the moment. The restaurant's warm stucco rooms make a welcome setting for the South American fare, which draws heavily from Peruvian and Argentine techniques. The food is delightful, from the ceviches (your choice of octopus, oyster, sea bass, tuna, or fluke) bursting with bold, fresh flavor to the excellent meats grilled on the South American *parilla*. The sides are equally delectable, especially the yummy yuca gratin and the crisp ñame pancakes, made from African yams. Sides are all ordered separately, so keep an eye on what you're ordering or the bill can skyrocket. I prefer to order dishes here tapas-style, which allows everyone in the party lots of tastes and keeps the tab reasonable. Both the exotic cocktails and the decadent desserts are also pleasing, even if they sometimes stray too far from the pan-Latino theme. Service is knowlegable and attentive. Unfortunately, this space is still too loud for comfortable dining, just as it was in its previous incarnation. Your best bet is to go for lunch on a break from browsing Bloomie's, which is just around the corner.

Caffe Grazie. 26 E. 84th St. (at Madison Ave.). ☎ **212/717-4407.** Reservations recommended. Main courses $12.50–$19.50; Sun brunch $12.95. AE, DC, MC, V. Mon–Sat 11:30am–11pm, Sun 11:30am–10pm. Subway: 4, 5, 6 to 86th St. ITALIAN.

This cheery, unpretentious Italian cafe is most notable for its convenient location near the Metropolitan Museum of Art, a neighborhood short of moderately priced, recommendable eats. It's perfect for sipping espresso between museum hops or lingering over an elegant dinner. Appetizers like the bruschetta assortment served with a small salad and the warm white-bean salad over prosciutto are generous enough to be a light meal in themselves. The pasta selection mixes staples (satisfying penne pomodoro and linguini pesto) with standouts (lasagna layered with grilled chicken, fresh tomatoes, cheese, and pesto). The entrees, like veal stuffed with prosciutto and spinach and jumbo shrimp with lemon-caper sauce, are fresh and flavorful. All in all, a hidden treasure in a needy neighborhood.

◐ Payard Patisserie & Bistro. 1032 Lexington Ave. (at 73rd St.). ☎ **212/717-5252.** Reservations recommended. Main courses $10–$25. AE, DC, MC, V. Mon–Sat noon–2:30pm and 6–11pm; tea Mon–Sat 3:30–5pm. Subway: 6 to 77th St. FRENCH BISTRO.

From Daniel Boulud, celebrity chef and owner of the highly acclaimed Daniel, and his former pastry chef, François Payard, comes this grand turn-of-the-century, Parisian-style cafe. Elegant cakes, pastries, and handmade chocolates fill glass cases in the pastry shop up front, while mirrors, mahogany, and straightforward bistro fare entice patrons to the cafe in back. The menu is unabashedly classic, with homemade duck confit, thick slabs of foie gras terrine, sublime steak frites, and fragrant bouillabaisse. The biggest problem with Payard? Choosing among the fabulous, beautifully presented desserts, which rank among the city's best. Everything is house-made, from the signature cakes, breads, and pastries to the delicate candies. Whether you go with the classic crème brûlée or something more decadent (anything chocolate is to die for), you're sure to be wowed. Feel free to come in just for afternoon tea or dessert if the entree prices are too rich for you.

INEXPENSIVE

In addition to the choices below, also consider the local branch of **Shabu Tatsu** (p. 147), at 114 York Ave., at 75th Street (☎ **212/472-3322**), which is well worth the trip to the far east side of town.

EJ's Luncheonette. 1271 Third Ave. (at 73rd St.). ☎ **212/472-0600.** Reservations not accepted. Main courses $3.95–$12. No credit cards. Mon–Thurs 8am–11pm, Fri–Sat 8am–11:30pm, Sun 8am–10:30pm. Subway: 6 to 77th St. AMERICAN DINER.

This retro diner is popular with Uptown yups and their kids who come for hearty American fare in a 1950s setting—turquoise vinyl booths, Formica tabletops, a soda fountain, and a lunch counter with stools that spin. The menu features a large selection of breakfasts so good you shouldn't be ashamed of indulging in a stack of banana-pecan pancakes for dinner. There's also a terrific selection of burgers (including a great veggie version), well-stuffed sandwiches, hearty green salads, and blue plate main dishes like meat loaf with mashed potatoes. Everything is well-prepared—better than you'd expect from a joint like this, in fact—and service is friendly. Don't miss the amazing sweet potato fries.

There are two other locations in addition to this one: On the Upper West Side at 447 Amsterdam Ave., between 81st and 82nd streets (☎ 212/873-3444); and in Greenwich Village at 432 Sixth Ave., between 9th and 10th streets (☎ 212/473-5555). Weekend brunch is a big deal at all three locations, but expect a wait.

Hi-Life Restaurant & Lounge. 1340 First Ave. (at 72nd St.). ☎ **212/249-3600.** Reservations accepted. Main courses $4.95–$8.50 at lunch, $8.95–$16.50 (including soup or salad) at dinner. AE, DC, DISC, MC, V. Mon–Fri 11am–4pm and 5pm–midnight, Sat–Sun 11:30am–4pm and 5pm–midnight. Subway: 6 to 68th St. AMERICAN/ECLECTIC.

Here's a page out of the days when men wore gray flannel suits, women looked like Myrna Loy, and everybody had a doozy of a before-dinner cocktail. Although it's a product of the '90s, the Hi-Life was designed in the tradition of pre-war restaurants

Pizza! Pizza!

Leave it to the chi-chi Upper East Side to specialize in designer pizza. **Sofia Fabulous Pizza**, 1022 Madison Ave., at 79th Street (☎ 212/734-2676), serves pricey but terrific Tuscan-style pizza, and there's even a wonderful alfresco rooftop setting. **Pintaile's Pizza**, at 26 E. 91st St., between Fifth and Madison avenues (☎ 212/722-1967), dresses their daintily crisp organic crusts with layers of plum tomatoes, extra virgin olive oil, and other fabulously fresh ingredients.

For something more traditional-style, head to **Totonno's Pizzeria Napolitano**, 1544 Second Ave., between 80th and 81st streets (☎ 212/327-2800), for killer coal-oven pies. Some naysayers consider this a pale comparison to the Coney Island original, but we think they're just hung up on the fancier digs. A little farther afield, at 408 E. 64th St. between First and York avenues, is a branch of **John's Pizzeria** (☎ 212/935-2895) that's worth checking out (p. 167).

and lounges, with a mahogany bar, comfy leather banquettes, neon signs, and stainless steel touches throughout. The bar prides itself on its excellent classic cocktails, particularly its martinis, and they are terrific. The food's not bad, either—good all-American fare at reasonable prices, with a little Asian flair here and there to keep you grounded in the present. The flame-grilled burgers, steaks, and chops are satisfying and fit the mood perfectly. The seafood selections also lean to Sinatra-era preparations such as grilled tuna in teriyaki and jumbo shrimp scampi, and they are better than I expected them to be. The menu also features a few pastas, entree-sized salads, and hearty noodle bowls for lighter tastes. There's a sushi and raw bar as well, but you can do better elsewhere in this department; stick with the standard menu.

The Hi-Life also has a more casual bar and grill on the Upper West Side at 477 Amsterdam Ave., at 83rd Street (☎ 212/787-7199).

Serendipity 3. 225 E. 60th St. (btw. Second and Third aves.). ☎ 212/838-3531. Reservations recommended for dinner. Main courses $5.50–$17.95; sweets and sundaes $4.50–$10. AE, DC, DISC, MC, V. Sun–Thurs 11:30am–midnight, Fri 11:30am–1am, Sat 11:30am–2am. Subway: 4, 5, 6 to 59th St.; N, R to Lexington Ave. AMERICAN.

You'd never guess that this whimsical place was once a top stop on Andy Warhol's agenda. Wonders never cease—and neither does the confection at this delightful restaurant and sweet shop. Tucked into a cozy brownstone a few steps from Bloomingdale's, Serendipity's small front-room curiosity shop overflows with odd objects, from jigsaw puzzles to silly jewelry. But the real action is behind the shop, where the quintessential American soda fountain still reigns supreme. Remember Farrell's? This is the better version (complete with candy to tempt the kids on the way out), and it's still going strong. Happy people gather at marble-topped ice-cream parlor tables for burgers and foot-long hot dogs, country meat loaf with mashed potatoes and gravy, and salads and sandwiches with cute names like "The Catcher in the Rye" (their own twist on the BLT, with chicken and Russian dressing—on rye, of course). The food isn't great, but the main courses aren't the point—just as they were at Farrell's, they're just an excuse to get to the desserts. The restaurant's signature is Frozen Hot Chocolate, a slushie version of everybody's cold weather favorite, but other crowd pleasers include dark double devil mousse, celestial carrot cake, lemon ice-box pie, and anything with hot fudge. So cast that willpower aside and come on in—Serendipity is a irony-free charmer to be appreciated by adults and kids alike.

14 Harlem

To locate Sylvia's, see the "Upper Manhattan Attractions" map (p. 257).

INEXPENSIVE

Sylvia's. 328 Lenox Ave. (btw. 126th and 127th sts.). ☎ **212/996-0660.** Reservations accepted for 10 or more. Main courses $8–$16. AE, DISC, MC, V. Mon–Thurs 8am–10:30pm, Fri–Sat 7:30am–10:30pm, Sun 11am–8pm. Subway: 2, 3 to 125th St. SOUL FOOD.

South Carolina–born Sylvia Woods is the last word in New York soul food. The place is so popular with both locals and visiting celebs that the dining room has spilled into the building next door. Since 1962, her Harlem institution has dished up the southern-fried goods: turkey with down-home stuffing; smothered chicken and pork chops; fried chicken and baked ham; collard greens and candied yams; and cavity-inducing sweet tea. And then of course there's "Sylvia's World Famous, Talked About, Bar-B-Que Ribs Special"—the sauce is sweet, with a potent afterburn. This Harlem landmark is still presided over by 72-year-old Sylvia, who's likely to greet you at the door herself. Some naysayers say that Sylvia's just isn't what it used to be, but chowing down here is still a one-of-a-kind New York experience. Sunday gospel brunch is a joyous time to go.

15 Waterfront Dining in Brooklyn & Queens

EXPENSIVE

✪ **The River Café.** 1 Water St. (at the East River), Brooklyn Heights. ☎ **718/522-5200.** Reservations required. Jacket required; tie preferred. Prix-fixe dinner $70; tasting menu $90. AE, CB, DC, MC, V. Mon–Fri noon–2:30pm and 6–11:30pm, Sat–Sun 11:30am–2:30pm and 6–11:30pm. Subway: A to High St./Brooklyn Bridge; 2, 3 to Clark St. CONTEMPORARY AMERICAN.

This magical restaurant is beautifully situated, on a barge festooned with twinkling lights tucked beneath the beautiful Brooklyn Bridge. The view of Lower Manhattan and New York Harbor is simply spectacular—the skyline looks close enough to reach out and touch. Even though lunch and weekend brunch are among the options, go for dinner—that's when the restaurant takes on a celebratory glow and the twinkling lights of the city are most bewitching. The dining room is glamorous, with touches evoking a stylish 1930s supper club (complete with pianist tinkling the ivories), and the beatifully prepared food fresh and seasonal. While there are choices for carnivores, including a wonderful boneless rack of lamb, this is really a seafood lovers' menu. Excellent appetizers may include sashimi-quality tuna and salmon tartares with roe, salmon smoked over fruitwood, or smoked duck foie gras terrine with quince and

For Steak Lovers

If you love steak enough to drag yourself out to Williamsburg, Brooklyn, then book a table and hop a cab to **Peter Luger Steakhouse,** 178 Broadway, at Driggs Avenue. (☎ **718/387-7400**). Expect loads of attitude and nothing in the way of decor or atmosphere (beer hall is the theme), but this century-old institution is porterhouse heaven. The first-rate cuts are dry-aged on the premises and cooked to order. Non-believers can order sole or lamb chops, but don't bother if you're not coming for the cow. Bring wads of cash, because this place is expensive and they don't take credit cards.

currant compote. (All smoked items are prepared in the restaurant's own smokehouse.) Entrees include braised Maine lobster with horseradish potatoes and portobellos; quick-seared yellowfin tuna with fennel, glazed cucumber, and 100-year-old balsamic vinegar; and crisp black sea bas in a red wine–butter sauce (as decadent and wonderful as it sounds) as well as the aforementioned rack of lamb and a grilled aged grilled prime sirloin. Desserts like a miniature Brooklyn Bridge sculpted from Valrhona marquise chocolate provide delightful finales.

Water's Edge. The East River at 44th Dr., Long Island City, Queens. ☎ **718/482-0033.** Reservations required. Jacket required. Main courses $22–$32; tasting menu $65; vegetarian tasting menu $45. AE, DC, JCB, MC, V. Mon–Fri noon–3pm and 6–11pm, Sat 6–11pm. Subway: E, F to 23rd St./Eli. Complimentary evening ferry from Manhattan (34th St. and the East River, at the heliport). CONTEMPORARY AMERICAN.

This sophisticated and somewhat formal dining room is warmed by a crackling fireplace, but all eyes are on the twinkling lights of midtown Manhattan. Both the food and service are as splendid as the stellar city view. Among the appetizing starters are a fricasse of wild mushrooms with asparagus and ricotta-sage dumplings, and sautéed foie gras with caramelized apples and macadamia nut brittle. Among the pleasing mains are a roast Chilean seabass in a rich bouillabaise broth served with poached mussels, fingerling potatoes, and calamata olives. The grilled breast of duck, loin of veal, steak, and roast free-range chicken are all excellent. Desserts are equally good; go with anything chocolate and you won't be disappointed (I especially like the bitter chocolate mousse). You really can't go wrong at this wonderful place—even the ferry ride across the East River is a delight. Ideal for a special occasion.

INEXPENSIVE

✪ **Patsy Grimaldi's Pizzeria.** 19 Old Fulton St. (btw. Front and Water sts.), Brooklyn Heights. ☎ **718/858-4300.** Reservations not taken. Pies $14 and up, depending on toppings. No credit cards. Fri 11:30am–11pm, Sat–Sun 2–11pm. Subway: 2, 3 to Clark St (use Henry St. exit); A, C to High St. PIZZA.

Here's New York's best pizza. You don't have to take it from me—just check Zagat's, which gives this Brooklyn classic a whopping 26 (out of 30) for food, a rating usually reserved for the likes of Lutèce. Thin coal-oven crust, crisp and smoky, is topped with perfectly seasoned red sauce, leafy basil, and only the freshest, whitest mozzarella. Crown this perfect pie with your choice of traditional toppings, including meaty pepperoni and house-roasted red peppers. And you don't have to suffer a greasy pizza joint to enjoy this sublime pizza: Grimaldi's is a surprisingly pleasant place, with red-checked tablecloths, photos of Sinatra covering the walls, and the Chairman of the Board himself crooning from the jukebox. Patsy is likely to greet you himself, warmly, with stogie in hand (despite the NO SMOKING signs). Otherwise, the service can be gruff, but that's how you'll know you've arrived—in Brooklyn, that is. The best time to come is in summer, when the restaurant sets up tables on the wide sidewalk outside, where you'll have the kind of spectacular views of the Brooklyn Bridge and twinkling lower Manhattan that usually only big money buys.

7

Exploring New York City

If this is your first trip to New York, face facts: It will be impossible to take in the entire city. Because New York is almost unfathomably big and constantly changing, you could live your whole life here and still make fascinating daily discoveries—we New Yorkers do. First-time visitors may find this daunting.

This chapter is designed to give you an overview of what's available in this multifaceted place, so you can narrow your choices to an itinerary that's digestible for the amount of time you'll be here—be it a day, a week, or something in between.

So don't try to tame New York—you can't. Decide on a few must-see attractions, and then let the city take you on its own ride. Inevitably, as you schlep around the city you'll be blown off course by unplanned diversions that are just as alluring as what you meant to see. After all, the true New York is in the details. As you dash from sight to sight, take time to admire a lovely detail on a prewar building, linger over a cup of coffee at a sidewalk cafe, or just idle away a few minutes on a bench watching New Yorkers parade through their daily lives.

GET LOST!

One of the best ways to experience New York is to pick a neighborhood and just stroll it. Bring a map for reference, but put it in your pocket—let yourself get lost. Walk the prime thoroughfares, poke your head into shops, park yourself on a bench or at an outdoor cafe, and just watch the world go by. For tips on where to go, how to get there, and what highlights to be on the lookout for, see "Manhattan's Neighborhoods in Brief" in chapter 4.

If getting lost isn't your style—or even if it is—you might consider taking an organized tour. That doesn't have to mean a big bus with an out-of-work-actor pointing out the Empire State Building (although general introductory tours are available, too). Many wonderful walking tours that really let you get to know a neighborhood or a particular aspect of New York are offered throughout the city. Walking tours are cheap, they're fun, and there's no better way to get to know a neighborhood than with an expert at the helm. For a complete rundown of operators and the kinds of tours they offer, see "Organized Sightseeing Tours" later in this chapter.

1 Sights & Attractions by Neighborhood

MANHATTAN

CHELSEA

Chelsea Piers Sports & Entertainment Complex (p. 248)

EAST VILLAGE & NoHo

Merchant's House Museum (p. 219)

THE FINANCIAL DISTRICT

American Museum of Financial History (p. 204)
Battery Park (p. 246)
Bowling Green Park (p. 206)
Brooklyn Bridge (p. 200)
City Hall & City Hall Park (p. 210)
Cunard Building (p. 206)
Ellis Island (p. 199)
Federal Hall National Memorial (p. 207)
Fraunces Tavern Museum (p. 206)
Group of Four Trees (p. 208)
Kalikow Building (p. 210)
Liberty Plaza (p. 209)
The Municipal Building (p. 212)
Museum of Jewish Heritage (p. 223)
National Museum of the American Indian (p. 226)
New York Stock Exchange (p. 201)
The Red Cube (p. 208)
South Street Seaport & Museum (p. 202)
Staten Island Ferry (p. 200)
Statue of Liberty (p. 198)
St. Paul's Chapel (p. 210)
Surrogate's Court (The Hall of Records) (p. 211)
Trinity Church (p. 208)
Tweed Courthouse (p. 211)
U.S. Customs House (p. 204)
Wall Street (p. 208)
Woolworth Building (p. 210)
World Trade Center (p. 203)

THE FLATIRON DISTRICT

Center for Jewish History (p. 218)
Flatiron Building (p. 233)
Theodore Roosevelt Birthplace (p. 227)
Union Square Park (p. 247)

GREENWICH VILLAGE

Forbes Magazine Galleries (p. 220)
Washington Square Park (p. 247)

LOWER EAST SIDE

Lower East Side Tenement Museum (p. 222)

MIDTOWN EAST

Bryant Park (p. 246)
Dahesh Museum (p. 220)
Chrysler Building (p. 227)
Empire State Building (p. 228)
Ford Foundation Building (p. 233)
Grand Central Terminal (p. 229)
Japan Society (p. 221)
Morgan Library (p. 222)
New York Public Library (p. 233)
New York Skyride (p. 228)
Roosevelt Island Tramway (p. 234)
Sony Wonder Technology Lab (p. 254)
St. Patrick's Cathedral (p. 234)
United Nations (p. 231)

MIDTOWN WEST

International Center of Photography—Midtown (p. 221)
Intrepid Sea-Air-Space Museum (p. 221)
Lever House (p. 232)
Madison Square Garden (p. 265)
Museum of Modern Art (p. 214)
Museum of Television and Radio (p. 226)
Rockefeller Center (p. 230)
Seagram Building (p. 232)
Sony Building (p. 232)
Times Square (p. 239)

SoHo

The Alternative Museum (p. 218)
Children's Museum of the Arts (p. 253)
Guggenheim Museum SoHo (p. 216)
Museum for African Art (p. 223)
New Museum of Contemporary Art (p. 226)

Downtown Attractions

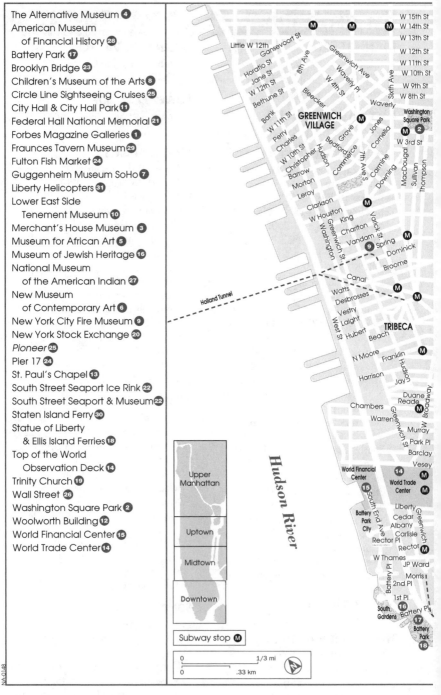

NA-0148

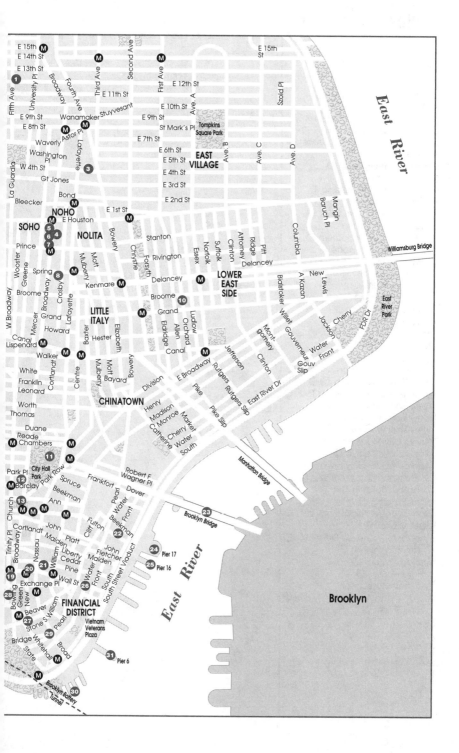

E 15th St
E 14th St
E 13th St
E 9th St
E 8th St
W 4th St
Fifth Ave
University Pl
Broadway
Fourth Ave
Third Ave
Second Ave
First Ave
E 12th St
E 11th St
E 10th St
E 9th St
St Mark's Pl
E 7th St
E 6th St
E 5th St
E 4th St
E 3rd St
E 2nd St
E 1st St
Ave. A
Ave. B
Ave. C
Ave. D
Szold Pl
E 15th St

Wanamaker
Astor Pl
Stuyvesant
Waverly
Washington Pl
La Guardia
Gt Jones
Bond
Bleecker
Lafayette

Tompkins Square Park
EAST VILLAGE

East River

NOHO
E Houston
SOHO
NOLITA
Prince
Spring
Wooster
Greene
Broome
W Broadway
Mercer
Grand
Howard
Crosby
Lafayette
Mulberry
Mott
Kenmare
Bowery
Chrystie
Forsyth
Stanton
Rivington
Delancey
Broome
Grand
Canal
Elizabeth
Hester
Baxter
Centre
Mott
Bayard
Bowery
LITTLE ITALY
CHINATOWN
Division
E Broadway
Henry
Madison
Monroe
Catherine
Cherry
Water
South
Norfolk
Suffolk
Clinton
Attorney
Ridge
Pitt
Columbia
Essex
Delancey
LOWER EAST SIDE
Ludlow
Orchard
Allen
Eldridge
Canal
Rutgers
Rutgers Slip
Jefferson
Clinton
Pike
Pike Slip
Market
East River Dr
Montgomery
Willet
Gouverneur
A Kazan
New
Lewis
Jackson
Cherry
Water
Front
Gouv Slip
Water
East River Dr
Mangin
Baruch Pl
Clinton

Williamsburg Bridge

East River Park

Manhattan Bridge

Brooklyn Bridge

East River

Brooklyn

Canal
Lispenard
Walker
White
Franklin
Leonard
Worth
Thomas
Duane
Reade
Chambers
Cortlandt

Park Pl
City Hall Park
Barclay
Church
Ann
Cliff
Beekman
Spruce
Frankfort
Dover
Pearl
Water
Front
Robert F Wagner Pl
Fulton
John
Platt
Maiden
William
Cedar
Liberty
Pine
Wall St
Water
Front
South
South Street Viaduct
John
Fletcher
Maiden
Pier 17
Pier 16
John
Nassau
Cortlandt
Trinity Pl
Broadway
Exchange Pl
New
Bowling Green
Beaver
Stone
S William
Pearl
Whitehall
Broad
Bridge
State
FINANCIAL DISTRICT
Vietnam Veterans Plaza
Pier 6
Brooklyn Battery Tunnel
Thomas

193

Midtown Attractions

Berlin Wall sections ⑩
Bryant Park ㉒
Carnegie Hall ②
Central Synagogue ⑫
Center for Jewish History ㊴
Chelsea Piers Sports
  & Entertainment Complex ㊵
Chrysler Building ⑱
Circle Line Sightseeing Cruises ㉖
Dahesh Museum ⑦
Empire State Building ㉟
Flatiron Building ㊱
Ford Foundation Building ⑰
Grand Central Terminal ⑲
Gray Line New York Tours ㉙
International Center of
  Photography–Midtown ㉓
Intrepid Sea-Air-Space
  Museum ㉕
Jacob Javits
  Convention Center ㉛
Japan Society ⑮
Liberty Helicopters ㉜
Lever House ⑬
Madison Square Garden ㉝
Morgan Library ㉞
Museum of Modern Art ③
Museum of Television & Radio ⑥
New York Apple Tours ⑭ ㉚
New York Double-Decker Tours ㉟
New York Public Library ㉑
New York Skyride ㉟
New York Waterway ㉘
Radio City Music Hall ④
Rockefeller Center ⑤
Roosevelt Island Tramway ①
St. Patrick's Cathedral ⑧
Seagram Building ⑭
Sony Building ⑪
Sony Wonder Technology Lab ⑪
Spirit Cruises ㊶
Theodore Roosevelt Birthplace ㊲
Union Square Park ㊳
United Nations ⑯
Villard Houses ⑨
Whitney Museum of
  American Art at Philip Morris ⑳
World Yacht ㉗

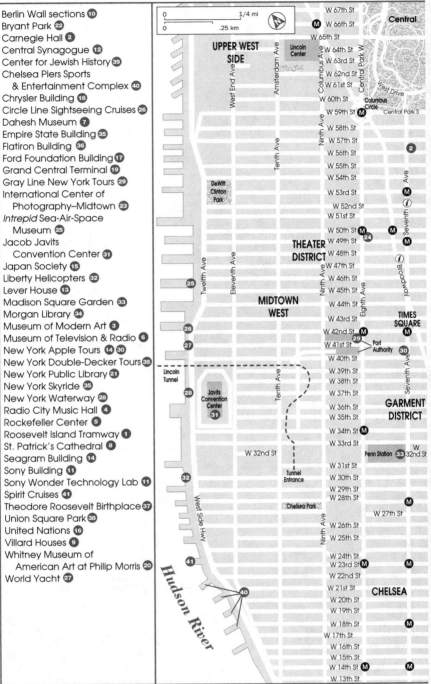

194

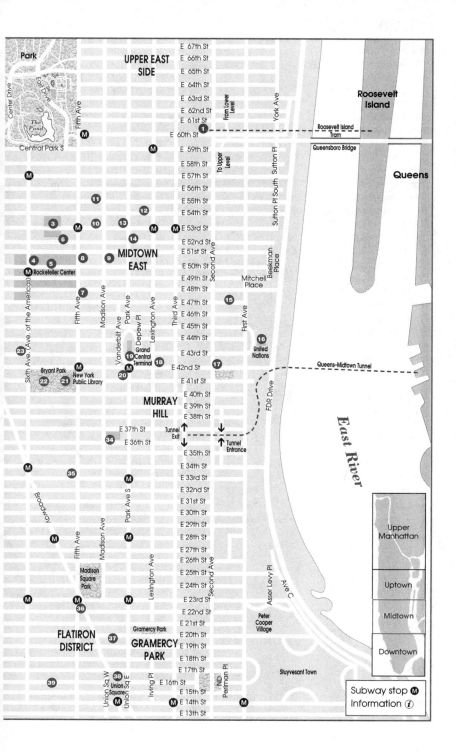

Park

UPPER EAST SIDE

E 67th St
E 66th St
E 65th St
E 64th St
E 63rd St
E 62nd St
E 61st St
E 60th St
E 59th St
E 58th St
E 57th St
E 56th St
E 55th St
E 54th St
E 53rd St
E 52nd St
E 51st St
E 50th St
E 49th St
E 48th St
E 47th St
E 46th St
E 45th St
E 44th St
E 43rd St
E 42nd St
E 41st St
E 40th St
E 39th St
E 38th St
E 37th St
E 36th St
E 35th St
E 34th St
E 33rd St
E 32nd St
E 31st St
E 30th St
E 29th St
E 28th St
E 27th St
E 26th St
E 25th St
E 24th St
E 23rd St
E 22nd St
E 21st St
E 20th St
E 19th St
E 18th St
E 17th St
E 16th St
E 15th St
E 14th St
E 13th St

Center Drive
East Drive
Fifth Ave
The Pond
Central Park S

From Lower Level
To Upper Level

York Ave

Roosevelt Island

Roosevelt Island Tram

Queensboro Bridge

Queens

Sutton Pl South
Sutton Pl

Beekman Place

Mitchell Place

MIDTOWN EAST

Rockefeller Center

Sixth Ave (Ave. of the Americas)
Fifth Ave
Madison Ave
Vanderbilt Ave
Park Ave
Depew Pl
Lexington Ave
Third Ave
Second Ave
First Ave

Grand Central Terminal

Bryant Park
New York Public Library

United Nations

FDR Drive

Queens-Midtown Tunnel

East River

MURRAY HILL

Tunnel Exit
Tunnel Entrance

Broadway
Fifth Ave
Madison Ave
Park Ave S
Lexington Ave
Second Ave

Madison Square Park

Asser Levy Pl
Ave C

Peter Cooper Village

Gramercy Park

FLATIRON DISTRICT

GRAMERCY PARK

Stuyvesant Town

Union Sq W
Union Sq E
Union Square
Irving Pl
ND Perlman Pl

Upper Manhattan

Uptown

Midtown

Downtown

Subway stop Ⓜ
Information ⓘ

195

Uptown Attractions

Abagail Adams Smith
  Museum & Gardens (24)
American Museum
  of Natural History (11)
The Ansonia (14)
Asia Society (17)
Beacon Theater (13)
Central Park Wildlife Center (22)
Children's Museum
  of Manhattan (10)
Cooper-Hewitt
  National Design Museum (5)
Dakota Apartments (15)
El Museo del Barrio (1)
The Frick Collection (18)
Goethe House of New York (8)
Gracie Mansion (7)
International Center
  of Photography (3)
The Jewish Museum (4)
Lincoln Center
  for the Performing Arts (20)
Metropolitan Museum of Art (9)
Museum of American Folk Art (21)
Museum of the
  City of New York (2)
New-York Historical Society (12)
Roosevelt Island Tramway (25)
Solomon R. Guggenheim
  Museum (6)
Spanish & Portuguese
  Synagogue (19)
Temple Emanu-El (23)
Whitney Museum
  of American Art (16)

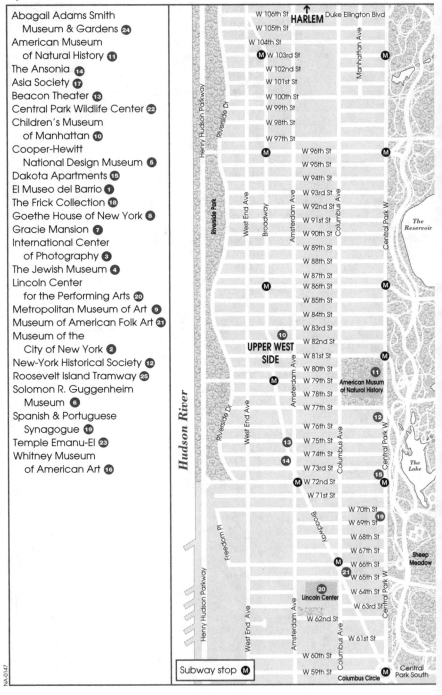

NA-0147

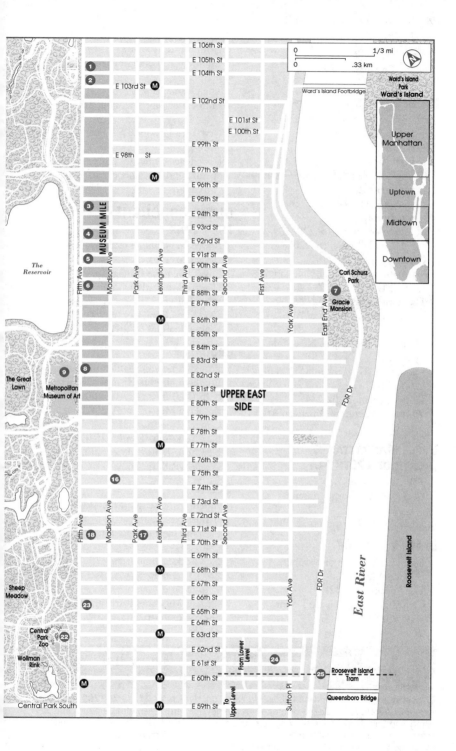

E 106th St
E 105th St
E 104th St
E 103rd St (M)
E 102nd St
E 101st St
E 100th St
E 99th St
E 98th St
E 97th St (M)
E 96th St
E 95th St
E 94th St
E 93rd St
E 92nd St
E 91st St
E 90th St
E 89th St
E 88th St
E 87th St
E 86th St (M)
E 85th St
E 84th St
E 83rd St
E 82nd St
E 81st St
E 80th St
E 79th St
E 78th St
E 77th St (M)
E 76th St
E 75th St
E 74th St
E 73rd St
E 72nd St
E 71st St
E 70th St
E 69th St (M)
E 68th St
E 67th St
E 66th St
E 65th St
E 64th St
E 63rd St (M)
E 62nd St
E 61st St
E 60th St (M)
E 59th St (M)

Ward's Island Footbridge
Ward's Island Park
Ward's Island

Upper Manhattan
Uptown
Midtown
Downtown

MUSEUM MILE

The Reservoir

Fifth Ave
Madison Ave
Park Ave
Lexington Ave
Third Ave
Second Ave
First Ave
York Ave
East End Ave

Carl Schurz Park
Gracie Mansion

FDR Dr

UPPER EAST SIDE

East River

Roosevelt Island

The Great Lawn
Metropolitan Museum of Art

Sheep Meadow

Central Park Zoo
Wollman Rink

Central Park South

From Lower Level
To Upper Level

Sutton Pl

Roosevelt Island Tram
Queensboro Bridge

0   1/3 mi
0   .33 km

197

TRiBeCa

New York City Fire Museum
(p. 253)

UPPER EAST SIDE

Abigail Adams Smith Museum
& Gardens (p. 217)
Asia Society (p. 218)
Central Park (p. 240)
Central Park Wildlife Center/Tisch
Children's Zoo (p. 244)
Cooper-Hewitt National Design
Museum (p. 219)
El Museo del Barrio (p. 220)
The Frick Collection (p. 220)
Gracie Mansion (p. 219)
International Center of Photography
(p. 221)
The Jewish Museum (p. 222)
Metropolitan Museum of Art
(p. 213)
Museum of the City of New York
(p. 225)
Solomon R. Guggenheim Museum
(p. 215)
Temple Emanu-El (p. 234)
Whitney Museum of American Art
(p. 216)

UPPER MANHATTAN
(NORTH OF 125TH ST.)

The Cloisters (p. 218)
Dyckman Farmhouse Museum
(p. 219)
Morris-Jumel Mansion (p. 219)

UPPER WEST SIDE

American Museum of Natural
History (p. 212)
The Ansonia (p. 232)
Cathedral of St. John the Divine
(p. 232)

Central Park (p. 240)
Children's Museum of Manhattan
(p. 253)
The Dakota (p. 232)
Museum of American Folk Art
(p. 223)
New-York Historical Society
(p. 227)
Rockefeller Center (p. 230)
Spanish and Portuguese Synagogue
(p. 234)

OUTER BOROUGHS
THE BRONX

Bronx Zoo Wildlife Conservation
Park (p. 258)
Edgar Allen Poe Cottage (p. 258)
New York Botanical Garden (p. 259)
Wave Hill (p. 259)
Woodlawn Cemetery (p. 260)
Yankee Stadium (p. 265)

BROOKLYN

Brooklyn Botanic Garden (p. 260)
Brooklyn Heights Historic District
(p. 263)
Brooklyn Museum of Art (p. 260)
Coney Island (p. 262)
New York Aquarium (p. 262)
New York Transit Museum (p. 262)
Prospect Park (p. 262)

QUEENS

American Museum of the Moving
Image (p. 264)
Flushing Meadows–Corona Park
(p. 254)
New York Hall of Science (p. 254)
P.S. 1 Contemporary Art Center
(p. 264)
Queens Museum of Art (p. 264)
Shea Stadium (p. 265)

2 In New York Harbor: Lady Liberty, Ellis Island & the Staten Island Ferry

✪ **Statue of Liberty.** On Liberty Island in New York Harbor. ☎ **212/363-3200** (general info) or 212/269-5755 (ticket/ferry info). www.nps.gov/stli. Ferry ticket/admission to Statue of Liberty and Ellis Island $7 adults, $6 seniors, $3 children under 17. Daily 9am–5pm; extended hours in summer. Subway: 4, 5 to Bowling Green; 1, 9 to South Ferry (the platform at this station is shorter than the train, so ride in the first 5 cars). From the station, walk south through Battery Park to Castle Clinton, the fort housing the ferry ticket booth.

For the millions who first came by ship to America in the last century—either as privileged tourists or needy, hopeful immigrants—Lady Liberty, standing in the Upper Bay, was their first glimpse of America. Few travel by boat anymore, so it probably won't be your first impression of New York, but you should make it one of the lasting ones. No monument so embodies the nation's, and the world's, notion of political freedom and economic potential. Even if you don't make it out to Liberty Island, you can get a spine-tingling glimpse from Battery Park, from the New Jersey side of the bay, or during a free ride on the Staten Island Ferry (see below). It's always reassuring to see her torch lighting the way.

The statue was designed by sculptor Frédéric-Auguste Bartholdi with the engineering help of Alexandre-Gustave Eiffel (responsible for the famed Paris tower), and unveiled on October 28, 1886. Despite the fact that Joseph Pulitzer had to make a mighty effort to attract donations on this side of the Atlantic for her pedestal, more than a million people watched as the French tricolor veil was pulled away. After nearly 100 years of wind, rain, and exposure to the harsh sea air, Lady Liberty received a resoundingly successful $70-million face-lift (including the replacement of the torch's flame) in time for its centennial celebration on July 4, 1986. Feted in fireworks, Miss Liberty became more of a city icon than ever before.

Touring Tips: Ferries leave daily every half hour to 45 minutes from 9:30am to 3:15pm, with more frequent ferries in the morning and extended hours in summer. Try to go early on a weekday to avoid the crowds that swarm in the afternoon, on weekends, and on holidays. Be sure to arrive by noon if your heart's set on experiencing everything; go later and you may not have time to make it to the crown. A stop at Ellis Island (see below) is included in the fare, but if you catch the last ferry, you can only visit the statue or Ellis Island, not both.

The ferry deposits you, in about 20 minutes, on Liberty Island, a short distance from the statue. Once on the island, you'll start to get an idea of the statue's immensity: She weighs 225 tons and measures 152 feet from foot to flame. Her nose alone is 4½ feet long, and her index finger is 8 feet long. You may have to wait as long as 3 hours to walk up into the crown (the torch is not open to visitors). If it's summer, or if you're just not in shape for it, you may want to skip it: It's a grueling 354 steps (the equivalent of 22 stories) to the crown, or you can cheat and take the elevator the first 10 stories up (an act I wholeheartedly endorse). But even if you take this shortcut, the interior is stifling once the temperature starts to climb. However, you don't have to go all the way up to the crown; there are a number of **observation decks** at different levels, including one at the top of the pedestal reachable by elevator. Even if you don't go inside, a stroll around the base is an extraordinary experience, and the views of the Manhattan skyline are stellar.

Note: If you're driving into the city to visit Lady Liberty, know that a much less-crowded ferry departs from Liberty State Park in Jersey City, NJ. Ferry fares are the same as from Battery Park. To get there, take the New Jersey Turnpike to Exit 14B. Parking is available at that site. For more information, call ☎ **201/435-9499.**

✪ **Ellis Island.** Located in New York Harbor. ☎ **212/363-3200** (general info) or 212/269-5755 (ticket/ferry info). www.ellisisland.org. For subway, hours, and ferry ticket details, see the Statue of Liberty, directly above (ferry trip includes stops at both sights).

Lost amid the hoopla of the Statue of Liberty reopening in 1986 was the fact that a much more fitting tribute to our nation was under renovation just next door. One of New York's most moving sights, the restored Ellis Island opened in 1990, slightly north of Liberty Island. Roughly 40% of Americans (myself included) can trace their heritage back to an ancestor who came through here. For the 62 years when it was America's main entry point for immigrants (it closed in 1954), Ellis Island processed some 12 million people. The greeting was often brusque—especially in the early years of the century, when as many as 12,000 came through in a single day. The statistics and their meaning can be overwhelming, but the **Immigration Museum** skillfully relates the story of Ellis Island and immigration in America by putting the emphasis on personal experience.

Today you enter the Main Building's baggage room, just as the immigrants did, and then climb the stairs to the **Registry Room,** with its dramatic vaulted tiled ceiling, where millions waited anxiously for medical and legal processing. A step-by-step account of the immigrants' voyage is detailed in the **"Through America's Gate"** exhibit, with haunting photos and touching oral histories. What might be the most poignant exhibit is **"Treasures from Home,"** 1,000 objects and photos donated by descendants of immigrants, including family heirlooms, religious articles, and rare clothing and jewelry. Outside, the **American Immigrant Wall of Honor** commemorates the names of hundreds of thousands of immigrants and their families, including George Washington's great-grandfather, John F. Kennedy's great-grandparents, Rudolph Valentino, Harry Houdini, and Marlene Dietrich (all catalogued on a computer registry as well). You can even research your own family's history at the **American Family Immigration History Center.** It's difficult to leave the museum unmoved.

Touring Tips: Ferries run daily to Ellis Island and Liberty Island from Battery Park and Liberty State Park at frequent intervals; see the Statue of Liberty (directly above) for details.

Staten Island Ferry. Departs from the Staten Island Ferry Terminal at the southern tip of Manhattan. ☎ **718/815-BOAT.** www.SI-Web.com/transportation/dot.htm. Free (fee charged for car transport). 24 hours; every 15–30 min weekdays, less frequently on off-peak and weekend hours. Subway: 1, 9, N, R to South Ferry.

Here's New York's best freebie—especially if you just want to glimpse the Statue of Liberty and not climb her steps. You get an enthralling hour-long excursion (round-trip) into the world's biggest harbor. This is not strictly a sightseeing ride, but commuter transportation to Staten Island (remember Melanie Griffith, in big hair and sneakers, heading to work in *Working Girl?*). As a result, during business hours, you'll share the boat with working stiffs reading papers and drinking coffee inside, blissfully unaware of the sights outside.

You, however, should go on deck and enjoy the busy harbor traffic. The old orange-and-green boats usually have open decks along the sides or at the bow and stern (try to catch one of these boats if you can; the newer white boats don't have decks). Go on a nice day if you can, as the outer decks are best. Grab a seat on the right side of the boat for the best view. On the way out of Manhattan, you'll pass the Statue of Liberty (the boat comes closest to Lady Liberty on the way to Staten Island), Ellis Island, and from the left side of the boat, Governor's Island; you'll see the Verranzano Narrows bridge spanning the distance from Brooklyn to Staten Island in the distance.

When the boat arrives at St. George, Staten Island, everyone must disembark. Follow the boat loading sign on your right as you get off; you'll circle around to the next loading dock, where there's usually another boat waiting to depart for Manhattan. The skyline views are simply awesome on the return trip. Well worth the time spent.

3 Historic Lower Manhattan's Top Attractions

Brooklyn Bridge. Subway: 4, 5, 6 to Brooklyn Bridge–City Hall; A, C to High St.

Its Gothic-inspired stone pylons and intricate steel-cable webs have moved poets like Walt Whitman and Hart Crane to sing the praises of this great span, the first to cross the East River and connect Manhattan to Brooklyn. Begun in 1867 and ultimately completed in 1883, the beautiful Brooklyn Bridge is now the city's best-known symbol of the age of growth that seized the city during the late 19th century. Walk across the bridge, and imagine the awe that New Yorkers of that age felt at seeing two boroughs joined by this monumental span. It's still astounding.

Designed by John Roebling, this massive engineering feat was plagued by death and disaster at its birth. Roebling was fatally injured in 1869 when a ferry rammed a waterfront piling on which he stood. His son, Washington, who was subsequently put in charge, contracted the bends in 1872 while working underwater to construct the bridge's towers, and oversaw the rest of the construction with a telescope from his bed at the edge of the East River in Brooklyn Heights (his wife relayed his instructions to the workers). Washington refused to attend the 1883 opening ceremonies, having had a bitter disagreement with the company that financed the construction. Though it was declared the "eighth wonder of the world" upon its completion, the bridge's troubles were not over: Twelve pedestrians were killed in a stampede when panic about its eminent collapse spread like wildfire on the day it opened to the public. Things are usually calmer now.

Walking the Bridge: Walking the Brooklyn Bridge is one of my all-time favorite New York activities. A wide wood-plank pedestrian walkway is elevated above the traffic, making it a relatively peaceful, and popular, walk. It provides a great vantage point from which to contemplate the New York skyline and the East River.

There's a sidewalk entrance on Park Row, just across from City Hall Park (take the 4, 5, or 6 train to Brooklyn Bridge–City Hall). But why do this walk *away* from Manhattan, toward the far less impressive Brooklyn skyline? For gorgeous Manhattan skyline views, take an A or C train to High Street, one stop into Brooklyn. From there, you'll be on the bridge in no time: Come above ground, then walk through the little park to Cadman Plaza East and head downslope (left) to the stairwell that will take you up to the footpath. (Following Prospect Place under the bridge, turning right onto Cadman Plaza East, will also take you directly to the stairwell.) It's a 20- to 40-minute stroll over the bridge to Manhattan, depending on your pace, the amount of foot traffic, and the number of stops you make to contemplate the spectacular views (there are benches along the way). The footpath will deposit you right at City Hall Park.

If you'd like to extend this walk a bit, I highly recommend pairing it with a quick tour of Brooklyn Heights and its wonderful Promenade; see "Highlights of the Outer Boroughs" later in this chapter for exact directions.

New York Stock Exchange. 20 Broad St. (between Wall St. and Exchange Place). ☎ **212/656-5165.** www.nyse.com. Free admission. Mon–Fri 9am–4:30pm (ticket booth opens at 8:45am). Subway: 2, 3, 4, 5 to Wall St.; J, M, Z to Broad St.

Wall Street—it's an iconic name, and ground zero for bulls and bears everywhere. This narrow 18th-century lane (you'll be surprised at how little it is) is appropriately monumental, lined with neo-classic towers that reach as far skyward as the dreams and greed of investors who built it into the world's most famous financial market. At the heart of the action is the New York Stock Exchange, the world's largest securities trader, where you can watch the billions change hands and get a fleeting idea of how the money merchants work.

While the NYSE is on Wall Street, the ticket kiosk is around the corner at 20 Broad St., where you'll be issued a ticket with a time on it; you must enter during the window of opportunity specified on your ticket. The staff starts handing out tickets at 8:45am, but get in line early if you want to be inside to see all hell break loose at the 9:30am opening bell. The 3,000 tickets issued per day are usually gone by noon; plan on having to return unless you're one of the first in line. Despite the number of visitors, things move pretty quickly.

Don't expect to come out with a full understanding of the market; if you didn't have one going in, you won't leave any more enlightened. Still, it's fun watching the action on the trading floor from the glass-lined, mezzanine-level **observation gallery** (look to the right, and you'll see the Bloomberg people sending their live reports back to the newsroom). You can stay as long as you like, but it doesn't really take more than 20 minutes or so to peruse the other jingoistic exhibits ("NYSE—our hero!"), which include a rather oblique explanation of the floor activities, interactive exhibits, and a short film presentation of the Exchange's history and present-day operations.

South Street Seaport & Museum. At Water and South sts.; museum is at 12–14 Fulton St. ☎ 212/748-8600. www.southstseaport.org. Museum admission $6 adults, $5 seniors, $3 children. Museum, Apr–Sept Fri–Wed 10am–6pm, Thurs 10am–8pm; Oct–Mar Wed–Sun 10am–5pm. Subway: 2, 3, 4, 5 to Fulton St. (walk east, or downslope, on Fulton St. to Water St.).

This landmark district on the East River encompasses 11 square blocks of historic buildings, a maritime museum, several piers, shops and restaurants (including the authentically old world North Star Pub; see chapter 6), and even a Best Western hotel (see chapter 5).

You can explore most of the Seaport on your own. It's an odd place. The 18th- and 19th-century buildings lining the cobbled streets and alleyways are beautifully restored but nevertheless have a theme-park air about them, no doubt due to the J. Crews, Brookstones, and Body Shops housed within. The height of the Seaport's cheesiness is **Pier 17,** a historic barge converted into a mall, complete with food court and cheap jewelry kiosks.

Despite its rampant commercialism, the Seaport is worth a look. There's a good amount of history to be discovered here, most of it around the **South Street Seaport Museum,** a fitting tribute to the sea commerce that once thrived here.

Including the galleries—which house paintings and prints, ship models, scrimshaw, and nautical designs, as well as frequently-changing exhibitions—there are a number of historic ships berthed at the pier to explore, including the 1911 four-masted *Peking* and the 1893 Gloucester fishing schooner *Lettie G. Howard.* A few of the boats are living museums and restoration works in progress; others are available for private charters. But you can actually hit the high seas on the 1885 cargo schooner *Pioneer* (☎ 212/748-8786), which offers two-hour public sails daily from early May through September. Tickets are $20 for adults, $15 for seniors and students, and $12 for children. Advance reservations are recommended, and can be made up to 14 days in advance; always call ahead to confirm sailing times.

Even **Pier 17** has its merits. Head up to the third-level deck overlooking the East River, where the long wooden chairs will have you thinking about what it was like to cross the Atlantic on the *Normandie.* From this level you can see south to the Statue of Liberty, north to the Gothic majesty of the Brooklyn Bridge, and Brooklyn Heights on the opposite shore.

Just to the north of Pier 17 is the famous **Fulton Fish Market,** on Fulton Street at the East River, the nation's largest wholesale fish market. If you're willing to come back down here at 4am, you can watch the catch of the day from all over the globe being tossed, traded, and sold the old-fashioned way. The city's great chefs and wholesale buyers from all over the country gather here daily to snap up untold pounds of fish.

At the gateway to the Seaport, at Fulton and Water streets, is the *Titanic* **Memorial Lighthouse,** a monument to those who lost their lives when the ocean liner sank on April 15, 1912. It was erected overlooking the East River in 1913, and moved to this spot in 1968, just after the historic district was so designated.

A variety of events take place in summer, ranging from street performers to concerts to fireworks. In winter, a petite but charming **Ice Rink** is erected on the waterfront, overlooking the historic ships and the wild river beyond. The rink is generally open from November to March; two hours of skating is $8 for adults, $6 for kids, and skate rentals are $5. Call ☎ **212/SEA-PORT** or 212/809-6080 for this year's schedule.

✪ **World Trade Center.** Bounded by Church, Vesey, Liberty, and West sts. ☎ **212/ 323-2340** for observation deck, 212/435-4170 for general information. www.wtc-top.com. Admission to observation deck $12 adults, $9 seniors, $6 children under 12. Sept–May daily 9:30am–9:30pm; June–Aug daily 9:30am–11:30pm. Subway: C, E to World Trade Center; 1, 9, N, R to Cortlandt St.

Nowhere near as romantic as the Empire State Building (see "Skyscrapers & Other Architectural Marvels" later in this chapter), the World Trade Center is nevertheless just as heroic, having withstood a bombing in its basement garage in 1993 without so much as a flinch. Built in 1970, the center is actually an immense complex of seven buildings on 16 acres housing offices, restaurants, a hotel, an underground shopping mall, and an outdoor plaza with fountains, sculpture, and summer concerts and performances. But the parts you'll be interested in are the Twin Towers, which usurped the Empire State to become New York's tallest structures.

The box-like buildings are so nondescript that the local Channel 11 once used them to represent that number in their commercials. Each is 110 stories and 1,350 feet high. The **Top of the World** observation deck is high atop 2 World Trade Center, to the south. On the 107th floor, it's like a mini theme park, offering (besides the views, of course) a 6-minute simulated helicopter tour over Manhattan, high-tech kiosks, a food court, and a nighttime light show. But the reason to come is for those incredible views. The enclosed top floor offers incredible panoramas on all sides, with windows reaching right down to the floor. Go ahead, walk right up to one, and look down—*scaaary.*

Come on a clear day. If you're lucky, you'll be able to go out on the **rooftop promenade,** the world's highest open-air observation deck. (It's only open under perfect conditions; I've only been able to go out once in a lifetime of visits.) You thought inside was incredible? Wait 'til you see this. While you're up here, look straight down and wonder what Frenchman Philippe Petit could've been thinking when in August 1974 he shot a rope across to tower no. 1, grabbed his balancing pole, and walked gingerly across, stopping to lie down for a moment in the center.

You can have a similar view in more convivial conditions by going to the top of One World Trade Center, where you can dine at elegant **Windows on the World** (see chapter 6) or linger over a drink and munchies—or put on some dancing shoes and Lindy to some hep-cat swing—at the **Greatest Bar on Earth** (see chapter 9).

Walking Tour: Wall Street & the Financial District

by Reid Bramblett

Start: Battery Park/U.S. Customs House.
Subway: Take the 5 to Bowling Green, the 1 or 9 to South Ferry, or the N or R to Whitehall Street.
Finish: The Municipal Building.
Time: Approximately 3 hours.
Best Time: Any weekday, when the wheels of finance are spinning and lower Manhattan is a maelstrom of frantic activity.
Worst Time: Weekends, when most buildings and all the financial markets are closed.

The narrow winding streets of the Financial District occupy the earliest-settled area of Manhattan, where the Dutch established the colony of Nieuw Amsterdam in the early 17th century. Before their arrival, downtown was part of a vast forest, a lush hunting

---
The Money Museum

Real money buffs (and who among us isn't?) may want to make a brief stop at the **American Museum of Financial History,** 28 Broadway, just north of Bowling Green Park (☎ **212/908-4110** or 212/908-4519; www.mafh.org). Exhibits housed in this little museum include numismatic and vintage ticker-tape displays; murals and photos depicting historic Wall Street scenes; and interactive financial news terminals, in partnership with CNNfn, so little bulls and bears can learn how to keep up with the market. The Crouch & Fitzgerald briefcase that Jackie gave JFK on their wedding day is also on display. Open Monday through Friday from 11:30am and 3:30pm, with limited hours on summer weekends.

At press time, the museum was scheduled to begin offering a Wall Street "World of Finance" walking tour, including a visit to the New York Stock Exchange, on Fridays; call for details.

---

ground for the Native Americans, inhabited by mountain lions, bobcats, beavers, white-tailed deer, and wild turkeys. A hunting path—which later evolved into Broadway—extended from the Battery to the present City Hall Park.

Today this section of the city, much like Nieuw Amsterdam, centers on commerce. Wall Street is America's most cogent symbol of money and power; bulls and bears have replaced the wild beasts of the forest, and conservatively attired lawyers, stockbrokers, bankers, and businesspeople have supplanted the Native Americans and Dutchmen who once traded otter skins and beaver pelts on these very streets.

A highlight of this tour is the Financial District's architecture, in which the neighborhood's modern manifestations and grand historical structures are dramatically juxtaposed: Colonial, 18th-century Georgian/Federal, and 19th-century neoclassical buildings stand in the shadow of colossal skyscrapers.

The subways all exit in or near **Battery Park,** an expanse of green at Manhattan's tip resting entirely upon landfill—an old strategy of the Dutch to expand their settlement farther into the bay. The original tip of Manhattan ran somewhere right along Battery Place, which borders the north side of the park. State Street flanks the park's east side, and stretched along it, filling the space below Bowling Green, squats the beaux arts bulk of the old:

1. **U.S. Customs House,** since 1994, home to the Smithsonian's National Museum of the American Indian (☎ **212/668-6624** or 212/514-3700). The giant statues lining the front of this granite 1907 structure personify *Asia* (pondering philosophically), *America* (bright-eyed and bushy-tailed), *Europe* (decadent, whose time has passed), and *Africa* (sleeping), and were carved by Daniel Chester French of Lincoln Memorial fame. The most interesting, if unintentional, sculptural statement—keeping in mind the building's new purpose—is the giant seated woman to the left of the entrance representing America. The young, upstart America is surrounded by references to Native America: Mayan pictographs adorning her throne, Quetzalcoatl under her foot, a shock of corn in her lap, and the generic plains Indian scouting out from over her shoulder. Look behind her throne for the stylized crow figure—an important animal in many native cultures, usually playing a trickster character in myths, which is probably why he's hiding back here.

The airy oval rotunda inside was frescoed by Reginald Marsh to glorify the shipping industry (and, by extension, the customs office once here). The free museum, open daily 10am to 5pm (to 8pm on Thursday), hosts a roster of well-curated

Walking Tour: Wall Street & the Financial District

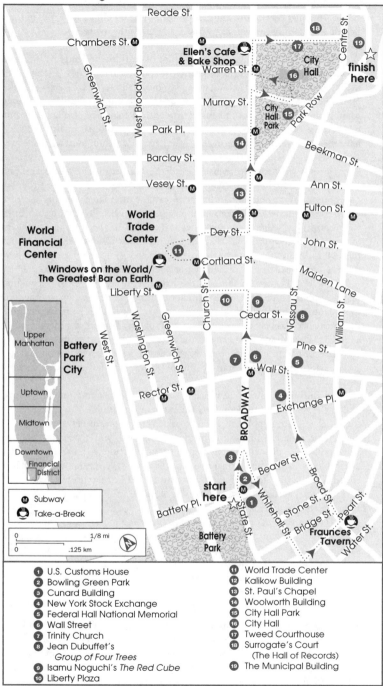

1. U.S. Customs House
2. Bowling Green Park
3. Cunard Building
4. New York Stock Exchange
5. Federal Hall National Memorial
6. Wall Street
7. Trinity Church
8. Jean Dubuffet's *Group of Four Trees*
9. Isamu Noguchi's *The Red Cube*
10. Liberty Plaza
11. World Trade Center
12. Kalikow Building
13. St. Paul's Chapel
14. Woolworth Building
15. City Hall Park
16. City Hall
17. Tweed Courthouse
18. Surrogate's Court (The Hall of Records)
19. The Municipal Building

M Subway

☕ Take-a-Break

0 — 1/8 mi
0 — .125 km

exhibits highlighting Native cultures, history, and contemporary issues in sophisticated and thought-provoking ways. For more information, see "More Manhattan Museums," later in this chapter.

As you exit the building, directly in front of you sits the pretty little oasis of:

2. **Bowling Green Park.** This is probably the spot, or at least near enough, where in 1626 Dutchman Peter Minuit gave glass beads and other trinkets worth about 60 Guilders ($24) to a group of Indians, and then claimed he had thereby bought Manhattan. Now the local Indians didn't consider that they owned this island—not because they didn't believe in property (that's a colonial myth), as they did have their own territories nearby. But Manhattan (which in local language means "hilly island") was considered communal hunting ground, shared by several different groups. So it isn't clear what the Indians thought the trinkets meant. Either (a) they just thought the exchange was a formal way, one to which they were accustomed, of closing an agreement to extend the shared hunting use of the island to this funny-looking group of pale people with yellow beards, or (b) they were knowingly selling land that they didn't own in the first place, thus performing the first shrewd real-estate deal of the Financial District. They probably then told Minuit they also had this bridge to sell, just up the river a ways, but he was too busy fortifying his little town of Nieuw Amsterdam to listen.

When King George III repealed the hated Stamp Act in 1770, New Yorkers magnanimously raised a statue of him here, although today it's just another lunch spot for stockbrokers. The statue lasted 5 years, until the day the Declaration of Independence was read to the public in front of City Hall (now Federal Hall) and a crowd rushed down Broadway to topple the statue, chop it up, melt it down, and transform it into 42,000 bullets, which they later used to shoot the British.

The park also marks the start of Broadway. Walk up the left side of Broadway; at no. 25 is the:

3. **Cunard Building,** now a post office but in 1921 the ticketing room for Cunard, one of the world's most glamorous shipping and cruise lines and proprietors of the *QEII*. Cunard established the first passenger steamship between Europe and the Americas, and in this still-impressive Great Hall, you once could book passage on any one of their famous fantastically unfortunate ships, from the *Lusitania* (blown up by the Germans) to the *Titanic* (well, you know how that one ended). The poorly lit and deteriorating churchlike ceiling inside is covered with Ezra Winter paintings of the ships of Columbus, Sir Francis Drake, and Leif Eriksson, among others.

As you exit the building, cross to the traffic island to pat the enormous bronze **bull,** symbol of a strong stock market, ready to charge up Broadway. This instant icon began as a practical joke by Italian sculptor Arturo DiModica, who originally stuck it in front of the New York Stock Exchange building in the middle of the night. The unamused brokers had it promptly removed, and it eventually got placed here.

🏛 **TAKE A BREAK** **Fraunces Tavern,** 54 Pearl St. (☎ 212/269-0144), is a great spot for a break, but it's also a legitimate stop on the tour. To reach Fraunces Tavern, head south again, around the left side of the U.S. Customs House on Whitehall Street. Take a left onto Pearl Street; just past Broad Street stretches a historic block lined with (partially rebuilt) 18th- and 19th-century buildings.

The two upper stories house the Fraunces Tavern Museum, where you can view the room in which Washington's historic farewell took place (today set up to represent a typical 18th-century tavern room) and see other American history exhibits. In late 1999–2000 new exhibits will include "Washington in Glory, American in Tears: The death of George Washington" and "Taverns, Coffeehouses and politics in Colonial New York." A small admission is charged. Hours are Monday through Friday from 10am to 4:45pm and Saturdays from noon to 4pm.

The main floor contains a posh, oak-paneled dining room with a working fireplace. Tables are set with pewter plates. The menu features steaks, seafood, pasta dishes, and colonial fare such as Yankee pot roast. A good buy here is the three-course fixed-price lunch for $17.76. Or you can opt for pub fare in the more moderately priced Tap Room, which has plush burgundy leather furnishings and walls hung with hunting trophies. Reservations are suggested for both. The restaurant is open weekdays for breakfast 7 to 10am, lunch 11:30am to 4pm, and dinner from 5 to 9:30pm; the Tap Room is open daily from 11:30am to 9:30pm.

From Fraunces Tavern, head straight up Broad Street. At no. 20, on the left, is the visitor's entrance to the:

4. **New York Stock Exchange (☎ 212/656-5165)**, which came into being in 1792, when merchants met daily under a nearby buttonwood tree to try and pass off to each other the U.S. bonds that had been sold to fund the Revolutionary War. By 1903, they were trading stocks of publicly held companies in this Corinthian-columned beaux arts "temple" designed by George Post. More than 3,000 companies are listed on the exchange, trading 253 billion shares valued around $11 trillion.

Inside you can learn all about stock trading, view exhibits and a short film on the history and workings of the stock market, and watch the frenzied action on the trading floor—color-coded capitalists oversee the changing of hands of more than 200 million stocks daily. The observation platform has been glassed in since the 1960s when Abbie Hoffman and Jerry Rubin created chaos by tossing dollar bills onto the exchange floor. Admission for this self-guided tour is free; for more information, see "Historic Lower Manhattan's Top Attractions" directly above.

After the New York Stock Exchange, continue north (left) up Broad St. At the end of the block you'll see the Parthenon-inspired:

5. **Federal Hall National Memorial.** 26 Wall St. at Nassau Street (☎ **212/ 825-6888**). Fronted by 32-foot fluted marble Doric columns, this imposing 1842 neoclassical temple is most famous for the history of the old British City Hall building, later called Federal Hall, that once stood here. Peter Zenger, publisher of the outspoken *Weekly Journal,* stood trial in 1735 for "seditious libel" against Royal Gov. William Cosby. Defended brilliantly by Alexander Hamilton, Zenger's eventual acquittal (based on the grounds that anything you printed that was true, even if it wasn't very nice, couldn't be construed as libel) set the precedent for freedom of the press, later guaranteed in the Bill of Rights, which was drafted and signed inside this building.

New York's first major rebellion against British authority occurred here when the Stamp Act Congress met in 1765 to protest King George III's policy of "taxation without representation." J.Q.A. Ward's 1883 statue of George Washington on the steps commemorates the spot of the first presidential inauguration, in 1789. Congress met here after the revolution, when New York was briefly the nation's capital.

Exhibits within (open daily 9am to 5pm mid-June to September, weekdays only from October to mid-June) elucidate these events along with other aspects of American history. Admission is free; call ahead if you'd like to hook up with one of the short guided tours, which usually take place on the half-hour between 12:30 and 3:30pm.

Facing Federal Hall, turn left up the road that has become the symbol of high finance the world over:

6. **Wall Street.** It is narrow, just a few short blocks long, and started out as a service road that ran along the fortified wall the Dutch erected in 1653 to defend against Indian attack. (Gov. Petyer Stuyvesant's settlers had at first played tribes off against each other in order to trick them into more and more land cessation, but the native groups quickly realized that their real enemies were the Dutch.)

Wall Street hits Broadway across the street from:

7. **Trinity Church** (☎ **212/602-0800**). Serving God and Mammon, this Wall Street house of worship—with neo-Gothic flying buttresses, beautiful stained-glass windows, and vaulted ceilings—was designed by Richard Upjohn and con-secrated in 1846. At that time its 280-foot spire dominated the skyline. Its main doors, embellished with biblical scenes, were inspired in part by Ghiberti's famed doors on Florence's Baptistery.

The first church on this site went up in 1697 and burned down in 1776. The church runs a brief tour daily at 2pm. There's a small museum at the end of the left aisle displaying documents (including the 1697 church charter from King William III), photographs, replicas of the Hamilton-Burr duel pistols, and other items. Capt. James Lawrence, whose famous last words were "Don't give up the ship," and Alexander Hamilton (against the south fence, next to steamboat inventor Robert Fulton) are buried in the churchyard, where the oldest grave dates from 1681.

Surrounding the church is a **churchyard** with monuments that read like an American history book: a tribute to Martyrs of the American Revolution, Alexander Hamilton, Robert Fulton, and many more. Lined with benches, this makes a wonderful picnic spot on warm days.

The church is open to the public weekdays 7am to 6pm, Saturday 8am to 4pm, and Sunday 7am to 4pm. Services are held weekdays at 8am and 12:05 and 5:15pm, Saturday at 9am, and Sunday at 9 and 11:15am. Trinity holds its Noonday Concert series of chamber music and orchestral concerts Thursdays at 1pm. Call ☎ **212/602-0747** or visit www.trinitywallstreet.org for details.

Take a left as you leave the church and walk two short blocks up Broadway. As you pass Cedar Street, look (don't walk) to your right, across Broadway, and down Cedar and you'll see, at the end of the street:

8. **Jean Dubuffet's** *Group of Four Trees,* installed in 1972 in the artist's patented style: amorphous mushroomlike white shapes traced with undulating black lines. Dubuffet considered these drawings in three dimensions "which extend and expand into space."

Closer at hand, in front of the tall black Marine Midlank Bank building on Broadway between Cedar and Libery streets, is:

9. **Isamu Noguchi's** 1967 *The Red Cube,* another famed outdoor sculpture of downtown Manhattan. Noguchi fancied that this rhomboid "cube"—balancing on its corner and shot through with a cylinder of empty space—represented chance, like the "rolling of the dice." It is appropriately located in the gilt-edged gambling den that is the financial district.

As you're looking at the Cube across Broadway, behind you is the tiny square called:

10. **Liberty Plaza,** a block off Liberty Street with some benches and shade for lunching CEOs. Turn left and walk through the park, heading east toward Trinity Place. Mingling among the flesh-and-blood office workers seated here is one in bronze, called *Double Check* (1982), by realist American sculptor J. Seward Johnson Jr.

At Trinity Place, take a right. A short block up on the left will open the grand plaza of the:

11. **World Trade Center (WTC),** bounded by Vesey, West, Liberty, and Church streets and best known for its famous 110-story twin towers. Still intact despite a terrorist bombing in early 1993, the WTC is an immense complex. Its 12 million square feet of rentable office space houses more than 350 firms and organizations. About 50,000 people work in its precincts, and some 70,000 others (tourists and businesspeople) visit them each day. The complex occupies 16 acres and includes, in addition to the towers, the sleek 22-story Marriott hotel, a plaza the size of four football fields, an underground shopping mall, and several restaurants, most notably the spectacular Windows on the World.

The plaza, like much of downtown, is rich in outdoor sculpture, including the polished black granite miniature mountains (as you enter) crafted by Japanese artist Masayuki Nagare (1972). Fritz Keonig's 25-foot-high bronze morphing sphere (1971) forms the centerpiece of the plaza's wide fountain. Hang a right here between two of the squat black glass buildings to get a glance of Alexander Calder's *Three Wings.* Take particular notice of the curving, metal, winglike flanges, riveted together and painted red.

Do an about-face to return to the central plaza. The left-hand of the twin towers is 2 World Trade Center. As you enter on the mezzanine level, to your left, you'll see a 1974 tapestry by Spanish artist Joan Miró and a TKTS booth if you want to pick up half-price tickets to one of tonight's Broadway or off-Broadway shows (for details, see chapter 9). The real thing to do, of course, is head around the elevator banks to the right to buy tickets and whiz up to the 107th-floor **Top of the World** Observation Deck, where you're treated to a 1,377-foot-high perspective of the city and New York Harbor. From there, be sure to ascend to the 110th-floor rooftop promenade, the world's highest open-air viewing platform, for even more magnificent views. Observation Deck facilities are open daily from 9:30am to 9:30pm (until 11:30pm June through August); for further information, see "Historic Lower Manhattan's Top Attractions" above.

☕ **TAKE A BREAK**   To enjoy those 107th-floor views to the fullest, consider dining "a quarter mile high in the sky" at the **Greatest Bar on Earth,** 1 World Trade Center (☎ **212/524-7000**), a casually conservative spot (no jeans or sneakers) with airy spaces, a trio of bars serving everything from wine to sushi, and a sweeping view of the East River. It serves lunch Monday to Friday noon to 3pm, with continuous bar and food service also until midnight Monday and Tuesday, to 1am Wednesday through Saturday, and to 10pm on Sunday; see chapter 9 for further details. There are also a handful of seats in the main restaurant, **Windows on the World,** open to nonmembers (reserve ahead; jacket required), featuring a sumptuous spread and a view of Manhattan; see chapter 6 for details.

For a quicker meal, there's a **Sbarro's** snack bar on the **107th-floor observation deck of WTC2** and a number of other casual choices on the main (street-level) concourse. In summer, you might want to bring your lunches to the tree-shaded tables on the plaza.

Walk out the front side of WTC plaza again the way you came in, cross Church Street, and head straight down Dey Street, which is in front of you, back to Broadway. Take a left, and on your left is the:

12. **Kalikow Building,** at 195 Broadway. This 1915–22 neoclassic tower, formerly AT&T headquarters, has more exterior columns than any other building in the world. The 25-story structure rests on a Doric colonnade, with Ionic colonnades above. The lobby evokes a Greek temple with a forest of massive fluted columns. The building's tower crown is modeled on the Mausoleum of Halicarnassus, the great Greek monument of antiquity. The bronze panels over the entranceway by Paul Manship (sculptor of Rockefeller Center's *Prometheus*) symbolize wind, air, fire, and earth.

Continue south on Broadway. The next block contains the small:

13. **St. Paul's Chapel,** between Vesey and Fulton streets, New York's only surviving prerevolutionary church, and now a transition shelter for homeless men. Under the east portico is a 1789 monument to Gen. Richard Montgomery, one of the first revolutionary patriots to die in battle. During the two years that New York was the nation's capital, George Washington worshiped at this Georgian chapel belonging to Trinity Church and dating from 1764; his "pew" is on the right side of the church. Built by Thomas McBean, with a templelike portico and fluted Ionic columns supporting a massive pediment, the chapel resembles London's St. Martin's-in-the-Fields. Explore the small **graveyard** where 18th- and early 19th-century notables rest in peace and modern businesspeople sit for lunch. Trinity's Noonday Concert series is held here on Mondays at noon; call the concert hotline at ☎ 212/602-0747 for details, or point your Web browser to **www. trinitywallstreet.org**.

Continue up Broadway, crossing Vesey and Barclay streets, and at 233 Broadway is the:

14. **Woolworth Building.** This soaring "Cathedral of Commerce" cost Frank W. Woolworth $13.5 million worth of nickels and dimes in 1913. Designed by Cass Gilbert, it was the world's tallest edifice until 1930, when it was surpassed by the Chrysler Building. At its opening, Pres. Woodrow Wilson pressed a button from the White House that illuminated the building's 80,000 electric lightbulbs. The neo-Gothic architecture is rife with spires, gargoyles, flying buttresses, vaulted ceilings, 16th-century–style stone-as-lace traceries, castlelike turrets, and a churchlike interior.

Step into the lofty marble entrance arcade to view the gleaming mosaic, Byzantine-style ceiling and gold-leafed, neo-Gothic cornices. The corbels (carved figures under the crossbeams) in the lobby include whimsical portraits of the building's engineer Gunwald Aus measuring a girder (above the staircase to the left of the main door), Gilbert holding a miniature model of the building, and Woolworth counting coins (both above the left-hand corridor of elevators). Stand near the security guard's central podium and crane your neck for a glimpse at Paul Jennewein's murals of *Commerce* and *Labor,* half hidden up on the mezzanine.

To get an overview of the Woolworth's architecture, cross Broadway. On this side of the street, you'll find scurrying city officials and greenery that together make up:

15. **City Hall Park,** a 250-year-old green surrounded by landmark buildings. A Frederick MacMonnies statue near the southwest corner of the park depicts Nathan Hale at age 21, having just uttered his famous words before execution: "I only regret that I have but one life to lose for my country." Northeast of City Hall in the park is a statue of Horace Greeley (seated with newspaper in hand) by

J.Q.A. Ward. This small park has been a burial ground for paupers and the site of public executions, parades, and protests.

It is the setting for:

16. City Hall, the seat of municipal government, housing the offices of the mayor and his staff, the city council, and other city agencies. City Hall combines Georgian and French Renaissance styles, designed by Joseph F. Mangin and John McComb Jr. in 1803–11. Later additions include the clock and 6,000-pound bell in the cupola tower. The cupola itself is crowned with a stately, white-painted copper statue of *Justice* (anonymously produced in a workshop).

Barring days when there are demonstrations or special hearings that draw large crowds, you can enter the building between 10am and 4pm, Monday to Friday. Several areas are open to the public, beginning with the Corinthian-columned lobby, which centers on a coffered and skylit rotunda. The elegant Governor's Room upstairs, where Lafayette was received in 1824, houses a museum containing Washington's writing desk, his inaugural flag, and artwork by well-known American artists. This room is closed from noon to 1pm. City Hall contains quite an impressive collection of American art; in your wanderings, you might note works by George Caitlin, Thomas Sully, Samuel B. Morse, and Rembrandt Peale, among others. If you'd like to take a tour, call ☎ **212/788-6865;** they're offered daily between 9am and 3pm, but you should call ahead to reserve.

☕ **TAKE A BREAK**   Grab a pastry or a diner meal at **Ellen's Cafe and Bake Shop,** 270 Broadway, at Chambers Street (☎ **212/962-1257**). Owner Ellen Hart won the Miss Subways beauty pageant in 1959, and her restaurant walls are lined with her own and other Miss Subways posters, plus photographs of all the politicians who have eaten here: Al D'Amato, Rudy Giuliani, Bella Abzug, Andy Stein, Mario Cuomo, and Geraldine Ferraro, to name just a few. Muffins, biscuits, and pastries are all oven-fresh, and full breakfasts of eggs, bacon, pancakes, and Belgian waffles are available. Open weekdays 6am to 7pm, Saturday 8am to 5pm.

Along the north edge of City Hall Park, on Chambers Street, sits the now-shabby:

17. Tweed Courthouse (New York County Courthouse, 52 Chambers St.). This 1872 Italianate courthouse was built during the tenure of William Marcy "Boss" Tweed, who, in his post on the board of supervisors, stole millions in construction funds. Originally budgeted as a $250,000 job in 1861, the courthouse project escalated to the staggering sum of $14 million. Bills were padded to an unprecedented extent—Andrew Garvey, who was to become known as the "Prince of Plasterers," was paid $45,966.89 for a single day's work! The ensuing scandal (Tweed and his cronies, it came out, had pocketed at least $10 million) wrecked Tweed's career; he died penniless in jail.

Across Chambers Street and to the right, at the corner of Elk Street, lies the turn-of-the-century:

18. Surrogate's Court (The Hall of Records), 31 Chambers St. Housed in this sumptuous beaux arts structure are all the legal records relating to Manhattan real estate deeds and court cases, some dating from the mid-1600s. Heroic statues of distinguished New Yorkers (Peter Stuyvesant, De Witt Clinton, and others) front the mansard roof, and the doorways, surmounted by arched pediments, are flanked by Philip Martiny's sculptural groups portraying *New York in Revolutionary Times* (to your left) and *New York in Its Infancy* (to your right). Above the entrance is a three-story Corinthian colonnade.

Step inside to see the vestibule's beautiful barrel-vaulted mosaic ceiling, embellished with astrological symbols, Egyptian and Greek motifs, and figures representing retribution, justice, sorrow, and labor. Continue back to the two-story skylit neoclassical atrium, clad in honey-colored marble with a colonnaded second-floor loggia and an ornate staircase adapted from the foyer of the Grand Opera House in Paris.

Exiting the Surrogate's Court from the front door, you'll see to your left, at the end of the block, that Chambers Street disappears under:

19. **The Municipal Building,** a grand civic edifice built between 1909 and 1914 to augment City Hall's government office space. It was designed by the famed architectural firm of McKim, Mead, and White (as in Stanford White), who used Greek and Roman design elements such as a massive Corinthian colonnade, ornately embellished vaults and cornices, and allegorical statuary. A triumphal arch, its barrel-vaulted ceiling adorned with relief panels, forms a magnificent arcade over Chambers Street; it has been called the "gate of the city." Sculptor Adolph Weinman created many of the building's bas reliefs, medallions, and allegorical groupings of human figures (they symbolize civic pride, progress, guidance, prudence, and executive power). The heroic hammered-copper statue of *Civic Fame*, Manhattan's largest statue, that tops the structure 582 feet above the street was also designed by Weinman, holding a crown whose five turrets represent New York's five boroughs.

See many lovey-dovey couples walking in and out? The city's marriage license bureau is on the second floor, and a wedding takes place about every 20 minutes.

4 The Top Museums

✪ **American Museum of Natural History.** Central Park West (btw. 77th and 81st sts.) ☎ **212/769-5100.** www.amnh.org. Suggested admission $8 adults ($13 with 1 IMAX movie, $16 with 2), $6 seniors and students ($9 with 1 IMAX movie, $12 with 2), $4.50 children 2–12 ($7 with 1 IMAX movie, $9 with 2). Sun–Thurs 10am–5:45pm, Fri–Sat 10am–8:45pm. Subway: B, C to 81st St.; 1, 9 to 79th St.

This four-block-square museum houses the world's greatest natural science collection in a group of buildings made of towers and turrets, pink granite and red brick—a mishmash of architectural styles, but overflowing with neo-Gothic charm. The diversity of the holdings is astounding: some 36 million specimens ranging from microscopic organisms to the world's largest cut gem, the Brazilian Princess Topaz (21,005 carats). It would take all day to see the entire museum, and then you still wouldn't get to everything. If you don't have a lot of time, you can see the best of the best on free **highlights tours** offered daily every hour at 15 minutes after the hour from 10:15am to 3:15pm. Free daily **spotlights tours,** thematic tours that change monthly, are also offered; stop by an information desk for the day's schedule. **Audio Expeditions,** high-tech audio tours that allow you to access narration in the order you choose, are also available to help you make sense of it all.

If you only see one exhibit, see the ✪ **dinosaurs,** which take up the entire fourth floor. Recent restorations and redesign put new life in these old bones, making this the best of what the museum has to offer by far. Start in the **Orientation Room,** where a short video gives an overview of the 500 million years of evolutionary history that led to you. Continue to the **Vertebrate Origins Room,** where huge models of ancient fish and turtles hang overhead, with plenty of interactive exhibits and kid-level displays on hand to keep young minds fascinated. Next come the great **dinosaur halls,** with mammoth, spectacularly reconstructed skeletons and more interactive displays. **Mammals**

Museum-Going Tip

Many of the city's top museums—including the Natural History Museum, the Met, and MoMA—have late hours on Friday and/or Saturday nights. Take advantage of them. Most visitors run out of steam by dinnertime, so even on jam-packed weekends you'll largely have the place to yourself by 5 or 6pm—which, in most cases, leaves you hours left to explore, unfettered by crowds or screaming kids.

and Their Extinct Relatives bring what you've learned in the previous halls home, showing how yesterday's prehistoric monsters have evolved into today's modern animals. Simply marvelous—you could spend hours in these halls alone.

Many other areas of the museum pale in comparison. The **animal habitat dioramas** and **halls of peoples** seem a bit dated but still have something to teach, especially the Native American halls. Other than peeking in to see the giant whale (viewable from the cafe below) skip the **ocean life** room altogether; let's hope this is next on the restoration agenda, because the current exhibit makes Disneyland's submarine ride look high-tech. The new **Hall of Biodiversity** is an impressive multimedia exhibit, but the doom-and-gloom story it tells about the future of rainforests and other natural habitats may be too much for the little ones. Kids five years and older should head to the **Discovery Room,** with lots of hands-on exhibits and experiments. (Be prepared, Mom and Dad—there seems to be a gift shop overflowing with fuzzy stuffed animals at every turn.)

The museum excels at **special exhibitions,** so I recommend checking to see what will be on while you're in town in case any advance planning is required. Highlights of the past year have included the magical Butterfly Conservatory, a walk-in enclosure housing nearly 500 free-flying tropical butterflies.

In addition, an **IMAX Theater** shows neat films like *Cosmic Voyage* and *Africa's Elephant Kingdom* on a four-story screen that puts you right in the heart of the action; you can buy tickets to screenings as part of your admission package (see above) IMAX tickets can also be ordered separately and in advance by calling ☎ **212/769-5200** or online at the museum's website. The **Hayden Planetarium** is closed in 1997 for demolition and reconstruction that should be completed in early 2000, but Beavis and Buttheads (and I say that fondly) can still see **laser light shows**—including U2 and Laser Zeppelin in 3D—Friday and Saturday at 9 and 10pm. Tickets are $9; call ☎ **212/769-5200** to reserve.

✪ **Metropolitan Museum of Art.** Fifth Ave. at 82nd St. ☎ **212/535-7710.** www.metmuseum.org. Suggested admission (includes same-day entrance to the Cloisters) $10 adults, $5 seniors and students, free for children under 12 when accompanied by an adult. Tues–Thurs and Sun 9:30am–5:15pm, Fri–Sat 9:30am–8:45pm. No strollers allowed Sun (back carriers available at 81st St. entrance coat-check area). Subway: 4, 5, 6 to 86th St.

Home of blockbuster after blockbuster exhibition, the Metropolitan Museum of Art attracts some 5 million people a year, more than any other spot in New York City. And it's no wonder—this place is magnificent. At 1.6 million square feet, this is the largest museum in the Western Hemisphere. Nearly all the world's cultures are on display through the ages—from Egyptian mummies to ancient Greek statuary to Islamic carvings to Renaissance paintings to Native American masks to 20th-century decorative arts—and masterpieces are the rule. You could go once a week for a lifetime and still find something new on each visit.

So unless you plan on spending your entire vacation in the museum (some people do), you cannot see the entire collection. My recommendation is to give it a good

Money- & Time-Saving Tip

CityPass just may be New York's best sightseeing deal. Pay one price ($27.50) for admission to six top attractions—the Top of the World observation deck at the World Trade Center, the Metropolitan Museum of Art, the Museum of Modern Art, the Empire State Building, the American Museum of Natural History, and the *Intrepid* Sea-Air-Space Museum—which would cost you fully twice as much if you paid for each one separately. More importantly, CityPass is not a coupon book; it contains actual admission tickets, so you can bypass lengthy ticket lines. CityPass is good for nine days from the first time you use it. It's sold at all participating attractions, and discounted rates are available for kids and seniors. If you want to avoid that first line, order your CityPass online at **www.citypass.net** or www.ticketweb.com. For phone orders, call Ticketweb at ☎ **212/269-4TIX.** Call CityPass at ☎ **707/256-0490** for further details.

day—or better yet, two half days so you don't burn out. One good way to get an overview is to take advantage of the little-known **Highlights Tour.** Even some New Yorkers who've spent many hours in the museum could profit from this once-over. Call ☎ **212/570-3711** (Monday to Friday from 9am to 5pm) or visit the museum's Web site for a schedule of this and subject-specific tours (French Impressionists, Arts of Japan, and so on).

The least overwhelming way to see the Met on your own is to pick up a map at the round desk in the entry hall and choose to concentrate on what you like, whether it's 17th-century paintings, American furniture, or the art of the South Pacific. Highlights include the American Wing's **Garden Court,** with its 19th-century sculpture, the lower-level **Costume Hall,** and the **Frank Lloyd Wright room.** The **Roman and Greek galleries** are overwhelming, but in a marvelous way, as is the collection of later **Chinese art.** The setting of the **Temple of Dendur** is dramatic, in a specially built glass-walled gallery with Central Park views. But it all depends on what your interests are. Don't forget the marvelous **special exhibitions,** which can range from "Jade in Ancient Costa Rica" to "Cubism and Fashion." If you'd like to plan your visit ahead of time, the museum's Web site is a useful tool; there's also a list of current exhibitions in the Friday and Sunday editions of the *New York Times.*

Special exhibits and programs abound. To purchase tickets for concerts and lectures, call ☎ **212/570-3949** (Mon–Sat 9:30am–5pm). The museum contains several dining facilities, including a **full-service restaurant** serving continental cuisine (☎ **212/570-3964** for reservations). The roof garden is worth visiting if you're here from spring to autumn, offering peaceful views over Central Park and the city.

On **Friday and Saturday evenings,** the Met remains open late not only for art viewing but also for cocktails in the Great Hall Balcony Bar (4–8:30pm) and classical music from a string quintet or trio. A slate of after-hours programs (gallery talks, walking tours, family programs) changes by the week; call for this week's schedule. The restaurant stays open until 10pm (last reservation at 8:30pm), and dinner is usually accompanied by piano music.

If you're interested in the medieval age, head to the **Cloisters,** a branch of the Met in Uptown Manhattan (see "More Manhattan Museums" below).

✪ **Museum of Modern Art.** 11 W. 53rd St. (btw. Fifth and Sixth aves.). ☎ **212/708-9400.** www.moma.org. Admission $9.50 adults ($13.50 with audio tour), $6.50 seniors and students ($10.50 with audio tour), free for children under 16 accompanied by an adult; pay as you wish Fri 4:30–8:15pm. Sat–Tues and Thurs 10:30am–5:45pm, Fri 10:30am–8:15pm. Subway: E, F to Fifth Ave.; B, D, F, Q to 47–50th sts./Rockefeller Center.

The Museum of Modern Art (or MoMA, as it's usually called) boasts the world's greatest collection of painting and sculpture ranging from the late 19th century to the present, including everything from van Gogh's *Starry Night,* Picasso's early *Les Demoiselles d'Avignon,* Monet's *Water Lilies,* and Klimt's *The Kiss* to later masterworks by Frida Kahlo, Edward Hopper, Andy Warhol, Robert Rauschenberg, and many others. Top that off with an extensive collection of modern drawings, photography, architectural models and furniture (including the Mies van der Rohe collection), iconic design objects ranging from tableware to sports cars, and film and video (including the world's largest collection of D.W. Griffith films), and you have quite a museum. If you're into modernism, this is the place to be.

While not quite Met-sized, MoMA is probably still more than you can see in a day. In true modern style, the museum is efficient and well organized, so it's easy to focus on your primary interests; just grab a museum map after you pay your admission. For an overview, take the **self-guided tour** that stops at the collection's highlights, chosen by the different departments' curators. The **sculpture garden**—an island of trees and fountains in which to enjoy the works of Calder, Moore, and Rodin—is particularly of note. In addition, there's usually at least one beautifully mounted **special exhibition** in house that's worth a special trip, whether it be the works of Finnish master architect Alvar Aalto, Julia Margaret Cameron's remarkable 19th-century photographs of women, or a celebration of sight gags in contemporary art.

MoMA boasts a good number of special programs. Hour-long family-oriented **gallery talks,** with such titles as "Music to My Eyes: Matisse and More," take place Saturdays at 10am. There's live jazz three evenings a week in **Sette MoMA** (☎ 212/ 708-9710), the museum's notable Italian restaurant overlooking the sculpture garden, or the Garden Cafe. A full slate of symposiums, gallery talks by contemporary artists, interactive family programs, and brown-bag lunches are always on offer; call ☎ 212/ 708-9781 or visit the museum's Web site to see what's on while you're in town. Additionally, there's always a multifaceted film and video program on the schedule; call the main number to see what's on. Films are included in the price of admission, but arrive early to make sure you get a seat.

Setting course for the 21st century, the Modern has embarked on a major expansion overseen by Japanese architect Yoshio Taniguchi that will attract worldwide attention and comparison to other recent museum projects, like Richard Meier's stunning Getty Center in Los Angeles and Frank Gehry's Guggenheim Museum in Bilbao, Spain. Don't look for this ambitious project to be completed anytime soon; but since it's expanding into adjacent space, it shouldn't appreciably affect your enjoyment of the museum as it currently exists.

Solomon R. Guggenheim Museum. 1071 Fifth Ave. (at 88th St.). ☎ **212/423-3500.** www.guggenheim.org. Admission $12 adults, $7 seniors, children under 12 free; Fri 6–8pm pay what you wish. Two-museum pass, which includes one admission to the SoHo branch valid for 1 week, $16 adults, $10 seniors. Sun–Wed 10am–6pm, Fri–Sat 10am–8pm. Subway: 4, 5, 6 to 86th St.

It has been called a bun, a snail, a concrete tornado, and even a giant wedding cake; bring your kids, and they'll probably see it as New York's coolest opportunity for skateboarding or in-line skating. Whatever descriptive you choose to apply, Frank Lloyd

---

Impressions

If you're bored in New York, it's your own fault.

—Myrna Loy

Wright's only New York building, completed in 1959, is best summed up as a brilliant work of architecture—so consistently brilliant that it competes with the art for your attention. If you're looking for the city's best modern art, head to MoMA or the Whitney first; come to the Guggenheim to see the house.

It's easy to see the bulk of what's on display in two to four hours. Inside, a spiraling rotunda circles over a slowly inclined ramp that leads you past changing exhibits, which can range from modern masterworks from the "Centre Pompidou" to the "Art of the Motorcycle." Usually the progression is counterintuitive: from the first floor up, rather than from the sixth floor down. If you're not sure, ask a guard before you begin. Permanent exhibits of 19th- and 20th-century art, including strong holdings of Kandinsky, Klee, Picasso, and French impressionists, occupy a stark annex called the **Tower Galleries,** an addition accessible at every level that some critics claimed made the original look like a toilet bowl backed by a water tank (judge for yourself—I think there may be something to that view).

The Guggenheim runs some interesting special programs, including free docent tours (there's a one-hour highlights tour daily at noon), a limited schedule of lectures, free family films (*The Red Balloon* and *Babar: The Movie* were among the choices at press time), avant-garde screenings for grown-ups, and the World Beat Jazz Series, which resounds through the rotunda on Friday and Saturday evenings from 5 to 8pm.

There's also a trendier downtown branch, the **Guggenheim Museum Soho,** 575 Broadway, at Prince St. (☎ **212/423-3500**), that generally houses temporary installations of high-tech multimedia works. However, this location has been suffering from financial troubles of late, and at press time had closed for renovations that included the shrinking of its square footage (some space was being turned over as separate retail space, a high-rent generator in superhot SoHo). It should reopen by the time you arrive, and post-modern enthusiasts might want to check it out.

✪ **Whitney Museum of American Art.** 945 Madison Ave. (at 75th St.). ☎ **212/ 570-3600** or 212/570-3676. www.echonyc.com/~whitney. Admission $9 adults, $7 seniors and students, free for children under 12; pay as you wish Thurs 6–8pm. Wed and Fri–Sun 11am–6pm, Thurs 11am–8pm. Subway: 6 to 77th St.

What is arguably the finest collection of 20th-century American art in the world belongs to the Whitney thanks to the efforts of Gertrude Vanderbilt Whitney. A sculptor herself, she organized exhibitions by American artists shunned by traditional academies, assembled a sizable personal collection, and founded the museum in 1930 in Greenwich Village.

Today's museum is an imposing presence on Madison Avenue—an inverted three-tiered pyramid of concrete and gray granite with seven seemingly random windows designed by Marcel Breuer, a leader of the Bauhaus movement. The rotating permanent collection consists of an intelligent selection of major works by Edward Hopper, George Bellows, Georgia O'Keeffe, Roy Lichtenstein, Jasper Johns, and other significant artists. A pleasing new fifth-floor exhibit space, the museum's first devoted exclusively to works from its permanent collection from 1900 to 1950, opened in 1998.

There are usually several simultaneous shows, usually all well curated and more edgy than what you'd see at the MoMA or the Guggenheim. Topics range from topical surveys, such as "American Art in the Age of Technology" and "The Warhol Look: Glamour Style Fashion" to in-depth retrospectives of famous or lesser-known movements (such as Fluxus, the movement that spawned Yoko Ono, among others) and artists (Mark Rothko, Keith Haring, Duane Hanson, Bob Thompson). From April 1999 to February 2000, a substantial mulitmedia exhibition called "The American Century: Art and Culture 1900–2000" showcases the Whitney's innovative cultural-technological partnership with Intel as it explores the changing nature of American identity. The next Biennial is scheduled for spring 2000. A major event on the national museum calendar, the Whitney Biennials serve as the premier launching pad for new American artists working on the vanguard in every media. The first to fall under Anderson's stewardship, the millennial edition promises to be an exciting and much-talked-about event.

The Whitney is also notable for having the best museum restaurant in town: **Sarabeth's at the Whitney** (☎ 212/560-3670), open for lunch Tuesday through Sunday and worth a visit in its own right (see chapter 6).

Free **gallery tours** are offered daily; call ☎ 212/570-3676 for the current schedule, or check at the Information desk when you arrive.

A Midtown branch, the **Whitney Museum of American Art at Philip Morris,** 120 Park Ave., at 42nd Street opposite Grand Central Terminal (☎ 212/875-2550; free admission; open Monday to Wednesday and Friday from 11am to 6pm, Thursday from 11am to 7:30pm), features an airy sculpture court and a small gallery that hosts changing exhibits, usually the works of living contemporary artists. Free hour-long gallery tours are offered Wednesday and Friday at 1pm.

5 More Manhattan Museums

In 1978, New York's finest cultural institutions located on Fifth Avenue from 82nd to 104th streets formed a consortium called **Museum Mile,** the name New York City officially gave to the stretch several years later. The "mile" begins at the **Metropolitan Museum of Art** (see "The Top Museums" above) and moves north to **El Museo del Barrio.** However, even the smallest museums along this stretch require some time, so don't plan on just popping into a few as you stroll along, or you'll be sorely disappointed by what you're able to see. Your best bet is to head directly to the museum that's tops on your list first, and then proceed to your second choice along the mile if you have time. If you're heading to the Metropolitan, forget trying to squeeze in anything else—as it is, you'll only see a portion of the collection there in a full day.

For details on **Federal Hall National Memorial** and **Fraunces Tavern Museum,** see the walking tour earlier in this chapter. For the **Brooklyn Museum of Art,** the **New York Transit Museum,** the **American Museum of the Moving Image,** the **Queens Museum of Art,** and the **P.S. 1 Contemporary Art Center,** see "Highlights of the Outer Boroughs" later in this chapter.

If you're traveling with the kids, also consider the museums listed under "Especially for Kids" later in this chapter, which include the **Children's Museum of Manhattan,** the **Sony Wonder Technology Lab,** the **New York Hall of Science,** and the **New York City Fire Museum.**

Abigail Adams Smith Museum & Gardens. 421 E. 61st St. (btw. First and York aves.). ☎ 212/838-6878. Admission $3 adults, $2 seniors, children under 12 free. Tues–Sun 11am–4pm; June and July, to 9pm Tues. Closed Aug. Subway: 4, 5, 6 to 59th St.; N, R to Lexington Ave.

It's a shock, a very pleasant one, to find such a little-known jewel on this otherwise thoroughly modern block. This rare survivor from the early American republic was built as a carriage house for Abigail Adams Smith, daughter of President John Adams, and her husband, William Stephens Smith, in 1799. It's been painstakingly restored by the Colonial Dames of America to its early 19th-century condition, when the house served as the Mount Vernon Hotel—a country hotel for bucolic overnights away from the city, if you can believe it. You can explore nine period rooms, outfitted in authentic Federal style, as well as the grounds, planted as a late 18th-century garden would be.

The Alternative Museum. 594 Broadway (btw. Houston and Prince sts.), 4th floor. ☎ **212/966-4444.** Suggested admission $3. Tues–Sat 11am–6pm. Subway: N, R to Prince St.; B, D, F, Q to Broadway–Lafayette St.

Here's the sharpest edge on the New York museum scene. This upstart (actually founded on the Lower East Side in 1975) focuses on lesser-known and emerging artists with high-concept or issue-oriented works, including many working in new media. Expect lots of explorations of race, class, and gender. What you see might not be good, but it will be thought provoking. There's also a jazz and new music program that has showcased such notables as the Kronos Quartet, among others.

American Craft Museum. 40 W. 53rd St. (btw. Fifth and Sixth Aves.). ☎ **212/956-3535.** $5 adults, $2.50 students and seniors, free for children under 12; pay as you wish Thurs 6–8pm. Tues–Wed and Fri–Sun 10am–6pm, Thurs 10am–8pm. Subway: E, F to Fifth Ave.

This small but aesthetically pleasing museum is the nation's top showcase for contemporary crafts. The collection focuses on objects that are prime examples of form and function, ranging from jewelry to baskets to vessels to furniture. You'll see a strong emphasis on material as well as craft, whether it be fiber, ceramics, or metal. Special exhibitions can range from hand-blown glass works to fine bookbinding. Stop into the gorgeous shop even if you don't make it into the museum, especially if you have some gift buying to do—but once you do, don't be surprised if you're tempted to peruse the permanent collection.

Asia Society. 725 Park Ave. (at 70th St.). ☎ **212/517-ASIA.** Gallery admission $4 adults, $2 seniors, children under 13 free; free Thurs 6–8pm. Tues–Sat 11am–6pm (to 8pm Thurs), Sun noon–5pm. Subway: 6 to 68th St./Hunter College.

The Asia Society was founded in 1956 by John D. Rockefeller III with the goal of increasing understanding between Americans and Asians through art exhibits, lectures, films, performances, and international conferences. The society is a leader in presenting contemporary Asian and Asian-American art; recent exhibits have included "Bamboo Masterworks," and "Sheer Realities: Body, Power and Clothing in the 19th-Century Philippines" was on the schedule for late '99 at press time.

Center for Jewish History. 17 W. 16th St. (btw. Fifth and Sixth aves.). ☎ **212/588-1253.** www.cjh.org. Admission and hours not determined at press time. Subway: L, N, R, 4, 5, 6 to 14th St./Union Sq.

Scheduled to open in fall 1999, the Center for Jewish History will occupy a new $40-million four-building complex. The Center brings together four of America's leading institutions of Jewish history: the **American Jewish Historical Society** (40 million documents and 30,000 books on Jewish Americana), the **Leo Baeck Institute** (documents, memoirs, and photos documenting German-speaking Jews), the **Yeshiva University Museum** (general-interest exhibits, plus a renowned collection of Judaica objects confiscated by the Nazis), and the **YIVO Institute for Jewish Research** (an academic institution concentrating on the civilization of Eastern European Jewry before the Holocaust). Besides offering a variety of public exhibits, the Center will feature special events in a 250-seat auditorium and a kosher eatery.

✪ The Cloisters. At the north end of Fort Tryon Park. ☎ **212/923-3700.** www.metmuseum.org/htmlfile/gallery/cloister/cloister.html. Suggested admission (includes same-day entrance to the Metropolitan Museum of Art) $8 adults, $4 seniors and students, free for children under 12. Nov–Feb Tues–Sun 9:30am–4:45pm; Mar–Oct Tues–Sun 9:30am–5:15pm. Subway: A to 190th St., then a 10-minute walk north along Margaret Corgan Drive, or pick up the M4 bus at the station. Bus: M4 Madison Ave. (FORT TRYON PARK–THE CLOISTERS).

If it weren't for this branch of the Metropolitan Museum of Art, many New Yorkers would never get to this northernmost point in Manhattan. This remote yet lovely spot

In Search of Historic Homes

New York's voracious appetite for change often means that older residential architecture is torn down so that money-earning high-rises can go up in its place. Surprisingly, however, the city maintains a truly fine collection of often-overlooked historic houses that are more than a tale of architecture—they're the stories of the people who passed their ordinary or extraordinary lives in buildings that range from humble to magnificent.

The **Historic House Trust of New York City** preserves 19 houses, located in city parks in all five boroughs. Those particularly worth seeking out include the **Morris-Jumel Mansion** (☎ 212/923-8008), built circa 1765 and Manhattan's oldest surviving house. The **Dyckman Farmhouse Museum** (☎ 212/304-9422) is the only Dutch Colonial farmhouse remaining in Manhattan, stoically and stylishly surviving the urban development that grew up around it. Built in 1809, Federal-style **Gracie Mansion** (☎ 212/570-4751) is now the official residence of "Hizzoner," the mayor of New York. The **Edgar Allan Poe Cottage** (☎ 718/ 881-8900) was the last home of the brilliant but troubled poet and author, who moved his wife to the Bronx because he thought the "country air" would be good for her tuberculosis. And the **Merchant's House Museum** (☎ 212/ 777-1089) is a rare jewel: a perfectly preserved 19th-century Greenwich Village home, complete with intact interiors, whose last resident is said to be the inspiration for Catherine Sloper in Henry James's *Washington Square*. Each of the 14 others has its own fascinating story to tell.

A brochure listing the locations and touring details of all 19 of the historic homes is available by calling ☎ 212/360-8282, and recorded information on special events at the houses is available at ☎ 212/360-3448. You'll also find complete information online at **www.ci.nyc.ny.us/html/dpr/html/nav.html**; click on HISTORIC HOUSES.

is devoted to the art and architecture of medieval Europe. Atop a magnificent cliff overlooking the Hudson River, you'll find a 12th-century chapter house, parts of five cloisters from medieval monasteries, a Romanesque chapel, and a 12th-century Spanish apse brought intact from Europe. Surrounded by peaceful gardens, this is the one place on the island that can even approximate the kind of solitude suitable to such a collection. Inside you'll find extraordinary works that include the famed Unicorn tapestries, sculpture, illuminated manuscripts, stained glass, ivory, and precious metalwork. Despite its remoteness, the Cloisters are extremely popular, especially in fine weather, so try to schedule your visit during the week rather than on a crowded weekend afternoon. A free guided tour is offered Tuesday through Friday at 3pm and Sunday at noon.

✪ **Cooper-Hewitt National Design Museum.** 2 E. 91st St. (at Fifth Ave.). ☎ **212/ 849-8300.** www.si.edu/ndm. Admission $5 adults, $3 seniors and students, free for children under 12; free to all Tues 5–9pm. Tues 10am–9pm, Wed–Sat 10am–5pm, Sun noon–5pm. Subway: 4, 5, 6 to 86th St.

Part of the Smithsonian Institution, the Cooper-Hewitt is housed in the Carnegie Mansion, built by steel magnate Andrew Carnegie in 1901. The museum underwent an ambitious $20-million renovation in 1996 that gave the building a long-overdue refreshening. Some 11,000 square feet of gallery space is devoted to changing exhibits that are invariably well conceived, engaging, and educational. Shows are both historic and contemporary in nature, and topics range from "Graphic Design· in the Mechanical Age" to "The Architecture of Reassurance: Designing the Disney Theme Parks." Many installations are drawn from the museum's own vast collection of industrial design, drawings, textiles, wall coverings, books, and prints. Exhibitions scheduled for late 1999–2000 include a retrospective on the work of Charles and Ray Eames and the National Design Triennial, featuring the work of both well-known and emerging talents as they address the pressing design issues of today.

On your way in, note the fabulous art nouveau–style .copper-and-glass canopy above the entrance. And be sure to visit the garden, ringed with Central Park benches from various eras.

Dahesh Museum. 601 Fifth Ave. (at 48th St.). ☎ **212/759-0606.** www.daheshmuseum. org. Free admission. Tues–Sat 11am–6pm. Subway: B, D, F, Q to 47–50th sts./Rockefeller Center.

If you consider yourself a classicist, this small museum is for you. It's dedicated to 19th- and early 20th-century European academic art, a continuation of Renaissance, Baroque, and Rococo traditions that were overshadowed by the arrival of Impressionism on the art scene. If you're not familiar with the academic school, expect lots of painstaking renditions of historical subjects and pastoral life. Artists represented include Jean-Léon Gérôme, Lord Leighton, and Edwin Long, whose *Love's Labour Lost* is a cornerstone of the permanent collection.

El Museo del Barrio. 1230 Fifth Ave. (at 104th St.). ☎ **212/831-7272.** www.elmuseo.org. Suggested admission $4 adults, $2 seniors and students, children under 12 free. Wed–Sun 11am–5pm. Subway: 6 to 103rd St.

What started in 1969 with a small display in a local school classroom in East Harlem is today the only museum in America dedicated to Puerto Rican, Caribbean, and Latin American art. The northernmost Museum Mile institution has a permanent exhibit ranging from pre-Columbian artifacts to historic photographs and handicrafts to a variety of paintings and sculpture. The display of *santos de palo*, wood-carved religious figurines, is especially worth noting. The well-curated changing exhibitions tend to focus on 20th-century artists and contemporary subjects.

Forbes Magazine Galleries. 62 Fifth Ave. (at 12th St.). ☎ **212/206-5548.** Free admission. Tues, Wed, Fri, Sat 10am–4pm. Subway: L, N, R, 4, 5, 6 to 14th St./Union Sq.

The late publishing magnate Malcolm Forbes may have been a self-described "capitalist tool," but he had esoteric, almost childish, tastes. He also had the altruism to share what he collected with the public for free. With its model boats, toy soldiers, old Monopoly game sets, presidential papers and memorabilia, and jewel-encrusted Fabergé eggs, this is a great museum for both you and the kids. Personal anecdotes explain why certain objects attracted Forbes's attention and turn the collection into an oddly interesting biographical portrait.

☉ The Frick Collection. 1 E. 70th St. (at Fifth Ave.). ☎ **212/288-0700.** www.frick.org. Admission $7 adults, $5 seniors and students. Children under 10 not admitted; children under 16 must be accompanied by an adult. Tues–Sat 10am–6pm, Sun and minor holidays 1–6pm (closed all major holidays). Subway: 6 to 68th St./Hunter College.

Henry Clay Frick could afford to be an avid collector of European art after amassing a fortune as a pioneer in the coke and steel industries at the turn of the century. To house his treasures and himself, he hired architects Carrère & Hastings to build this 18th-century-French–style mansion (1914), one of the most beautiful remaining on Fifth Avenue.

Most appealing about the Frick is its intimate size and setting. This is a living testament to New York's vanished Gilded Age: The interior still feels like a private home (albeit a really, really rich guy's home) graced with beautiful paintings, rather than a museum. Come here to see the classics, by some of the world's most famous painters: Titian, Bellini, Rembrandt, Turner, Vermeer, El Greco, and Goya, to name only a few. A highlight of the collection is the **Fragonard Room,** graced with the sensual rococo series *The Progress of Love.* The portrait of Montesquieu by Whistler is also stunning. Sculpture, furniture, Chinese vases, and French enamels complement the paintings and round out the collection. Included in the price of admission, the AcousticGuide audio tour is particularly useful, because it allows you to follow your own path rather than a proscribed route.

In addition to the permanent collection, the Frick regularly mounts small, well-focused temporary exhibitions, such as "Victorian Fairy Painting" and "Constable, A Master Draughtsman."

Free **chamber music concerts** are held twice a month, generally every other Sunday at 5pm; call or visit the Web site for the current schedule and ticket information.

International Center of Photography and ICP—Midtown. Uptown branch: 1130 Fifth Ave. (at 94th St.) ☎ **212/860-1777.** Midtown branch: 1133 Sixth Ave. (at 43rd St.). ☎ **212/768-4682.** www.icp.org. Admission (includes both uptown and midtown locations) $6 adults, $4 seniors, $1 children under 13; Tues 5–8pm pay what you wish. Tues–Thurs 10am–5pm, Fri 10am–8pm, Sat and Sun 10am–6pm. Subway: 6 to 96th St. to ICP Uptown; B, D, F, Q to 42nd St. to ICP Midtown.

The ICP is one of the world's premier collectors and exhibitors of photographic art, mounting some of the most interesting changing art exhibits in the city. The original ICP is also worth a look, but the Midtown branch is the place to start since it's twice the size of the original and usually has two mounted exhibitions rather than just one. The emphasis is on contemporary photographic works, but historically important photographers aren't ignored. Topics can range from "Man Ray: Photography and Its Double" to "Soul of the Game: Images and Voices of Street Basketball." A must on any photography buff's list. Call or check the Web site for current exhibitions.

Intrepid **Sea-Air-Space Museum.** Pier 86 (W. 46th St. at Twelfth Ave.). ☎ **212/245-0072.** www.intrepid-museum.com. Admission $10 adults; $7.50 veterans, seniors, and students; $5 children 6–11; first child under 6 free, each extra child $1. May–Sept, Mon–Sat 10am–5pm (last admission 4pm), Sun 10am–6pm (last admission 5pm); Oct–Apr, Wed–Sun 10am–5pm (last admission 4pm). Subway: A, C, E to 42nd St. Bus: M42 crosstown.

The most astonishing thing about the aircraft carrier USS *Intrepid* is how it can be simultaneously so big and so small. It's a few football fields long, holds 40 aircraft, and sometimes doubles as a ballroom for society functions. But stand there and think about landing an A-12 jet on the deck and suddenly, it's miniscule. Furthermore, in the narrow passageways below, you'll find it isn't quite the roomiest of vessels. Now a National Historic Landmark, the entire exhibit also includes the destroyer USS *Edison,* the submarine USS *Growler,* and the lightship *Nantucket,* as well as a collection of vintage and modern aircraft, including the A-12 Blackbird, the world's fastest spy plane. Special exhibits are often mounted, such as 1998's tribute to 200 years of naval service by African-Americans. Kids just love this place. But think twice about going in winter—it's almost impossible to heat an aircraft carrier.

Japan Society. 333 E. 47th St. (btw. First and Second aves.). ☎ **212/832-1155.** Suggested admission to gallery $5. Tues–Sun 9am–5:30pm. Subway: 6 to 51st St.; E, F to Lexington Ave.

In a striking modern building by Junzo Yoshimuro (1971), the U.S. headquarters of the Japan Society mounts highly regarded exhibits of Japanese art in a suitably serene gallery, plus changing displays whose subjects have included "Japanese Theater in the World." The society also hosts a wide variety of lectures, films, concerts, and classes throughout the year.

The Jewish Museum. 1109 Fifth Ave. (at 92nd St.). ☎ **212/423-3230.** www. jewishmuseum.org. Admission $8 adults, $5.50 seniors and students, free for children under 12; pay as you wish Tues 5–8pm. Check Web site for special online admission discounts (50% off at press time). Sun, Mon, Wed, Thurs 11am–5:45pm, Tues 11am–8pm. Subway: 4, 5 to 86th St.; 6 to 96th St.

Housed in a Gothic-style mansion renovated in the early '90s by AIA Gold Medal winner Kevin Roche, this wonderful museum now has the world-class space it deserves to showcase its remarkable collections, which chronicle 4,000 years of the Jewish experience. The two-floor permanent exhibit, "Culture and Continuity: The Jewish Journey," is the museum's centerpiece. Artifacts range from ancient daily objects that might have served the authors of the books of Genesis, Psalms, and Job to a wonderful collection of classic TV programs (as any fan of television's Golden Age knows, its finest comic moments were Jewish comedy). There's also a great assemblage of intricate Torahs. The scope of the exhibit is phenomenal, and its story an enlightening— and intense—one. In addition, there's a rotating calendar of special exhibitions that range from antiquities to contemporary Jewish art, plus a design store showcasing contemporary Jewish crafts.

✪ **Lower East Side Tenement Museum.** Visitors' Center at 90 Orchard St. (at Broome St.). ☎ **212/431-0233.** www.wnet.org/tenement. $8 adults, $6 seniors and students for 1 tenement tour; $14 adults, $10 seniors and students for any 2 tours; $20 adults, $14 seniors and students for all 3 tours. Tenement tours depart Tues–Fri at 1pm and every half-hour to 4pm; Thurs hourly 6pm–9pm; Sat–Sun every half-hour 11am–4:30pm. Subway: F to Delancey St.; B, D, Q to Grand St.

Awarded the prized designation just last year, this decade-old museum is the first-ever National Trust for Historic Preservation site that was not the home of someone rich or famous. This one is something quite different: A five-story tenement that 10,000 people from 25 countries called home between 1863 and 1935—people who had come to the United States looking for the American dream, and made 97 Orchard St. their first stop. This living history museum tells the story of the great immigration boom of the late 19th and early 20th centuries, when the Lower East Side was considered the "Gateway to America." A visit here makes a good follow-up to an Ellis Island trip— what happened to all the people who passed through that famous waystation?

The only way to see the museum is by guided tour. At press time, three tours, each lasting about one hour, were on offer: two tenement tours, each showcasing the tenement during different decades, and one neighborhood walking tour. One tenement tour and the neighborhood tour are only offered on weekends, so it's wise to plan ahead if you'd like to see and do everything. However, the primary tenement tour, offered on all open days, offers a satisfying exploration of the museum. A knowledgeable guide leads you into the dingy urban time capsule, where several apartments have been faithfully restored to their exact lived-in condition, and recounts the real-life stories of the families who occupied them in fascinating detail. Tours are limited in number, so it pays to reserve ahead. The Visitors' Center has several small exhibits, including photos, videos, and a model tenement.

✪ **Morgan Library.** 29 E. 36th St. (at Madison Ave.). ☎ **212/685-0008.** www.shop. morganlibrary.org. Admission $7 adults, $5 seniors, children under 12 free. Tues–Thur 10:30am–5pm, Fri 10:30am–8pm, Sat 10:30am–6pm, Sun noon–6pm. Subway: 6 to 33rd St.

Here's an undiscovered New York treasure, boasting one of the world's most important collections of original manuscripts, rare books and bindings, master drawings, and personal writings. Among the remarkable artifacts on display under glass are stunning illuminated manuscripts (including Gutenberg bibles), a working draft of the U.S. Constitution bearing copious handwritten notes, Voltaire's personal household

Did You Know?

You can find five sections of the **Berlin Wall,** graffiti intact, in a small park behind 520 Madison Ave., on the north side of 53rd Street, between Madison and Fifth avenues.

account books, and handwritten scores by the likes of Beethoven, Mozart, and Puccini. The collection of mostly 19th-century drawings—featuring works by Seurat, Degas, Rubens, and other great masters—have an excitement of immediacy about them that the artists' more well-known paintings often lack. This rich repository originated as the private collection of turn-of-the-century financier J. Pierpont Morgan and is housed in a landmark Renaissance-style palazzo building (1906) he commissioned from McKim, Mead & White to hold his masterpieces. Morgan's library and study are preserved virtually intact, and worth a look unto themselves for their landmarked architecture (particularly the rotunda) and richly detailed fittings. The special exhibitions are particularly well chosen and curated; subjects can range from medieval bookbinding techniques to the literary genesis of the mystery novel and pulp fiction. Exhibitions scheduled for the coming year include "The Great Experiment: George Washington and the American Republic," tracing the first U.S. president's development from loyal British subject to leader of a radical revolution. A reading room is available by appointment.

Museum for African Art. 593 Broadway (btw. Houston and Prince sts.). ☎ **212/966-1313.** www.africanart.org. Admission $5 adults, $2.50 seniors/children. Tues–Fri 10:30am– 5:30pm, Sat noon–8pm, Sun noon–6pm. Subway: N, R to Prince St.

This captivating museum (whose interior was designed by architect Maya Lin, best known for her Vietnam Veterans Memorial in Washington, D.C.) is a leading organizer of temporary exhibits dedicated to historic and contemporary African art and culture. Exhibitions on the calendar for late 1999–2000 include "Liberated Voices: Contemporary Art from South Africa," focusing on works created since the end of Apartheid in 1994; an intricate look at hair and hair dressing in African art and culture, from artistic, social, and religious perspectives; and a look at great African dynasties in "African Nobility and Their Objects of Power." In addition, an excellent museum shop showcases contemporary African crafts.

Museum of American Folk Art. 2 Lincoln Sq. (Columbus Ave. between 65th and 66th sts.). ☎ **212/977-7298** or 212/595-9533. www.folkartmuse.org. Free admission. Tues–Sun 11:30am–7:30pm. Subway: 1, 9 to 66th St.

This museum displays a wide range of works from the 18th century to the present, reflecting the breadth and vitality of the American folk-art tradition. The textiles collection is the museum's most popular, highlighted by a splendid variety of quilts. The gift shop is filled with one-of-a-kind objects.

In 1998, the museum started construction on its new larger home on West 53rd Street, just down the block from the Museum of Modern Art. The new building, four times larger than the current space, is scheduled to open in 2001.

Museum of Jewish Heritage—A Living Memorial to the Holocaust. 18 First Place (at Battery Place), Battery Park City. ☎ **212/968-1800.** www.mjhnyc.org. Admission $7 adults, $5 seniors and students, children under 5 free. Sun–Wed 9am–5pm, Thurs 9am–8pm, Fri and evenings of Jewish holidays 9am–2pm. Subway: 1, 9 to South Ferry; 4, 5 to Bowling Green.

The Museum of Jewish Heritage was dedicated in fall 1997, more than 50 years after the idea of such a museum was first proposed. Located in the south end of Battery

Art for Art's Sake: The Gallery Scene

The biggest news in the art gallery world has been the decreasing importance of SoHo as the capital of contemporary art. With the increasing commercialization of SoHo as a trendy shopping district, major showrooms have fled either Uptown or to far West Chelsea. But the all this commotion may just be the result of natural cycles of change, evidence of which is SoHo's increasing prominence on the museum scene. Now that Broadway has turned into a veritable museum row—with the Museum of African Art, the Guggenheim SoHo, the Alternative Museum, and the increasingly high-profile New Museum of Contemporary Art all calling the stretch between Houston and Prince streets home—it may be just simply that art has taken root in SoHo. So those opposed to such permanence—namely, cutting-edge artists—have fled elsewhere.

All this movement only serves to underline that Manhattan is the undisputed capital of art—or, more significantly, art sales. The island has more than 500 private art galleries, selling everything from old masters to tomorrow's news. Galleries are open free to the public, generally Tuesday through Saturday from 10am to 6pm. Saturday-afternoon gallery hopping, in particular, is a favorite pastime—nobody will expect you to buy, so don't worry. The best way to winnow down your choices is by perusing the Friday and Sunday *New York Times, Time Out New York, New York* magazine, or the *New Yorker.* I suggest picking the neighborhood that sounds best to you and just browsing. But if you want to plan your gallery visits before you arrive, go online at **www.gallery-guide.com/ content/current/ny** for the latest exhibition listings. You can also pick up a hard copy of the *Gallery Guide* at most galleries around town.

Although Uptown tends to be more traditional and Downtown more contemporary, there are constant surprises in both neighborhoods. Although I've included below the names of artists or art periods in which these dealers usually trade, note that these can change with the whims of the market.

Several important dealers showing contemporary painting and sculpture are playing both sides of the deck, with galleries in more than one location: **Gagosian** (works by Francesco Clemente, Howard Hodgkin, David Salle, Mark di Suvero) is at 980 Madison Ave. (☎ 212/744-2313) and 136 Wooster St. (☎ 212/228-2828); **PaceWildenstein** (Jim Dine, Lucas Samaras, Julian Schnabel, Kiki Smith, as well as Picasso and Henry Moore) is at 32 E. 57th St. (☎ 212/421-3292) and 142 Greene St. (☎ 212/431-9224); and **Leo Castelli** (Jasper Johns, Roy Lichtenstein, James Rosenquist) is at 420 W. Broadway (☎ 212/431-5160) and 578 Broadway (☎ 212/941-9855).

UPTOWN   Uptown galleries are clustered in and around the glamorous crossroads of Fifth Avenue and 57th Street as well as on and off stylish Madison

Park City, it occupies a strikingly spare six-sided building designed by award-winning architect Kevin Roche, with a six-tier roof alluding to the Star of David and the 6 million murdered in the Holocaust. The permanent exhibits—"Jewish Life a Century Ago," "The War Against the Jews," and "Jewish Renewal"—recount the daily prewar lives, the unforgettable horror that destroyed them, and the tenacious renewal experienced by European and immigrant Jews in the years from the late 19th century to the present. Its power derives from the way it tells that story: through the objects, photographs, documents, and, most poignantly, through the videotaped testimonies

Avenue in the 60s, 70s, and 80s. Unlike their upstart West Chelsea counterparts, these blue-chip galleries maintain their quiet white-glove demeanor. They include **Mitchell-Innes & Nash,** 1018 Madison Ave. (☎ 212/744-7400); **Richard Gray,** 1018 Madison Ave. (☎ 212/472-8787); **Winston Wachter Fine Art,** 39 E. 78th St. (☎ 212/327-2526); and **James Danziger,** 851 Madison Ave. (☎ 212/734-5300), a dealer in fine photographs who left SoHo after 8 years.

Other major galleries include **Mary Boone,** 745 Fifth Ave. (☎ 212/752-2929), a major relocation from SoHo, known for success with the works of Ross Bleckner, Eric Fischl, and Malcolm Morley; **Hirschl & Adler,** 21 E. 70th St. (☎ 212/535-8810), 18th- to 20th-century European and American painting; **Leonard Hutton,** 41 E. 57th St. (☎ 212/751-7373), German expressionism, Italian futurism, Russian constructivism; **Kennedy,** 730 Fifth Ave., 2nd floor. (☎ 212/541-9600), 18th- to 20th-century American painting; **Knoedler,** 19 E. 70th St. (☎ 212/794-0550), Helen Frankenthaler, Nancy Graves, David Smith, Frank Stella; **Marlborough,** 40 W. 57th St. (☎ 212/541-4900), Fernando Botero, Red Grooms, Alex Katz; **Spanierman,** 45 E. 58th St. (☎ 212/832-0208), 19th- to early 20th-century American, Mary Cassatt, Childe Hassam, Winslow Homer; **Wildenstein,** the classical big brother of PaceWildenstein, 19 E. 64th St. (☎ 212/879-0500), old masters and Renaissance paintings and drawings.

DOWNTOWN   Don't count **SoHo** out yet. The neighborhood does remain colorful, if less edgy than it used to be, just south of Houston Street, north of Chinatown, and centered on West Broadway. In far **West Chelsea,** north and south of West 23rd Street and mostly between Tenth and Eleventh avenues, are a number of galleries, often in the large open spaces of former garages and abandoned warehouses. If you're interested in the cutting edge, it's worth coming down just to browse around.

O. K. Harris, 383 W. Broadway (☎ 212/431-3600), shows a wide and fascinating variety of contemporary painting, sculpture, and photography; **Louis K. Meisel,** 141 Prince St. (☎ 212/677-1340), photorealism and other contemporary works; **Holly Solomon,** 172 Mercer St. (☎ 212/941-5777), mixed-media pieces and works by emerging artists; and other dealers in contemporary art from Cy Twombly to Nan Goldin, like **Paula Cooper,** 534 W. 21st St. (☎ 212/255-1105), **Morris Healey,** 530 W. 22nd St. (☎ 212/243-3753), **Matthew Marks,** 522 W. 24th St. (☎ 212/243-1650), **Barbara Gladstone,** 515 W. 24th St. (☎ 212/206-9300), and **Alexander & Bonin,** 132 Tenth Ave. (☎ 212/367-7474).

of Holocaust victims, survivors, and their families, all chronicled by Steven Spielberg's Survivors of the Shoah Visual History Foundation.

Advance tickets are highly recommended to guarantee admission, and can be purchased by calling ☎ **212/786-0820,** ext. 111 or Ticketmaster (☎ **800/307-4007** or 212/307-4007; www.ticketmaster.com).

Museum of the City of New York. 1220 Fifth Ave. (at 103rd St.). ☎ **212/534-1672.** www.mcny.org. Suggested admission $5 adults, $4 seniors, students and children, $10 families. Wed–Sat 10am–5pm, Sun noon–5pm. Subway: 6 to 103rd St.

It's the nearest thing to heaven we have in New York.

—Deborah Kerr to Cary Grant in *An Affair to Remember,*
on the Empire State Building

A wide variety of objects—costumes, photographs, prints, maps, dioramas, and memorabilia—traces the history of New York City from its beginnings as a humble Dutch
colony in the 16th century to its present-day prominence. Two outstanding permanent exhibits are the re-creation of John D. Rockefeller's master bedroom and dressing
room, and the space devoted to the history of New York theater. The permanent "Furniture of Distinction, 1790–1890" displays 33 elegant pieces representing New York's
central role in American cabinetmaking that will have you eyeing your IKEA with new
contempt. Kids will love "New York Toy Stories," a permanent exhibit showcasing toys
and dolls owned and adored by centuries of New York children.

Museum of Television & Radio. 25 W. 52nd St. (btw. Fifth and Sixth aves.). ☎ **212/ 621-
6800.** Admission $6 adults, $4 seniors and students, $3 children under 13. Tues, Wed, and
Fri–Sun noon–6pm, Thurs noon–8pm. Subway: B, D, F, Q to 47–50th sts./Rockefeller Center;
N, R to 49th St.

If you can resist the allure of this museum, I'd wager you've spent the last 70 years in
a bubble. You can watch and hear all the great personalities of TV and radio—from
Uncle Miltie to Johnny Carson to Jerry Seinfeld—at a private console (available for 2
hours). And amazingly, you can also conduct computer searches to pick out the great
moments of history, viewing almost anything that made its way onto the airwaves,
from the the Beatles' first appearance on *The Ed Sullivan Show* to the crumbling of the
Berlin Wall (the collection consists of 75,000 programs and commercials). The
museum was founded by former CBS head William Paley, in a building designed by
Philip Johnson. Selected programs are also presented on large screens, which can range
from "Barbra Streisand: The Television Performances" to little-seen Monty Python
episodes; check to see what's on while you're in town.

National Museum of the American Indian, George Gustav Heye Center. 1 Bowling
Green (btw. State and Whitehall sts.). ☎ **212/668-6624.** www.si.edu/nmai. Free admission.
Sun–Wed and Fri–Sat 10am–5pm, Thurs 10am–8pm. Subway: 1, 9 to South Ferry; 4, 5 to
Bowling Green.

Part of the Smithsonian Institution, this collection is the oldest of its kind in the
country. It's housed in the beautiful 1907 beaux arts U.S. Customs House, a National
Historic Landmark that's worth a look in its own right. The bulk of the extensive collection is due to move yet again, in 2002, to the new Museum on the Mall in Washington, D.C. Until then, enjoy items from the spiritual to the quotidian, collected
mainly by New York banking millionaire George Gustav Heye in the beginning of this
century. Despite the wealth of material here, it's poorly organized and that curse of
modern museums—video displays—vie for your attention when the exhibits themselves would suffice. Exhibitions scheduled for late 1999–2000 include "Spirit Capture: Native Americans and the Photographic Image." The museum also hosts
interpretive programs plus free storytelling, music, and dance presentations. For a calendar of current programs, call ☎ **212/514-3888** or 212/825-6922.

New Museum of Contemporary Art. 583 Broadway (btw. Houston and Prince sts.).
☎ **212/219-1222.** www.newmuseum.org. $5 ($3 seniors, students, and artists); free Thurs
6–8pm. Thurs–Sat noon–8pm, Sun and Wed noon–6pm. Subway: N, R to Prince St.; B, D, F,
Q to Broadway–Lafayette St.

With 33,000 new square feet of space on Broadway, SoHo's burgeoning museum row (also home to the Guggenheim SoHo, the Museum of African Art, and the Alternative Museum), and the former curator of contemporary art at the Whitney as its brand-new director, the New Museum is now a prime contender on the museum scene. This contemporary arts museum has moved closer to the mainstream in recent years, but it's only a safety margin in from the edge as far as most of us are concerned, so expect some adventurous and well-curated exhibitions. Subject matter on the schedule for late 1999–2000 includes "The Time of Our Lives," examining the concept of age and aging in Western society; "Picturing the Modern Amazon," a show devoted to representations of hypermuscular and physically strong women; and retropective of such artists as Brazilian artist Cildo Meireles and video artist/feminist Martha Rosler.

New-York Historical Society. 2 W. 77th St. (at Central Park West). ☎ **212/873-3400.** www.nyhistory.org. Admission $5 adults, $3 seniors and students, free for children 12 and under. Tues–Sun 11am–5pm. Subway: B, C to 81st St.; 1, 9 to 79th St.

Launched in 1804, the New-York Historical Society is a major repository of American history, culture, and art, with a special focus on the New York region. The grand neo-classical edifice is finally undergoing major renovations, expected to be complete in early 2000, that will transform the fourth floor into a state-of-the-art study facility and gallery displaying highlights from the fine- and decorative-arts collections. In the meantime, check the schedule of temporary exhibits, which has featured subjects as wide-ranging as "New York's Finest: A History of the NYPD" to "Secrets of a Beautiful Face: Beauty Product Advertisements." On the second floor, a small selection of colorful Tiffany lamps is on display, and paintings from Hudson River School artists Thomas Cole, Asher Durand, and Frederic Church, and others hang in the Luman Reed Gallery.

Theodore Roosevelt Birthplace. 28 E. 20th St. (btw. Broadway and Park Ave. South). ☎ **212/260-1616.** Admission $2 adults, free for children under 17. Wed–Sun 9am–5pm. Subway: 6 to 23rd St.; N, R to Broadway/23rd St.

The present building is a faithful reconstruction, inside and out, on the same site of the brownstone where Theodore Roosevelt was born on October 27, 1858. Period rooms appear as they did in Teddy's youth. The powder-blue parlor is in the rococo revival style popular at the time, the stately green dining room boasts horsehair-covered chairs, and the children's nursery has a window that leads to a small gymnasium built to help the frail young Teddy become more "bully." About 40% of the furniture is original (another 20% belonged to family members). Tours are given every hour until 3:30pm. There's also a collection of Roosevelt memorabilia.

6 Skyscrapers & Other Architectural Marvels

THE TOP STRUCTURES

For details on the **World Trade Center,** see p. 203, and the **Brooklyn Bridge,** see section 3, "Historic Lower Manhattan's Top Attractions," earlier in this chapter; the **Woolworth Building** is also discussed in the walking tour at the end of that section.

Chrysler Building. 405 Lexington Ave. (at 42nd St.). Subway: 4, 5, 6, 7, S to 42nd St./Grand Central.

Built as Chrysler Corporation headquarters in 1930 (they moved out decades ago), this is perhaps the 20th century's most romantic architectural achievement, especially at night, when the lights in its triangular openings play off its steely crown. A recent cleaning added new sparkle. As you admire its facade, be sure to note the gargoyles reaching out from the upper floors, looking for all the world like streamline-Gothic hood ornaments.

There's a fascinating tale behind this building. While it was under construction, its architect, William Van Alen, hid his final plans for the spire that now tops it. Working at a furious pace in the last days of construction, the workers assembled in secrecy the elegant pointy top—and then they raised it right through what people had assumed was going to be the roof, and for one brief moment it was the world's tallest tower (a distinction stolen by the Empire State Building only a few months later). Its exterior chrome sculptures are magnificent and spooky. Its lavish ground-floor interior, which you can visit, is art deco to the max. The ceiling mural depicting airplanes and other early marvels of the first decades of the 20th century evince the bright promise of technology. The elevators are works of art, masterfully covered in exotic woods (especially note the lotus-shaped marquetry on the doors). Although the observation deck closed long ago, developers have tossed around plans to turn the upper floors into a luxury hotel.

✪ **Empire State Building.** 350 Fifth Ave. (at 34th St.). ☎ **212/736-3100.** www.esbnyc. com. Observatory admission $6 adults, $3 seniors and children under 12, free for children under 5. Daily 9:30am–midnight (tickets sold until 11:30pm). Subway: B, D, F, Q, N, R to 34th St.; 6 to 33rd St.

King Kong climbed it in 1933. A plane slammed into it in 1945. The World Trade Center superseded it in 1970 as the island's tallest building. And in 1997, a gunman ascended it to stage a deadly shooting. But through it all, the Empire State Building has remained one of the city's favorite landmarks, and its signature high-rise. Completed in 1931 on what had been the site of the first Waldorf Astoria and, before that, Caroline Astor's mansion, it climbs 102 stories (1,454 feet) and now harbors the offices of fashion firms and, in its upper reaches, a jumble of high-tech broadcast equipment.

Always a conversation piece, the Empire State Building glows every night, bathed in colored floodlights to commemorate events of significance (red, white, and blue for Independence Day; green for St. Patrick's Day; red, black, and green for MLK Day; even lavender and white for Gay Pride Day). The familiar silver spire can be seen from all over the city; my favorite view of the building is from 23rd Street, where Fifth Avenue and Broadway converge. On a lovely day, stand at the base of the Flatiron Building (see below) and gaze up Fifth; the crisp, gleaming deco tower jumps out, soaring above the sooty office buildings that surround it.

But the views that keep nearly 3 million visitors coming every year are the ones from the 86th- and 102nd-floor **observatories.** The lower one is best—you can walk out on a windy deck (even inside at this height you feel the air whistling through the building) and look through coin-operated viewers (bring quarters!) over what, on a clear day, can be as much as an 80-mile visible radius. The citywide panorama is magnificent. One surprise is the flurry of rooftop activity, an aspect of city life that thrives unnoticed from our everyday sidewalk vantage point. The higher observation deck is glass-enclosed and cramped.

Light fog can create an admirably moody effect, but it goes without saying that a clear day is best. Dusk brings the most remarkable views, and the biggest crowds. Consider going in the morning, when the light is still low on the horizon, keeping glare to a minimum. Starry nights are pure magic.

In your haste to go up, don't rush through the beautiful three-story-high marble **lobby** without pausing to admire its features, which include a wonderful streamline mural.

In case you haven't had enough of the real thing, **New York Skyride** (☎ **888/ SKYRIDE** or 212/279-9777; www.skyride.com) offers a short, motion-flight

Empire State Ticket-Buying Tip

Lines can be frightfully long at the concourse-level ticket booth, so be prepared to wait—or consider purchasing **advance tickets** online using a credit card at **www.esbnyc.org**. You'll pay a $2 service charge for the privilege, but it's well worth it, especially if you're visiting during a busy season, when the line can be shockingly long. You're not required to choose a time or date for your tickets in advance; they can be used on any regular open day. However, order them well before you leave home, because they're sent only by regular mail. Expect them to take 7 to 10 days to reach you (longer if you live out of the country). With tickets in hand, you're allowed to proceed directly to the second floor—past everyone who didn't plan as well as you did!

simulation sightseeing tour of New York on the second floor of the building. You sit on a platform that tilts and lurches to thunderous sound effects while the film takes you around and "through" New York's major landmarks (just like Star Tours). A high point: It lets you feel what it's like to fall from the building—what fun! Tickets are $11.50 for adults, $9.50 for kids, and the ride is open daily from 10am to 10pm—but unless the kids insist, skip it.

✪ **Grand Central Terminal.** 42nd St. at Park Ave. www.grandcentralterminal.com. Subway: 4, 5, 6, 7, S to 42nd St./Grand Central.

After more than two years and $175 million, Grand Central Terminal has come out from under the tarps and scaffolding. Rededicated with all the appropriate pomp and circumstance on October 1, 1998, the 1913 landmark (originally designed by Warren & Wetmore with Reed & Stem) has been reborn as one of the most magnificent public spaces in the country. The restoration, by the New York firm of Beyer Blinder Belle, is an utter triumph. Their work has reanimated the genius of the station's original intent: to inspire those who pass through this urban meeting point with lofty feelings of civic pride and appreciation for Western architectural traditions. In short, they've put the "grand" back into Grand Central.

By all means, come and visit, even if you're not catching one of the subway lines or Metro North commuter trains that rumble through the bowels of this great place. And even if you arrive and leave by subway, be sure to exit the station, walking a couple of blocks south, to about 40th Street, before you turn around to admire Jules-Alexis Coutan's neo-classical sculpture *Transportation* hovering over the south entrance, with a majestically buff Mercury, the Roman god of commerce and travel, as its central figure.

The greatest visual impact comes when you enter the vast **main concourse.** Cleaned of decades of grime and cheesy advertisements, it boasts renewed majesty. The high windows once again allow sunlight light to penetrate the space, glinting off the half-acre Tennessee marble floor. The brass clock over the central kiosk gleams, as do the gold- and nickel-plated chandeliers piercing the side archways. The masterful **sky ceiling,** again a brilliant greenish blue, depicts the constellations of the winter sky above New York. They're lit with 59 stars, surrounded by dazzling 24-karat-gold and emitting light fed through fiber-optic cables, their intensities roughly replicating the magnitude of the actual stars as seen from Earth. Look carefully, and you'll see a patch near one corner left unrestored as a useful reminder of the neglect once visited on this splendid overhead masterpiece. On the east end of the main concourse is a grand **marble staircase** where there had never been one before, but as the original plans had always intended.

This dramatic beaux arts splendor serves as a hub of social activity as well. New retail shops and restaurants have taken over the mezzanine and lower levels. The highlight of the mezzanine is **Michael Jordan's—The Steak House,** a gorgeous art deco space that allows you to dine within view of the sky ceiling (see chapter 6). Off the main concourse at street level there's a nice mix of specialty shops and national retailers, including **Banana Republic** and **Kenneth Cole.** The **lower concourse** houses newsstands, a food court offering everything from deli sandwiches to caviar, and the famous **Oyster Bar,** also restored to its original old-world glory (see chapter 6).

✪ **Rockefeller Center.** Between 47th and 50th sts., from Fifth to Sixth aves. ☎ **212/ 632-3975.** Subway: B, D, F, Q to 47th–50th sts./Rockefeller Center.

A streamline moderne masterpiece, Rockefeller Center is one of New York's central gathering spots for visitors and New Yorkers alike. A prime example of the city's skyscraper spirit and historic sense of optimism, it was erected mainly in the 1930s, when the city was deep in a depression as well as its most passionate art deco phase. Designated a National Historic Landmark in 1988, it's now the world's largest privately owned business-and-entertainment center, with 18 buildings on 21 acres.

For a dramatic approach to the entire complex, start at Fifth Avenue between 49th and 50th streets. The builders purposely created the gentle slope of the Promenade, known here as the **Channel Gardens** because it's flanked to the south by La Maison Française and to the north by the British Building (the Channel, get it?). You'll also find a number of attractive shops along here, including a big branch of the **Metropolitan Museum of Art Store,** a good stop for elegant gifts. The Promenade leads to the **Lower Plaza,** home to the famous ice-skating rink in winter (see next paragraph) and alfresco dining in summer in the shadow of Paul Manship's gilded bronze statue *Prometheus,* more notable for its setting than its magnificence as an artwork. All around the flags of the United Nations' member countries flap in the breeze. Just behind *Prometheus,* in December and early January, towers the city's official and majestic Christmas tree.

The **Rink at Rockefeller Plaza** (☎ 212/332-7654), is tiny but positively romantic, especially during the holidays, when the giant Christmas tree's multicolored lights twinkle from above. It's open from mid-October to mid-March, and you'll skate under the magnificent tree for the month of December.

The focal point of this "city within a city" is the **GE Building,** at 30 Rockefeller Plaza, a 70-story showpiece towering over the plaza. It's still one of the city's most impressive buildings; walk through for a look at the granite marble lobby, lined with monumental sepia-toned murals by José Maria Sert. You can pick up a walking-tour brochure highlighting the center's art and architecture at the main information desk in this building.

NBC television maintains studios throughout the complex. *Saturday Night Live,* the *Rosie O'Donnell Show,* and *Late Night with Conan O'Brien* originate in the GE Building (see "Talk of the Town: TV Tapings" later in this chapter for tips on getting tickets). If you're a fan of NBC's ***Today Show,*** the glass-enclosed studio from which the show is broadcast live weekdays from 7 to 9am is on the southwest corner of 49th Street and Rockefeller Plaza; come early if you want a visible spot, and bring your HI MOM! sign. Who knows? If it's a nice day, you may even get to chat with Katie, Matt, or Al in a segment. One-hour **NBC Studio Tours** (☎ 212/664-7174) run every 15 minutes daily from 9:15am to 4:30pm from Easter through Labor Day and Thanksgiving through New Year's, and every half-hour Monday through Saturday at other times of the year. Tickets are $10 per person, and children under 6 are not admitted.

Other notable buildings throughout the complex includes the **International Building,** on Fifth Avenue between 50th and 51st streets, worth a look for its Atlas statue out front; and the **McGraw-Hill Building,** on Sixth Avenue between 48th and 49th streets, with its 50-foot sun triangle on the plaza.

But **Radio City Music Hall,** 1260 Sixth Ave., at 50th Street (☎ **212/247-4777**), is perhaps the most impressive architectural feat of the complex. Designed by Donald Donald Deskey, it's one of the largest indoor theaters, with 6,200 seats. But its true grandeur derives from its magnificent art deco appointments. The crowning touch is the stage's great proscenium arch, which from the distant seats evokes a faraway sun setting on the horizon of the sea. The men's and women's lounges are also splendid. The theater is currently under renovation, but is scheduled to reopen in October 1999, in plenty of time for the season's **Christmas Spectacular,** starring the Rockettes. At this time, the illuminating one-hour **Grand Tour** (☎ **212/632-4041**) will also be reintroduced; call for the latest schedule and prices.

United Nations. At First Ave. and 46th St. ☎ **212/963-8687.** www.un.org. Guided tours $7.50 adults, $5.50 seniors, $4.50 students, $3.50 children (those under 5 not permitted). Daily tours every half-hour 9:15am–4:45pm; closed weekends Jan–Feb. Subway: 4, 5, 6, 7, S to 42nd St./Grand Central.

In the midst of what some consider the world's most cynical city is this working monument to world peace. The U.N. headquarters occupies 18 acres of international territory—neither New York City nor the United States has jurisdiction here—along the East River from 42nd to 48th streets. Designed by an international team of architects (led by American Wallace K. Harrison and including Le Corbusier) and finished in 1952, the complex weds the 39-story glass slab Secretariat with the free-form General Assembly on beautifully landscaped grounds donated by John D. Rockefeller, Jr., along the East River. One hundred eighty nations use the facilities to arbitrate worldwide disputes.

Guided one-hour tours take you to the General Assembly Hall and the Security Council Chamber and introduce the history and activities of the United Nations and its related organizations. Along the tour you'll see donated objects and artwork, including charred artifacts that survived the atomic bombs at Hiroshima and Nagasaki, stained-glass windows by Chagall, a replica of the first *Sputnik*, and a colorful mosaic called *The Golden Rule,* based on a Norman Rockwell drawing, which was a gift from the United States in 1985.

If you take the time to wander the beautifully landscaped **grounds,** you'll be rewarded with lovely views and some surprises. The mammoth monument *Good Defeats Evil*, donated by the Soviet Union in 1990, fashioned a contemporary St.

Story Time

Wowed by the sheer verticality in this town? Awed by the architectural marvel that is the high-rise? You're not alone. If you'd like to learn more about the technology, culture, and sheer muscle behind it all, seek out the **Skyscraper Museum** (☎ **212/ 968-1961;** www.skyscraper.org). This itinerant museum first set up shop in an abandoned bank in lower Manhattan in 1997, committed to telling the multi-faceted story of the multi-story high-rise. Next came "Building the Empire State," celebrating the design and construction of the city's signature skyscraper in another Wall Street space. The museum is slated to get a permanent home in a new Battery Park City high-rise (natch) in the next few years; in the meantime, call or go online to see where you can find the latest installation.

George slaying a dragon from parts of a Russian ballistic missile and an American Pershing missile.

The **Delegates' Dining Room** (☎ 212/963-7625), which affords great views of the East River, is open to the public on weekdays for lunch 11:30am to 2:30pm (reserve in advance). The **gift shop** sells flags and unusual handcrafted items from all over the world, and the **post office** sells unique United Nations stamps that can be purchased and posted only here.

OTHER NOTABLE STRUCTURES & ENGINEERING FEATS

For **City Hall,** see the walking tour under "Historic Lower Manhattan's Top Attractions" earlier in this chapter.

In addition to the landmarks below, architecture buffs may also want to seek out these notable buildings: The **Lever House,** built in 1952 at 390 Park Ave., between 53rd and 54th streets, and the neighboring **Seagram Building** (1958), at 375 Park Ave., are the city's best examples of the form-follows-function, glass-and-steel International style, with the latter designed by master architect Mies van der Rohe himself. Also in Midtown East is the **Sony Building,** at 550 Madison Ave., designed in 1984 by Philip Johnson with a pretty rose-granite facade and a playful Chippendale-style top that puts it a cut above the rest on the block.

The Upper West Side is home to two of the city's prime examples of residential architecture. On Broadway, taking up the block between 73rd and 74th streets, is the **Ansonia,** looking for all the world like a flamboyant architectural wedding cake. This splendid beaux arts building has been home to the likes of Stravinsky, Toscanini, and Caruso, thanks to its virtually soundproof apartments; it was also featured prominently as the thrill-a-minute residence of Bridget Fonda and Jennifer Jason Leigh in *Single White Female.* Even more notable is the **Dakota,** at 72nd Street and Central Park West. Legend has it that the angular 1884 apartment house—accented with gables, dormers, and oriel windows that give it a brooding appeal—earned its name when its forward-thinking developer, Edward S. Clark, was teased by friends that he was building so far north of the city that he might he might as well be building in the Dakotas. The building's most famous resident, John Lennon, was gunned down outside the 72nd Street entrance on December 8, 1980, by Mark David Chapman; Yoko Ono still lives inside, while the all-grown-up Sean has since relocated to a downtown loft.

♻ **Cathedral of St. John the Divine.** 1047 Amsterdam Ave. (at 112th St.). ☎ 212/ 316-7540 or 212/932-7347 for tour information and reservations. www.stjohndivine.org. Suggested admission $2; tour $3; tower tour $10. Mon–Sat 8am–6pm, Sun 7am–7:30pm. Tours offered Tues–Sat 11am, Sun 1pm; tower tours 1st and 3rd Sat of the month at noon and 2pm. Services Mon–Sat 7:15am and 12:15 and 5:30pm; Sun 8, 9, and 11am and 7pm. Subway: 1, 9, B, C to Cathedral Pkwy.

The world's largest Gothic cathedral, St. John the Divine has been a work in progress since 1892. Its sheer size is amazing enough—a nave that stretches two football fields and a seating capacity of 5,000—but keep in mind that there is no steel structural support. The church is being built using traditional Gothic engineering; blocks of granite and limestone are carved out by master masons and their apprentices (some from the surrounding Harlem neighborhood). Perhaps that's why the construction is still going on, more than 100 years after it began, with no end in sight. But what makes this place so wonderful is that finishing isn't necessarily the point.

Though the seat of the Episcopal Diocese of New York, St. John's embraces an interfaith tradition. Internationalism is a theme found throughout the cathedral's iconography; each chapel is dedicated to a different national or ethnic group. You can explore it on the **Public Tour,** offered six days a week, or on the twice-monthly **Vertical Tour,** which takes you on hike up the 11-flight circular staircase to the top, for spectacular views. The cathedral is known for presenting outstanding musical events and important speakers. The free **New Year's Eve concert** draws thousands of New Yorkers; so, too, does its annual **Blessing of the Animals,** held in early October (see the "Calendar of Events" in chapter 2). Call ☎ **212/662-2133** for event information and tickets.

If you need a snack after your tour, stop into the lovely, worn **Hungarian Pastry Shop,** 1030 Amsterdam Ave., between 110th and 111th streets (☎ **212/866-4230**), a favorite among Columbia University students. Order a plateful of crumbly, buttery cookies from the display case up front, then set up camp; this is another place you won't be rushed out of.

Flatiron Building. 175 Fifth Ave. (at 23rd St.). Subway: R to 23rd St.

This triangular masterpiece was one of the first skyscrapers. Its knife-blade wedge shape is the only way the building could fill the triangular property created by the intersection of Fifth Avenue and Broadway, and that happy coincidence created one of the city's most distinctive buildings. Built in 1902 and fronted with limestone and terra cotta (not iron), the Flatiron measures only 6 feet across at its narrow end. So called for its resemblance to the laundry appliance, it was originally named the Fuller Building, then later "Burnham's Folly" (since folks were certain that architect Daniel Burnham's 21-story structure would fall down). It didn't. There's no observation deck, and the building mainly houses publishing offices, but a few shops do grace the ground floor. The building's existence has served to name the neighborhood around it—the Flatiron District, home to a bevy of smart new restaurants and shops (see "Manhattan's Neighborhoods in Brief" in chapter 4 for more on the surrounding 'hood).

Ford Foundation Building. 320 E. 43rd St. (at Second Ave.). ☎ **212/573-5000.** Subway: 4, 5, 6, 7, S to 42nd St./Grand Central.

On your way to or from the United Nations, stop in the Ford Foundation Building for a stroll in its magnificent interior garden (open to the public weekdays from 9am to 5pm). The ⅓-acre landscape thrives with a small pond, greenery, and full-grown trees rising up under the 12-story glass-enclosed greenhouse. This is a fine example of what modern public spaces should be like. As if the Kevin Roche design weren't pleasing enough, a visit would be in order if only for the peace it affords.

New York Public Library. Fifth Ave. and 42nd St. ☎ **212/869-8089** (exhibits and events) or 212/661-7220 (library hours). www.nypl.org. Free admission to all exhibitions. Main Reading Room and exhibition halls, Mon and Thurs–Sat 10am–6pm, Tues–Wed 11am–6pm. Subway: B, D, F, Q to 42nd St.; 4, 5, 6, 7, S to Grand Central/42nd St.

The New York Public Library, adjacent to Bryant Park (see "Central Park & Other Parks & Places to Play" below) and designed by Carrère & Hastings (1911), is one of the country's finest examples of beaux arts architecture, a majestic structure of white Vermont marble with Corinthian columns and allegorical statues. Before climbing the broad flight of steps to the Fifth Avenue entrance, take note of the famous lion sculptures—*Fortitude* on the right, and *Patience* on the left—so dubbed by whip-smart former mayor Fiorello La Guardia. At Christmastime they don natty wreaths to keep warm.

This library is actually the **Humanities and Social Sciences Library,** only one of the research libraries in the New York Public Library system. The interior is one of the finest in the city and features **Astor Hall,** with high arched marble ceilings and grand staircases. The stupendous **Main Reading Rooms** have now reopened after a massive restoration and modernization that both brought them back to their stately glory and moved them into the computer age (goodbye, card catalogs!).

Even if you don't stop in to peruse the periodicals, you may want to check out one of the **exhibitions,** which can range from "The Drawings of Charles Addams" to "Netherlandish Prints at the New York Public Library" to a private collection of 17th-century maps, atlases, charts, and globes. There's also a full calendar of **lecture programs,** with past speakers ranging from Tom Stoppard to Cokie Roberts; popular speakers often sell out, so it's a good idea to purchase tickets in advance.

There are three other research libraries in the NYPL system: The **Schomburg Center for Research in Black Culture,** at 515 Malcolm X Blvd. in Harlem (☎ 212/491-2200); the high-tech **Science, Industry, and Business Library,** 188 Madison Ave., 34th Street (☎ 212/592-7700); and the **New York Public Library for the Performing Arts,** normally located at 40 Lincoln Center Plaza (☎ 212/870-1630), but the collection is currently housed in different locations as the building undergoes renovations. Call the general number or visit the Web site to locate branch libraries throughout the five boroughs.

Roosevelt Island Tramway. Departing Second Ave. at 60th St. ☎ 212/832-4543. www.rioc.com. $1.50 each way; seniors and disabled travelers pay 1 way only; children under 5 ride free. Sun–Thurs 6am–2am, Fri–Sat 6am–3:30am. Departures every 7½ minutes during rush hours; every 15 minutes at other times. Subway: 4, 5, 6 to 59th St.; N, R to Lexington Ave.

Gliding 250 feet over the East River, alongside the 59th Street Bridge, you have a unique view of Midtown Manhattan. On the other side of the 4- to 5-minute ride is Roosevelt Island, a small strip of land two miles in length and at most 800 feet wide. The eerie ruins of a hospital haunt the south end, where lunatics, criminals, and other undesirables were exiled in the 19th and early 20th centuries. Today, the island is a planned community with spacious parks, city views, and a few historic buildings—and, on average, a much higher class of tenant.

St. Patrick's Cathedral. Fifth Ave. (btw. 50th and 51st sts.) ☎ 212/753-2261. Free admission. Mon–Fri and Sun 7am–8:30pm, Sat 8am–8:30pm. Mass Mon–Fri 7, 7:30, 8, and 8:30am, noon, and 12:30, 1, and 5:30pm; Sat 8 and 8:30am, noon, and 12:30 and 5:30pm; Sun 7, 8, 9, and 10:15am, noon, and 1, 4, and 5:30pm. Subway: B, D, F, Q to 47–50th sts./Rockefeller Center.

The largest Catholic cathedral in the United States is also the seat of the Archdiocese of New York. The congregation is still presided over by John Cardinal O'Connor, who received a special dispensation to continue past the age of retirement from Pope John Paul II. Designed by James Renwick, begun in 1858, and consecrated in 1878, St. Patrick's wasn't completed until 1906. Strangely, Irish Catholics picked one of the city's WASPiest neighborhoods for this Gothic church, constructed of white marble and stone. Look for Mother Elizabeth Seton, the first American-born saint, among the statues in the nave.

Spanish and Portuguese Synagogue (Congregation Shearith Israel). 2 W. 70th St. (at Central Park West). ☎ 212/873-0300. Free admission. Call synagogue for service schedule. Subway: 1, 2, 3, 9, B, C to 72nd St.

This is the oldest Jewish congregation in the United States, dating back to 1654, when the first refugees fleeing the Spanish Inquisition arrived in New Amsterdam. The interior of the 1897 classic revival building is impressive, especially for the Tiffany windows. The congregation follows Sephardic tradition.

Temple Emanu–El. 1 E. 65th St. (at Fifth Ave.). ☎ 212/744-1400. www.emanuelnyc.org. Free admission. Daily 10am–5pm. Services Sun–Thurs 5:30pm, Fri 5:15pm, Sat 10:30am. Subway: 6 to 68th St.; N, R to Fifth Ave.

Many of New York's most prominent and wealthy families are members of this congregation, housed in the city's most famous synagogue. The largest Reform synagogue in the world is a blend of Moorish and Romanesque styles, symbolizing the mingling of Eastern and Western cultures. The **Bernard Museum** houses a small but remarkable collection of Judaica, including a collection of Hanukkah lamps with examples ranging from the 14th to the 20th centuries. There are also three galleries telling the story of the congregation Emanu–El from 1845 to the present.

7 Organized Sightseeing Tours

Reservations are required on some of the tours listed below, but even if they're not it's always best to call ahead to confirm prices, times, and meeting places.

DOUBLE-DECKER BUS TOURS

Taking a narrated sightseeing tour is one of the best ways to see and learn quickly about New York's major sights and neighborhoods. However, keep in mind that the commentary is only as good as the guide, who is seldom an expert. Tour guides tend toward hyperbole, and might get a few of the facts wrong. Clyde Haberman of the *New York Times* recently found tour-bus guides spouting the following inaccuracies: 65 people were killed in the World Trade Center blast (it was 6); New York has the oldest subway system in the world (third, behind London's—41 years before New York—and Boston's, the first in the U.S.); Frank Sinatra was born in Jersey City (it was Hoboken); and Herald Square was named after the founder of the *New York Herald Tribune* (there was no Mr. Herald). But the idea is to see the highlights, not write a dissertation from this stuff. So enjoy the ride—and take the "facts" you hear along the way with a grain of salt.

✪ **Gray Line New York Tours.** In the Port Authority Bus Terminal, Eighth Ave. and 42nd St. ☎ **212/397-2600.** www.graylinenewyork.com. Hop-on, hop-off bus tours from $22 adults, $13 children 5–11; basic full-city tour $33 adults, $21 children. Check Web site for online booking discounts (10% at press time). Operates daily. Subway: A, C, E to 42nd St.

Gray Line offers just about every sightseeing tour option and combination you could want. There are double-decker bus tours by day and by night that run uptown, downtown, and all around the town, as well as bus combos with Circle Line cruises, helicopter flights, museum entrances, and guided visits of sights. Two-day options are available, as are some out-of-town day trips (even a full day at Woodbury Commons, if you can't resist an opportunity for outlet shopping).

There's no real point to purchasing some combination tours—you don't need a guide to take you to the top of the World Trade Center or to the Statue of Liberty, and you don't save any money on admission by buying the combo ticket—but others, such as the Sunday Harlem Gospel tour, which features a tour of Harlem's top sights and a gospel service, is well worth the $33 price tag ($24 for kids 5–11). I've found Gray Line to put a higher premium on accuracy than the other big tour-bus operators, so this is your best bet among the biggies. There's also a sales office in the **Times Square Visitors Center,** 1560 Broadway, between 46th and 47th streets.

New York Apple Tours. Eighth Ave. at 53rd St.; tours also depart from 3 other stops in midtown. ☎ **800/876-9868** (information) or 212/944-9200 (reservations). Multi-tour booking discounts available. www.nyappletours.com. Hop-on, hop-off bus tours from $21 adults, $12 children under 12; full-city tour $35 adults, $22 children. 10% discount if tickets purchased in advance with major credit card. Operates daily. Subway: C, E to 50th St.

This company operates a smaller slate of tours than competitor Gray Line, all aboard double-decker buses, but they do have a few twists, such as a tour of Brooklyn's major attractions. Most tours allow you to hop on and off as much as you like along your purchased route for two days. New York Apple is the least reliable when it comes to the facts, so I suggest sticking with Gray Line instead.

HARBOR CRUISES

If you'd like to sail the New York Harbor aboard the 1885 cargo schooner *Pioneer,* see the listing for South Street Seaport & Museum earlier in this chapter, under "Historic Lower Manhattan's Top Attractions."

⊙ Circle Line Sightseeing Cruises. Departing from Pier 83, at W. 42nd St. and Twelfth Ave. and Pier 16 at South Street Seaport. ☎ **212/563-3200.** Also departing from Pier 16 at South Street Seaport, 207 Front St. ☎ **212/630-8888.** www.circleline.com. Cruises from $12 adults, $6 children under 12; 3-hour Full Island cruise $22 adults, $12 children. Operates daily. Subway to Pier 83: A, C, E to 42nd St. Subway to Pier 16: J, M, Z, 2, 3, 4, 5 to Fulton Street.

Circle Line is the only tour company that circumnavigates the entire 35 miles around Manhattan, and I love this ride. It takes three hours and passes by the World Trade Center, the Statue of Liberty, Ellis Island, the Brooklyn Bridge, the United Nations, Yankee Stadium, the George Washington Bridge, and more, including Manhattan's wild northern tip. The panorama is riveting, and the commentary isn't bad. The big boats are basic but fine, with lots of deck room for everybody to enjoy the view. Snacks, soft drinks, coffee, and beer are available on-board for purchase.

If three hours is more than you or the kids can handle, go for either the 1½-hour **Semi-Circle** or **Sunset** cruise ($18 adults, $10 kids), both of which show you the highlights of the skyline. There's also a 1-hour **Seaport Liberty** version ($12 adults, $6 kids) that sticks close to the south end of the island. But of all the tours, the kids might like **The Beast** best, a thrill-a-minute speedboat ride offered in summer only ($15 adults, $10 kids).

In addition, a number of adults-only **Music Cruises** are regularly on offer in summer. Depending on the night of the week, you can groove to the sounds of jazz, Latin, gospel, or a DJ spinning dance tracks as you sail along the skyline. Call, check the Web site, or stop into the sales office in the Times Square Visitors Center, 1560 Broadway (between 46th and 47th streets), for details.

New York Waterway. Most tours departing from Pier 78, at W. 38th St. and Twelfth Ave. (Free bus pickup from 3 midtown locations.) ☎ **800/533-3779**. www.nywaterway.com. Cruises from $11.50 adults, $5.50 children under 13. 90-min harbor cruises $18 adults, $9 children. Operates daily late Mar–Dec; limited service Jan–Mar. Subway: A, C, E to 42nd St.

New York Waterway offers similar 1½-hour narrated cruises to those offered by Circle Line. Their primary cruise is a **New York Harbor** trip showcasing the skyline's highlights **Twilight** cruises are also offered from May to November, including Broadway show tune and disco versions that the kids are welcome on (unlike Circle Line's themed cruises). Additionally, New York Waterways offers a **Lower Harbor** cruise, a short-and-sweet, 45-minute tour around the Statue of Liberty, the Brooklyn Bridge, and lower Manhattan, from Pier 17 at South Street Seaport. Land-and-sea combo packages are also available with New York Apple Tours (see "Double-Decker Bus Tours" above).

Their city cruises may have little that's new to offer, but New York Waterways also offers two exceptional day-long Hudson River cruises (from May to November; $60 per person), which combine with historic sightseeing in the Hudson River Valley: the **Sleepy Hollow Cruise,** featuring a working 17th-century Dutch-Colonial farm and then Sunnyside, the riverside home of Washington Irving; and the **Kykuit Cruise,** which includes a tour of Kykuit, a Rockefeller family estate that's a Hudson Valley gem. There's also a two-hour **North Hudson** river-only cruise ($15 adults, $8 kids) that's particularly wonderful in early autumn. The Kykuit Cruise is immensely popular and must be reserved well in advance. You can also spend the day at the beach at **Sandy Hook,** located in the Gateway National Recreation Area ($25 adults, $12.50 kids); this is a great way to beat the shore traffic.

Lastly, you can pair a cruise with a ball game by taking either the **Yankee Clipper** or the **Mets Express** from various points in Manhattan to the stadium; call or go online for details.

Spirit Cruises. Departing from Pier 61 (at Chelsea Piers), W. 23rd St. ☎ **212/727-2789.** 2 to 2½-hour lunch cruises $26.65–$33.80; 3-hour dinner cruises $50.70–$61.40. Inquire about children's rates. Operates daily May–Nov. Subway: C, E to 23rd St.

Spirits Cruises' three modern ships are floating cabarets that combine sightseeing in New York Harbor with freshly prepared meals, musical revues, and dancing to live bands. The atmosphere is festive and fun, and a touch more relaxed than aboard World Yacht (below). The buffet meals are nothing special, but they're fine.

If you live or are staying outside of the city, there's no need to drive in to board your cruise. Spirit cruises also depart from Lincoln Harbor Marina in Weehawken, NJ; call ☎ **201/867-6201** for details.

✪ **World Yacht.** Departing from Pier 81, at W. 41st St. and Twelfth Ave. ☎ **800/498-4270** or 212/630-8100. 3-hour dinner cruise $67 per person Mon–Thurs, $75–$79 Fri–Sat; 2-hour brunch cruise $39.95 per person. Dinner cruises daily Apr–Dec, weekends only Jan–Mar; brunch cruises Wed and Sat–Sun May–Oct, Sun only Mar–May and Nov–Dec. Subway: A, C, E to 42nd St.

If you want a more elegant cruise than what Spirit offers, go with World Yacht. They offer dressy, high-quality cruises with a touch of class and fair-to-middling continental cuisine. Still, come for the experience, which is romantic to the max. There's a 2-hour Sunday brunch cruise with live piano music, and a 3-hour dinner cruise featuring a 4-course meal, live entertainment, dancing, and spectacular views. A great way to celebrate a special occasion. You can buy yourself a higher level of food, seating, and service with Ambassador Service ($25 extra per person). A jacket is required at dinner, and sneakers and jeans aren't permitted at any time.

AIR TOURS

Liberty Helicopters. Departing from VIP Heliport at W. 30th St. and Twelfth Ave., or the Downtown Heliport on Pier 6. ☎ **212/967-6464,** 212/967-4550, or 212/487-4777. www. libertyhelicopters.com. Pilot-narrated tours $46–$159. VIP heliport daily 9am–9pm (last flight 8:30pm); Downtown heliport Mon–Fri 9am–7pm (last flight 6:30pm). Reservations required for 3 or more. Subway to VIP: A, C, E, to 34th St. Subway to Downtown: 2, 3 to Wall St.

How about a bird's-eye view of Manhattan? These flightseeing trips are pricey, so if you only want a taste, choose your heliport carefully: 4½-minute tours from Midtown's VIP Heliport take in the USS *Intrepid,* midtown skyscrapers, and Central Park, while those from the Wall Street area's Downtown Heliport focus on the Statue of Liberty and lower Manhattan. Longer tours last 10 or 15 minutes, and the routes are similar no matter which departure point you choose. If you opt for the longest tour, you'll fly far enough uptown to take in the George Washington Bridge and Yankee Stadium. Singles or duos aren't required to book ahead, but you'll save by doing so—tickets purchased at the heliport are subject to a $5 surcharge.

SPECIALTY TOURS
✪ MUSEUMS & CULTURAL ORGANIZATIONS

The **Municipal Art Society** (☎ 212/935-3960; www.mas.org) offers excellent historical and architectural walking tours aimed at intelligent, individualistic travelers, not the mass market. Each is led by a highly qualified guide who gives insights into the significance of buildings, neighborhoods, and history. Topics range from the urban history of Greenwich Village to "Money Matters: The Interiors of Wall Street." On Wednesdays at 12:30pm, the society sponsors a free tour of **Grand Central Terminal** (call for meeting place; donations accepted). Weekday walking tours are $10, $8 for students and seniors, and reservations are not usually necessary; prices for weekend walking tours vary, and reservations are highly recommended. A full schedule of upcoming tours is available online.

The **92nd Street Y** (☎ 212/415-5628 or 212/415-5420; www.92ndsty.org) offers a wonderful variety of **walking tours,** many with featuring funky themes or behind-the-scenes visits. Subjects can range from "Diplomat for a Day at the U.N" to "Secrets of the Chelsea Hotel" to "Artists of the Meatpacking District" to "Jewish Harlem." Prices range from $18 to $60, but many include ferry rides, afternoon tea, dinner, or whatever suits the program. Guides are well-chosen experts on their subjects, ranging from highly respected historians to an East Village poet, mystic, and art critic (for "Allen Ginsberg's New York" and "East Village Night Spots"), and many routes travel into the outer boroughs. The 92nd Street Y also offers a full range of day-long **bus tours** beyond Manhattan, which are equally as compelling; prices generally range from $50 to $90. Advance registration is required for all walking and bus tours. Schedules are planned out a few months in advance, so check the Web site for tours that might interest you.

INDEPENDENT OPERATORS

One of the most highly praised sightseeing organizations in New York is ✪ **Big Onion Walking Tours** (☎ 212/439-1090; www.bigonion.com). Enthusiastic Big Onion guides (all hold an advanced degree in American history from Columbia or New York universities) peel back the layers of history to reveal the city's inner secrets. The two-hour tours are offered mostly on weekends, and subjects include the "The Bowery," "Presidential New York," "Irish New York," "Central Park," "Greenwich Village in Twilight," "Historic Harlem," and numerous historic takes on Lower Manhattan. One of the most popular programs is the "Multi-ethnic Eating Tour" of the Lower East Side, where you munch on everything from dim sum and dill pickles to fresh mozzarella. Big Onion also conducts exclusive visits to Ellis Island and Roosevelt Island. Tour prices range from $10 to $16 for adults, $8 to $14 for students and seniors. No reservations are necessary, but Big Onion strongly recommends that you call to verify schedules.

All tours offered by ✪ **Joyce Gold History Tours of New York** (☎ 212/242-5762; www.nyctours.com) are offered by Joyce Gold herself, an instructor of Manhattan history at New York University and the New School for Social Research, who has been conducting history walks around New York since 1975. Her tours can really cut to the core of this town; Joyce is full of fascinating stories about Manhattan and its people. Tours are arranged around themes like "The Colonial Settlers of Wall Street," "The Genius and Elegance of Gramercy Park," "Downtown Graveyards," and "TriBeCa: The Creative Explosion." Tours are offered most weekends March to December and last from 2 to 4 hours, and the price is $12 per person; no reservations are required. Private tours are available if you're traveling with a group.

Alfred Pommer has conducted **New York City Cultural Walking Tours** (☎ 212/979-2388) in nearly every Manhattan neighborhood for more than 15 years. He focuses on history and architecture, making the past come alive via photographs and stories. A number of his tours focus on specific subjects, like "Gargoyles in Manhattan" and "Rockefeller Center's Public Art." His 2- to 2½-hour tours take place Sundays at 2pm from March through December; the charge is $10 per person. Private tours are available at $15 per hour for one to three people or $25 per hour for four or more.

Behind the scenes is the focus of **Adventure on a Shoestring** (☎ 212/265-2663), a membership organization that offers 1¼-hour public walking tours on weekends year-round for just $5. One of the earliest entrants in the now-burgeoning walking tour market, Howard Goldberg has provided unique views of New York since 1963, exploring Manhattan's neighborhoods with a breezy, man-of-the-people style. Past tours have featured more offbeat adventures such as backstage tours of Broadway shows, visits to handwriting analysts, and lessons in flamenco dancing. If you're going to be in the city for awhile, you may want to pay the $40 membership fee for access to some of the more unusual activities. Call for reservations.

Self-proclaimed "radical historian" Bruce Kayton leads unconventional **Radical Walking Tours** (☎ 718/492-0069) to conventional tourist sights. A tour of Harlem covers the Black Panthers, the Communist Party, and Malcolm X in addition to the Apollo Theater and the Schomburg Center. A Greenwich Village tour focuses on riots, folk singers, and Prohibition, and a visit to the Lower East Side is incomplete without mention of radical Jews such as Abraham Cahan (founder of the influential newspaper *Forward* in 1897). Tour prices are $10, and tours last about 2½ hours; no reservations are required.

Harlem Spirituals (☎ 212/391-0900; www.munditickets.com/english/harlem. htm) specializes in gospel and jazz tours of Harlem that can be combined with a traditional soul food meal. A variety of options is available, including a tour of Harlem sights with gospel service, and soul food lunch (brunch on Sunday) as an add-on ($35 adults, $27 children 12 and under; $65 adults, $55 children with lunch or brunch). The Harlem jazz tour ($80 per person) includes a neighborhood tour, dinner at a family-style soul-food restaurant, and a visit to a local jazz club. Additional options include evening tours of Harlem paired with a "behind the scenes" gospel choir rehearsal. All tours leave from Harlem Spirituals' midtown office (690 Eighth Ave., between 43rd and 44th), and all transportation is included.

For 18 years Larcelia Kebe, owner of **Harlem Your Way! Tours Unlimited** (☎ 212/690-1687; www.harlemyourway.com), has been leading visitors around Harlem on bus and walking tours that take you beyond the snapshot stops at major sights (though they're all included). She shares Harlem's distinct culture—peppered with her own social commentary—on spirited tours of brownstones, churches, jazz clubs, and soul-food restaurants. Regularly scheduled tours include the Harlem "Sights and Sounds" tour, offered Monday through Saturday; the Wednesday-night "Champagne Safari to the Apollo;" the club-hopping "Champagne Jazz Safari," Friday and Saturday nights; and the Sunday Gospel Tour. Walking tours are $25 to $48 per person, and bus tours are $35 to $55. Tours generally meet at the company's home base, an 1882 brownstone at 129 W. 30th St. Custom tours are also available.

FREE NEIGHBORHOOD TOURS

The **34th Street Tour,** sponsored by the 34th Street Partnership (☎ 212/868-0521), reveals the stories behind the buildings under the guidance of architectural historian Francis Morron and architect Alan Neumann. Tours are Thursdays at 12:30pm; meet at the Fifth Avenue entrance to the Empire State Building.

The **Times Square Tour,** sponsored by the Times Square Visitors Center, 1560 Broadway, between 46th and 47th streets (☎ 212/768-1560; www.timessquarebid. org), offers a behind-the-scenes look at the Theater District's architecture, history, and current trends. Led by an actor, the tours are animated and enlightening. Tours meet at the center Friday at noon.

If you're looking to tour a specific neighborhood with an expert guide, call **Big Apple Greeter** (☎ 212/669-8159; www.bigapplegreeter.org). This non-profit organization is comprised of specially-trained New Yorkers who volunteer to take visitors around town for a free 2- to 4-hour tour of a particular neighborhood. Reservations must be made in advance, preferably at least 1 week ahead of your arrival. Big Apple Greeter is also well-suited to accommodating disabled travelers; see "Tips for Travelers with Special Needs" in chapter 2 for details.

But Was There a *Real* Puffy Shirt?

Now that *Seinfeld* lives only in syndication, Kenny Kramer, former across-the-hall neighbor of *Seinfeld* co-creator Larry David and the real-life inspiration for Cosmo Kramer ("Giddy-up!"), hopes his 3-hour **Kramer's Reality Tour for Seinfeld Fans** can fill the void. The tour starts out kind of hokey, but really gets going once you board the van (equipped with TV monitors for seeing clips of the show) and hit the road. Among the many stops are the real Monk's, Tom's Restaurant (also immortalized in song by Suzanne Vega); the office building where Elaine worked, Kramer had his coffee-table book published, and George had sex with the cleaning lady on his desk; and the vegetable stand where Kramer was banned for squeezing fruit. There's lots of trivia and entertaining anecdotes along the way, and Kenny does a good job keeping the crowd entertained. He's an official guide licensed by the city, so expect a good dose of general New York trivia, too. Tours are offered Saturday and Sunday at noon, and tickets are $37.50—a little pricey, but fun for die-hard fans and casual viewers alike. Reservations are required (☎ **800/KRAMERS** or 212/268-5525; www.kennykramer.com). Tip: Buy some soup if the Soup Nazi's open, because the pizza is less than inspiring.

The **Orchard Street Bargain District Tour,** sponsored by the Lower East Side Business Improvement District (☎ **888/VALUES-4-U** or 212/226-9010), explores the general history and long-standing retail culture of this historic neighborhood. This is a particularly good bet for bargain-hunters, who will learn all about the famous Old World shops and newer outlet stores in this discount-shopping destination. The free tours are offered Sundays at 11am from April to December, rain or shine, and no reservation is required. Meet up with the guide in front of Katz's Delicatessen, 205 E. Houston St., at Ludlow Street.

8 Central Park & Other Places to Play

✪ CENTRAL PARK

Without this miracle of civic planning, Manhattan would be a virtual unbroken block of buildings. Instead, smack in the middle of Gotham, an 843-acre natural retreat provides a daily escape valve and tranquilizer for millions of New Yorkers.

While you're in the city, be sure to take advantage of the park's many charms—not the least of which is its sublime layout. Frederick Law Olmstead and Calvert Vaux won a competition with a plan that marries flowing paths with sinewy bridges, integrating them into the natural rolling landscape with its rocky outcroppings, man-made lakes, and wooded pockets. The park's construction, between 1859 and 1870, provided much-needed employment during an economic depression and drew the city's population into the upper reaches of the island, which at that time were still quite rural. Nevertheless, designers predicted the hustle and bustle to come, and tactfully hid traffic from the eyes and ears of parkgoers by building roads that are largely hidden from the bucolic view.

On just about any day, Central Park is crowded with New Yorkers and visitors alike. On nice days, especially weekend days, it's the city's party central. Families come to play in the snow or the sun, depending on the season; in-line skaters come to fly through the crisp air and twirl in front of the bandshell; couples come to stroll or paddle the lake; dog people come to hike and throw frisbees to Bowser; and just about everybody comes to sunbathe at the first sign of summer. On beautiful days, the crowds are part of the appeal—everybody's come here to peel off their urban armor

Central Park

Alice in Wonderland statue ⑪
The Bandshell ⑭
Belvedere Castle ⑥
Bethesda Terrace
   & Bethesda Fountain ⑬
Bow Bridge ⑧
Carousel ⑱
Central Park Wildlife Center ㉒
Charles A. Dana
   Discovery Center ❶
Conservatory ⑫
Conservatory Garden ❶
The Dairy Information Center ⑲
Delacorte Clock ㉑
Delacorte Theater ⑤
Diana Ross Playground ❸
Hans Christian Anderson
   Statue ⑩
Harlem Meer ❶
Hecksher Playground ㉔
Henry Luce
   Nature Observatory ⑥
Imagine Mosaic ⑮
Loeb Boathouse ⑧
The Mall ⑯
The Obelisk
   (Cleopatra's Needle) ❹
Pat Hoffman Friedman
   Playground ❼
Park View at the Boathouse ❾
Rustic Playground ⑳
Shakespeare Garden ⑥
Spector Playground ❷
Swedish Cottage
   Marionette Theatre ⑥
Tavern on the Green ⑰
Tisch Children's Zoo ⑳
Wollman Rink ㉓

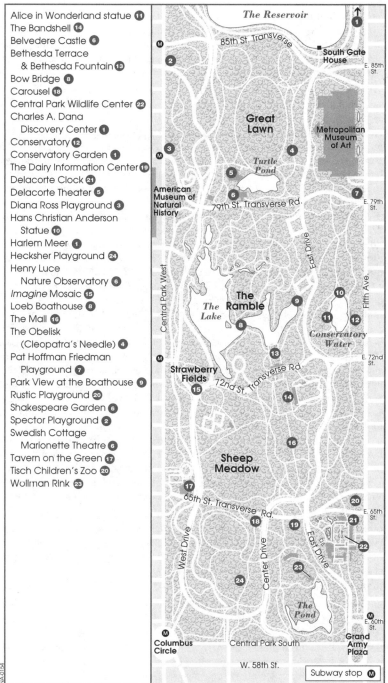

NA-0154

241

and relax, and the common goal puts a general feeling of comeraderie in the air. On these days, the people-watching is more compelling than anywhere else in the city. But one of Central Park's great appeals is that even on the most crowded days, there's always somewhere to get away from it all, if you just want a little peace and quiet, and a moment to commune with nature.

ORIENTATION & GETTING THERE   Look at your map—that great green swath in the center of Manhattan is Central Park. It runs from 59th Street (also known as Central Park South) at the south end to 110th Street at the north end, and from Fifth Avenue on the east side to Central Park West (the equivalent of Eighth Avenue) on the west side. A 6-mile rolling road, **Central Park Drive,** circles the park, and has a lane set aside for bikers, joggers, and in-line skaters. A number of **transverse** (crosstown) **roads** cross the park at major points—at 65th, 79th, 86th, and 97th streets—but they're built down a level, largely out of view, to minimize intrusion on the bucolic nature of the park.

A number of subway stops and lines serve the park, and which one you take depends on where you want to go. To reach the southernmost entrance on the west side, take an A, B, C, D, 1, or 9 to 59th Street/Columbus Circle. To reach the southeast corner entrance, take the N, R to Fifth Avenue; from this stop, it's an easy walk into the park to the Information Center in the **Dairy** (☎ **212/794-6564;** open daily 11am to 5pm, to 4pm in winter), midpark at about 65th Street. Here you can ask questions, pick up park information, and purchase a good park map. If your time for exploring is limited, I suggest entering the park at 72nd or 79th streets for maximum exposure (subway: B, C to 72nd St. or 81st St–Museum of Natural History). From here, you can pick up park information at the visitor center at **Belvedere Castle** (☎ **212/ 772-0210;** open Wed–Sun 11am–4pm), mid-park at 79th Street. There's also a third Visitor Center at the **Charles A. Dana Discovery Center** (☎ **212/ 860-1370;** open daily 11am–5pm, to 4pm in winter), at the northeast corner of the park at Harlem Meer (subway: 2, 3 to Central Park North/110th St.). The Dana Center also hosts workshops, music programs, and park tours, and lends fishing poles for fishing in Harlem Meer (park policy is catch-and-release).

Food carts and vendors are set up at all of the park's main gathering points, selling hot dogs, pretzels, and ice cream, so finding a bite to eat is never a problem. You'll also find a fixed food counter at the **Conservatory,** on the east side of the park north of the 72nd Street entrance, and both casual snacks and more sophisticated dining at **Park View at the Boathouse** (for details on this and **Tavern on the Green,** see chapter 6).

GUIDED TOURS   **Trolley tours** of the park are offered weekdays from May through November; call ☎ 212/397-3809 for details. The Dana Center hosts ranger-guided tours on occasion (☎ **212/860-1370**). Also consider a private walking tour; many of the companies listed under "Organized Sightseeing Tours" earlier in this chapter offer guided tours.

FOR FURTHER INFORMATION   Call the main number at ☎ **212/360-3444** for recorded information, or 212/794-6564 to talk to a real person at the Dairy Information Center. The park also has a comprehensive Web site that's worth checking out before you go at **www.centralpark.org**.

SAFETY TIP   Even though the park has the lowest crime rate of any of the city's precincts, be wary, especially in the more remote northern end. It's a good idea to avoid the park entirely after dark, unless you're heading to one of the restaurants for dinner or to a Summerstage or Shakespeare at the Park event (see chapter 9), when you should stick with the crowds. For more safety tips, see "Playing It Safe" in chapter 4.

EXPLORING THE PARK

The best way to see Central Park is to wander along the park's 58 miles of winding pedestrian paths, keeping in mind the following highlights.

Before starting your stroll, stop by the **Information Center** in the Dairy, midpark in a 19th-century–style building overlooking Wollman Rink at about 65th Street, to get a good park map and other information on sights and events, and to peruse the kid-friendly exhibit on the park's history and design.

The southern part of Central Park is more formally designed and heavily visited than the relatively rugged and remote northern end. Not far from the Dairy is the **carousel** with 58 hand-carved horses (open daily 10:30am to 6pm, to 5pm in winter; rides are 90¢); the zoo (see "Central Park Wildlife Center" below), and the Wollman Rink for roller- or ice-skating (see "Activities" below).

The **Mall,** a long formal walkway lined with elms shading benches and sculptures of sometimes forgotten writers, leads to the focal point of Central Park, **Bethesda Fountain** (along the 72nd Street transverse road). **Bethesda Terrace** and its grandly sculpted entryway border a large **lake** where dogs fetch sticks, rowboaters glide by, and dedicated early-morning anglers try their luck at catching carp, perch, catfish, and bass. You can rent a rowboat at or take a gondola ride from **Loeb Boathouse,** on the eastern end of the lake (see "Activites" below). Boats of another kind are at **Conservatory Water** (on the east side at 73rd Street), a stone-walled pond flanked by statues of both **Hans Christian Andersen** and **Alice in Wonderland.** On Saturdays at 10am, die-hard yachtsmen race remote-controlled sailboats in fierce competitions following Olympic regulations. (Sorry, model boats aren't for rent.)

If the action there is too intense, **Sheep Meadow** on the southwestern side of the park is a designated quiet zone, where Frisbee throwing and kite flying are as energetic as things get. Another respite is **Strawberry Fields,** at 72nd Street on the West Side. This memorial to John Lennon, who was murdered across the street at the Dakota apartment building (72nd Street and Central Park West, northwest corner), is a gorgeous garden centered around an Italian mosaic bearing the title of the lead Beatle's most famous solo song, and his lifelong message: IMAGINE. In keeping with its goal of promoting world peace, the garden has 161 varieties of plants, donated by each of the 161 nations in existence when it was designed in 1985. This is a wonderful place for peaceful contemplation.

Bow Bridge, a graceful lacework of cast-iron designed by Calvert Vaux, crosses over the lake and leads to the most bucolic area of Central Park, the **Ramble.** This dense 38-acre woodland with spiraling paths, rocky outcroppings, and a stream is the best spot for bird-watching and feeling as if you've discovered an unimaginably leafy forest right in the middle of the city.

North of the Ramble, **Belvedere Castle** is home to the **Henry Luce Nature Observatory** (☎ 212/772-0210), worth a visit if you're with children. From the castle, set on Vista Rock (the park's highest point at 135 feet), you can look down on the **Great Lawn,** which has emerged lush and green from renovations, and the **Delacorte Theater,** home to Shakespeare in the Park (see chapter 9). The small **Shakespeare Garden** south of the theater is scruffy, but it does have plants, herbs, trees, and other bits of

Where's Balto?

The people at Central Park say that the question they're asked almost more than any other these days is "Where is the statue of Balto?" The heroic dog is just northwest of the zoo, mid-park at about 66th Street.

greenery mentioned by the playwright. Behind the Belvedere Castle is the Swedish **Cottage Marionette Theatre** (☎ **212/988-9093**), hosting various marionette plays for children throughout the year; call to see what's on.

At the northeast end, **Conservatory Garden** (at 105th Street and Fifth Avenue), Central Park's only formal garden, is a magnificent display of flowers and trees reflected in calm pools of water. (The gates to the garden once fronted the Fifth Avenue mansion of Cornelius Vanderbilt II.) **Harlem Meer** and its boathouse were recently renovated, and look beautiful. The boathouse now berths the **Dana Discovery Center** (☎ **212/860-1370**), where children learn about the environment and borrow fishing poles at no charge; see "Orientation & Getting There" under "Central Park & Other Places to Play" earlier in this chapter for further details.

GOING TO THE ZOO

Central Park Wildlife Center/Tisch Children's Zoo. At Fifth Ave. and E. 64th St. ☎ **212/861-6030.** www.wcs.org/zoos. Admission $3.50 adults, $1.25 seniors, 50¢ children 3–12, under 3 free. Apr–Oct, Mon–Fri 10am–5pm, Sat–Sun 10:30am–5:30pm; Nov–Mar, daily 10am–4:30pm. Subway: N, R to Fifth Ave.

It has been nearly a decade since the zoo in Central Park was renovated, making it in the process both more human and more humane. Lithe sea lions frolic in the central pool area with beguiling style. The gigantic but graceful polar bears (one of whom, by the way, made himself a true New Yorker when he began regular visits with a shrink) glide back and forth across a watery pool that has glass walls through which you can observe very large paws doing very smooth strokes. The monkeys seem to regard those on the other side of the fence with knowing disdain. In the hot and humid Tropic Zone, large colorful birds swoop around in freedom, sometimes landing next to nonplussed visitors.

Because of its small size, the zoo is at its best with its displays of smaller animals. The indoor, multi-level Tropic Zone is a real highlight, its steamy rainforest home to everything from black-and-white Colobus monkeys to Emerald tree boa constrictors to a leaf-cutter ant farm. So is the large penguin enclosure in the Polar Circle, which is better than the one at San Diego's Sea World. In the Temperate Territory, look for the Asian red pandas (cousins to the big black-and-white ones), which look like the world's most beautiful raccoons. Despite their pool and piles of ice, however, the polar bears still look sad.

The entire zoo is good for short attention spans; you can cover the whole thing in 1½ to 3 hours, depending on the size of the crowds and how long you like to linger. It's also very kid-friendly, with lots of well-written and -illustrated placards that older kids can understand. For the littlest ones, there's the $6-million **Tisch Children's Zoo.** With pigs, llamas, potbellied pigs, and more, this new (in fall 1997) petting zoo and playground is a real blast for the five-and-under set.

ACTIVITIES

The 6-mile rolling road circling the park, **Central Park Drive,** has a lane set aside for bikers, joggers, and in-line skaters. The best time to use it is when the park is closed to traffic: Monday to Friday 10am to 3pm (except Thanksgiving to New Year's) and 7 to 10pm. It's also closed from 7pm Friday to 6am Monday, but when the weather is nice, the crowds can be hellish.

BIKING   Off-road mountain biking isn't permitted; stay on Central Park Drive or your bike may be confiscated by park police.

You can rent 3- and 10-speed bikes as well as tandems in Central Park at the **Loeb Boathouse,** midpark near 74th Street and East Drive (☎ **212/861-4137** or 517-3623); at **Metro Bicycles,** 1311 Lexington Ave., at 88th Street (☎ **212/427-4450**);

at **Pedal Pushers,** 1306 Second Ave., between 68th and 69th streets (☎ **212/ 288-5592**); and at **Toga Bike Shop,** 110 West End Ave., at 64th Street (☎ **212/ 799-9625**).

Bite of the Big Apple Tours (☎ **212/606-2270**) conducts leisurely 2-hour guided bicycle tours of the southern half of Central Park daily. The price is $30 adults and $20 children 15 and under, including bicycle rental.

BIRD WATCHING   Because New York is on the Atlantic flyway, Central Park is one of the top birding places in the country, drawing an impressive number and variety of birds. To add to your "life list," bring your binoculars to the wooded **Ramble** for the best birding. Bird-watching walks are organized by the **urban park rangers** (☎ **888/NYPARKS** or 212/360-1406) and the **New York City Audubon Society** (☎ **212/691-7483**). For recorded information on what has been seen where, call the **Rare Bird Alert** at ☎ **212/979-3070.**

BOATING   From spring to fall, gondola rides and canoe rentals are available at the **Loeb Boathouse,** midpark near 74th Street and East Drive (☎ **212/517-3623**). Rentals are $10 for the first hour, $2.50 every 15 minutes thereafter, and a $30 deposit is required.

HORSE-DRAWN CARRIAGE RIDES   At the entrance to the park at 59th Street and Central Park South, you'll see a line of **horse-drawn carriages** waiting to take passengers on a ride through the park or along certain of the city's streets. Horses belong on city streets as much as chamber pots belong in our homes. You won't need me to tell you how forlorn most of these horses look; if you insist, a ride is about $50 for two for a half-hour, but I suggest skipping it.

IN-LINE SKATING   Central Park is the city's most popular place for blading. See the top of this section for details on Central Park Drive, main drag for skaters. On weekends, head to West Drive at 67th Street, behind Tavern on the Green, where you'll find trick skaters weaving through an NYRSA slalom course at full speed, or the Mall in front of the bandshell (above Bethesda Foutain) for twirling to tunes. In summer, **Wollman Rink** converts to a hot-shot roller rink, with half-pipes and lessons available (see "Ice Skating" below).

You can rent skates for $15 a day weekdays and $25 a day weekends from **Blades East,** 160 E. 86th St. (☎ **212/996-1644**), and **Blades West,** 120 W. 72nd St. (☎ **212/787-3911**), April to October. Wollman also rents in-line skates for park use at similar rates.

ICE SKATING   Central Park's **Wollman Rink,** at 59th Street and Sixth Avenue (☎ **212/396-1010**), is the city's best outdoor skating spot. It's open for skating generally from mid-October to mid-April, depending on the weather. Rates are $7 for adults, $3.50 for seniors and kids under 12, and skate rental is $3.50; lockers are available.

PLAYGROUNDS   Nineteen Adventure Playgrounds are scattered throughout the park, perfect for jumping, sliding, tottering, swinging, and digging. At Central Park West and 81st Street is the **Diana Ross Playground,** voted the city's best by *New York* magazine. Also on the west side is the **Spector Playground,** at 85th Street and Central Park West, and, a little farther north, the **Wild West Playground** at 93rd Street. On the east side is the **Rustic Playground,** at 67th Street and Fifth Avenue, a delightfully landscaped space rife with islands, bridges, and big slides; and the **Pat Hoffman Friedman Playground,** right behind the Metropolitan Museum of Art at East 79th Street, is geared towards older toddlers.

RUNNING   Marathoners and wannabes regularly run in Central Park along the 6-mile **Central Park Drive,** which circles the park (run toward traffic to avoid being mowed down by wayward cyclists and in-line skaters). For a shorter loop, try the mid-park 1.58-mile track around the **Reservoir,** recently renamed for Jacqueline Kennedy Onassis, who often enjoyed a jog here (keep your eyes ready for spotting Madonna and other famous bodies). It's safest to jog only during daylight hours and where everybody else does. Avoid the small walks in the Ramble and at the north end of the park.

TENNIS Of the 50 or so municipal tennis courts maintained by the New York City Parks Department, Central Park's 30 Har-Tru outdoor courts are the best. The verdant setting is beautiful and the atmosphere friendly, making it easy to find a partner. Single-play is generally $5; call the **Central Park Tennis Center** at ☎ 212/280-0201 for more information. Courts are assigned on a first-come, first-served basis by sign-up sheets put out every half-hour for the next hour's play. When the U.S. Open is in town, stop by to try to catch the athletes warming up already-hot backhands.

OTHER PARKS

For parks in Brooklyn and Queens, see "Highlights of the Outer Boroughs" later in this chapter. For more information on these and other city parks, point your Web browser to **www.ci.nyc.ny.us/html/dpr.**

Battery Park. From State Street to New York Harbor. Subway: N, R to Whitehall St.; 1, 9 to South Ferry; 4, 5 to Bowling Green.

As you traverse Manhattan's concrete canyons, it's sometimes easy to forget you're actually on an island. But here, at Manhattan's southernmost tip, you get the very real sense that just out past Liberty, Ellis, and Staten islands is the vast Atlantic Ocean.

The 21-acre park is named for the cannons built to defend residents after the American Revolution. **Castle Clinton National Monument** (the place to purchase tickets for the Statue of Liberty and Ellis Island ferry; see section 2 earlier in this chapter) was built as a fort before the War of 1812, though it was never used as such. You'll most likely recognize Battery Park for the prominent role it played in *Deperately Seeking Susan,* Madonna's first movie. Besides the requisite T-shirt vendors and hot-dog carts, you'll find several statues and memorials scattered throughout the park. This is quite the civilized park, with lots of STAY OFF THE GRASS! signs and Wall Streeters eating deli sandwiches on the many park benches. Pull up your own bench for a good view out across the harbor.

Bryant Park. Behind the New York Public Library, at Sixth Ave. between 40th and 42nd sts. Subway: B, D, F, Q to 42nd St.; 7 to Fifth Ave.

Another success story in the push for urban redevelopment, Bryant Park is the latest incarnation of a 4-acre site that was, at various times in its history, a graveyard and a reservoir. Named for poet and *New York Evening Post* editor William Cullen Bryant (look for his statue on the east end), the park actually rests atop the New York Public Library's many miles of underground stacks. Another statue is also notable: a squat and evocative stone portrait of Gertrude Stein, one of the few outdoor sculptures of women in the city.

This simple green swath, just east of Times Square, is welcome relief from midtown's concrete, taxi-choked jungle, and good weather attracts brownbaggers from neighboring office buildings. Just behind the library is **Bryant Park Grill** (☎ 212/840-6500), an airy bistro with New American food and service that doesn't live up to its fine setting (or high prices). Still, the grill's two summer alfresco restaurants—**The Terrace,** on the Grill's roof; and the casual **Cafe,** with small tables beneath a canopy of trees—are worth a peek if you're in the park on a nice day.

Additionally, the park plays host to New York's **Seventh on Sixth** fashion shows, set up in billowy white tents (open to the trade only) in the spring and fall. If you're visiting in summer, bring a picnic supper to the free Monday-night **Bryant Park Film Festival,** where you'll see classic and kitschy flicks under the stars—just like a drive-in, but without the car. Call ☎ **212/512-5700** for this season's film schedule.

✪ **Union Square Park.** From 14th to 17th sts., btw. Park Ave. South and Broadway. Subway: L, N, R, 4, 5, 6 to 14th St./Union Sq.

Here's a delightful place to spend an afternoon. Reclaimed from drug dealers and abject ruin in the late '80s, Union Square Park is now one of the city's best assets. The seemingly endless subway work should no longer be disturbing the peace by the time you're here. This patch of green remains, with or without the construction, the focal point of the newly fashionable Flatiron and Gramercy Park neighborhoods. Don't miss the grand equestrian statue of George Washington at the south end or the bronze statue (by Bartholdi, the sculptor of the Statue of Liberty) of the marquis de Lafayette at the eastern end, gracefully glancing toward France.

This charming square is now best known as the site of New York's premier **Green-market.** Every Monday, Wednesday, Friday, and Saturday, vendors come down from upstate, Long Island, and as far away as Pennsylvania to hawk fresh veggies and fruits, organic baked goods, cider, wine, and even fresh fish and lobsters in booths that flank the north and west sides of the square. Fresh-cut flowers and plants are also for sale, as are books and postcards. During summer and fall, you can graze the bazaar and easily assemble a cheap and healthy lunch to munch under the trees, or at the picnic tables at the park's north end. Musical acts regularly play the small pavilion at the north end of the park, and in-line skaters take over the market space in the after-work hours. At the north end of the park, a small cafe called **Luna Park** (☎ **212/475-8464**) is open in warm weather. A number of hip restaurants and superstores rim the small park—so on a nice day, pop in to **Barnes & Noble** superstore for a book or a magazine, stop into the **Virgin Megastore** for some new tunes for your walkman, pick a bench in the park, and you'll be happy as a clam for a few hours.

Washington Square Park. At the southern end of Fifth Ave. (where it intersects Waverly Place btw. Macdougal and Wooster sts.). Subway: A, B, C, D, E, F, Q to West 4th St./Washington Sq.

You'll be hard-pressed to find much "park" in this mainly concrete square—once a burial ground in the late 18th century—but it's undeniably the focal point of Greenwich Village. Chess players, skateboarders, street musicians, New York University students, gay and straight couples, the occasional film crew, and not a few homeless people compete for attention throughout the day, and most of the night. (If anyone issues a friendly challenge to play you in the ancient and complex Chinese game of Go, don't take any of them up on it—you'll lose money.)

The lively scene belies a macabre past. Once marshland traversed by Minetta Brook, it became in 1797 a potter's field (most green and fertile downtown parks were originally graveyards), and the remains of some 10,000 bodies are buried here. In the early 1800s the square, or more specifically the infamous Hanging Elm in the northwest corner where MacDougal Street meets the park, was used for public executions. It wasn't until the 1830s that the elegant Greek Revival town houses on Washington Square North known as "The Row" (note especially nos. 21–26) attracted the elite. Stanford White designed Washington Arch (1891–92) to commemorate the centenary of George Washington's inauguration as first president. While in the neighborhood, peek down charming MacDougal Alley and Washington Mews, both lined with delightful old carriage houses.

Despite a city cleanup and increased police presence, it's a good idea to stay out of the park after dark.

CHELSEA PIERS

One of the city's biggest—and most successful—private urban development projects of the last few years has been the 30-acre **Chelsea Piers Sports and Entertainment Complex** (☎ 212/336-6666; www.chelseapiers.com). Jutting out into the Hudson River on four huge piers between 17th and 23rd streets, it's a terrific multi-functional recreational facility.

The ✪ **Sports Center** (☎ 212/336-6000), a three-football-fields-long mega-facility, does health clubs one better. It offers not only the usual cardiovascular training, weights, and aerobics but also a four-lane, quarter-mile indoor running track, a boxing ring, basketball courts, a sand volleyball court, a gorgeous 25-yard indoor pool with a whirlpool and sundeck, the world's most challenging rock-climbing wall plus a bouldering wall, and the **Origins Feel-Good Spa** (☎ 212/336-6780), which offers massage, reflexology, facials, and the like. Day passes to the Sports Center are $36 for nonmembers; spa treatments are extra, of course.

The **Golf Club** (☎ 212/336-6400), has 52 all-weather, fully automated hitting stalls on four levels, and a 200-yard net-enclosed turf fairway jutting out over the water, the Piers is the best place in the city to hit a few. It's $15 for 100 balls at off-peak hours, $15 for 68 balls at peak times; club rentals are $2 each, or $3 for five.

The **Sky Rink** (☎ 212/336-6100), the city's latest ice spot, has twin around-the-clock indoor rinks for recreational skating and pickup hockey games with Hudson River views. Skating is $10.50 for adults, $8 for seniors and kids; skate rental is $5.

If wheels are your thing, there are two outdoor **Roller Rinks** (☎ 212/336-6200) for in-line skating and roller hockey games. General skating is $5 for adults, $4 for kids; skate rentals are $13.50 for adults, $8 for kids, and a $150 cash or credit-card deposit is required. The **Skate School** offers instruction if you'd like to learn.

The **Field House** (☎ 212/336-6500) is mainly for team sports, but young rock climbers will enjoy the 30-foot indoor **climbing wall,** designed to be suitable for kids as well as grown-ups. Adult open climbs are $15, and children's lessons are available. **Batting cages** are also available ($1 per 10 pitches).

Feeling like a little 10-pin tonight? State-of-the-art **AMF Chelsea Piers Bowling** (☎ 212/835-2695) offers 40 lanes of fun. Games are $6.50 per person, and shoe rental is $4.

Beyond its athletics, the complex is a destination in and of itself. The 1.2-mile **esplanade** has benches and picnic tables with terrific river views; they serve as the

Washington Square's Literary Landmarks

The square at the heart of Greenwich Village is rich with literary lore. It's become the center of bohemia and university life, but Washington Square was a bastion of patrician gentility at the turn of the century, one that resident Edith Wharton recounted in such novels as *Age of Innocence*. Edith Wharton herself lived at no. 7 **Washington Square North,** where Alexander Hamilton also resided about a century earlier. Wharton maintained a close friendship with Henry James, a fellow traveler in Manhattan's highest social circles, whose grandmother lived at no. 19, now destroyed. (The no. 19 that exists today is a different house, the numbering system having changed since James's day.) This Gilded Age setting became the inspiration for James's *Washington Square*. Most recently, Washington Square North was the fictional home of John Schuyler Moore, the turn-of-the-century crime reporter in Caleb Carr's best-seller, *The Alienist*, which transported contemporary readers back to turn-of-the-century New York.

We Can Work It Out

Your hotel doesn't have a gym, and walking around New York just isn't enough of a workout for you? Never fear: The city has a number of health clubs that are open to out-of-towners on a day-to-day basis.

For sweating with the yuppies and their personal trainers in state-of-the-art facilities, head to the **Equinox Fitness Club,** at 897 Broadway (☎ **212/780-9300**), or 344 Amsterdam Ave. (☎ **212/721-4200**), where a day pass is $36.40. A more down-to-earth, iron-pumping crowd can be found at **Crunch Fitness,** 404 Lafayette St. (☎ **212/614-0120**), 160 W. 83rd St. on the Upper West Side (☎ **212/875-1902**), and at other locations throughout Manhattan (check the Yellow Pages). Crunch charges a per-day drop-in fee of $22, and the Lafayette Street location is open 24 hours per day. And don't forget about the fabulous **Sports Center at Chelsea Piers** (directly above), the best health club in the city available to day members.

Two favorites of Midtown office workers are the **Midtown YWCA,** 610 Lexington Ave. (☎ **212/755-4500;** $15 drop-in fee), and **Vanderbilt YMCA,** 224 E. 47th St. (☎ **212/756-9600;** $20 drop-in fee), both with pools.

---

perfect vantage point for watching the *QEII* head out to sea, or the navy and Coast Guard ships sailing in for Fleet Week each May. For waterfront dining there's New York's largest microbrewery/restaurant, the **Chelsea Brewing Company** (☎ **212/336-6440**), on Pier 59, serving up very good brews and okay food on a terrific waterfront terrace.

Getting There: Chelsea Piers is accessible by taxi and the M23 crosstown bus. The nearest subway is the C and E at 23rd Street and Eighth Avenue, then pick up the M23 and walk 4 long blocks west. Another option is to take the A, C, E to 14th Street or the L train to Eighth Avenue, walk to the river, then follow the walking/riding/running path along the river north.

9 Talk of the Town: TV Tapings

The trick to getting tickets for TV tapings in this city is to be from out of town. You visitors have a much better chance than we New Yorkers; producers are gun-shy about filling their audiences with obnoxious locals, and see everybody who's not from New York as being from the heartland—and therefore their target TV audience. Whatever. This means good news for you, as long as you don't live in the city. If you do, my best advice is to use Uncle Phil's address in Boise when you send in your postcard for tickets.

If your heart's set on getting tickets to a show, be sure to request them as early as possible—six months ahead isn't too early, and even earlier is better for the most popular shows. You're usually asked to send a postcard. Always include the number of tickets you want, your preferred dates of attendance (be as flexible as you can with this one), and your address *and* phone number. Tickets are always free. The shows tend to be pretty good about trying to meet your specific date requests, but don't be surprised if Maury Povich is far more responsive than, say, Dave. And even if you send in your response extra-early, don't be surprised if tickets don't show up at your house until one or two weeks before tape date.

If you come to town without any tickets, all hope is not lost. Because they know that every ticket holder won't make it, many studios give out a limited number of standby tickets on the day of taping. If you can just get up a little early and don't mind standing in line for a couple (or a few) hours, you have a good chance of getting one. Now, the bad news: Only one standby ticket per person is allowed, so everybody who wants to get in has to get up at the crack of dawn and stand in line. And even if you get your hands on a standby ticket, it doesn't guarantee admission; they usually only start seating standbys after the regular ticketholders are in. Still, chances are good.

For additional information on getting tickets to tapings, call ☎ **212/484-1222,** the New York Convention and Visitors Bureau's 24-hour hot line. And remember—you don't need a ticket to be on the *Today* show. *Good Morning America* will also have a street-facing studio, in Times Square on Broadway between 43rd and 44th streets, by the time you read this—but it will be on the second floor (just like the MTV studios across the street, at 1515 Broadway), so you won't be able to peer in.

Cosby Tapings of this legendary funnyman's CBS sitcom are Thursdays at 4 and 7:30pm at Kaufman-Astoria Studios in Queens, and you must be 16 or older to attend. Send a postcard requesting tickets to *Cosby* Tickets, c/o Kaufman Astoria Studios, 34-12 36th St., Astoria, NY 11106 (☎ **718/706-5389**).

If you do attend a taping, be sure to bring a sweater, even in winter. As anybody who watches Letterman knows, it's an icebox in those studios. And bring ID, as proof of age may be required.

The Daily Show with Jon Stewart Comedy Central's boldly irreverent, often hilariously funny mock newscast tapes every Monday through Thursday at 5:45pm, at 513 W. 54th St. Call ☎ **212/586-2477** at least 2 months in advance (no postcards), or check with them on Fridays for any cancellation tickets for the upcoming week.

Late Night with Conan O'Brien Conan tix might not quite have the cachet of a Dave ticket yet, but they're a hot commodity nevertheless—so start planning now. Tapings are Tuesday through Friday at 5:30pm (plan on arriving by 4:45pm if you have tickets), and you must be 16 or older to attend. Send your postcard to NBC Tickets/*Late Night*, 30 Rockefeller Plaza, New York, NY 10112 (☎ **212/664-3056,** 212/664-3057 or 212/664-4000). Fifty same-day standby tickets are distributed at the page desk at NBC Studios at 30 Rockefeller Plaza at 9am, but come much earlier if you actually want to get one.

The Late Show with David Letterman Here's the most in-demand TV ticket in town—so planning nine months ahead isn't too soon. Tapings are Monday through Thursday at 5:30pm (arrive by 4:15pm), with a second taping Thursday at 8pm (arrive by 6:45pm). You must be 16 or older to attend. Send your postcard at least six months early (two tickets max; one request only, or all will be disregarded), to *Late Show* Tickets, Ed Sullivan Theater, 1697 Broadway, New York, NY 10019 (☎ **212/ 975-5853**). On tape days, call ☎ **212/247-6497** at 11am for standby tickets (no in-line standbys anymore); start dialing early, because the machine will kick in as soon as all standbys are gone.

Live! with Regis and Kathie Lee Here's the *other* hottest ticket in town. Tapings of this popular couple are Monday to Friday at 9am at the ABC Studios at 7 Lincoln Square (Columbus Avenue and West 67th Street) on the Upper West Side. You must be 10 or older to attend (under 18s must be accompanied by a parent). Send your postcard (four tickets max) a *full year* in advance to *Live!* Tickets, Ansonia Station, P.O. Box 777, New York, NY 10023-0777 (☎ **212/456-3054** or 212/456-3537). Standby tickets are sometimes available. Arrive at the studio no later than 8am and request a standby number; they're handed out on a first-come, first-served basis, so earlier is better. You might also have a chance at last-minute tickets by calling ☎ **212/ 456-2410** or 212/456-3055, but this is a longer shot than standby.

The Maury Show   Tapings of Maury Povich's talkfest are generally Tuesday through Thursday at 8:30am and 11:30am, at 15 Penn Plaza, 33rd Street between Seventh Avenue and Broadway. You must be 18 or over to attend. Mr. Connie Chung doesn't exactly have the best ratings in town, so getting in isn't that difficult; just call ☎ 212/244-7545.

The Montel Williams Show   Tapings are generally Wednesday and Thursday at 10:30am and 1:30 and 3:30pm, at 356 W. 58th St. You must be 18 or older to attend. Order tickets by calling ☎ 212/989-8101.

The Ricki Lake Show   Tapings are generally Tuesday at 1pm, Wednesday and Thursday at 3pm and 5:30pm, and Friday 1pm and 3pm. You must be 18 or older to attend. Order tickets by sending a postcard one month in advance to the *Ricki Lake Show*, 226 W. 26th St. 4th Floor, New York, NY 10001 (☎ 800/GO-RICKI or 212/352-3322; e-mail requests: rltickets@aol.com). Standby tickets are usually available 1 to 1½ hours before taping; just show up at the studio, 26th Street and Seventh Avenue (call to confirm that a taping is on first).

The Rosie O'Donnell Show   Rosie is so popular right now that ticket requests have been suspended at press time. Take heart, however, because they're scheduled to start up again by the time you read this. The schedule varies, but in general Rosie tapings are Monday through Thursday at 10am and Wednesday at 2pm. No children under 5 are allowed, and under 18s must be accompanied by an adult. Send your postcard a year in advance (two per request) to NBC Tickets/ *The Rosie O'Donnell Show,* 30 Rockefeller Plaza, Suite 800E, New York, NY 10112 (☎ 212/506-3288 or 212/664-4000). Standby tickets, if available, are distributed at 7:30am outside 30 Rockefeller Plaza, on 49th Street side of the building; it's a random lottery system, so it doesn't help to show up too early.

The Sally Show   You can see Sally Jesse Raphaël in action twice daily Monday through Wednesday (usually 10am and 3pm), at 15 Penn Plaza, 33rd Street between

Celluloid Moments

There are so many streets and sites that recall movie scenes in this town that I couldn't recount them all without writing an encyclopedia. For the best celluloid overview, try Woody Allen's **Hannah and Her Sisters,** in which the Woodman gives us, via Sam Waterston, a wonderful tour of city highlights (notably omitting the Empire State Building; even Woody, as Mia Farrow would no doubt agree, can make a mistake).

One unforgettable Manhattan movie memory, an icon in modern times, took place at the northwest corner of 52nd Street and Lexington Avenue: Above a subway grate—there's still one there—a great white dress billowed up on the fine young form of Marilyn Monroe. (Monroe was still Mrs. Joe DiMaggio at the time of filming; word is that the very public filming of this revealing scene gave the late Yankee Clipper more than a touch of agita.) To relive the moment on screen, rent the wonderful comedy **The Seven-Year Itch.**

More recently, the Upper West Side got the Hollywood treatment in the Tom Hanks–Meg Ryan romantic comedy **You've Got Mail.** Moviegoers will find that much of the neighborhood—in which filmmaker Nora Ephron really lives—will look familiar, from famous grocer Zabar's to the 91st Street Garden in Riverside Park. To relive a movie moment, stop in to **Cafe Lalo,** on West 83rd Street between Broadway and Amsterdam Avenue (☎ 212/496-6031), where Meg Ryan's character nervously awaits her first face-to-face meeting with her cyberbeau.

Seventh Avenue and Broadway. You must be 18 or older to attend. Call ☎ **800/411-7941** or 212/244-3595 for tickets.

Saturday Night Live Everything about the show may change, but one thing remains the same—SNL's enduring popularity. This is another extremely hard ticket to come by. Tapings are Saturdays 11:30pm (arrival time 10pm); there's also a full dress rehearsal (arrival time 7pm). You must be 16 or older to attend. Send your postcard to arrive *in the month of August only* to NBC Tickets/*Saturday Night Live*, 30 Rockefeller Plaza, New York, NY 10112 (☎ **212/664-4000**). Lotteries for pairs of tickets are held during the season; if you're a winner, you'll be notified with only one to two weeks' advance notice. Standby tickets may be a better bet: They're available at 9:15am on Saturday morning of tape day at the 49th Street entrance to Rockefeller Plaza.

Spin City Taping days vary for Michael J. Fox's hit sitcom, but filming always takes place at Pier 61 at Chelsea Piers, 23rd Street and the Hudson River. You must be 18 or older to attend. Send your request (two tickets max) at least 4 weeks in advance to *Spin City* Tickets, London Terrace Post Office, P.O. Box 20241, New York, NY 10011-0003 (☎ **212/336-6993**). Since ticket requests are often suspended early in the season, standbys may be a better bet: Show up at the studio by 5pm on tape day; standby tix are handed out at 6:45pm. Taping begins at 7:30pm and generally lasts four hours. Call for the current taping schedule.

The *Today* Show As most of you know, anybody can be on TV with Katie, Matt, and cuddly weatherman Al Roker. All you have to do is show up outside the *Today* show's glass-walled studio at Rockefeller Center, on the southwest corner of 49th Street and Rockefeller Plaza, with your very own HI, MOM! sign. Tapings are Monday through Friday at 7am sharp, but come at the crack of dawn if your heart's set on being in front. Who knows? If it's a nice day, you may even get to chat with Katie, Matt, or Al in a segment.

The View ABC's girl power gabfest tapes live Monday through Friday at 11am, and you must be at least 18 to attend. Requests, which should be send about 3 to 4 months in advance, can be submitted online (**www.abc.go.com/theview**) or via postcard to Tickets, *The View*, 320 W. 66th St., New York, NY 10023 (☎ **212/579-1167**). Since date requests are not usually accommodated, try standby: Arrive before 10am and put your name on the standby list; earlier is better, since tickets are handed out on a first-come, first-served basis.

10 Especially for Kids

You don't have to worry about how you'll keep your kids occupied in New York. This action-packed, neon-bright urban jungle has always been able to keep kids enthralled. These days, it's better than ever for the under-16 set—just ask Disney, which has turned Times Square into a pint-sized person's paradise. For general tips and other resources for visiting the city with the kids, see "For Families" under "Tips for Travelers with Special Needs" in chapter 2.

Some of New York's sights and attractions are designed specifically with kids in mind, and I've listed those below. But many of those I've discussed in the rest of this chapter are terrific for kids as well as adults; I've also included cross-references to the best of them below.

Probably the best place of all to entertain the kids is in ✪ **Central Park,** which has kid-friendly diversions galore, including the **Central Park Wildlife Center** with its **Tisch Children's Zoo** for the little ones; rides aboard magical old-fashioned **carousel;** canoe rides on the lake at **Loeb Boathouse;** the statue of heroic movie pup **Balto;** and

19 separate playgrounds, including the **Diana Ross Playground,** voted the city's best by *New York* magazine. For details on all of Central Park's delights, see the section earlier in this chapter.

MUSEUMS

In addition to the museums designed specifically for kids below, also consider the following, discussed elsewhere in this chapter: The **American Museum of Natural History** (p. 212), whose dinosaur displays are guaranteed to wow both you and the kids; the *Intrepid* **Sea-Air-Space Museum** (p. 221), on a real battleship with an amazing collection of vintage and high-tech airplanes; the **Forbes Magazine Galleries** (p. 220), whose wacky collection includes a number of vintage toys and games; the **Museum of Television & Radio** (p. 226), where you and the kids can pull up episodes of *Sesame Street* and other classic kids' TV shows to watch; the **American Museum of the Moving Image** (p. 264), where you and the kids can learn how movies are actually made; the **Lower East Side Tenement Museum** (p. 222), whose living-history approach really intrigues school-age kids; the **New York Transit Museum** (p. 262), where kids can explore vintage subway cars and other hands-on exhibits; and the **South Street Seaport & Museum** (p. 202), which little ones will love for its theme park–like atmosphere and old boats bobbing in the harbor.

Children's Museum of the Arts. 182 Lafayette St. (btw. Broome and Grand sts.). ☎ **212/ 941-9198** or 212/274-0986. Admission $4 weekdays, $5 weekends for adults under 65 and children over 18 months. Wed noon–7pm, Thurs–Sun noon–5pm. Subway: B, D, G, Q to Broadway–Lafayette St.; 6 to Spring St.

Interactive workshop programs for children 18 months to 10 years are the attraction here. Kids dabble in puppet making and computer drawing or join in sing-alongs and live performances, which may include improvisational storytelling from "The Brothers Grin." Call for the current schedule.

✪ **Children's Museum of Manhattan.** 212 W. 83rd St. (btw. Broadway and Amsterdam Ave.). ☎ **212/721-1234.** www.cmom.org. Admission $5 children and adults, $2.50 seniors. Wed–Sun 10am–5pm. Subway: 1, 9 to 86th St.

Here's a great place to take the kids when they're tired of being told not to touch. Designed for kids 2 to 12, this museum is strictly hands-on. Interactive exhibits and activity centers encourage self-discovery—and a recent expansion means that there's now more than ever before to keep the kids busy and learning. The Time Warner Media Center takes children through the world of animation and helps them produce their own videos. Brand-new in 1999 is the Body Odyssey, a zany, scientific journey through the human body (just like Will Robinson on *Lost in Space* or *Sabrina the Teenage Witch,* depending what TV generation you belong to). This isn't just a museum for the five-and-up set—there are exhibits especially designed for babies and toddlers, too. The busy schedule also includes daily art classes and storytellers, and a full slate of entertainment on weekends.

New York City Fire Museum. 278 Spring St. (btw. Varick and Hudson sts.). ☎ **212/ 691-1303.** www.nyfd.com/museum.html. Suggested donation $4 adults, $2 seniors and students, $1 children under 12. Tues–Sun 10am–4pm. Subway: C, E to Spring St.; 1, 9 to Houston St.

What's better than fire trucks when you're a little kid? Not much. If your kids are like my nephew, they will *love* this museum. Housed in a real three-story 1904 firehouse, this museum displays include vintage fire trucks and equipment all the way back to the horse-drawn days. Look for the leather hoses, fire boats, poles, bells, Currier & Ives prints, and even a stuffed firehouse dog. Tours with an emphasis on fire safety are available for small groups by calling ahead.

☼ **New York Hall of Science.** 4701 111th St., in Flushing Meadows–Corona Park, Queens. ☎ **718/699-0005.** www.nyhallsci.org. Admission $6 adults, $4 children and seniors; free Thurs–Fri 2–5pm. Mon–Wed 9:30am–2pm, Thurs–Sun 9:30am–5pm. Subway: 7 to 111th St.

Children of all ages will love this huge, hands-on museum, which bills itself as New York's only Science Playground. This place is amazing for school-age kids—it's just like Beakman's World come to life. Exhibits let them be engulfed by a giant soap bubble (shades of Veruca Salt, Mom and Dad?), float on air in an antigravity mirror, compose music by dancing in front of light beams, and explore the more-than-miniature world of microbes. There are even video machines that kids can use to retrieve astronomical images, including pictures taken by the *Galileo* in orbit around Jupiter. There's even a Preschool Discovery Place for the really little ones. But probably best of all is the summertime Outdoor Science Playground for kids six and older—ostensibly lessons in physics, but really just a great excuse to laugh, jump, and play on jungle gyms, slides, seesaws, spinners, and more.

The museum is located in **Flushing Meadows–Corona Park,** where kids can enjoy even more fun beyond the Hall of Science. Not only are there more than 1,200 acres of park and playgrounds, but there's also a zoo, a carousel, an indoor ice-skating rink, an outdoor pool, and bike and boat rentals. Kids and grown-ups alike will love getting an up-close look at the Unisphere steel globe, which was not really destroyed in *Men in Black.* The park is also home to the **Queens Museum of Art** (see "Highlights of the Outer Boroughs," below) as well as Shea Stadium and the U.S. Open Tennis Center.

Sony Wonder Technology Lab. Sony Plaza, 550 Madison Ave. (at 56th St.). ☎ **212/833-8100.** Free admission. Tues, Wed, Fri, Sat 10am–6pm; Thurs 10am–8pm; Sun noon–6pm. Subway: 4, 5, 6 to 59th St.; E, F, to Fifth Ave.

Not as much of an infomercial as you'd expect. Both kids and adults love this high-tech science and technology center, which explores communications and information technology. You can experiment with robotics, explore the human body through medical imaging, edit a music video, mix a hit song, design a video game, and save the day at an environmental command center. The lab also features the first high-definition interactive theater in the United States.

THEATER FOR KIDS

The theater scene for kids is flourishing. There's so much going on that it's best to check *New York* magazine, *Time Out New York,* or the Friday *New York Times* for current listings. Besides larger-than-life Broadway shows, the following are some dependable entertainment options.

The **New Victory Theater,** 209 W. 42nd St. (☎ 212/382-4020), reopened a few years back as the city's first full-time family-oriented performing-arts center and has offered such events as a colorful performance by the Fred Garbo Inflatable Theater Co. that incorporated gymnastics, dance, juggling, and magic into one amusing show.

The **Paper Bag Players,** called "the best children's theater in the country" by *Newsweek,* perform funny tales for children 4 to 9 in a set made from bags and boxes, in winter only, at Hunter College's Sylvia and Danny Kaye Playhouse, 68th Street between Park and Lexington avenues (☎ 212/362-0431 or 212/772-4448).

TADA!, 120 W. 28th St. (☎ 212/627-1732), is a youth ensemble for kids ages 5 to 12 that performs musicals and plays with a multiethnic perspective for family audiences.

Also, don't forget the **Swedish Cottage Marionette Theatre,** which puts on marionette shows for kids at its Central Park theater; see "Central Park" earlier in this chapter for details.

OTHER KID-FRIENDLY DIVERSIONS

In addition to the choices below, don't forget New York's fabulous theme restaurants, which are all playgrounds unto themselves for visiting kids; see "Theme Restaurant Thrills!" in chapter 6.

ZOOS & AQUARIUMS   Bigger kids will love the legendary **Bronx Zoo** (p. 258), while the **Central Park Wildlife Center** with its Tisch Children's Zoo (p. 244) is particularly suitable to younger kids. At the **New York Aquarium** at Coney Island (p. 262), kids can touch starfish and sea urchins and watch bottlenose dolphins and California sea lions stunt-swim in the outdoor aquatheater.

SKY-HIGH VIEWS   Kids of all ages can't help but turn dizzy with delight incredible views from atop the **Empire State Building** (p. 228) and the **World Trade Center** (p. 203). The Empire State Building also offers the **New York Skyride,** which offers a stomach-churning virtual tour of New York—just in case the real one isn't enough for them.

SHOPPING   Everybody loves to shop in New York—even kids. Don't forget to take them to **Books of Wonder,** that temple of sneakerdom **Niketown,** and **FAO Schwarz,** the best toy store in the world—just ask Tom Hanks (remember *Big?*). See chapter 8 for details.

SPECIAL EVENTS   Children's eyes grow wide at the year-long march of **parades** (especially Macy's Thanksgiving Day Parade), **circuses** (Big Apple, and Ringling Bros.and Barnum & Bailey), and **holiday shows** (the Rockettes' Christmas and Easter performances). See the "Calendar of Events" in chapter 2 for details.

11 Attractions in Upper Manhattan

The area north of 110th Street, Upper Manhattan is comprised of **Harlem,** the country's most famous and fabled African-American community, and its northern neighbors, **Washington Heights** and **Inwood.** This area is drawing crowds of visitors who once trod only the usual Midtown precincts.

You can find in these pages much of what you need to know about Upper Manhattan's sights. Still, since distances between the attractions are long, and there are some unsafe areas between them. Therefore, I recommend that all visitors, especially first-timers, join a group tour; a number of good tours of Harlem and the rest of Upper Manhattan are discussed under "Organized Sightseeing Tours" earlier in this chapter.

IN HARLEM

Over the past several years, the press has heralded the Second Harlem Renaissance. With all kinds of new projects in the works or on the boards, the neighborhood—from about 110th Street to 155th Street, from about St. Nicholas Avenue to the East River—has begun to dispel its reputation as a symbol of declining urban America. Those who've lived in Harlem for many years no doubt find this talk a little suspect and remember that much of what's being "discovered" has been there all along. Nonetheless, there's truth in the notion that the neighborhood has become a kind of "sleeper" hit—rediscovered first by visitors (especially Europeans and Japanese) and now by New Yorkers who head up on weekends to its music clubs, something few would've even thought of just a few years ago.

Harlem has always had more than its share of historic treasures. To find the treasures that still grace Harlem, pay a call on the **Astor Row Houses,** 130th Street between Fifth and Lenox avenues, a fabulous series of 28 redbrick town houses built in the 1880s and graced with wooden porches, generous yards, and ornamental ironwork.

Equally impressive is **Strivers' Row,** West 138th to 139th street, between Adam Clayton Powell Jr. and Frederick Douglass boulevards, a group of 130 houses built in 1891 by a man named David King, who'd already developed the base of the Statue of Liberty and the original Madison Square Garden. On the north side of 139th Street are neo-Italian Renaissance residences by McKim, Mead & White. Across the street are Georgian-inspired homes. Once the original white owners had moved out, these lovely houses attracted the cream of the Harlem population, the "strivers" (hence the name) like Eubie Blake and W. C. Handy.

Handsome brownstones, limestone town houses, and row houses are sprinkled atop **Sugar Hill,** 143rd to 155th streets, between St. Nicholas and Edgecombe avenues, named for the "sweet life" enjoyed by its residents. At 409 Edgecombe Ave. lived such prominent people as W. E. B. Du Bois.

Besides its bounty of architectural wealth, Harlem has several important cultural institutions. The **Schomburg Center for Research in Black Culture,** 515 Malcolm X Blvd., between 135th and 136th streets (☎ **212/491-2200;** www.nypl.org; open Monday to Wednesday noon to 8pm, Thursday to Saturday 10am to 6pm, and Sunday 1 to 5pm; admission free), is a research branch of the New York Public Library that played a central role in the Harlem Renaissance. Arthur Schomburg, a Puerto Rican black, set himself to accumulating materials about blacks in America, and his collection is now housed and preserved here. The center hosts changing exhibits related to black culture, such as "Black New York Artists of the 20th Century," and performing arts events. Make an appointment—it'll be worth your while—to see the 1930s murals by Harlem Renaissance artist Aaron Douglas.

The **Studio Museum,** 144 W. 125th St. (☎ **212/864-4500;** open Wednesday to Friday 10am to 5pm, Saturday and Sunday 1 to 6pm; admission $5 adults, $3 seniors and students, $1 children under 12), is devoted to the historical and contemporary works fo black artists. It also exhibits historic photographs of Harlem and has in its permanent collection fascinating works by James VanDerZee of the Harlem Renaissance. Both places offer a variety of special concerts, readings, and the like.

The legendary **Apollo Theater,** 253 W. 125th St. (☎ **212/749-5838**), which launched or abetted the careers of so many musical icons (Bessie Smith, Billie Holiday, Dinah Washington, Duke Ellington, Count Basie, Aretha Franklin) and is in large part responsible for the development and worldwide popularization of African-American music, was reserved for whites only until relatively late in Harlem history. It wasn't until 1934 that blacks were allowed into the audience. Since the 1980s, after years of deterioration, it has been revived, especially its famous Wednesday Amateur Night at the Apollo show at 7:30pm. For more, see the entry under "Major Concer Halls & Landmark Venues" in chapter 9.

In a mixed blessing for the congregations, **Sunday-morning gospel services** at Harlem's many churches have become so popular that bus tour groups sometimes outnumber parishioners. At **Abyssinian Baptist Church,** 132 W. 138th St., between Seventh and Lenox avenues (☎ **212/862-7474**), services are at 9 and 11am. Another resounding service takes place at the **First Corinthian Baptist Church,** 1912 Seventh Ave., at West 116th Street (☎ **212/864-5976**), at 11am. Remember these are religious services first, not gospel shows.

Another essential aspect of Harlem is its food, and it doesn't get any better than what drifts out of the soulful kitchens of **Sylvia's Restaurant** (see chapter 6). If the devil gets the better of you, try the sinfully sweet but heavenly glazed donuts at **Georgie's,** 50 W. 125th St.

Upper Manhattan Attractions

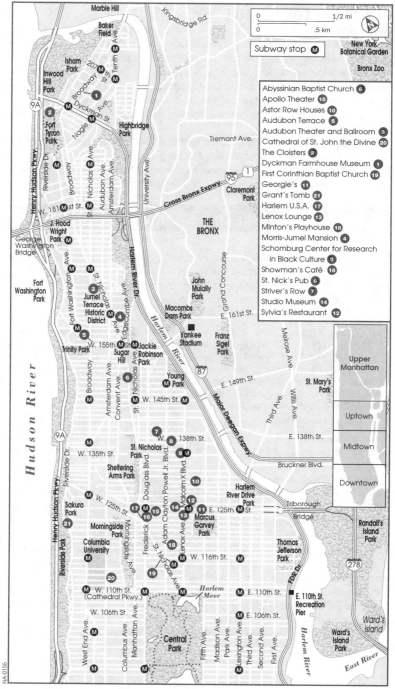

Subway stop Ⓜ

New York Botanical Garden

Bronx Zoo

Abyssinian Baptist Church ⑧
Apollo Theater ⑮
Astor Row Houses ⑩
Audubon Terrace ⑤
Audubon Theater and Ballroom ③
Cathedral of St. John the Divine ⑳
The Cloisters ②
Dyckman Farmhouse Museum ①
First Corinthian Baptist Church ⑲
Georgie's ⑪
Grant's Tomb ㉑
Harlem U.S.A. ⑰
Lenox Lounge ⑬
Minton's Playhouse ⑱
Morris-Jumel Mansion ④
Schomburg Center for Research
    in Black Culture ⑨
Showman's Café ⑯
St. Nick's Pub ⑥
Striver's Row ⑦
Studio Museum ⑭
Sylvia's Restaurant ⑫

Upper Manhattan

Uptown

Midtown

Downtown

IN WASHINGTON HEIGHTS

North of Harlem is Washington Heights, 155th Street to Dyckman Street, a neighborhood whose westernmost fringe, past Broadway and to the Hudson, is a quiet residential district with many attractive art deco and faux Tudor apartment houses. (East of Broadway, the neighborhood is often inappropriate for foot tourism.) For most travelers, the main attraction here is the **Cloisters** (see "More Manhattan Museums" earlier in this chapter), the Metropolitan Museum of Art's Uptown branch housing a magnificent medieval art collection in a complex that incorporates authentic medieval architecture.

The **Jumel Terrace Historic District,** west of St. Nicholas Avenue, between 160th and 162nd streets, is centered on the **Morris-Jumel Mansion,** while in adjacent Inwood is the Dutch Colonial **Dyckman Farmhouse Museum** (see the "In Search of Historic Homes" box earlier in this chapter).

12 Highlights of the Outer Boroughs

IN THE BRONX

In addition to the choices below, literary buffs might also want to consider the **Edgar Allan Poe Cottage,** at the Grand Concourse and East Kingsbridge Road (☎ 718/ 881-8900), the final home for the brilliant but troubled author of *The Raven, The Tell-Tale Heart,* and other masterworks. For more information, see the box called "In Search of Historic Homes" earlier in this chapter.

✪ **Bronx Zoo Wildlife Conservation Park.** Fordham Rd. and Bronx River Pkwy., the Bronx. ☎ **718/367-1010.** www.wcs.org. Admission Jan 4–Mar, $4 adults, seniors and children under 12 $2; Apr–Oct, $7.75 adults, $4 seniors and children under 12; Nov–Jan 3, $6 adults, $3 seniors and children under 12; free Wed year-round. There may be small additional charges for some exhibits. Jan–Mar daily 10am–4:30pm; Apr–Oct Mon–Fri 10am–5pm, Sat–Sun 10am–5:30pm; Nov 1–Nov 20 daily 10am–4:30pm; Nov 20–Dec 31 Sun–Thu 10am–9pm, Fri and Sat 10am–9:30pm. Transportation: See "Getting There" below.

Founded in 1899, the Bronx Zoo is the largest metropolitan animal park in the United States, with more than 4,000 animals living on 265 acres. Most of the old-fashioned cages have been replaced by more natural settings—this is quite a progressive zoo as zoos go.

One of the zoo's most impressive exhibits is the **Wild Asia Complex.** This zoo-within-a-zoo comprises the **Wild Asia Plaza** education center; **Jungle World,** an indoor re-creation of Asian forests with birds, lizards, gibbons, and leopards; and the **Bengali Express Monorail** (open May to October), which takes you on a narrated ride high above free-roaming Siberian tigers, Asian elephants, Indian rhinoceroses, and other non-native New Yorkers (keep your eyes peeled—the animals aren't as interested in seeing you). But you don't have to undertake a Peter Matthiessen–style journey to catch a glimpse of the beautiful and extremely rare (estimates indicate fewer than 1,000 in nature) snow leopard. The Bronx Zoo, where 74 cubs have been born, has re-created a **Himalayan Highlands Habitat** that's home to some 17 snow leopards, as well as red pandas and white-naped cranes.

The **Children's Zoo** (open April to October) allows young humans to learn about their wildlife counterparts. Kids can compare their leaps to those of a bullfrog, slide into a turtle shell, climb into a heron's nest, see with the eyes of an owl, and hear with the acute ears of a fennec fox. There's also a farmlike area were children feed domestic animals.

A popular exhibit, open from spring to September, is the **Butterfly Zone,** aflutter with 1,000 colorful specimens flying all around you inside a 170-foot-long tent—

amusingly resembling a caterpillar. Call ahead to check if it will be around when you get to the zoo. New in 1999 is the **Congo Gorilla Forest,** a 6½-acre exhibit that will be home to Western lowland gorillas, okapi, red river hogs, and other African rainforest animals.

If the natural settings and breeding programs aren't enough to keep zoo residents entertained, they can always choose to ogle the 2 million annual visitors. But there are ways to beat the crowds. Try to visit on a weekday or on a nice winter's day. In summer, come early in the day, before the heat of the day sends the animals back into their enclosures. And you can always schedule an **Insider's Hour** tour (January to March and July to September) by calling ☎ **718/220-5141.**

Getting There: The easiest way to get to the Bronx Zoo is by Liberty Line's BxM11 express bus running from various stops on Madison Avenue to the park entrance; call ☎ **718/652-8400** for a schedule. By subway, take the no. 2 train to Pelham Parkway and then walk 2 blocks west.

New York Botanical Garden. 200th St. and Southern Blvd., the Bronx. ☎ **718/817-8700.** www.nybg.org. Admission $3 adults, $2 seniors and students, $1 children 2–12; free all day Wed and Sat 10am–noon. Extra charges for Everett Children's Adventure Garden, Enid A. Haupt Conservatory, and T. H. Everett Rock Garden and Native Plant Garden. Apr–Oct Tues–Sun and Mon holidays 10am–6pm; Nov–Mar Tues–Sun and Mon holidays 10am–4pm. Transportation: See "Getting There" below.

A National Historic Landmark, the 250-acre New York Botanical Garden was founded in 1891 and today is one of America's foremost public gardens. The setting is spectacular—a natural terrain of rock outcroppings, a river with cascading waterfall, hills, ponds, and wetlands.

Highlights of the Botanical Garden are the 27 **specialty gardens** (the Peggy Rockefeller formal rose garden, the Nancy Bryan Luce herb garden, and the restored rock garden are my favorites), an exceptional **orchid collection,** and 40 acres of **uncut forest** as close as New York gets to its virgin state before the arrival of Europeans. Natural exhibits are augmented by year-round educational programs, musical events, bird-watching excursions, lectures, special family programs, and many more activities. Snuff Mill, once used to grind tobacco, has a charming cafe on the banks of the Bronx River.

A major beneficiary of capital improvements in 1997 was the **Enid A. Haupt Conservatory**, a stunning series of Victorian glass pavilions that recall London's former Crystal Palace, sheltering a rich collection of tropical, subtropical, and desert plants as well as seasonal flower shows. In 1998, a brand-new **Children's Adventure Garden** debuted.

There are so many ways to see the garden—tram, golf cart, walking tours—that it's best to call for more information.

Getting There: The easiest way is by Garden Shuttle that operates weekends, April through October, between the American Museum of Natural History, the Metropolitan Museum of Art, and the Botanical Garden; call ☎ **718/817-8700** for reservations and information. By train, take Metro North (☎ **212/532-4900**) from Grand Central Terminal to the New York Botanical Garden station. By subway, take the D or 4 train to Bedford Park Boulevard and walk east 8 long blocks.

Wave Hill. 675 W. 252nd St. (at Independence Ave.), Bronx. ☎ **718/549-3200.** www.wavehill.org. Tues–Sun 9am–4:30pm; extended in summer (check ahead). Admission $4 adults, $2 seniors and students; free in winter, and on Sat mornings and Tues in summer. Transportation: See "Getting There" below.

Formerly a private estate with panoramic views of the Hudson River and the Palisades, Wave Hill has, at various times in its history, been home to a British U.N. ambassador as well as Mark Twain and Theodore Roosevelt. Its 28 acres were bequeathed to the city of New York for use as a public garden that is now one of the most beautiful spots in the city. Programs range from horticulture to environmental education, visual and performing arts, landscape history, and forestry—more than enough to justify a visit.

Getting There: Take the 1 or 9 subway to 231st St., then take Bx7 or BX10 bus at the northwest corner of 231st Street; Wave Hill is a short walk from the 252nd Street stop. Metro-North trains (☎ 212/532-4900) to the Riverdale stop, then walk up 254th Street and turn right on Independence Ave. Or take Liberty Lines' Manhattan-Riverdale Express (☎ 718/652-8400) bus BxM1 or BxM2 to 252nd Street and walk west across the parkway bridge, following the signs.

Woodlawn Cemetery. Main gate is at Webster Ave. and 233rd St., the Bronx. ☎ **718/920-0500.** Daily 9am–4:30pm. Subway: 2, 5 to 233rd St. Metro North: to Woodlawn.

This 313-acre cemetery is the final earthly mansion of F. W. Woolworth, the dime-store millionaire; Jay Gould, of the Erie and Union Pacific railroads; Fiorello La Guardia, beloved mayor of New York City, who charmed and distracted its residents by reading the comic strips over the radio during a newspaper strike; suffragist Elizabeth Cady Stanton; and jazz great Duke Ellington, to name only a few. Pick up a map at the main entrance to steer you through the extravagant mausoleums, including the one of horse lover Oliver Hazard Perry Belmont modeled after the chapel at France's Château d'Amboise.

IN BROOKLYN

For details on walking the **Brooklyn Bridge,** see "Historic Lower Manhattan's Top Attractions" earlier in this chapter.

It's easy to link visits to the Brooklyn Botanic Garden, the Brooklyn Museum of Art, and Prospect Park, since they're all an easy walk from one another, just off **Grand Army Plaza.** Designed by Frederick Law Olmsted and Calvert Vaux as a suitably grand entrance to their Prospect Park, it boasts a grand Civil War memorial arch designed by John H. Duncan (1892–1901) and the main **Brooklyn Public Library,** an art deco masterpiece completed in 1941 (the garden and museum are just on the other side of the library, down Eastern Parkway). If you don't want to walk, a **free trolley** loops the area once an hour weekends and holidays noon to 5pm; for information, call ☎ 718/965-8967. The entire area is a half-hour subway ride from midtown Manhattan.

✪ **Brooklyn Botanic Garden.** 1000 Washington Ave. (at Eastern Pkwy.), Brooklyn. ☎ **718/623-7200.** www.bbg.org. Admission $3 adults, $1.50 seniors and students, 50¢ children 6–16. Admission free Tues and Sat 10am–noon. Free tours Sat–Sun 1pm. Apr–Sept Tues–Fri 8am–6pm, Sat–Sun 10am–6pm; Oct–Mar Tues–Fri 8am–4:30pm, Sat–Sun 10am–4:30pm. Subway: 2, 3 to Eastern Pkwy./Brooklyn Museum; D to Prospect Park.

Just down the street from the Brooklyn Museum of Art (below) is the most popular botanic garden in the city. This peaceful, 52-acre sanctuary is at its most spectacular in May, when thousands of deep-pink blossoms of cherry trees are abloom. In addition to the **rose garden,** the **Shakespeare Garden** with plants mentioned in his writings, a **Children's Discovery Garden,** and the **Fragrance Garden,** designed for the blind but appreciated by all noses. Inside the Steinhardt Conservatory is the world-renowned **Bonsai Museum.** Much-needed restoration was just beginning on the extraordinary **Japanese Hill-and-Pond Garden** at press time, and is scheduled to be completed in January 2000.

✪ **Brooklyn Museum of Art.** 200 Eastern Pkwy. (at Washington Ave.), Brooklyn. ☎ **718/638-5000.** www.brooklynart.org. Suggested admission $4 adults, $1.50 seniors and students, children under 12 free. Wed–Fri 10am–5pm; first Sat of the month 11am–11pm, each Sat thereafter 11am–6pm; Sun 11am–6pm. Subway: 2, 3 to Eastern Pkwy.–Brooklyn Museum.

Brooklyn Heights Attractions

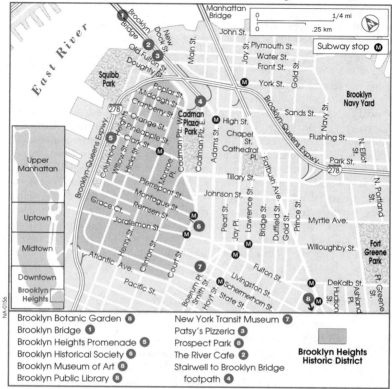

Brooklyn Botanic Garden **8**

Brooklyn Bridge **1**

Brooklyn Heights Promenade **5**

Brooklyn Historical Society **6**

Brooklyn Museum of Art **8**

Brooklyn Public Library **8**

New York Transit Museum **7**

Patsy's Pizzeria **3**

Prospect Park **8**

The River Cafe **2**

Stairwell to Brooklyn Bridge footpath **4**

Brooklyn Heights Historic District

One of the nation's premier art institutions, the Brooklyn Museum of Art rocketed back into the public consciousness with a blockbuster a couple of years ago: "Monet and the Mediterranean" attracted 225,000 visitors. It's now best known for its consistently remarkable temporary exhibitions, which have included "The Jewels of the Romanovs," "Impressionists in Winter," and "From Hip to Hip Hop: Black Fashion and the Culture of Influence," as well as its excellent permanent collection. Among the exhibitions scheduled for late 1999–2000 are "Vital Forms: American Art in the Atomic Age, 1940–1960," "Maxfield Parrish 1870–1966," and "Masterpieces of Fashion" from the museum's outstanding costume collection.

The museum's grand beaux arts building, designed by McKim, Mead & White (1897), befits its outstanding holdings, most notably the Egyptian collection of sculpture, wall reliefs, and mummies. The distinguished decorative arts collection includes 28 American period rooms from 1675 to 1928 (the extravagant Moorish-style smoking room from John D. Rockefeller's 54th Street mansion is my favorite). Other highlights are the African and Asian arts galleries, 58 works by Rodin, and a diverse collection of both American and European painting and sculpture that includes works by Homer, O'Keeffe, Monet, Cézanne, and Degas.

First Saturday is the museum's ambitious—and popular—program that takes place on the first Saturday of each month. It runs from 5 to 11pm and includes free admission and a slate of live music, films, dancing, and and other entertainment that can get pretty esoteric (think karaoke, lesbian poetry, silent film, experimental jazz, and disco dancing). Weekly **Insider's Hour** gallery talks are offered on weekends; call for schedule.

New York Aquarium. West 8th St. and Surf Ave., Coney Island, Brooklyn. ☎ **718/ 265-3400.** www.wcs.org. Admission $8.75 adults, $4.50 seniors and children 2–12, free for children under 2. Daily 10am–5pm. Subway: D, F to W. 8th St. in Brooklyn.

Because of the long subway ride (about an hour's ride from midtown Manhattan) and its proximity to the Coney Island boardwalk, this one is really for summer. The Aquarium is home to hundreds of sea creatures. Taking center stage are Atlantic bottle-nose dolphins and California sea lions that perform daily during summer at the **Aquatheater.** Also basking in the spotlight are seven beluga whales, gangly Pacific octopuses, and Bertha the sand tiger shark. Black-footed penguins, California sea otters, and a variety of seals live at the **Sea Cliffs exhibit,** a re-creation of a Pacific coastal habitat. Children love the hands-on exhibits at **Discovery Cove.** There's an indoor oceanview cafeteria and an outdoor snack bar, plus picnic tables.

If you've made the trip out, you simply must check out the human exhibits on nearby **Coney Island**'s 2.7-mile-long boardwalk. Not much is left from its heyday, and it can be a little eerie when the crowds aren't around. But you can still use the beach, drop some cash at the boardwalk arcade, and ride the famed wooden Cyclone roller coaster (still a terrifying ride, if only because it seems so . . . rickety). You can't leave without treating yourself to a Nathan's Famous hot dog (just off the boardwalk at Surf and Stillwell avenues)—this is the *original* location where the term "hot dog" was coined back in 1906.

New York Transit Museum. Boerum Place and Schermerhorn St., Brooklyn. ☎ **718/ 243-8601.** www.mta.nyc.ny.us/museum. Admission $3 adults, $1.50 seniors/children under 18, free Wed noon–4pm. Tues–Fri 10am–4pm, Sat–Sun noon–5pm. Subway: 2, 3, 4, 5 to Borough Hall; C, F to Jay St.; N, R to Court St.

This underground museum, housed in a real (decommissioned) subway station, is a wonderful place to spend an hour or so, especially if you're a transit or social history buff. The museum is small but very well done, with good multimedia exhibits exploring the history of the subway from the first shovelful of dirt scooped up at groundbreaking (March 24, 1900) to the present. Kids and parents alike will enjoy the interactive elements—you even get to lift a wheelbarrow full of rocks just like the ones that the turn-of-the-century tunnel blasters had to move—as well as the vintage subway cars, old wooden turnstiles, and beautiful station mosaics of yesteryear. All in all, a minor but remarkable tribute to an important development in the city's history, and to a time when mass transit was a thing of sophistication and civic pride—a remarkable contrast for those of us who only know the grimy MTA of today.

Prospect Park. At Grand Army Plaza, bounded by Prospect Park West, Parkside Ave., and Flatbush Ave., Brooklyn. ☎ **718/965-8951.** www.prospectpark.org. Subway: 2, 3 to Grand Army Plaza (walk down Plaza Street West 3 blocks to Prospect Park West and the entrance) or Eastern Pkwy./Brooklyn Museum.

Designed by Frederick Law Olmsted and Calvert Vaux after their great success with Central Park, this 562 acres of woodland, meadows, bluffs, and ponds is considered by many to be their masterpiece and the pièce de résistance of Brooklyn.

The best approach is from Grand Army Plaza, presided over by the monumental **Soldiers' and Sailors' Memorial Arch** (1892) honoring Union veterans. For the best view of the lush landscape, follow the path to Meadowport Arch, and proceed through to the Long Meadow, following the path that loops around it (it's about an hour's walk). Other park highlights include the 1857 Italianate mansion **Litchfield Villa** on Prospect Park West; the **Friends' Cemetery** Quaker burial ground (where Mont-gomery Clift is eternally prone—sorry, it's fenced off to browsers); the **carousel** with white wooden horses salvaged from a famous Coney Island merry-go-round; and

Lefferts Homestead (☎ 718/965-6505), a 1783 Dutch farmhouse with a museum of period furniture and exhibits geared toward children. There's a map at the park entrance that you can use to get your bearings.

On the east side of the park is the **Prospect Park Wildlife Conservation Center** (☎ 718/399-7339). Major renovations completed in 1993 have made it a thoroughly modern children's zoo where kids can walk among wallabies, explore a prairie-dog town, and much more. Admission is $2.50 for adults, $1.25 for seniors, 50¢ for children under 12, free for those under 3. April through October, it's open Monday through Friday 10am to 5pm, 5:30pm on weekends and holidays; November through March, hours are daily from 10am to 4:30pm.

✪ BROOKLYN HEIGHTS HISTORIC DISTRICT

Just across the Brooklyn Bridge is a peaceful neighborhood of tree-lined streets, more than 600 historic houses built before 1860, landmark churches, and restaurants. Even with its magnificent promenade providing sweeping views of Lower Manhattan's ragged skyline, it feels more like its own village than part of the larger urban expanse.

This is where Walt Whitman lived and wrote *Leaves of Grass,* one of the great accomplishments in American literature. And in the 19th century, fiery abolitionist Henry Ward Beecher railed against slavery at **Plymouth Church** of the Pilgrims on Orange Street between Henry and Hicks streets (his sister wrote *Uncle Tom's Cabin*). If you walk down **Willow Street** between Clark and Pierrepont, you'll see three houses (nos. 108–112) in the Queen Anne style that was fashionable in the late 19th century, as well as an attractive trio of Federal-style houses (nos. 155–159) built before 1829. Also visit lively **Montague Street,** the main drag of Brooklyn Heights and full of cafes and shops. And don't forget about **Patsy Grimaldi's Pizzeria,** nearby on historic Old Fulton Street, serving up the city's best pizza (see chapter 6).

GETTING THERE   Bounded by the East River, Fulton Street, Court Street, and Atlantic Avenue, the Brooklyn Heights Historic District is one of the most outstanding and easily accessible sights beyond Manhattan. The neighborhood is reachable via a number of subway trains: the A, C, F to Jay St.; the 2, 3, 4, 5 to Clark Street or Borough Hall; and the N, R to Court Street.

It's easy to link a walk around Brooklyn Heights and along its Promenade with a walk over the **Brooklyn Bridge** (p. 200), a tour that makes for a lovely afternoon on a nice day. Take a 2 or 3 train to **Clark Street** (the first stop in Brooklyn). Turn right out of the station and walk toward the water, where you'll see the start of the waterfront **Brooklyn Promenade.** Stroll along the promenade admiring both the stellar views of lower Manhattan to the left and the gorgeous multi-million-dollar brownstones to the right, or park yourself on a bench for awhile to contemplate the scene.

The promenade ends at Columbia Heights and Orange Street. To head to the bridge from here, turn left and walk toward the Watchtower Building. Before heading downslope, turn right immediately after the playground onto Middagh Street. After four or five blocks, you'll reach a busy thoroughfare, Cadman Plaza West. Cross the street and follow the walkway through little **Cadman Plaza Park;** veer left at the fork in the walkway. At Cadman Plaza East, turn left (downslope) toward the underpass, where you'll find the stairwell up to the Brooklyn Bridge footpath on your left.

IN QUEENS

For details on the **New York Hall of Science** and **Flushing Meadows–Corona Park** (also home to the Queens Museum of Art, below), see "Especially for Kids," earlier in this chapter.

☉ American Museum of the Moving Image. 35th Ave. at 36th St., Astoria, Queens. ☎ **718/784-0077** or 718/784-4777. www.ammi.org. Admission $8.50 adults, $5.50 seniors and college students, $4.50 children 5–18. Tues–Fri noon–5pm, Sat–Sun 11am–6pm. Subway: R to Steinway St.

If you truly love movies, come here instead of Planet Hollywood. Unlike Manhattan's Museum of Television and Radio (see "More Manhattan Museums" earlier in this chapter), which is more of a library, this is a thought-provoking museum examining how moving images—film, video, and digital—are made, marketed, and shown; it encourages you to consider their impact on society as well. It's housed in part of the Kaufman Astoria Studios, which once were host to W. C. Fields and the Marx Brothers, and more recently have been used by Martin Scorsese (*The Age of Innocence*), Woody Allen (*Radio Days*), Bill Cosby (his *Cosby* TV series), and *Sesame Street.* (For details on getting tickets to a *Cosby* taping, see "Talk of the Town: TV Tapings" earlier in this chapter.)

The museum's core exhibit, **"Behind the Screen,"** is a thoroughly engaging two-floor installation that takes you step-by-step through the process of making, marketing, and exhibiting moving images. There are more than 1,000 artifacts on hand, from technological gadgetry to costumes, and interactive exhibits where you can try your own hand at sound-effects editing or create your own animated shorts, among other simulations. Special-effects benchmarks from the mechanical mouth of *Jaws* to the blending of past and present in *Forrest Gump* are explored and explained. And in a nod to Hollywood nostalgia, memorabilia that wasn't swept up by the Planet Hollywood chain is displayed, including a Hopalong Cassidy lunch box, an E.T. doll, celebrity coloring books, and Dean Martin and Jerry Lewis hand puppets.

The museum hosts **film and video screenings,** usually accompanied by artist appearances, lectures, or panel discussions. Silent films are presented with live music. Free **exhibition tours** are offered Tuesday through Satuday at 3pm.

P.S. 1 Contemporary Art Center. 22–25 Jackson Ave., at 46th Ave., Long Island City, Queens. ☎ **718/784-2084.** www.queensmuse.org. Suggested admission $4 adults, $2 seniors and students. Wed–Sun noon–6pm. (Hours vary in summer, so call ahead.) Subway: E, F to 23rd St.–Ely Ave.; 7 to 45th Rd.–Court House Sq.

If you're interested in contemporary art that's too cutting–edge for most museums, don't miss P.S. 1. Reinaugurated in 1997 after a 3-year, $8.5-million renovation of the Renaissance Revival building that was originally a public school, this is the world's largest institution exhibiting contemporary art from America and abroad. You can expect to see a kaleidoscopic array of works from artists ranging from Jack Smith to Julian Schnabel; the museum is particularly well-known for large-scale exhibitions by artists such as James Turrell. In early 1999 a high-profile merger with the Museum of Modern Art was announced, so P.S. 1 should start getting the kind of attention it so richly deserves.

Queens Museum of Art. Next to the Unisphere in Flushing Meadows–Corona Park, Queens. ☎ 718/592-9700. www.queensmuse.org. Suggested admission $4 adults, $2 seniors and children, free for children under 5. Wed–Fri 10am–5pm, Sat–Sun noon–5pm. Subway: 7 to Willets Point–Shea Stadium.

One way to see New York in the shortest time (albeit without the street life) is to visit the Panorama, an enormous building-for-building architectural model of New York City complete with an airplane that takes off from La Guardia Airport. The 9,335-square-foot Gotham City is the largest model of its kind in the world, with 895,000 individual structures built on a scale of 1 inch = 100 feet. Constructed for the 1964–65 world's fair, today it mirrors most of the current cityscape thanks to a 2-year rebuilding and refurbishing in the early '90s.

13 Spectator Sports

For details on the **New York City Marathon,** see the "Calendar of Events," in chapter 2.

BASEBALL With two baseball teams in town, you can catch a game almost any day from opening day in April to beginning of playoffs in October. (Don't bother trying to get subway series tix, though—they're the hottest seats in town. Ditto for Opening Day or any playoff game.) Know that rooters for the **New York Mets** or the **New York Yankees** are fanatical and can't seem to understand why they don't win every year (perhaps a by-product of the Yankees' winning ways, which produced a 24th World Championship in 1998).

The Mets, playing at dreary **Shea Stadium** in Queens (Subway: 7 to Willets Point/Shea Stadium), haven't been as productive, but seem to warm the city's heart more when they've been successful. Prospects look bright for the Amazin' Mets now that they've acquired superstar Mike Piazza. For tickets and information, call the **Mets Ticket Office** at ☎ **718/507-8499,** or point your Web browser to **www.mets.com**.

The Yankees play at the House That Ruth Built, otherwise known as Yankee Stadium (Subway: 4, C, D to 161st St./Yankee Stadium). For tickets, call **TicketMaster** (☎ **212/307-1212** or 212/307-7171; www.ticketmaster.com) or **Yankee Stadium** (☎ **718/293-6000;** www.yankees.com). After the game, check into one of the rowdy sports bars across the street to down a brew and relive the action with fellow fans. Serious baseball fans might check the schedule and try to catch **Old Timers' Day,** usually held in July, when pinstriped stars of years past return to the stadium to take a bow. This is your chance to cheer for legends like Whitey Ford and Reggie Jackson in person.

You can decide to catch a game a couple of hours before game time, hop on the subway, and buy your tickets at the stadium. At Yankee Stadium, upper tier box seats, especially those behind home plate, give you a great view of all the action. Upper tier reserve seats are directly behind the box seats, and are significantly cheaper. Bleacher seats are even cheaper, and the rowdy commentary from that section's roughneck bleacher creatures is absolutely free. Most of the expensive seats (field boxes) are sold out in advance to season ticket holders. You can often purchase these very same seats from scalpers, but you'll pay a premium for them.

BASKETBALL Three teams call **Madison Square Garden,** Seventh Avenue between 31st and 33rd streets (☎ **212/465-6741** or www.thegarden.com; **212/307-7171** or www.ticketmaster.com for tickets; Subway: 1, 2, 3, 9, A, C, E to 34th St.), home court: Patrick Ewing and the **New York Knicks** (☎ **212/465-JUMP** or www.nba. com/ knicks), who traded crowd-pleaser John Starks for Golden State bad boy Latrell Sprewell at the start of 1999's strike-shortened season; the **New York Liberty** (www. wnba.com/ liberty), who have electrified fans with their tough-playing defense and star players—like Rebecca Lobo, Richie Audubato, and Teresa Weatherspoon—since the WNBA's inaugural season; and, in college hoops, **St. John's Red Storm.** Knicks tickets are hardest to come by, of course, so plan ahead if you want a front-row seat near first fan Spike Lee.

The hapless **New Jersey Nets** play at Continental Airlines Arena, Meadowlands Sports Complex, East Rutherford, N.J. (☎ **800/7NJ-NETS** or www.nba.com/nets; 212/307-7171 or www.ticketmaster.com for tickets). Take the NJ Transit bus from Manhattan's Port Authority Bus Terminal, Eighth Avenue between 40th and 42nd streets (☎ **212/564-8484**).

FOOTBALL Though they both play in New Jersey, both local teams, the **Jets** and the **Giants** are claimed by New York, especially after the Jets came *thisclose* to snaring a Super Bowl berth in '99. Their regular season schedule is played out from September

---

Year-Round Yankee Tip

For a taste of Yankee glory at any time of year, take the **Insider's Tour of Yankee Stadium** (☎ 718/579-4531). This official tour of the House That Ruth Built will take you out onto the field, to Monument Park, into the pressbox and the dugout. You'll even learn how to run the scoreboard and—if you're lucky—take a peek inside the clubhouse. The guide peppers the tour with lots of Yankee history and anecdotes as you go. And who knows? You might even spot that cutie Derek Jeter as you make the rounds. Tours are offered Monday through Saturday at noon (other times are available for groups of 12 or larger). Tickets are $8 for adults, $4 for seniors and kids under 14. No reservations are required; all you need to do is show up at the ballpark's press gate just before tour time, but it's still a good idea to call and confirm.

---

to December at **Giants Stadium** in the Meadowlands Sports Complex, East Rutherford, NJ (☎ 201/935-3900 or www.meadowlands.com; 212/307-7171 or www.ticketmaster.com for tickets). The best way to get to see a game is to know someone who's holding a season ticket; almost all the seats are sold out far in advance. Chances are you'll have to catch these teams from a sports bar, but if you do manage to go, the best way to get there is by New Jersey Transit bus from Manhattan's Port Authority Bus Terminal, Eighth Avenue and 41st Street (☎ 212/564-8484).

ICE HOCKEY   The **New York Rangers** play at Madison Square Garden, Seventh Avenue between 31st and 33rd streets (☎ 212/308-NYRS or www.newyorkrangers.com; Subway: 1, 2, 3, 9, A, C, E to 34th St.). The memories of the Mark Messier–led 1994 Stanley Cup team linger on, much to the chagrin of the present underachieving team, which suffered another serious blow when Wayne Gretzky retired in April 1999. Tickets are hard to get nevertheless, so plan well ahead.

The 1995 Stanley Cup Champion **New Jersey Devils** play at Continental Airlines Arena, Meadowlands Sports Complex, East Rutherford, N.J. (☎ 201/935-6050 or www.newjerseydevils.com). Take the NJ Transit bus from Manhattan's Port Authority Bus Terminal, Eighth Avenue between 40th and 42nd streets (☎ 212/564-8484).

For tickets to either Rangers or Devils games, call ☎ 212/307-7171, or point your Web browser to www.ticketmaster.com for online orders.

If you'd rather head out to the Island to see the New York Islanders, call ☎ 888/ETM-TIXS or visit **www.xice.com**.

SOCCER   The **New York/New Jersey MetroStars** play at Giants Stadium, in the Meadowlands Sports Complex, East Rutherford, N.J. (☎ 201/935-3900 for the box office, or 212/307-7171 for TicketMaster; www.metrostars.com or www.ticketmaster.com). Take the NJ Transit bus from Manhattan's Port Authority Bus Terminal, Eighth Avenue between 40th and 42nd streets (☎ 212/564-8484).

TENNIS   From late August to early September, the hottest ticket in town is to the **U.S. Open Tennis Championships** at the National Tennis Center in Flushing Meadows–Corona Park (☎ 718/760-6200 for information, or 888/673-6849 or 212/239-6200 for tickets; www.usopen.org; Subway: 7 to Willets Point/Shea Stadium). Tickets go on sale in June. While it's next to impossible to cop final-round tickets, early-round seats are relatively abundant and just as entertaining; for more ticket-scoring tips, see the "Calendar of Events" in chapter 2.

The **Chase Championships of the Corel WTA Tour** at Madison Square Garden, Seventh Avenue between 31st and 33rd streets (☎ 212/465-6741), in mid-November, attracts the top 16 singles players and top eight doubles teams.

Shopping 8

Calling New York a shopper's delight is like saying you caught a little flick last night called *Lawrence of Arabia*. An understatement, to say the least.

At first glance, the size and breadth of the city's shopping scene seems more overwhelming than anything else. The range of possibilities could test the limits of even the most die-hard shopaholic. Even as more and more big chains lay down roots in the city (what New Yorkers like to refer to as the "mallification" of Manhattan), the world's most unique crop of specialty shops continues to thrive right alongside them. From dinosaur fossils to duck eggs, platform shoes to Chanel suits, love potions to love seats—you'll find a world's worth of merchandise in the Big Apple.

1 The Top Shopping Streets & Neighborhoods

Here's a rundown of New York's most interesting shopping areas, from first-class to fabulously funky, with some highlights of each to give you a feel for the neighborhood. If addresses and phone numbers are *not* given here, refer to the store's more expanded listing by category below under "Shopping A to Z" later in this chapter.

DOWNTOWN
LOWER MANHATTAN
The Financial District and environs are home to two kinds of shopping: discount shopping à la **Century 21** department store and **J&R** for electronics galore; and mall-style retail shopping.

National chains and standard mall stores are housed in **South Street Seaport** (☎ 212/732-7678; subway: 2, 3, 4, 5 to Fulton St.) on Pier 17 and on Fulton Street, the Seaport's main cobbled drag; in the **World Financial Center** across the West Side Highway from the World Trade Center in Battery Park City (☎ 212/945-0505); and on the ground level of the **World Trade Center** (☎ 212/435-4170; subway: 1, 9, N, R to Cortlandt St.; C, E to World Trade Center). The World Trade Center makes a good bet for standards like the **Gap, Banana Republic,** and **J.Crew,** plus branches of **Coach,** the **Body Shop, Nine West** for shoes, the **Limited,** and the neighborhood's only bookstore, a terrific branch of **Borders Books & Music.**

Sales Tax

New York City sales tax is 8.25%. For the last couple of years, however, the city has experimented with a few highly successful tax-free weeks on clothing purchases of less than $500—usually in January and again in late August or early September, just before the beginning of the school year. There has been much talk about eliminating sales tax on such purchases altogether.

If you're visiting from out of state, consider having your purchases shipped directly home to avoid paying sales tax.

CHINATOWN

Don't expect to find the purchase of a lifetime on Chinatown's streets, but there's some fun browsing to be had. The fish markets along Canal, Mott, Mulberry, and Elizabeth streets are fun to browse for their bustle and exotica. Dispersed among them (especially along Canal), you'll find an astounding (and sometimes astoundingly bad) collection of knock-offs: sunglasses, designer bags, and watches. Mott Street, between Pell Street and Chatham Square, boasts the most interesting of Chinatown's off-Canal shopping, with an antique shop or two dispersed among the tiny storefronts selling blue-and-white Chinese dinnerware.

But the definite highlight of Chinatown shopping is ✪ **Pearl River Mart,** 277 Canal St., at Broadway (☎ 212/431-4770; subway: N, R to Canal St.), a three-floor Chinese mall overflowing with affordable Asian exotica, from paper lanterns to Chinese snack foods to Mandarin-collared silk pajamas to mah jongg sets to Hong Kong action videos. This fascinating place can keep you occupied for hours.

THE LOWER EAST SIDE

The bargains aren't quite what they used to be in the **Historic Orchard Street Shopping District**—which basically runs from Houston to Canal along Allen, Orchard, and Ludlow streets, spreading outward along both sides of Delancey Street—but prices on leather bags, shoes, luggage, fabrics on the bolt, and men's and women's clothes are still quite good. Be aware, though, that the hard sell on Orchard Street can be pretty hard to take. Still, the Orchard Street Bargain District is a nice place to discover a part of New York that's disappearing. Come during the week, since most stores are Jewish-owned, and therefore close Friday afternoon and all day Saturday. Sundays tend to be a madhouse.

Stop in first at the **Lower East Side's Visitor Center,** 261 Broome St., between Orchard and Allen streets (☎ 888/825-8374 or 212/226-9010; open Sun–Fri 10am–4pm; subway: F to Delancey St. or B, D, Q to Grand St.) for a shopping guide to the bargain district. There's also a free walking tour offered Sundays at 11am from April to December; see p. 240 for details.

The artists and other trendsetters who have been turning this neighborhood into a hopping club scene have also added a cutting edge to its shopping scene in recent years, too. You'll find a handful of mainly kitschy alterna-shops tucked between the bars and clubs mostly along Ludlow Street in the couple of blocks south of Houston, and also on Rivington Street. Highlights include the funky junk at **Lucky Wang,** 100 Stanton St., between Orchard and Ludlow streets (☎ 212/353-2850); **Yu,** 151 Ludlow St., between Stanton and Rivington streets (☎ 212/979-9370), a consignment shop specializing in vintage wear and Japanese designer labels; **Patch,** 155 Rivington St., between Suffolk and Clinton streets (☎ 212/533-9995), with witty new designs for young hipsters; and **Have a Seat,** 37 Clinton St, between Stanton and

Rivington streets (☎ 212/353-9550), a groovy modern furnishings store featuring wild '50s, '60s, and '70s designs.

A little farther west, the stretch of the Bowery (Third Avenue) from Canal to Houston streets is considered the "light-fixture district" for its huge selections and great bargains on light fixtures, lamps, and ceiling fans. The best of the bunch is **Lighting by Gregory,** 158 Bowery, between Delancey and Broome streets (☎ 212/226-1276).

SoHo

People love to complain about super-fashionable SoHo—it's become too trendy, too tony, too Mall of America. True, **J. Crew,** 99 Prince St. (☎ 212/966-2739), is only one of many big names that have supplanted the artists and galleries who used to inhabit its historic cast-iron buildings. But SoHo is still one of the best shopping 'hoods in the city—and few are more fun to browse. It's the epicenter of cutting-edge fashion, and still boasts plenty of unique boutiques. The streets are chock-full of tempting stores, so your best bet is to just come and browse.

SoHo's prime shopping grid is from Broadway east to Sullivan Street, and from Houston down to Broome, although Grand Street, on block south of Broome, has been sprouting shops of late. Broadway is the most commercial strip, with such recognizable names as **Pottery Barn, Victoria's Secret, Banana Republic,** and **A/X Armani Exchange.** Most compelling along here are gourmet supermarket **Dean and Deluca, Canal Jean Co.,** and **Kenneth Cole** for shoes (see "Shopping A to Z" later in this chapter).

Among the designers in residence in SoHo are **Anna Sui,** 113 Greene St. (☎ 212/941-8406), whose slinky fashions have a glammy edge; wild, colorful retro-inspired designs from golden boy **Todd Oldham,** 123 Wooster St. (☎ 212/226-4668); **Marc Jacobs,** 163 Mercer St. (☎ 212/343-1490), who has brought whole new meaning to "body-conscious" with his risqué designs; trend-busting British designs from the legendary **Vivienne Westwood,** 71 Greene St. (☎ 212/334-5200); austerely beautiful Japanese design from **Yohji Yamamoto,** 103 Grand St. (☎ 212/966-9066); pretty and playful Asian motifs from **Vivienne Tam,** 99 Greene St. (☎ 212/966-2398); Prada offshoot **Miu Miu,** 100 Prince St. (☎ 212/334-5156); plus sleek-chic from **Cynthia Rowley** and wild club clothes from Patricia Field at **Hotel Venus.** Additionally, uptown names like **Louis Vuitton,** 116 Greene St. (☎ 212/274-9090), have been migrating downtown of late.

If you're less interested in designer fashions and more interested in reasonable wearables, consider **Harriet Love,** 126 Prince St. (☎ 212/966-2280), for women who like a lacy, Stevie Nicks-ish retro look; the incomparable **Eileen Fisher**'s new flagship; and **Phat Farm** for upscale hip hop wear. Hat lovers shouldn't miss the wonderful **Hat Shop,** 120 Thompson St. (☎ 212/219-1445), a full-service milliner for women.

SoHo is also fabulous for shoes. The cobbled streets boast stores galore, from chic **Calvin Klein Shoes,** 133 Prince St. (☎ 212/505-3549), and **Omari,** 132 Prince St. (☎ 212/219-0619), to trendier styles at **Otto Tootsi Plohound,** 413 W. Broadway (☎ 212/925-8931), **Giraudon,** and **John Fluevog.**

Fashion is only half the story at **Anthropologie,** 375 W. Broadway (☎ 212/343-7070), whose funky-chic affordable wearables mix with fun gifts and home decorating items—much like Urban Outfitters for grown-ups.

High-end home stores are another huge part of the SoHo scene, from **Smith & Hawken,** at 394 W. Broadway (☎ 212/925-1190), and **Portico Bed & Bath** for fresh and fancy linens to such high-end antiques and design dealers as **Depression Modern** for glamorous art deco and **Moss** for cutting-edge industrial design. Hot potter **Jonathan Adler** has a cool new shop at 465 Broome St. (☎ 212/941-8950)—anybody who has been reading shelter mags over the last year will recognize his bold vases instantly. **Global Table,** 107 Sullivan St. (☎ 212/431-5839), is a great source for beautiful tableware from around the world (including lots of Japanese stuff), much of it affordable.

NoLiTa

Less than a handful of years ago, **Elizabeth Street** was a nondescript adjunct to Little Italy and the no-man's land east of SoHo. Today it's the grooviest shopping strip in town, star of the neighborhood known as NoLiTa. Elizabeth and neighboring Mott and Mulberry streets are dotted with an increasing number of shops between Houston and Spring streets, with a few pushing one more block south to Kenmare. It's an easy walk from the Broadway-Lafayette stop on the B, D, F, Q line to the neighborhood, since it starts just east of Lafayette Street.

This may be a burgeoning neighborhood, but don't expect cheap—NoLiTa is clearly the stepchild of SoHo. Its boutiques are largely the provence of sophisticated shopkeepers specializing in high-quality, fashion-forward products and design. Highlights include **Calypso Enfants,** 284 Mulberry St. (☎ 212/965-8910), for stylish kidswear with a tropical flair. Next door, at no. 280, is **Jade** (☎ 212/925-6544), for reinterpretations of traditional Asian and Indian fashions in sumptuous jewel-toned silks (gorgeous accessories, too). Farther down, at no. 209, is animated young fashion designer **Tracy Feith** (☎ 212/334-3097), a favorite among downtown fashionistas.

Mott Street is an accessories bonanza, with **Jamin Puech,** no. 252 (☎ 212/334-9730), for some of the most beautiful and unusual daytime and evening bags I've ever seen, all handmade in France by a husband-and-wife design team; **Sigerson Morrison** for eyepopping original shoe designs (see "Shopping A to Z" below); and **Calypso St. Barths,** no. 280 (☎ 212/965-0990), for grown-up haute island style. On Prince Street, there's **Cocoon & Co.** at no. 25 (☎ 212/966-8680) for a charmingly quirky mix of vintage housewares and contemporary gifts, and **Gates of Morocco,** at no. 8 (☎ 212/ 925-2650), for traditional Moroccan imports.

While not exactly reaching SoHo standards yet, the boutique density is most intense on Elizabeth. Offerings range from **Daily 235,** at no. 235 (☎ 212/334-9728), a candy store for artsy grown-ups, to ✪ **Shì,** no. 233 (☎ 212/334-4330), dedicated to new artists with an eye for innovation in home decor. **Area I.D.** (☎ 212/219-9903) and **Ace** (☎ 212/226-5123), vintage modern furniture neighbors at no. 262 and no. 269, both have a predisposition for sleek Danish design.

THE EAST VILLAGE

The East Village remains the international standard of bohemian hip. **Kmart,** Astor Place at 770 Broadway (☎ 212/673-1540), between 8th and 9th streets, is so out of place it's marvelous camp: Japanese kids stare and marvel at gargantuan boxes of laundry detergent as if they were Warhol designed, and the sale prices on trash food like chips and cookies are rock-bottom.

The easiest subway access is the 6 train to Astor Place, which lets you right out at Kmart and **Astor Wines & Spirits;** from here, it's just a couple blocks east to the prime hunting grounds. Note that some East Village shops don't open until 2pm, so your best bet is to come in the afternoon; most stay open until 8pm, some later.

East 9th Street between Second Avenue and Avenue A has become one of my favorite shopping strips in the entire city. Lined with an increasingly smart collection of boutiques, it proves that the East Village isn't just for kids anymore. Up-and-coming designers selling good-quality and affordably priced original fashions for women have

Additional Sources for Serious Shoppers

If you're looking for a specific item, your best bet is to peruse the online shopping listings at **www.timeoutny.citysearch.com** or at **www.newyork.citysearch.com** before you go. The Time Out shopping site is more limited, but it's unsullied by advertising like the more extensive main CitySearch site is. (CitySearch takes payment for Web site space from shops, and lists advertisers first in any given shopping category, such as "Antiques" or "Children's Clothing.") There's also shopping coverage at **www.newyork.sidewalk.com**, but it's an odd mix of New York stores and net shopping that can be confusing to navigate.

For the latest sales, visit **www.inshop.com**, where you can search for sales by merchandise type, store name, or designer name. The information is extremely detailed, such as, "Kate Spade is having a two-day sale at her SoHo store. All her fab handbags from the Fall/Winter collection will be 40% off. For example, her classic tote handbag in winter's wool fabrics are now $120 to $150, regularly $200 to $250." This tip comes accompanied by exact dates and store location and hours. An excellent source for bargain hunters.

Hard information about current sales, new shops, and special art, craft, and antique shows is best found in the "Check Out" section of *Time Out New York* or the "Sales & Bargains" and "Best Bets" sections of *New York* magazine (*New York* doesn't usually cover shows).

If you're coming in search for sample sales, check out the box "Scouring the Sample Sales" later in this chapter.

---

set up shop along here, including **Lisa Tsai,** 436 E. 9th St. (☎ 212/529-8231), a bright, cheery shop with wonderful retro-inspired designs and accessories; **Mark Montano,** next door at no. 434 (☎ 212/505-0325), who harkens back to styles from Victoria to Jackie O as inspiration for his line of wonderful wearables and handbags; **Between the Sheets,** at no. 315 (☎ 212/677-7586), for ultra-feminine lingerie; plus **Meghan Kinney Studio,** the utterly fabulous **Jill Anderson,** and a small branch of **Eileen Fisher.** Vintage runs the gamut from the pristine '60s and '70s wear at **Argosy** to kitschy 20th-century collectibles at the charming **Cha Cha Tchatchka,** 437 E. 9th St. (☎ 212/674-9242) and **Atomic Passion,** across the street at no. 430 (☎ 212/533-0718).

For stylish gifts and little luxuries, there's **Paper Rock Scissors,** 436 E. 9th St. (☎ 212/358-1555), specializing in handmade treasures; **Mascot Studio,** whose remarkable one-of-a-kind picture frames are sold at no. 328 (☎ 212/228-9090); **Geomancy,** at no. 337 (☎ 212/777-2733), a serene store with a warm country vibe selling Asian and African collectibles and furnishings; and ✪ **H,** at no. 335 (☎ 212/477-2631), with wonderful Japanese-inspired and other collectibles, from slinky vases to rice-paper coasters. There's also the factory store for super-hip **Manhattan Portage,** if you're looking for something to stash your booty in. If you're really enjoying this neighborhood, check out the offerings on surrounding blocks, too, which aren't quite as mature yet, but it won't take long.

If it's strange, illegal, or funky, it's probably available on **St. Marks Place,** which takes over for 8th Street, running east from Third Avenue to Avenue A. This skanky strip is a permanent street market, with countless T-shirt and boho jewelry stands. The height of the action is between Second and Third avenues, which is prime hunting grounds for used-record collectors. For details on the top shops to browse, see "Music" under "Shopping A to Z" later in this chapter.

LAFAYETTE STREET FROM SOHO TO NOHO

Lafayette Street has a retail character all its own, distinct from the rest of SoHo even south of Houston. It has grown into a full-fledged Antique Row, especially strong in mid-century modern furniture. Prices are high, but so is quality. Dispersed among the furniture and design stores are a number of cutting-edge clothiers—this is where skateboard fashion got its start down the catwalks.

The stretch to stroll is between Astor Place to the north and Spring Street to the south. Either take the 6 train to Astor Place and work your way south, get off at Spring Street and walk north, or take the B, D, F, or Q to Broadway-Lafayette and get dropped off in the heart of the action. Highlights include **Art & Industrial Design,** 399 Lafayette St. (☎ 212/477-0116), for sculptural furniture (lots from the '60s), Italian glass, and movie props (the mechanical penguins from the second Batman movie were on sale here for awhile). **Guéridon,** 359 Lafayette St. (☎ 212/677-7740; www.gueridon.com), features sophisticated 20th-century European pieces, mainly French. **Lost City Arts,** at no. 275 (☎ 212/941-8025; www.lostcityarts.com), offers vintage furnishings and a particularly quirky selection of accessories (gas station signs, 3-D photos, and the like), plus their own three excellent lines of mid-century-inspired furnishings and accessories, including one inspired by the otherwise forbiddingly expensive custom designs of Machine Age genius Warren MacArthur. **City Barn Antiques,** at no. 269 (☎ 212/941-5757), is one of the nation's foremost specialists in Heywood-Wakefield; and **Ruby,** just off Lafayette at 70 Spring St. (☎ 212/941-4145), is less notable for its furniture than its impressive assemblage of vintage cameras and small but stellar collection of quality vintage clothing. There's much, much more—furniture hunters and design lovers will be enthralled for hours. Most dealers are well-versed in shipping worldwide.

Among the fashion outlets worth noting are **Bond 07,** just off Lafayette at 7 Bond St. (☎ 212/677-8487), and **Spooly D's,** 51 Bleecker St., at Lafayette (☎ 212/598-4415), both featuring artfully displayed collections of classic vintage fashions and accessories (Bond 07 often features homewares, too); **Daryl K.,** 21 Bond St. (☎ 212/777-0713), for sleek, sexy wear for men and women; and **Screaming Mimi's,** the city's most famous—and maybe its best—vintage clothing outlet. South of Houston is **X-Large,** 267 Lafayette St. (☎ 212/334-4480), for upscale hip-hop wear (the Beasties' Mike D is a co-owner); and **Swell,** 240 Lafayette St. (☎ 212/966-0215), for funky streetwear from L.A.-based designers as well as a terrific collection of funkier Hush Puppies. And don't forget the wonderful **Pop Shop,** which sells cool casual wear emblazoned with Keith Haring's distinctive modern art (see "Logo Stores" under "Shopping A to Z" later in this chapter).

A block over from Lafayette in NoHo, on the Bowery just north of Houston Street, is the place to find restaurant-supply-quality kitchenware.

GREENWICH VILLAGE

The West Village is great for browsing and gift shopping. Specialty book- and record stores, antiques and craft shops, and gourmet food markets dominate. (Attention gourmands: Don't miss **Balducci's** if you can help it.) The best **Tower Records** in the country is at West 4th Street and Broadway. Except for NYU territory—8th Street between Broadway and Sixth Avenue for trendy footwear and affordable fashions, and Broadway from 8th Street south to Houston, anchored by **Urban Outfitters** at 628 Broadway (☎ 212/475-0009) and dotted with skate and sneaker shops—the Village isn't much of a destination for fashion hunters. Clothes hounds looking for volume shopping are better off elsewhere.

The prime drag for strolling is bustling **Bleecker Street,** where you'll find lots of leather shops and record stores (see "Shopping A to Z" later in this chapter) interspersed with a good number of interesting and artsy boutiques. Just a few of the highlights include **Old Japan,** 382 Bleecker St. (☎ 212/633-0922), for Japanese gifts, including cool vests fashioned out of vintage kimonos; **Barr-Magill,** at no. 333 (☎ 212/ 741-0656), whose black-and-white photography—much of it featuring the city as subject—makes a great souvenir; **Davis & Gardner,** at no. 318 (☎ 212/ 229-0660), for an eclectic mix of antiques with a real romantic bent; **Condomania,** at no. 351 (☎ 212/691-9442), everybody's favorite creative condom store; and a branch of **An American Craftsman** for fine gifts. Newer on the scene is **Sleek on Bleecker,** at no. 361 (☎ 212/243-0284), for fashionable but affordable fashions for working women with style.

Narrow **Christopher Street** is another fun street to browse, because it's loaded with genuine Village character. Here you'll find such highlights as **Amalgamated Home** for groovy household goods; **Li-Lac Chocolates** for sweets made the old-fashioned way; and the **Oscar Wilde Bookshop,** which bills itself as the world's oldest gay and lesbian bookstore.

Those who really love to browse should also wander **west of Seventh Avenue,** where charming boutiques are tucked among the brownstones. Highlights include **The End of History** for retro Murano and other European glass; the unpronounceable ❂ **Mxyplyzyk,** 125 Greenwich Ave., at 13th Street, a block from 14th Street and Eighth Avenue (☎ 212/989-4300), for one of the city's best collections of cool, one-of-a-kind homewares and gifts; and any number of boutiques along Hudson Street, including the utterly charming **Tootsie's** for an usual selection of children's books and discovery toys.

MIDTOWN
THE FLATIRON DISTRICT & UNION SQUARE

When 23rd Street was the epitome of New York Uptown fashion more than a hundred years ago, the major department stores stretched along **Sixth Avenue** for about a mile from 14th Street up. These elegant stores stood in huge cast-iron buildings that were long ago abandoned and left to rust. In the last few years, however, the area has been rezoned and turned into the city's discount shopping center, with superstores and off-pricers filling up the renovated spaces: **Filene's Basement, TJMaxx,** and **Bed Bath & Beyond,** are all at 620 Sixth Ave., while witty **Old Navy,** the cheaper version of the Gap, is next door, and **Barnes & Noble** is just a couple of blocks away at Sixth Avenue near 22nd Street.

On Broadway just a few blocks north of Union Square is **ABC Carpet & Home,** a magnet for aspiring Martha Stewarts. If it's actually a rug you're looking for, you'll find a whole slew of imported carpet dealers lining Broadway from ABC north to about 25th Street.

Upscale retailers who have rediscovered the architectural majesty of **lower Fifth Avenue** include retro-inspired **Restoration Hardware,** at 22nd Street (☎ 212/ 260-9479); **Joan & David,** 104 Fifth Ave., at 15th Street (☎ 212/627-1780), for fine footwear; plus city and national mainstays like **Kenneth Cole, Banana Republic,** and **Victoria's Secret.** You won't find too much that's new along here, but it's a pleasing stretch nonetheless.

HERALD SQUARE & THE GARMENT DISTRICT

Herald Square—where 34th Street, Sixth Avenue, and Broadway converge—is dominated by **Macy's,** the self-proclaimed world's biggest department store, and other famous-name shopping, like **Toys "Я" Us** at 34th Street and Broadway (☎ 212/ 594-8697). At Sixth Avenue and 33rd Street is the **Manhattan Mall** (☎ 212/ 465-0500), anchored by unremarkable Stern's department store and home to mall standards like Foot Locker and Radio Shack.

A long block over on Seventh Avenue, not much goes on in the grimy, heavily industrial Garment District. This is, however, where you'll find that quintessential New York experience, the sample sale; see the box called "Scouring the Sample Sales," later in this chapter.

TIMES SQUARE & THE THEATER DISTRICT

This neighborhood has become increasingly family-oriented: hence, **Disney** and **Warner Bros.** outposts at the crossroads of Times Square, Richard Branson's rollicking **Virgin Megastore,** and **Skechers** for teenybopping tennies on Seventh Avenue just south of 42nd Street (☎ 212/354-8110). **The Gap** is already here at 42nd and Broadway, and word is that **Old Navy** is moving in, too.

At first glance it may be hard to tell, but there's more to offer here than these high-style theme stores and an array of tacky souvenir shops. **West 48th Street** between Sixth and Seventh avenues is *the* place to shop if you want to make your own music. Like ducks in a row you'll find friendly **Sam Ash,** 160 W. 48th St. (☎ 212/719-2299), and **Manny's Music,** 156 W. 48th St. (☎ 212/819-0576), both offering a wide range of instruments. On the same block you'll find custom axes from **Carlo Greco Custom Guitars** at no. 165 (☎ 212/704-2042), and—even better for browsing—**48th Street Custom Guitars,** no. 170 (☎ 212/764-1364).

West 47th Street between Fifth and Sixth avenues is the city's famous **Diamond District.** Apparently, more than 90% of the diamonds sold in the United States come through this neighborhood first, so there are some great deals to be had if you're in the market for a nice rock or another piece of fine jewelry. Be ready to wheel and deal with the largely Hasidic dealers, who offer quite a juxtaposition to the crowds that people the rest of the area. For a complete introduction to the district, including smart buying tips, point your Web browser to **www.47th-street.com**. For semiprecious stones, head one block over to the **New York Jewelry Mart,** 26 W. 46th St. (☎ 212/575-9701). Virtually all of these dealers are open Monday through Friday only.

You'll also notice a wealth of electronics stores throughout the neighborhood, many suspiciously trumpeting GOING OUT OF BUSINESS sales. These guys have been going out of business since the Stone Age. That's the bait and switch; pretty soon you've spent too much money for not enough stereo. If you want to check out what they have to offer, go in knowing what going prices are on that PDA or digital camera you're interested in. You can make a good deal if you know exactly what the market is, but these guys will be happy to suck you dry given half a chance.

FIFTH AVENUE & 57TH STREET

The heart of Manhattan retail is the corner of Fifth Avenue and 57th Street. Time was, only the very rich could make this sacred crossroads their ground-zero shopping site. Not anymore, now that **Tiffany & Co.,** which has long reigned supreme here, sits a stone's throw from a huge **Original Levi's Store** and a **Warner Bros. Studio Store,** with **Niketown** and the **NBA Store** just down the street. In addition, a good number of mainstream retailers, like **Banana Republic** and **Liz Claiborne** have set up their flagships along Fifth, further democratizing the avenue.

Fifth Avenue has only a few big-name designer boutiques left in the 50s, although the opening of the **Gianni Versace** shop at 647 Fifth Ave. (☎ 212/317-0224) just before his death has heralded a new era of respect for the avenue. Other deluxe designer tenants are **Fendi,** at no. 720 (☎ 212/767-0100); **Ferragamo,** no. 725 (☎ 212/759-3822); **Gucci,** no. 685 (☎ 212/826-2600); and **Christian Dior,** no. 703 (☎ 212/223-4646). You'll also find big-name jewelers like **Harry Winston, Cartier,** and **Van Cleef & Arpels** along here, as well as chi-chi department stores like

Open Hours

Keep in mind that open hours can vary significantly from store to store—even different branches of the Gap can keep different schedules depending on location and management. As a general rule of thumb, stores open at 10 or 11am from Monday through Saturday, and 7pm is the most common closing hour (although sometimes it's 6pm); both opening and closing hours tend to get later as you move downtown to SoHo and the Village. The department stores, and shops along major strips like Fifth Avenue, usually stay open later one night a week (oftentimes Thursday) until 8 or 8:30pm, although not all shops may comply. Sunday hours are usually noon to 5 or 6pm. Most shops are open seven days a week, but smaller boutiques may close one day a week, and some whole neighborhoods virtually shut down—namely the Lower East Side on Saturday and most of the Financial District for the weekend. Your best bet is to call ahead if your heart's set on visiting a particular shop, especially late in the day or on Sunday. At holidaytime, anything goes: Macy's often stays open to midnight for the last couple of weeks before Christmas!

Bergdorf Goodman, Henri Bendel, and **Saks Fifth Avenue,** all of which have helped the avenue maintain its classy cachet.

While 57th Street has similarly changed in the last few years, many big names are still hanging on. Italian knit queen **Laura Biagiotti** is at 4 W. 57th St. (☎ 212/399-2533); **Chanel** is at 15 E. 57th St. (☎ 212/355-5050); menswear and cigar specialist **Alfred Dunhill,** at 450 Park Ave., at the corner of 57th (☎ 212/888-4003); as well as **Prada, Hermès,** and **Louis Vuitton** (see "Leather Goods, Handbags & Luggage" under "Shopping A to Z" later in this chapter). Look for Hermès to defect to tonier Madison Avenue in the future, where Prada already has another store.

UPTOWN
MADISON AVENUE

Madison Avenue from 57th to 79th streets has usurped Fifth Avenue as *the* tony shopping street in the city. In fact, in 1998, it vaunted ahead of Hong Kong's Causeway Bay to become so most expensive retail real estate in the world. Bring lots of plastic.

This strip of Madison is home to the most luxurious designer boutiques in the world, with **Barneys New York** as the anchor. **Calvin Klein** is all chrome and clean edges at 654 Madison Ave., between 60th and 61st streets (☎ 212/292-9000), hawking magnificent threads for men and women with megabucks, plus home furnishings. **Giorgio Armani** holds minimalist court at 760 Madison Ave. (☎ 212/988-9191). Glamorous **Valentino** is at 747 Madison Ave. (☎ 212/72-6969), while Italian super-chic is at home at **Dolce & Gabanna,** no. 825 (☎ 212/249-4100); **Versace,** no. 815 (☎ 212/744-6868); and **Prada,** no. 841 (☎ 212/327-4200). Other sophisticated names lining the strip are **Ungaro** at no. 792 (☎ 212/249-4090) for body-conscious sophisticates; **Max Mara** at no. 813 (☎ 212/879-6100) for luxurious understatement; **Givenchy** at no. 954 (☎ 212/772-1040) for the ultimate in haute Parisian style; plus **Vera Wang** for chic bridal wear and **Ralph Lauren**'s stunner of a store for the ultimate in all-American style. Look for **Donna Karan** to open a flagship on Madison between 68th and 69th; her more accessible **DKNY** store at Madison and 60th will be open by the time you arrive.

For those of us without unlimited fashion budgets, the good news is that stores like **Crate & Barrel** and the fabulous **Ann Taylor** flagship make the untouchable Madison Avenue seem approachable and affordable. Shoe freaks from budget to deluxe should

be on the lookout for wallet-friendly **Unisa,** 701 Madison Ave. (☎ 212/753-7474);
Joan & David at no. 816 (☎ 212/772-3970) and **Cole-Haan** at no. 667
(☎ 212/421-8400), where style triumphs over trendiness; **Timberland,** at no. 709
(☎ 212/754-0434), for the best in rugged footwear; **Patrick Cox,** no. 702 (☎ 212/
759-3910), for more cutting-edge fashions; and **Sergio Rossi,** no. 835 (☎ 212/
396-4814), for glamorous mules, sexy slingbacks, and classic pointy-toe pumps.

The other big news is that upper Madison, from about 72nd to 86th streets, is
becoming the domain of cozy-chic home stores for the uptown Martha Stewart set.
Between 80th and 82nd streets, look for beautiful all-cotton fabrics on the bolt at
Maison Decor, no. 1094 (☎ 212/744-7079); sophisticated country French imports
at **A La Maison,** no. 1078 (☎ 212/396-1020); and bath and beauty products from
around the world at **Fresh,** no. 1061 (☎ 212/396-0344).

The Upper West Side

The Upper West Side's best shopping street is **Columbus Avenue**. Small shops
catering to the neighborhood's white-collar mix of young hipsters and families line
both sides of the pleasant avenue from 66th Street (where you'll find an excellent
branch of **Barnes & Noble**) to about 86th Street. Highlights include branches of
Eileen Fisher for comfortably chic womenswear, and **Kenneth Cole** for stylish
footwear and leather. For comfort over style (these city streets can be murder on the
feet!), try **Aerosoles,** 310 Columbus Ave. (☎ 212/579-8659), or **Sacco** for women's
shoes that offer a bit of both. Other highlights include **La Belle Epoque,** at no. 280
(☎ 212/362-1770), for vintage posters, mostly pre-war European advertisements;
Housing Works Thrift Shop, at no. 306 (☎ 212/579-7566), an excellent not-for-
profit thrift store whose sales go to support those living with HIV and AIDS; **Robert
Marc Opticians,** at no. 190 (☎ 212/799-4600), for fashionable eyewear; and **Maxilla & Mandible** for groovy natural science-based gifts (see "Museum Stores" under
"Shopping A to Z" later in this chapter).

There's also a few shops lining main drag Broadway, but it's most notable for its terrific gourmet edibles at **Zabar's** and **Fairway** markets, both legends in their own right.

2 The Big Department Stores

All of the big department stores are open seven days a week. However, unlike department stores in suburban malls, most of these stores don't keep a regular 10am to 9pm
schedule, so your best bet is to call ahead if you're planning on a late afternoon visit.
Virtually all keep extended hours during the Christmas season, which tend to get
longer as the holiday grows nearer.

Barneys New York. 660 Madison Ave. (at 61st St.). ☎ **212/826-8900.** Subway: N, R to
Fifth Ave.

New York's self-made temple of chic has been plagued with financial woes (and the
accompanying publicity storm) over the last few years, so severe that they forced the
closure of the original Chelsea location. You wouldn't know it by walking into the
Madison Avenue store, though—its eight floors of menswear and eight floors of
womenswear and accessories exude impeccable high style. While the store focuses on
hot-off-the-runway womenswear, its menswear runs the gamut from classic to cutting-
edge. The fragrance department has worked hard to be the place to find offbeat and
unusual scents as well as the classics. Chelsea Passage, the gift/tabletop department, is
one of the world's best such spaces. Bring your platinum card, because nothing comes
cheap here. The Tuscan food is fine, if overpriced (you expect otherwise?), at basement
boite and celebrity magnet **Fred's.**

Bergdorf Goodman. 754 Fifth Ave. (at 57th St.). ☎ **212/753-7300.** Subway: E, F to Fifth Ave.

Once the fanciest specialty store in New York, Bergdorf's is a museum of haute couture. The store is beautifully designed on an intimate scale, and many claim that it lacks the nouveaux-riche feel of the Bendel's crowd, but its formality and quiet just makes me feel uncomfortable (or maybe it's just that I can't afford anything here?). The customer base is primarily composed of ladies who lunch and businesswomen with gobs of money but little time for nonsense. Still, there's an unparalleled gift and tabletop floor, worth a browse alone, as well as some finely tuned designer salons. Just across the street is **Bergdorf Goodman Man,** a palace of fine men's fashion.

✪ **Bloomingdale's.** 1000 Third Ave. (Lexington Ave. at 59th St.). ☎ **212/705-2000.** Subway: 4, 5, 6 to 59th St.

This is my favorite of New York's big department stores. It's more accessible than Barneys or Bergdorf's and more affordable than Saks, but still has the New York pizzazz that Macy's and Lord and Taylor now largely lack. Taking up the space of a city block, Bloomie's has just about anything you could want, from clothing (both designer and everyday basics) and fragrances to housewares and furniture. It pays to make a reconnaissance trip to get the overview, then move in for the kill. The main entrance is on Third Avenue, but pop up to street level from the 59th Street station and you'll be right at the Lexington Avenue entrance. On the sixth floor is **Le Train Bleu,** a favorite for afternoon tea that offers an elegant escape from the bustle.

✪ **Century 21.** 22 Cortlandt St. (btw. Broadway and Church St.). ☎ **212/227-9092.** Subway: 1, 9, N, R to Cortlandt St.; 4, 5 to Fulton St.; C, E to World Trade Center.

Just across from the World Trade Center, Century 21 long ago achieved legend status as *the* designer discount store. If you don't mind wrestling with the aggressive, ever-present throngs, this is where you'll find those $20 Todd Oldham pants or the $50 Bally loafers you've been dreaming of—not to mention underwear, hosiery, and ties so cheap that they're almost free. Don't think that $250 Armani blazer is a bargain? Look again at the tag—the retail price on it is upwards of $800.

Henri Bendel. 712 Fifth Ave. (at 56th St.). ☎ **212/247-1100.** Subway: N, R to Fifth Ave.

This beautiful Fifth Avenue store is a lot of fun to browse. It feels like you're shopping in the town house of a confident, monied old lady who doesn't think twice about throwing on a little something by Anna Sui and an outrageously wide-brimmed hat to go out shopping for the day—and she's got the panache to pull it off. It's a super-stylish, high-ticket collection, but the sales are good, and there's always some one-of-a-kind accessories that make affordable souvenirs (and earn you one of black-and-white striped shopping bags, the best in town). The interior is so divine that you should remember to take a break from perusing the racks to look up, down, and around every once in awhile. The pretty **tea room** looks out on Fifth Avenue through Lalique windows.

Lord & Taylor. 424 Fifth Ave. (at 39th St.). ☎ **212/391-3344.** Subway: B, D, F, Q to 42nd St.

Okay, so maybe Lord & Taylor isn't the first place you'd go for a vinyl miniskirt. But I like Lord & Taylor's understated, elegant mien. Long known as an excellent source for women's dresses and coats, L&T stocks all the major labels for men and women, with a special emphasis on American designers. Their house-brand clothes (khakis, blazers, turtlenecks, and summer sportswear) are well made and a great bargain. Sales, especially around holidays, can be stellar. The store is big enough to have a good selection (especially for petites), but doesn't overwhelm—I wish the lighting were better, though, but it's a minor complaint. The Christmas window displays are an annual delight.

Macy's. At Herald Square, W. 34th St. and Broadway. ☎ **212/695-4400.** Subway: 1, 2, 3, 9, B, D, F, Q, N, R to 34th St.

A four-story sign on the side of the building trumpets, "MACY'S, THE WORLD'S LARGEST STORE"—a hard fact to dispute, since the ten-story behemoth covers an entire city block, even dwarfing Bloomie's on the other side of town. Macy's is a hard place to shop: The size is unmanageable, the service is dreadful, and the incessant din from the crowds on the ground floor alone will kick your migraine into action. But they do sell *everything.* Massive renovation over the past few years has redesigned many departments into more manageable "mini-stores"—there's a Metropolitan Museum Gift Shop, a Swatch boutique, and cafes and make-up counters on several floors—but the store's one-of-a-kind flair that I remember so well from my childhood is just a memory now. Still, sales run constantly, holiday or no (one-day sales are popular on Wednesdays and Saturdays), so bargains are guaranteed. And because so many feel adrift in this retail sea, the store provides personal guides/shoppers at absolutely no charge. My advice: Get the floor plan, and consult it often to avoid wandering off into the sportswear netherworld. At Christmastime, come as late as you can manage (the store is usually open until midnight in the final shopping days).

Saks Fifth Avenue. 611 Fifth Ave. (btw. 49th and 50th sts.). ☎ **212/753-4000.** Subway: B, D, F, Q to 47–50th sts.–Rockefeller Center; E, F to Fifth Ave.

There are branches of Saks all over the country now, but this is it: The Saks *Fifth Avenue.* This legendary flagship store is well worth an hour or two of your time, and the smaller-than-most size makes it manageable in that amount of time. Saks carries a wide range of clothing; departments err on the pricey designer side (stay out of the lingerie department if you're looking for basics) but run the gamut to affordable housebrand basics. As department stores go, there's something for everyone here. Some call this men's department the finest in the city. The cosmetics and fragrance departments on the main floor are justifiably noteworthy, since they carry many hard-to-find and brand-new brands. And the store's location, right across from Rockefeller Center, makes it a convenient stop for those on the sightseeing circuit. Don't miss the holiday windows. On the eighth floor is **Cafe S.F.A.,** serving yuppiefied salads and sandwiches in a stylish dining room with a fabulous view over St. Patrick's Cathedral.

Takashimaya. 693 Fifth Ave. (btw. 54th and 55th sts.). ☎ **212/350-0100.** Subway: E, F to Fifth Ave.

This petite branch of the Japan's most famous department store chain doesn't resemble the domestic branches. Rather, this Fifth Avenue outpost exudes an appealingly austere, Japanese-tinged French country charm. Paris's most famous florist, Christian Tortu, has a main-floor boutique that's a work of art in its own right. The serenely elegant **Tea Box** specializes in delicate bento box lunches and beautiful sweets. Aesthetes shouldn't miss this place.

3 Shopping A to Z

ANTIQUES & COLLECTIBLES

Looking for glass? Then don't miss **Galileo,** which boasts a small but stellar collection of vintage glassware; see "Home Fashions & Housewares" below. Mid-century modern furniture lovers should be sure to browse **Lafayette Street;** see "The Top Shopping Streets & Neighborhoods" above.

Most call it the 26th Street flea market; the famous **Annex Antiques Fair and Flea Market** (☎ 212/243-5343) is an outdoor emporium of nostalgia, filling a few parking lots along Sixth Avenue between 24th and 27th streets on weekends year-round. The assemblage is hit or miss—some days you'll find treasures galore, and others it seems like there's nothing but junk. A few quality vendors are almost always on hand, though. The truly dedicated arrive at 6:30am, but the browsing's still plenty good as late as 4pm. Sunday is always best, since there's double the booty on hand. One lot charges $1 admission both days. Die-hards can continue the hunt at the Garage, an indoor two-story parking garage on 25th Street between Sixth and Seventh avenues, then proceed to 26th Street and Seventh Avenue, where another lot fills up with dealers on Sunday.

Real collectibles hounds should also consider the regular calendar of antiques shows, the best of which is the twice-annual **Triple Piers Expo,** always in March and again in November; see the "Calendar of Events" in chapter 2 for details.

Chelsea Antiques Building. 110 W. 25th St. (btw. Sixth and Seventh aves.). ☎ **212/929-0909.** www.chelseaantiques.com. Subway: F to 23rd St.

Right around the corner from New York's best flea market (above), this 12-floor building is filled with dealers both weekdays and weekends. Goods are priced more reasonably than at Uptown addresses, and shoppers are the type who love to prowl, touch everything, and sniff out a deal. Highlights include **Waves** (☎ 212/989-9284; www.wavesradio.com) for antique radios and phonographs, including a good selection of 78s and Edison cylinders; **Jerome Wilson** (☎ 212/352-1370) for fine vintage linens, porcelain, and glass; **Julian's Books** (☎ 212/929-3620; www.julianbook.com), for first, signed, and rare editions; **Retro-Metro/The Missing Link** (☎ 212/645-6928) for cufflinks, handbags, and other vintage jewelry and accessories; and **Toys from the 50s** (☎ 212/352-9182; www.toys-50s.com), specializing in classic TV show toys and memorabilia.

Depression Modern. 150 Sullivan St. (btw. Houston and Prince sts.). ☎ **212/982-5699.** Subway: N, R to Prince St.

Depression Modern specializes in restoring art deco furnishings, and their pieces are always gorgeous. The selection is new every Saturday, so go on the weekend for the best pickings. Gorgeous streamline tabletop items, too.

✪ **The End of History.** 548½ Hudson St. (btw. Perry and Charles sts.). ☎ **212/647-7598.** Subway: 1, 9 to Christopher St.–Sheridan Square.

This marvelous shop specializes in Murano, Blenko, Holmegaard, and other European glass, with a strong emphasis on the '60s. The constantly changing collection features lots of dazzling shapes and colors, all fetchingly displayed on select pieces of for-sale furnishings, which often have a Scandinavian or mod flair. This shop is so creatively put together that you'll have a blast browsing even if their collectibles aren't your thing.

Form & Function. 95 Vandam St. (1 block north of Spring St., btw. Hudson and Greenwich sts.). ☎ **212/414-1800.** Subway: 1, 9 to Houston St.

This newish gallery, co-owned by Fred Schneider of the B-52s, specializes in lesser-known designers and design trends from 1945 to 1975—a boon to those of us who have seen enough Heywood-Wakefield to last a lifetime. This is a serious gallery, not a mid-century kitschfest, so come for the high quality of the home designs. Vintage electronics are featured, too.

Kentshire Galleries. 37 E. 12th St. (btw. University Place and Broadway). ☎ **212/673-6644.** Subway: 4, 5, 6, N, R, L to 14th St.–Union Square.

Going . . . Going . . . Sold!

Auctions specialize in anything collectible, from animation cels to fine wines to Chinese ceramics to Academy Awards fashions. The two major auction houses are **Christie's,** at 502 Park Ave. (☎ **212/546-1000;** www.christies.com), and 219 E. 67th St. (☎ **212/606-0400**); and **Sotheby's,** 1334 York Ave. (☎ **212/606-7000;** www.sothebys.com). Every now and then a celebrity estate (like Jackie O's and the Duke and Duchess of Windsor's so famously did) goes up for auction. No matter what the auction, viewings are free and open to the public. If you plan to participate, be sure to review the catalog for price estimates beforehand, and attend the sale preview for an advance look at the merchandise.

Here's the city's prime stop for 18th- and 19th-century English antiques, ranging from jewelry and tabletop items to formal furnishings.

Manhattan Art & Antiques Center. 1050 Second Ave. (btw. 55th and 56th sts.). ☎ **212/355-4400.** www.glenwoodmanagement.com/maac. Subway: N, R to Lexington Ave.

This three-floor antiques center represents just about every genre of collecting on the map, from perfume bottles and porcelain to arms and armor. Once you've toured the more than 100 stalls, stroll along 60th Street, where about two dozen dealers selling higher-end goods line both sides of the street.

Mood Indigo. 181 Prince St. (btw. Sullivan and Thompson sts.). ☎ **212/254-1176.** Subway: C, E to Spring St.; N, R to Prince St.

Looking for the perfect vintage cocktail shaker? How about some hip martini glasses for those Cosmopolitans you just learned to make? Maybe a certain piece of Jadite or Fiestaware to complete your collection? Then come to this dandy of a shop, the city's top dealer in glassware, dishware, and kitchen accessories from the 1930s through the 1950s. The charming shopkeepers also specialize in bakelite jewelry and 1939 World's Fair memorabilia, and boast a whopping collection of salt-and-pepper shakers. Everything is pristine, so expect to pay accordingly.

Newel Art Galleries. 425 E. 53rd St. (btw. First Ave. and Sutton Place). ☎ **212/758-1970.** Subway: 6 to 51st St.

This wonderful gallery houses six floors of the best furniture from ages past—be it a throne that would make King Arthur proud or an art deco vanity that Carole Lombard might've loved. Browsing hardly gets better.

ART

For a complete look at the art scene, see "Art for Art's Sake: The Gallery Scene" in chapter 7.

BOOKS
THE BIG CHAINS

Barnes & Noble Booksellers. 22 E. 17th St. (at Union Square). ☎ **212/253-0810** or 212/727-4810 (for New York–area B&N information). www.barnesandnoble.com. Subway: 4, 5, 6, N, R, L to Union Square.

With locations throughout the city, B&N is the undisputed king of city bookstores. The Union Square location is my favorite: The selection is huge and well organized, the store is comfortable and never feels too crowded, and you're welcome to browse— or nab a comfy chair and read—for as long as you like. There's a cafe, of course, and an extensive magazine stand.

There's another superstore at 1972 Broadway, at 66th Street (☎ 212/595-6859), plus additional good-sized locations at 4 Astor Place, between Broadway and Lafayette Street (☎ 212/420-1322); 675 Sixth Ave., near 22nd Street (☎ 212/727-1227); 160 E. 54th St. (☎ 212/750-8033); at Rockefeller Center, 600 Fifth Ave., at 48th St. (☎ 212/765-0590); 2289 Broadway, at 82nd Street (☎ 212/362-8835); and 240 E. 86th St., at Second Avenue (☎ 212/794-1962). Look for an extensive calendar of readings at most locations; featured luminaries have included Martin Amis, Peter Jennings, and Elmore Leonard.

Borders Books & Music. 5 World Trade Center (at Church and Vesey sts.). ☎ **212/839-8049.** www.bordersstores.com. Subway: 1, 9, N, R to Cortlandt St.; C, E to World Trade Center.

After several years with no decent bookstore representation anywhere in the neighborhood, Borders is a welcome addition to the Financial District. The selection of both books and music is extensive, service is great, and the store hosts a wealth of in-store events, including appearances from best-selling authors to musicians like Lou Reed and Jonathan Brooke. There's a second location at 461 Park Ave., at 57th Street (☎ 212/980-6785), and, at press time, a third was scheduled to open soon.

SPECIALTY BOOKSTORES

New York has more terrific specialty bookstores than I can possibly recount here. These are just *some* of the best. In addition to these choices, also consider **Tower Books,** a branch of the mega-music chain (see "Music" below).

Academy Book Store. 10 W. 18th St. (btw. Fifth and Sixth aves.). ☎ **212/242-4848.** Subway: 4, 5, 6, N, R, L to 14th St.–Union Square.

Academy is best-known for its record store (see "Music" below), but adjacent is this friendly neighborhood used book store. Their inventory is quite deep, focusing on literature, history, art, humanities, and philosophy. Best of all, the prices are scrupulously fair.

Archivia. 944 Madison Ave. (btw. 74th and 75th sts.). ☎ **212/439-9194.** Subway: 6 to 77th St.

Here you'll find new, imported, and rare books on architecture, the decorative arts, gardening, and interior design, some quite rare. A book and design lover's dream.

If you like Archivia, you might also check out the Municipal Art Society's **Urban Center Books,** 457 Madison Ave., between 50th and 51st streets (☎ 212/935-3595), which has a terrific selection of books on architecture, design, and urban planning.

Argosy Books. 116 E. 59th St. (btw. Park and Lexington aves.). ☎ **212/753-4455.** Subway: 4, 5, 6 to 59th St.

In addition to Academy, rare and used-book hounds should also check out this stately store, with high ceilings, packed shelves, a quiet intellectual air, and an outstanding collection of rarities, including 18th- and 19th-century prints.

Books of Wonder. 16 W. 18th St. (btw. Fifth and Sixth aves.). ☎ **212/989-3270.** www.booksofwonder.com. Subway: 4, 5, 6, N, R, L to 14th St.–Union Square.

You don't have to be a kid to fall in love with this charming bookstore, which served as the model for Meg Ryan's shop in *You've Got Mail* (Meg even worked here a spell to train for the role). Kids will love BOW's story readings, which take place every Sunday at 11:45am.

✪ **Coliseum Books.** 1771 Broadway (at 57th St.). ☎ **212/757-8381.** Subway: 1, 9, A, B, C, D to 59th St.–Columbus Circle.

This big, well-stocked independent is a must on any book lover's list—and it's well located for visitors, right on the edge of the Theater District, a stone's throw from Central Park. It may not be Barnes & Noble cozy, but you'll find an excellent selection of fiction and literature (both contemporary and the classics), along with great travel, art, and coffee-table books. Staff, poised atop a raised platform in the middle of the store, are on hand to answer questions or proffer a literary opinion. Coliseum also stocks a selection of notecards, greeting cards, and journals.

Complete Traveller. 199 Madison Ave. (at 35th St.). ☎ **212/685-9007.** Subway: 6 to 33rd St.

Whether your destination is Texas or Tibet, you'll find what you need in this, possibly the world's best travel bookstore. There are maps and travel accessories as well, plus a rare collection of antiquarian travel books whose facts may be outdated but whose writers' perceptions continue to shine. The staff is attentive.

A Different Light Bookstore. 151 W. 19th St. (btw. Sixth and Seventh aves.). ☎ **212/989-4850.** www.adlbooks.com. Subway: 1, 9 to 18th St.

The city's largest gay and lesbian bookstore stocks just about every category—fiction, nonfiction, biography, travel, gay/lesbian studies, and more—plus cassettes, calendars, you name it. There's also a cafe. Check the Web site for a full calendar of readings and video nights.

Forbidden Planet. 840 Broadway (at 13th St.). ☎ **212/473-1576.** Subway: 4, 5, 6, N, R, L to 14th St.–Union Sq.

Here's the city's largest collection of sci-fi, comics, and graphic-illustration books. The prices aren't low, but the range of products can't be beat, and the proudly geeky staff really knows what's what. Great sci-fi-themed toys, too.

۞ Gotham Book Mart. 41 W. 47th St. (btw. Fifth and Sixth aves.). ☎ **212/719-4448.** Subway: B, D, F, Q to 47–50th sts./Rockefeller Center.

Paris may have had its Sylvia Beach, but New York was lucky enough to have Frances Steloff. She opened Gotham Book Mart in 1920, and quickly became a defender of the First Amendment rights of authors. She championed such once-banned works as Henry Miller's *Tropic of Cancer*, and numbered among her admirers Ezra Pound, Saul Bellow, and Jackie Kennedy Onassis. Frances has since passed on, but her aura lives on. As always, the emphasis is on poetry, literature, and the arts. This is New York's undisputed literary landmark; look for the sign that says, WISE MEN FISH HERE.

Hagstrom Map & Travel Center. 57 W. 43rd St. (btw. Fifth and Sixth aves.). ☎ **212/398-1222.** Subway: B, D, F, Q to 42nd St.

This bookstore sells travel guides and an incredible selection of cartography to meet just about any map need. There's a second location in lower Manhattan at 125 Maiden Lane, at Water Street (☎ **212/785-5343**).

Kitchen Arts & Letters. 1435 Lexington Ave. (btw. 93rd and 94th sts.). ☎ **212/876-5550.** Subway: 6 to 96th St.

Foodies take note: Here's the ultimate cook's and food-lover's bookstore. You'll be wowed by the depth of the selection, which includes rare and out-of-print cookbooks. The staff will conduct free searches for hard-to-find titles. The shop is an overstuffed jumble, but if this is your bag, you'll be browsing for hours.

Murder Ink. 2486 Broadway (at 92nd St.). ☎ **212/362-8905.** www.murderink.com. Subway: 1, 9 to 96th St.

Murder, she wrote, he wrote, they wrote. This is the ultimate specialty bookstore—as much fun as a good mystery. They claim to sell every mystery in print, and also carry a huge selection of out-of-print paperbacks, hard-to-find imported titles, and rare signed first editions. You can even keep buying over the Web site or toll-free line (☎ **800/488-8123**) from home; have your name added to the catalog mailing list.

Mystery and true-crime fans will also enjoy the **Mysterious Book Shop,** 129 W. 56th St., between Sixth and Seventh avenues (☎ **212/765-0900;** www.mysteriousbookshop. com), another store specializing in current and rare whodunits.

Oscar Wilde Bookshop. 15 Christopher St. (btw. Sixth and Seventh aves.) ☎ **212/ 255-8097.** www.OscarWildeBooks.com. Subway: 1, 9 to Christopher St.–Sheridan Sq.

The world's oldest gay and lesbian bookstore is still going strong. It's much smaller than A Different Light (above), but a recent renovation allows for more titles and ancillary merchandise than ever before, and the nice staff makes this landmark a pleasure.

Rand McNally Travel Store. 150 E. 52nd St. (btw. Lexington and Third aves.). ☎ **212/ 758-7488.** www.randmcnallystore.com. Subway: 6 to 51st St.; E, F to Lexington Ave.

Sheet maps, globe maps, city maps, international maps, laminated maps—so many maps, in fact, you might never get lost again. In addition to cartography, Rand McNally sells a wide range of travel guides, atlases, and such travelers' aids as voltage converters and inflatable pillows. There's a second location in the Garment District at 555 Seventh Ave. (☎ **212/944-4477**).

Rizzoli. 31 W. 57th St. (btw. Fifth and Sixth aves.). ☎ **212/759-2424.** Subway: N, R to Fifth Ave.

This clubby Italian bookstore is the classiest—and most relaxing—spot in town to browse for the best visual art and design books, plus quality fiction, gourmet cookbooks, and other upscale reading. There's also a decent selection of foreign-language, music, and dance titles as well. Two more locations: in SoHo at 454 West Broadway, just south of Houston (☎ **212/674-1616**), and at 3 World Financial Center (☎ **212/385-1400**).

Shakespeare & Co. 716 Broadway (at Washington Place). ☎ **212/529-1330.** Subway: N, R to 8th St.

A boutique-like bookstore in the Village stocks the latest fiction (and non-) bestsellers, and has a generally well-rounded inventory. The displays are quite enticing if you're looking for something new to read. Another branch is uptown, at 939 Lexington Ave., between 68th and 69th streets (☎ **212/570-0201**).

✪ **St. Mark's Bookshop.** 31 Third Ave. (at 9th St.). ☎ **212/260-7853.** Subway: 6 to Astor Place.

This left-of-center East Village bookshop is a great place to browse. You'll find lots of terrific alternative and small-press fiction and literature, plus cultural criticism and mainstream literature with an edge. You'll also find art and design books as well as an alternative 'zine rack.

✪ **The Strand.** 828 Broadway (at 12th St.). ☎ **212/473-1452.** Subway: 4, 5, 6, N, R, L to 14th St.–Union Sq.

Something of a New York legend, The Strand is worth a visit for its staggering "eight miles of books" as well as its extensive inventory of review copies and bargain titles at up to 85% off list price. It's unquestionably the city's best book deal—there's almost nothing marked at list—and the selection is phenomenal in all categories (there's even a rare book department on the third floor). Still, you'll work for it: The narrow aisles mean you're always getting bumped; the books are only roughly alphabetized; and there's no air-conditioning in summer. Nevertheless, a used-book lover's paradise. There's a smaller Strand downtown, at 95 Fulton St., between William and Gold streets (☎ 212/732-6070).

BEAUTY & BATH

In addition to the choices below, **Floris,** the London fragrance house, is at 703 Madison Ave., between 62nd and 63rd streets (☎ 212/935-9100).

Cosmetics Plus. 1601 Broadway (at 48th St.). ☎ 212/757-3122. Subway: N, R to 49th St.

This chain sells a wide range of perfumes, health and beauty aids, cosmetics from Cover Girl to Lancôme and Borghese, and high-end hair-care products, all at discounted prices. Check the Yellow Pages for additional locations throughout the city.

Kiehl's. 109 Third Ave. (at 13th St.). ☎ 212/475-3400. Subway: 4, 5, 6, N, R, L to 14th St.–Union Sq.

Kiehl's is more than a store: It's a virtual cult. Models, stockbrokers, foreign visitors, and just about everyone else stops by this always-packed old-time apothecary for its simply packaged, wonderfully formulated products for women and men. Lip Balm no. 1 is the perfect antidote for the biting winds of city or slope.

MAC. 113 Prince St. (btw. Mercer and Greene sts.). ☎ 212/334-4641. Subway: N, R to Prince St.

What began as a Canadian-based, custom-designed modeling makeup line has become a super-successful retail operation thanks to a chic color line, eco-friendly packaging, and decent prices (considering the quality). The downtown-chic, don't-hate-me-because-I'm-beautiful unisex staff is dressed in perennially hip all black. Lighter and more sheer than most, the lipsticks are particularly popular; I buy redwood practically by the gross. Another, smaller branch is in the Village at 14 Christopher St. (☎ 212/243-4150), plus counters at Saks, Bloomingdale's, and Henri Bendel.

CLOTHING
RETAIL FASHIONS
The Top Designers
You'll find the classic designer names—**Chanel, Hermès, Alfred Dunhill, Gucci,** and friends—lined up like haute couture soldiers along Fifth Avenue and 57th Street. The biggest names in clean-lined modern design—**Calvin Klein, Donna Karan, Armani, Dolce & Gabbana**—call super-chic Madison Avenue home. For established but still cutting-edge designers—**Anna Sui, Yohji Yamamoto, Marc Jacobs, Vivienne Westwood, Todd Oldham, Vivienne Tam**—hang out in SoHo, while talented up-and-comers have set up shop in NoHo, NoLiTa, and along 9th Street in the East Village. See "The Top Shopping Streets & Neighborhoods" earlier in this chapter.

Fashion Flagships
Some New York flagship stores of the major brands are an experience you won't catch in your nearest mall. These stores are display cases for the complete line of fashions, so you'll often find much more to choose from than in your at-home branch. You'll also find other locations throughout the city, but these are meant to be the biggest and best: Check out the gorgeous **Ann Taylor,** at 645 Madison Ave., at 60th Street (☎ 212/832-2010); **Banana Republic,** 655 Fifth Ave., at 52nd Street (☎ 212/644-6678); **Eddie Bauer,** 1976 Broadway, at 67th Street (☎ 212/877-7629), which also carries the AKA Eddie Bauer line and the sports and mountaineering line; **Liz Claiborne,** 650 Fifth Ave., at 50th Street (☎ 212/956-6505), which carries every one of Liz's lines; the **Original Levi's Store** at 3 E. 57th Street, between Fifth and Madison

(☎ 212/838-2125); and **Victoria's Secret,** 34 E. 57th St., between Madison and Park avenues (☎ 212/758-5592). **Old Navy** has a huge flagship featuring its affordable basics and signature sense of humor at 610 Sixth Ave., at 18th St. (☎ 212/645-0663). **Diesel** sells its casual, youthful streetwear at its vibrant superstore across from Bloomingdale's, at Lexington and 60th Street (☎ 212/755-9200). **J. Crew** has a big bi-level SoHo store at 100 Prince St., between Mercer and Greene (☎ 212/966-2739).

For Men & Women

agnès b. 116 Prince St. (btw. Wooster and Greene sts.). ☎ **212/925-4649.** Subway: N, R to Prince St.

Wanna look like Catherine Deneuve in *The Umbrellas of Cherbourg* or Belmondo in *Breathless?* Then look no further than agnès b., whose French fashions are at once superstylish and classically cool. This location is the women's store, where the emphasis is on breezy, silky styles; the men's store, **agnès b homme,** is nearby at 79 Greene St., at Spring Street. The striped shirts are timeless, and the leather car coat (about $1,200) is thoroughly mod.

Brooks Brothers. 346 Madison Ave. (at 44th St.). ☎ **212/682-8800.** www.brooksbrothers. com. Subway: 4, 5, 6, 7, S to 42nd St.–Grand Central.

The perfect definition of all that is preppy lies behind this clubby storefront. The label is synonymous with quality, quiet taste, and classic tailoring. The cut of the man's suit is a tad boxy, making it great for the full American body but not quite right for the skinny European guy. There's a second location, appropriately enough, at Church and Liberty streets in the Financial District (☎ 212/267-2400).

Canal Jean Co. 504 Broadway (btw. Spring and Broome sts.). ☎ **212/226-1130.** Subway: N, R to Prince St.; 6 to Spring St.

This big, bright store almost single-handedly started the SoHo shopping revolution nearly two decades ago. You'll find scads of well-priced jeans (low-riders, bellbottoms, and just plain regular), midriff-baring T-shirts, and flannels, with the requisite vinyl purses/backpacks, and clunky costume jewelry thrown in. Go downstairs for vintage wear, but know that the stuff they have is geared to the skateboard set and tends to be a tad shopworn.

Cynthia Rowley. 112 Wooster St. (btw. Prince and Spring sts.). ☎ **212/334-1144.** Subway: N, R to Prince St.

Rowley is one of Downtown Manhattan's big fashion guns, and her work has been heralded by all the major magazines. Once you see her dynamite, slim-cut designs, you'll sing her praises too. Modern without being supertrendy, her clothes are beautifully made, witty, sophisticated, and cool. She now carries a men's line, too.

Patricia Field. 10 E. 8th St. (btw. Fifth Ave. and University Place). ☎ **212/254-1699.** Subway: 6 to Astor Place.

The wildest club kids and trendiest trendsetters know Patricia Field as *the* place to shop. Pat Field has been the leading doyenne of cutting-edge chic and downtown cool for more than two decades now, and she still is. Her shop sports the city's grooviest, most outrageous men's and women's clubwear. The store's wild makeup counter will appear tame once you see the outlandish 'dos in the wacky wig and hair salon. There is nothing understated about this place—it's a hoot to browse. Pat Field's SoHo location, **Hotel Venus,** 382 West Broadway, between Spring and Broome streets (☎ 212/966-4066), is a bit more upscale, but no less funky.

Phat Farm. 129 Prince St. (btw. West Broadway and Wooster St.). ☎ **212/533-PHAT.** Subway: N, R to Prince St.

For the most stylish hip-hop clothes on the market, head to music impresario Russell Simmons's SoHo boutique, which sells his label exclusively. Extra-puffy down jackets, extra-baggy pants, logo Ts—you'll find it all here.

Polo/Ralph Lauren. 867 Madison Ave. (at 72nd St.). ☎ **212/606-2100.** Subway: 6 to 68th St.

Among all the high-ticket designers whose shops line Madison Avenue (see "The Top Shopping Streets & Neighborhoods" earlier in this chapter), Ralph Lauren deserves special mention for the stunning beauty of this shop, housed in a landmark Rhinelander mansion. While **Polo Sport,** his store across the street at 888 Madison (☎ 212/434-8000), is also snazzy and worth a look, this particular mansion was one of New York's first important freestanding American designer shops and has continued to wear as well as the classics Ralph churns out. Housewares and infants' clothing as well as women's and men's clothes are for sale. The activewear and sporty country looks are across the street.

Shanghai Tang. 667 Madison Ave. (at 61st St.). ☎ **212/888-0111.** Subway: 4, 5, 6 to 59th St.; N, R to Fifth Ave.

This Hong Kong clothier boasts one of the loveliest, wittiest stores on Madison Avenue. The designs are irreverent takes on Chinese classics—Mandarin-collared jackets, ankle-length cheung sams—done in a vibrant palette that runs the gamut from the hot pink to electric blue (plus black, for those of us who prefer to tone down rather than up). Done in shimmering silks, lustrous velvets, and rich jacquards, the clothes are well worth a look even if you don't buy—but don't be surprised if you walk out with a piece or two.

Tristan & America. 1230 Sixth Ave. (at 49th St.). ☎ **212/246-2354.** Subway: B, D, F, Q to 47–50th sts./Rockefeller Center.

This Canadian retailer sells affordable, nicely tailored clothing in muted palettes to men and women who love Banana Republic's clothes, but need a break from the high prices there. Look for great men's sweaters, affordable women's suits, and nicely cut trousers and A-line skirts. Also in SoHo at 560 Broadway, at Prince Street (☎ 212/965-1810).

Just Women

Betsey Johnson. 248 Columbus Ave. (at 72nd St.). ☎ **212/362-3364.** Subway: 1, 2, 3, 9 to 72nd St.

Betsey has been working the same ditzy, stretchy New Wave look (think early Cyndi Lauper) forever—and on petite, madcap, slightly eccentric women, it still looks good. Also at 138 Wooster St. in SoHo (☎ 212/995-5048); 251 E. 60th St., at Second Avenue (☎ 212/319-7699); and 1060 Madison Ave., between 80th and 81st streets (☎ 212/734-1257).

○ **Eileen Fisher.** 395 West Broadway (btw. Spring and Broome sts.). ☎ **212/431-4567.** Subway: C, E to Spring St.

Slowly making their way around the nation in her own shops and through outlets like Saks and the Garnet Hill catalog, Eileen Fisher's separates are a dream come true for stylish women looking for easy-to-wear classic pieces that transcend the latest fads. She designs fluid clothes in a pleasing neutral palette and uses natural fibers that don't sacrifice comfort for chic. The A-line styles look a bit droopy on shorter women, but otherwise suit all figure types well. Prices are on the high side, but the superior quality, fabrics, and style make them worth every penny. This beautifully austere SoHo location is Fisher's prime showcase. Also at 314 E. 9th St., between First and Second avenues (☎ 212/529-5715); 103 Fifth Ave., near 18th Street (☎ 212/924-4777);

Scouring the Sample Sales

Welcome to the ultimate New York bargain: the sample sale. At a sample sale, top-notch designers recoup some losses by selling off the sample outfits they make to show to store buyers. Often, they throw in canceled orders, overstock, and discontinued styles as well. Prices are rock-bottom, even better than what you'd pay at TJ Maxx and other such discounters. What's the drawback? Such sales aren't advertised, because fashion designers don't want to alienate the big retailers by stealing their customers.

So how do you get the inside scoop? The **weekly columns** "Sales & Bargains" in *New York* magazine and "Check Out" in *Time Out New York* list current and future sales. A Web site, **www.samplesale.com**, posts information on sales in New York City as well as other cities. And **www.newyork.sidewalk.com/shopping** is a great source for the latest sales (click on "weekly sales sheet"); you can even register to be notified on a weekly basis. If you're in the Garment District (especially along Broadway and Seventh Avenue) in the morning or at lunchtime, you'll probably be handed several **flyers** advertising the sales going on that day.

A few tips as you venture into bargain land:

- Though some designers do accept credit cards, don't chance it; cash is the preferred method of payment.
- *Don't* go during lunch hour—you'll be elbow-to-elbow with harried, rushed office workers.
- Few, if any, of these spaces have dressing rooms, so be prepared to try things on over your clothes (or cross your fingers and hope it fits). Furthermore, since these garments are samples, they don't always come in a wide array of sizes. A man who is a 40 regular, for instance, is in like Flynn. If you're a 46 extra long, you're going to have rougher going.
- All items are sold "as is," and every sale is final, so inspect merchandise carefully before forking over your dough.

521 Madison Ave., at 53rd Street (☎ **212/759-9888**); and 341 Columbus Ave., near 77th Street (☎ **212/362-3000**). The closet-sized East 9th Street location basically functions as an outlet store, with lots of sale merchandise and seconds on hand.

✪ **Jill Anderson.** 311 E. 9th St. (btw. First and Second aves.). ☎ **212/253-1747.** Subway: 6 to Astor Place.

Finally, a New York designer who designs affordable clothes for real women to wear for real life—not just for 22-year-old size-2s to match with a pair of Pradas and wear out clubhopping. This narrow, peaceful shop and studio is lined on both sides with Jill's simple, clean-lined designs, which drape beautifully and accentuate a woman's form without clinging. They're wearable for all ages and many figure types (her small sizes are small enough to fit petites, and her larges generally fit a full-figured size 14). Her clothes are feminine without being frilly, retro-reminiscent but completely modern, understated but utterly stylish. If Jill's clothes sound appealing to you, don't miss her shop—you won't regret it.

Meghan Kinney Studio. 312 E. 9th St. (btw. First and Second aves.). ☎ **212/260-6329.** Subway: 6 to Astor Place.

Just across the street from Jill Anderson, Meghan Kinney specializes in elegant fashions of another kind: gorgeous, figure-flattering separates with elegantly straight lines in fabrics that cling just a bit, but not too much. Her well-priced clothes transcend constantly changing trends—pieces you buy today are likely to become wardrobe basics for years to come. If Audrey Hepburn were alive today, this is probably where she'd shop.

Nicolina. 247 W. 46th St. (btw. Broadway and Eighth Ave.). ☎ **212/302-NICO.** Subway: 1, 2, 3, 9, N, R, S to 42nd St.–Times Square.

This charming and sophisticated shop is a Theater District anomaly. Come for fashionable basics in high-quality natural materials: wide-legged linen pants, flowing A-line and princess-cut dresses in silk and cotton, sweaters from labels like Beyond Threads and Sarah Arizona in fine wools, cotton, and silk. Great accessories, too, plus a small selection of contemporary and vintage gifts. A joy to browse.

Vera Wang. 991 Madison Ave. (at 77th St.). ☎ **212/628-3400.** Subway: 6 to 77th St.

The lady who designed that white frock for Nancy Kerrigan to wear in the 1994 Olympics is still *the* hottest name in bridal fashions. Vera clothes scads of top stars (particularly petite ones with great figures) on their big day or for the Oscars in her simple, elegant designs. Vera's studio is open by appointment only, so brides-to-be looking for the best should call ahead. If you don't have big bucks, ask about the annual warehouse sale, usually in September.

Just Men
Paul Smith. 108 Fifth Ave. (at 16th St.). ☎ **212/627-9770.** Subway: F to 14th St.

This temple of new English fashion is another can't-miss. When it comes to menswear that's at once of-the-moment and undisputedly classic, Paul Smith wins the prize. Jackets, suits, pants, shoes (among the handsomest in town), sportswear, and accessories that are super-pricey but worth every cent.

Paul Stuart. Madison Ave. (at 45th St.). ☎ **212/682-0320.** Subway: 4, 5, 6, 7, S to 42nd St.–Grand Central.

If Brooks Brothers is your cup of tea, then Paul Stuart is probably a touch too hip for you. Stuart is the quintessential European men's haberdasher—gorgeous fabrics, impeccable tailoring, and high price tags. You'll find everything from suits to weekend wear; there's womenswear too, but I find Paul Stuart to be all about the man. This is a way-of-life store for those who subscribe.

Thomas Pink. 520 Madison Ave. (at 53rd St.). ☎ **212/838-1928.** Subway: E, F to Fifth Ave.; 6 to 51st St.

One of London's most revered shirtmakers has set up camp on a prime Madison Avenue corner. This shop specializes in beautifully made, pre-sized cotton shirts, crafted from the finest quality two-fold pure cotton poplin. While the name Thomas Pink bespeaks tradition to anyone who knows fine shirtmaking, don't expect stuffy: The tailors work in a broad and lively palette, in both classic and modern styles. The huge selection of ties is equally eye-catching, with some of the richest jewel tones I've seen. Pricey, but worth it.

Just Kids
If you need the basics, you'll find branches of **Gap Kids** and **Baby Gap** all over town—it's harder to avoid one than to find one. The department stores are also great sources, of course.

Greenstones et Cie. 442 Columbus Ave. (between 81st and 82nd sts.). ☎ **212/580-4322.** Subway: 1, 9 to 79th St.

This store specializes in funky cute. Many of the clothes are one-of-a-kind or hand-crafted items, so expect to pay accordingly. Also at 1184 Madison Ave., between 86th and 87th streets (☎ **212/427-1665**).

OshKosh B'Gosh. 586 Fifth Ave. (btw. 47th and 48th sts.). ☎ **212/827-0098.** Subway: E, F to Fifth Ave.

Wisconsin's most famous name in fashion has a store decked out with train compartments to display the clothes: infants in the rear, boys on the left, and girls on the right. Prices are affordable, especially for European shoppers who pay upward of $100 for overalls at home. The store gives away size-conversion charts at the center desk/cashier.

The Stork Club. 142 Sullivan St. (btw. Houston and Prince sts.). ☎ **212/505-1927.** Subway: C, E to Spring St.

This charming SoHo store overflows with gorgeous, one-of-a-kind children's wear. You'll find a wonderful collection of vintage toys, too.

VINTAGE CLOTHING

In addition to the shops below, you'll find lots more in the **East Village,** along **Lafayette Street,** and on and around Bleecker Street in the **West Village;** see "The Top Shopping Streets & Neighborhoods" earlier in this chapter.

✪ **Allan & Suzi.** 416 Amsterdam Ave. (at 80th St.). ☎ **212/724-7445.** Subway: 1, 9 to 79th St.

Make it past the freaky windows and inside you'll find one of the best consignment shops in the city. Allan and Suzi have specialized in gently worn 20th-century designer wear for well more than a decade now, and their selection is marvelous. Their extensive vintage and contemporary couture collection—which ranges from conservative Chanel to over-the-top Halston, Mackie, and Versace—is so well priced that it's well within reach of the average shopper looking for something extra-glamorous to wear. The wild one-of-a-kind pieces (for ogling only) are worth a look unto themselves.

Antique Boutique. 712 Broadway (btw. 4th St. and Astor Place). ☎ **212/460-8830.** Subway: 6 to Astor Place.

With a techno soundtrack and a huge array of less formal duds like bowling shirts, Hawaiian shirts, and hiphuggers among the vintage wear, this store targets the teen and nightclubbing crowd who want to look retro-sharp when they make the scene.

Argosy. 428 E. 9th St. (btw. First Ave. and Ave. A). ☎ **212/982-7918.** Subway: 6 to Astor Place.

This narrow shop offers a small but utterly pristine collection of '60s and '70s fashions, including an excellent collection of stylish leather jackets. Prices are reasonable considering the quality.

Love Saves the Day. 119 Second Ave. (at 7th St.). ☎ **212/228-3802.** Subway: 6 to Astor Place.

This is the store made famous in Madonna's big film break, *Desperately Seeking Susan* (she bought those groovy boots here). In the more than 10 years since the movie's release, LSD hasn't changed much, except the prices keep going up. In addition to the big and entertaining collection of tacky vintage clothes, there's another good reason to fall in Love here: the impressive assortment of Donny and Marie memorabilia and other collectible kitsch.

Metropolis. 43 Third Ave. (btw. 9th and 10th sts.). ☎ **212/358-0795.** Subway: 6 to Astor Place.

It's rumored that some of the biggest names in the fashion world scout this clean, orderly vintage shop for street fashion ideas. With good reason, too: Some of the coolest old clothes in the world turn up here, from skater pants and micro-cords to gingham-checked Western shirts perfect for your very own hoe-down or hullabaloo.

✪ **Screaming Mimi's.** 382 Lafayette St. (btw. 4th and Great Jones sts.). ☎ **212/ 677-6464.** Subway: 6 to Astor Place.

Think you hate vintage shopping? Think again: Screaming Mimi's is as neat and well organized as any high-priced boutique. The clothes are a little pricier than in some competing shops, but it's worth paying for the well-chosen selection and top-notch display. The vintage housewares department offers a cornucopia of kitschy old stuff, and the selection of New York memorabilia is a real hoot. Good accessories, too.

EDIBLES

New York boasts the finest gourmet markets in the world. Below are my favorites, but foodies will also have a ball at **Chelsea Market,** a big, dazzling food mall at 75 Ninth Ave., between 15th and 16th streets (☎ 212/243-5678); and **Fairway,** 2127 Broadway, at 74th Street (☎ 212/595-1888), an excellent and completely unpretentious gourmet food market down the street from Zabar's (see below). There's also the **Vinegar Factory,** 431 E. 91st St., between First and York avenues (☎ 212/ 987-0885), a high-end food emporium from the Zabar family, this time with a chic uptown vibe; a pleasant brunch is served on a loft overlooking the bustling store on weekends from 8am to 4pm. And don't forget about the **Union Square Greenmarket;** see p. 247.

✪ **Balducci's.** 424 Sixth Ave. (at 9th St.). ☎ **212/673-2600.** www.balducci.com. Subway: A, B, C, D, E, F, Q to W. 4th St. (use 8th St. exit).

Though you'll need a yuppified income to afford anything here, this gourmet grocery is a foodie's dream come true. It's relatively small (the shopping carts are even scaled down) and always packed, but the store overflows with imported foodstuffs; the best and freshest meats, fish, and breads; picture-perfect fruits and veggies, including international exotica like hard-to-find starfruit and enoki mushrooms; and deli, cheese, and dessert counters to die for. The knowledgeable staff manages to keep its collective cool even at the height of the holiday bustle. You can put together a gourmet take-out meal at the prepared foods counter, but I suggest heading across the street to the new **Cafe Balducci,** at Sixth Avenue and West 10th Street, where you can order from the extensive selection of sandwiches, salads, and other prepared foods and enjoy your meal at one of the pleasant cafe tables.

Dean & Deluca. 560 Broadway (at Prince St.). ☎ **212/431-1691.** www.dean-deluca.com. Subway: N, R to Prince St.

Another gourmet supermarket, though this one is a little too self-consciously hip. Still, it's hard to argue with quality. In addition to the excellent butcher, cheese, and dessert counters (check out the stunning cakes and the great character cookies) and beautiful fruits and veggies, you'll find a dried fruit and nut bar, a huge coffee bean selection, a gorgeous cut-flower selection, lots of imported waters and beers in the refrigerator case, and a limited but quality selection of kitchenware in back. There's a small cafe up front, too. Other **cafe-only** locations include a roomy branch at 9 Rockefeller Center, across from the *Today* show studio, and at the Paramount hotel, 235 W. 46th St., between Broadway and Eighth Avenue.

Gourmet Garage. 453 Broome St. (at Mercer St.). ☎ **212/941-5850.** Subway: N, R to Prince St.

This SoHo store features a neighborhood-appropriate loft-like setting and some of the tastiest gourmet products in town (the produce is particularly impressive). The Garage supplies many of the city's best restaurants, including Le Cirque 2000, and sells to the public at wholesale, about 40% off the retail of fancier stores. You'll find additional locations at 301 E. 64th St., between First and Second avenues (☎ 212/535-6271);

and 2567 Broadway, between 96th and 97th streets (☎ **212/663-0656**), the latter featuring an extensive department of Kosher foods.

✪ **Zabar's.** 2245 Broadway (at 80th St.). ☎ **212/787-2000.** Subway: 1, 9 to 79th St.

More than any other of New York's gourmet food stores, Zabar's is an institution. This giant deli sells prepared foods, packaged goods from around the world, coffee beans, excellent fresh breads, and much more. This is the place for lox, and the rice pudding is the best I've ever tasted. You'll also find an excellent selection of cooking and kitchen gadgets on the second floor, and a never-ending flow of Woody Allen film stock characters who shop here daily. Prepare yourself for serious crowds, though.

BAGELS

No one should visit New York without tasting a real New York bagel. They come in all flavors, from plain to "everything" (sesame, poppy seeds, garlic, onion, *and* salt). H&H, below, is my (and most New Yorkers') favorite, but for excellent bagels and sit-down service, head to **Ess-A-Bagel** (p. 174) instead.

H&H Bagel. 2239 Broadway (at 80th St.). ☎ **212/595-8003.** Subway: 1, 9 to 79th St.

H&H is the king of New York bagel makers. Stop in to this barebones shop for a piping-hot bagel, so good it needs no accompaniment. If you prefer the traditional toppings—cream cheese, lox, and the like—they're sold in refrigerator cases for take-home use. Other locations: 639 W. 46th St., at Twelfth Avenue, across from the *Intrepid* (☎ **212/595-8000**); and 1551 Second Ave., between 80th and 81st streets (☎ **212/734-7441**). All locations are open around the clock, so come by for a bagel fix anytime. If you crave more H&H when you get home, call ☎ **800/NY-BAGEL** to order; they ship almost anywhere.

CHOCOLATES

Black Hound. 170 Second Ave. (btw. 10th and 11th sts.). ☎ **212/979-9505.** Subway: 6 to Astor Place; L to Third Ave.

This charming shop specializes in beautifully made truffles, cookies, and cakes. This is a terrific choice for those who like their chocolates not too frilly or too sweet. Just about everything comes packaged in a blond-wood box tied with a velveteen ribbon, making them simple but elegant gifts for chocolate lovers.

La Maison du Chocolat. 1018 Madison Ave. (btw. 78th and 79th sts.). ☎ **212/744-7117.** Subway: 6 to 77th St.

The most famous chocolatier in Paris has a small shop in New York. It's hard to decide which is more fabulous—the sweets themselves (flown in from Paris) or the gorgeous ribbon on the boxes, exactly like the ones made for Hermès (only brown, of course).

Li-Lac Chocolates. 120 Christopher St. (btw. Bleecker and Hudson sts.). ☎ **212/ 242-7374.** www.citysearch.com/nyc/lilacchocolates. Subway: 1, 9 to Christopher St.–Sheridan Sq.

Li-Lac is one of the few chocolatiers anywhere still making its sweets by hand. In business in the same location since 1923, this supremely charming Village shop whips up its chocolate and maple-walnut fudge fresh every day, and it's about the best this city has seen. If fudge isn't your bag, they also make a selection of pralines, caramels, and other hand-dipped chocolates, including specialty sweets for the holidays (hollow bunnies and chocolate eggs for Easter, chocolate Santas for Christmas, and so on).

Richart Design et Chocolat. 7 E. 55th St. (btw. Fifth and Madison aves.). ☎ **212/ 371-9369.** Subway: E, F to Fifth Ave.

Vogue called these sophisticated Parisian sweets "the most beautiful chocolates in the world." Dark-chocolate lovers, in particular, will find themselves in heaven in this jewel box of a store, where the chocolates are displayed like the precious gems they are. Extremely expensive, but per-piece pricing means that everybody can afford to indulge in these marvelous treats.

Teuscher Chocolates of Switzerland. 620 Fifth Ave. (at the Channel Gardens in Rockefeller Center). ☎ **212/246-4416.** Subway: B, D, F, Q to 47–50th sts./Rockefeller Center. Also at 25 E. 61st St. (just east of Madison Ave.). ☎ **212/751-8482.** Subway: 4, 5, 6 to 59th St.; N, R to Lexington Ave.

At $49 a pound, you'd think they were selling gold bouillon. Teuscher makes mints, pralines, and wondrous marzipan, but it's the truffles that folks write home about. Splurge on one or two justifiably famous champagne truffles, and you'll weep with joy.

ELECTRONICS

J&R Music World/Computer World. Park Row (at Ann St., opposite City Hall Park). ☎ **800/221-8180** or 212/238-9100. www.jandr.com. Subway: 2, 3 to Park Place.

Midtown may be overrun with electronics dealers, but it's the Financial District's J&R that's the city's top discount computer, electronics, and small appliance retailer. J&R takes up almost the whole block of Park Row, with separate storefronts for small appliances, computers, music (jazz, pop, and classical), audio and video, and office equipment. The sales staff is knowledgeable but can get pushy if you don't buy at once or know exactly what you want. Don't succumb—take your time and find exactly what you need. Or better yet, peruse the store's copious catalog or extensive Web site, both of which make advance research, mail order, and comparison shopping easy.

Sony Style. 550 Madison Ave. (btw. 55th and 56th sts.). ☎ **212/833-8000.** Subway: E, F to Fifth Ave.

This all-Sony retail store doesn't offer any bargains, but electronics buffs will enjoy perusing the full line of company products. On street level is the gadget store, full of small electronics from Sony PlayStations to bookshelf stereo systems. Downstairs is the "Home Entertainment Lounge," a stylish setting for Sony's complete line of audio components and home-entertainment systems.

GIFTS

If you're looking for a special gift for a creative spirit, be sure to check out the shops that line **East 9th Street** between Second Avenue and Avenue A in the East Village; the side streets of **SoHo,** where a good number unusual boutiques still survive; new **NoLiTa;** and Greenwich Village, especially in the wonderful cadre of one-of-a-kind shops in the **West Village.** For details, see "The Top Shopping Streets & Neighborhoods" earlier in this chapter.

For first-rate Fifth Avenue gifts, don't forget **Tiffany & Co.,** whose upper level boasts wonderful, and surprisingly affordable, small gifts like money clips, key rings, picture frames, and more, all crafted in signature Tiffany silver and wrapped in the unmistakable blue box; see "Jewelry & Accessories" below.

An American Craftsman. 790 Seventh Ave. (at 52nd St.) ☎ **212/399-2555.** Subway: 1, 9 to 50th St.

This pleasing shop sells wood furniture and crafts, decorative glassware, silver jewelry, and other fine-quality gift items—all, as the name implies, hand-crafted by American artists. They also sell the highly prized glass handmade by Vermont-based Simon Pearce, and their wooden jewelry box and humidor collection is stunning. Other branches: In the Village at 317 Bleecker St. (☎ **212/727-0841**) and 478 Sixth Ave.

(☎ 212/243-0245); in the Financial District at 60 Broad St. (☎ **212/480-3945**); in Gramercy Park at 77 Irving Place (☎ **212/598-4248**); and on the East Side at 1222 Second Ave. (☎ **212/794-3440**).

And Bob's Your Uncle. 137 W. 22nd St. (btw. Sixth and Seventh aves.). ☎ **212/ 627-7702.** Subway: 1, 9, F to 23rd St.

Who cares who Bob is? He's a genius for whimsy, kitsch, and clutter, turning it all into creative and eco-friendly gift items. Practically everything is artfully made from stuff that the rest of us throw away: lampshades from vintage clothing and electrical piping, mirrors framed in mosaics of broken bottle glass. Some pieces are surprisingly beautiful, and the whole vintage-meets-postmodernism take is tons of fun.

La Maison Moderne. 144 W. 19th St. (btw. Sixth and Seventh aves.). ☎ **212/691-9603.** Subway: 1, 9 to 18th St.

This lovely little shop is filled with a beautiful, affordable mix of both vintage and contemporary gift items. Lots of care went into assembling this charming Parisian-inspired store, and it shows. My favorite part of the store is the basement, where you'll find one-of-a-kind homewares like handcrafted velvet pillows and the cutest collection of teapots in town.

HOME FASHIONS & HOUSEWARES

There's a mammoth **Crate & Barrel** at Madison Avenue and 59th Street (☎ **212/ 308-0011**), and discount superstore **Bed Bath & Beyond** at Sixth Avenue and 18th Street (☎ **212/255-3550**).

The second floor of **Zabar's** (see "Edibles" above) is an excellent source for high-end kitchenware galore, as is **Broadway Panhandler,** at 477 Broome St., between Greene and Wooster in SoHo (☎ **212/966-3434**).

If you're looking for high-quality linens, **Portico Bed & Bath,** 139 Spring St., at Wooster, in SoHo (☎ **212/941-7722**) and 584 Broadway at 20th Street in the Flatiron District (☎ **212/328-4343** or 212/473-6662), is my favorite outlet for luxurious linens, ultra-plush towels, and well-designed bath accessories. **Pratesi,** the excellent Italian linen maker, is at 829 Madison Ave., at 69th St. (☎ **212/288-2315**).

✪ ABC Carpet & Home. 888 Broadway (at 19th St.). ☎ **212/473-3000.** www. abccarpet.com. Subway: N, R, 4, 5, 6, L to 14th St.–Union Square.

This two-building emporium is the ultimate home fashions and furnishings department store. On the west side of the street is the ten-floor home emporium, which is a dream come true for aspiring Martha Stewarts. Shopping ABC has often been compared to taking a fantasy tour of your ancestor's attic: The goods run the gamut from mosaic-tile end tables to hand-painted Tuscan pottery to Tiffanyish lamps to distressed bed frames made up with Frette linens to much, much more, all carefully chosen and exquisitely displayed. There's a whole floor of on-the-bolt upholstery fabrics to die for. Prices aren't bad comparatively speaking, but these are high-end goods. Some of the smaller items are quite affordable, though, and their occasional sales yield substantial discounts. In back is the **ABC Parlour Cafe,** serving lunch fare, tea, and elegant desserts. Across the street is the multi-floor carpet store, which boasts a remarkable collection of area rugs in particular.

Amalgamated Home. 9–19 Christopher St. (btw. Sixth and Seventh aves.). ☎ **212/ 255-4160** (furniture and lighting), 212/989-6538 (hardware), or 212/691-8695 (household sundries). Subway: 1, 9 to Christopher St.–Sheridan Square.

This trio of home shops stocks eye-catching household goods you won't see anywhere else. Looking for brushed metal switchplates for your groovy new stainless-steel

Street Shopping

New York has a very active street culture. Along main thoroughfares throughout the city, you'll see street merchants selling everything from fresh fruit to knapsacks to art books to baseball cards. Many are legitimate, licensed vendors, but some aren't. Chances are, if there's a suitcase involved or a blanket that can be rolled up and carted away quickly, or the collection of stuff for sale is a little too eclectic (like it could be the contents of somebody's apartment or a traveler's bag, say), the vendor shouldn't be there.

The museum streets of **West 53rd and 54th** are peppered with vendors selling their own art. Book vendors line Broadway on the **Upper West Side,** especially on weekends. If you encounter a vendor selling just-published hardcover books on the street, chances are they've been stolen. And paperback books sold without covers are considered returned goods and aren't meant for resale. Hawkers with faux Chanel and Prada handbags and "designer" watches are most prolific in **Times Square.** The quality is questionable, so don't even think about shelling out more than $20 for a counterfeit watch. **SoHo** is popular with high-end street peddlers, mostly legitimate, hawking hand-crafted silver jewelry, coffee-table books, and their own art, mainly along Prince Street. **St. Marks Place** (8th Street) in the East Village is big on cheap sunglasses and the kind of chunky silver jewelry Marilyn Manson would love. At the city's immensely popular weekly **outdoor flea markets,** particularly those that congregate 26th Street and Sixth Avenue, you'll find all kinds of stuff, from trash-worthy junk to highly collectible antiques. (See "Antiques & Collectibles" earlier in this section.) Most flea-market vendors are perfectly legitimate, but on occasion you'll run across one that's clearly hawking stolen goods.

When it comes to this type of alternative retail, the best rule of thumb is this: Use your best judgement, and let your conscience be your guide. But if you choose to buy what are clearly stolen goods, keep in mind that you're encouraging this kind of resale with your wallet—and the next set of stuff for sale on the street could be yours.

---

kitchen? How about a purple velvet love seat straight out of a Looney Tunes cartoon? Or the hippest rice bowls in town? You'll find it all and more at Amalgamated. Don't miss the terrific matte-white dinnerware shaped like Chinese takeout containers from Swid Powell.

Fishs Eddy. 889 Broadway (at 19th St.). ☎ **212/420-9020.** www.fishseddy.com. Subway: N, R, 4, 5, 6, L to 14th St.–Union Square.

What a great idea—selling remainders of kitschy, custom-designed china leftover from yesteryear. Ever wanted a dish that *really* says "Blue Plate Special?" Or how about a coffee mug with the terse logo "Cup o' Joe To Go?" The store is Browse Heaven, and prices are low enough. Other items for sale include basic vintage and retro-inspired flatware, heavy crockery bowls, and classic restaurant-supply glassware that can be hard to find in regular stores, like soda-fountain and pint glasses. There's also a branch at 2176 Broadway, at 77th Street (☎ **212/873-8819**).

✪ **Galileo.** 37 Seventh Ave. (at 13th St.). ☎ **212/243-1629.** Subway: 1, 2, 3, 9 to 14th St.

This eclectic shop features an excellent mix of contemporary wares and 20th-century vintage pieces. The selection of fine-quality linens and kitchen towels is small but smart. There are usually a few pieces of furniture scattered about, often blond-wood post-war pieces from the likes of Heywood-Wakefield or Paul McCobb. Gorgeous accessories galore abound here, as well as the most pristine selection of vintage glassware I've seen. Not kitsch—an excellent collection of tumblers, highballs, cocktails, and more. Registry is available.

Moss. 146 Greene St. (btw. Houston and Prince sts.). ☎ **212/226-2190.** Subway: N, R to Prince St.

This sleek, brightly lit store is a temple to modern design. All kinds of everyday object are reinvented by cutting-edge European designers, from staplers to flatware to shelving units. It may sound out there, but the products (mostly by European designers) were designed with 21st-century homes in mind, so they're surprisingly utilitarian and space-efficient. If you have any interest in contemporary industrial design, don't miss this place.

Totem Design Group. 71 Franklin St. (btw. Church St. and Broadway). ☎ **212/925-5506.** Subway: 1, 9 to Franklin St.

If you're interested in finding out what's new in contemporary design, look no further than Totem, which is dedicated to manufacturing and distributing furniture and objects by talented young domestic and international designers. Designs range from minimalist to whimsical to super-swanky, but the three-fold theme of form, function, and affordability is common throughout.

JEWELRY & ACCESSORIES

Every big-name international jewelry merchant has a shop on Fifth Avenue in the 50s: **Cartier,** at no. 653 (☎ 212/446-3400); **Bulgari,** at no. 730 (☎ 212/315-9000); royal jeweler **Asprey,** at no. 725 (☎ 212/688-1811); ultra-glamorous **Harry Winston** at no. 718 (☎ 212/245-2000); and, best of all, **Van Cleef & Arpels,** at no. 744 (☎ 212/644-9500). Some of the smaller boutique names of Europe are on Madison Avenue in the '60s. **Fred Leighton,** 773 Madison Ave., at 66th Street (☎ 212/288-1872), specializes in magnificent estate jewelry.

Bargain hunters shouldn't miss the **Diamond District,** the nation's leading wholesale gem and jewelry center, on West 47th Street; see "The Top Shopping Streets & Neighborhoods" earlier in this chapter.

Vintage jewelry fans will find that signed costume pieces from the 1950s and 1960s are hot items at the flea markets. Also check the vintage clothing and collectibles stores as well as **Antique Addiction,** 436 West Broadway, just south of Prince Street (☎ 212/925-6342), a charming SoHo shop chock full of vintage genuine and costume jewelry (including a great selection of cufflinks), plus classic eyewear and lighters.

Fortunoff. 681 Fifth Ave. (btw. 53rd and 54th sts.). ☎ **212/758-6660.** Subway: E, F to Fifth Ave.

Despite the high-ticket facade, Fortunoff is a good resource for Swatch watches and a nice place to start pricing classic pieces: gold earrings, necklaces, bracelets, and the like. The styles aren't innovative, but the store tries to keep up an image as a discounter, and prices are low. Great for wedding gifts, too.

Reinstein/Ross. 29 E. 73rd St. (btw. Fifth and Madison aves.). ☎ **212/772-1901.** Subway: 6 to 77th St.

If you're looking for an engagement ring or another piece of finely crafted jewelry but find yourself thoroughly bored with standard settings, check out the unusual designs at Reinstein/Ross. Many of their gold and silver pieces are done with beautiful matte finishes, and they also specialize in unusual gems. Also at 122 Prince St., between Greene and Wooster streets, in SoHo (☎ 212/226-4513).

Robert Lee Morris. 400 West Broadway (btw. Spring and Broome sts.). ☎ **212/431-9405.** Subway: C, E to Spring St.

Smooth gold matte jewelry is Robert Lee Morris's thing, but he's always got something new and original in his SoHo store.

○ **Stuart Moore.** 128 Prince St. (at Wooster St.). ☎ **212/941-1023.** Subway: N, R to Prince St.

Those interested in sleek, minimal, angular modern design should head for this sizable store, which showcases the works of Stuart Moore and other supremely talented contemporary designers. Ultra-modern, elegant, and simply terrific—I could browse here for hours.

○ **Tiffany & Co.** 727 Fifth Ave. (at 57th St.). ☎ **212/755-8000.** Subway: N, R to Fifth Ave.

The most famous jewelry store in New York—and maybe the world—deserves all the kudos. This wonderful multi-level store offers a breathtaking selection of jewelry, signature watches, and a handful of surprisingly affordable gift items. I particularly like the whimsical designs, like butterfly brooches and other playful shapes. The store is so full of tourists at all times that it's easy to browse without having any intention of buying. If you do indulge, anything you buy—even a $35 key chain—comes wrapped in that unmistakable blue box and presented with flair.

Tourneau Time Machine. 12 E. 57th St. (at Madison Ave.). ☎ **212/758-7300.** Subway: N, R to Fifth Ave.

There are two more Tourneau locations, but this snazzy three-floor emporium is the one to visit. It's almost like a watch theme store, with entertaining displays at every turn. The mind-boggling selection runs the gamut from Swatch to Rolex.

LEATHER GOODS, HANDBAGS & LUGGAGE

The big names of European luxury leather goods have their stores on Fifth Avenue in the '50s or Madison Avenue in the '60s. **Hermès,** 11 E. 57th St. (☎ **212/751-3181**), begins a parade of big-name purveyors of luxury leathers from Fifth Avenue to Park Avenue that includes **Prada,** 45 E. 57th St. (☎ **212/308-2332**), and **Louis Vuitton,** 49 E. 57th St. (☎ **212/371-6111**).

Greenwich Village is the place to go for funkier and more affordable leather looks, especially along Christopher and Bleecker streets in the West Village. Worth seeking out are **Bleecker House,** at 182 Bleecker St. (☎ **212/358-1442**), for leather jackets, and the **Village Tannery,** at 173 Bleecker (☎ **212/673-5444**), for bags, wallets, and organizers.

The Lower East Side's bargain district is a great source for discount handbags and luggage. The best of the bunch is **Fine & Klein,** 119 Orchard St., near Delancey (☎ **212/674-6720**), offering good discounts (usually 20%) on name-brand handbags.

Coach. 595 Madison Ave. (at 57th St.). ☎ **212/754-0041.** Subway: 4, 5, 6 to 59th St; N, R to Lexington Ave.

Traditionally super-preppy, this New York-based bag manufacturer has become more high-styled of late, and the line is all the better for it. Pricey, but the quality is top-notch—these bags last almost forever. Great men's briefcases and new accessory lines, too. Also at 5 World Trade Center (☎ **212/488-0080**), and other locations throughout the city.

Crouch & Fitzgerald. 400 Madison Ave. (at 48th St.). ☎ **212/755-5888.** Subway: 4, 5, 6 to 42nd St.

This long-time specialist in leather goods is an excellent source for the big names in luggage as well as its own top-quality house brands.

Kate Spade. 454 Broome St. (at Mercer St.). ☎ **212/274-1991.** Subway: N, R to Prince St.

Kate Spade revolutionized the high-end handbag market with her practical yet chic rectangular handbags. They come in a wide range of fabrics and sizes, from pretty seer-suckers to groovy prints to fashionable flannel to basic black, plus a wide range of solids. The daintier evening line is charming, particularly the grosgrain silks.

Manhattan Portage Ltd. Store. 333 E. 9th St. (btw. First and Second aves.). ☎ **212/ 995-1949.** www.manhattanportageltd.com. Subway: 6 to Astor Place.

Come here for the hippest nylon and canvas carry-alls in town. True to its name, Man-hattan Portage manufactures all its bags right in the city, and they're made from hard-wearing materials that can stand up to an urban lifestyle. Popular styles include all-purpose messenger bags, DJ bags, and backpacks in a range of colors from irides-cent yellow to camouflage. Manhattan Portage bags are also sold at a number of other stores in the city and throughout the world (all listed on the Web site), but you're unlikely to find such a complete selection elsewhere.

LOGO STORES

Coca-Cola Fifth Ave. 711 Fifth Ave. (btw. 55th and 56th sts.). ☎ **212/418-9261.** Subway: E, F, N, R to Fifth Ave.

The one that began the Fifth Avenue theme-store invasion. T-shirts, jackets, baseball caps, keychains, glassware—if they can slap a Coke logo on it, it's probably for sale here. You'll also find vintage vending machines—and, of course, Coke.

The Disney Store. 711 Fifth Ave. (at 55th St.). ☎ **212/702-0702.** Subway: E, F or N, R to Fifth Ave.

Disney burst onto Manhattan's retail scene with this monster three-story emporium. Bring the kids in, and just *try* to get out without buying something. As a corollary to the Disney-led Times Square redevelopment, you'll find another big branch at 210 W. 42nd St., at Seventh Avenue (☎ 212/221-0430). There's yet another on the Upper West Side at Columbus Avenue and 66th Street (☎ 212/362-2386), worth men-tioning for its collection of ABC TV souvenirs (the studio is right next door), from Regis and Kathie Lee Ts to a range of souvenirs spouting those wry black-on-yellow "TV is Good" messages.

NBA Store. 666 Fifth Ave. (at 52nd St.). ☎ **212/515-NBA1.** Subway: B, D, F, Q to 47–50th sts./Rockefeller Center.

For all things NBA and WNBA, head to this three-level mega-store, a multimedia cel-ebration of pro basketball, complete with a bleacher-seated arena for player appear-ances and signings.

Niketown. 6 E. 57th St. (btw. Fifth and Madison aves.). ☎ **212/891-6453.** Subway: N, R to Fifth Ave.

More multimedia advertorial than sportswear store, Niketown opened in the fall of 1996 with much to-do. It's actually surprisingly low-key and attractive, with five floors of shoes and athletic wear displayed in stark, Lucite-and-polished-metal surroundings. "Museum" cases display Sneakers of the Rich and Famous, and everywhere you're assailed by images of celebrity pitchmen and women, with his Airness prevalent above all others, of course (retirement? what retirement?). No sales or bargains here—plan on paying top dollar for the high-style athletic wear. Somebody's gotta pay for this place!

✪ **The Pop Shop.** 292 Lafayette St. (at Prince St.). ☎ **212/219-2784.** www.haring.com. Subway: B, D, F, Q to Broadway–Lafayette St.

For affordable and wearable art that makes super-cool souvenirs, come to the Pop Shop. This groovy store is chock-full of items based on designs by artist Keith Haring, who died in 1990. T-shirts, posters, calendars, stationery, toys, notebooks, neat transparent backpacks—all sport the vivid primary colors and loopy stick-figure drawings that Haring made famous. Best of all, the Pop Shop is a non-profit organization, offering continued support to the AIDS-related and children's charities that the young artist championed in life.

Warner Bros. Studio Store. 1 E. 57th St. (at Fifth Ave.). ☎ **212/754-0300.** Subway: N, R to Fifth Ave.

This mega-theme store sits right near both Van Cleef & Arpels and Tiffany—wouldn't Bugs have a field day in those joints! Another three-story shop with cartoon-character everything, including animation cels for sale. For the short-attention-span crowd, Looney Tunes play continuously on store monitors. There's now an equally monolithic branch at 1 Times Square, at 42nd Street between Broadway and Seventh Ave. (☎ **212/840-4040**).

Yankees Clubhouse Shop. 393 Fifth Ave. (btw. 36th and 37th sts.). ☎ **212/685-4693.** Subway: 6 to 33rd St.

For all your Bronx Bombers needs—hats, jerseys, jackets, and so on, including souvenirs from the Yanks' '96 and '98 World Series wins. Tickets for regular-season home games are also for sale, and there's a limited selection of other New York team jerseys as well. Also at 110 E. 59th St., between Park and Lexington avenues (☎ **212/ 758-7844**); and at Fulton and South streets in the South Street Seaport (☎ **212/ 514-7182**).

MUSEUM STORES

American Craft Museum. 40 W. 53rd St. (btw. Fifth and Sixth Aves.). ☎ **212/956-3535.** Subway: E, F to Fifth Ave.

The nation's top showcase for contemporary crafts boasts an impressive collection of crafts in its museum store, too. Come for exquisite handblown glassware, one-of-a-kind jewelry, original pottery, and other artistic treasures, all beautifully displayed.

Metropolitan Museum of Art Store. Fifth Ave. at 82nd St. ☎ **212/570-3894.** www.metmuseum.org. Subway: 4, 5, 6 to 86th St.

Given the scope of the museum itself, it's no wonder that the gift shop is outstanding. Many treasures from the museum's collection have been reproduced as jewelry, china, and other objets d'art. The range of art books is dizzying, and upstairs is an equally comprehensive selection of posters and inventive children's toys. The notecards, calendars, and wrapping paper also make fun, affordable gifts. And you don't even have to go uptown to indulge: Other branches can be found on the plaza at Rockefeller Center (☎ **212/332-1360**), in SoHo at 113 Prince St. (☎ **212/614-3000**), and on the mezzanine level at Macy's (☎ **212/268-7266**).

Maxilla & Mandible. 451-5 Columbus Ave. (btw. 81st and 82nd sts.). ☎ **212/724-6173.** Subway: B, C to 81st St.

This shop is not affiliated with the American Museum of Natural History, but a visit here makes a good adjunct to your trip to the museum (which is right around the corner). It may look like a freakshop at first glance, but it's really a fascinating natural history emporium. Inside you'll find unusual rocks and shells from around the world, luminescent butterflies in display boxes, even surprisingly affordable real fossils containing prehistoric fish and insects that come with details on their history and where they were excavated. There's also a good variety of natural history-themed toys for the kids.

✪ **MOMA Design Store.** 44 W. 53rd St. (btw. Fifth and Sixth aves.). ☎ **212/767-1050.** www.moma.org. Subway: E, F to Fifth Ave.; B, D, F, Q to 47–50th sts./Rockefeller Center.

Across the street from the Museum of Modern Art is this terrific shop, whose stock ranges from museum posters and clever toys for kids to fully licensed reproductions of many of the classics of modern design, including free-form Alvar Aalto vases, Frank Lloyd Wright chairs, and Eames recliners. If these high-design items are out of your reach, there are plenty of more affordable outré home accessories to choose from.

Even if you don't check out the permanent collection, pop in across the street at the museum's main gift shop for a stellar collection of gift books, artsy notecards, and the like, all with a modern twist.

Museum of American Folk Art. 2 Lincoln Sq. (Columbus Ave. between 65th and 66th sts.). ☎ **212/496-2966.** www.folkartmuse.org. Subway: 1, 9 to 66th St.

This charming gift shop is filled with one-of-a-kind objects that make wonderful take-home gifts. It's especially good with gifts for children, and homespun holiday ornaments at Christmastime.

MUSIC

In addition to the choices below, music buffs will find a wealth of new-and-used shops in the West Village on **Bleecker Street** between Sixth and Seventh avenues as well as on side streets like Carmine and Christopher. Standouts include **Rebel Rebel,** 319 Bleecker St. (☎ 212/989-0770), for British and Japanese imports and New Wave and glam classics; and **Rockit Scientist,** just off Bleecker at 43 Carmine St. (☎ 212/242-0066). Unfortunately, **Bleecker Bob's Golden Oldies,** 118 W. 3rd St., between Sixth Avenue and MacDougal Street (☎ 212/475-9677), has outlived its legend; it's now a dirty little hole-in-the-wall with lots of worn, badly organized vinyl and a rude staff.

Grungy **St. Marks Place** between Third and Second avenues in the East Village is another great bet. **Venus Records** (☎ 212/598-4459) is a standout, as are **Sounds** (☎ 212/677-3444), the dirt-cheap granddaddy of the St. Marks shops, and **Mondo Kim's** (☎ 212/598-9985) for indie music, video, and 'zines. Farther down, just off of St. Marks at 131 Ave. A, is **Accidental Records and Tapes** (☎ 212/995-2224), a friendly junkpile of a store noteworthy for its good, cheap collection of used CDs and "we never close" policy.

In the Financial District, **J&R Music World** has a big selection of classical, jazz, and rock, and brand-new releases are almost always on sale; see "Electronics" above for details.

For musical instruments, see "Times Square & the Theater District" under "The Top Shopping Streets & Neighborhoods" earlier in this chapter.

Academy Records & CDs. 12 W. 18th St. (btw. Fifth and Sixth aves.). ☎ **212/242-3000.** www.academy-records.com. Subway: 4, 5, 6, N, R, L to 14th St.–Union Square.

This Flatiron District shop has a cool intellectual air that's more reminiscent of a good used-book store than your average used-record store. Academy is always filled with classical, opera, and jazz junkies perusing the extensive and well-priced collection of used CDs and vinyl. In addition to the extensive classical and jazz collection is a variety of other audiophile favorites, from rare '60s pop songsters to spoken word. Adjacent is the actual used-book store.

○ **Bleecker St. Records.** 239 Bleecker St. (near Carmine St., just west of Sixth Ave.). ☎ **212/255-7899.** Subway: A, B, C, D, E, F, Q to W. 4th St.

This sizable, well-lit space is great for one-stop shopping. The clean, well-organized CD and LP collections run the gamut from rock, oldies, jazz, folk, and blues to Oi! punk. You'll find lots of imports, collectible, and out-of-print records (including singles), a terrific collection of used CDs, and a mix of casual listeners and serious collectors cruising the bins.

○ **Colony Record & Tape Center.** 1619 Broadway (at 49th St.). ☎ **212/265-2050.** www.colonymusic.com. Subway: 1, 9 to 50th St.; N, R to 49th St.

This longlived Theater District shop is housed in the legendary Brill Building, basically the Tin Pan Alley of '50s and '60s pop, where legendary songwriters like Goffin and King and producers like Don Kirschner and Phil Spector crafted the soundtrack for a generation. It's the perfect home for Colony, a nostalgia emporium filled with a pricey but excellent collection of vintage vinyl and CDs. You'll find a great collection of Broadway scores and cast recordings, plus decades worth of recordings by pop song stylists both legendary and obscure. There's also one of the best collections of sheet music in the city (including some hard-to-find international stuff), and a great selection of original theater and movie posters. You can stock up your in-home karaoke machine here, too.

If you like Colony, also visit **Footlight,** 113 E. 12th St., between Third and Fourth avenues (☎ **212/533-1572;** www.footlight.com), whose dreamy collection of vintage vinyl is strong in jazz and pop vocalists, soundtracks, and showtunes.

Generation Records. 210 Thompson St. (btw. Bleecker and 3rd sts.). ☎ **212/254-1100.** Subway: A, B, C, D, E, F, Q to W. 4th St.

This tidy little store sells mostly CDs and is an excellent source for "import" live recordings. Originally specializing in hardcore, punk, and heavy metal, the new collection upstairs still has a heavy edge but has since diversified appreciably. Downstairs is a well-organized and well-priced used CD selection that's not as picked over as most and runs the genre gamut; there's also a good selection of used LPs. Despite the help's tough look, they're actually quite friendly and helpful.

Jazz Record Center. 236 W. 26th St. (btw. Seventh and Eighth aves.), 8th floor. ☎ **212/ 675-4480.** Subway: 1, 9 to 28th St.

Jazz Record Center is *the* place to find rare and out-of-print jazz records. In addition to the extensive selection of CDs and vinyl (including 78s), videos, books, posters, and other memorabilia are available. Prices can be high, as befits the rarity of the stock. Owner Frederick Cohen is extremely knowledgeable, so come here if you're trying to track down something obscure (Cohen does mail-order business as well).

NYCD. 426 Amsterdam Ave. (btw. 80th and 81st sts.). ☎ **212/724-4466.** Subway: 1, 9 to 79th St.

This neat, narrow little store is home to one of the city's bet collections of used rock CDs thanks to its off-the-beaten-track Upper West Side location. Downtown trollers simply don't make it this far uptown to prune the selection, so it's easy to find lots of top titles among the pickings.

○ **Other Music.** 15 E. 4th St. (btw. Broadway and Lafayette St.). ☎ **212/477-8150.** Subway: 6 to Astor Place; B, D, F, Q to Broadway–Lafayette St.

Head to Other Music for the wildest sounds in town. You won't find a major label here (that's what Tower is for across the street). This shop focuses exclusively on small international labels, especially those on the cutting edge (you can find records on the

Knitting Factory label here). The bizarro runs the gamut from underground Japanese spin doctors to obscure Irish folk; needless to say, the world music selection is terrific. Fascinating, and bound to be filled with music you've never heard of. The sales staff really knows their stuff, so ask away.

Throb. 211 E. 14th (btw. Second and Third aves.). ☎ **212/533-2328.** www.throb.com. Subway: L to Third Ave.

Throb is home to CDs and 12" vinyls of not-even-close-to-mainstream genres: house, ambient, jungle, drum-and-bass, trance, trip hop. Imports are also big business here. Not surprisingly, considering the cutting-edge inventory, it's a popular stop for dance-club DJs. Test drive the trippy sounds in a listening booth. You'll also find record bags and T-shirts.

If the music at Throb is your thing, you might also want to hike out to **Temple Records,** 29A Ave. B, between 2nd and 3rd streets, in the East Village (☎ **212/ 475-7552**).

Tower Records. 692 Broadway (at W. 4th St.). ☎ **212/505-1500.** Subway: N, R to 8th St.; 6 to Astor Place.

As mighty of a chain as it may be, it's hard to complain about Tower. Both the Village location and the Upper West Side branch (2107 Broadway, at 66th St.; ☎ **212/ 799-2500**) are huge multimedia superstores brimming with an encyclopedic collection of music—classical, jazz, rock, world, you name it. The Village location also stocks a very good selection of indie and alternative labels. Just behind it at West 4th and Lafayette is **Tower Books** (☎ **212/228-5100**), where you'll find videos, books, and magazines; and the **Tower Clearance Outlet** (☎ **212/228-7317**), selling out-of-print and cut-out CDs for a song. Look for in-stores by big names in music, usually advertised in the *Time Out New York* and *Village Voice* music sections.

Virgin Megastore. 1540 Broadway (at 45th St.). ☎ **212/921-1020.** Subway: 1, 2, 3, 7, 9, N, R to 42nd St.–Times Square.

Right in the heart of Times Square, this superstore bustles day and night. For the size of it, the selection isn't as wide as you'd think; still, you're likely to find what you're looking for among the two levels of domestic and imported CDs and cassettes (there's also a limited vinyl selection). Other plusses are an extensive singles department, a phenomenal number of listening posts, plus a huge video department. There's also a bookstore, a cafe, and multiplex movie theater, and you can even arrange airfare on Virgin Atlantic with the on-site travel agent. The new Union Square location, 52 E. 14th St., at Broadway (☎ **212/598-4666**), is brand new but equally hopping. As at Tower, look for a busy schedule of in-stores at both locations.

PAPER & STATIONERY

Kate's Paperie. 561 Broadway (btw. Prince and Spring sts.). ☎ **212/941-9816.** Subway: N, R to Prince St.

Three cheers to Kate's for keeping the art of letter writing alive in our computer age. I could browse for hours among this delightful shop's handmade stationery and wrap, innovative invitation and thank you's, imported notebooks, writing tools, and other creative paper products, including cool paper lampshades. Lovely art cards, too—perfect for writing the folks back home. A joy! Also at 8 W. 13th St., between Fifth and Sixth avenues (☎ **212/633-0570**), and 1282 Third Ave., between 73rd and 74th streets (☎ **212/396-3670**), but the SoHo location is best.

Kate Spade Paper. 59 Thompson St. (btw. Broome and Spring sts.). ☎ **212/965-8654.** Subway: C, E to Spring St.

The très hip SoHo bagmaker (see "Leather Goods, Handbags & Luggage" above) now sells her own charming line of preprinted notecards and stationery in this cute little store.

SHOES

Designer shoe shops start on **East 57th Street** and amble up **Madison Avenue,** becoming pricier as you move uptown. **SoHo** is an excellent place to search for the latest styles; the streets are overrun with terrific shoe stores. Cheaper copies of the trendiest styles are sold in the tiny shops along **8th Street** between Broadway and Sixth Avenue in the Village, which some people call Shoe Row. Most department stores have two sizable shoe departments—one for designer stuff and one for daily wearables. See "The Top Shopping Streets & Neighborhoods" and "The Big Department Stores" earlier in this chapter. For **Niketown,** see "Logo Stores" above.

Billy Martin's. 810 Madison Ave. (at 68th St.). ☎ **212/861-3100.** Subway: 6 to 68th St.

Baseball's most notorius manager was also an urban cowboy, and his shop brings the Santa Fe look to Madison Avenue. It's a good source for fantasy cowboy boots. Rhinestones optional.

Giraudon. 339 West Broadway (at Grand St.). ☎ **212/334-9867.** Subway: C, E to Spring St.

Giraudon makes fashionable, well-made street shoes for hip men and women who want something fashionable but not too chunky or trendy. Not cheap, but not overpriced—these shoes last forever. Also at 152 Eighth Ave. (between 17th and 18th streets) in Chelsea (☎ **212/633-0999**).

John Fluevog Shoes. 104 Prince St. (btw. Mercer and Greene sts.). ☎ **212/431-4484.** www.fluevog.com. Subway: N, R to Prince St.

John Fluevog's funky, chunky footwear has proven itself stylish enough to make the brand a mainstay among usually fickle young trendsetters. Some of the styles border on the ridiculous (check out the super-silly space-age Lift-Offs, with lucite heels) but others, like the beautifully retro-styled Buick loafers, are a dream. Offering a more stylized take on the Dr. Marten look, the longstanding Angels line are the ultimate in sturdy comfort for urban feet.

Kenneth Cole. 95 Fifth Ave. (at 17th St.). ☎ **212/675-2550.** www.kencole.com. Subway: N, R to 23rd St.

Kenneth Cole may be hitting the runway these days with a complete line of stylish clothing, but it's footwear that he'll always be most famous for. An ideal blend of comfort and glamour for both men and women—a tad pricey, but worth it. Great leather jackets and accessories, too. Also at 353 Columbus Ave, near 77th Street (☎ **212/873-2061**); 597 Broadway in SoHo (☎ **212/965-0283**); and street level at Grand Central Terminal, 107 E. 42nd St. (☎ **212/949-8079**).

Manolo Blahnik. 31 W. 54th St. (btw. Fifth and Sixth aves.). ☎ **212/582-3007.** Subway: E, F to Fifth Ave.

If you make only one wild and crazy purchase in your life, it may well be a pair of Manoloes—wildly sexy women's shoes notorious for the cut and sway of the shoe and the way they shape the leg. Most famous are the catch-me-if-you-can high heels, but there are plenty of flats and low heels, too. Custom shoes in your own fabric are also a possibility. Cinderella never had it so good.

Manolo fans might also want to check out the similarly sexy but slightly trendier styles from **Jimmy Choo,** whose brand-new three-floor emporium is at 645 Fifth Ave., at 51st Street (☎ **212/593-0800**).

Sacco. 324 Columbus Ave. (btw. 75th and 76th sts.). ☎ **212/799-5229.** Subway: B, C to 81st St.

This city shoe chain specializes in women's shoes that cross style with supreme comfort. I especially love their fall and winter boots, comfortable enough to carry me around the city on even the most arduous of research days. Lots of terrific basic blacks and browns. Good sales, too. Also at 111 Thompson St. in SoHo (☎ **212/925-8010**); 94 Seventh Ave., at 16th Street, in Chelsea (☎ **212/675-5180**); and 2355 Broadway, at 86th Street (☎ **212/874-8362**).

✪ **Sigerson Morrison.** 242 Mott St. (btw. Houston and Prince sts.). ☎ **212/219-3893.** Subway: B, D, F to Broadway–Lafayette St.

Women who love shoes and are willing to pay in the neighborhood of $200 or $250 for something really special should make a beeline for this NoLiTa shop. These fashion-forward originals wow with their immaculate details, bright color palette, and sexy, strappy retro appeal. Worth every penny.

SPORTING GOODS

For **Niketown,** see "Logo Stores" above.

Eastern Mountain Sports. 611 Broadway (at Houston St.). ☎ **212/505-9860.** Subway: B, D, F, Q to Broadway–Lafayette St.

This one-stop sporting shop is famous for all-weather, high-tech camping, hiking, and climbing gear at prices well below those of Patagonia (see below). This is an excellent, affordable source for Polartec pullovers, waterproof shells, and the like. You'll also find hardware like compasses, cookwear, and Swiss Army knives. There's another location at West 61st Street and Broadway (☎ **212/397-4860**).

Paragon Sporting Goods. 867 Broadway (at 18th St.). ☎ **212/255-8036.** Subway: 4, 5, 6, N, R, L to 14th St.–Union Square.

Paragon is an excellent all-purpose sporting goods store. The emphasis here is on equipment and athletic wear for virtually every sport, from tennis to biking to mountain climbing. End-of-the-season sales, especially on sneakers and outdoor clothing, bring serious discounts.

Patagonia. 101 Wooster St. (btw. Prince and Spring sts.). ☎ **212/343-1776.** Subway: N, R to Prince St; 6 to Spring St.

Expensive though it may be, Patagonia deserves kudos for its commitment to producing eco-friendly sportswear and adventure gear (fleece pullovers made from recycled plastic soda bottles, organic-cotton-only T-shirts). This retail outlet stocks all the climbing and camping stuff you'll find in their catalog.

TOYS

If your kids love to read, don't miss **Books of Wonder;** see "Books" earlier in this section.

FAO Schwarz. 767 Fifth Ave. (at 58th St.). ☎ **212/644-9400.** Subway: N, R to Fifth Ave.

The best-loved toy store in America was designed with an eye for fun: The elevator is shaped like a huge toy soldier, and there are plenty of hands-on displays to keep the little ones occupied for hours. Entire areas are devoted to specific toy makers (Lego, Fisher Price, *Star Wars* action figures, Barbie). You and the kids will find plenty of affordable little gifts to take home as souvenirs (the front-left corner specializes in prewrapped gifts for Moms and Dads on business trips).

Kidding Around. 60 W. 15th St. (btw. Fifth and Sixth aves.). ☎ **212/645-6337.** Subway: F to 14th St.

This boutique stocks pricey high-quality toys, many imported from Europe. The emphasis is on the old-fashioned—low-tech goodies like puzzles, rocking horses, and tops. One wall is devoted exclusively to tub toys, windups, and other stocking stuffers. There's a second store at 68 Bleecker St., between Broadway and Lafayette Street (☎ **212/598-0228**).

Penny Whistle. 448 Columbus Ave. (btw. 81st and 82nd sts.). ☎ **212/873-9090.** Subway: B, C to 81st St.

The merchandise at this upscale shop is geared toward slightly older kids, and there's a brace of silly doodads adults will get a kick out of, too. Also at 1283 Madison Ave., between 91st and 92nd streets (☎ **212/369-3868**).

Tootsie's Children's Books. 554 Hudson St. (btw. Perry and 11th sts.). ☎ **212/242-0182.** Subway: A, C, E to 14th St.

Despite the name, books are only part of the inventory at Tootsie's. This cute-as-a-button shop also carries a creative selection of toys (with an emphasis on learning toys) and games. Look for the Space Puppies, the grooviest stuffed animals around.

WINE & SPIRITS

Acker Merrall & Condit Co. 160 W. 72nd St. (btw. Amsterdam and Columbus aves.). ☎ **212/787-1700.** Subway: 1, 2, 3, 9 to 72nd St.

This attractive little store is the Upper West Side's best wine source. There are no bad bottles here. The careful selection is well-displayed, with opinionated cards attached to each bin to help you choose. A supremely knowledgeable staff is on hand if you'd like additional assistance.

Astor Wines & Spirits. 12 Astor Place (at Lafayette St.). ☎ **212/674-7500.** Subway: 6 to Astor Place.

This large store is the source for excellent values on liquor and wine; their stock is deep, and ranges far and wide. The knowledgeable staff is always willing to recommend a vintage.

Morrell & Company. 1 Rockefeller Plaza (at 49th St.). ☎ **212/688-9370.** www.winesbymorrell.com. Subway: B, D, F, Q to 47th–50th sts./Rockefeller Center.

One of the leading stockists in America, Morrell is scheduled to be relocated from Madison Avenue to a fabulous new space on Rockefeller Center's main plaza by the time you read this. The store boasts a friendly, helpful staff, and their Fine Wine Division hosts four high-profile auctions per year. It was unclear at press time if the phone number would change, so call information at ☎ **411** if you can't get through at the above number. Also look for the new Morrell Wine Bar & Cafe, scheduled to be located adjacent to the retail store.

Sherry-Lehmann. 679 Madison Ave. (btw. 61st and 62nd sts.). ☎ **212/838-7500.** Subway: 4, 5, 6 to 59th St; N, R to Lexington Ave.

Zagat's has called Sherry-Lehmann one of the finest wine shops *in the world.* Their vast inventory is mind-boggling, and includes ritzy gift baskets that make luxurious gifts. Service is excellent, and free wine tastings are often on hand.

New York City After Dark 9

New York's nightlife scene is an embarrassment of riches. There's so much to see and do in this city after the sun goes down that your biggest problem is likely going to be choosing among the many temptations.

There's no way that I can tell you in these pages what's going to be on the calendar while you're in town. So for the latest, most comprehensive nightlife listings, from classic and cutting-edge theater and performing arts to live rock, jazz, and dance club coverage, *Time Out New York* is my favorite weekly source; a new issue hits newsstands every Thursday. The free weekly *Village Voice,* the city's legendary alterna-paper, is available late Tuesday downtown and early Wednesday in the rest of the city. The arts and entertainment coverage couldn't be more extensive, and just about every live music venue advertises its shows here. Another great weekly is *New York* magazine; flip to the "Cue" section at the back for the latest happenings. The *New York Times* features terrific nightlife coverage, particularly in the two-part Friday "Weekend" section. The cabaret, classical music, and theater guides are particularly useful.

Some of your best, most comprehensive and up-to-date information sources for what's going on about town are in cyberspace, of course. An excellent source is **www.newyork.sidewalk.com**, which is particularly good for nightlife—most club listings even feature day-to-day schedules, and there's a Select-a-Bar page to help you find the drink shop that's exactly right for you. Done in cooperation with the *Daily News* and *Time Out,* **www.newyork.citysearch.com** is another complete online source, while **www.nytoday.com** is an expanded version of the the *New York Times's* already terrific cultural coverage. Hipster monthly the *Paper* boasts opinionated coverage of the downtown club and bar scenes at **www.papermag.com**.

Sponsored by the Theatre Development Fund and supported by American Express, **NYC/Onstage** (☎ **212/768-1818;** www.tdf.org) is a recorded and online service providing schedules, descriptions, and other details on theater and the performing arts. The bias is toward Broadway and off-Broadway plays, but NYC/Onstage is a good source for concerts, chamber and orchestral music (including all Lincoln Center events), dance, opera, cabaret, and family entertainment, too. Once you've listened to your options, you can choose to be transferred to the appropriate ticket-selling outlet, which may be TicketMaster, Tele-charge, or the theater's box office.

For more on these and other general information sources, see "Visitor Information" in chapter 2 and "Orientation" in chapter 4. I'll also discuss subject-specific information sources in the appropriate sections below.

In addition to the wealth of choices below, you might want to consider one of the **sunset** or **dinner cruises** that circle Manhattan, taking in the twinkling lights of the skyline from all sides. The cruises offered by **World Yacht** are particularly romantic. See "Harbor Cruises" under "Organized Sightseeing Tours" in chapter 7.

1 All the City's a Stage: The Theater Scene

Nobody does theater better than New York. No other city—not even London—has a theater scene with so much breadth and depth, with so many wide-open alternatives. Broadway, of course, gets the most ink and the most airplay, and deservedly so: Broadway is where you'll find the big stage productions and the moneymakers, from crowd-pleasing warhorses like *Cats* to phenomenal newer successes like *The Lion King*. But today's scene is thriving beyond the bounds of just Broadway—smaller, "alternative" theater has taken hold of the popular imagination, too. With bankable stars on stage, crowds lining up for hot tickets, and hits popular enough to generate major-label cast albums, off-Broadway isn't just for culture vultures anymore.

With such a vital scene, it's no wonder that it's the promise of the stage, more than anything else, that draws visitors from all over the world to New York City. Despite this vitality, plays and musicals close all the time, often with little warning. Even the most basic production is expensive to mount, and ticket sales must be robust to keep it in business. So I can't tell you precisely what will be on while you're in town. Your best bet is to check the publications and Web sites listed at the start of this chapter before you go, or even once you reach town to get an idea of what you might like to see. A particularly useful source is the **Broadway Line** (☎ **888/BROADWAY** or 212/302-4111; www.broadway.org), where you can obtain details and descriptions on current Broadway shows, hear about special offers and discounts, and choose to be transferred to Tele-charge to buy tickets. There's also **NYC/Onstage** (☎ **212/768-1818;** www.tdf.org), providing the same kind of service for both Broadway and off-Broadway productions. (Don't buy tickets, though, until you read "Top Ticket-Buying Tips" below!)

Even though I can't guarantee what'll be on stage when you're visiting, the likelihood is good that you'll find lots of large-scale musicals and revivals on Broadway, and more original drama and offbeat musicals on the off-Broadway stage. If you find new drama on Broadway, it's likely to be the transcontinental transfer of a London stage hit, similar to Yasmina Reza's for-thinking-theatergoers-only *Art* in 1998, and David Hare's *Amy's View* in 1999. If you're coming to see the big hits, chances are extremely good that you'll still find *Cats* (the longest-running show in Broadway history) at the Winter Garden, *Les Misérables* at the Imperial, *Miss Saigon* at the Broadway Theater, and *Phantom* at the Majestic. Kids will be enchanted by Disney's one-two punch of *Beauty and the Beast* and, if you can get tickets (call now!), *The Lion King*. Off-Broadway is more volatile, but you're likely to still find the ridiculously fun *Blue Man Group* at the Astor Place Theater, and the percussion sensation *Stomp!* at the Orpheum Theatre; both are performance art pieces that are more palatable than you'd expect, and have been pleasing kids and grown-ups alike for years now. And I'd pretty much stake my life on the fact that the legendary show *The Fantasticks* will still be alive and kicking at the Sullivan Street Playhouse—it opened on May 3, 1960, and is now the longest-running musical in the world. (For tickets, see "Top Ticket-Buying Tips," below.)

The Theater District

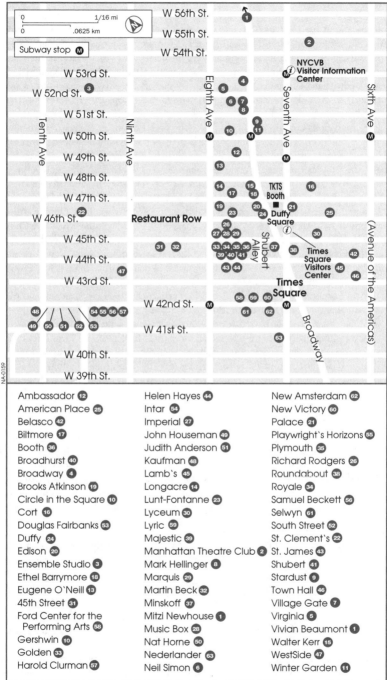

0 1/16 mi
0 .0625 km

Subway stop Ⓜ

W 56th St.
W 55th St.
W 54th St.
W 53rd St.
W 52nd St. ③
W 51st St.
W 50th St.
W 49th St.
W 48th St.
W 47th St.
W 46th St. ㉒
W 45th St.
W 44th St.
W 43rd St.
W 42nd St. Ⓜ
W 41st St.
W 40th St.
W 39th St.

Eighth Ave.
Seventh Ave.
Sixth Ave.
Tenth Ave.
Ninth Ave.
(Avenue of the Americas)

NYCVB
Visitor Information
Center

TKTS
Booth

Duffy
Square

Restaurant Row

Shubert Alley

Times
Square
Visitors
Center

Times
Square

Broadway

NA-0159

Ambassador ⑫	Helen Hayes ㊹	New Amsterdam ㉖
American Place ㉕	Intar ㊴	New Victory ㉠
Belasco ㊷	Imperial ㉗	Palace ㉑
Biltmore ⑰	John Houseman ㊾	Playwright's Horizons �
Booth ㊱	Judith Anderson ㊿	Plymouth ㉟
Broadhurst ㊵	Kaufman ㊽	Richard Rodgers ㉖
Broadway ④	Lamb's ㊺	Roundabout ㊳
Brooks Atkinson ⑲	Longacre ⑭	Royale ㉞
Circle in the Square ⑩	Lunt-Fontanne ㉓	Samuel Beckett ㊶
Cort ⑯	Lyceum ㉚	Selwyn ㉖
Douglas Fairbanks ㊾	Lyric ㊾	South Street ㉒
Duffy ㉔	Majestic ㊴	St. Clement's ㉒
Edison ⑳	Manhattan Theatre Club ②	St. James ㊸
Ensemble Studio ③	Mark Hellinger ⑧	Shubert ㊶
Ethel Barrymore ⑱	Marquis ㉙	Stardust ⑨
Eugene O'Neill ⑬	Martin Beck ㉜	Town Hall ㊻
45th Street ㉛	Minskoff ㊲	Village Gate ⑦
Ford Center for the	Mitzi Newhouse ①	Virginia ⑤
Performing Arts ㊺	Music Box ㉘	Vivian Beaumont ①
Gershwin ⑩	Nat Horne ㊿	Walter Kerr ⑮
Golden ㉝	Nederlander ㊽	WestSide ㊼
Harold Clurman ㊼	Neil Simon ⑥	Winter Garden ⑪

307

Helping to assure the recent success of the New York theater scene has been the presence of A-list Hollywood stars. Whoopi Goldberg, Glenn Close, Holly Hunter, Alan Alda, Quentin Tarantino, and Liam Neeson are just some of the famous names that have appeared on Broadway marquees in the last few years. Natasha Richardson wowed audiences and won a Tony as Sally Bowles in *Cabaret*, and returned in 1999's *Closer*. Christian Slater received the best reviews of his career (well, second to *Heathers*, perhaps) in *Side Man*. Academy Award winner Kevin Spacey got raves for 1999's revival of Eugene O'Neill's *The Iceman Cometh*. Dame Judi Dench brought David Hare's marvelous London hit *Amy's View* to the Broadway stage and was rewarded with a Tony. But no one made a bigger splash than Nicole Kidman, who bared it all in Hare's otherwise fundamentally disappointing *The Blue Room*. And Broadway hasn't been the only call to stage: Amanda Plummer, *The Right Stuff*'s Scott Glenn, and Fairuza Balk all did runs in the wild *Killer Joe*; Molly Ringwald appeared in the disturbing but marvelous *How I Learned to Drive*; and Billy Crudup and Frances MacDormand played screwed-up son and mother in a 1998 version of *Oedipus*. All this star power has brought in lots of theatergoers who would've otherwise stayed home. Keep in mind, though, that stars' runs are often very short, and tickets tend to sell out fast. If you hear that there's a celeb you'd like to see coming to the New York stage, don't put off your travel and ticket-buying plans. (The box office can tell you how long a star is contracted for a role.)

Lastly, keep in mind that while "Off-Broadway" may mean experimental and therefore be riskier, it doesn't have to mean lower-quality in any way. These days, the best off-Broadway shows don't need to move to Broadway to be legitimized. In fact, in many ways, especially with dramas, being away from Broadway can mean they're freer to be hits without being huge draws. Witness such recent powerhouse hits as Margaret Edson's *Wit*, with a tour-de-force performance by Kathleen Chalfont, and John Cameron Mitchell's *Hedwig and the Angry Inch* (step aside, *Rent*—here's a musical that really rocks!), plus the aforementioned longrunners *Blue Man Group* and *Stomp!* And remember—*Rent* is just one of many phenomenons that made its debut off-Broadway.

In addition to *Blue Man Group* and *Stomp!*, off-Broadway theaters that deserve a special look include particularly good reputations include **The Public Theater**, 425 Lafayette St. (☎ **212/260-2400**), Joseph Papp's legacy, home to the New York Shakespeare Festival as well as the launching pad for such hits as *Bring in 'da Noise, Bring in 'da Funk*. (For details on the Public Theater's summertime **Shakespeare in the Park** in Central Park—probably the city's best outdoor arts event—see the box called "Park It! Shakespeare, Music & Other Free Fun" later in this chapter.)

THE BASICS

The terms **Broadway, Off-Broadway,** and **Off-Off-Broadway** refer to theater size, pay scales, and other arcane details, not location—or, these days, even star wattage. Most of the Broadway theaters are in Times Square, huddled around the thoroughfare the scene is named for, but not directly on it: Instead, you'll find them dotting the side streets that intersect Broadway, mostly in the mid-40s between Sixth and Eighth avenues (44th and 45th streets in particular) but running north as far as 53rd Street. There's even a Broadway theater outside Times Square: The Vivian Beaumont in Lincoln Center, at Broadway and 65th Street.

Off-Broadway, on the other hand, is not that exacting an expression. Frankly, with the increasing popularization of off-the-beaten-track productions, the distinction between off- and off-off-Broadway productions has become fuzzier. Off-off-Broadway shows tend to be more avant-garde, experimental, and/or nomadic. Off- and off-off-Broadway productions tend to be based around Greenwich Village, but pockets show up in the East Village, around Midtown, in SoHo, and even on the Upper West Side. And there are off-Broadway theaters in Times Square and even *on* Broadway. Needless to say, carefully check the address where your production is playing.

Broadway shows tend to keep pretty regular **schedules.** There are usually eight performances a week: Evening shows Tuesday through Saturday, plus matinees on Wednesday, Saturday, and Sunday. Evening shows are usually at 8pm, while matinees are usually at 2pm on Wednesday and Saturday, and 3pm on Sunday. Schedules do vary, however; both *Cats* and *Les Misérables,* for instance, also stage a Monday show to accommodate the seemingly endless tourist demand. And times often vary depending on the show's length; the 1999 staging of *The Iceman Cometh* starring Kevin Spacey, for instance, started nightly at 7pm to accommodate the marathon 4¼-hour running time. Shows usually start right on the dot, or within a few minutes of starting time; if you arrive late, you may have to wait until after the first act to take your seat, which can really be a drag.

Off-Broadway shows tend to follow a similar daily schedule and time clock, but you'll find more variations. Off-Broadway theaters usually stage an additional Sunday evening show. Some, such as the rock musical *Hedwig and the Angry Inch,* also stage 11:30pm shows on Friday and Saturday to accommodate the downtown crowds who could care less about the late hour (this is the exception, not the rule).

Ticket prices for Broadway shows vary dramatically. Expect to pay for good seats; the high end for any given show is likely to be between $60 and $100. The cheapest end of the price range can be as low as $15 or as high as $50, depending on the theater configuration. If you're buying tickets at the very low end of a wide available range, be aware that you may be buying obstructed-view seats. If all tickets are the same price or the range is small, you can pretty much count on all of the seats being pretty good. Otherwise, price is your barometer. Note that leg room can be tight in these old theaters, and you'll usually get more in the orchestra seats.

Off-Broadway and off-off-Broadway shows tend to be cheaper, with tickets often as low as $10 or $15. However, seats for the most established shows (such as Margaret Edson's phenomenal *Wit*) and those with star power (like the 1999 production of Molière's *The Misanthrope* starring Uma Thurman and Roger Rees) can command prices as high as $50.

Don't let price be a deterrent to enjoying the theater. There are ways to pay less if you're willing to make the effort and be flexible, with a few choices at hand as to what you'd like to see. Read on.

Top Ticket-Buying Tips

Phone ahead or go online for tickets to the most successful or popular shows as far in advance as you can—in the case of shows like *The Lion King* and, thus far, *Cabaret,* it's never too early.

Buying tickets can be simple, if the show you want to see isn't sold out. You need only call such general numbers as **Tele-Charge** (☎ 212/239-6200; www.telecharge. com), which handles most Broadway and off-Broadway shows and some concerts; or **TicketMaster** (☎ 212/307-4100; www.ticketmaster.com), which also handles Broadway and off-Broadway shows and most concerts. If you use the **Broadway Line** (☎ 888/411-BWAY or 212/302-4111) or **NYC/Onstage** (☎ 212/768-1818; www. tdf.org) services discussed above to select your show, you can be automatically transferred to the appropriate ticket agency.

If you're an American Express gold card holder, check to see if tickets are being sold through **American Express Gold Card Events** (☎ 800/448-TIKS;

www.americanexpress.com/gce). You'll pay full price just as you would through Tele-Charge or TicketMaster. But AmEx has access to blocks of preferred seating that are specifically set aside for gold-card holders, so you may be able to get tickets to a show that's otherwise sold out, or better seats than you would be able to buy through other outlets.

Owned by Cameron Mackintosh (producer behind such megahits as *Cats, Phantom of the Opera, Les Misèrables,* and *Miss Saigon*), **Theatre Direct International (TDI)** is a ticket broker that sells tickets to select Broadway and off-Broadway shows direct to individuals and travel agents. Check to see if they have seats to the shows you're interested in by calling ☎ 800/334-8457 or pointing your Web browser to **www.theatredirect.com**. (Disregard the discounted prices, unless you're buying for a group of $20 or more; tickets are full price for smaller quantities.) With a service charge of $12.50 per ticket, you'll do a bit better by trying TicketMaster or TeleCharge first; but because they act as a consolidator, TDI may have tickets left for a specific show even if the major outlets don't. It's also worth checking for VIP packages, which throw in extras like dinner, souvenir programs, and/or cast recordings along with preferred seating and ticket-cancellation insurance for a value-priced additional premium.

Other reputable ticket brokers include **Keith Prowse & Co.** (☎ 800/669-8687; www.keithprowse.com) and **Edwards & Edwards Global Tickets** (☎ 800/223-6108). For a complete list of other licensed ticket brokers recommended by the NYCVB, get a copy of the "Big Apple Visitor's Kit" (see "Visitor Information" in chapter 2 for details). All kinds of ticket brokers list ads in the Sunday *New York Times* and other publications, but don't take the risk. Stick with a licensed broker recommended by the NYCVB. You should be aware that state law limits the amount the premium brokers can charge to $5 or 10%, whichever is less, but if you believe they all stick to that, I know of this bridge in Brooklyn. . . .

If you want to secure tickets before you come to New York but don't want to pay a service charge, try calling the **box office** directly. Broadway theaters don't sell tickets over the telephone, but a good number of off-Broadway theaters do.

Also, before you resort to calling broker after broker to snag tickets to a hot show, consider calling the **concierge** at the hotel where you'll be staying. If you've chosen a hotel with a well-connected concierge, he or she may be able to have tickets waiting for you when you check in—for a premium, of course. For more on this, see "When You Arrive," below.

Good Tickets for a Good Deed

One option for finding hard-to-get tickets is more expensive than most, but good for your self-esteem. **Broadway Cares/Equity Fights AIDS** gets producers, theater owners, celebrities, and other Broadway types to donate their coveted house seats to Broadway and off-Broadway shows. They sell these tickets for double the face value ($120 for a $60 ticket, for example), with the proceeds donated to people living with the disease. Not only do you get what are probably the best seats in the house, but 50% of your purchase is tax deductible. Call ☎ 212/840-0770 for ticket choices, which are limited in number but can also include some performances at Radio City Music Hall. Ticket requests are taken the month prior to the dates you're interested in on the first day of the month (starting March 1 if you're interested in seeing a show in April, for instance); mark your calendar if you're trying to snag coveted tix like *The Lion King* or *Cabaret.* For other shows, call at least 48 hours in advance.

WHEN YOU ARRIVE

Once you arrive in the city, getting your hands on tickets can take some street smarts—and failing those, good hard cash. Even if it seems unlikely that seats are available, always **call the box office** before attempting any other route. Single seats are often easiest to obtain, so people willing to sit apart may find themselves in luck.

You should also try the **Broadway Ticket Center,** run by the League of American Theaters and Producers (the same people behind the Broadway Line, above) at the Times Square Visitors Center, 1560 Broadway, between 46th and 47th streets (open daily 8am to 8pm). They often have tickets available for otherwise sold-out shows, and only charge $4 extra per ticket.

Even if saving money isn't an issue for you, check the boards at the **TKTS Booth** in Times Square; more on that under "Reduced-Price Ticket Deals" below.

In addition, your **hotel concierge** may be able to arrange tickets for you. These are usually purchased through a broker and a premium will be attached, but they're usually good seats and you can count on them being legitimate. If you want to deal with a licensed broker direct, **Global Tickets Edwards & Edwards** has a local office that accommodates drop-ins at 1270 Sixth Ave. between 50th and 51st streets on the 24th floor (☎ **212/332-2435;** open Mon–Sat 9am–9pm, Sun noon–7pm).

If you buy from one of the **scalpers** selling tickets in front of the theater doors, you're taking a risk. They may be perfectly legitimate—a couple from the 'burbs whose companions couldn't make it for the evening, say—but they could be swindlers passing off fakes for big money. It's a risk that's not worth taking.

One preferred **insiders' trick** is to make the rounds of Broadway theaters at about 6pm, when unclaimed house seats are made available to the public. These tickets—reserved for VIPs, friends of the cast, the press, or other hangers-on—offer great locations and are sold at face value.

Also, note that **Mondays** are often good days to cop big-name show tickets. Though most theaters are dark on that day, some of the most sought-after choices aren't. Locals are at home on the first night of the work week, so all the odds are in your favor. Your chances will always be better on weeknights, or for Wednesday matinees, rather than weekends.

REDUCED-PRICE TICKET DEALS

If you're visiting the city early in the year, be sure to look into the **Passport to Off Broadway.** The Alliance of Resident Theaters/New York sponsors this campaign, which offers 10 to 50% discounts on tickets to more than 200 off- and off-off-Broadway shows from February through April. You can download the discount coupon as many times as you want by pointing your Web browser to **www.newyork.sidewalk.com/passport**. Note, however, that some restrictions may apply: Some theaters don't accept the coupons for Friday or Saturday night performances, and some will accept them only for cash purchases. Still, the inconveniences are minimal, and it's a great deal.

Even blockbusters can have a limited number of cheaper tickets for **students and seniors,** and they may even be available at the last minute; call the box office direct to inquire. In the past, the Roundabout offered half-price tickets to those 17 and under. *Rent* has offered all kinds of bargains to keep younger theatergoers coming.

The best deal in town on **same-day tickets** for both Broadway and off-Broadway shows is at the ✪ **Times Square Theatre Centre,** better known as the **TKTS booth** run by the nonprofit Theatre Development Fund in the heart of the Theater District at Duffy Square, 47th Street and Broadway (open 3 to 8pm for evening performances, 10am to 2pm for Wednesday and Saturday matinees, from 11am on Sunday for all performances). Tickets for that day's performances are usually offered at half price, with a few reduced only 25%, plus a $2.50 per ticket service charge. Boards outside the ticket windows list available shows; you're unlikely to find certain perennial or out-size smashes, but most other shows turn up. Cash and traveler's checks only are accepted. There's often a huge line, so show up early for the best availability and be prepared to wait—but frankly, the crowd is all part of the fun. If you don't care much what you see and you'd just like to go to a show, you can walk right up to the window later in the day and something's always available.

Run by the same group and offering the same discounts is the **TKTS Lower Manhattan Theatre Centre,** on the mezzanine of Two World Trade Center (open Monday to Friday 11am to 5:30pm, Saturday 11am to 3:30pm). All the same policies apply. The advantages to coming down here is that the lines are generally shorter; your wait is sheltered indoors; and matinee tickets are available the day before, so you can plan ahead.

Many theater shows, particularly long-running shows like *Miss Saigon* and *Cats,* offer special coupons that allow you to buy **two-fers**—two tickets for the price of one certain nights of the week. You can find these coupons at many places in the city: hotel lobbies, in banks, even at restaurant cash registers. A guaranteed bet is the Times Square Visitors Center, 1560 Broadway, between 46th and 47th streets; they're also likely to be available at the new NYCVB Visitor Information Center at 810 Seventh Avenue, between 52nd and 53rd streets.

2 Opera, Classical Music & Dance

While Broadway is the Big Apple's greatest hit, many other performing arts also flourish in this culturally rich and entertainment-hungry town.

In addition to the listings below, be sure to check out what's happening at **Carnegie Hall** and the **Brooklyn Academy of Music,** two of the most respected—and enjoyable—multi-functional performing arts venues in the city. The marvelous **92nd Street Y** also regularly hosts events that are worth considering. I've listed the operatic and symphonic companies housed at **Lincoln Center** below; also check the center's full calendar for all offerings. For complete details on these four venues, see "Major Concert Halls & Landmark Venues" later in this chapter.

OPERA

New York has grown into an important center in the opera world. Stars from Luciano Pavarotti to Kathleen Battle to Roberto Alagna regularly take the stage at one of the city's renowned venues, where they're warmly welcomed by a packed house. The season generally runs from September to May, but there's usually something going on at any time of year.

In addition to the choices below, the **New York Grand Opera** (☎ 212/245-8837; www.csis.pace.edu/newyorkgrandopera) puts on free productions of Verdi operas at Central Park's Summerstage in July and August; for more on Summerstage, see the "Park It! Shakespeare, Music & Other Free Fun" box later in this chapter.

Amato Opera Theatre. 319 Bowery (at 2nd St.). ☎ **212/228-8200.** www.amato.org. Subway: 6 to Bleecker St.; F to Second Ave.

This cozy, off-the-beaten-track venue for mostly Italian opera is run by husband-and-wife team Anthony and Sally Amato and functions as a showcase for talented young American singers. The intimate 100-plus-seat house celebrated its 50th season last year amid a rising reputation and increasing ticket sales. The staple is full productions of Italian classics—Verdi, Puccini, Rossini, with an occasional Mozart tossed in—at great prices (usually $20 to $25). Performances, usually held on Saturday and Sunday, now regularly sell out, so it's a good idea to reserve three weeks in advance. Once a month at the 11:30am on Saturday, "Opera in Brief" offers fully costumed, kid-length versions of the classics interwoven with narration so Mom and Dad have a palatable forum in which to introduce the little ones to the music form. At $12 or so per ticket, these matinee performances are wallet-friendly, too.

✪ **Metropolitan Opera.** At the Metropolitan Opera House, Lincoln Center, Broadway and 64th St. ☎ **212/362-6000.** www.metopera.org. Subway: 1, 9 to 66th St.

Tickets can cost a small fortune (anywhere from $30 to $250), but for its full productions of the classic repertory and schedule packed with world-class grand sopranos and tenors, the Metropolitan Opera ranks first in the world. Millions are spent on fabulous stagings, and the venue itself is a wonder of acoustics. Among the notable events of the 1999–2000 calendar are the world premiere of *The Great Gatsby,* with libretto by noted American composer John Harbison, and exciting new productions of Boito's *Mefistofele* and Wagner's *Tristan und Isolde.*

To guarantee that its audience understands the words, the Met has outfitted its seat backs with screens for subtitles. James Levine continues his role as the brilliant and popular conductor of the orchestra. Associate conductor Valery Gergiyev helps fill in for the peripatetic Levine (who also conducts the Munich Philharmonic), bringing needed experience in the Russian repertory to the Met.

✪ **New York City Opera.** At the New York State Theater, Lincoln Center, Broadway and 64th St. ☎ **212/870-5570,** or 212/307-4100 for tickets (online purchases at www.ticketmaster.com). www.nycopera.com. Subway: 1, 9 to 66th St.

The New York City Opera is a superb company, with a delightful duality to its approach: It not only attempts to reach a wider audience than the Metropolitan with its more "human" scale and significantly lower prices ($22 to $82) but it's also committed to adventurous premieres, newly composed operas, the occasional avant-garde work, American musicals presented as operettas (Stephen Sondheim's *Sweeney Todd* is an example), and even obscure works by mainstream or lesser-known composers. Its mix stretches from the "easy" works of Puccini and Verdi and Gilbert & Sullivan to the more challenging oeuvres of the likes of Arnold Schönberg and Philip Glass.

New York Gilbert and Sullivan Players. At Symphony Space, Broadway and 95th St. ☎ **212/864-5400** or 212/769-1000. www.nygasp.org. Subway: 1, 2, 3, 9 to 96th St.

If you're in the mood for light-hearted operetta, try this lively company, which specializes in Gilbert and Sullivan's 19th-century English comic works. Tickets are affordable, in the $25 to $50 range. This year's calendar, which generally runs from October through April, is scheduled to include *The Pirates of Penzance, Princess Ida,* and *The Mikado.*

CLASSICAL MUSIC

Just about any grand interpreter of the classics comes through New York. The many concert halls throughout the city—ranging from the expected, like **Carnegie Hall,** to the surprising, like the **92nd Street Y**—book the best of the best (see "Major Concert Halls & Landmark Venues" later in this chapter).

The following is a select list of particularly important companies and venues. Additionally, you might wish to see what's on at the Metropolitan Museum of Art's **Grace Rainey Rogers Auditorium** (☎ 212/570-3949), an elegant venue that presents recitals, chamber music, and orchestral concerts throughout the year. Many other venues also offer performances, so be sure to check one of the publications or Web sites mentioned at the start of this chapter before you come to town.

✪ **Bargemusic.** At the Fulton Ferry Landing (just south of the Brooklyn Bridge), Brooklyn. ☎ **718/624-2083** or 718/624-4061. www.bargemusic.org. Subway: 2, 3 to Clark St.

Many thought Olga Bloom peculiar, if not deranged, when she transformed a 40-year-old barge into a chamber-music concert hall. More than 20 years later, Bargemusic is an internationally renowned recital room boasting more than 100 first-rate chamber music performances a year. Olga trawls from the pool of visiting musicians who love the chance to play in such an intimate setting, so the roster regularly includes highly respected international musicians as well as local stars like violinist Cynthia Phelps. There are two shows per week, on Thursday evening and Sunday afternoon; from June through August, there's also a Friday-evening performance. The musicians perform on a small stage in a cherry-paneled, fireplace-lit room accommodating 130. Bloom herself places name cards on the red-velvet cushions of the folding chairs, and there's bread and cheese, cakes and cookies, and wine and coffee. The barge may creak a bit and an occasional boat may speed by, but the music rivals what you'll find in almost any other New York concert hall—and the panoramic view through the glass wall behind the stage can't be beat. Neither can the price: Tickets are just $23 ($20 seniors, $15 students). Reserve well in advance.

The Juilliard School. 60 Lincoln Center Plaza (Broadway at 65th St.). ☎ **212/769-7406.** www.juilliard.edu. Subway: 1, 9 to 66th St.

During its school year, the nation's premier music education institution sponsors about 550 performances of the highest quality—at the lowest prices. With most concerts free and $15 as a maximum ticket price, Juilliard is one of New York's greatest cultural bargains. Though most would assume that the school presents only classical-music concerts, Juilliard also offers other music as well as drama, dance, opera, and interdisciplinary works. The best way to find out about the wide array of productions is to call, visit the school's Web site (click on CALENDAR OF EVENTS), or consult the bulletin board in the building's lobby. Watch for master classes and discussions open to the public featuring celebrity guest teachers.

✪ **New York Philharmonic.** At Avery Fisher Hall, Lincoln Center, Broadway and 64th St. ☎ **212/875-5030,** or 212/721-6500 for tickets. www.newyorkphilharmonic.org, or www.lincolncenter.org for online purchases. Subway: 1, 9 to 66th St.

Symphony-wise, you'd be hard-pressed to do better than the New York Philharmonic. The country's oldest philharmonic orchestra is under the strict but ebullient guidance of music director Kurt Masur. Since he has announced that he'll retire in 2002, don't miss this chance to see the master conductor leading his orchestra. Highlights of the 1999–2000 season include the Completely Copland Festival throughout December, Anne-Sophie Mutter in residence in January, an all-Mozart night led by guest conductor Sir Colin Davis in May, and Mahler's *Symphony no. 9* to close the season in early June. There's a summer season in July, when themed classics brighten the hall, as well as summer concerts in Central Park that are worth checking into.

Tickets range from $12 to $88; opt for a rush-hour concert or a matinee for the lowest across-the-board prices. If you can afford it—and if the tickets are available—it's well worth it to pay for prime seats. The acoustics of the hall are such that, at the mid-range price points, I prefer the second tier (especially the boxes) over the more expensive rear orchestra seats. Go cheap if you have to; you're sure to enjoy the program from any vantage.

DANCE

In general, dance seasons run September to February and then March to June, but there's almost always something going on. In addition to the major troupes below,

Last-Minute Ticket-Buying Tips

Most seats at **New York Philharmonic** performances are sold to subscribers, with just a few left for the rest of us. But there are still ways to get tickets. When subscribers can't attend, they may turn their tickets back to the theaters, which then resell them at the last moment. These can be in the most coveted rows of the orchestra. The hopeful form "cancellation lines" two hours or more before curtain time for a crack at returned tickets on a first-come, first-served basis. And periodically, a number of **same-day orchestra tickets** are set aside at the philharmonic, and sold first thing in the morning for $25 a pop (maximum 2). **Senior/student/ disabled rush tickets** may be available for $10 (maximum 2) on concert day, but never at Friday matinees or Saturday evening performances. To check availability for all New York Philharmonic performances, call the **Audience Services Department** at ☎ 212/875-5656.

Note that Lincoln Center's **Alice Tully Hall** (where the Chamber Music Society peforms and other concerts are held), the **Metropolitan Opera,** and **Carnegie Hall** offer similar last-minute and discount programs. It makes sense to call the box office first to check on same-day availability before heading to the theater— or, if you're willing to risk coming away empty-handed, be there at opening time for first crack.

some other names to keep in mind are the **Brooklyn Academy of Music** (see "Major Concert Halls & Landmark Venues" below), and the **Dance Theatre of Harlem** (☎ 212/690-2800), which performs throughut the city and holds an open house one Sunday a month. For particularly innovative works, see what's on at the **Merce Cunningham Studio,** 55 Bethune St. (☎ 212/691-9751; www.merce.org); the **Dance Theater Workshop,** in the Bessie Schönberg Theater, 219 W. 19th St. (☎ 212/ 924-0077; www.dtw.org); and **Danspace Project,** at St. Mark's Church, 131 E. 10th St. (☎ 212/674-8194), whose performances lean toward the seriously avant-garde. Also see if Pilar Rioja is perfoming at the **Repertorio Español,** Gramercy Arts Theater, 138 E. 27th St. (☎ 212/889-2850); her classic Spanish movements mix awesome restraint with explosive passion.

In addition to regular appearances at City Center (below), the **American Ballet Theatre** (www.abt.org), takes up residence at Lincoln Center's Metropolitan Opera House (☎ 212/362-6000) for eight weeks each spring; their recent reinterpretation of *Swan Lake* caused quite a stir. The same venue also hosts such visiting companies as the Kirov, Royal, and Paris Opéra ballets.

City Center. 131 W. 55th St. (btw. Sixth and Seventh aves.). ☎ **212/581-7907.** Subway: N, R or B, Q to 57th St.; B, D, E to Seventh Ave.

Modern dance usually takes center stage in this Moorish dome-topped performing arts palace. Regular performances by the companies of Merce Cunningham, Martha Graham, Paul Taylor, Trisha Brown, Alvin Ailey, Twyla Tharp, and the American Ballet Theatre are often on the calendar. Don't expect cutting edge—but do expect excellence. Sightlines are terrific from all corners.

۞ Joyce Theater. 175 Eighth Ave. (at 19th St.). ☎ **212/242-0800.** www.joyce.org. Subway: C, E to 23rd St.; 1, 9 to 18th St.

Housed in an old art deco movie house, the Joyce has grown into one of the world's greatest modern dance institutions. You can see everything from Native American ceremonial dance to Maria Benites Teatro Flamenco to the innovative works of Pilobolus to the Martha Graham Dance Company. In residence annually is Eliot Feld's ballet company, Ballet Tech, which WQXR radio's Francis Mason called "better than a whole month of namby-pamby classical ballets." The Joyce now has a second space, **Joyce SoHo,** at 155 Mercer St., between Houston and Prince streets (☎ 212/431-9233), where you can see rising young dancers and experimental works in the intimacy of a 70-seat performance space.

New York City Ballet. At the New York State Theater at Lincoln Center, Broadway and 64th St. ☎ **212/870-5570** or 212/307-4100. www.nycballet.com or www.ticketmaster.com. Subway: 1, 9 to 66th St.

Highly regarded for its unsurpassed technique, the New York City Ballet is the world's best. The company renders with happy regularity the works of two of America's most important choreographers: George Balanchine, its founder, and Jerome Robbins. Under the direction of former dancer Peter Martins, the troupe continues to expand its repertoire and performs to a wide variety of classical and modern music. The cornerstone of the annual season is the Christmastime production of *The Nutcracker,* for which tickets usually become available starting in early October. Ticket prices for most events run $16 to $70.

3 Major Concert Halls & Landmark Venues

Apollo Theater. 253 W. 125th St. (btw. Adam Clayton Powell and Frederick Douglass blvds.). ☎ **212/749-5838** or 212/864-0372. Subway: 1, 9 to 125th St.

Built in 1914, the Apollo had its heyday in the 1930s when Count Basie, Duke Ellington, Ella Fitzgerald, and Billie Holiday were on the bill. By the 1970s it had fallen on hard times, but a 1986 restoration breathed new life into the historic Harlem landmark. Today the Apollo is again internationally renowned for its African-American acts of all musical genres, from hip-hop acts to B.B. King to Wynton Marsalis's "Jazz for Young People" events. Wednesday's "Amateur Night at the Apollo" are loud, fun-filled nights that draw in young talents from all over the country with high hopes of making it big (a very young Lauryn Hill started out here—and didn't win!).

✪ Brooklyn Academy of Music. 30 Lafayette Ave., Brooklyn. ☎ **718/636-4100.** www. bam.org. Subway: 2, 3, 4, 5, D, Q to Atlantic Ave.; B, M, N, R to Pacific Ave.

BAM, as it's known, is the city's most renowned contemporary arts institution, presenting cutting-edge theater, opera, dance, and music. Offerings have included historically informed presentations of baroque opera by William Christie and Les Arts Florissants; pop opera from Lou Reed; Marianne Faithfull singing the music of Kurt Weill; dance by Mark Morris, Merce Cunningham, and Mikhail Baryshnikov; music by Laurie Anderson and Philip Glass; the Royal Dramatic Theater of Sweden directed by Ingmar Bergman; and many more experimental works by both renowned and lesser-known international artists as well as visiting companies from all over the world. Of particular note is the **Next Wave Festival,** from September through December, this country's foremost showcase for new experimental works (for further details, see the "Calendar of Events" in chapter 2). The new **BAM Rose Cinemas** show first-run independent films, with such offerings as Brazil's *Central Station* and Iran's *The Apple.* There's also free live music every Friday and Saturday night at **BAMcafé,** which can range from atmospheric electronica from coronetist Graham Haynes to Harlem-style swing by the Yallopin' Hounds.

✪ Carnegie Hall. 881 Seventh Ave. (at 57th St.). ☎ **212/247-7800.** www.carnegiehall. org. Subway: N, R or B, Q to 57th St.

Perhaps the world's most famous performance space, Carnegie Hall offers everything from grand classics to the music of Ravi Shankar. The 2,804-seat main hall welcomes visiting orchestras from across the country and the world. Many of the world's premier soloists and ensembles give recitals. The legendary hall is both visually and acoustically brilliant; don't miss an opportunity to experience it if there's something on that interests you. There's also the intimate 284-seat **Weill Recital Hall,** usually used to showcase chamber music and vocal and instrumental recitals. Carnegie Hall has also reclaimed an ornate underground concert hall, occupied by a movie theater for 38 years, and plans to turn it into an intermediate-size third stage by the 2001–02 season. For last-minute ticket-buying tips, see the feature on p. 315.

✪ **Lincoln Center for the Performing Arts.** 70 Lincoln Center Plaza (at Broadway and 64th St.). ☎ **212/546-2656.** www.lincolncenter.org. Subway: 1, 9 to 66th St.

New York is the world's premier performing arts city, and Lincoln Center is its premier institution. Whenever you're planning an evening's entertainment, check the offerings here—which can include opera, dance, symphonies, jazz, theater, film, and more, from the classics to the contemporary. Lincoln Center's many buildings serve as permanent homes to their own companies as well major stops for world-class performance troupes from around the globe.

Resident companies include: The **Chamber Music Society of Lincoln Center** (☎ 212/875-5788; www.chamberlinc.org), which performs at Alice Tully Hall or the Daniel and Joanna S. Rose Rehearsal Studio, often in the company of such high-caliber guests as Anne Sofie Von Otter and Midori. The **Film Society of Lincoln Center** (☎ 212/875-5600; www.filmlinc.com) screens a daily schedule of movies at the Walter Reade Theater, and hosts a number of important annual film and video festivals as well as the Reel to Real program for kids, pairing silent screen classics with live performance. **Jazz at Lincoln Center** (☎ 212/875-5299; www.jazzatlincolncenter. org) is led by the incomparable Wynton Marsalis, with the orchestra usually performing at Alice Tully Hall; the new "Jazz at the Penthouse" program, where great jazz pianists like Ellis Marsalis and Tommy Flanagan play in a spectacular candlelit setting overlooking the Hudson River, is the hottest ticket in town. **Lincoln Center Theater** (☎ 212/501-3100; www.lct.org) consists of the Vivian Beaumont Theater, a modern and comfortable venue with great sightlines that has been home to much good Broadway drama, and the Mitzi E. Newhouse Theater, a well-respected off-Broadway house that has also boasted numerous theatrical triumphs. Past seasons have included excellent productions of Tom Stoppard's *Arcadia, Carousel* in revival, and David Hare's one-man show, *Via Dolorosa.* For details on the **Metropolitan Opera,** the **New York City Opera,** the **New York City Ballet,** the **Juilliard School,** the phenomenal **New York Philharmonic,** led by master conductor Kurt Masur, and the **American Ballet Theatre,** which takes up residence here every spring, see "Opera, Classical Music & Dance" earlier in this chapter.

Most of the companies' **major seasons** run from about October to May or June. **Special series** like Great Performers and the new American Songbook, showcasing classic American show tunes, help round out the calendar. Indoor and outdoor events are held in warmer months: Spring blooms with the **JVC Jazz Festival;** July sees **Midsummer Night's Swing** with partner dancing, lessons, and music on the plaza; **Mostly Mozart** attracts talents like Alicia de Larrocha and André Watts; the three-year-old **Lincoln Center Festival,** celebrating the best of the performing arts; **Lincoln Center Out-of-Doors,** a series of free alfresco music and dance performances in August in September; the **New York Film Festival,** and more. Check the "Calendar of Events" in chapter 2 or Lincoln Center's Web site to see what special events will be on while you're in town.

Park It! Shakespeare, Music & Other Free Fun

As the weather warms, New York culture comes outdoors to play.

Shakespeare in the Park, held at Central Park's Delacorte Theater, is by far the city's most famous alfresco arts event. Organized by the Joseph Papp Public The-ater, the schedule consists of summertime productions of usually two of the Bard's plays (although the 1997 season also saw restaging of the 1944 musical *On the Town*). Productions usually feature big names, and range from traditional inter-pretations (Andre Braugher as an armor-clad *Henry V*) to avant-garde presenta-tions (Morgan Freeman, Tracey Ullman, and David Alan Grier in *Taming of the Shrew* as a wild-west showdown). Patrick Stewart's role as Prospero in *The Tempest* a few years back was so popular that the show was propelled onto Broadway for an award-winning run. The theater itself, next to Belvedere Castle near 79th Street and West Drive, is a dream—on a beautiful starry night, there's no better stage in town. Tickets are given out free on a first-come, first-served basis (two per person), at 1pm on the day of the performance at the theater. The Delacorte Theater might have 1,881 seats, but each is a hot commodity, so people generally line up on the baseball field next to the theater about two to three hours in advance. You can also pick up tickets between 1 and 3pm at the Joseph Papp Public Theater, at 425 Lafayette St., where the Shakespeare Festival continues throughout the year. For more information, call the Public Theater at ☎ **212/539-8500** or the Delacorte at ☎ **212/861-7277,** or go online at **www.publictheater.org.**

With summer also comes the sound of music to Central Park, where the **New York Philharmonic** and the **Metropolitan Opera** regularly entertain beneath the stars; for the current schedule, call ☎ **212/360-3444** or 212/875-5709. But the most active music stage in the park is **SummerStage,** at Rumsey Playfield, mid-park around 72nd Street, which has featured everyone from the Godfather of Soul, James Brown, to the angel poet of punk, Patti Smith. Recent offerings have included concerts by Yoko Ono, Rocket from the Crypt, and Peter, Paul, and Mary; readings by authors Grace Paley, Paul Auster, and Tom Robbins; and

Tickets for all performances at Avery Fisher and Alice Tully halls can be purchased through **CenterCharge** (☎ 212/721-6500) or online at www.lincolncenter.org (click on BOX OFFICE & SCHEDULE in the upper right corner). Tickets for all Lincoln Center Theater performances can be purchased thorough **TeleCharge** (☎ 212/ 239-6200; www.telecharge.com). Tickets for New York State Theater productions (New York City Opera and Ballet companies) are available through **TicketMaster** (☎ 212/307-4100; www.ticketmaster.com), while tickets for films showing at the Walter Reade Theater can be bought via **Movie Phone** (☎ 212/777-FILM; www.777film. com; the theater code is 954). For last-minute ticket-buying tips, see the feature on p. 315.

Lincoln Center is normally home to the **New York Public Library for the Per-forming Arts** (☎ 212/870-1630), but the collection is currently pieced out to disparate locations as the library undergoes renovations.

Offered daily, one-hour **guided tours** of Lincoln Center tell the story of the great performing arts complex, and even offer glimpses of rehearsals; call ☎ 212/875-5370.

Madison Square Garden. On Seventh Ave. from 31st to 33rd sts. ☎ 212/465-**MSG1.** www.thegarden.com. Subway: 1, 2, 3, 9, A, C, E to 34th St.; B, D, G, F, N, R to Herald Square.

"Viva, Verdi!" festival performances by the New York Grand Opera. The season usually lasts from mid-June to early August. Tickets aren't usually required, but donations are warmly accepted. For the latest concert and performance info, call the SummerStage hot line at ☎ **212/360-2777** or visit **www.summerstage.org**.

Central Park may be the most happening park in town, but the calendar of free events heats up throughout the city's parks in summertime. You can find out what's happening by calling ☎ **212/360-3456,** or visiting **www.ci.nyc.ny.us/html/dpr** online.

The **Bryant Park Film Festival** takes place every Monday night throughout July and August, starting at sunset. This charming block-square park is blanket-to-blanket as crowds come to watch classic and family-friendly films such as *Breakfast at Tiffany's* screened under the stars. The crowds can get thick, especially for popular titles, so stake out your spot early. Rain dates are Tuesday. Call ☎ **212/512-5700** for this season's schedule.

A full slate of free concerts (Philip Glass and Robert Fripp have been among recent performers), modern and classical dance performances, family events, and more are regularly offered year-round in Winter Garden and on the Plaza of the **World Financial Center** (☎ **212/945-0505;** www.worldfinancialcenter.com) in Battery Park City. Events are regularly held at the **South Street Seaport** (☎ **212/732-7678;** www.southstseaport.org) indoors at Pier 17 in winter, outdoors on Pier 16 in summer.

Additionally, most of the city's top museums offer free music and other programs after regular hours on Friday, Saturday, and other nights of the week. The **Metropolitan Museum of Art,** in particular, has an extensive slate of offerings each week, but there's lots of fun to be had at others as well, including the **Museum of Modern Art** and the **Brooklyn Museum of Art,** which hosts the remarkably eclectic **First Saturday** program monthly. For details, see the museum listings in chapter 7.

Kiss, The Who, the Smashing Pumpkins, Springsteen, Tina Turner, Lauryn Hill, and other monsters of rock and pop regularly fill this 20,000-seat arena, which is also home to the Knicks and Rangers. A cavernous concrete hulk, it's better suited to sports than to concerts. End up in the back, and you'd better bring binoculars.

You'll find far better sightlines at **The Theater at Madison Square Garden,** an amphitheater-style auditorium with 5,600 seats that has also played host to some major pop stars, from Barbra Streisand to Oasis. Watch for possibly annual stagings of *The Wizard of Oz,* which has starred Roseanne and Eartha Kitt in past productions, and *A Christmas Carol,* with Roger Daltrey as last season's Scrooge.

The box office is located at Seventh Avenue and 32nd Street. Or you can purchase tickets through **TicketMaster** (☎ **212/307-7171;** www.ticketmaster.com).

✪ **92nd Street Y.** 1395 Lexington Ave. (at 92nd St.). ☎ **212/996-1100.** www.92ndsty. org. Subway: 4, 5, 6 to 86th St.; 6 to 96th St.

This community center offers a phenomenal slate of top-rated cultural happenings. Just because you see "Y," don't think this place is small potatoes: The greatest classical performers—Isaac Stern, Janos Starker, Nadja Salerno-Sonnenberg—give recitals here. In addition, the full concert calendar often includes musical programs from luminaries such as Max Roach, John Williams, and Judy Collins; Jazz at the Y from Dick Hyman and guests; the long-standing Chamber Music at the Y series; the new Music from the Jewish Spirit series; and regular cabaret programs. The lectures and literary readings calendar is unparalleled, with featured speakers ranging from Lorne Michaels to David Halberstam to Edgar Bronfman, Jr., to Ann Richards to Susan Sontag to Charles Frazier to Edward Albee to . . . the list goes on and on. Past poetry readings have included new British poets (Gwyneth Lewis, Glyn Maxwell) and a commemorative reading of Allen Ginsberg's *Howl*. Best of all, readings and lectures are usually priced between $10 and $15 for non-members (although select lectures can be priced as high as $30), and concert tickets generally go for $25 to $35—half or a third of what you'd pay at comparable venues.

Radio City Music Hall. 1260 Sixth Ave. (at 50th St.). ☎ **212/247-4777** or 212/307-1000 for tickets. www.radiocity.com. Subway: B, D, F, Q to 49th St./Rockefeller Center.

This stunning 6,200-seat art deco theater, with interior design by Donald Deskey, opened in 1932. Radio City continues to be a choice venue, where the theater alone adds a dash of panache to any performance. Star of the Christmas season is the **Radio City Music Hall Christmas Spectacular,** starring the legendary Rockettes. Visiting pop chart-toppers, from Stevie Nicks to Radiohead, also perform here. Thanks to perfect acoustics and uninterrupted sightlines, there's hardly a bad seat in the house. The theater also hosts a number of annual awards shows—such as the ESPYs, the GQ Man of the Year Awards, and anything MTV is holding in town—so this is a good place to celeb-spot on show nights.

The theater is currently under renovation, mainly to bring it up to ADA accessibility code, and is scheduled to reopen by October 1999. In the meantime, the box office remains open.

Town Hall. 123 W. 43rd St. (btw. Sixth and Seventh aves.). ☎ **212/840-2824.** www.the-townhall-nyc.org. Subway: 1, 2, 3, 7, 9, N, R, S to Times Square; B, D, F, Q to 42nd St.

This intimate landmark theater is blessed with outstanding acoustics, making it an ideal place to enjoy many kinds of performances, including theater, dance, and pop and world music. The calendar regularly includes such offerings as American tap and Brazilian tango exhibitions; Native American music and global rhythms; comedy from Chicago City Limits or Bill Maher; live tapings of "A Prairie Home Companion" with Garrison Keillor; concerts by the likes of Sarah MacLachlan or the reunited Blondie; and much more. The grade is extremely steep, so unless Lurch sits in front of you, fellow audience members shouldn't block your view.

4 Live Rock, Jazz, Blues & More

I discuss the top venues, both large and small, below. But there are far more than these, and new ones are popping up all the time. For the latest, be sure to check the publications and online sources discussed at the opening of this chapter.

LARGER VENUES

For coverage of **Madison Square Garden,** the **Theater at MSG,** and **Town Hall,** see "Major Concert Halls & Landmark Venues" above.

Beacon Theatre. 2124 Broadway (at 74th St.). ☎ **212/496-7070.** Subway: 1, 2, 3, 9 to 72nd St.

This pleasing midsize Upper West Side venue—a 1928 art-deco movie palace with an impressive lobby, stairway, and auditorium seating about 2,700—hosts mainly pop-music performances. Featured acts have ranged from street-smart pop diva Sheryl Crow to befuddled Beach Boy Brian Wilson. You'll also find such special events as the bodybuilding "Night of Champions" on the mix-and-match calendar.

Hammerstein Ballroom. At the Manhattan Center, 311 W. 34th St. (btw. Eighth and Ninth aves.). ☎ **212/564-4882.** Subway: A, C, E to 34th St.–Penn Station.

In the past couple of years, this midsize venue has become one of the city's most popular rock stages, hosting such acts as Sonic Youth, the Verve, Ben Folds Five, and Jonny Lang and Chris Whitley on a double bill; Oasis and Marilyn Manson both debuted their last American tours here. The sound system is very good, and the stage is mounted high enough that sightlines are decent even from the main floor. The side balconies are always reserved for VIPs, but the main balcony level, graded for good views and boasting comfortable theater-style seating, is usually open to regular Joes and Janes like us. However, you have to have a mezzanine-level ticket to gain access, so request one when you're buying if you want one (there's usually no cost difference). Otherwise, you'll end up on the general-admission, standing-room-only floor, which some (not me!) prefer.

Roseland. 239 W. 52nd St. (btw. Broadway and Eighth Ave.). ☎ **212/247-0200.** Subway: 1, 9, C, E to 50th St.

This old warhorse of a venue, a 1919 ballroom gone to seed, has been under threat of the wrecking ball for years now. Everybody has played at this too-huge-for-its-own-good general admission hall, from Big Bad Voodoo Daddy to Busta Rhymes to Nine Inch Nails to Jeff Beck. Bands who tend to inspire mosh pits like to book here (think Sugar Ray, Offspring), since there's plenty of space for slamming and surfing at the front of the stage. Thankfully, there's also lots of room to steer clear and still enjoy the show. Advance tickets can be purchased at the Irving Plaza box office (see p. 322) without service charge. Take a moment on your way through the lobby to check out the cases memorializing Roseland's post-war heydays as the city's premier dance hall.

MID-SIZED & MULTI-GENRE VENUES

In addition to the venues below, see what's on at the **Supper Club,** 240 W. 47th St. (☎ 212/921-1940). This stylin' venue is home to big band swing on the weekends (see "It Might as Well Be Swing" later in this chapter), but often hosts easygoing rock shows throughout the week; Pete Townshend, Van Morrison, and Rufus Wainwright are among the artists who have played here. Rock and pop musicians also occasionally set up at the **Westbeth Theater,** 151 Bank St. in the far West Village (☎ 212/741-0391), which has, among other things, played host to VH1's *Storytellers* series.

Ticket-Buying Tips

Tickets for events at all larger theaters as well as at Hammerstein Ballroom, Roseland, Irving Plaza, Coney Island High, S.O.B.'s, and Tramps can be purchased through **TicketMaster** (☎ 212/307-7171; www.ticketmaster.com).

Advance tickets for an increasing number of shows at smaller venues—including CBGB's (and CB's 313 Gallery), Bowery Ballroom, Mercury Lounge, Iridium, Knitting Factory, and Manny's Car Wash—can be purchased through **Ticketweb** (☎ 212/269-4TIX; www.ticketweb.com). Do note, however, that Ticketweb sells out in advance of actual ticket availability. Just because Ticketweb doesn't have tickets left for an event doesn't mean it's completely sold out, so be sure and check with the venue directly.

Even if a show is sold out doesn't mean you're out of luck. There's usually a number of people hanging around at showtime trying to get rid of extra tickets for friends who didn't show, and they're usually happy to pass them off for face value. You'll also see professional scalpers, who are best avoided—it doesn't take a rocket scientist to tell the difference. Be aware, of course, that all forms of resale are illegal.

The Bottom Line. 15 W. 4th St. (at Mercer St.). ☎ **212/228-7880** or 212/228-6300. Subway: N, R to Astor Place; A, B, C, D, E, F, Q to W. 4th St.

The Bottom Line built its reputation by serving as showcase for the likes of Bruce Springsteen and the Ramones, and it remains one of the city's most well-respected venues. With table seating, wait service, decent burgers and fries, and a no-smoking policy, it's one of the city's most comfortable, too. The Bottom Line is renowned for its excellent sound and bookings of the best rock and folk singer/songwriters in the business. Loudon Wainwright, Marshall Crenshaw, Robyn Hitchcock, Lucinda Williams, Jimmy Webb, Lyle Lovett, Emmylou Harris, and David Johansen (and alter-ego Buster Poindexter, natch) are among the many artists that make this their favored venue for area appearances. There are usually two shows nightly.

✪ **Bowery Ballroom.** 6 Delancey St. (at Bowery). ☎ **212/533-2111.** Subway: F, J, M, Z to Delancey St.

New in 1998, this marvelous space is run by the same people behind the pleasing Mercury Lounge (see below). The Bowery space is bigger, accommodating a crowd of 500 or so, and even better. The stage is big and raised to allow good sightlines from every corner. The sound couldn't be better, and art deco details give the place a sophistication that doesn't come easy to general-admission halls. My favorite spot is on the balcony, which has its own bar and seating alcoves. Quickly becoming a favorite with alt-rockers like Afghan Whigs, Cracker, and Shudder to Think as well as more established acts (Neil Finn, Patti Smith) who thrive in an intimate setting. Save on the service charge by buying advance tickets at Mercury's box office.

Irving Plaza. 17 Irving Place (at 15th St.). ☎ **212/777-6800.** www.irvingplaza.com. Subway: 4, 5, 6, L, N, R to Union Square.

This high-profile mid-sized music hall is the prime stop for national-name rock bands that aren't quite big enough yet (or anymore) to sell out Hammerstein, Roseland, or the Beacon. Think Shawn Mullins ("Lullaby"), Squirrel Nut Zippers, Kula Shaker, Lemonheads, Run DMC, Cheap Trick. From time to time, big-name artists also perform—Bob Dylan and Trent Reznor have both played "secret" shows here. All in all, a very nice place to see a show, with a well-elevated stage and lots of open space even on sold-out nights. There's an upstairs balcony that offers unparalleled views, but come early for a spot.

The Knitting Factory. 74 Leonard St. (btw. Broadway and Church St.). ☎ **212/219-3006.** www.knittingfactory.com. Subway: 1, 9 to Franklin St.

New York's premier avant-garde music venue has four separate spaces, each showcasing performances ranging from experimental jazz and acoustic folk to spoken-word and poetry readings to out-there multimedia works. Regulars who use the Knitting Factory as their lab of choice include former Lounge Lizard John Lurie; around-the-bend experimentalist John Zorn; guitar gods Vernon Reid, Eliot Sharp, and David Torn; innovative sideman (to Tom Waits and Elvis Costello, among others) Marc Ribot; and Television's Richard Lloyd. (If these names mean nothing to you, chances are good that the Knitting Factory is not for you.) The schedule is peppered with edgy star turns from the likes of Yoko Ono, Taj Mahal, Faith No More's Mike Patton, and folky charmer Jill Sobule ("I Kissed a Girl"). There are often two showtimes a night in the remarkably pleasing main peformance space, so it's easy to work a show around other activities. The Tap Bar offers an extensive list of microbrews and free live music, often soundtracking obscure silent films.

Tramps. 51 W. 21st St. (btw. Fifth and Sixth aves.). ☎ **212/544-1666.** Subway: F to 23rd St.; N, R to 23rd St.

This loft space is a happening spot for roots music, zydeco, reggae, funk, blues, and blues-tinged classic rock. Anything goes here, from Jerry Lee Lewis pounding out sets of 1950s oldies to Shawn Colvin singing her latest laments to George Clinton and the P-Funk All Stars rocking the house 'til dawn. This place gets packed, and the grown-up audience can really cut up the floor when things get going. Stake out a spot behind the railing near the elevated bar if you'd like a view over the crowd. The adjacent **Tramps Cafe** serves up decent Cajun food and live music from 11:30 on Monday through Saturday.

(MOSTLY) ROCK CLUBS

In addition to the choices below, you might also want to see what's happening at **Meow Mix,** a friendly lesbian bar that's been booking a quality local rock calendar of late (see "The Lesbian & Gay Scene" later in this chapter). Also see what's on at **Don Hill's,** a multi-dimensional party scene showcasing live bands on some nights, as well as the increasingly eclectic **Baby Jupiter,** which hosts live music in its back coffee-house-like room; see "Dance Clubs & Party Scenes" below.

○ **Arlene Grocery.** 95 Stanton St. (btw. Ludlow and Orchard sts.). ☎ **212/358-1633.** www.arlene-grocery.com. Subway: F to Second Ave.

Live music is always free at this Lower East Side club, which boasts a friendly bar and a good sound system. Arlene Grocery primarily serves as a showcase for hot bands looking for a deal or promoting their self-pressed record. On occasion, bigger names like Mark Eitzel and Richard X. Heyman take the stage to exercise their chops, but it's far more likely that the act on stage will be brand new to you. Still, there's little risk involved thanks to the no-cover policy, and bookers who know what they're doing. The crowd is an easygoing mix of club hoppers, rock fans looking for a new fix, and industry scouts looking for new blood. The new **Arlene Grocery Cafe** was scheduled to open next door at press time.

The Bitter End. 147 Bleecker St. (btw. La Guardia Place and Thompson St.). ☎ **212/ 673-7030.** www.bitterend.com. Subway: A, B, C, D, E, F, Q to W. 4th St.

This old-time club has been a Village mainstay since the '60s, when it launched many an early folk career. The Bitter End now features five rock, blues, and/or R&B bands nightly for a cover charge that seldom tops $5. Thanks to the high music-for-dollar ratio, expect a crowd chock full students from nearby NYU.

Brownie's. 169 Ave. A (btw. 10th and 11th sts.). ☎ **212/420-8392.** Subway: L to First Ave.

This unpretentious bar has grown into a well-respected alt-rock club. The crowd is half music-savvy scenesters and half carefree college students, with a few A&R types in the mix. The sound system is very good, but the layout could be better. Still, expect a packed bill—and a full crowd—just about any night of the week. Shows generally start at 8 or 9pm, and a DJ cranks out tunes after 11pm on weeknights.

Cafe Wha? 115 MacDougal St. (btw. Bleecker and W. 3rd sts.). ☎ **212/254-3706.** Subway: A, B, C, D, E, F, Q to W. 4th St.

You'll find a carefree crowd dancing in the aisles of this casual basement club just about any night of the week. From Wednesday through Sunday, the stage features the house's own Wha Band, which does an excellent job cranking out crowd-pleasing covers of familiar rock-and-roll hits from the '70s, '80s, and '90s. Monday night is the hugely popular Brazilian Dance Party, while Tuesday night is Funk Night. Expect to be sur-rounded by lots of Jersey kids and out-of-towners on the weekends, but so what? You'll be having as much fun as they are.

CBGB's. 315 Bowery (at Bleecker St.). ☎ **212/982-4052,** or 212/677-0455 for CB's 313 Gallery. www.cbgb.com. Subway: 6 to Bleecker St.; F to Second Ave.

Don basic black, not because you'll be doing the right thing fashionwise but because you'll leave without visible residue. The original downtown rock club has seen much better days, but no other spot is so rich with rock-and-roll history. This was the launching pad for New York punk and New Wave: the Ramones, Blondie, the Talking Heads, Television, the Cramps, Patti Smith, Stiv Bators and the Dead Boys—everybody got started here. The occasional names still show up (at press time, Tom Tom Club was doing a special 25th Anniversary show) but most acts performing here these days you've never heard of. Never mind—CB's still rocks. Expect loud and cynical, and you're unlikely to come away disappointed. Come early if you have hopes of actually seeing the stage, and avoid the bathrooms at all costs.

More today than yesterday is ✪ **CB's 313 Gallery,** a welcome spin-off that showcases alternative art on the walls and mostly acoustic singer/songwriters on stage. The music tends toward smoother rock, folk, blues, and acoustic. Within striking distance of the history, but much more pleasant all the way around.

Coney Island High. 15 St. Mark's Place (btw. Second and Third aves.). ☎ **212/674-7959.** Subway: 6 to Astor Place.

If you're over 30, you're likely to just consider this place a trial—even if you still love rock shows—but younger fans looking for the East Village edge will be in their glory. Founded by Jesse Malin (lead singer for local heroes D Generation), Coney Island High is the star of the East Village's skankiest strip, St. Mark's (known as 8th Street elsewhere in the city). With two main spaces, expect lots of loud, obnoxious rock and neo-punk, plus occasional alt-star (Spacehog, Alex Chilton) turn. A few theme nights pop up here and there, including the Green Door, a monthly Saturday-night glam-fest.

The Cooler. 416 W. 14th St. (btw. Ninth and Tenth aves.). ☎ **212/229-0785.** www. thecooler.com. Subway: A, C, E to 14th St.; L to Eighth Ave.

A former meatlocker in the heart of the meatpacking district has been transformed into this marvelously moody alternative music club with a discriminating taste for the eclectic—anything goes, as long as it's good. Offerings can range from Afrika Bambaataa to the acid-jazz Groove Collective to any number of local boy Thurston Moore's numerous side projects (when he isn't busy with Sonic Youth, of course). DJ nights can range from ambient to 100% hip-hop. There's no sign, so look for the metal doors and the staircase leading to the subterranean entrance. Advance tickets can be purchased at X-Large, 267 Lafayette St. (at Prince Street) in SoHo.

Fez Under Time Cafe. 380 Lafayette St. (at Great Jones St.). ☎ **212/533-2680.** Subway: 6 to Bleecker St.

You have to reserve a seat a few days ahead for the wildly popular Thursday-night Mingus Big Band, when the low-ceilinged basement performance space is filled with the cool sounds of jazz and well-dressed see-and-be-seensters for two sets. The rest of the week brings an eclectic live music-and-performance art mix, which can range from Combustible Edison to esoteric local acts. The stage is fronted by tightly packed picnic-style tables and a few coveted booths. Time Cafe's pleasing, well-priced menu is served during performances (see chapter 6 for details). I would love this sophisticated space if it were just better ventilated; if you need to escape the rampant cigarette smoke, head upstairs to Fez, a relaxing lounge and bar with an *Arabian Nights* ambiance.

✪ **Mercury Lounge.** 217 E. Houston St. (at Essex St./Ave. A). ☎ **212/260-4700.** Subway: F to Second Ave.

The Merc is everything a top-notch live music venue should be: unpretentious, extremely civilized, and outfitted with a killer sound system. The rooms themselves are nothing special: a front bar and an intimate back-room performance space with a low stage and a few tables along the wall. The calendar is filled with a mix of accomplished local rockers and national acts like Del Amitri and Art Alexakis from Everclear. The crowd is grown-up and easygoing. The only downside is that it's consistently packed thanks to the high quality of the entertainment and all-around pleasing nature of the experience.

Rodeo Bar. 375 Third Ave. (at 27th St.). ☎ **212/683-6500.** www.rodeobar.com. Subway: 6 to 28th St.

Here's New York's oldest—and finest—honky-tonk. Hike up your Wranglers and head those Fryes inside, where you'll find longhorns on the walls, peanut shells underfoot, and Tex-Mex on the menu. But this place is really about the music: urban-tinged country, foot-stompin' bluegrass, swinging rockabilly, Southern-flavored rock. While bigger names like Rosie Flores and up-and-comers on the tour circuit occasionally grace the stage, regular acts like Dixieland swingers the Flying Neutrinos and Simon and the Bar Sinisters usually supply the free music, keeping the urban cowboys plenty happy. A ten-gallon hat full o' fun.

Wetlands. 161 Hudson St. (at Laight St.). ☎ **212/966-4225.** www.wetlands-preserve.org. Subway: 1, 9, A, C, E to Canal St.

This environmentally conscious club isn't just for Deadheads anymore. Sure, Phish is worshipped by most of the crowd and you'll still find Haight-Ashbury scenesters like Jorma Kaukonen on the schedule every once in awhile, but the club's musical focus has really broadened in recent years. Wetlands regularly offers hip-hop, global funk, and other groovy world music in addition to mind-bending, indie, and roots rock. Also look for frequent sets from tribute bands honoring the likes of Bob Marley (Cannabis Cup), Pink Floyd (The Machine), and the Doors (Soft Parade).

JAZZ, BLUES, LATIN & WORLD MUSIC

Be aware that a night at a top-flight jazz club can be expensive. Cover charges can vary dramatically—from as little as $10 to as high as $65, depending on who's taking the stage—and there's likely to be an additional two-drink minimum (or a dinner requirement, if you choose an early show). Call ahead so you know what you're getting into; reservations are also an excellent idea at top spots.

For those of you who like your jazz with an edge, see what's on at the **Knitting Factory** (see "Mid-Size & Multi-Genre Venues," under "Live Rock, Jazz, Blues & More" above). Trad fans should also consider the Thursday Mingus Big Band Workshop at **Fez Under Time Cafe,** those wearing their dancing shoes should check out the Monday-night Brazilian big band and Tuesday-night funk at **Cafe Wha?,** and look for groovy world music at **Wetlands;** for details, see "(Mostly) Rock Clubs," above. You also might want to see what's on at the Lower East Side's **Tonic,** 107 Norfolk St., between Delancey and Rivington streets (☎ **212/358-7503**), whose downstairs lounge is becoming quite the avant-garde jazzerie.

Also, don't forget to see what's on at **Jazz at Lincoln Center,** the city's—and the nation's—premier forum for the traditional and developing jazz canon; see "Major Concert Halls & Landmark Venues" earlier in this chapter. Serious jazz fans may also want to plan their visit around the **JVC Jazz Festival;** see the "Calendar of Events" in chapter 2 for details.

Birdland. 315 W. 44th St. (btw. Eighth and Ninth aves.). ☎ **212/581-3080.** Subway: A, C, E to 42nd St.

Take the A Train

Harlem's jazz scene has taken on new energy in recent years, serving up top-notch music without the high cover charges and drink/food minimums that downtown clubs often require. **Showman's Cafe,** 2321 Frederick Douglass Blvd., between 124th and 125th streets (☎ 212/864-8941; subway: A, B, C, D to 125th St.), has one of the few organ rooms left in the Harlem jazz scene; the nightly music ranges from soulful jazz to funky bebop. **Lenox Lounge,** 288 Lenox Ave., between 124th and 125th streets (☎ 212/427-0253; subway: 2 or 3 to 125th St.), is a great art deco bar with live jazz quintets on weekends, as well as a lively Monday night jam session featuring trumpeter Roy Campbell. And **St. Nick's Pub,** 773 St. Nicholas Ave., at 149th Street (☎ 212/283-9728; subway: A, B, C, D to 145th St.), is an older Sugar Hill closet that's being rediscovered by a younger crowd for its great jazz five nights a week. The Monday jazz jams attract music lovers and players from all walks of life, and the service is just as friendly whether you come from the neighborhood, downtown, or out of town.

This legendary club abandoned its distant uptown roost in 1996 for a more convenient midtown nest, where it has established itself once again as one of the city's premier jazz spots. While the legend of Parker, Monk, Gillespie, and other bebop pioneers still holds sway, this isn't a crowded, smoky joint of yesteryear. The big room is spacious, comfy, and classy, with an excellent sound system and top-notch talent roster any night of the week. Expect lots of big-band swing, plus occasional appearances by stars like Tito Puente and his Latin Jazz Ensemble. You can't go wrong with the regular Sunday-night show, starring Chico O'Farrell's smokin' Afro-Cuban Jazz Big Band. The Southern-style food is even pretty good.

✪ Blue Note. 131 W. 3rd St. (at Sixth Ave.). ☎ 212/475-8592. www.bluenote.net. Subway: A, B, C, D, E, F, Q to W. 4th St.

Blue Note attracts the biggest names in jazz to its intimate setting. Those who've played here include just about everyone of note: Lionel Hampton, Dave Brubeck, Ray Charles, B. B. King, Manhattan Transfer, Dr. John, George Duke, and the superb Oscar Peterson. Dizzy Gillespie even celebrated his 81st birthday here. The sound system is excellent, and every seat in the house has a sightline to the stage. A night here can get expensive, but how often do you get to enjoy jazz of this caliber? Dinner is served (main courses are $19 to $29); also consider a Sunday brunch show.

Chicago B.L.U.E.S. 73 Eighth Ave. (btw. 13th and 14th sts.). ☎ 212/924-9755. Subway: A, C, E, L to 14th St.

Here's the best blues joint in the city, with a genuine Windy City flair. The contrived decor makes the place feel more theme-park than roadhouse, but the music is the real thing. Kick back on the comfortable couches for some of the best unadulterated blues around, which can include big names like Buddy Miles and Lonnie Brooks.

✪ Iridium. 44 W. 63rd St. (at Columbus Ave., below the Merlot Bar & Grill). ☎ 212/582-2121. www.iridiumjazz.com. Subway: 1, 9 to 66th St.; 1, 9, A, B, C, D to Columbus Circle.

This well-respected and snazzily designed basement boîte across from Lincoln Center books accomplished acts that play crowd-pleasing standards and transfixing new compositions. The Les Paul Trio still plays every Monday night, and other top-notch performers who often appear include the Frank Foster Quintet, the Charlie Haden Duo, McCoy Tyner and Bobby Hutcherson, and the excellent Jazz Messengers. In addition to just-fine cuisine from the upstairs restaurant, there's an extensive wine list.

The Jazz Standard. 116 E. 27th St. (btw. Park Ave. South and Lexington Ave.) ☎ **212/576-2232.** Subway: 6 to 28th St.

Kudos to the Jazz Standard, where both the food and music meet all expectations: This is the only combination restaurant/jazz club to be awarded two stars by the *New York Times*. You can order the highly regarded New American cuisine in both the airy street-level dining room (known as 27 Standard) and the spacious basement jazz lounge. Boasting a sophisticated retro-speakeasy vibe, the Jazz Standard is one of the city's largest jazz clubs, with well-spaced tables seating 150. The rule is straightforward, mainstream jazz by new and established musicians. You really can't go wrong here.

Manny's Car Wash. 1558 Third Ave. (btw. 87th and 88th sts.). ☎ **212/369-BLUES.** www.mannyscarwash.com. Subway: 4, 5, 6 to 86th St.

Some come to this friendly Upper East Side joint for the top-notch blues, while others come for the scene (yuppie love seekers on Monday for ladies night, frat-pack types on weekends). Fans know Manny's best for its excellent Windy City sounds, but the schedule also features Louisiana bayou blues and zydeco. Don't be surprised if you spot a star or two on the bill, such as Hiram Bullock. The cover charge is remarkably low for the quality of the music: It's often less than $10, and I've never seen it go higher than $15. Look for the legendary free Sunday-night blues jam, and don't miss Popa Chubby's rockin' Blues Band if he's on the bill.

Small's. 183 W. 10th St. (at Seventh Ave.). ☎ **212/929-7565.** Subway: 1, 2, 3, 9 to W. 14th St.

Here's a great destination for committed jazzophiles: If you just don't want to stop grooving after the other clubs close, head to this cozy basement hideaway, which stays open all night. Scheduled performers, which often include cutting-edge unsigned acts or overlooked talents, play from around 10pm to 2am, followed by a nightly jam session until dawn (and often beyond). No alcohol is served, but that doesn't keep the crowds away—they're happy to come just for the music. Drinks are free with the $10 cover, and all ages are welcome.

۞ S.O.B.'s. 204 Varick St. (at W. Houston St.). ☎ **212/243-4940.** Subway: 1, 9 to Houston St.

If you like your music hot, hot, hot, S.O.B.'s is the place for you. This is the city's top world-music venue, specializing in Brazilian, Caribbean, and Latin sounds. The packed house dances and sings along nightly to calypso, samba, mambo, African drums, reggae, or other global grooves, united in the high-energy, feel-good vibe. Bookings include top-flight performers from around the globe; luminaries who have graced the stage include Marc Anthony, Astrud Gilberto, Ruben Blades, King Sunny Ade, and the unsurpassed Celia Cruz. The room's Tropicana Club style has island pizzazz that carries through to the Caribbean-influenced cooking and extensive tropical drinks menu. This place is so popular that it's an excellent idea to book in advance, especially if you'd like table seating. At press time, free before-show dance lessons were offered on Mondays so you could be ready to strut your stuff once the band takes the stage.

Sweet Basil. 88 Seventh Ave. South (btw. Grove and Bleecker sts.). ☎ **212/242-1785.** www.sweetbasil.com. Subway: 1, 9 to Christopher St.–Sheridan Square.

The choice runs from fusion to traditional at this intimate but excellent jazz club. You can count on finding top names playing top-notch music. Pricey, but you'll get your money's worth—the food is even better than you'd expect. The Sunday brunch is so popular that they've added a Saturday version as well.

⭘ **The Village Vanguard.** 178 Seventh Ave. South (just below 11th St.). ☎ **212/255-4037.** Subway: 1, 2, 3, 9 to 14th St.

What CBGB's is to rock, the Village Vanguard is to jazz. One look at the photos on the walls will show you who's been through: John Coltrane, Miles Davis, Thelonious Monk, Wynton Marsalis, and many, many more. Thankfully, this legendary club is just as vital as ever. Expect a mix of established names and high-quality local talent, including the Vanguard's own jazz orchestra. The sound is great but sightlines are terrible, so come early for a front table. The crowd can seem either overly serious or overly touristy, but don't let that stop you—you'll always find great music.

5 Cabaret & Comedy

A evening spent at a sophisticated cabaret just might be the quintessential New York night on the town. It isn't cheap: Most of the following clubs have high covers that vary by the entertainer, but can be anywhere from $10 to $50, or even more. Some also have two-drink or dinner-check minimums, higher prices on weekends, and other qualifications. Always reserve ahead, and get the complete lowdown when you make reservations.

I'm sad to report the closing of **Rainbow & Stars,** the cabaret room next to the Rainbow Room high atop Rockefeller Center. As you can see from the list below, however, there are plenty of other swellegant venues to pick up the slack.

⭘ **Cafe Carlyle.** In the Carlyle hotel, 781 Madison Ave. (at 76th St.). ☎ **212/744-1600.** Subway: 6 to 77th St. Closed July–Aug.

Cabaret doesn't get any better than this. First of all, this is where you'll find Bobby Short—and that's all those who know cabaret need to know. Nothing evokes the essence of Manhattan more than an evening with this quintessential interpreter of Porter and the Gershwins. When he's not in residence, you'll find such rarified talents as Eartha Kitt, Betty Buckley, and Michael Feinstein. The room is intimate and as swanky as they come. Expect a high tab—admission is $50 with no minimum, but add dinner and two people could easily spend $300—but if you're looking for the best of the best, look no further. On most Mondays, Woody Allen joins the Eddy Davis New Orleans Jazz Band on clarinet to swing Dixie style.

Don't Tell Mama. 343 W. 46th St. (btw. Eighth and Ninth aves.). ☎ **212/757-0788.** Subway: 1, 2, 3, 9, N, R to Times Square; A, C, E to 42nd St.; C, E to 50th St.

Singing waitresses go from tips to tunes when their turn in the spotlight comes. You'll find an evening of torch songs, comedy, and much more in a friendly, and affordable, atmosphere. The piano bar is particularly lively. Drinks only, no dinner.

Duplex Cabaret. 61 Christopher St. (at Seventh Ave. So). ☎ **212/255-5438.** Subway: 1, 9 to Christopher St.–Sheridan Square.

Expect a high camp factor and lots of good-natured fun in this multi-level space. A mixed gay/straight crowd of locals and curious out-of-towners sit at outdoor tables for drinks, gather around the downstairs piano (sing-alongs from around 9pm), or head upstairs to the cabaret for shows that run from mini-musicals to drag revues to stand-up comedy.

Eighty Eights. 228 W. 10th St. (btw. Bleecker and Hudson sts.). ☎ **212/924-0088.** Subway: 1, 9 to Christopher St.–Sheridan Square.

This attractive, informal downtown spot offers affordable, top-quality cabaret that ranges from torch songs to musical comedy to stand-up. Two shows nightly, drinks only. Downstairs is a friendly piano bar where both patrons and staff aren't afraid to sing along loudly.

✪ **Joe's Pub.** At the Joseph Papp Public Theater, 425 Lafayette St. (btw. Astor Place and 4th St.). ☎ **212/539-8777** or Telecharge at 212/239-6200 (for advance tickets). www. publictheater.org. Subway: 6 to Astor Place.

The newest entry on the cabaret circuit is a beautiful new cabaret and supper club eloquently named for the legendary Joseph Papp. It's everything a New York cabaret should be: an elegant retro-style, multi-level space serving up a classic American menu (think burgers, shrimp cocktail, baked Alaska) and top-notch entertainers. The sophisticated crowd comes for music and spoken word that ranges from legendary Broadway duo Betty Comden and Adolph Green to Cuban troubadour Pedro Luis Ferrer to fiery flamenco dancing to performance poets to pop golden boy Duncan Sheik. Don't be surprised if Broadway actors show up on off-nights to exercise their substantial chops.

✪ **The Oak Room.** At the Algonquin hotel, 59 W. 44th St. (btw. Fifth and Sixth aves.). ☎ **212/840-6800.** Subway: B, D, F, Q to 42nd St.

Recently refurbished to recall its glory days, the Oak Room is one of the city's most intimate, elegant, and sophisticated spots for cabaret. Headliners include such first rate talents as Andrea Marcovicci, Steve Ross, Julie Wilson, and cool-cat jazz guitarist John Pizzarelli, plus occasional lesser names that are destined for greatness. Monday night is Spoken Word night at the Oak Room, with speakers as diverse as Spalding Gray, Stanley Tucci, and Paul Theroux.

6 Stand-Up & Sketch Comedy

Cover charges are generally in the $10 to $20 range, with all-star Caroline's going as high as $25 on occasion. Many clubs also have a two-drink minimum. Be sure to ask about the night's cover when you make reservations.

In addition to the choices below, you might also want to see what's on at **Don't Tell Mama, Eighty Eights,** and **Duplex,** cabarets that tend to tickle the funny bone on a regular basis; see directly above.

Caroline's. 1626 Broadway (btw. 49th and 50th sts.). ☎ **212/757-4100.** Subway: 1, 9 to 50th St.; N, R to 49th St.

Caroline Hirsch presents today's hottest headliners in her upscale Theater District showroom. You're bound to recognize at least one or two of the established names and hot up-and-comers on the bill in any given week, like Dave Chapelle, Colin Quinn, Kathy Griffin, Gilbert Gottfried, or Caroline Rhea. The celebrated Robert Klein even takes the stage on occasion. Monday is New Talent Night, while kids take center stage Saturday and Sunday afternoon at Caroline's Kids Klub.

✪ **Comedy Cellar.** 117 MacDougal St. (btw. Bleecker and W. 3rd sts.). ☎ **212/254-3480.** Subway: A, B, C, D, E, F, Q to W. 4th St. (use 3rd St. exit).

This intimate subterranean club is the club of choice for stand-up fans in the know, thanks to the best, most consistently impressive lineups in the business. I'll always love the Comedy Cellar for introducing an uproariously funny unknown comic named Ray Romano to me a few years back.

Comic Strip Live. 1568 Second Ave. (btw. 81st and 82nd sts.). ☎ **212/861-9386.** www.comicstriplive.com. Subway: 4, 5, 6 to 86th St.

This was *the* comedy club of the '80s, launching such careers as Jerry Seinfeld, Eddie Murphy, Carol Leifer, Paul Reiser, Adam Sandler, and Chris Rock. The big, boisterous room is still very well respected as a forum for new talent, and greatful superstars often return to the old homestead for surprise appearances.

Dangerfield's. 1118 First Ave. (btw. 61st and 62nd sts.). ☎ **212/593-1650.** Subway: N, R to 60th St.; 4, 5, 6, to 59th St.

Dangerfield's is the nightclub version of the comedy club, with a mature crowd and a straight-outta-Vegas atmosphere. The comedians are all veterans of the comedy-club and late-night talk-show circuit. An affordable dinner menu is served.

✪ **Gotham Comedy Club.** 34 W. 22nd St. (btw. Fifth and Sixth aves.). ☎ **212/367-9000.** www.citysearch.com/nyc/gothamcomedy. Subway: N, R or F to 23rd St.

Here's the city's trendiest and most sophisticated comedy club. The young talent—Tom Rhodes, Jeff Ross, Paul Mercurio, Lynn Harris—is red-hot. Look for theme nights like the lovelorn laugh riot "Breakup Girl Live!" and "A Very Jewish Thursday."

Stand-Up New York. 236 W. 78th St. (at Broadway). ☎ **212/595-0850.** Subway: 1, 9 to 79th St.

The Upper West Side's premier stand-up comedy club hosts some of the brightest young comics in the business, and drop-in guests have included Dennis Leary, Robin Williams, and Mr. Upper West Side himself, Jerry Seinfeld.

✪ **Upright Citizen's Brigade Theater.** 161 W. 22nd St. (btw. Sixth and Seventh aves.) ☎ **212/366-9176.** www.uprightcitizens.com. Subway: 1, 9 to 23rd St.

You've seen their twisted, highly original sketch comedy on Comedy Central—now you can see the Upright Citizen's Brigade, New York's premier sketch comedy troupe, live. The biggest success to come out of New York's late '90s alternative comedy explosion, the UCB now has its very own showcase. The best of the non-stop hilarity is *A.S.S.S.C.A.T.*, the troupe's extremely popular long-form improv show. At press time, it was being offered twice on Sundays; make your reservations for the 7:30pm show well in advance. The 9:30pm show is free, but come extra-early to stand in line. For everything else, you won't pay more than $5.

7 Bars & Cocktail Lounges

If you want even more bars and lounges to choose from, pick up the pocket-sized *Shecky's Bar, Club & Lounge Guide*, available in most city bookstores.

SOUTH STREET SEAPORT & THE FINANCIAL DISTRICT
✪ **The Greatest Bar on Earth.** 1 World Trade Center, 107th floor (on West St., btw. Liberty and Vesey sts.) ☎ **212/524-7000.** www.windowsontheworld.com. Subway: 1, 9, C, E to Church St.; N, R to Cortlandt St.

High atop the World Trade Center sits the Greatest Bar on Earth, whose name is only a slight exaggeration. This is a magical spot for cocktails, decent à la carte dining (finger foods and gourmet munchies mostly), and dancing. No matter how many times I come up here, I'm wowed by the incredible views. The place is huge, but intimate nooks and a separate back room bring the scale down to comfortable proportions. The crowd is a lively mix of in-the-know locals and stylish out-of-towners. This is a great place to come with a group; the music is loud, and the joint really jumps as the night goes on. Quintessentially—and spectacularly—New York. Look for swing on Friday and Saturdays, plus mambo, funk, and R&B other nights of the week. Wednesday is home to the super-hip Mondo 107 strato-lounge DJ party. See "It Might as Well Be Swing" later in this chapter for more on the swing scene.

North Star Pub. At South Street Seaport, 93 South St. (at Fulton St.). ☎ **212/509-6757.** www.northstarpub.com. Subway: 2, 3, 4, 5 to Fulton St.

In addition to an excellent selection of bottled and on-tap brews, this genuine British pub boasts one of the finest single-malt scotch menus in the city. Owner Devon Black is very serious about his potables: He carries no fewer than 75 single malts, conducts regular tasting seminars, and specializes in British-style ales, bitters, ciders, and stouts. The North Star is warm, friendly, and affordable—the perfect place to linger over an Imperial pint or a wee dram for connoisseurs and casual drinkers alike. Great pub grub, too.

Wall St. Kitchen & Bar. 70 Broad St. (btw. Beaver and S. William sts., about 1½ blocks south of New York Stock Exchange). ☎ **212/797-7070.** Subway: 4, 5 to Bowling Green; J, M, Z to Broad St.

Want to rub elbows with some genuine bulls and bears after a hard day of downtown sightseeing? Head to this surprisingly appealing and affordable bar, housed (appropriately enough) in a spectacular former bank in the heart of the financial district. Like its sister hangout, Soho Kitchen & Bar (below), Wall St. Kitchen specializes in on-tap beers (around 50 are on offer at any given time) and "flight" menus of wines and microbrews for tasting. The familiar bar food is well prepared and reasonably priced. Come on a weekday to enjoy the crowd.

TRIBECA

Bubble Lounge. 228 W. Broadway (btw. Franklin and White sts.). ☎ **212/431-3443.** www.bubblelounge.com. Subway: 1, 9 to Franklin St.

From the first cork that popped, this wine bar dedicated to the bubbly was an effervescent hit. There are hundreds of champagnes and sparkling wines, 25 of them by the glass, to pair with caviar, foie gras, and desserts. The crowd is appropriately sophisticated for the elegant surroundings and offerings, but you don't have to spend a fortune to enjoy this swanky place: Champagne starts at $8 a glass. There's live music (usually jazz) every Monday.

El Teddy's. 219 W. Broadway (btw. Franklin and White sts.). ☎ **212/941-7070.** Subway: 1, 9 to Franklin St.

This upscale South-of-the-Border restaurant is a great place to pony up to the bar for a cocktail. The food's a bit pricey for what you get, but the bathtub-sized margaritas are terrific, and you have about two dozen to choose from. All the fashionistas left years ago, but the kitschy decor is still retro-hip. You can't miss this place—just look for the enormous Statue of Liberty crown suspended over the sidewalk.

Riverrun. 176 Franklin St. (btw. Greenwich Ave. and Hudson St.). ☎ **212/996-3894.** Subway: 1, 9 to Franklin St.

Down-to-earth as ever, this neighborhood pioneer is now a refreshing find in an increasingly haute 'hood. Before Nobu, before Miramax, before JFK Jr. and Sean Lennon grew up and moved downtown, there was this quiet, unpretentious, unassuming bar-restaurant. Like a lot of vintage joints, the decor is more clutter than clean lines, but the friendly bar does a great job of keeping the easygoing crowd happy. There's a sensible wine list, a good selection of beers on tap, a respectable single-malt selection, and satisfying comfort food. The crowd morphs from traders to locals as the evening wears on. A relaxing stop for those tired of New York's high prices and lofty pretensions.

✪ The Sporting Club. 99 Hudson St. (btw. Franklin and Leonard sts.). ☎ **212/ 219-0900.** www.thesportingclub.net. Subway: 1, 9 to Franklin St.

The city's best sports bar is a guy's joint if there ever was one. The space is as big as a linebacker, with giant TV screens at every turn tuned to just about every game on the planet. (Wall Streeters bring their international cohorts here to catch everything from English football to Japanese sumo.) The menu is what you'd expect: wings, burgers, club sandwiches, and *lots* of beer. There's no better place for sports fans to get crazy at Super Bowl time and during March Madness. When the big games are over, this turns into a surprisingly popular singles place.

Walker's. 16 North Moore St. (at Varick St.). ☎ **212/941-0142.** Subway: 1, 9 to Franklin St.

Like Riverrun, Walker's is an old holdout from pre-fabulous TriBeCa. It's surprisingly charming, with a tin ceiling, a long wooden bar, oldies on the sound system, and cozy tables where you can dine on affordable meat-and-potatoes fare. The bartenders are a friendly bunch, but do yourself a favor and don't get fancy with your drink orders.

CHINATOWN & LITTLE ITALY

✪ **Double Happiness.** 173 Mott St. (at Broome St.). ☎ **212/941-1282.** Subway: 6 to Spring St.; B, D, Q to Grand St.

This new kid on a new block has already shown itself to be quite a star. The only indicator to the subterranean entrance is a vertical WATCH YOUR STEP sign. Once through the door, you'll find a beautifully designed lounge with artistic nods to the neighborhood throughout the stylish decor. The space is large, but a low ceiling and intimate nooks enhance its romantic vibe (although the loud funkified music mix may deter true wooing). Don't miss the green tea martini, an inspired house creation.

Mare Chiaro. 176½ Mulberry St. (at Broome St.). ☎ **212/226-9345.**

This authentic corner of Little Italy now hosts a bizarro mix of slumming NoLiTa hipsters, uptown singles, and neighborhood holdovers from an age when this was just a drinkingman's bar. But Mare Chiaro still works its crusty magic, transporting you back to another era with its gentrification-resistant vibe. A great place for a cheap beer at a crossroads of city life.

SOHO

Casa La Femme. 150 Wooster St. (btw. Houston and Prince sts.) ☎ **212/505-0005.** Subway: N, R to Prince St.

Welcome to the Casbah, man. This swank restaurant and bar is gloriously *Arabian Nights*–themed, complete with private tents and an Egyptian/Moroccan menu in the dining room. Alas, the cuisine doesn't live up to the setting, but no matter— come for cocktails. They're pricey, but the ambiance is worth the extra dough. Comfy pillow seating around low tables in the bar area make perfect snuggle spots; arrive early in the evening or the week to nab one. If you inhale, go full Middle Eastern luxe and order up a hookah, which comes filled with apple-cured tobacco (about $20).

Merc Bar. 151 Mercer St. (btw. Prince and Houston sts.). ☎ **212/966-2727.** Subway: N, R to Prince St.; B, D, F, Q to Broadway–Lafayette St.

Notable for its long tenure in the fickle world of beautiful-people bars, Merc Bar has mellowed nicely. You'll still find a good-looking crowd in the a small, superbly appointed lounge, but now it's a confident rather than a trend-happy one. The decor bespeaks civilized rusticity—think SoHo meets the Sundance catalog. A great place to nestle into a comfortable couch with your honey and enjoy the scene. Look carefully, because there's no sign.

Ñ. 33 Crosby St. (btw. Grand and Broome sts.). ☎ **212/219-8856.** Subway: 6 to Spring St.; N, R to Prince St.

On a charming cobbled street that somehow escaped gentrification, Ñ (pronounced like the Spanish letter, *enyay*) is long, narrow, candlelit, and hip. Despite its cool, the staff is warm, and the many sherries for sale are excellent. There's also a nice, fruity sangria, plus a full bar for non-Spanish tastes. You can order some of the city's best tapas, which come out of a very tiny kitchen in back. Flamenco dancers heighten the appeal on select Wednesday nights.

Pravda. 281 Lafayette St. (btw. Prince and Houston sts.). ☎ **212/226-4696** or 212/226-4944. Subway: B, D, F, Q to Broadway–Lafayette St.

If you were prowling New York's watering holes looking for Boris and Natasha, this is where you'd most likely find them. This Soviet-chic lounge makes pricey but perfect martinis for a classy crowd drawn in by the romantic pre-Gorbachev revolutionary vibe. There's plenty of Russian caviar on hand to wash down with those pricey cocktails, plus a full humidor for the cigar-bar crowd.

Soho Kitchen & Bar. 103 Greene St. (btw. Spring and Prince sts.). ☎ **212/925-1866.** Subway: N, R to Prince St.; C, E to Spring St.

This fun, easygoing bar and restaurant is a nice antidote to the standard SoHo pretensions. The large, lofty space attracts an animated after-work and late-night crowd to its central bar, which dispenses more 21 beers on tap, a whole slew of microbrews by the bottle, and more than 100 wines by the glass, either individually or in "flights" for comparative tastings.

Veruka. 525 Broome St. (btw. Thompson St. and Sixth Ave.). ☎ **212/625-1717.** Subway: C, E to Spring St.

Lounges just don't get more 21st-century swellegant than this impeccably designed bi-level hotspot. The mark-ups on the cocktails and haute bar food are ridiculous, but that's the price you pay to rub elbows with such a sleek, super-chic crowd. Don't be surprised if you spot a famous face or two. Dress to impress and arrive early for your best chance of making it past the velvet rope.

LOWER EAST SIDE

✪ **Idlewild.** 145 E. Houston St. (btw. First and Second aves., on the south side of Houston). ☎ **212/477-5005.** Subway: F to Second Ave.

It may look unapproachable from the street, with nothing but an unmarked stainless-steel facade, but inside you'll find a fun, easygoing bar that's perfect for lovers of retro-kitsch. The interior is a larger-scale repro of a jet airplane, complete with reclining seats, tray tables, and too-small bathrooms that will transport you back to your favorite mid-air moments in no time. There are booths in back for larger crowds, and an Austin Powers–style bar to gather around at center stage. The DJ spins a listener-friendly mix of light techno, groovy disco in the Funkadelic vein, and '80s tunes from the likes of the Smiths and the Cure.

Lansky Lounge. 138 Delancey St. (entrance on Norfolk St., between Rivington and Delancey sts.). ☎ **212/677-9489.** Subway: F to Delancey St.

A doorman stands on the sidewalk to point patrons down a flight of stairs, through an alley, and back up a staircase into this faux speakeasy. Fashionistas lament that Lansky Lounge has been "discovered" (read: ruined), but it's still one of the Lower East Side's coolest scenes. The special martinis and infused vodkas are terrific. Come on a weeknight, when the crowd is more local than bridge-and-tunnel. *Note:* The bar is closed on Friday night in observance of the Jewish Sabbath.

Ludlow Bar. 165 Ludlow St. (btw. Stanton and Houston sts.). ☎ **212/353-0536.** Subway: F to Second Ave.

This friendly little lounge manages to avoid the pretensions of its hipper-than-thou neighbors. Still, in keeping with the lounge trend, you'll find cozy furniture, a purple-felt pool table, and a DJ spinning funky jazz and trip-hop for an artsy crowd that's slightly older than neighborhing Max Fish's.

Max Fish. 178 Ludlow St. (at Houston St.). ☎ **212/529-3959.** Subway: F to Second Ave.

Max Fish has been the cornerstone of this now-trendy strip of the Lower East Side. If grungy kitsch is more your style than loungey sleek, then Max Fish is the place for you. You'll find a great jukebox, video games, and a pool table that's best left to the locals unless you can live up to the challenge. The crowd is a curious mix of serious neighborhood artists (shows hang here periodically) and twentysomethings seriously on the make.

Orchard. 200 Orchard St. (btw. Houston and Stanton sts.). ☎ **212/673-5350.** Subway: F to Second Ave.

This super-cool lounge is the best of the Lower East Side crop. The postmodern-goes-organic decor is at once funky and serene, the friendly barstaff knows how to mix a cocktail, and the crowd is more relaxed than at neighboring pickup spots. DJs spin a smart, eclectic mix that creates a nice aural backdrop but doesn't overwhelm. A terrific place for a casual drink on a weeknight, but skip it on the weekend unless you can stand the tight squeeze (I can't).

THE EAST VILLAGE & NOHO

In addition to the choices below, also consider the magical **Fez,** 380 Lafayette St., at Great Jones St. (☎ **212/533-2680**), a dimly lit Moroccan-themed bar and lounge that I much prefer to the downstairs performance space; see "Live Rock, Jazz, Blues & More" above for further details.

Barmacy. 538 E. 14th St. (btw. Avenues A and B). ☎ **212/228-2240.** Subway: L to First Ave.

Barmacy is just what you'd guess—a bar housed in a vintage pharmacy, complete with shelves of classic toiletries and a drugstore counter that would make Lana Turner smile. On an otherwise desolate stretch of East 14th, it's really a fun place to spend an evening, complete with youngish party-hearty crowd and happening DJ spinning groovy tunes in the back room that range from earnest Britpop to modern funk to makeout music, depending on the evening.

✪ **B Bar & Grill.** 40 E. 4th St. (at Bowery). ☎ **212/475-2220.** Subway: 6 to Bleecker St.

As Bowery Bar, this place was *the* celebrity hotspot a few years back. Reincarnated a year or so ago as B Bar, it managed to survive the limelight, and now makes an appealing spot for cocktails and/or a casual late-night bite. Originally a Gulf gas station, the cavernous dining room is '60s modern and attractive, with high ceilings, comfy booths, retro-style mood lighting, a large central bar, and the latest alterna-hits on the sound system. But it's the giant tree-filled courtyard that's the biggest draw. The bar offers a regular selection of signature drinks, including a Ketel One martini that even Bond could love.

✪ **dba.** 41 First Ave. (btw. 2nd and 3rd sts.). ☎ **212/475-5097.** Subway: F to Second Ave.

Along with Temple Bar (below), this is my other favorite bar in the city. It has completely bucked the loungey trend that has taken over the city, instead remaining firmly and resolutely an unpretentious neighborhood bar that's as comfy as your favorite shirt, where everyone is welcome and at home. Most importantly, dba is a beer- and scotch-lover's paradise, with a massive drink menu on the giant chalkboards behind the bar. Owner Ray Deter specializes in British-style cask-conditioned ales (the kind that you pump by hand) and stocks a phenomenal collection of 90 single-malt scotches. The relaxed crowd is a pleasing mix of connoisseurs and casual drinkers who like the unlimited choices and egalitarian vibe. Excellent jukebox, too.

Flamingo East. 219 Second Ave. (btw. 13th and 14th sts.). ☎ **212/533-2860.** Subway: 6 to Astor Place; L to Third Ave.

Here's the East Village's most sophisticated hangout, drawing a mixed gay/straight crowd. Downstairs is a votive-lit, black-and-white bar and restaurant peopled by a fashionable crowd that's Euro without the trash, while upstairs is a white-washed art gallery with changing exhibits and a following that's just as cool, if a touch younger. The lounge party changes from burlesque to gay salon to '80s-themed, depending on the night. Best of all is the outdoor terrace, open in summer.

✪ **KGB Bar.** 85 E. 4th St. (btw. Second and Third Aves.) ☎ **212/505-3360.** Subway: 6 to Astor Place.

This former Ukranian social club still boasts its Soviet-themed decor, but it now draws creative intellectual types who like the low-key boho vibe. Sunday nights are the biggest draw thanks to the success of KGB's excellent reading series, where an increasingly talented pack of up-and-coming and published writers read from their prose works to a receptive crowd starting at 7pm. Past readers have included Rick Moody (*The Ice Storm*), Catherine Texier (*Breakup*), and Kathryn Harrison (*The Kiss*). For a preview, pick up a copy of *The KGB Bar Reader,* a 28-story anthology edited by the curator of KGB's reading series. The Red Room also stages theatrical productions.

Lucky Cheng's. 24 First Ave. (btw. 1st and 2nd sts.). ☎ **212/473-0516.** Subway: F to Second Ave.

You gotta have a gimmick if you want to get ahead, according to *Gypsy*—so why not go the RuPaul route? The Asian fusion food is beside the point at this silly place, so come simply to be entertained by the fabulous drag queens in the brand-new six-screen, state-of-the-art karaoke lounge with a goldfish pond under the plexiglass stage. It's pure camp—like stepping into a production of *The King and I* cast in a New Orleans bordello. You'll find a mixed crowd, suits and jeans, yuppies and gays, with bemused out-of-towners spicing the brew.

McSorley's Old Ale House. 15 E. 7th St. (btw. Second and Third aves.). ☎ **212/ 473-9148.** Subway: 6 to Astor Place.

Shrine Time—and they want you to worship their way. In business for more than 140 years, McSorley's window proudly claims "WE WERE HERE BEFORE YOU WERE BORN," and their original fixtures hint at a history that includes Abe Lincoln and JFK. Only McSorley's Ale is served, light or dark and two at a time. Come to bask in the old-time New York glory, not to nurse a Diet Coke. This is an ale-sodden madhouse most nights, and an Irish Armageddon on St. Patrick's Day. While it's also a McSorley's tradition to urinate on the wall outside, they prefer you honor that one in the breach, not in the commission.

✪ **Temple Bar.** 332 Lafayette St. (just north of Houston St., on the west side of the street). ☎ **212/925-4242.** Subway: B, D, F, Q to Broadway/Lafayette St.; 6 to Bleecker St.

Temple Bar is, hands down, my favorite lounge in the city. Members of the It crowd will tell you it's passe, which only serves to increase its appeal as far as I'm concerned—it's easy to get in now and, on weeknights at least, you can even usually manage to find a comfy seat. One of the first comers to New York's lounge scene, Temple Bar is still a gorgeous art deco hangout, with a long L-shaped bar leading to a lovely seating area with velvet drapes, romantic backlighting, and Sinatra softly crooning in the background. Cocktails simply don't get any better than the classic martini (with just a kiss of vermouth, of course) or the smooth-as-penoir silk Rob Roy (Johnnie Walker Black, sweet vermouth, bitters). Elegant finger foods provide a reason to never leave. Bring a date—and feel free to invite me along anytime. Temple Bar is a little inconspicuous, so look for the petroglyph-like lizards on the facade.

GREENWICH VILLAGE

Bar d'O. 29 Bedford St. (at Downing St.). ☎ **212/627-1580.** Subway: A, B, C, D, E, F, Q to W. 4th St. (use 3rd St. exit).

This intimate space is home to the Village's best lounge scene—which unfortunately makes it crowded, but still cozy and appealing. A different DJ sets the scene for the mixed gay/straight crowd nightly in this low-slung, candlelit space, but the real show is drag diva Joey Arias, who wows the crowd twice weekly (Tuedays and Saturdays at press time) with her spot-on Billie Holliday renditions. Call ahead to check the schedule.

✪ Chumley's. 86 Bedford St. (btw. Grove and Barrow sts.). ☎ **212/675-4449.** Subway: 1, 9 to Christopher St.–Sheridan Square.

A classic. Many bars in New York date their beginnings to Prohibition, but Chumley's still has the vibe. The circa college-age crowd doesn't date back nearly as far, however. Come to warm yourself by the fire and indulge in a once-forbidden pleasure: beer. The door is unmarked, with a metal grille on the small window; another entrance is at 58 Barrow St., which takes you in through a back courtyard.

Hudson Bar & Books. 636 Hudson St. (btw. Horatio and Jane sts.). ☎ **212/229-2642.** Subway: A, C, E to 14th St.; L to Eighth Ave.

This former exclusive gentleman's club maintains a similar appeal as an elegant cigar bar. Among the draws are cool jazz, a magnificent copper-topped marble bar, comfortable seating, and an extensive—and expensive—cocktails, cognacs, and malts menu. A great date place, as long as you don't mind the smoke. There are also three tony uptown locations, all requiring jackets for men (this downtown branch does not): **Beekman Bar & Books** (a.k.a. Cigar Bar at Beekman), 889 First Ave., at 50th Street (☎ **212/980-9314**); **Lexington Bar & Books,** 1020 Lexington Ave., at 73rd Street (☎ **212/717-3902**); and **Carnegie Bar & Books,** 156 W. 56th St., between Sixth and Seventh avenues (☎ **212/957-9676**).

Moomba. 133 Seventh Ave. South (btw. Charles and W. 10th sts.). ☎ **212/989-1414.** Subway: 1, 9 to Christopher St.–Sheridan Square.

This relatively tiny lounge, on the upper floor of the too-hot restaurant of the same name, has managed to outlive its fifteen minutes of fame, cashing in another fiver to remain *the* nightspot of the moment for just a bit longer. It's so crammed with names and faces you know from TV and the movies that it seems like a gossip page come to life. Pretty boy Leonardo DiCaprio still shows up whenever he's in town, Marilyn Manson has been known to make the scene, and Madonna's always dropping by, as are Mick, Gwyneth, Ellen—you get the point. You probably won't get past the vigilant bouncer if you're just regular folks, but give it a shot. Who knows? You may be rubbing elbows with Leo or The Donald in no time. Best of luck to you.

THE FLATIRON DISTRICT, UNION SQUARE & GRAMERCY PARK

Cibar. At the Inn at Irving Place, 56 Irving Place (btw. 17th and 18th sts.). ☎ **212/460-5656.** Subway: 4, 5, 6, N, R to Union Square.

Late-Night Bites

All this bar-hopping and clubbing really works up an appetite. Where to eat?

Open until 4am nightly, **Blue Ribbon,** 97 Sullivan St., between Prince and Spring streets in SoHo (☎ 212/274-0404), is where the city's top chefs come to unwind after they close their own kitchens for the night. Thanks to a top-drawer oyster bar and excellent comfort food, this cozy bistro is always packed, so expect a wait.

For sophisticated New American late-night dining, head to **Clementine** (p. 148), which serves up a pleasingly casual, lighter late-night menu for loungers. Other great choices for after-hours eats include the funky Francophile diner **Florent** (p. 151), in the far West Village meatpacking district, and **Cafeteria** (p. 159), the glam version of a 24-hour greasy spoon in the heart of the West Village. In the East Village, head to **Veselka** (p. 147), a comfortable and appealing diner offering authentic Eastern European fare at rock bottom prices. A quintessential late-night choice in far west Chelsea is the **Empire Diner** (p. 160), a throwback shrine to the slicked-up all-American diner where the after-hours crowd may be the best people-watching in town.

Also, remember that many of the bars and cocktail lounges listed in this chapter serve food, from full meals to munchies, well into the wee hours.

Pick your perch carefully at this stylish amber-lit, art nouveau–accented lounge, Gramercy Park's bid for the cocktail crowd. If you aren't lucky enough to get a couch near the fireplace or one of the cushy chairs, you'll be subjected to chairs that put form before function. Still, Cibar is a romantic place to enjoy pricey but terrific martinis and expensive cigars, all served by aspiring models who'd rather be elsewhere.

Heartland Brewery. 35 Union Sq. W. (16th St.). ☎ **212/645-3400.** Subway: 4, 5, 6, N, R, L to 14th St./Union Square.

The food leaves a bit to be desired, but the house-brewed beers are first-rate. Brewmaster Jim Migliorini's two-time award-winner, Farmer Jon's Oatmeal Stout, is always on hand, as are four other hand-crafted brews (usually a lager and two stouts). The wood-paneled, two-level bar is big and appealing, but expect a loud, boisterous after-work crowd. There's now a second location, in Midtown at 1285 Sixth Ave., at 51st Street (☎ **212/582-8244**).

✪ Old Town Bar & Restaurant. 45 E. 18th St. (btw. Broadway and Park Ave. South). ☎ **212/529-6732.** Subway: 4, 5, 6, N, R, L to 14th St./Union Sq.

This genuine tin-ceilinged, 19th-century bar is a terrific place to soak up some old New York atmosphere. You'll find lots of beers on tap, great pub grub, a youngish singles crowd packing the joint just about every night of the week, plus a blissfully smoke-free upstairs room. I like this place so much that I also listed it among my favorite restaurants; for a more complete description, see chapter 6.

Pete's Tavern. 129 E. 18th St. (at Irving Place). ☎ **212/473-7676.** Subway: 4, 5, 6, N, R, L to 14th St./Union Square.

Here's another old-timer. There's a sidewalk for summer imbibing, Guinness on tap, and a St. Patrick's Day party that makes the neighbors crazy. But the best thing in Pete's (opened in 1864—while Lincoln was still president!) is the happy hour, where drinks are cheap and the crowd is a mix of locals from ritzy Gramercy Park and more down-to-earth types.

Getting Beyond the Velvet Rope

If your heart's set on getting into an exclusive club or lounge, here are a few pointers that may help to tip the scale in your favor:

- **Dress well and fashionably.** Like it or not, the doorman is sizing you up to decide if you're hip enough to make the scene. If you want to get in, you have to play along.
- **Arrive early.** This is an especially good tip for getting into bars like Moomba, Veruka, or Lot 61. Frankly, the bouncers are just not as vigilant at 9pm, when the place is half empty, as they are at 11pm—and once you're inside, you're in for the night if you wish. Weeknights are also a better bet. Clubbers may tell you that eager beavers are disdained for arriving too early at party scenes like Life, but I find earlier to almost always be more successful than later.
- **Be polite.** No matter how obnoxious the doorman may be, giving attitude back won't help. And who knows? You might just charm him with your winning personality.
- **Don't try to talk your way in.** Don't drop names or make up some story to get in the door. These guys have heard it all. If you're not wanted, why bother? Take your business to a friendlier establishment, where you'll be happier in the long run.

CHELSEA

Ciel Rouge. 176 Seventh Ave. (btw. 20th and 21st sts.). ☎ **212/929-5542.** Subway: 1, 9 to 23rd St.

This is a haven for hip Francophiles in need of a shot of Left Bank lounging. Completing the red-hued scene are well-mixed drinks, decent food, and live music: either jazz, classical, or Piaf and Brel types conjuring up Gallic memories, depending on the night.

Justin's. 31 W. 21st St. (btw. Fifth and Sixth aves.). ☎ **212/352-0599.** Subway: N, R, or F to 23rd St.

Surprise, surprise—Sean "Puffy" Combs's tony soul fooder is the hangout of choice for hip-hop stars and music industry execs. Dine elsewhere and come for the late-night scene in the sophisticated lounge if you're up for some top-notch people-watching. Be prepared for the velvet rope on busy nights.

✪ **Lot 61.** 550 W. 21st St. (near 11th Ave.). ☎ **212/243-6555.** Subway: C, E to 23rd St.

This cavernous hotspot in far west Chelsea is my favorite of the fashionista hangouts. The fabulous warehouse-meets-*Wallpaper* design is so humorously high style that you just gotta love it—where else are you going to recline on rubber sofas rescued from upstate mental hospitals surrounded by oversized art from contemporary bad boys like Damien Hirst and Sean Landers? Nowhere else but Lot 61, natch. So as not to find yourself cramped into the front bar, make a reservation in the lounge, where you can sip Cosmopolitans and graze from a surprisingly terrific menu of finger foods and other light dishes. Earlier is better; let the Kate Mosses in training fill up the room around you. Take a taxi, and look carefully for the door (the logo is faint). It's easy to catch a cab on the way out, as there's a garage on the same block.

Merchant's New York. 112 Seventh Ave. (at 17th St.). ☎ **212/366-7267.** Subway: 1, 9 to 18th St.

New York's young working crowd just loves this place, and for good reason: It's attractive, comfortable, and mixes a great martini. On the ground floor is a stylish bar, with a mezzanine for dinner. In the downstairs lounge a fireplace roars even in a heat wave, while air-conditioning delivers a polar blast. The crowd is a pleasing mix: yuppies looking for love, smart folks on dates, gays and straights, friends chatting on the couches and chairs downstairs.

TIMES SQUARE & MIDTOWN WEST

In addition to the choices below, also consider the genuinely terrific bar at the original theme restaurant, the **Hard Rock Cafe,** 221 W. 57th St., between Broadway and Seventh Avenue (☎ 212/459-9320), where you can groove to classic rock while you peruse a truly astounding collection of memorabilia (see "Theme Restaurant Thrills!" in chapter 6). There's also a second branch of **Heartland Brewery** at 1285 Sixth Ave., at 51st Street (☎ 212/582-8244); see "The Flatiron District, Union Square & Gramercy Park" earlier in this chapter. If you're the cigar bar type, **Carnegie Bar & Books,** 156 W. 56th St., between Sixth and Seventh avenues (☎ 212/957-9676), is similar to Hudson Bar & Books in Greenwich Village (p. 336).

⊙ **The Algonquin.** 59 W. 44th St. (btw. Fifth and Sixth aves.), New York, NY 10036. ☎ **212/840-6800.** Subway: B, D, F, Q to 42nd St.

The past isn't just a memory anymore at this venerable literary landmark—a complete 1998 restoration returned it to its full Arts and Crafts splendor. The splendid oak-paneled lobby is the comfiest and most welcoming in the city, made to linger over pre- or post-theater cocktails. You'll feel the spirit of Dorothy Parker and the legendary Algonquin Round Table that pervades the room. Adjacent is the pubby, clubby **Blue Bar,** home to a rotating collection of Hirschfeld drawings that's well worth checking out.

Flute. 205 W. 54th St. (btw. Seventh Ave. and Broadway). ☎ **212/265-5169.** Subway: 1, 9 to 50th St.; B, D, E to Seventh Ave.

This swanky subterranean champagne lounge is a terrific place to linger over a glass of the bubbly and fancy finger foods. The sexy, intimate space is punctuated with cozy seating nooks and sofas that are ideal for nuzzling. A DJ spins a funky dance mix later in the evening that makes conversation difficult, but that gives you a perfect excuse to cuddle even closer. I'd love to award Flute a star, if only the service weren't so lackadasical. Still, a much-needed addition to the Theater District. Look carefully for the stairs leading to the entrance; they're on the north side of the street, about mid-block.

Joe Allen. 326 W. 46th St. (btw. Eighth and Ninth aves.). ☎ **212/581-6464.** Subway: A, C, E to 42nd St.

An upscale pub peopled with Broadway types gives this atmospheric place the edge on Restaurant Row. More than 30 bottled beers are on the shelves. The bar is always hopping, but the American food is reliable and well-priced if you'd rather sit down at a table for a bite. You'll thoroughly enjoy perusing the walls, which are covered with posters and other memorabilia from legendary Broadway flops. The waiters might be actors-in-waiting, but don't be surprised if you spot a star or two among the clientele.

Mickey Mantle's. 42 Central Park South (btw. Fifth and Sixth aves). ☎ **212/688-7777.** Subway: B, Q to 57th St.

Of course, it's terribly sad that the Mick, who gave his life to the bottle, should have his name on a bar. But if you're a fan, it's definitely worth a visit to his sports bar and restaurant, which chronicles his life and career in photos. A great place to watch the game, too. Don Imus, a self-styled sports expert, has been known to wander in on occasion.

⊙ **The Royalton.** 44 W. 44th St. (btw. Fifth and Sixth aves.). ☎ **212/869-4400.** Subway: B, D, F, Q to 42nd St.

The arch Philippe Starck–designed lobby of this Ian Schrager hotel is still a major hangout for the fashionable crowd. The Starck-Schrager team really knows how to generate a social scene: The sunken lounge space features comfy seating nooks, an extensive martini list, and a light menu of excellent finger foods. In the back is restaurant 44, filled with editorial powerhouses from nearby Condé Nast, which is just about as glam as the publishing world gets. Come early to nab a seat in the marvelous Round Bar, a 20-seat circular enclave done in high *Jetsons* style (on your right just past the invariably cute doorman).

Whiskey Park. 100 Central Park South (at Sixth Ave.). ☎ **212/307-9222.** Subway: B, Q to 57th St.

Here's a social scene extraordinaire courtesy of Mr. Cindy Crawford, bar-and-lounge impresario Rande Gerber. This sleek cocktail lounge is a terrific addition to a chic neighborhood that needed some updating in the nightlife department. The space is gorgeous, featuring all dark woods, mohair upholstery, and mood lighting. This isn't the place to show up in jeans and tennies—the beautiful crowd is super-successful and super-stylish. Come early in the week to really enjoy the place. Be forewarned, however: The attitude can swing unpredicatably between friendly and condescending.

The View Lounge. On the 48th floor of the New York Marriott Marquis, 1535 Broadway (btw. 45th and 46th sts.). ☎ **212/398-1900.** Subway: 1, 2, 3, 9, N, R to Times Square; N, R to 49th St.

If it's a clear night, head up to this aptly named three-story revolving rooftop bar and restaurant for great views and decent cocktails. Grab a window seat if you can; it takes about an hour to see the 360-degree view of Times Square go by.

MIDTOWN EAST & MURRAY HILL

If you'd just love a single malt and a stogie, don a jacket (required for men) and head to **Beekman Bar & Books** (a.k.a. Cigar Bar at Beekman), 889 First Ave., at 50th Street (☎ 212/980-9314), the Midtown East version of Hudson Bar & Books (p. 336), which caters primarily to a Wall Street crowd looking for love.

British Open. 320 E. 59th St. (btw. First and Second aves.). ☎ **212/355-8467.** Subway: 4, 5, 6 to 59th St.

Here's the perfect pub for golf lovers, or anybody who pines for a well-pulled pint and some good English grub. This charming local is more sophisticated than most, with a mahogany bar polished to a high sheen, a pretty dining room in back, and friendly, attentive service from an imported staff. I just love this place; last time I was in, the Scottish bartender and an English regular were debating the merits of Brad Pitt's Irish accent in *The Devil's Own.* You'll find Guinness, Bass, Fullers ESB, and other British imports on tap, and golf and other sports on the telly at all hours.

Divine Bar. 244 E. 51st St. (btw. Second and Third aves.). ☎ **212/319-9463.** Subway: 6 to 51st St.; E, F to Lexington Ave.

This glowing hacienda-style wine bar is a big hit with a cute and sophisticated under-40 crowd (think up-and-coming media types and you'll get the picture), with a few older patrons in the mix who come for the excellent selection of wines and microbrews rather than the pick-up scene. I prefer the second, fireplace-lit level over the first floor. The DJ plays a familiar, radio-friendly mix, and there's live acoustic music on Sundays. Good tapas and an extensive humidor round out the appeal.

The Ginger Man. 11 E. 36th St. (btw. Fifth and Madison aves.). ☎ **212/532-3740.** Subway: 6 to 33rd St.

The big bait at this appealing and cigar-friendly beer bar is the 66 gleaming tap handles lining the wood-and-brass bar, dispensing everything from Sierra Nevada and

Hoegaarden to cask-conditioned ales. The cavernous space has a clubby feel, as Cohiba-toking Wall Streeters and the young men and women they flirt with lounge on sofas and chairs. The limited menu is well prepared, and prices are better than you'd expect from an upmarket place like this.

✪ **King Cole Room.** At the St. Regis hotel, 2 E. 55th St. (at Fifth Ave.). ☎ **212/339-6721.** Subway: E, F to 53rd St.

The birthplace of the Bloody Mary, this theatrical spot may just be New York's best hotel bar. The Maxfield Parrish mural alone is worth the price of a classic cocktail (ask the bartender to tell you about the "hidden" meaning of the painting). The sophisticated setting demands proper attire, so be sure to dress for the occasion. The *New York Times* calls the bar nuts "the best in town," but there's an elegant bar food menu if you'd like something more substantial.

✪ **Mica Bar.** 252 E. 51st St. (btw. Second and Third aves.). ☎ **212/888-2453.** Subway: 6 to 51st St.; E, F to Lexington Ave.

This cool, Japanese-inspired bar is one of my favorite places in the city for a romantic cocktail, or relaxed drinks with a small group of friends. You'll find comfortable, low-slung furniture and votives throughout the intimate bi-level space, with petite bonsai tucked into wall niches. The friendly staff serves up a terrific cocktail menu; try the Sake-tini (Finlandia, sake, dry vermouth, cucumber) for a neat twist on the original. You'll also find good selections of beer, wine, sake, single malts, and brandies. Pan-Asian finger foods are also available. A bamboo open-air terrace adds extra appeal in warm weather.

Oak Bar. At the Plaza Hotel, 768 Fifth Ave. (at 59th St.). ☎ **212/546-5330.** Subway: N, R to 60th St.

And they do mean oak! The warm wood sets an elegant tone throughout this clubby beer hall. Sumptuous red chairs and old-time waiters set the right mood for the after-work power crowd. The bar gets very crowded after 5pm, but the atmosphere always remains sophisticated and old world.

Park Avenue Country Club. 381 Park Ave. So. (at 27th St.). ☎ **212/685-3636.** Subway: 6 to 28th St.

This place bills itself as a "sports cafe," and it is indeed more polished than your average beer-and-pretzels sports bar. That said, it's a very comfortable place to hunker down over a club sandwich and a beer to watch the game. There are TVs at every turn, and a nice mahogany central bar serves up an extensive list of bottled and on-tap brews.

✪ **Pen-Top Bar & Terrace.** On the 23rd floor of the Peninsula hotel, 700 Fifth Ave. (at 55th St.). ☎ **212/956-2888.** Subway: E, F to Fifth Ave.

This petite penthouse bar offers some of Midtown's most dramatic views, straight down fabulous Fifth Avenue in both directions. Best of all is the huge rooftop patio—much bigger than the bar itself—which is midtown's best open-air spot on warm evenings. Expect an extremely well-heeled crowd that doesn't mind the big tab that follows cocktails here. This place is extremely popular, so don't be surprised if you can't get in, especially on nights when the weather isn't accommodating to alfresco revelers.

Top of the Tower. On the 26th floor of Beekman Tower, 3 Mitchell Place (First Ave. at 49th St.). ☎ **212/355-7300.** Subway: 6 to 51st St.

Location is everything, and this lounge has a great one from which to preside over glorious Manhattan. The art deco room sets the mood for the view, which includes the romantic Empire State Building. A simply wonderful place to escape the urban bustle for a quiet, elegant drink. A pianist keeps the tone hushed and romantic after 9pm. Pricey but well-respected continental cuisine is served if you'd like to stay for dinner.

THE UPPER WEST SIDE

✪ **All State Cafe.** 250 W. 72nd St. (btw. Broadway and West End Ave.). ☎ **212/ 874-1883.** Subway: 1, 2, 3, 9 to 72nd St.

Despite its proximity to Broadway, this subterranean pub is one of Manhattan's undiscovered treasures. It's easy to miss from the street, and the regulars like it that way. The All State attracts a grown-up neighborhood crowd drawn in by the casual ambiance, the great burgers, and an outstanding jukebox. Peter the bartender serves a smooth house wine and a variety of single-malt scotches. A fireplace makes it even more homey and inviting in cold weather.

Boomer's Sports Club. 349 Amsterdam Ave. (btw. 76th and 77th sts.). ☎ **212/362-5400.** Subway: 1, 9 to 79th St.

Surprise, surprise: Jets quarterback Boomer Esiason's pub is a sports bar. Come here if you like to watch, talk, eat, and drink sports. The youngish yuppie crowd doesn't mind that the food menu is no great shakes, since the beer selection is extensive.

Hi-Life Bar & Grill. 477 Amsterdam Ave. (at 83rd St.). ☎ **212/787-7199.** Subway: 1, 9 to 86th St.

During the week, expect a few quiet drinks with a slightly older crowd in this casual retro-style bar and restaurant. Come the weekend, youth reigns, the volume cranks up, and the dating game zooms into full gear. The classic martinis couldn't be better, and there's a nice outdoor deck for summer evenings.

O'Neal's. 49 W. 64th St. (btw. Broadway and Central Park West). ☎ **212/787-4663.** Subway: 1, 9 to 66th St.

O'Neal's easygoing, old-time atmosphere makes it a favorite among a grown-up neighborhood crowd as well as students from nearby Juilliard. Lincoln Center is a stone's throw away, making this a great place for a pre-theater cocktail or a reasonably priced, if unremarkable, bite to eat.

Shark Bar. 307 Amsterdam Ave. (btw. 74th and 75th sts.). ☎ **212/874-8500.** Subway: 1, 2, 3, 9 to 72nd St.

This perennially popular upscale spot is well known for its good soul food and even better singles' scene. It's also a favorite hangout for sports celebs, so don't be surprised if you spot a New York Knick or two.

THE UPPER EAST SIDE

If you'd like a sophisticated cigar bar, **Lexington Bar & Books,** 1020 Lexington Ave., at 73rd Street (☎ **212/717-3902**), the tonier uptown branch of Hudson Bar & Books (p. 336), caters to a well-heeled older crowd (jackets required for men).

✪ **Bemelmans Bar.** At the Carlyle hotel, 35 E. 76th St. (at Madison Ave.). ☎ **212/744-1600.** Subway: 6 to 77th St.

Named after children's book illustrator Ludwig Bemelmans, who created the Madeline books after he painted the whimsical mural here, is a supremely luxurious spot for cocktails. Tuck into a dark, romantic corner and nurse a classic martini (both house bartenders have been on the job for 40 years) as you eye the best-heeled crowd in town. A pianist tinkles the ivories throughout the evening.

Brandy's Piano Bar. 235 E. 84th St. (btw. Second and Third aves.). ☎ **212/650-1944.** Subway: 4, 5, 6 to 86th St.

A mixed crowd—Upper East Side locals, waiters off work, gays, straights, all ages—comes to this intimate, old-school piano bar for the friendly atmosphere and nightly entertainment. The talented waitstaff does most of the singing while waiting for their big break, but enthusiastic patrons join in on occasion. An appealing and affordable night on the town.

✪ **Elaine's.** 1703 Second Ave. (btw. 88th and 89th sts.). ☎ **212/534-8103.** Subway: 4, 5, 6 to 86th St.

The Big Chill claimed that Elaine's was over and done with way back when. They were dreaming. Glittering literati still come here for dinner and book parties. Look for such regulars as writer Norman Mailer, Woody Allen, and other A-list types. If you can't get a table, you can always scan the room from the up-front bar.

Madison Pub. 1043 Madison Ave. (btw. 79th and 80th sts.). ☎ **212/650-1809.** Subway: 6 to 77th St.

Near the Metropolitan Museum of Art, Madison Pub is neighborhood place that you'd dismiss as a workingman's watering hole if it weren't for the tony address. A fine place to nurse a Rolling Rock and rest your museum-weary feet. The jukebox is a few decades out of date, but that only adds to the appeal.

Mark's Bar. In the Mark hotel, 25 E. 77th St. (btw. Fifth and Madison aves.). ☎ **212/ 744-4300.** Subway: 6 to 77th St.

If the more high-profile luxe hotel bars like Bemelmans or the King Cole are just too full, head to this lesser-known but equally appealing compatriot. The space is outfitted like an elegant living room with a romantic flair. The crowd tends to be older, and quite used to sipping expensive cocktails like the house Bloody Mary, a worthy challenger to the King Cole's original. Sophisticated nibbles are also served.

Subway Inn. 143 E. 60th St. (just east of Lexington Ave.). ☎ **212/223-8929.** Subway: 4, 5, 6 to 59th St.; N, R to Lexington Ave.

Now, here's a dive bar if there ever was one—and that's precisely the Subway Inn's appeal. Every time I go to Bloomingdale's, I get a perverse joy at seeing this hole-in-the-wall surviving in the shadow of the great department store, as the high-rent neighborhood around it grows more and more upscale and out-of-reach to the average Joes inside. A great spot for hubbys to nurse a cheap beer while their wives exercise the plastic next door. Note to film buffs: This was Montgomery Clift's local—he lived just down the street for years.

8 Dance Clubs & Party Scenes

No slice of the New York nightlife pie is as mutable as the club scene. In this world, hotspots don't even get 15 minutes of fame—their time in the limelight is usually more like a commercial break.

First things first: Finding and going to the latest hotspot is not worth agonizing over. Clubbers spend their lives obsessing over the scene. My rule of thumb is that if I know about a place, it must not be hip anymore. Even if I could tell you where the hippest club kids hang out today, they'll have moved on by the time you arrive in town. One big trend in recent years that makes the scene so hard to chart is that "clubs" as actual, physical spaces don't mean much anymore. The hungry-for-nightlife crowd now follows events of certain party "producers" who switch venues and times each week. As the scene becomes more and more amorphous, venues become less and less traditional. Lots of the bars and lounges listed in the previous section host "club" scenes on various nights of the week, such as—at press time, at least—Koncrete Jungle on Monday nights at **Coney Island High,** the loungey Beige on Tuesdays at **B Bar,** and the Big '80s–themed Reagan Death Watch at **Barmacy** on Sundays.

The tracking game is best left to the perennial party crowd who know the rest of the crowd as well as the guy at the door (who lets them in for free) and someone at the bar (who comps them drinks). You're just not likely to get that well-connected in your week of vacation. Even if you manage to make your way into the club du jour (after groveling to a meatheaded doorman, no doubt), you'll find out that everyone looks supremely bored, because to admit you were having a good time would be to announce that you're hopelessly square. Just find someplace that amuses you, and enjoy the crowd that enjoys it with you.

In the listings below, I've concentrated on a wide variety of club scenes, from performance arty to perennially popular discos, most of which are generally easy to make your way into. You can find listings for the most current hotspots and moveable parties in the publications and online sources listed at the start of this chapter. You might also want to pick up a copy of *Shecky's Bar, Club & Lounge Guide,* available in most city bookstores. Another good bet is to cruise hip boutiques in SoHo, the East Village, and the Lower East Side, where party planners usually leave flyers advertising the latest goings-on. No matter what, **always call ahead,** because schedules change constantly, and can do so at the last minute.

Keep in mind that New York nightlife starts late. With the exception of places that have scheduled performances, it's almost useless to show up anywhere before about 11pm. Don't depend on plastic—bring cash, and plan on dropping a wad at most places. Cover charges often start out high—anywhere from $10 to $25—and often get more expensive as the night wears on. Some venues and select nights, such as Sunday's Shout! at 13, are free. For tips that may help you get past vigilant bouncers, see the feature called "Getting Beyond the Velvet Rope" on page 338.

In addition to the choices below, lovers of Brazilian, Afro-Caribbean, and other world music should seriously consider ✪ **S.O.B.'s,** where top-notch live bands keep the party sizzling nightly. For S.O.B.'s and details on other club scenes with live music, see "Live Rock, Jazz, Blues & More" earlier in this chapter.

Baby Jupiter. 170 Orchard St. (at Stanton St.). ☎ **212/982-BABY.** Subway: F to Second Ave.

This funny, funky place may look like a '60s-style retro-diner restaurant, but it's actually becoming increasingly popular for its club scene. The weekly calendar features an ever-changing and increasingly eclectic mix of live music and DJ nights. At press time, the best of the bunch was Wednesday's Jungle Jazz, a wild mix of dub, jazz, jungle, and—that's right—tap lines led by a high-BPM DJ and one-armed Italian trumpeter Fabio Morgera. You'd think the other nights would pale in comparison, but Thursday's funky soul and Saturday's tribal house offer equally esoteric fun. The schedule here is far from fixed, however, so call ahead to see what's on—or better yet, show up with an open mind and let yourself be surprised. Leave your Prada at home—this place caters to working arts and other edgy Lower East Side types. It's best to come early if you actually want to eat first.

Cheetah. 12 W. 21st St. (btw. Fifth and Sixth aves.). ☎ **212/206-7770.** Subway: F, N, R to 23rd St.

With ultrasuede on the walls and cheetah prints everywhere, this excruciatingly glam club is reminiscent of Studio 54. The Euro-trash crowd loves it. In the words of owner Robert Shalom, "Anyone who wants to have a good time and has $100 to spend will feel welcome." If the glitz quotient becomes too much for you, head to the more laid-back basement lounge. Parties worth seeking out include Monday's female-fueled hip-hop party Purr.

China Club. 268 W. 47th St. (btw. Broadway and Eighth Ave.). ☎ **212/398-3800.** Subway: 1, 9, C, E to 50th St.; N, R to 49th St.

The China Club has been a top choice for club hoppers for years now, and it's still a great place to shake your booty. This huge club caters to both celebs and mere mortals drawn in by the top-flight sound system, high-style fiber-optic lighting, and a good, accessible dance music mix. Live acts perform once in awhile. Trendy types gravitate to the bar and VIP lounge, where Broadway hopefuls mix with famous faces like Christy Turlington and Rod Stewart on occasion.

The Copacabana. 617 W. 57th St. (btw. Eleventh and Twelfth aves.). ☎ **212/582-2672.** Subway: 1, 9, A, B, C, D to Columbus Circle.

The Copa isn't exactly the hippest spot in town these days, but it does once again elicit images of retro-glamour among a grown-up crowd that likes to groove to the hottest Latin music in town. There's a high cheese factor in the glittery Big '80s vibe, but it's all part of the fun. Take a cab to the far-west location.

Decade. 1117 First Ave. (at 61st St.). ☎ **212/835-5979.** Subway: 4, 5, 6 59th St.; N, R to Lexington Ave.

Finally—somewhere to dance until nearly dawn for the baby boomers. This hybrid supper club/dance club attracts well-dressed, well-heeled thirty-, forty-, and fifty-somethings who lounge in the cigar and champagne bars in between boogie downs to a fun mix of tunes from the '60s, '70s, and '80s. The service is top-notch, too, making this an all-around terrific (and expensive) place to spend an evening.

Don Hill's. 511 Greenwich St. (at Spring St.). ☎ **212/219-2850.** Subway: 1, 9 to Canal St.; C, E to Spring St.

This big and eclectic place changes faces constantly: Sometimes it's a rock performance space featuring top-notch local talent, others it plays host to party nights. Squeezebox on Friday nights is a rollicking gay/straight party with a drag edge, but the best night of the bunch is the Thursday night '80s Night (a.k.a. BeavHer), when the cool kids join the rest of us to dance to a groovy blend of retro hits.

Life. 158 Bleecker St. (Sullivan & Thompson sts.). ☎ **212/420-1999.** Subway: A, B, C, D, E, F, Q to W. 4th St.

A $12-million renovation of what used to be the venerable Village Gate jazz club instantly established this velvet-drenched, faux-deco nightclub as *the* clubbers' hotspot a few years back, and it just keeps on going. The formula changes every night: Lifestyle Fridays draws a fabulous fashion crowd always dotted with a few famous faces; Wednesdays offer the star-studded house party Legends as well as retro-campy Lust for Life, which books '80s throwbacks like the Human League alongside local glam acts; and Boy's Life Sundays draws beautiful Chelsea boys looking for the same.

✪ **Mother.** 432 W. 14th St. (at Washington St.). ☎ **212/366-5680.** Subway: A, C, E to 14th St.

Fabulous hipsters, both gay and straight, crowd this joint for a variety of hugely popular events. On Tuesday it's Jackie 60 (☎ **212/929-6060;** www.echonyc.com/~interjackie), which *Paper* magazine calls "the mother of all freak fests." Boys and girls dress up in drag based on the night's theme, which can get pretty twisted (witness the recent "Daddy's Little Prostitute: The JonBenet Ramsey Story"), yet the party always manages an upbeat, enthusiastic vibe thanks to the untiring talents of husband and wife Chi-Chi Valenti and Johnny Dynell (she's the hostess, he's the DJ). Almost as popular is Saturday's Click + Drag, a futuristic techno-fetish party from the same team. Performance art, poetry readings, and other multimedia fun round out the goings-on. Call to check if a strict dress code is being enforced the night you go.

✪ **Nell's.** 246 W. 14th St. (btw. Seventh and Eighth aves.). ☎ **212/675-1567.** Subway: 1, 2, 3, 9, A, C, E to 14th St.

It Might as Well Be Swing

It may have taken some time for the swing thing to make its way to the right coast, but New York has taken to it with a vengeance. It's a zoot suit riot, man.

Swing is a nightly affair at **Swing 46,** a jazz and supper club on the Theater District's Restaurant Row at 349 W. 46th St. (☎ 212/262-9554). There's live swing every night at 10pm from big bands with names like the Flipped Fedoras and the Crescent City Maulers, as well as the club's own 15-piece Make-Believe Ballroom Orchestra. The young, enthusiastic crowd dresses to the nines, '40s style, and really knows the moves. Even if you're a first-timer, you can join in, too: Just come early for free swing lessons at 7 and 9pm.

On weekends, probably the best place to get jiggy is the **Supper Club,** 240 W. 47th St., between Broadway and Eighth Avenue (☎ 212/921-1940), an ultra-plush dance hall and supper club that's been dressed and waiting for the swing trend to come along for a few years now. The 16-piece house band plays old-school swing every Friday and Saturday night early on for an older supper crowd. Later in the evening, around 11pm, the tables are cleared and the neo-swingers show up to strut their stuff to an ultra-hot visiting jump band like Zoot Suit Revue, Harlem's Yallopin' Hounds, or Swingerhead. The joint jumps 'til 4am.

Another terrific spot for swing is **The Greatest Bar on Earth,** high atop 1 World Trade Center on the 107th floor (☎ 212/524-7000). The live jive from circuit bands like the Camaros and the Blue Saracens starts Friday and Saturdays at 9pm; there's also a mambo party on Thursdays for a little Latin-flavored swing. The dance floor is big enough for everybody to enjoy but small enough that you don't

---

After Freud came Nell's in the popularization of the couch in modern life. Nell's was the first to establish a loungelike atmosphere years ago. It has been endlessly copied by restaurateurs and nightclub owners, who have since realized that if people wanted to stay home, why not make "out" just as comfy as "in?" Nell's attracts everyone from homies to Wall Streeters. Most of the parties have a soulful edge. Look for the hugely popular laid-back Voices, sort of a sophisticated weekly *Star Search* that's a showcase for a surprising number of new talents.

Polly Esther's. 1487 First Ave. (btw. 77th and 78th sts.). ☎ **212/628-4477.** www.pollyesthers.com. Subway: 6 to 77th St. Also at 186 W. 4th St. (btw. Sixth and Seventh aves.). Subway: 1, 9 to Christopher St.–Sheridan Square.

Here's the ultimate '70s theme bar and club, where you can groove to the sounds of K.C., Gloria Gaynor, the Bee Gees, ABBA, and every other band you loved when you still listened to AM radio and turned the dial on the TV set. Decor runs along Brady Bunch and Partridge Family lines, with tons of Me decade movie, TV, and music memorabilia throughout. This place is really targeted to tourists, but who cares? Dig out those bellbottoms, tie on those platform shoes, and hustle on over to Polly Esther's for a nostalgic good time.

If you're more of a Karma Chameleon than a Dancing Queen, then head to **Culture Club,** 179 Varick St., between King and Charlton streets (☎ 212/243-1999), where the big '80s come to life. From the same team behind Polly Esther's, this new dance club is similarly silly, but lots of retro fun for those with a touch of nostalgia for Duran Duran, Pac Man, Boy Toy–era Madonna, and *Miami Vice.*

Roxy. 515 W. 18th St. (at Tenth Ave.). ☎ **212/645-5156.** Subway: 1, 9 to 18th St.

feel like you're on display like you are at the Supper Club—a blessing for those of us who don't exactly have our moves down pat. And no dance floor has more spectacular views.

For the latest on the local neo-swing scene from the man behind the Supper Club's swinging success, "Lo-Fi" Lee Sobel, check out **www.nycswing.com**. Lo-Fi Lee always has a swing party going on, and at press time had just introduced Tatou Swings! to the ultra-tony **Tatou Supper Club**, 151 E. 50th St., between Lexington and Third avenues (☎ **212/753-1144**). Tatou Swings! is set to feature live first-rate bands, DJ, and dance lessons every Thursday night.

In the Village, do the swing thing at the **Louisiana Community Bar & Grill**, 622 Broadway, at Houston Street (☎ **212/460-9633**), which is booking more and more swing bands on its weekly schedule.

Serious folks who know that swing transcends its fad status belong to the **New York Swing Society** (☎ **212/696-9737**), which holds its weekly Savoy Sundays at Irving Plaza. This event is for all ages and abilities and there's no dress code, so you don't have to worry about impressing the cool cats around you—you're free to strictly enjoy yourself. Expect to see a good number of original swingers at this event. Free dance lessons are offered once a month.

In July and August, Lincoln Center sponsors **Midsummer Night's Swing.** Dancing duos head to the Lincoln Center Fountain Plaza for romantic evenings of big band swing, salsa, and tango under the stars to the sounds of top-flight bands. Dance lessons are offered with the purchase of a ticket. Call ☎ **212/ 875-5766,** or visit **www.lincolncenter.org**.

This could be the single best place to see the Manhattan night mix. You'll find fashion models, city-club kids, wide-eyed kids from the 'burbs, straights and gays of every color, plus lights, sound, and action. Glamour is in the air, the space is monumental, and the beehive wigs reach for the stars. There's in-line roller disco on Tuesday (predominantly gay) and Wednesday (mixed). Friday nights draw a big Hispanic crowd with salsa and merengue, while Saturdays bring in a committed mixed gay/straight crowd in love with DJ Victor Calderone's tribal house mix. There's also a martini lounge, a cigar bar, and two VIP rooms.

✪ **13.** 35 E. 13th St. (btw. Broadway and University Place), 2nd floor. ☎ **212/979-6677.** www.citysearch.com/nyc/13. Subway: 4, 5, 6, N, R, L to Union Square.

This little lounge is a great place to dance the night away. It's stylish but unpretentious, with a steady roster of fun weekly parties. I'm thrilled that Sunday night's Britpop fest Shout! lives on, as popular as ever—just goes to show that you can't put a good pop song down. Other regular highlights include Wednesday night's Beep, a friendly progressive beat party; and DJ Cadet spinning an appealing classic dance mix that ranges from '70s disco to current hip-hop on Friday and Saturday. Monday is poetry and spoken-word night. Arrive extra-early, between 4 and 8pm, for two-for-one Happy Hour.

Twilo. 530 W. 27th St. (btw. Tenth and Eleventh aves.). ☎ **212/268-1600.** Subway: C, E to to 23rd St.

Go west—way west—to this mega-size dance factory, on the site of the legendary Sound Factory. Superstar DJ Junior Vasquez still spins pulsating dance music marathons, called Juniorverse, for an adoring, mostly gay crowd on Saturdays. Twilo Fridays draws an energized straight crowd with imported international DJs.

XIT. 511 Lexington Ave. (btw. 47th and 48th sts.). ☎ **212/371-1600.** Subway: 4, 5, 6, 7 to Grand Central.

If Decade sounds fun but just too fancy—or expensive—for your tastes, head to XIT instead. The former home of urban hoedown Denim & Diamonds has been transformed into another baby-boomer hangout spinning a mainstream mix of tunes ranging from the '60s to the top hits of today. Wednesday is salsa night, with a live band providing the beat. The club owners have issued a "no attitude" promise to the press, so everyone should feel comfortable here. There's a pool room in back.

Vinyl. 6 Hubert St. (btw. Hudson and Collister sts.). ☎ **212/343-1379.** Subway: 1, 9 to Canal St.

This commodious TriBeCa club welcomes a big, mixed black/white, gay/straight crowd to hip hop- and house-flavored party nights ruled by a terrific crop of DJs. Best of all is the long-lived Body and Soul, a Sunday afternoon acid-garage-house party that's on its way to becoming a legend. Also look for Planet V, a hugely popular monthly jungle party.

Webster Hall. 125 E. 11th St. (btw. Third and Fourth aves.). ☎ **212/353-1600.** www. webster-hall.com. Subway: 6 to Astor Place.

Five floors and a seemingly endless warren of rooms mean that there's something for everyone at this old warhorse of a nightclub. Theme nights range from Swing Mania to Psychedelic Thursdays (ladies free); live local and national acts also perform on occasion. Weekends are a great time to come if you're just looking for a straightforward crowd and music mix. Even though it's dominated by a bridge-and-tunnel crowd, Webster Hall is still a plenty interesting place to hang. Expect to wait in line to get in.

9 The Lesbian & Gay Scene

To get a thorough, up-to-date take on what's happening in gay and lesbian nightlife, pick up a free copy of *Homo Xtra (HX)* or *HX for Her,* by far the best guides to the gay scene; another choice is *Next.* They're available for free in bars and clubs or at the Lesbian and Gay Community Center (see "Tips for Travelers with Special Needs" in chapter 2). Both mags also have information online at **www.hx.com**. *Time Out New York* also boasts a terrific gay and lesbian section, and the Web sites at the start of this chapter also serve as good sources. Always remember that asking people in one bar can lead you to discover another that fits your tastes.

These days, many bars, clubs, cabarets, and cocktail lounges are neither gay nor straight but a bit of both, either catering to a mixed crowd or to varying orientations on different nights of the week. In addition to the choices below, most of the clubs listed under "Dance Clubs & Party Scenes," above, cater to a gay crowd, some predominately so. Be sure to see what's happening at **Don Hill's, Life, Mother, Roxy, Twilo,** and **Vinyl.** The **Duplex Cabaret** is at the heart of the gay cabaret scene (see

"Supper Clubs & Cabarets," above). Among the bars and cocktail lounges, consider **Flamingo East, Lucky Cheng's,** and **Bar d'O** (particularly on nights the phenomenal Joey Arias is performing) if you're looking for a predominately gay crowd.

Axis. 17 W. 19th St. (btw. Fifth and Sixth aves.). ☎ **212/633-1717.** Subway: 1, 9 to 18th St.; F to 23rd St.

If your idea of masculine beauty is buffed bodies and beefed go-go boys, Axis is your idea of a club. Very big, very popular, very cruisy. Watch for the weekly DJ parties, the best of which is Subliminal, probably the hottest house party in town.

✪ **Barracuda.** 275 W. 22nd St. (btw. Seventh and Eighth aves.). ☎ **212/645-8613.** Subway: 1, 9 or C, E to 23rd St.

Chelsea is now central to gay life—and gay bars. This trendy, loungy place was voted "Best Bar" by *HX* and *New York Press* magazines, while *Paper* singles out the hunky bartenders. There's a sexy bar for cruising out front, and a comfy lounge in back. Look for the regular drag shows.

Boiler Room. 86 E. 4th St. (btw. First and Second aves.). ☎ **212/254-7536.** Subway: F to Second Ave.

This East Village dive is a serious cruising scene for well-sculpted beautiful boys who just love to pose. Girls who like girls take over the house once a month, usually on a Sunday.

Crazy Nanny's. 21 Seventh Ave. South (at Leroy St.). ☎ **212/366-6312.** Subway: 1, 9 to Houston St.

This longstanding lesbian bar is huge and hugely popular with women on the make. There's two floors, two bars, dancing, and a variety of theme nights. Especially popular with out-of-towners.

g. 223 W. 19th St. (btw. Seventh and Eighth aves.). ☎ **212/929-1085.** Subway: 1, 9 to 18th St.

Big crowds of muscular, designer-dressed men have made this lovely lounge a popular style scene for meeting dream dates. Excellent DJs set the stage.

Hangar Bar. 115 Christopher St. (btw. Bleecker and Bedford sts.). ☎ **212/627-2044.** Subway: 1, 9 to Christopher St.–Sheridan Square.

Across from Ty's (below), this easygoing men's hangout has a big window that lets you watch who's walking Christopher. Excellent happy-hour drink specials make this a significant pick-up scene from early in the evening.

Hell. 59 Gansevoort St. (btw. Washington and Greenwich sts.). ☎ **212/727-1666.** Subway: A, C, E to 14th St.

This glamorous lounge is a sexy haven for a predominately gay crowd in a sketchy section of the meatpacking district. The cocktails are well mixed, and plenty of comfy sofas are on hand for getting cozy. Do yourself a favor and take a cab.

Henrietta Hudson. 438 Hudson St. (at Morton St.). ☎ **212/924-3347.** Subway: 1, 9 to Houston St.

This friendly and extremely popular women's bar is known for drawing in an attractive crowd that comes for the great jukebox and videos as well as the pleasingly low-key atmosphere.

✪ **Meow Mix.** 269 E. Houston St. (btw. Avenues A and B) ☎ **212/254-0688.** Subway: F to Second Ave.

This funky two-level East Villager is the city's best, and probably its most popular, lesbian hangout. It draws in a young, attractive, arty crowd with nightly diversions like groovy DJs and the hugely popular Xena Night. Meow Mix is also booking an increasing number of good local bands, with most nights dedicated to the girls but one night set aside for all-boy bands.

Stella's. 266 W. 47th St. (btw. Broadway and Eighth Ave.). ☎ **212/575-1680.** Subway: 1, 9, C, E to 50th St.; N, R to 49th St.

This Midtown scene is hot, hot, hot. Behind the dark glass windows, go-go boys dance, sometimes upstairs, sometimes downstairs (mainly weekends, always after 10:30pm). The regulars are friendly, and some of them are looking for a good time.

Stonewall. 53 Christopher St. (just east of Seventh Ave. South). ☎ **212/463-0950.** Subway: 1, 9 to Christopher St./Sheridan Square.

A new bar at the spot where it all started. A mixed male crowd—old and young, beautiful and great personalities—makes this an easy place to begin.

Ty's. 114 Christopher St. (at Bedford St.). ☎ **212/741-9641.** Subway: 1, 9 to Christopher St./Sheridan Square.

Here's a very friendly, unassuming gay bar that's been a part of the Christopher Street men's cruise scene for about a million years.

The Web. 40 E. 58th St. (btw. Madison and Park aves.) ☎ **212/308-1546.** Subway: 4, 5, 6, N, R to 59th/60th sts.

This subterranean complex offers many different events throughout the week, sometimes with a door charge (call for specifics). You might find go-go boys, drag shows, and other diversions for the heavily Asian crowd (and the Western men who love them). The dance floor gets crowded on weekends after midnight. Go late or it's Dullsville.

✪ **Wonder Bar.** 505 E. 6th St. (btw. Avenues A and B). ☎ **212/777-9105.** Subway: 6 to Astor Place.

The "sofa look" has lent a loungier, more stylish tone to this packed-on-weekends East Village hangout. There's some male cruising, but fun and friendly Wonder Bar gets points for making staights feel welcome, too. DJs now spin a listener-friendly mix from the revamped back room.

Frommer's Online Directory

by Michael Shapiro
Michael Shapiro is the author of *Internet Travel Planning*
(The Globe Pequot Press).

Frommer's Online Directory is a new feature designed to help you take advantage of the Internet to better plan your trip. Part I lists some general Internet resources that can make any trip easier, such as sites for booking airline tickets. It's not meant to be a comprehensive list; it's a discriminating selection of useful sites to get you started. In Part II you'll find some top online guides specifically for New York, which cover local lodging, the top attractions, and getting around.

1 The Top Travel-Planning Web Sites

Among the most popular sites are online travel agencies. The top agencies, including Expedia, Preview Travel, and Travelocity, offer an array of tools that are valuable even if you don't book online. You can check flight schedules, hotel availability, car rental prices, or even get paged if your flight is delayed.

While online agencies have come a long way over the past few years, they don't always yield the best price. Unlike a travel agent, for example, they're unlikely to tell you that you can save money by flying a day earlier or a day later. On the other hand, if you're looking for a bargain fare, you might find something online that an agent wouldn't take the time to dig up. Because airline commissions have been cut, a travel agent may not find it worthwhile spending half an hour trying to find you the best deal. On the Net, you can be your own agent and take all the time you want.

Online booking sites aren't the only places to book airline tickets— all major airlines have their own Web sites and often offer incentives, such as bonus frequent-flyer miles or Net-only discounts, for buying online. These incentives have helped airlines capture the majority of the online booking market.

Below are the Web sites for the major airlines serving New York's airports. These sites offer schedules and flight booking, and most have pages where you can sign up for e-mail alerts on weekend deals.

Aer Lingus: www.aerlingus.ie
Air Canada: www.aircanada.ca
America West: www.americawest.com
American: www.americanair.com
British Airways: www.british-airways.com
Canadian Airlines: www.cdair.ca

Continental: www.flycontinental.com
Delta: www.delta-air.com
Northwest: www.nwa.com
TWA: www.twa.com
US Airways: www.usairways.com
United: www.ual.com
Virgin Atlantic: www.fly.virgin.com

WHEN SHOULD YOU BOOK ONLINE?

Online booking is not for everyone. If you prefer to let others handle your travel arrangements, one call to an experienced travel agent should suffice. But if you want to know as much as possible about your options, the Net is a good place to start, especially for bargain hunters.

The most compelling reason to use online booking is to take advantage of last-minute specials, such as American Airlines' weekend deals or other Internet-only fares that must be purchased online. Another advantage is that you can cash in on incentives for booking online, such as rebates or bonus frequent-flyer miles.

Online booking works best for trips within North America; for international tickets, it's usually cheaper and easier to use a travel agent or consolidator.

Online booking is certainly not for those with a complex international itinerary. If you require follow-up services, such as itinerary changes, use a travel agent. Though Expedia and some other online agencies employ travel agents available by phone, these sites are geared primarily for self-service.

LEADING BOOKING SITES

Below are listings for the top travel-booking sites. The starred selections are the most useful and best designed sites.

Cheap Tickets. www.cheaptickets.com
Essentials: Discounted rates on domestic and international airline tickets and hotel rooms.

Sometimes discounters such as Cheap Tickets have exclusive deals that aren't available through more mainstream channels. Registration at Cheap Tickets requires inputting a credit card number before getting started, which is one reason many people elect to call the company's toll-free number rather than booking online. Cheap Tickets actually regards this policy as a selling point, arguing that "lookers" who don't intend to buy will be scared off and won't bog down the site with their queries. If Cheap Tickets is serious about getting people to use its online booking service, it should abolish this credit card–first approach.

Despite its misguided credit card policy, Cheap Tickets is worth the effort because its fares can be substantially lower than those offered by its competitors.

Factoid

Far more people *look* online than *book* online, partly from fear of putting their credit cards through on the Net. Though secure encryption has made this fear less justified, there's no reason you can't find a flight online and then book it by calling a toll-free number or contacting your travel agent. To be sure you're in secure mode when you book online, look for a little icon of a key (in Netscape) or a padlock (Internet Explorer) at the bottom of your Web browser.

Take a Look at Frommer's Site

We highly recommend **Arthur Frommer's Budget Travel Online** (**www. frommers.com**) as an excellent travel-planning resource. Of course, we're a little biased, but you will find indispensable travel tips, reviews, monthly vacation giveaways, and online booking.

Subscribe to Arthur Frommer's Daily Newsletter (**www.frommers.com/ newsletters**) to receive the latest travel bargains and inside travel secrets in your mailbox every day. You'll read daily headlines and articles from the dean of travel himself, highlighting last-minute deals on airfares, accommodations, cruises, and package vacations. You'll also find great travel advice by checking our Tip of the Day or Hot Spot of the Month.

Search our Destinations archive (**www.frommers.com/destinations**) of more than 200 domestic and international destinations for great places to stay, tips for traveling there, and what to do while you're there. Once you've researched your trip, you might try our online reservation system (**www.frommers.com/ booktravelnow**) to book your dream vacation at affordable prices.

✪ **Expedia. expedia.com**
Essentials: Domestic and international flights, plus hotel and rental car booking; late-breaking travel news, destination features, and commentary from travel experts; deals on cruises and vacation packages. Free registration is required for booking.

Expedia makes it easy to handle flight, hotel, and car booking on one itinerary, so it's a good place for one-stop shopping. Expedia's hotel search offers crisp, zoomable maps to pinpoint most properties; click on the camera icon to see images of the rooms and facilities. But like many online databases, Expedia focuses on the major chains, such as Hilton and Hyatt, so don't expect to find too many one-of-a-kind boutique hotels or B&Bs here.

Once you're registered (it's only necessary to do this once from each computer you use), you can start booking with the Roundtrip Fare Finder box on the home page, which expedites the process. After selecting a flight, you can hold it until midnight the following day or purchase online. If you think you might do better through a travel agent, you'll have time to try to get a lower price. And you may do better with a travel agent because Expedia's computer reservation system does not include all airlines. Most notably absent are some leading budget carriers, such as Southwest Airlines, which doesn't serve New York's major airports, but has begun service to Long Island. (*Note:* At press time, Travelocity was the only major booking service that includes Southwest.)

Expedia's World Guide, offering destination information, is a glaring weakness; it takes lots of page views to get very little information. However, Expedia compensates by linking to other Microsoft Network services, such as its Sidewalk city guides, which offer entertainment and dining advice.

Preview Travel. www.previewtravel.com
Essentials: Domestic and international flights, plus hotel and rental car booking; Travel Newswire lists fare sales; deals on cruises and vacation packages. Free (one-time) registration is required for booking. Preview offers express booking for members, but at presstime, this feature was buried below the fold on Preview's reservation page.

Preview features the most inviting interface for booking trips, though the wealth of graphics involved can make the site somewhat slow to load. Use Farefinder to quickly find the lowest current fares on flights to dozens of major cities. Carfinder offers a similar service for rental cars, but you can search only airport locations, not city pick-up sites. To see the lowest fare for your itinerary, input the dates and times for your route and see what Preview comes up with.

In recent years Preview and other leading booking services have added features such as Best Fare Finder, so after Preview searches for the best deal on your itinerary, it will check flights that are a bit later or earlier to see if it might be cheaper to fly at a different time. While these searches have become quite sophisticated, they still occasionally overlook deals that might be uncovered by a top-notch travel agent. If you have the time, see what you can find online and then call an agent to see if you can get a better price.

With Preview's Fare Alert feature, you can set fares for up to three routes and you'll receive e-mail notices when the fare drops below your target amount. For example, you could tell Preview to alert you when the fare from Chicago to New York drops below $250. If it does, you'll get an e-mail telling you the current fare.

Minor quibbles: When you search for a fare or hotel (at least when we went to press), Preview launches an annoying little "Please Wait" window that gets in the way of the main browser window, even when your results begin to appear. The hotel search feature is intuitive, but the images and maps aren't as crisp as those at Expedia. Also, all sorts of information that's irrelevant to travelers (such as NYC public school locations) is listed on the maps.

Note to AOL Users: You can book flights, hotels, rental cars and cruises on AOL at keyword: Travel. The booking software is provided by Preview Travel and is similar to Preview on the Web. Use the AOL "Travelers Advantage" program to earn a 5% rebate on flights, hotel rooms, and car rentals.

Priceline.com. www.priceline.com

Even people who aren't familiar with too many Web sites have heard about Priceline.com, which lets you "name your price" for domestic and international airline tickets. In other words, you select a route and dates, guarantee with a credit card, and make a bid for what you're willing to pay. If one of the airlines in Priceline's database has a fare that's lower than your bid, your credit card will automatically be charged for a ticket.

But you can't say when you want to fly—you have to accept any flight leaving between 6am and 10pm, and you may have to make a stopover. No frequent-flyer miles are awarded, and tickets are non-refundable and can't be exchanged for another flight. So if your plans change, you're out of luck. Priceline can be good for travelers who have to take off on short notice (and who are thus unable to qualify for advance purchase discounts). But be sure to shop around first—if you overbid, you'll be required to purchase the ticket and Priceline will pocket the difference.

Travelocity. www.travelocity.com

Essentials: Domestic and international flight, hotel and rental car booking; deals on cruises and vacation packages. Travel Headlines spotlights latest bargain airfares. Free (one-time) registration is required for booking.

Travelocity almost got it right. Its Express Booking feature enables travelers to complete the booking process more quickly than they could at Expedia or Preview, but Travelocity gums up the works with a page called "Featured Airlines." Big placards of several featured airlines compete for your attention. If you want to see the fares for *all* available airlines, click the much smaller box at the bottom of the page labeled "Book a Flight."

Some have worried that Travelocity, which is owned by American Airlines' parent company AMR, directs bookings to American. This doesn't seem to be the case—I've booked there dozens of times and have always been directed to the cheapest listed flight, for example on Tower or ATA. But this "Featured Airlines" page seems to be Travelocity's way of trying to cash in with ads and incentives for booking certain airlines. (*Note:* It's hard to blame these booking services for trying to generate some revenue. Many airlines have slashed commissions to $10 per domestic booking for online transactions so these virtual agencies are groping for revenue streams.) There are rewards for choosing one of the featured airlines. You'll get 1,500 bonus frequent-flyer miles if you book through United's site, for example, but the site doesn't tell you about other airlines that might be cheaper. If the United flight costs $150 more than the best deal on another airline, it's not worth spending the extra money for a relatively small number of bonus miles.

On the plus side, Travelocity has some leading-edge techie tools. Exhibit A is Fare Watcher E-mail, an "intelligent agent" that keeps you informed of the best fares offered for the city pairs (round-trips) of your choice. Whenever the fare changes by $25 or more, Fare Watcher will alert you by e-mail. Exhibit B is Flight Paging: If you own an alphanumeric pager with national access that can receive e-mail, Travelocity's paging system can alert you if your flight is delayed. Finally, though Travelocity doesn't include every budget airline, it does include Southwest, the leading U.S. budget carrier, which now flies into Long Island's Islip airport.

FINDING LODGINGS ONLINE

While the services above offer hotel booking, it can be best to use a site devoted primarily to lodging; you may find properties that aren't listed on more general online travel agencies. Some lodging sites specialize in a particular type of accommodation, such as B&Bs, which you won't find on the more mainstream booking services. Other services, such as TravelWeb, offer weekend deals on major chain properties, which cater to business travelers and have more empty rooms on weekends.

All Hotels on the Web. www.all-hotels.com
Well, this site doesn't include *all* the hotels on the Web, but it does have tens of thousands of listings throughout the world. Bear in mind that each hotel listed has paid a small fee of ($25 and up) for placement, so it's not an objective list but more like a book of online brochures.

Hotel Reservations Network. www.180096hotel.com
Bargain on room rates at hotels in more than two dozen U.S. cities. The cool thing is that HRN pre-books blocks of rooms in advance, so sometimes it has rooms—at discount rates—at hotels that are "sold out." Select a city, input your dates, and you'll get a list of best prices for a selection of hotels. Descriptions include an image of the property and a locator map (to book online, click the "Book Now" button). HRN is notable for some deep discounts, even in cities where hotel rooms are expensive. The toll-free number is printed all over this site; call it if you want more options than are listed online.

InnSite. www.innsite.com
B&B listings for inns in all 50 U.S. states and dozens of countries around the globe.
Find an inn at your destination, have a look at images of the rooms, check prices and availability, and then e-mail the innkeeper if you have further questions. This is an extensive directory of B&Bs, but includes listings only if the proprietor submitted one (*Note:* It's free to get an inn listed). The descriptions are written by the innkeepers, and many listings link to the inn's own Web sites, where you can find more information and images.

Places to Stay. www.placestostay.com
Mostly one-of-a-kind places in the U.S. and abroad that you might not find in other directories, with a focus on resorts. Again, listing is selective—this isn't a comprehensive directory, but can give you a sense of what's available at different destinations.

Quikbook. www.quikbook.com
Though Quikbook lists hotels in only seven U.S. cities (including New York), it offers some good rates on these properties, such as rooms for under $200 at Manhattan's Omni, where the rack rate is as high as $389. Lists of amenities and expandable images of the hotel, rooms, and lobby round out Quikbook's listings.

✪ **TravelWeb. www.travelweb.com**
TravelWeb lists more than 16,000 hotels worldwide, focusing on chains such as Hyatt and Hilton, and you can book almost 90% of these online. TravelWeb's Click-It Weekends, updated each Monday, offers weekend deals at many leading hotel chains. TravelWeb is the online home for Pegasus Systems, which provides transaction processing systems for the hotel industry.

LAST-MINUTE DEALS & OTHER ONLINE BARGAINS

There's nothing airlines hate more than flying with lots of empty seats. The Net has enabled airlines to offer last-minute bargains to entice travelers to fill those seats. Most of these are announced on Tuesday or Wednesday and are valid for travel the following weekend, but some can be booked weeks or months in advance. You can sign up for weekly e-mail alerts at airlines' sites (see above) or check sites such as WebFlyer (see below) that compile lists of these bargains. To make it easier, visit a site (see below) that will round up all the deals and send them in one convenient weekly e-mail. But last-minute deals aren't the only online bargains; some of the sites below can help you find value even if you can't wait until the eleventh hour.

✪ **1travel.com. www.1travel.com**
Deals on domestic and international flights, cruises, hotels, and all-inclusive resorts such as Club Med. 1travel.com's Saving Alert compiles last-minute air deals so you don't have to scroll through multiple e-mail alerts. A feature called "Drive a little using low-fare airlines" helps map out strategies for using alternate airports to find lower fares. And Farebeater searches a database that includes published fares, consolidator bargains, and special deals exclusive to 1travel.com. *Note:* The travel agencies listed by 1travel.com have paid for placement.

BestFares. www.bestfares.com
Budget seeker Tom Parsons lists some great bargains on airfares, hotels, rental cars, and cruises, but the site is poorly organized. News Desk is a long list of hundreds of bargains, but they're not broken down into cities or even countries, so it's not easy trying to find what you're looking for. If you have time to wade through it, you might find a good deal. Some material is available only to paid subscribers.

Go4less.com. www.go4less.com
Specializing in last-minute cruise and package deals, Go4less has some eye-popping offers, such as off-peak Caribbean cruises for under $100 per day. The site has a clean design but the bargains aren't organized by destination. However, you avoid sifting through all this material by using the Search box and entering vacation type, destination, month, and price.

Moment's Notice. www.moments-notice.com
As the name suggests, Moment's Notice specializes in last-minute vacation and cruise deals. You can browse for free, but if you want to purchase a trip, you have to join Moment's Notice, which costs $25.

Smarter Living. www.smarterliving.com
Best known for its e-mail dispatch of weekend deals on 20 airlines, Smarter Living also keeps you posted about last-minute bargains on everything from Windjammer Cruises to flights to Iceland.

✪ **WebFlyer. www.webflyer.com**
WebFlyer is the ultimate online resource for frequent flyers and also has an excellent listing of last-minute air deals. Click on "Deal Watch" for a round-up of weekend deals on flights, hotels, and rental cars from domestic and international suppliers.

TRAVELER'S TOOLKIT

✪ **CultureFinder. www.culturefinder.com**
Up-to-date listings for plays, opera, classical music, dance, film, and other cultural events in more than 1,300 U.S. cities. Enter the dates you'll be in a city and get a list of events; you can also purchase tickets online.

Intellicast. www.intellicast.com
Weather forecasts for all 50 states and cities around the world.

✪ **MapQuest. www.mapquest.com**
Specializing in U.S. maps, MapQuest enables you to zoom in on a destination, calculate step-by-step driving directions between any two U.S. points, and locate restaurants, hotels, and other attractions on maps.

✪ **Net Café Guide. www.netcafeguide.com**
Locate Internet cafes at hundreds of locations around the globe. Catch up on your e-mail, log onto the Web, and stay in touch with the home front, usually for just a few dollars per hour.

TheTrip: Airport Maps and Flight Status. www.trip.com
A business travel site where you can find out when an airborne flight is scheduled to arrive. Click on "Guides and Tools" to peruse airport maps for more than 40 domestic cities.

Visa. www.visa.com/pd/atm/

MasterCard. www.mastercard.com/atm
Find Cirrus and Plus ATMs in hundreds of cities in the U.S. and around the world. Both include maps for some locations and both list airport ATM locations, some with maps. Remarkably, MasterCard lists ATMs on all seven continents (there's one at Antarctica's McMurdo Station). *Tip:* You'll usually get a better exchange rate using ATMs than exchanging traveler's checks at banks.

Handy Tip

While most people learn about last-minute weekend deals from e-mail dispatches, it can be best to find out precisely when these deals become available and check airlines' Web sites yourself at this time. To find out when bargains will be announced, check the pages devoted to these deals on airlines' Web pages. Because these offerings are limited, seats can vanish within hours (sometimes even minutes), so it pays to log on as soon as they're available. An example: Southwest's specials are posted at 12:01am Tuesdays (Central time). So if you're looking for a cheap flight, stay up late and check Southwest's site to grab the best new deals.

Check Your E-mail While You're on the Road

Until a few years ago, most travelers who checked their e-mail while traveling carried a laptop, but this posed some problems. Not only are laptops expensive, but they can be difficult to configure, incur expensive connection charges, and are attractive to thieves. Thankfully, Web-based free e-mail programs have made it much easier to stay in touch.

Just open an account at a free-mail provider, such as Hotmail (hotmail.com) or Yahoo! Mail (mail.yahoo.com), and all you'll need to check your mail is a Web connection, easily available at Net cafes and copy shops around the world. After logging on, just point the browser to www.hotmail.com, enter your username and password and you'll have access to your mail.

Internet cafes have become ubiquitous, so for a few dollars an hour you'll be able to check your mail and send messages back to colleagues, friends and family. If you already have a primary e-mail account, you can set it to forward mail to your free-mail account while you're away. Free-mail programs have become enormously popular (Hotmail claims more than 10 million members), because they enable everyone, even those who don't own a computer, to have an e-mail address they can check wherever they log onto the Web.

2 The Top Web Sites for New York City

CITY GUIDES

City guides are a good way to get acquainted with what's going on in New York. While some are geared toward residents, they can still be excellent for travelers who want to read a theatrical review, see what's on at the Met, or get ideas about what to see and do.

✪ CitySearch: New York. www.newyork.citysearch.com
Reviews and listings for arts and entertainment, restaurants, shopping, hotels, and attractions.

Like Sidewalk, CitySearch is part of a national network of city guides, and has editorial reviews as well as paid Web pages from restaurants and other businesses. CitySearch clearly labels its links "editorial profile" or "advertiser's web site." Use CitySearch's Event Finder to search for sports, opera, comedy, and much more—just choose a date and see what's available. The extensive shopping listings range from clothing to wine. Along with New York Sidewalk, CitySearch is the leading directory for arts and dining in New York (but New York Today, backed by the *New York Times,* is quickly catching up).

MiningCo.com: New York City for Visitors. www.about.com
The core of this site is its collections of New York links, on topics ranging from accommodations to zoos. Features (all with Net links) cover dining, dancing, and attractions, as well as unusual topics such as where to go when you gotta go.

New York City! www.nycvisit.com
The Web site for the New York Convention & Visitors Bureau. Fast Facts, fantastic photos, an events calendar, and online hotel booking. Boosterish, as expected, but not overdone.

New York City Reference. www.panix.com/clay/nyc
Almost 2,000 links to sites about the Big Apple, organized by category. Hunt for gems such as the quirky New York Trash (www.nytrash.com), a rant on everything trashy about New York.

The keyword "New York" leads to **Digital City New York,** a site that's similar in scope to CitySearch and Sidewalk. You'll find reviews and listings for restaurants, arts, sports, and much more. If you search for the term "New York" in AOL's Find box, you'll come up with a list of other resources for New York, including an adventure/ outdoor guide, B&B listings, New York vacation packages, and AOL's New York Message Board, an online bulletin board that's open to any AOL member who wants to browse or ask a question. Digital City: New York is also available on the Web at **newyork.digitalcity.com**.

○ **New York Sidewalk. newyork.sidewalk.com**
Reviews and listings for restaurants, shopping, movies, nightlife, and other things to do. New York Sidewalk is one of about 18 Sidewalk sites that maintains a local editorial staff—so it's superior to those relying primarily on content from Sidewalk's national edition. All Sidewalk reviews are written by its editorial staff; other listings are paid for by businesses. Sidewalk's restaurant reviews are particularly strong, with lists of the top choices for romance, bargains, late-night meals and many more. You can also use the excellent block-by-block guide to find more restaurants and other attractions.

○ **New York Today. www.nytoday.com**
Arts, restaurant, and entertainment reviews and listings from the *New York Times.* At press time, New York Today was the only major city guide to offer an easy-to-use calendar format on its home page (don't be surprised if other sites soon emulate this). While much of NY Today's content comes from the *Times,* it also has some content found only on this site, including some arts reviews.

○ **Time Out New York. www.timeoutny.com**
Reviews and listings for restaurants, shops, and nightlife, with tips from TONY's critics. Time Out is a lively guide with a young, hip approach but has features for everyone, such as "Got Beer," a roundup of the best microbreweries in town. See "Essential New York" for off-the-beaten-track suggestions, such as free kayaking or the Greater New York Orchid Show.

NEWSPAPERS & MAGAZINES

New York Magazine. **www.newyorkmag.com**
Insightful features on the city. But they don't give it all away—some articles are available only in the print magazine. Click on "Cue" for arts listings.

○ **The New York Times Online. www.nytimes.com**
The authoritative scoop from the paper of record: sports, arts, restaurants, and much more.

The Village Voice. **www.villagevoice.com**
Features, columns, and reviews from New York's venerable, left-leaning alternative newspaper. Click on "Listings" for efficient searches of art, dance, music, and theater events by date and borough.

DINING GUIDES
Get a taste of the restaurants at your destination with online reviews.

CuisineNet. **www.cuisinenet.com**
Listings and reviews for New York and 15 other U.S. cities. Each restaurant has a capsule review compiled by CuisineNet and ratings based on surveys received from site

users. For many restaurants, only two or three people have bothered to submit ratings, so they may not be statistically significant. However comments can be instructive, as CuisineNet's readers discuss service, parking, free birthday desserts, and a host of other insightful observations.

Zagat Restaurant Survey. cgi.pathfinder.com/cgi-bin/zagat/homepage
Reviews of top restaurants for New York and dozens of U.S. cities. Zagat has made a name for itself as the people's choice, as its listings are based on extensive surveys. As this book went to press, Zagat (after several years on Pathfinder's site) was launching its own site at **www.zagat.com.**

THE TOP ATTRACTIONS

American Museum of Natural History. www.amnh.org
Exhibition information and an online tour of the one place on earth where massive dinosaur skeletons still rule.

Carnegie Hall. www.carnegiehall.org
A concert calendar, a box office, and a virtual tour.

Central Park. www.centralpark.org
Maps, upcoming events, and a tour of the park.

Circle Line. www.circleline.com
Tickets and information on how to see the world's most famous skyline in a 3-hour cruise around Manhattan island.

Ellis Island. www.ellisisland.org
An online tour of the former immigration center that was the gateway to the U.S. for millions of immigrants.

Empire State Building. www.esbnyc.com
Tour information, facts, history, and kid stuff.

Lincoln Center. www.lincolncenter.org
A calendar of upcoming performances, plus online ticket purchasing for many events.

Madison Square Garden. www.thegarden.com
Home to the Knicks and Rangers, the Garden offers a site that lists upcoming games, concerts, the circus, and more, plus how to buy tickets.

Metropolitan Museum of Art. www.metmuseum.org
A taste of the million-plus works of art, plus a calendar of exhibitions.

Museum of Modern Art. www.moma.org
Calendar and exhibition information for one of the world's leading modern-art collections.

New York Mets. www.mets.com
New York Yankees. www.yankees.com
Tickets, schedules, stadium information, and player profiles.

**NY.com: Museums in New York City. http://ny.com/nyc/museums/
all.museums.html**
An extensive listing of city museums.

NYC Museums. www.go-newyorkcity.com/museums/index.html
A guide to the city's leading museums and current exhibitions.

Radio City Music Hall. www.radiocity.com
A schedule of events and an online tour.

Rockefeller Center. www.nyctourist.com/rock_center1.htm
This art deco marvel, graced by a statue of Prometheus, comes alive during the holidays with its famous Christmas tree and ice rink.

South Street Seaport. www.southstreetseaport.com
A guide to shopping, dining, and special events on Manhattan's waterfront.

Statue of Liberty. www.nyctourist.com/liberty1.htm
An online photo tour of America's enduring symbol of freedom.

Top of the World. www.wtc-top.com
Visitor information and sample views from atop the World Trade Center.

United Nations. www.un.org
Information on how to watch diplomats from dozens of nations try to keep the peace.

GETTING TICKETS

Remember, you can buy tickets through the venues themselves, or through **Culture-finder.com.**

Ticket Depot. www.ticketdepot.com
A broker for tickets to Tri-state area sports, theater, concerts and more.

TicketMaster. events.ticketmaster.com
A national outlet, TicketMaster sells tickets for sports, theater, and concerts—all with a hefty service charge. You can also reach TicketMaster through CitySearch.

TicketWeb. www.ticketweb.com
TicketWeb also sells theater and concert tickets, but usually with a much lower service charge than TicketMaster. TicketWeb is best for events at smaller venues such as CBGB—many of the larger arenas and halls are locked into exclusive deals with large ticket sellers and do not sell through other outlets.

GETTING AROUND

New York Transportation. www.newyorktransportation.com
A guide to the city's buses, subway, taxis, and airports. You'll also find information on ground transportation from the airports to downtown.

✪ Subway Navigator. metro.ratp.fr:10001/bin/cities/english
An amazing site with detailed subway route maps for more than 60 cities around the world. Select a city and enter your departure and arrival points. Subway Navigator maps out your route and tells you how long the trip should take. It will even show your route on a subway map.

Index

See also separate Accommodations and Restaurant indexes, below. Page numbers in *italics* refer to maps.

General Index

Restaurant Index

FROMMER'S® COMPLETE TRAVEL GUIDES

Alaska
Amsterdam
Arizona
Atlanta
Australia
Austria
Bahamas
Barcelona, Madrid & Seville
Beijing
Belgium, Holland & Luxembourg
Bermuda
Boston
Budapest & the Best of Hungary
California
Canada
Cancún, Cozumel &
  the Yucatán
Cape Cod, Nantucket & Martha's Vineyard
Caribbean
Caribbean Cruises & Ports of Call
Caribbean Ports of Call
Carolinas & Georgia
Chicago
China
Colorado
Costa Rica
Denmark
Denver, Boulder & Colorado Springs
England
Europe
Florida
France
Germany
Greece
Greek Islands
Hawaii
Hong Kong
Honolulu, Waikiki & Oahu
Ireland
Israel
Italy
Jamaica & Barbados
Japan
Las Vegas
London
Los Angeles
Maryland & Delaware
Maui
Mexico
Miami & the Keys

Montana & Wyoming
Montréal & Québec City
Munich & the Bavarian Alps
Nashville & Memphis
Nepal
New England
New Mexico
New Orleans
New York City
Nova Scotia, New Brunswick &
  Prince Edward Island
Oregon
Paris
Philadelphia & the
  Amish Country
Portugal
Prague & the Best of the Czech Republic
Provence & the Riviera
Puerto Rico
Rome
San Antonio & Austin
San Diego
San Francisco
Santa Fe, Taos &
  Albuquerque
Scandinavia
Scotland
Seattle & Portland
Singapore & Malaysia
South Africa
Southeast Asia
South Pacific
Spain
Sweden
Switzerland
Thailand
Tokyo
Toronto
Tuscany & Umbria
USA
Utah
Vancouver & Victoria
Vermont, New Hampshire
  & Maine
Vienna & the Danube Valley
Virgin Islands
Virginia
Walt Disney World & Orlando
Washington, D.C.
Washington State

FROMMER'S® DOLLAR-A-DAY GUIDES

Australia from $50 a Day
California from $60 a Day
Caribbean from $70 a Day
England from $70 a Day
Europe from $60 a Day
Florida from $60 a Day

Hawaii from $70 a Day
Ireland from $50 a Day
Israel from $45 a Day
Italy from $70 a Day
London from $85 a Day ·
New York from $80 a Day

New Zealand from $50 a Day
Paris from $85 a Day
San Francisco from $60 a Day
Washington, D.C.,
   from $60 a Day

FROMMER'S® PORTABLE GUIDES

Acapulco, Ixtapa &
   Zihuatanejo
Alaska Cruises & Ports of Call
Bahamas
Baja & Los Cabos
Berlin
California Wine Country
Charleston & Savannah
Chicago

Dublin
Hawaii: The Big Island
Las Vegas
London
Maine Coast
Maui
New Orleans
New York City
Paris

Puerto Vallarta, Manzanillo
   & Guadalajara
San Diego
San Francisco
Sydney
Tampa & St. Petersburg
Venice
Washington, D.C.

FROMMER'S® NATIONAL PARK GUIDES

Family Vacations in the
   National Parks
Grand Canyon

National Parks of the
   American West
Rocky Mountain

Yellowstone & Grand Teton
Yosemite & Sequoia/
   Kings Canyon
Zion & Bryce Canyon

FROMMER'S® GREAT OUTDOOR GUIDES

New England
Northern California

Southern California & Baja
Washington & Oregon

FROMMER'S® MEMORABLE WALKS

Chicago
London

New York
Paris

San Francisco
Washington D.C.

FROMMER'S® IRREVERENT GUIDES

Amsterdam
Boston
Chicago
Las Vegas

London
Los Angeles
Manhattan

New Orleans
Paris
San Francisco

Seattle & Portland
Vancouver
Walt Disney World
Washington, D.C.

FROMMER'S® BEST-LOVED DRIVING TOURS

America
Britain
California

Florida
France
Germany

Ireland
Italy
New England

Scotland
Spain
Western Europe

THE COMPLETE IDIOT'S TRAVEL GUIDES

Boston
Chicago
Cruise Vacations
Planning Your Trip to Europe
Florida
Hawaii

Ireland
Las Vegas
London
Mexico's Beach Resorts
New Orleans
New York City

Paris
San Francisco
Spain
Walt Disney World
Washington, D.C.

THE UNOFFICIAL GUIDES®

Bed & Breakfast in
  New England
Bed & Breakfast in
  the Northwest
Beyond Disney
Branson, Missouri
California with Kids
Chicago

Cruises
Florida with Kids
The Great Smoky &
  Blue Ridge
  Mountains
Inside Disney
Las Vegas

London
Miami & the Keys
Mini Las Vegas
Mini-Mickey
New Orleans
New York City
Paris

San Francisco
Skiing in the West
Walt Disney World
Walt Disney World
  for Grown-ups
Walt Disney World
  for Kids
Washington, D.C.

SPECIAL-INTEREST TITLES

Born to Shop: France
Born to Shop: Hong Kong
Born to Shop: Italy
Born to Shop: New York
Born to Shop: Paris
Frommer's Britain's Best Bike Rides
The Civil War Trust's Official Guide
  to the Civil War Discovery Trail
Frommer's Caribbean Hideaways
Frommer's Europe's Greatest Driving Tours
Frommer's Food Lover's Companion to France
Frommer's Food Lover's Companion to Italy
Frommer's Gay & Lesbian Europe
Israel Past & Present
Monks' Guide to California

Monks' Guide to New York City
The Moon
New York City with Kids
Unforgettable Weekends
Outside Magazine's Guide
  to Family Vacations
Places Rated Almanac
Retirement Places Rated
Road Atlas Britain
Road Atlas Europe
Washington, D.C., with Kids
Wonderful Weekends from Boston
Wonderful Weekends from New York City
Wonderful Weekends from San Francisco
Wonderful Weekends from Los Angeles

WHEREVER YOU TRAVEL, *H*ELP IS NEVER FAR AWAY.

From planning your trip to providing travel assistance along the way, American Express® Travel Service Offices are always there to help you do more.

New York City

American Express Travel Service
420 Lexington Ave.
Betwn 43rd and 44th Sts.
212/687-3700

American Express Travel Service
822 Lexington Ave.
Corner of 63rd St.
212/758-6510

American Express Travel Service
Macy's Herald Square
35th St. Balcony
212/695-8075

American Express Travel Service
374 Park Avenue
At 53rd St.
212/421-8240

American Express Travel Service
American Express Tower
World Financial Center
Lobby Level
200 Vesey St.
212/640-5130

American Express Travel Service
65 Broadway
Betwn Rector St. & Exchange Place
212/493-6500

American Express Travel Service
1185 Sixth Avenue
At 47th St.
212/398-8585

American Express Travel Service
200 Fifth Avenue
At 23rd St.
212/691-9797

do more AMERICAN EXPRESS
Travel

www.americanexpress.com/travel

American Express Travel Service Offices are located throughout the United States. For the office nearest you, call 1-800-AXP-3429.